ARCTIC OCEAN

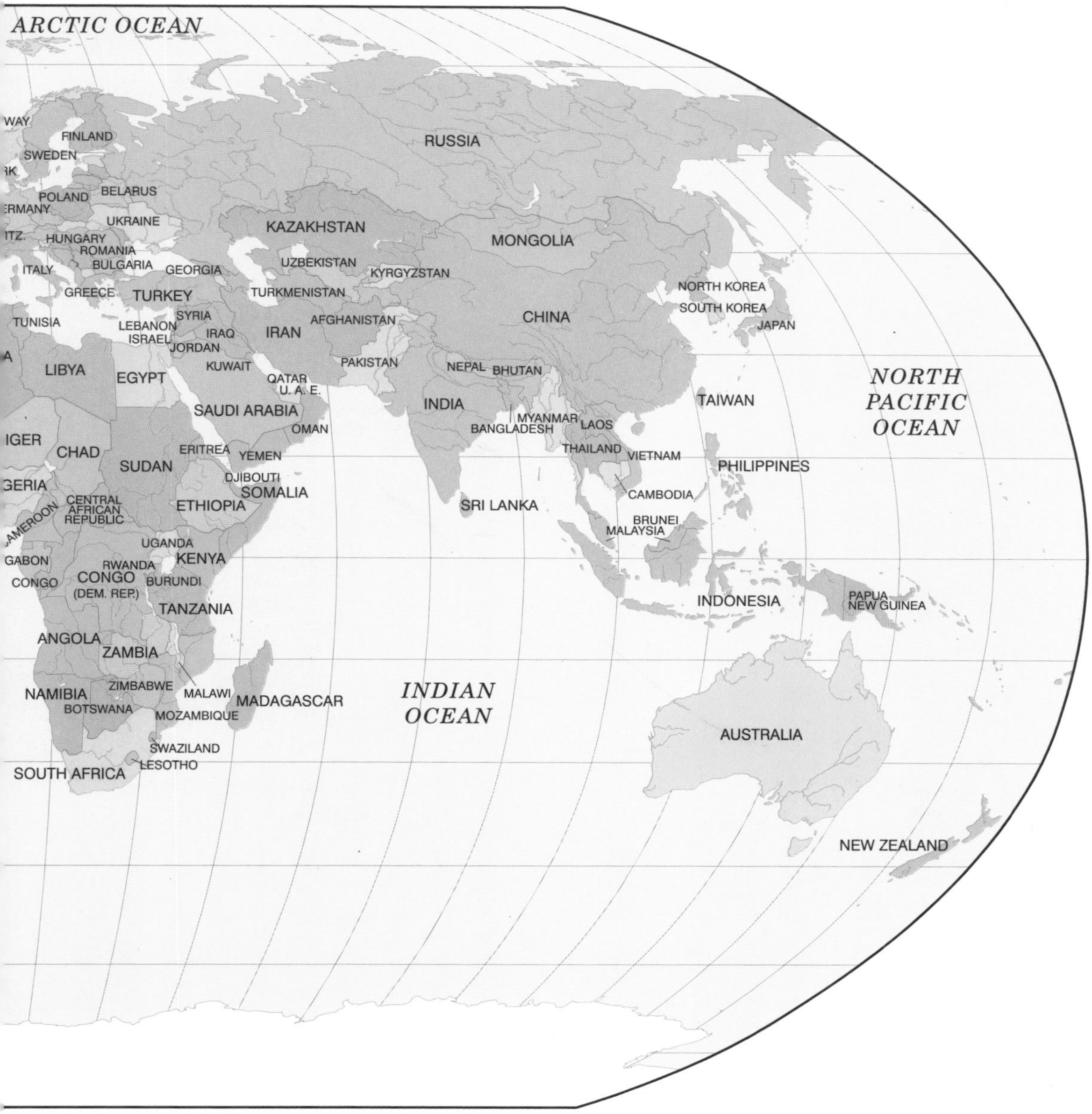

WAY
FINLAND
SWEDEN
RK
RUSSIA
POLAND
BELARUS
ERMANY
UKRAINE
KAZAKHSTAN
ITZ.
HUNGARY
ROMANIA
BULGARIA
MONGOLIA
ITALY
GEORGIA
UZBEKISTAN
KYRGYZSTAN
GREECE
TURKEY
TURKMENISTAN
NORTH KOREA
SOUTH KOREA
TUNISIA
SYRIA
LEBANON
ISRAEL
IRAQ
IRAN
AFGHANISTAN
CHINA
JAPAN
JORDAN
A
LIBYA
EGYPT
KUWAIT
PAKISTAN
NEPAL
BHUTAN
QATAR
U. A. E.
NORTH PACIFIC OCEAN
SAUDI ARABIA
INDIA
TAIWAN
MYANMAR
BANGLADESH
LAOS
OMAN
IGER
CHAD
ERITREA
YEMEN
THAILAND
VIETNAM
SUDAN
PHILIPPINES
DJIBOUTI
GERIA
SOMALIA
CENTRAL AFRICAN REPUBLIC
ETHIOPIA
SRI LANKA
CAMBODIA
AMEROON
BRUNEI
MALAYSIA
UGANDA
KENYA
GABON
RWANDA
CONGO
CONGO (DEM. REP.)
BURUNDI
INDONESIA
PAPUA NEW GUINEA
TANZANIA
ANGOLA
ZAMBIA
INDIAN OCEAN
NAMIBIA
ZIMBABWE
MALAWI
MADAGASCAR
BOTSWANA
MOZAMBIQUE
AUSTRALIA
SWAZILAND
SOUTH AFRICA
LESOTHO
NEW ZEALAND

Understanding God's World Series

Understanding God's World Series

Understanding
THE OLD WORLD

—A Christian Perspective—

Grade 7

Rod and Staff Publishers, Inc.
P.O. Box 3, Hwy. 172
Crockett, Kentucky 41413-0003
Telephone: (606) 522-4348

ACKNOWLEDGMENTS

We are indebted first of all to God who created the world and who upholds all things by the Word of His power. We are grateful that He has enabled the many who worked on this project. David Martin wrote the basic text, Bennie Hostetler and Michael Martin served as editors. The artwork (other than the old prints listed with the photo credits) was drawn by Donna Kauffman, Lester Miller, and Barbara Schlabach. Others spent many hours writing some of the exercises, reviewing the material, giving helpful suggestions, and preparing the manuscript for publication.

We thank Digital Wisdom and Cartesia for the use of their maps. Dale Yoder also drew some maps for this book. We are also grateful for the permissions that were granted for use of photos. See pages 572 and 573 for credits.

—The Publishers

Printed in U.S.A.

ISBN 978-07399-0652-1

Catalog no. 19701

4 5 6 7 8 — 23 22 21 20 19 18 17 16 15 14

Introduction

Earth: The Arena of History and Geography

Spinning through space is a tiny oasis, the planet called Earth. Glowing blue-green in the black vastness, it journeys 583 million miles (939 million km) around the sun every year. What keeps the earth from flinging itself into the starry reaches of outer space? Scientists say it is gravity from the sun that holds the earth in its path. No man knows what causes this force, but God knows. Job tells us that God is the one who "hangeth the earth upon nothing" (Job 26:7).

Among all the bodies that circle the sun, only on earth has God created the conditions needed to sustain life. These conditions are so balanced that even fairly small changes would destroy life on earth as we know it. For example, if the earth were closer to the sun, temperatures might climb to the 850°F (455°C) of Venus. If it were farther out, temperatures might drop to the -100°F (-73°C) of Mars. Some planets have very little atmosphere; other planets have a thick layer of poisonous gases; but the earth has a life-supporting atmosphere. The earth alone has colorful flowers, swaying trees, and creatures that live, move, and praise their Maker. "O LORD, . . . thou hast done wonderful things" (Isaiah 25:1).

Here, on the small planet where God has placed man, seasons come and go. Men live out their days in a flash of time and then go to meet their Maker. After they leave this earth, they must give account for what they have done; and it is too late then to go back and change anything. The story of what people have done in their lifetime here on earth is what we call history.

A knowledge of history is valuable because it helps us to understand ourselves. By studying history, we may avoid making the mistakes other people have made, and our lives will be more profitable here on earth.

When we study history, we must remember that our understanding is limited and our ideas about the past may be mistaken. The Bible says, "The fear of the LORD is the beginning of knowledge" (Proverbs 1:7). Only those who see God as the Creator and Sustainer of all things can begin to properly understand history. God has given us the Bible, the only completely accurate history book. As we study history in light of the Bible, we have a better understanding of life.

In this book you will study both history and geography. History is the story of man and his deeds. Geography is a study of the earth. (*Geo* means "earth" and *graphy* means "writing"; therefore *geography* means "writing about the earth.") You will study geography first, to gain an understanding of the earth—its mountains, rivers, and seas; its continents and countries. Then you will study history to see what man has done on the earth. As you pursue these studies, may you see the work of God, who created the earth and gave man the privilege to live upon it.

Front cover: The Romans were the greatest engineers of their time in building roads and bridges. For nearly 2,000 years, this Roman-built bridge (called Pont du Gard) near Nîmes, France, has supported an aqueduct. The Romans designed miles of slightly sloping aqueducts to carry water from rivers and mountain springs to satisfy thirsty cities.

Table of Contents

SECTION 1

GEOGRAPHY OF THE OLD WORLD—
EUROPE, ASIA, AFRICA, AND THE MIDDLE EAST

Europe, northern Africa, and part of Asia glow in brilliant colors in this satellite image taken from far above the earth. Note how the dry areas appear brown. Above Italy, snow crowns the high Alpine peaks.

1 Map Skills

History of Globes

Advantages of Globes

Advantages of Flat Maps

Kinds of Maps

Map Grids

The Earth's Grid

Hemispheres

"The earth is the L*ORD'S, and the fulness thereof; the world, and they that dwell therein. For he hath founded it upon the seas, and established it upon the floods."*

Psalm 24:1, 2

Map Skills

History of Globes

The Earth as a Sphere. "It is he that sitteth upon the circle of the earth, and the inhabitants thereof are as grasshoppers" (Isaiah 40:22).

Who first discovered that the earth is round? Apparently Isaiah knew this fact when God inspired him to write about the circle of the earth. Perhaps men had learned this even before Isaiah's day. We know that some 550 years later (about 150 B.C.), the Greeks made the first known globe. They not only understood that the earth is a ***sphere*** but also that they could also compute the approximate circumference of the sphere. They defined the poles and the equator, and they thought there must be undiscovered land to the west.

Later in history, many of the Greeks' ideas were forgotten and their map-making skills were lost. Some people believed that the earth was flat and that if one sailed far enough in any direction, he would fall off the earth!

By the time of Christopher Columbus, some scholars believed that the earth is round. In 1492, Martin Behaim (BAY hym) of Germany made the oldest globe in existence today. But this globe had a serious flaw. It showed the earth as being much smaller than it really is, and it did not include the undiscovered New World.

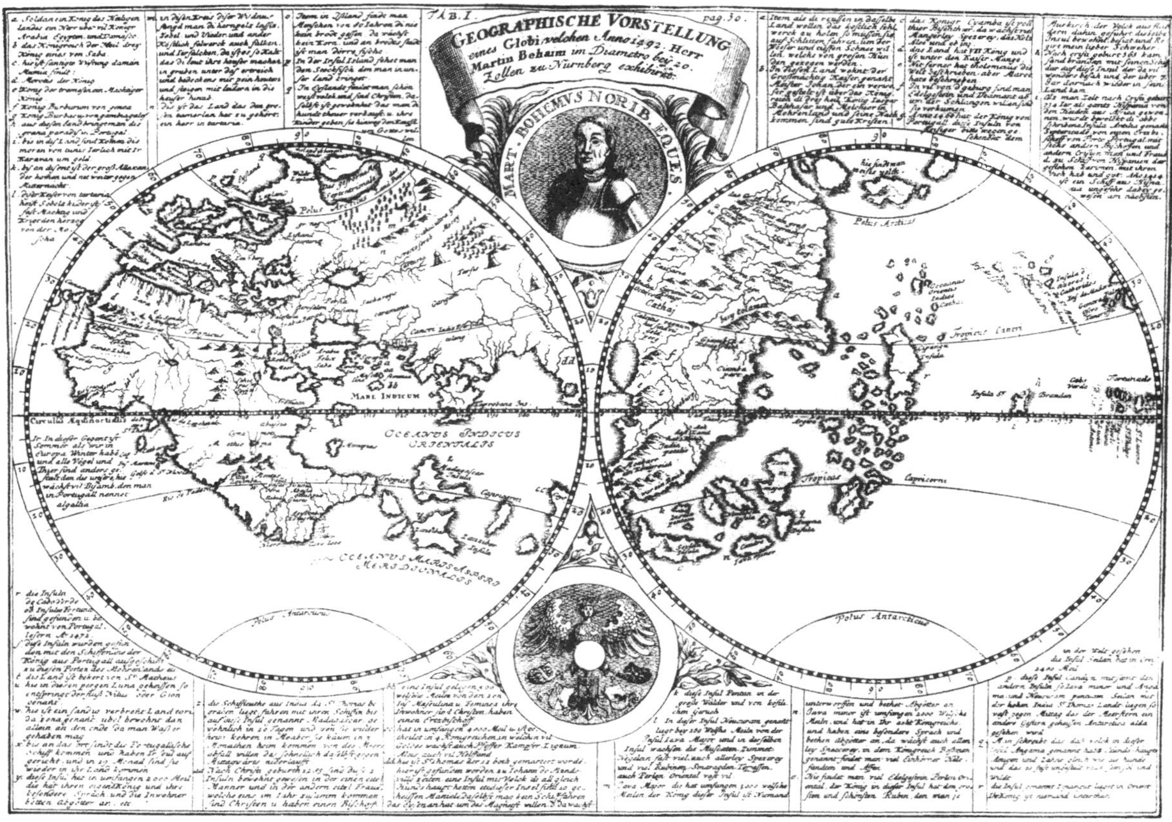

Martin Behaim studied geography, arithmetic, and ship navigation. He constructed this globe in 1492. At that point he knew nothing of the new lands that Columbus discovered in October of the same year. This globe shows only Europe, Africa, and Asia.

Behaim's globe quite likely influenced Columbus, and it may have contributed to his mistaken calculations about the size of the earth. Columbus believed he could land in Japan by sailing about 3,000 miles (4,800 km) west of the Canary Islands. Japan is actually about 12,000 miles (19,300 km) west; and besides, the Americas lie between.

Today, aided by photographs from space and by computers and other instruments, men can measure the earth very precisely. Modern globes are the most accurate way of representing the earth on a map.

Advantages of Globes

Maps come in various shapes and sizes. A globe is one kind of map. There are also flat maps, such as the ones in this book. Each kind of map has its advantages. The advantages of a globe are its accuracy in showing direction, distance, and the shape of land and water bodies.

Direction. A globe shows direction more accurately than a flat map does. This is because there is no way to show the surface of a round globe on a flat map without pulling it out of its true shape. Every flat map has ***distortions.*** On maps of small areas, the distortions are barely noticeable; but on world maps such as those in Figure 1:2, distortions can be very great. This is not the mapmaker's fault; it happens because a round world cannot be shown on a flat surface without being distorted.

Distance. Globes also show distance more accurately than flat maps do. To illustrate, find the shortest route between Mexico City

Figure 1:2

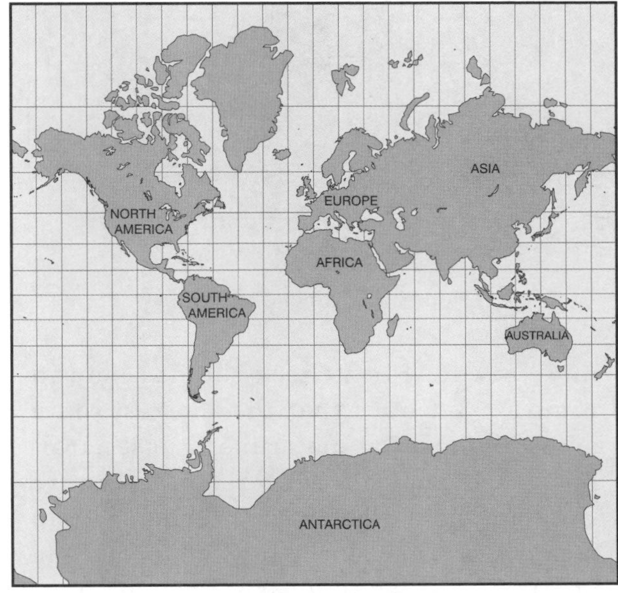

Mercator Projection

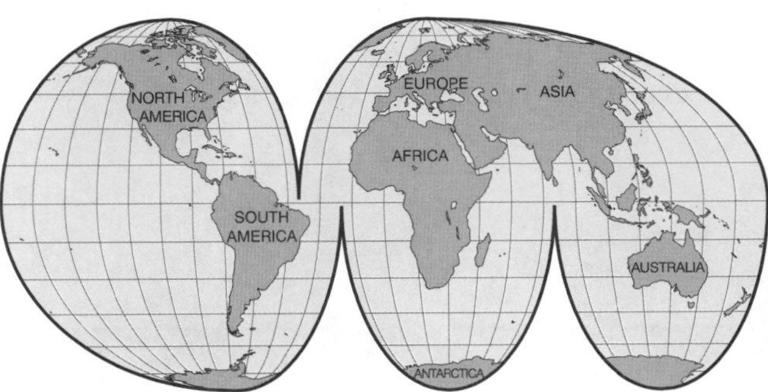

Mollweide Interrupted Projection

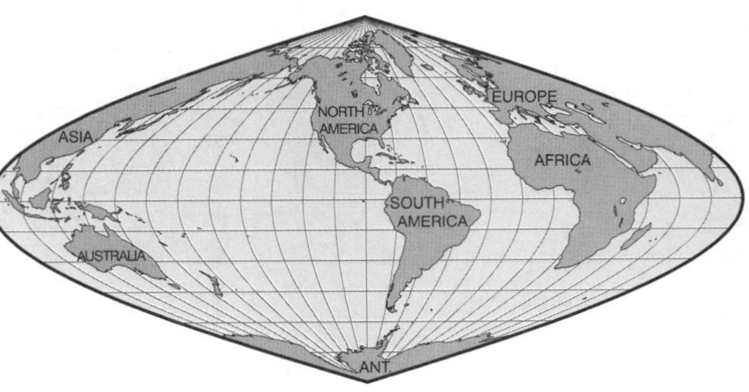

Sinusoidal Projection

Figure 1:2. What is the general shape of the seven continents? How large is Greenland in comparison to other bodies of land? Does Asia extend north farther than North America? The answers to these questions seem to depend on the map you use. Compare these maps with the globe.

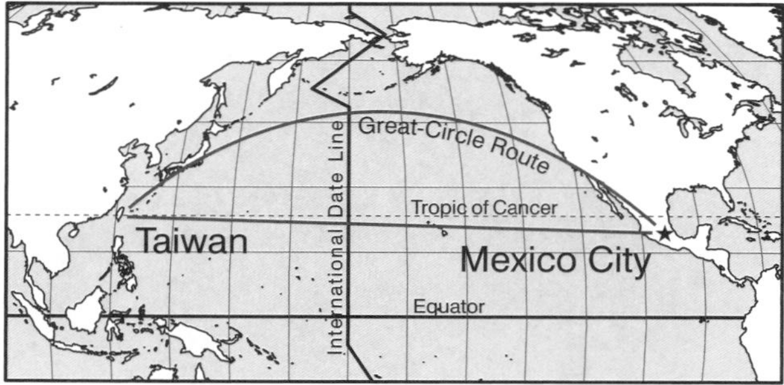

Figure 1:3. Great-Circle Route

and Taiwan. First check the flat map in Figure 1:3. Notice that the shortest route according to a flat map runs almost parallel to the Tropic of Cancer. Now measure the route on a globe with a string, a strip of paper, or a measuring tape. Place one end on Mexico City and measure the distance to Taiwan, keeping your string parallel to the Tropic of Cancer. Your string should cross the Hawaiian Islands.

Then pull the string tight enough so that it marks the most direct route between the two points. Is the string shorter now? Does it cross the Hawaiian Islands?

Because of the curve on the earth's surface, the shortest routes often appear circular on a flat map. Such routes are called ***great-circle routes.*** See Figure 1:3.

Size and Scale. Besides showing direction and distance more accurately than flat maps do, globes also give a more precise picture of the size and shape of land and water areas. The reason again is distortion. Flat maps exaggerate the size and the shape of areas near the poles. The closer an area is to a pole, the greater the exaggeration.

Greenland is a good illustration. Compare the general shape of Greenland as it is shown on the sinusoidal projection in Figure 1:2 with the way it is shown on a globe. Observe the difference in the shapes.

Now compare the sizes of South America and Greenland on the Mercator projection, and then on a globe. South America is about eight times as large as Greenland, but on some flat maps they appear about the same size. South America is distorted much less than Greenland because most of South America is close to the equator.

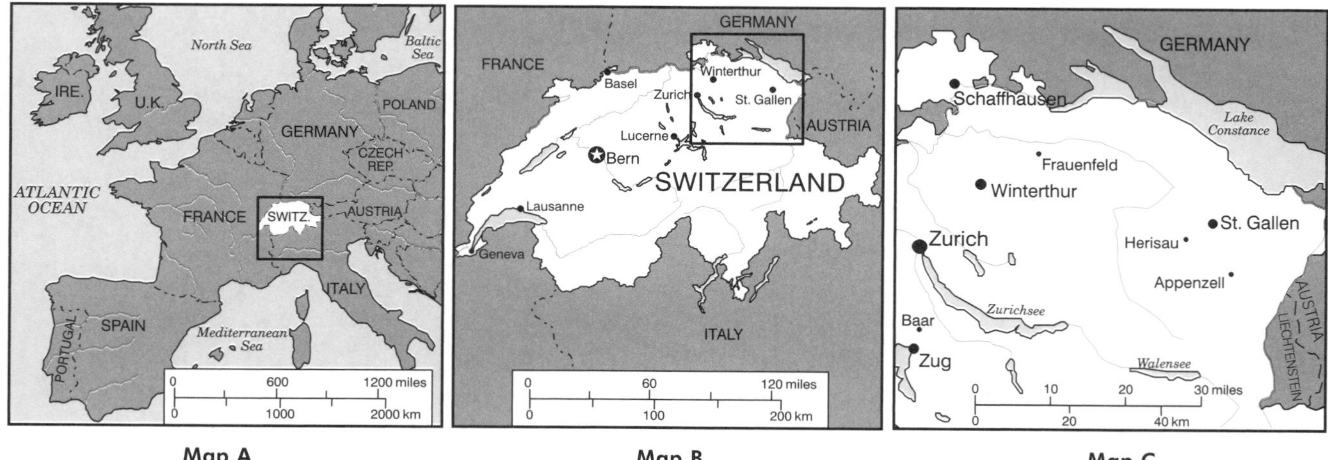

Figure 1:4. Map B is an enlargement of the boxed area of Map A. In the same way, Map C is an enlargement of Map B. On which map does one inch represent the longest distance? Is this a large-scale or a small-scale map?

Study Exercises

1. What is a sphere?
2. (a) When was the first known globe made? (b) How old is the oldest preserved globe?
3. In what three ways is a globe more accurate than a flat map?
4. On a flat map of the earth, which areas are distorted the most?

Advantages of Flat Maps

Although globes are more accurate than flat maps in many ways, flat maps also have some advantages over globes. Flat maps are more convenient to hold, they can be folded, and they can be printed in books. Most important, flat maps can show an area in large scale.

Map Scale. Look at the size of Switzerland on a globe. Compare this with the size of Switzerland on Map B of Figure 1:4. If Switzerland were shown to the same scale on a globe as it is on this map, it would take a globe almost 7 feet (2.1 m) in diameter to do so!

The scale of a globe is limited because it must show the entire earth. But a flat map can show any amount of area—as much as the entire earth, or as little as the area covered by your schoolroom. The scale to which a map is drawn determines how large an area the map will show.

On a small-scale map, the same area is smaller than it would be on a large-scale map. Compare the scales used for the maps in Figure 1:4. The scale used on the globe is much smaller than the one used in Map C of Figure 1:4.

Scales are shown in several ways. Some maps simply have a statement like "one inch equals 500 miles" or "one centimeter equals 300 kilometers." On others, the scale is shown by a line resembling a ruler (like the ones in Figure 1:4) or having alternate black and white spaces. To use such a scale, lay a paper on the map so that its edge passes over two specific places. Make marks to show how far apart the places are, and then hold the paper along the scale. It will show how many miles or kilometers are between the two places.

Still another method of showing scale is by using a fraction to show the ratio. For example, 1/24,000,000 means that one unit of measurement on the map indicates a distance 24,000,000 times as large. One inch would equal 24,000,000 inches or about 379 miles. One centimeter would equal 24,000,000 centimeters or 240 kilometers. This simple method of showing scale can be used with any unit of measure.

Map Symbols. A picture can often tell you more than many words. Maps are the same way. They give you a picture or representation of an area. They can give you an idea of its shape and size, and show the location of mountains and rivers. A map could show as many other details as the mapmaker could put on it.

Mapmakers must be careful not to include too many details, or the map becomes cluttered. They often use symbols to simplify the details they want to show. Some symbols are small pictures of the objects they stand for. Other symbols have no resemblance to the features they represent. For example, a dot may stand for a city and a circled star for a capital. Different colors may stand for different altitudes above sea level.

Maps usually have a ***legend*** or key to interpret the symbols. Note the legend in Figure 1:5, and use it to interpret the symbols on the maps.

Map symbols are like the words of a language. When you understand the symbols, you can read a map as you would read a book. Map symbols can tell us much about the features of the earth. They can show both the natural features made by God

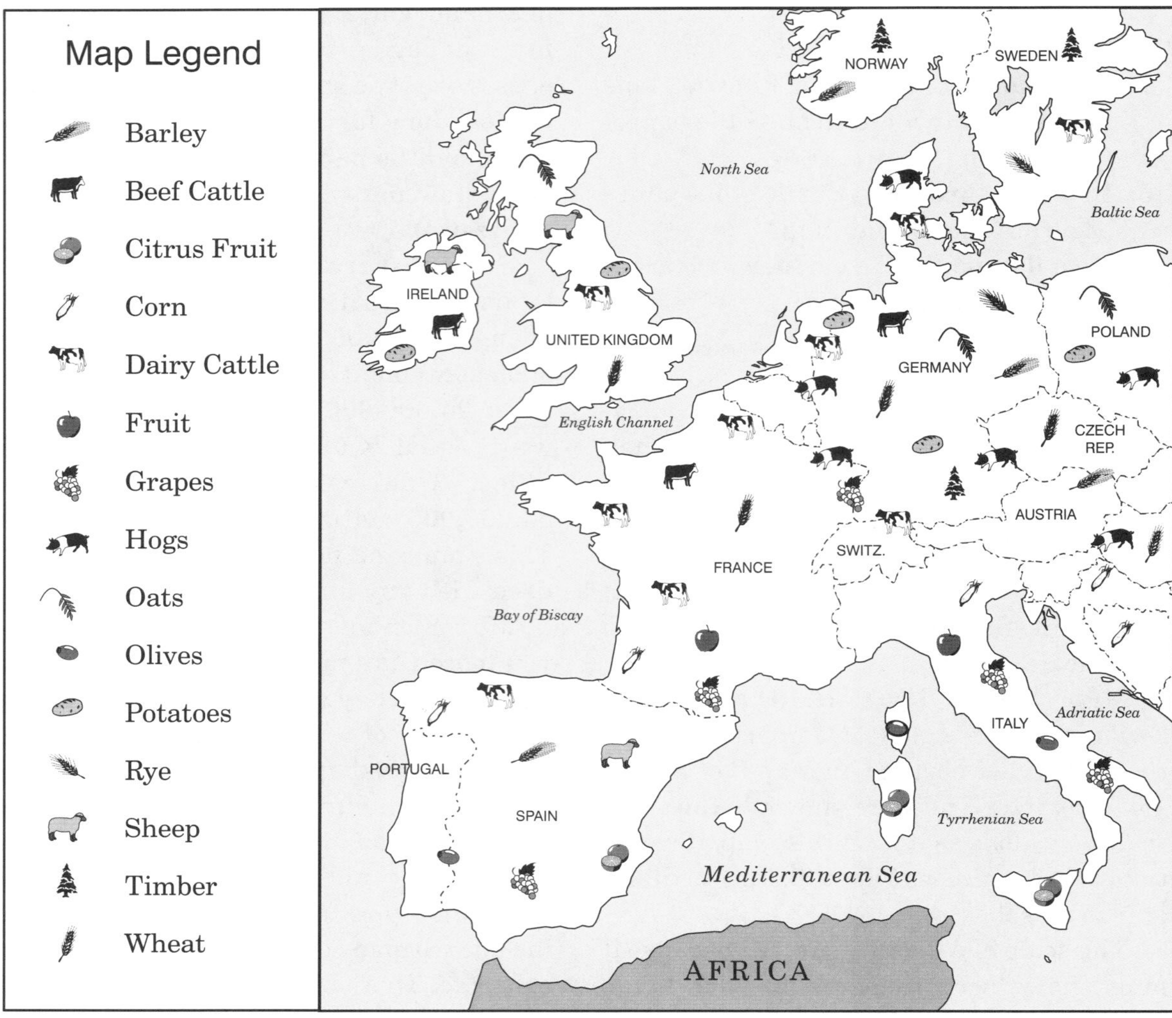

Figure 1:5. Western European Agricultural Products and Timber

(rivers, mountains, lakes) and manmade features (cities, roads, reservoirs).

Kinds of Maps

Maps are tools; and like tools, there are many different kinds. Just as a carpenter or mechanic uses different tools for different jobs, so the geographer uses different kinds of maps for different purposes.

Physical Relief Maps. A ***physical relief map*** shows the surface features of the earth. Shading of various colors shows different elevations above sea level. Mountains and other natural features are shaded to give a visual idea of what the land is like. Some physical relief maps show the depth of ocean water. The map legend explains what the different colors represent. Examples of physical relief maps are found on pages 15 and 29.

Political Maps. A physical relief map mainly shows the natural features God gave to the earth, while a ***political map*** shows the things men have done. Political maps tell how people have divided the earth into countries, states, provinces, and even smaller parts. They show cities, roads, and other manmade features.

Figure 1:6. Physical relief map of Germany

Political maps often use standard symbols. Dotted lines may show the boundaries of states or countries. Different types of lines show different kinds of roads. The size of type used for the name of a town or city can give an idea of its population and importance. The larger the type, the larger and more important the city. The map legend explains the symbols. Most globes and some flat maps show both political and physical features.

Special-Purpose Maps. Special maps are useful tools to find special information, such as yearly rainfall, population density, natural resources, or ocean currents. They are helpful because we can clearly and accurately compare these statistics for different parts of the earth.

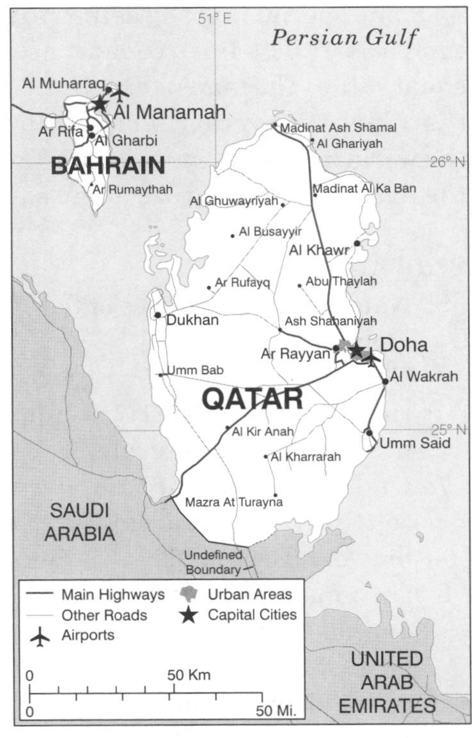

Figure 1:7. Political map of Bahrain and Qatar

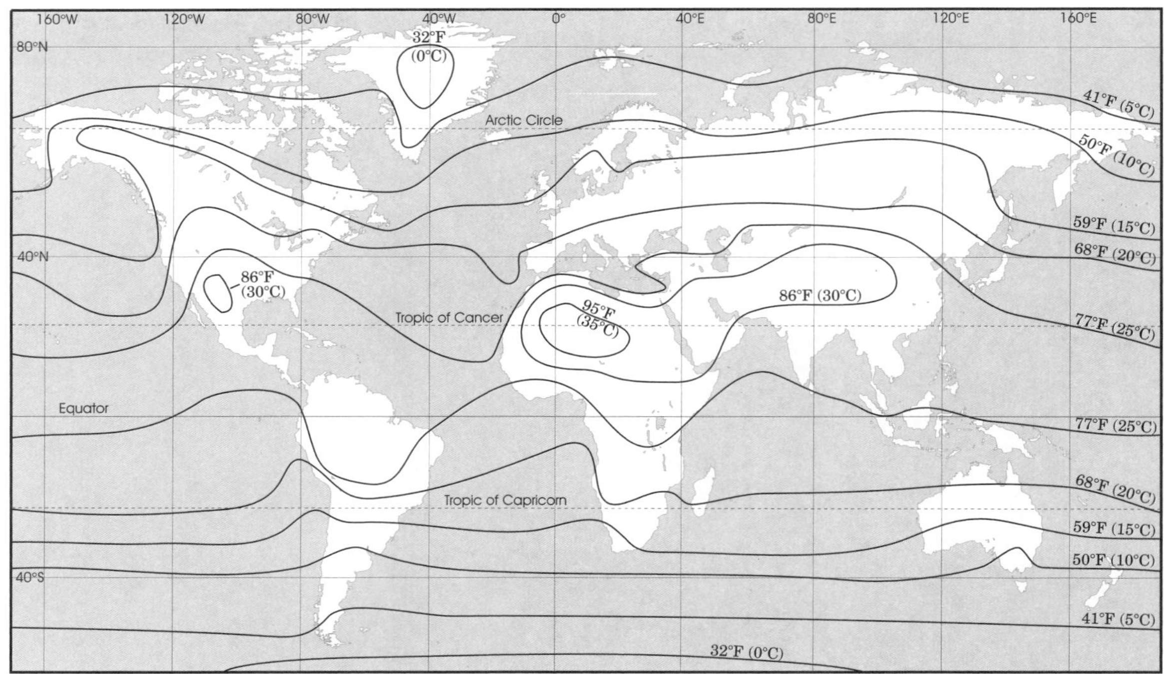

Figure 1:8. Average Global Temperature in July.

Some special maps use lines to show the comparison. The lines connect all places of equal value. The map in Figure 1:8 has lines that show the average temperature around the world in July. Wherever each line passes, the average temperature is the same.

Study Exercises

5. Name four advantages of flat maps over globes.
6. Compare the map in Figure 1:6 with the one in Figure 1:7. Which map is drawn on a larger scale?
7. On Map B in Figure 1:4, use the scale to find the approximate distance between Bern and St. Gallen.
8. On a map drawn to a scale of 1:50,000, one centimeter of measurement would represent (*a*) 50,000 inches. (*b*) 50,000 centimeters. (*c*) 50,000 miles. (*d*) 50,000 kilometers.
9. Use the map of Figure 1:5 to tell which two statements are true.
   a. Much corn is grown in northern Europe.
   b. Many grapes are grown in France, Italy, and Spain.
   c. More sheep are raised in the United Kingdom than in Germany.
   d. Citrus fruit grows well in all parts of Europe.
10. (*a*) Which kind of map shows natural features? (*b*) List at least three features that would appear on this kind of map.
11. (*a*) Which kind of map shows manmade features? (*b*) List at least five features that would appear on this kind of map.
12. What is the average July temperature of central Australia? (See Figure 1:8.)

Important Plants of the Old World

In a series of articles throughout this book, some cereal grains and other important plants that originated in the Old World will be discussed. Many other food plants could be mentioned, such as sorghum, but we will only cover those that are mentioned in the text. Corn (maize) will not be covered, as it is a New World plant brought to the Old World by Spanish conquerors in the 1500s.

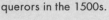

In our world today, about 70 percent of the agricultural land is used for the growing of cereal grasses, and more than 50 percent of the calories consumed come from the edible seeds (grains) of these grasses. Within each seed is a baby plant called an embryo (or germ), which contains protein, oil, and some vitamins. The bulk of the seed contains the endosperm, a carbohydrate-rich food for the embryo after it germinates. An edible protective seed coat called bran surrounds the embryo and endosperm, and all of these parts are enclosed in an inedible protective layer called a husk (or chaff). The woody husk is separated from the grains by threshing.

Since it is our tendency to be unthankful even if we have so many good foods to eat, it is well for us to consider the warning given in Deuteronomy 8:10–18: "When thou hast eaten and art full, then thou shalt bless the Lord thy God for the good land which he hath given thee. Beware that thou forget not the Lord thy God, in not keeping his commandments, and his judgments, and his statutes, which I command thee this day: lest when thou hast eaten and art full, and hast built goodly houses, and dwelt therein; . . . and all that thou hast is multiplied; then thine heart be lifted up, and thou forget the Lord thy God, . . . and thou say in thine heart, My power and the might of mine hand hath gotten me this wealth. But thou shalt remember the Lord thy God: for it is he that giveth thee power to get wealth."

Map Grids

Maps often have an index listing countries, cities, towns, and other features. But a map index cannot give you a page number to tell you where a place is on a map. Maps need a grid system to locate places.

Suppose you want to find Limerick on the map of Ireland in Figure 1:9. Look at the index below the map. You will find "Limerick, C6." At the top of the map you find letters, and on the side you find numbers. Find *C* at the top and *6* on the side. Follow the rows of squares until they cross. In this square you will find Limerick. Use the grid to find the other towns listed in the index.

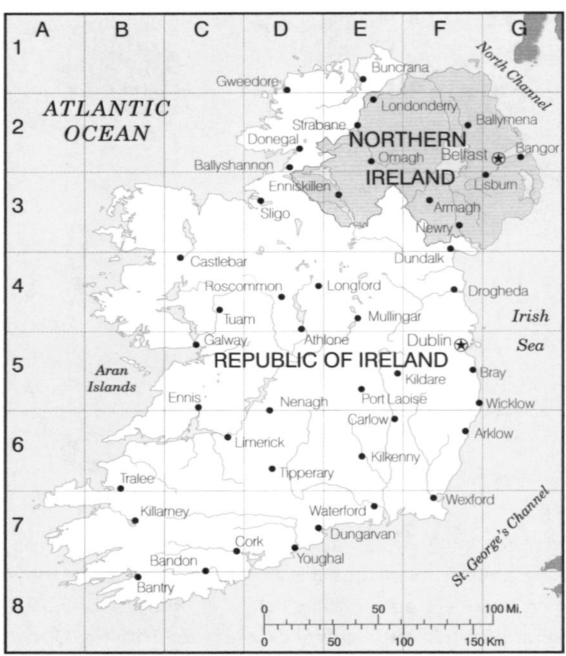

Figure 1:9

Index

Belfast G2
Cork C7
Dublin F5
Galway C5
Limerick C6
Wicklow F5

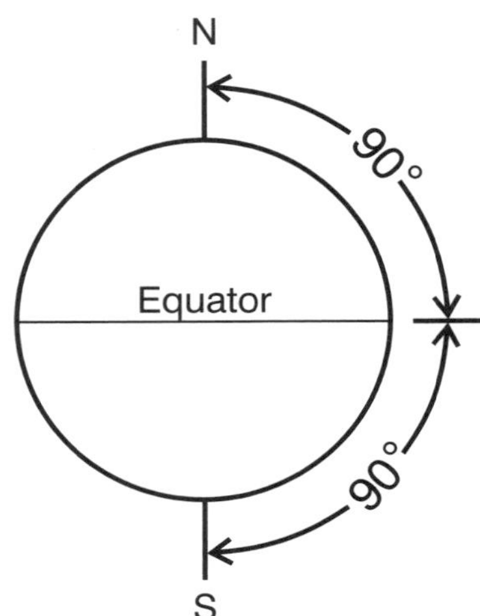

Figure 1:10

The Earth's Grid

The earth also has a grid. Men have devised a pattern of crisscrossing lines that help us to locate places on earth. Because of the exactness with which God established time and measurement, men have learned to locate places precisely.

Since the globe is round, it can be divided into degrees. If you have learned about the degrees of a circle, you may remember that a circle has 360 degrees (written 360°). One-half of a circle has 180°, and one-fourth of a circle has 90°.

If you imagine the poles of the globe as being vertical, then the equator is horizontal. From the equator to the poles is one-fourth of a circle, or 90°. (See Figure 1:10.)

The equator is a natural starting point for measuring degrees of ***latitude.*** Beginning at the equator, 90° of latitude are measured to the North Pole and 90° to the South Pole. There are about 69 miles (111 km) in each degree of latitude.

The imaginary lines that circle the earth at different degrees of latitude are called ***parallels*** because they run parallel with the equator. Most globes do not show a parallel for every degree. They may show parallels for every ten or fifteen degrees.

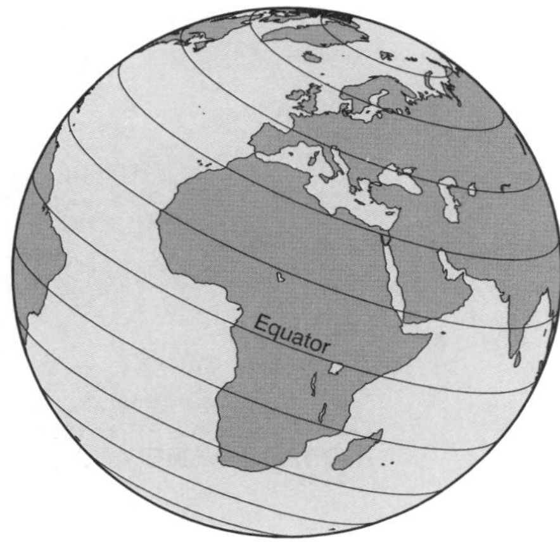

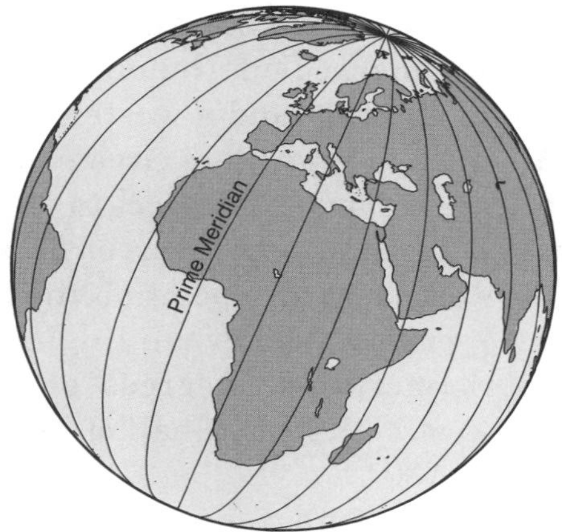

Figure 1:11. Parallels run east and west around the earth. They measure distance north and south of the equator. Meridians run north and south between the poles. They measure distance east and west of the prime meridian.

To distinguish the degrees of latitude north of the equator from the degrees of latitude south of the equator, geographers refer to them as degrees north and degrees south. Someone in North America might live at 40° north (N), whereas someone in South America might live at 40° south (S).

Geographers use degrees of latitude to show how far north or south of the equator a place is. They also need a way to show how far east or west a place is. To do this, they use degrees of ***longitude*** (LAHN jih tood). The lines that mark these degrees are called ***meridians*** (muh RIHD ee uhnz) of longitude.

Where do meridians of longitude start? Since there is no natural starting point as with the equator, an international conference was held in 1884 to determine where the zero meridian should be. It was decided that the Royal Greenwich Observatory (GREHN ihch) just outside London, England, would be the starting point, or the ***prime meridian.***

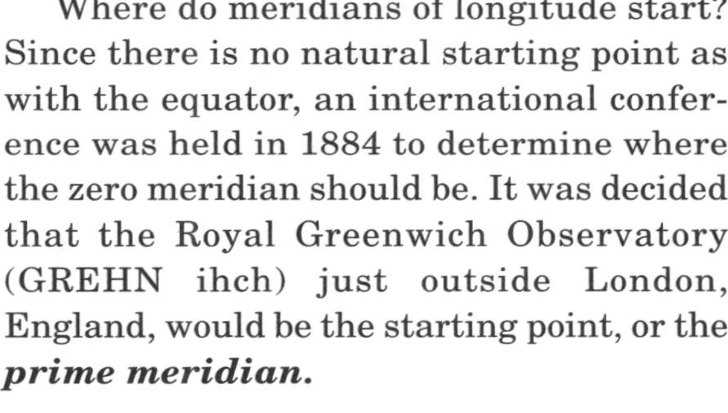

This monument marks the equator line, just a few miles from Quito, Ecuador. Tourists like to pose here with a foot in each hemisphere.

The Royal Greenwich Observatory was originally used to determine time and to locate heavenly bodies more accurately, thereby improving ship navigation. It was established in 1675 at Greenwich, England, now a borough of London. In 1990, it was moved to its present location at Cambridge, north of London.

With Greenwich as zero, degrees of longitude were marked off around the earth, in both an easterly and a westerly direction. Degrees to the east of Greenwich are called degrees east, and degrees to the west are called degrees west. Degrees east and degrees west meet at a point on the earth exactly opposite Greenwich, England, at the 180th meridian. Degrees east and degrees west both form a half circle, each containing 180°.

Because the 180th meridian runs through much less land area than the prime meridian does, it was decided that each new day would begin at the 180th meridian. This line where a new day begins is called the ***International Date Line.*** The International Date Line closely follows the 180th meridian, except in a few places where it zigzags to avoid dividing land areas or island groups.

The date just west of the International Date Line is always one full day later than the date just east of the line. On a globe or map, find the Tonga and Samoa Islands in the Pacific Ocean (about 15°S 175°W). When it is Sunday noon on the Tonga Islands, it is Saturday noon on the Samoa Islands.

Unlike parallels of latitude, meridians of longitude do not run parallel with each other. Notice in Figure 1:11 that they meet at the poles and are farthest apart at the equator. A man would need to travel about 69 miles (111 km) at the equator to cross one degree of longitude. At the poles he could cross one degree by moving his foot.

To pinpoint locations, degrees of latitude and longitude are further divided into minutes and seconds. Each minute is one-sixtieth (1/60) of a degree, and each second is one-sixtieth (1/60) of a minute. This book uses only minutes.

The abbreviation for minutes is a single mark (′). The Tropic of Cancer is located at 23°27′N. (The capital letter shows direction.) Galway, Ireland, is located at 53°16′N and 9°03′W. See Figure 1:12.

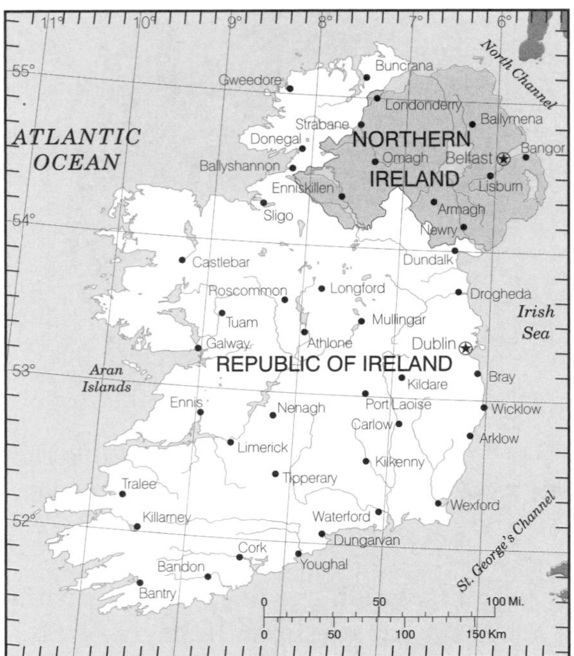

Figure 1:12

On this map, the space between each degree of latitude or longitude is marked off in divisions of ten minutes each.

Index

Belfast........................54°40′N 5°50′W
Cork ....51°54′N 8°28′W
Dublin........................53°20′N 6°15′W
Galway.......................53°16′N 9°03′W
Limerick.....................52°40′N 8°38′W
Londonderry..............55°N 7°19′W
Wicklow.....................52°59′N 6°03′W

Notice that parallels and meridians form a grid that shows the location of Galway, Ireland. This system allows the geographer to locate any place on the earth. *N* or *S* tells whether it is north or south of the equator, and *E* or *W* tells whether it is east or west of the prime meridian. The number of the degree and the minute further helps to pinpoint the exact location.

Some map indexes use the letter and number grid system, but many indexes use

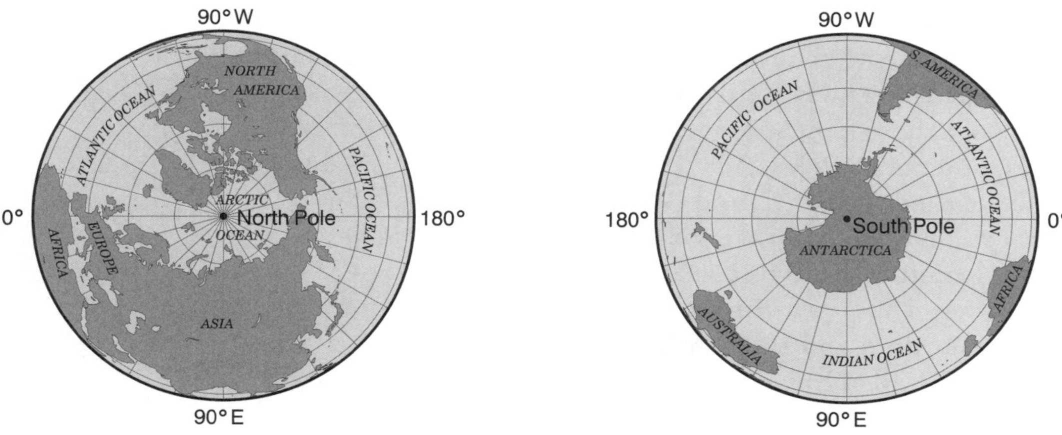

Figure 1:13. Northern and Southern Hemispheres. Compare the amount of land area in the Northern Hemisphere with the amount in the Southern Hemisphere. Which hemisphere has the most water?

latitude and longitude. A letter and number grid can be used only on the map for which it was made, whereas latitude and longitude are the same on all maps, including the globe. This makes it a more useful method.

See if you can locate the places in Ireland listed in the index in Figure 1:12.

Hemispheres

What is a ***hemisphere***? You already know that a sphere is a round object such as the earth. The prefix *hemi-* means half. A hemisphere is half of a sphere.

If you live in North America, you live in the Northern Hemisphere and in the Western Hemisphere. You can live in more than one hemisphere because the globe can be divided differently depending on how you look at it.

Actually, there can be any number of hemispheres. From whatever angle you look at a globe, you can always see a hemisphere. But only four of these possible hemispheres—the Northern, Southern, Eastern, and Western Hemispheres—are important in geography.

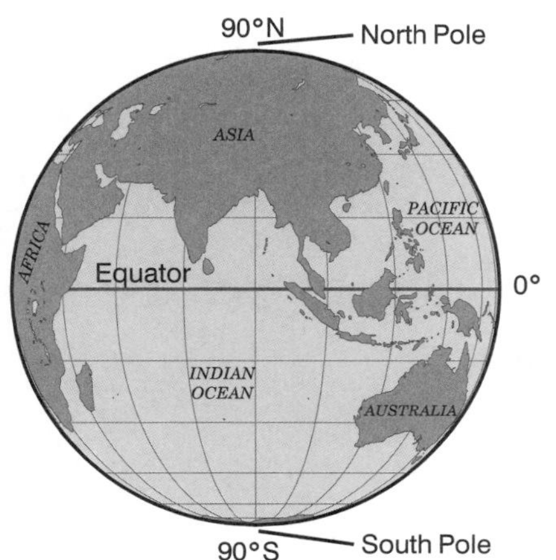

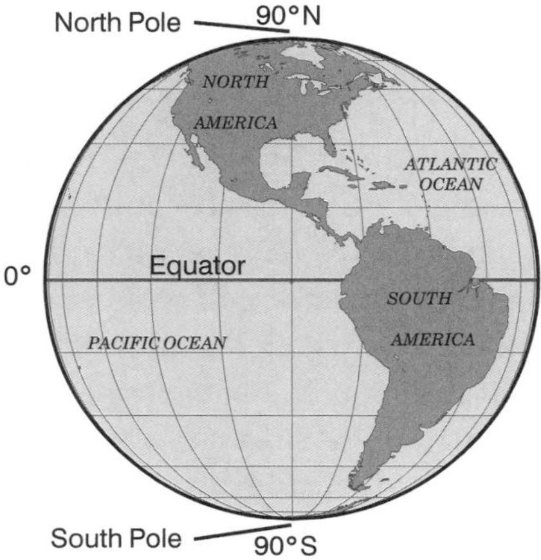

Figure 1:14. The Eastern and Western Hemispheres. Which hemisphere has the most land area?

The equator is a natural dividing line between the Northern and Southern Hemispheres. The center points from which you would see these hemispheres would be the North and South Poles.

The so-called Eastern and Western Hemispheres have no natural dividing line. Degrees of longitude could be used to divide the Eastern and Western Hemispheres at the prime meridian and the 180th meridian. But usually all of Europe, Asia, Africa, and Australia are considered as the Eastern Hemisphere, even though small parts of Europe, Asia, and Africa are actually west longitude. When the Eastern Hemisphere is defined in this more general way, it is separated from the Western Hemisphere by the Atlantic and Pacific Oceans. The Western Hemisphere includes North and South America.

The division of "East" and "West" is largely a result of history. During the centuries when this idea developed, European nations ruled the seas. To them the Americas were to the west. If the Japanese or Chinese had been the world's main traders during that period, perhaps today the Americas would be the "East" and Europe and Asia the "West."

Study Exercises

13. Why are degrees of latitude also called parallels?
14. (*a*) What is the starting point for degrees of latitude? (*b*) for degrees of longitude?
15. State how many degrees there are for each of these.
    a. degrees north
    b. degrees south
    c. degrees west
    d. degrees east
16. (*a*) What line marks the beginning of a new day? (*b*) Which meridian does this line closely follow?
17. What divides the Northern Hemisphere from the Southern Hemisphere?
18. (*a*) Find Spain on a map of Europe. Is Madrid, Spain, about 4°E or 4°W? (*b*) Why is Spain usually considered part of the Eastern Hemisphere?
19. In which two of these hemispheres do you live: Eastern, Western, Northern, Southern?
20. Find the approximate latitude and longitude of your home.

Clinching the Chapter

Multiple Choice

Write the word or phrase least *associated with the first item.*

1. Globe: atlas, accurate, sphere, small scale
2. Physical maps: rivers, altitude, ocean depth, population
3. Flat maps: distortion, convenient, true shapes, many scales
4. Political maps: cities, mountains, countries, roads
5. Latitude: south, degrees, parallels, elevation
6. Longitude: meridians, west, equator, Greenwich
7. Parallels: latitude, equator, meet at poles, 0° to 90°
8. Meridians: longitude, International Date Line, not parallel, 0° to 360°
9. Prime meridian: zero, parallel, Greenwich, longitude
10. International Date Line: Pacific Ocean, straight, 180th meridian, new day

Matching

For each clue, write the correct term from the right-hand column.

1. Made the oldest globe still in existence	Columbus
2. Wrote about the "circle of the earth"	distortion
3. Correctly computed the earth's circumference	great-circle route
4. Sailed west in search of the East	Greeks
5. Half of a sphere	hemisphere
6. Interprets map symbols	Isaiah
7. Most direct path between two points	legend
8. Used to locate places on a map	map grid
9. A disadvantage of flat maps	map scale
10. Used to compute actual distance	Martin Behaim

Geographical Skills

1. Look up the maps on these pages, and state whether they are physical relief maps, political maps, or special maps: page 30, page 54, page 83, page 87.
2. On a globe, measure the distance between Cuba and Taiwan. Tie a knot in a string and tape it to Cuba. Stretch the string along Cuba and Taiwan's latitude (the Tropic of Cancer), and mark the distance on the string. Then stretch the string up across the globe to find the shortest route (the great-circle route) between the two countries, and mark the string again. Use the globe scale to find the actual length of each route in miles or kilometers. How much difference is there?
3. On the maps of Switzerland in Figure 1:4, use the scale to find the distance between Zurich and the following cities.
   a. Bern b. Winterthur c. Geneva
4. Suppose you were flying around the world and were stopping at the cities named below. Use a globe to find the total distance that you would travel. (First list the cities and the distances between them, and then find the total.)
   a. New York City, New York, to London, England
   b. London to Rome, Italy
   c. Rome to Jerusalem, Israel
   d. Jerusalem to Calcutta, India
   e. Calcutta to Manila, Philippines
   f. Manila to Tokyo, Japan
   g. Tokyo to Seattle, Washington
   h. Seattle to New York City
5. Use the physical relief map of Germany in Figure 1:6 to choose the correct answers.
   a. Part of Germany with the lowest elevation: north, central, south
   b. Three cities in hilly or mountainous regions: Berlin, Freiburg, Kiel, Munich, Nuremberg
   c. Region of Germany with the highest elevation: Bavarian Alps, Franconian Mountains, Taunus Mountains
   d. Shortest of these three rivers: Elbe, Ems, Rhine

6. Name the capital cities found at the following locations.
   a. 48°52′N 2°20′E
   b. 55°45′N 37°42′E
   c. 15°45′S 47°57′W
   d. 35°40′N 139°45′E
   e. 45°25′N 75°43′W
   f. 9°12′N 7°11′E
   g. 14°37′N 120°58′E
   h. 12°03′S 77°03′W
7. Using the map of Asia on page 54, give an approximate figure of latitude and longitude for these capital cities.
   a. Kabul, Afghanistan
   b. Islamabad, Pakistan
   c. New Delhi, India
   d. Katmandu, Nepal
   e. Dhaka, Bangladesh
   f. Colombo, Sri Lanka

Further Study

Use reference sources and your knowledge about hemispheres to answer these questions. Give two answers for each.

1. Which hemispheres have the largest land area?
2. Which hemispheres have the highest population?
3. Which hemispheres have the highest mountains?
4. Which hemispheres have the longest river?
5. Which hemispheres have the largest river?
6. Which hemispheres have the largest island?
7. Which hemispheres have the smallest continent?

The gently rolling hills of southern Poland contain much of the country's best farmland. Corn, potatoes, and wheat grow in the rich soil. (The wooden building above is a farmhouse.)

On Portugal's rolling plains and plateaus south of the Tagus River, hardworking farmers raise grain for their nation. Many farms in this region of Portugal are huge estates where the owners employ as many as 100 workers.

2 Europe

Where Is Europe?

What Is Europe?

The Shape of Europe

Europe's Climate

Europe's Highland and Lowland Regions

Europe's Waterways

Europe's Natural Resources

Industry in Europe

What About Farming?

Trade in Europe

Europe's Many Cultures

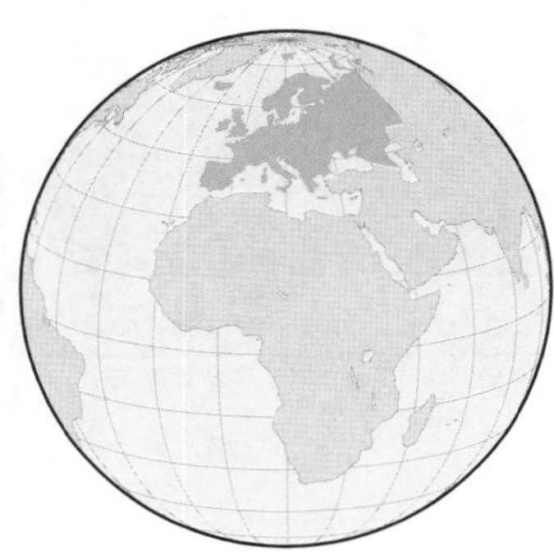

Albania • Andorra • Austria • Belarus • Belgium • Bosnia-Herzegovina • Bulgaria • Croatia • Czech Republic • Denmark • Estonia • Finland • France • Germany • Greece • Hungary • Iceland • Ireland • Italy • Kazakhstan • Latvia • Liechtenstein • Lithuania • Luxembourg • Macedonia • Malta • Moldova • Monaco • Netherlands • Norway • Poland • Portugal • Romania • Russia • San Marino • Slovakia • Slovenia • Spain • Sweden • Switzerland • Ukraine • United Kingdom • Yugoslavia

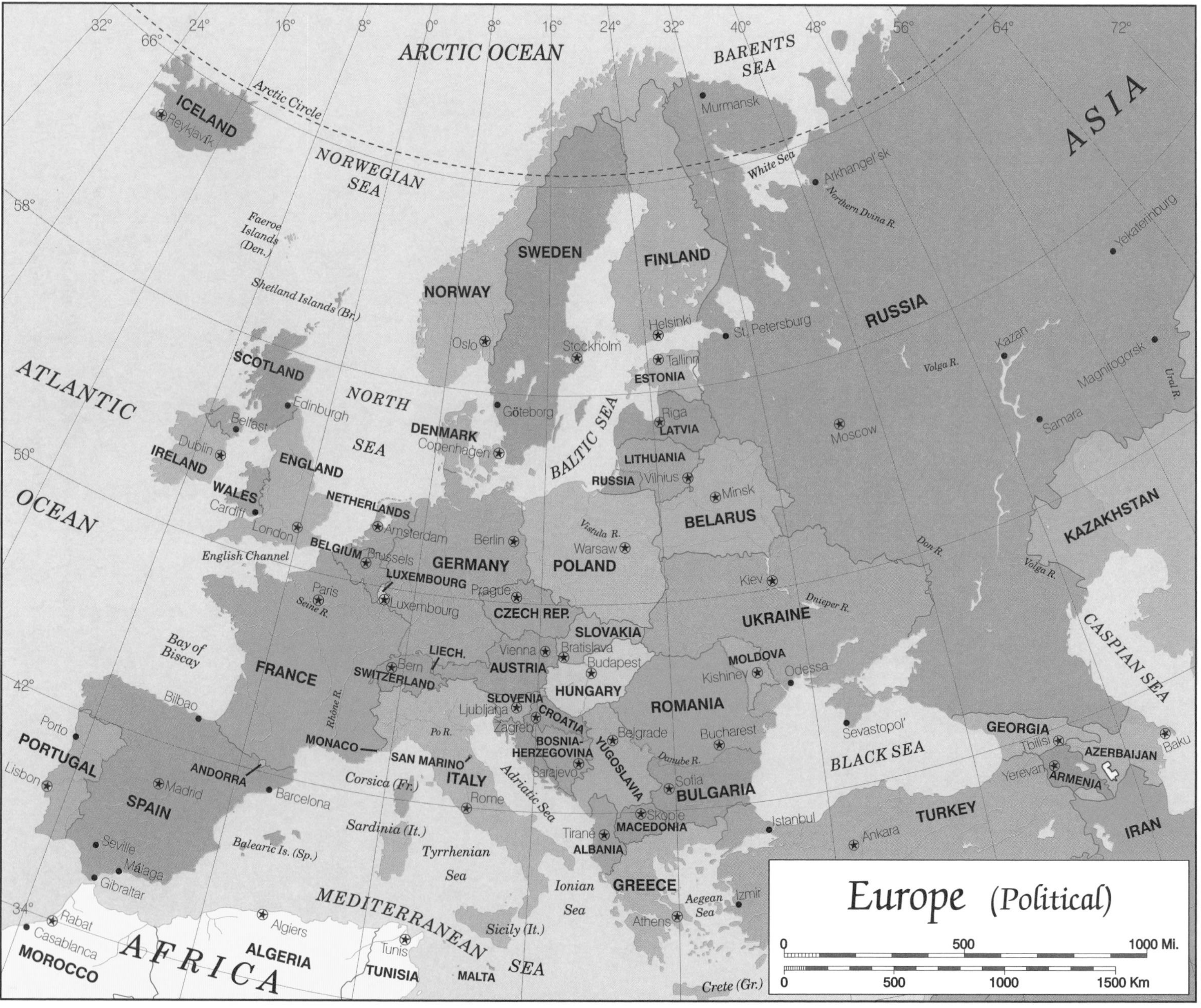
Europe (Political)
0
500
1000 Mi.
0
500
1000
1500 Km
ARCTIC OCEAN
BARENTS SEA
ASIA
Arctic Circle
NORWEGIAN SEA
White Sea
NORTH SEA
BALTIC SEA
ATLANTIC OCEAN
Bay of Biscay
English Channel
CASPIAN SEA
BLACK SEA
MEDITERRANEAN SEA
Tyrrhenian Sea
Ionian Sea
Adriatic Sea
Aegean Sea
AFRICA
ICELAND
Reykjavík
Faeroe Islands (Den.)
Shetland Islands (Br.)
IRELAND
Dublin
Belfast
SCOTLAND
Edinburgh
WALES
Cardiff
ENGLAND
London
NORWAY
Oslo
SWEDEN
Stockholm
Göteborg
FINLAND
Helsinki
DENMARK
Copenhagen
NETHERLANDS
Amsterdam
BELGIUM
Brussels
LUXEMBOURG
Luxembourg
GERMANY
Berlin
FRANCE
Paris
Seine R.
Rhône R.
MONACO
SWITZERLAND
Bern
LIECH.
AUSTRIA
Vienna
CZECH REP.
Prague
POLAND
Warsaw
Vistula R.
SLOVAKIA
Bratislava
HUNGARY
Budapest
SLOVENIA
Ljubljana
CROATIA
Zagreb
BOSNIA-HERZEGOVINA
Sarajevo
YUGOSLAVIA
Belgrade
MACEDONIA
Skopje
ALBANIA
Tiranë
GREECE
Athens
Crete (Gr.)
BULGARIA
Sofia
Danube R.
ROMANIA
Bucharest
MOLDOVA
Kishinev
UKRAINE
Kiev
Odessa
Dnieper R.
Sevastopol'
BELARUS
Minsk
LITHUANIA
Vilnius
RUSSIA
LATVIA
Riga
ESTONIA
Tallinn
RUSSIA
St. Petersburg
Moscow
Murmansk
Arkhangel'sk
Northern Dvina R.
Volga R.
Don R.
Volga R.
Ural R.
Kazan
Samara
Magnitogorsk
Yekaterinburg
KAZAKHSTAN
GEORGIA
Tbilisi
ARMENIA
Yerevan
AZERBAIJAN
Baku
IRAN
TURKEY
Ankara
Istanbul
Izmir
ITALY
Rome
Po R.
SAN MARINO
Corsica (Fr.)
Sardinia (It.)
Sicily (It.)
MALTA
SPAIN
Madrid
Barcelona
Bilbao
Seville
Málaga
Gibraltar
ANDORRA
Balearic Is. (Sp.)
PORTUGAL
Lisbon
Porto
MOROCCO
Rabat
Casablanca
ALGERIA
Algiers
TUNISIA
Tunis

Figure 2:1

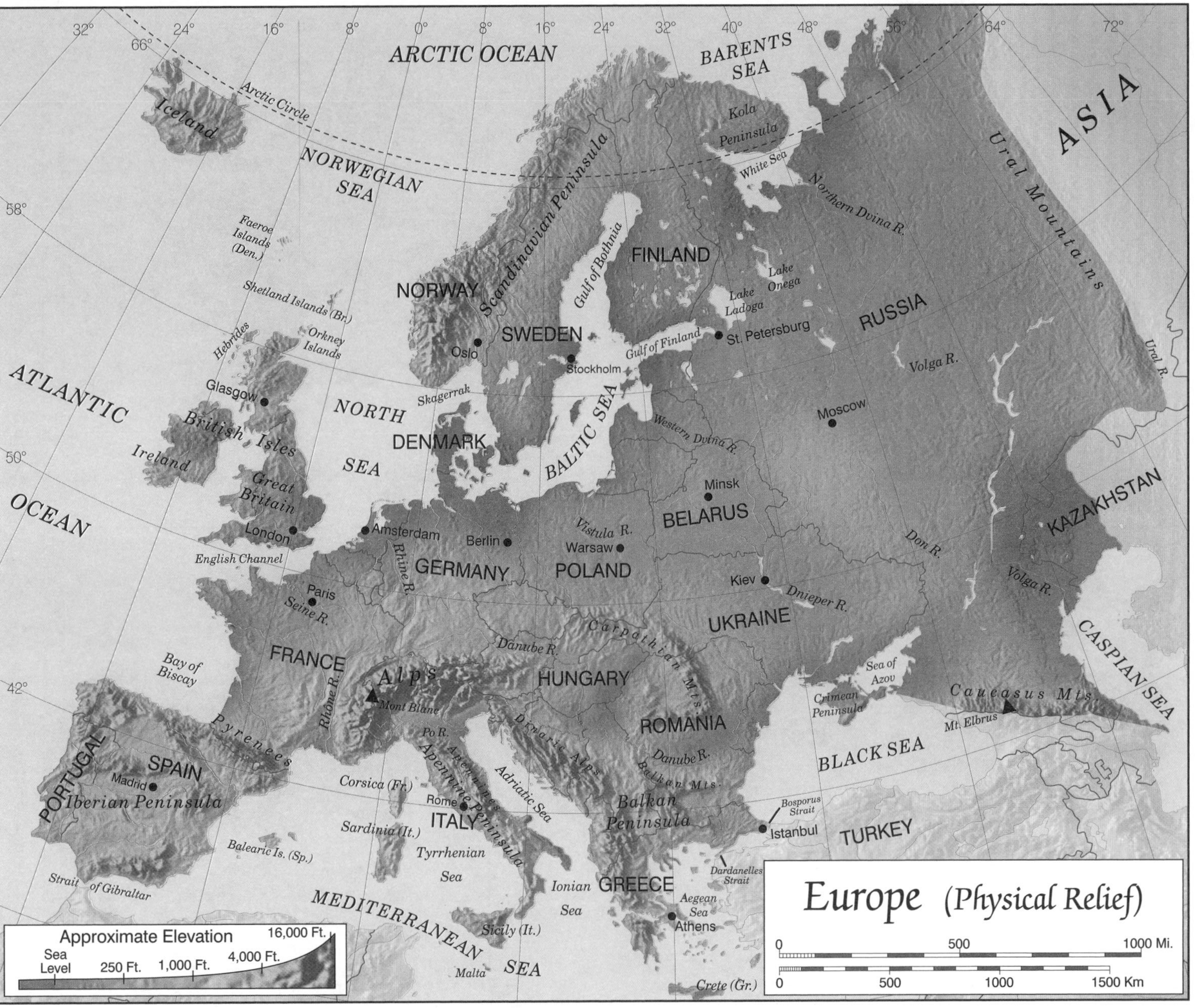
Europe (Physical Relief)
0 500 1000 Mi.
0 500 1000 1500 Km
Approximate Elevation
Sea Level
250 Ft.
1,000 Ft.
4,000 Ft.
16,000 Ft.
ASIA
ARCTIC OCEAN
BARENTS SEA
NORWEGIAN SEA
NORTH SEA
ATLANTIC OCEAN
BALTIC SEA
BLACK SEA
CASPIAN SEA
MEDITERRANEAN SEA
Adriatic Sea
Ionian Sea
Tyrrhenian Sea
Aegean Sea
Sea of Azov
White Sea
Bay of Biscay
English Channel
Skagerrak
Gulf of Bothnia
Gulf of Finland
Strait of Gibraltar
Bosporus Strait
Dardanelles Strait
Arctic Circle
Ural Mountains
Caucasus Mts.
Mt. Elbrus
Carpathian Mts.
Balkan Mts.
Dinaric Alps
Alps
Mont Blanc
Apennines
Pyrenees
Scandinavian Peninsula
Kola Peninsula
Crimean Peninsula
Balkan Peninsula
Apennine Peninsula
Iberian Peninsula
British Isles
Great Britain
Ireland
Iceland
Faeroe Islands (Den.)
Shetland Islands (Br.)
Orkney Islands
Hebrides
Corsica (Fr.)
Sardinia (It.)
Sicily (It.)
Malta
Crete (Gr.)
Balearic Is. (Sp.)
Lake Onega
Lake Ladoga
Ural R.
Volga R.
Don R.
Northern Dvina R.
Western Dvina R.
Dnieper R.
Vistula R.
Danube R.
Rhine R.
Rhone R.
Seine R.
Po R.
RUSSIA
KAZAKHSTAN
FINLAND
SWEDEN
NORWAY
DENMARK
BELARUS
UKRAINE
POLAND
GERMANY
HUNGARY
ROMANIA
TURKEY
GREECE
ITALY
FRANCE
SPAIN
PORTUGAL
Moscow
St. Petersburg
Minsk
Kiev
Warsaw
Stockholm
Oslo
Berlin
Amsterdam
London
Glasgow
Paris
Rome
Madrid
Athens
Istanbul
32°
24°
16°
8°
0°
8°
16°
24°
32°
40°
48°
56°
64°
72°
66°
58°
50°
42°

Figure 2:2

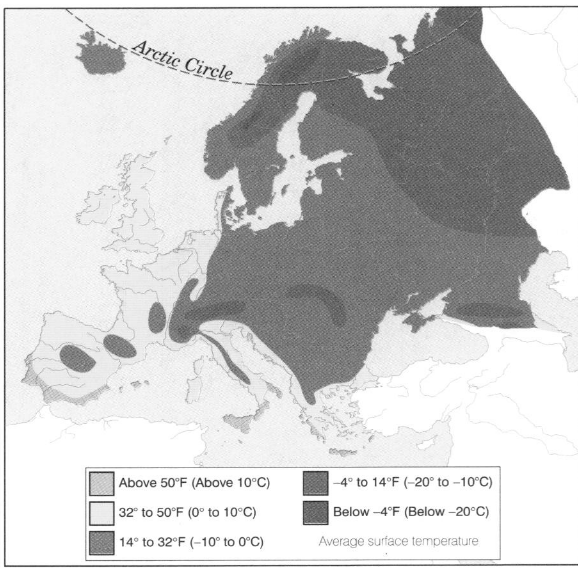

Figure 2:3. Average January Temperature

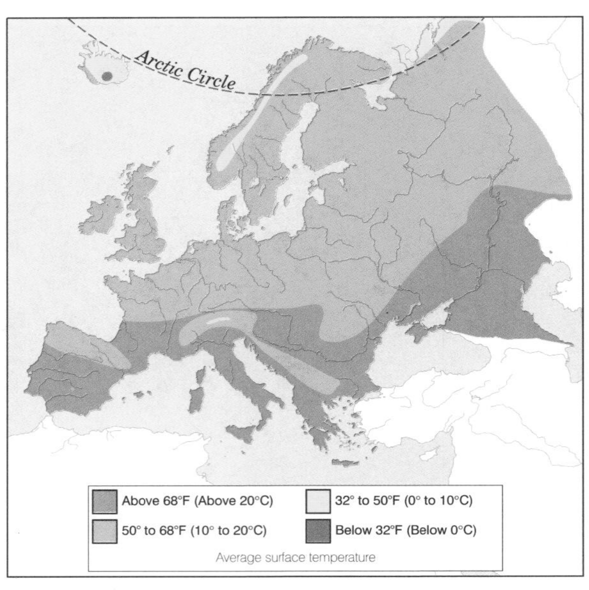

Figure 2:4. Average July Temperature

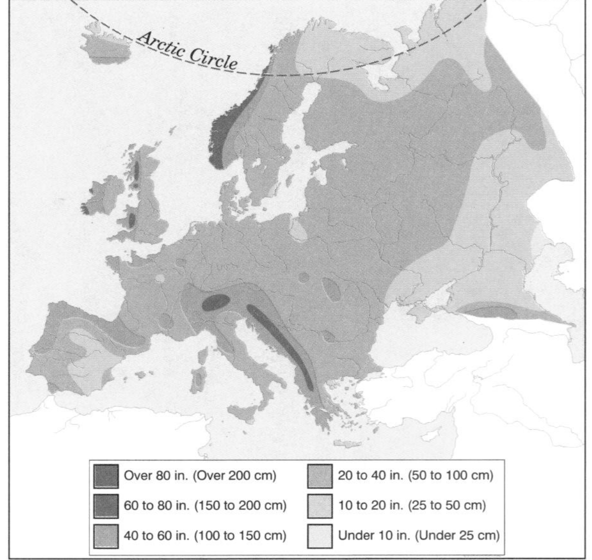

Figure 2:5. Average Annual Rainfall

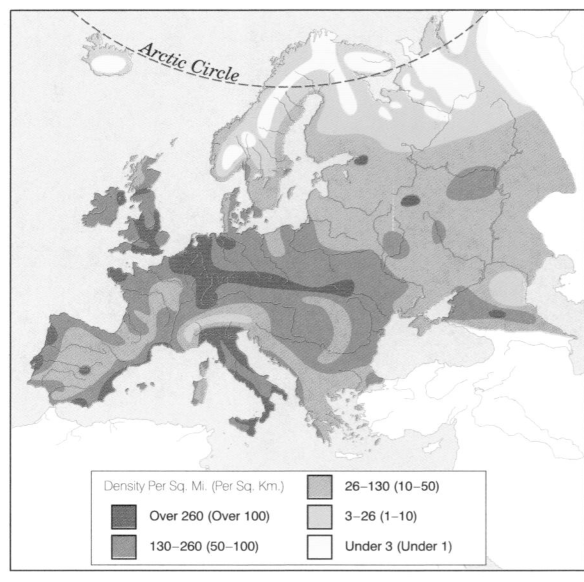

Figure 2:6. Population Distribution

EUROPE

Where Is Europe?

Europe is one of the smallest continents, yet its people and way of life have spread to many parts of the world. The location of Europe is one reason this happened. If you hold a globe so that you can see most of the world's land, Europe is in the center.

Europe lies between the Arctic Ocean in the north and the Mediterranean Sea in the south. It reaches from the Atlantic Ocean in the west to deep within Russia in the east.

Europe is close to Bible lands, where mankind began. The Gospel of Christ was first heard in Europe when the apostle Paul went to Philippi in Macedonia. Paul later visited other parts of Europe, such as Athens, Corinth, Rome, and possibly Spain. The Gospel spread throughout Europe and from there to America and around the world.

What Is Europe?

As you begin studying the continent of Europe, a small problem immediately turns up. Why is it called a continent? A glance at a map suggests that it is about as reasonable to call Europe a separate continent from Asia as to call Canada a separate continent from the United States. Sometimes Europe and Asia are considered as one huge continent called Eurasia.

Yet the division of Europe and Asia is reasonable. The people of Europe are so different in ***culture*** from the people of Asia that the two areas can properly be called two continents. Europe is considered part of the West, and its lifestyle, religion, and customs are called Western culture. The lifestyle, religion, and customs of Asia are called Eastern culture.

Dividing Europe from Asia is an old tradition. The ancient Greeks and Romans, not having accurate maps, thought that Europe and Asia were connected only by a narrow neck of land. Since that time, geographers have built on this two-continent idea, even drawing an official line along the Ural Mountains (YUR uhl) where they thought it seemed logical to divide the two.

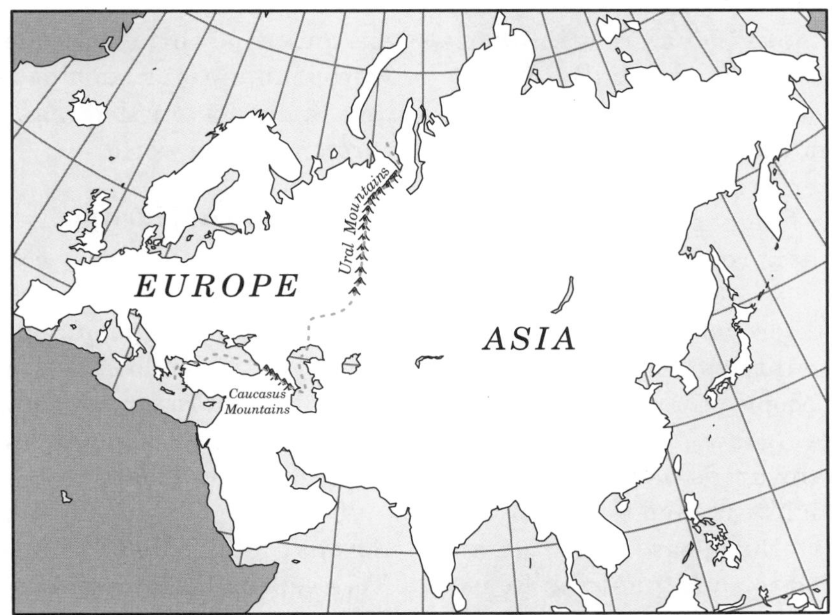

Figure 2:7 Eurasia

In London, crowded Piccadilly Road is a reminder that this important city was around long before the days of automobiles. The narrow, winding streets in the old section of the city are a driver's nightmare.

The entire city, called Greater London, covers about 620 square miles (1,606 sq. km) and houses around 8 million inhabitants. The ancient heart of the metropolis, called the City of London, is about 1 square mile (2.59 sq. km). About half a million people work daily in the great banks and financial centers that dominate this square mile.

Europeans have had a great influence on modern history, especially in the Americas. Most Americans have ancestors who came from Europe. It is from Europe that most Americans have received their customs, their languages, their religious beliefs, and their respect for individual freedom.

Europe is a crowded continent with many small countries. It has more than twice as many people per square mile as the world average. A few places are almost empty, but many areas have great cities, traffic-filled highways, and busy markets. Although most European countries are small compared to such giants as Russia and Canada, some of the small countries are quite powerful. In the past, small European nations such as Great Britain and Spain have ruled many other lands throughout the world.

The Shape of Europe

Europe is not an easy continent to picture in your mind. How much easier it is to remember the shape of South America or Africa! But if you look at a map of Europe, you will see a roughly triangular shape—broad to the east, and narrowing to a point toward the southwest.

The large, triangle-shaped peninsula of Europe contains many smaller peninsulas. Note especially four important ones: the Scandinavian (skan duh NAY vee uhn)

Peninsula, containing Norway and Sweden; the Iberian (eye BEER ee uhn) Peninsula, containing Spain and Portugal; the Balkan (BAWL kuhn) Peninsula, containing Greece, Bulgaria, and their neighbors; and the Apennine (AP uh nyn) Peninsula, containing the boot-shaped country of Italy.

Notice on the map the many islands God placed around Europe. Remember to look for Iceland, far to the northwest. In the Mediterranean Sea, locate Crete and Sicily (SIHS uh lee). Which European countries own them?

The islands most important in European history are the British Isles, which contain Ireland and the United Kingdom. (The United Kingdom includes England, Wales, Scotland, and Northern Ireland.) Being located on islands, these nations have a natural protection against invading armies. The narrow English Channel, separating England from France, has played an important part in a number of wars.

Some small European islands have also made their mark in history. During a severe storm on the Mediterranean, the apostle Paul was shipwrecked on Melita, now called Malta. The apostle John was banished to an island called Patmos, now belonging to Greece. There he received the visions recorded in the Book of Revelation.

Study Exercises

1. Why is it reasonable to study Europe and Asia separately?
2. Name four things that North American culture received from European culture.
3. (*a*) What mountains form the eastern boundary of Europe? (*b*) In what country are they?
4. Of the four European peninsulas mentioned, which one is (*a*) farthest to the east? (*b*) farthest to the north? (*c*) farthest to the west? (See a map of Europe.)
5. What large islands lie just far enough away from the mainland of Europe to help keep invading armies out, yet close enough for easy transportation and communication? (See a map of Europe.)

A small town in northwestern France nestles in the hillside along the English Channel.

Europe's Climate

God gave western Europe a mild, moist climate. A globe shows that much of Europe lies as far north as Canada. Yet western Europe has warmer temperatures than most of Canada does. A warm ocean current from the Caribbean Sea, called the ***North Atlantic Drift,*** flows across the Atlantic toward Europe. Winds in Europe are usually from the west. These west winds, warmed by the North Atlantic Drift, keep temperatures in western Europe moderate. Even Norway, whose shores stretch north beyond the Arctic Circle, does not have much trouble with ice in her harbors.

Farther inland the climate becomes more severe; the winters are colder, and the

In chilly, forested northern Finland, a reindeer sleigh caravan moves through the snow. Northern areas of European countries such as Finland have long summer days. At the northernmost point in Finland, continuous daylight lasts for about two and a half months during the summer, and continuous darkness for about two months during the winter.

summers are hotter. Russia is well known for having cold winters. Moscow (MAHS kow), the capital of Russia, has an average January temperature of 14°F (-10°C). In contrast to this, Edinburgh (EHD uhn bur uh), Scotland (a bit farther north), has an average January temperature of 38°F (3°C). The difference is that Moscow is far inland, while Edinburgh is warmed by the North Atlantic Drift.

The climate of Europe also is drier farther inland. The broad ***steppes*** (STEHPS) of Russia have just enough rain for wheat, and some parts are too dry even for wheat.

The climate along the Mediterranean Sea is entirely different from that in the rest of Europe. In parts of Spain, France, Italy, and Greece, the winters are rainy and warm, and the summers are hot and dry. The growing season for grain is during winter, and harvest comes in early summer! This type of climate is called a ***Mediterranean climate*** because it is found in lands along the Mediterranean Sea, including Bible lands.

In autumn, a farmer in south-central Spain levels the rough ground in his field, preparing to plant a crop and take advantage of the winter rains.

Norway is known for its beautiful mountains, coasts, and rivers. Because of the mountainous, forested terrain and the cool climate, agriculture only accounts for about 4 percent of the nation's economy. Most of the farms lie in narrow inland valleys or along the coast. In order to supplement their income, many farmers are also loggers or fishermen.

Europe's Highland and Lowland Regions

God created a complex array of mountains, valleys, and plains in Europe. Yet if you look at a map that shows the landforms of Europe, you can see three main regions: northern mountains, central plains, and southern mountains.

The Northern Mountains. First notice the northern hills and mountains. A range of mountains runs most of the length of Norway and Sweden, through the western part of the Scandinavian Peninsula (The term *Scandinavia* usually refers to Norway, Sweden, and Denmark.). Similar, smaller hills are in Scotland, England, and Wales, just across the North Sea.

Norway is famous for the long, crooked fingers of the sea called ***fiords*** (FYAWRDZ) that reach in among the coastal mountains. Norway's longest fiord is more than 100 miles (160 km) long. The fiords make good harbors—especially since they remain free of ice all year. Norway is one of the great shipping and fishing countries of the world.

The mountain streams of Norway and Sweden provide ***hydroelectricity*** for power-hungry industries that ***smelt*** metal and make chemicals. Sweden produces high-quality steel for products such as ball bearings and precision instruments.

Evergreen forests, which are also known as ***coniferous*** (koh NIHF ur uhs) forests, cover much of Norway and Sweden. Logging is an important industry in these countries.

The British Isles are even milder than Norway. Though Ireland is as far north as Labrador, Canada, it has little snow during the winter. Warm winds from off the North Atlantic Drift are full of moisture, bringing many rainy days to the islands. Only in the higher mountains of Scotland is there much snowfall. The mild, rainy climate of the British Isles encourages grass to grow for grazing.

The Central Plain. This is the most important and most densely populated part of Europe. The plain begins in France along the Atlantic Ocean. It extends north and east, narrowing to about 50 miles (80 km) in Belgium, and then becoming broader again farther east.

Moving slowly across Europe's central plain, combines harvest wheat. With its wheat, corn, and potato production, the central plain somewhat resembles the American Midwest.

WHEAT

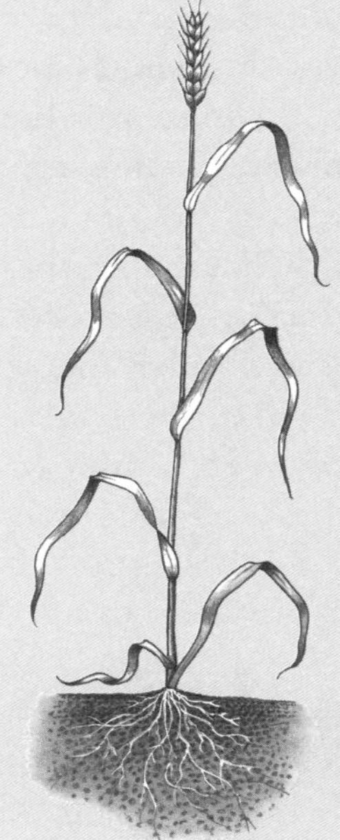

To many, wheat is the most important food plant in the world. It has been grown since ancient times and is mentioned often in the Bible. Wheat is an annual cereal grass that is highly nutritious, can tolerate a wide range of growing conditions, and has grain that is quite easy to harvest and store.

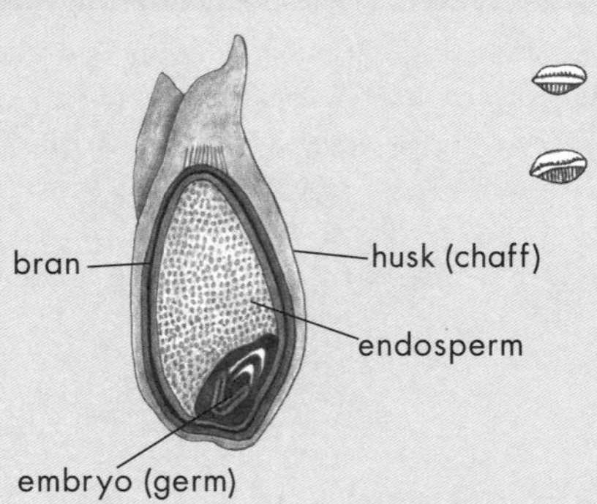

Wheat usually produces an even number of grains (an average of fifty) on each hollow stalk. On poor ground, a wheat plant may only produce one stalk, with perhaps fifty or less grains in the seed head. But on good ground, a plant can produce from six to twelve stalks, each with a full seed head. The parable of the sower illustrates this: "But other fell into good ground, and brought forth fruit, some an hundredfold, some sixtyfold, some thirtyfold" (Matthew 13:8). Crossbreeding wheat varieties that have desirable characteristics has produced new strains that mature in a shorter time, have a higher yield, and have resistance to wheat diseases.

Winter wheats (usually soft wheats) are planted in autumn in areas that are generally humid and do not have severely cold winters. The wheat comes up, but does not grow much until spring. It is harvested in early summer. Spring wheats (usually hard wheats) are sown as early as possible in the spring in dry areas where winter wheat plants would freeze.

More of the world's farmland is used to grow wheat than to grow any other crop: an estimated 570,000,000 acres (230,000,000 hectares) are sown annually. China, India, France, Russia, and Turkey are leading wheat producers in the Old World.

Of the fourteen main types of wheat, three of the most important types (and main uses) are: common (bread), durum (pasta), and club (cakes, crackers, pies, and more). Each type has many varieties. Wheats are classified as *hard* or *soft* wheats. Hard wheats are good for making bread, for they have more gluten (protein) in their grains than soft wheats. Gluten gives the elastic quality to bread dough, which produces a high, light loaf. Soft wheats are best for pies, cakes, biscuits, and cookies. Compare the uses and amount of protein of wheat flours on the chart.

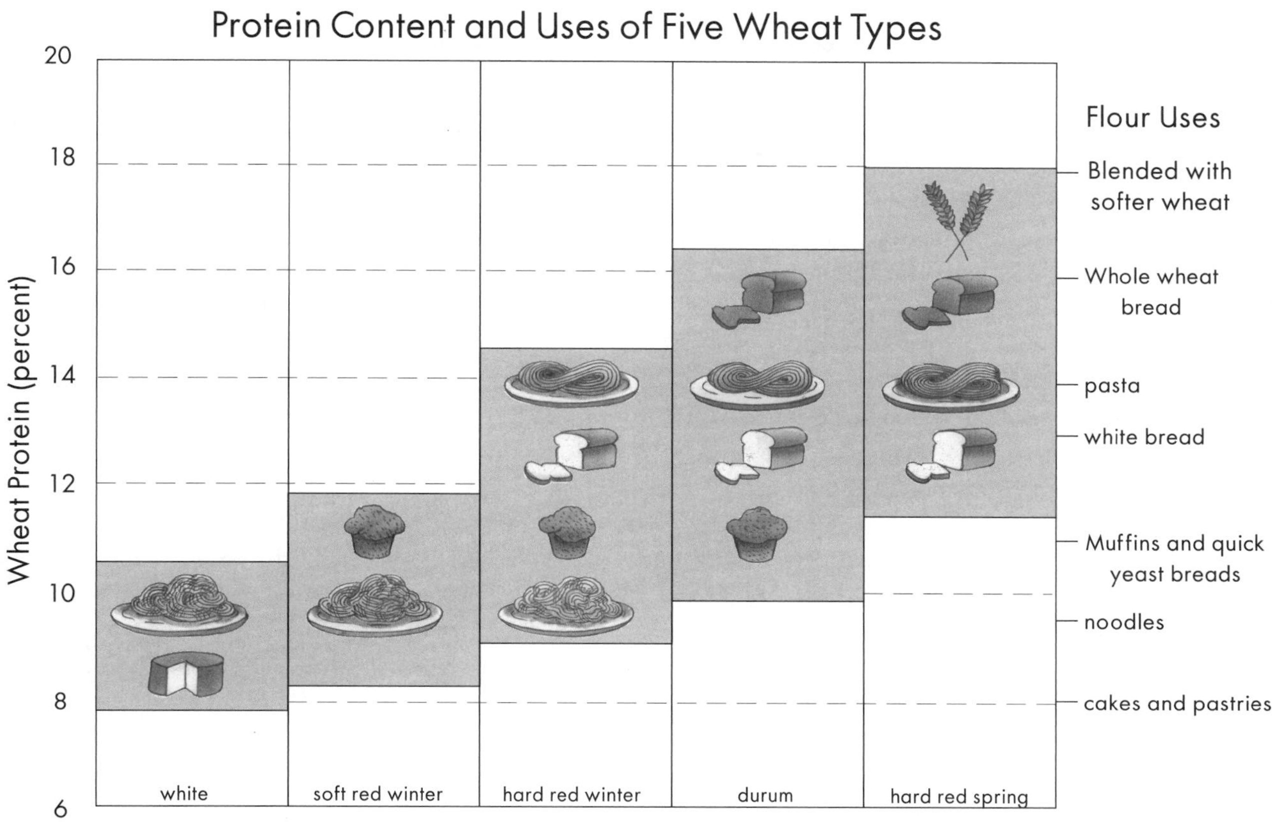

The central plain passes through the Netherlands, Denmark, Germany, Poland, Belarus (BEHL uh roos), and other nearby countries; and it ends at the Ural Mountains deep in Russia. At this eastern edge its width is more than 1,500 miles (2,410 km) from north to south and includes most of eastern Russia. On the plains lie grassy meadows and fields of wheat, potatoes, and vegetables.

Good farmland is not the only thing that attracts people to the central plain. Rich deposits of coal and iron ore have been discovered in this region. Factories use these minerals to make steel and steel products. Many other goods are also manufactured there.

Good transportation is another advantage of the plains. Roads and railroads can be built almost anywhere. Deep, broad rivers flow slowly along, making good highways for heavy loads. Where there are no rivers, canals can be dug.

The central plain offers so many advantages that big cities have grown up there, especially in the narrow western part. You have probably heard of Paris, Amsterdam, and Berlin. The broad eastern part of the plain is not nearly as densely populated, but it is still an important region with some large cities, including Moscow. Because of its importance, the central plain is sometimes called the Heart of Europe.

The Southern Mountains. To the south of the plains lie hills, and farther south, the snow-capped Alps. When most people think of the Alps, they think first of Switzerland and perhaps of her most famous mountain peak, the Matterhorn. But Switzerland's neighbors, such as Austria, contain Alps too. France has the highest peak of the Alps—Mont Blanc (mawn BLAHN), 15,771 feet high (4,807 m). Through this mountain runs the longest highway tunnel in the world, having a length of 7.2 miles (11.6 km).

Scenic farms nestle in the Alpine valleys. During the summer, goats graze in steep meadows above the tree line. But the rugged, cool Alps are not very good for farming. The people earn more by taking advantage of their tumbling rivers to produce hydroelectricity. They make small, finely crafted products such as watches in their factories.

The Alps make up only a part of the huge mountain system that God formed across southern Europe. The southern ranges include the Pyrenees (PIHR uh neez) that separate France from Spain, the Apennines (AP uh nynz) in Italy, the jumble of mountain chains in the Balkan Peninsula, and even the Caucasus Mountains (KAW kuh suhs) far to the east between the Black Sea and the Caspian Sea. Mount Elbrus (EHL broos), the highest mountain in Europe, is in the Caucasus range. Its peak rises 18,510 feet (5,642 m) above sea level. Throughout southern Europe there are many plains and hilly areas too—not just mountains.

During much of history, the Alps formed a massive barrier separating various regions of Europe from each other. They even hemmed in the Roman Empire for a while until the Romans built roads through them. Today, with modern roads and tunnels, people can easily travel through the Alps.

Study Exercises

6. Explain why western Europe has warmer temperatures than other lands at the same latitude.
7. In general, the climate is (drier, wetter) and (more, less) severe farther inland in Europe.
8. If an area is too dry for most grains, what grain might farmers try to grow?
9. What are the four most important industries in the northern mountain region of Europe?
10. Name three advantages of the central plains.
11. How did the Alps affect the settlement of Europe?

The snow-capped peak of the Matterhorn rises 14,692 feet (4,478 m) above sea level on the border between Switzerland and Italy.

From the 800s to the 1500s, remnants of Bible-believing people who tried to escape persecution lived in cool valleys high in the Alps. Among them were people called Waldenses. Some Waldenses fought their persecutors, but others peacefully gave their lives for their faith. Many of their persecutors lost their lives as they pursued the Christians in the cold and rugged mountains.

Rye

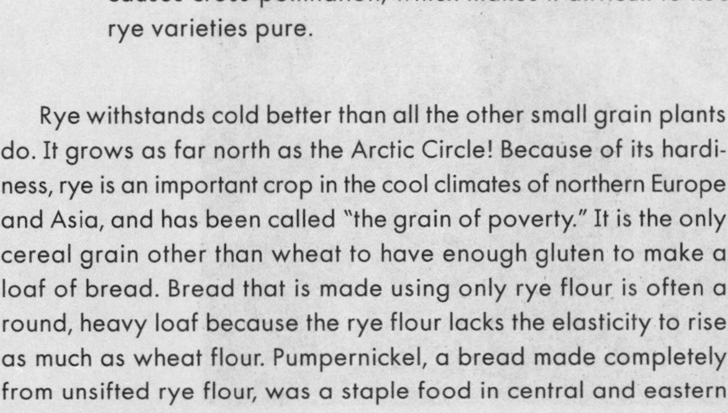

Rye (spelled *rie* in the Bible) has been grown since ancient times and ranks second to wheat as a bread flour. The dark-colored grains grow in pairs on slender seed spikes with long, stiff awns (also called beards) and are threshed like wheat. One difference between rye and some of the other cereal grains is the fact that rye flowers open for pollination. Their pollen is spread by the wind. This causes cross-pollination, which makes it difficult to keep rye varieties pure.

Rye withstands cold better than all the other small grain plants do. It grows as far north as the Arctic Circle! Because of its hardiness, rye is an important crop in the cool climates of northern Europe and Asia, and has been called "the grain of poverty." It is the only cereal grain other than wheat to have enough gluten to make a loaf of bread. Bread that is made using only rye flour is often a round, heavy loaf because the rye flour lacks the elasticity to rise as much as wheat flour. Pumpernickel, a bread made completely from unsifted rye flour, was a staple food in central and eastern Europe for centuries. Because of its dark brown color, it is called black bread. The familiar, lighter-colored rye bread contains a mixture of rye, wheat, and other flours.

Pumpernickel (bread)

Rye bread

Rye protects the soil when grown as a cover crop; as a green manure crop, it improves the soil. In Europe, people eat most of the rye crop, whereas in North America much of the rye crop is fed to livestock. However, Europeans often use rye hay and milling by-products in mixed animal feed. Rye straw has many uses: as packing material, for stuffing mattresses, and to make paper, mats, and straw hats. Also, rye straw is preferred for thatched roofs because decay is less rapid for rye thatch than for thatch made from most other kinds of straw.

Rye grain is often destroyed by a poisonous fungus called ergot. A horn-like blackish body replaces the grain, and poisons livestock and people who eat the infected rye or a food made from it. However, ergot has been used to make a valuable drug to help people, not hurt or kill them.

Ergot fungus on rye stalk

Over one-third of the world's rye is grown in Russia and Ukraine. Poland, Germany, and Belarus are also important rye-producing nations.

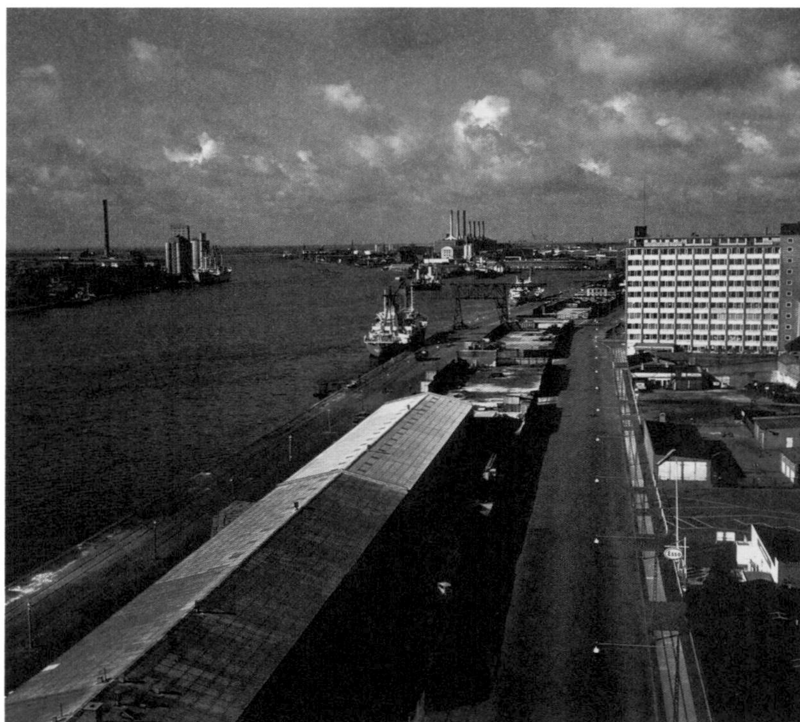

Through its busy harbors, small, productive Denmark sends breakfast to millions of Europeans. Denmark is one of the world's largest exporters of meats, butter, eggs, and cheese. Textiles, clothing, and chemical products are also important exports. Copenhagen is pictured here.

Europe's Waterways

God blessed Europe with many waterways. Because the coastline of Europe is so crooked, no place in western Europe is more than 500 miles (800 km) from a sea. The many bays and gulfs along the coastline make good seaports. Businessmen and traders can easily transport goods to and from these ports.

Notice on the map in Figure 2:1 that nearly all the countries of Europe have good access to the ocean. The Baltic Sea reaches deep into the continent, giving the northern countries an outlet to the Atlantic Ocean. The countries of southern Europe border the Mediterranean Sea. From there, ships can sail out to the Atlantic Ocean. Ships can also sail from the Black Sea into the Mediterranean Sea, and out into the Atlantic Ocean.

The ***straits*** of Europe have also played an important part in history. The country that controls a strait can regulate the shipping that goes through it, and can even require ships to pay a toll. For hundreds of years, Denmark did just that to ships sailing from the North Sea to the Baltic Sea. England controls Gibraltar (juh BRAWL tur), the strait between the Mediterranean Sea and the Atlantic Ocean.

The Bosporus (BAHS pur uhs) and

The Rock of Gibraltar dominates a small, narrow peninsula on Spain's southern Mediterranean coast. About 30,000 people live there and make their living mainly from tourism and by servicing many ships that pass through the narrow strait which connects the Atlantic Ocean and the Mediterranean Sea.

A barge travels on the Rhine River between terraced slopes dotted with ancient castles and towns. The river also flows through heavily industrialized areas that take advantage of cheap water transportation to ship their products. Barges must be narrow to navigate the many canals that connect the Rhine to other European waterways.

Dardanelles (dahr duhn EHLZ), controlled by Turkey, are straits connecting the Black Sea with the Mediterranean. Romania, Bulgaria, Ukraine (yoo KRAYN), and Russia must use these straits to reach the Mediterranean Sea and the Atlantic Ocean.

The river with the heaviest traffic is the Rhine in northern Europe. Barges haul coal, iron ore, grain, and lumber up and down the river or turn into the canals that join

Leaving London on the Thames River, a British naval ship passes under the famous Tower Bridge.

it. The Rhine gives Switzerland and parts of France and Germany a highway to the Atlantic.

The Danube (DAN yoob) begins not far from where the Rhine begins. Instead of flowing northward, it flows eastward through the central and eastern European countries of Austria, Hungary, Yugoslavia (yoo goh SLAH vee uh), Romania, and even the corner of Slovakia (sloh VAH kee uh). It also forms part of the boundary of Bulgaria, Croatia, and Ukraine. (As a memory device, note that most of these countries end with *ia*.) The Danube has been deepened so that large boats can travel from far inland to the Black Sea.

The longest European river is the Volga (VAHL guh) in Russia. It flows into the Caspian Sea. Since the Caspian Sea has no outlet to the ocean, canals have been dug to let boats travel from the Volga to the Black Sea in the south and to the Baltic Sea in the north.

Other rivers that are not as long, but are well known, include the Thames (TEHMZ) that flows through London, and the Seine (SAYN) that flows through Paris.

France, Germany, and their neighbors have a large network of canals that connect rivers and cities to each other. For example, riverboats can travel up the Rhine River, pass through canals to the Danube River, and sail into the Black Sea.

Study Exercises

12. (*a*) What sea reaches far into northwestern Europe, giving access to the Atlantic? (*b*) What two seas do the same for southern Europe?
13. Why is it an advantage for a country to control a strait?
14. (*a*) Into what body of water does the Rhine River flow? (*b*) the Danube?

Europe's Natural Resources

Europe's natural resources are not as plentiful as they once were. The population of Europe has been high for many years, and the people have used up many of the natural resources that God placed on the continent. But today Europeans are being more careful with their resources than they had been in the past.

Forests. At one time, most of Europe was covered with forests. Now many of the forests are gone—cleared for fields or paved with city streets. Some countries have noticed their forests diminishing and have taken steps to preserve what they have left. Norway, Sweden, and Finland are good examples of this. They manage their forests carefully and make sure they grow as much wood in their forests as they cut down. A vast belt of evergreen trees, called the ***taiga*** (TY guh), stretches across Russia. Large areas of this forest have barely been touched.

Minerals. Some of Europe's most important minerals are coal, iron ore, and ***bauxite*** (BAWK syt). England and Germany, having both coal and iron ore, are big steel producers. These minerals helped them to become great industrial powers.

Nearby nations also produce steel, but most of them do not have both coal and iron ore in large amounts. France, for example, has large deposits of iron ore, but needs to import some of the coal it uses. Most European nations must import either coal or iron ore for their factories.

Europeans also import much of the petroleum that they need. However, after oil was discovered in the North Sea during the 1960s, Europeans became more self-sufficient in this natural resource than they had been.

Fishing. Like northeastern North America, Europe has a broad ***continental shelf*** along its shoreline. Many fish feed and spawn in this shallow water. Western Europeans catch more fish than North Americans catch along all their shores put together.

Industry in Europe

Some countries in northern and western Europe are involved in ***heavy industry.*** Heavy industry is the manufacture of large products from steel, such as cars, trucks, locomotives, and machinery. France, England, Germany, Poland, and Russia have much heavy industry. They have either the iron ore or coal, or both, that it takes to produce steel. An area called the Ruhr in Germany has high-grade coal and many factories. The whole Ruhr area resembles one huge city, and it contains one of the greatest concentrations of industry in the world.

Car manufacturers in Europe send their products around the world. People in almost any country might drive a Volvo made in Sweden, a Fiat made in Italy, a Renault made in France, or a Volkswagen made in Germany.

If car manufacturing is heavy industry, what is ***light industry***? Light industry is the production of goods such as food, ***textiles,*** and electrical appliances. The Netherlands, Belgium, and Switzerland specialize in light industry.

Of course a country with heavy industry has some light industry too, and vice versa. Belgium, for example, produces much iron and steel. Paris is known for producing luxuries and fashionable clothes, but it is also the most important car manufacturing center in France. Germany and England, which have much heavy industry, also employ thousands of people to work in light industry.

The greatest amount of industry is found in the countries of northwestern Europe. Eastern and southern Europe are less industrialized. More people farm in southern Europe, yet even the farm production

Europeans produce a great variety of goods. A few are shown here: electric locomotives, watches, cars, tractors, food products, appliances, textiles, clothing, and carpets.

there is not as great as in northern Europe. One reason is that farmers in northwestern Europe use more modern machinery.

But there are some exceptions to this general observation. Italy, in southern Europe, is a great industrial country. And Russia, in eastern Europe, is the biggest industrial giant of all Europe. The less developed countries of southern and eastern Europe are working to catch up. They have more industry now than they had thirty years ago.

Study Exercises

15. Name a natural resource that Europeans used up too rapidly at one time but that they have learned to manage carefully.
16. What is heavy industry?
17. In what general area of Europe can many highly industrialized countries be found?
18. How is Italy an exception to this fact (number 17)?

What About Farming?

Because Europe is crowded, Europeans farm every acre of cropland as well as they can to get as much food from it as possible. This is especially true in northern and western Europe.

Farmers in Europe have much less land than North American farmers do. The average farm in western Europe has about 30 acres (12 ha), while the average farm in the United States has more than 450 acres (182 ha). European farmers fertilize their land to keep the soil productive. They rotate their crops, not raising the same crop on the same field year after year. Working hard on a few acres, farmers in western Europe usually raise more per acre than farmers do in North America.

Many farmers in Europe live in villages instead of living on farmland. Their farmland surrounds the village, and they travel out to their land every day to do their work. This settlement pattern dates from the days when people lived together for protection from their enemies. Even today it has the advantage of making it easier for people to work together on their farms.

Europe does not have a corn belt as the United States does. Wheat is Europe's most important crop, especially in some eastern countries like the Ukraine. But wheat will not grow well in northern Europe, where summers are cool and the soil is poor. Farmers in these areas must raise crops that can grow in cool weather and poor soil, such as rye, oats, barley, or potatoes. Many people in Poland, Russia, and nearby countries eat dark bread made from rye. In Ireland, Germany, Poland, and Norway, potatoes are as important to people as grains.

Many farmers in northern Europe also raise animals, which can make use of the fodder crops and grass that grow well there. Butter, cheese, bacon, and wool come from countries like the United Kingdom, Ireland, Denmark, and the Netherlands.

Not surprisingly, some of the popular breeds of American livestock come from Europe. Suffolk horses and Yorkshire hogs are both named for the counties in England where they originated. Holstein cattle come from the Holstein district of Germany, and Jerseys come from tiny Jersey Island in the English Channel. Can you guess where Brown Swiss cattle come from?

The farms in some countries are especially colorful. Some Dutch farmers raise fields of tulips and sell the flower bulbs. In Bulgaria, farmers raise fields of roses that are used to make perfume.

Farmers that live near large cities often raise vegetables such as cabbages, potatoes, and carrots. They can easily sell them because of the many people living nearby. Early in the season, when vegetables are

Colorful fields of flowers cover the countryside near Haarlem in the Netherlands. Haarlem is a major trading center for flower-bulbs.

Lands in southern Europe are not as green or as forested as northern Europe. These dry, rolling pastures in northern Spain look much like some of the North American Great Plains, or like some areas in central Africa.

Oats

Oats are not mentioned in the Bible, perhaps because they grow in cooler climates than the Bible lands have. Oats are second only to rye in the ability to survive in poor soils. Before World War I, the world oat crop was larger than the world wheat crop, but wheat production has surpassed oat production since then. However, oats are still a favorite grain in Scotland. The story is told of an Englishman traveling in Scotland who met a Scot carrying a bag of oats. The Englishman said, "In England we use those for feeding horses, but in Scotland they are eaten by men." "Yes," replied the Scot. "No doubt that is why in England you have such fine horses, and in Scotland we have such fine men."

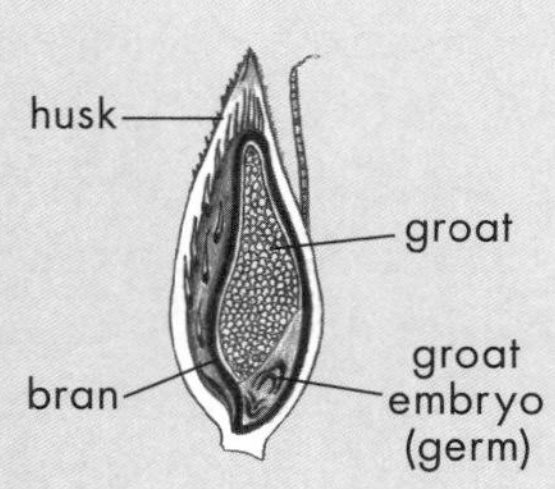

The oat plant is different from most other cereal grains because each grain hangs down on a thread-like attachment from a branching head instead of the grains growing in a close seed head. Also, oats put out such long, branching roots that scientists have proved that if all the root parts of a single oat plant were to be joined into one long strand, the strand would reach over 150 feet (46 m)!

Oats have a higher food value than any other cereal grain, and contain more oil than any cereal grain but corn. After the husk is removed (for human consumption) the kernel is called a groat. When flattened, groats are the familiar rolled oats that are often eaten as a breakfast food such as oatmeal or ready-to-eat cereals. Oat flour is used to make pancakes, cookies, and puddings. Most of the world's oat crop (husks left on) is used for animal feed. Oats are the best grain to feed horses.

Like wheat, farmers plant either spring oats or winter oats, depending on climate. Spring oats are the most common type. Oat plants provide good hay and silage. The straw is used for animal feed and bedding. The leading Old World oat-producing countries are Russia, Sweden, France, Ukraine, Poland, and Finland.

not yet ready in northern Europe, farmers in southern Europe send their vegetables north, just as is done in North America.

In the southernmost part of Europe, lands with a Mediterranean climate have no thick forests of broad-leaved trees or lush fields of vegetables (except where they are irrigated). Here and there, leathery-leaved trees dot the countryside. Olives and figs grow well, just as in Bible lands, and so do oranges and other citrus fruits. France, Italy, and Spain are well known for their grapes.

Study Exercises

19. Why do farmers in western Europe produce more per acre, on the average, than farmers in the United States?
20. Name four crops (other than grass) that a farmer could raise if his climate is too cool and damp for wheat.
21. The type of vegetation growing along the Mediterranean Sea tells us something about the climate. Is it mainly wet or mainly dry?

Trade in Europe

Most countries of Europe do not have enough land or resources to produce all the food and raw materials they need. They must buy goods from their neighbors. They must sell other goods to buy what they need.

England, for example, has far too little farmland to feed her many people. The people work in factories to produce goods to sell. This provides them with money to buy food from other countries. England's factories themselves depend on imported raw materials. Cotton and wool from other parts of the world supply her big textile factories.

Other European countries also depend on each other. In some ways the European countries would feel more secure if they had their own raw materials and could raise their own food. Then if other nations said "We do not like what you are doing, so we will not sell you our goods anymore," they could still live comfortably. As it is, the various countries must work hard to keep peace among themselves.

A number of European nations have joined in a trade association called the European Community, or the European Common Market. They have agreed to do away with taxes on goods that come into their countries from other members of the European Common Market. This free trade has helped to keep prices low because customers do not have to pay an added tax on their purchases. More goods flow from country to country because of this trade agreement.

Besides trading among themselves, the nations of Europe also trade with countries in other parts of the world.

Europe's Many Cultures

Europe is a continent of many cultures. In the United States and Canada there are only two official languages (French and English), but in Europe there are dozens of languages. Many languages also have several dialects (local forms of the same language).

One reason for this is that Europe was settled long ago when travel was slow. There were no automobiles or trains or modern bridges and tunnels. Mountain ranges made travel difficult. People mostly stayed where they had settled. Each community developed a language and culture quite different from those in nearby countries, or even in the next valley.

With different languages and customs,

Much of the farmland in Poland was owned by the government during the years of communist rule. Now this farmer can grow and sell his own crop of potatoes without government interference. Such farmers are willing to work hard to improve their land for future crops, even though they do not have much modern machinery.

it was easy for the peoples of Europe to misunderstand and distrust each other. Down through the centuries, Europeans have fought many wars with each other. World War I and World War II, the two worst wars in history, began in Europe.

Yet in some ways the people of Europe are similar. Most have light-colored skin. Most can read and write. (This contrasts with some countries in other parts of the world, where only one or two out of ten people can read and write.) Most Europeans have enough to eat and wear, and they live in comfortable houses. Many Europeans make their living by working in businesses or factories. If they farm, they do it to earn money, not just to raise food for themselves. All this sets them apart from people in other places who live in poverty and farm only to feed their own families.

One of the most serious divisions among Europeans during the 1900s was the ***Iron Curtain.*** This guarded border separated the free countries of western Europe from the ***communist*** countries of eastern Europe. The Soviet Union (made up of Russia and fourteen other republics) was the biggest communist country, and it controlled most of the smaller ones nearby. These smaller communist countries were called ***satellite*** countries. In the 1950s and 1960s, the people of East Germany, Hungary, Poland, and Czechoslovakia (now the Czech Republic and Slovakia) each tried to gain more freedom, but Soviet tanks and soldiers overpowered them.

Christians living in communist countries endured additional trials. Although communist governments usually claimed to allow religious freedom, they placed many restrictions on the worship of God. Communists promote atheism—the belief that there is no God. Christians often were not allowed freedom to hold church services or to have Christian schools.

Part of the former Iron Curtain, this fence between former East and West Germany demonstrated the measures that communist leaders took to keep their people from escaping to other countries. Many people tried to escape anyway. Some made it to freedom, and some lost their lives. True Christians are always free, no matter how the world treats them. "If the Son therefore shall make you free, ye shall be free indeed" (John 8:36).

The communists failed in their efforts to stop the worship of God. Hundreds of people in communist countries continued to worship in secret. Many went to prison rather than give up their faith. These believers could enjoy peace in their hearts and freedom from sin, even if their bodies were imprisoned and tortured.

Finally, in the late 1980s, the Soviet Union leaders began allowing great political changes to take place in the satellite countries, and even within the Soviet Union itself. Soon the communist governments were replaced with governments promising more freedoms. Communist leaders who had seemed strong suddenly lost their power, and some even lost their lives. The Soviet Union was broken up into Russia and many smaller countries. But the Word of God, which the communists tried to suppress for almost seventy years, is still as true and powerful as ever.

Jesus told His disciples, "Ye shall be hated of all nations for my name's sake" (Matthew 24:9). Only God knows how much Christians in Europe, North America, and the rest of the world might need to suffer in the future. But we should remember that Jesus also said, "Blessed are they which are persecuted for righteousness' sake: for theirs is the kingdom of heaven" (Matthew 5:10).

Study Exercises

22. How does the European Common Market help to keep prices lower?
23. Name two ways in which Europeans differ from each other and two ways in which they are similar.
24. For many years, what kept the small communist countries of eastern Europe from becoming free countries?
25. Why did communists try to hinder the worship of God?

Clinching the Chapter

Use the text and maps to complete these exercises.

Multiple Choice

A. *Choose the country* least *associated with the first item.*

1. Central plain: Hungary, Belgium, Poland, Belarus
2. Coniferous forests: Norway, Finland, Spain, Russia
3. Alps: Switzerland, Ireland, France, Austria
4. Mediterranean Sea: Italy, Spain, Greece, Poland
5. Heavy industry: Poland, Russia, Albania, Germany
6. Black Sea: Russia, Romania, Slovakia, Bulgaria
7. Rhine: Switzerland, France, Portugal, the Netherlands
8. Baltic Sea: Romania, Finland, Sweden, Lithuania
9. Potatoes: Ireland, Norway, Poland, Italy
10. Olives and figs: Spain, Italy, Russia, Greece

B. *Write the correct words.*

1. Which part of the United Kingdom is separated from the rest by water? (England, Northern Ireland, Wales, Scotland)
2. Which word does not name a peninsula? (Iberian, Balkan, Scandinavian, Hungarian)
3. Which is least common in Europe's central plain? (cities, factories, sawmills, canals)
4. Which do we associate least with mountains? (goats, factories, hydroelectricity, large farms)
5. Which is the highest mountain in Europe? (Elbrus, Matterhorn, Mont Blanc, Jungfrau)
6. Which is a product of light industry? (ice cream, cars, trucks, locomotives)
7. Which term does not describe the farms of northwestern Europe? (small, productive, Mediterranean climate, cool summers)
8. What does England export? (wool, cotton, food, textiles)

9. What part of Europe has its growing season in the winter? (northern, southern, eastern, western)
10. What did the former communist governments of Europe restrict? (atheism, the Iron Curtain, worship of God, Russian soldiers)

Matching

A. *For each clue, write the correct term from the right-hand column.*

1. Largest country in Europe (and the world)	British Isles
2. Iberian Peninsula	Iceland
3. Most important islands in European history	Italy
4. Island far northwest of the mainland	Malta
5. Island visited by the apostle Paul	the Netherlands
6. Fiords	Norway
7. Bosporus and Dardanelles	Russia
8. Matterhorn	Spain
9. Great industrial nation in southern Europe	Switzerland
10. Tulip bulbs	Turkey

B. *Match as in Part A.*

1. Separate Europe from Asia	central plain
2. Separates British Isles from the mainland	English Channel
3. Separate France from Spain	North Atlantic Drift
4. Island owned by Italy	Pyrenees
5. Warms western Europe	Rhine
6. Busiest river in Europe	Ruhr
7. Heart of Europe	Sicily
8. Flows through London	Thames
9. Longest river in Europe	Urals
10. Industrial complex in Germany	Volga

Completion

1. Where soil is black beneath our feet,
   And clouds are few, the crop is ———.
2. A briny, narrow water gate
   Between two seas is called a ———.
3. The fisherman supports himself
   Upon the ——— ———.
4. Where several countries can agree
   To withhold taxing, trade is ———.
5. A country under Soviet might
   Was called a Russian ———.

Thought Questions

The geography and climate of a land greatly influence its history. Think of how this is true as you answer the first three questions.

1. What geographical fact explains why France has been invaded more often than England?
2. How might the history of the Roman Empire have been different without the Alps?

3. In what ways might the history of western Europe have been different if the North Atlantic Drift were cold instead of warm?
4. Which is better for a country—an irregular coastline or a straight one? Give two reasons.
5. In the American West, mountains cut off moisture-bearing winds, creating desert. Europe also has mountains. Then why is there so little desert?
6. (*a*) How do the Alps discourage farming? (*b*) How do they encourage manufacturing?
7. What basic industry must powerful countries have?
8. What do buyers of foreign goods appreciate about the European Common Market?
9. Although North Americans from different regions speak with different accents, they have not developed different dialects as Europeans have. Why not?
10. What is one good reason that communists have not been able to stop the worship of God?

Geographical Skills

A. Would you expect a European country such as the United Kingdom to be at about the same latitude as your home, farther north, or farther south? Check your estimate on the globe. Then find which four of these cities are farthest north by comparing their latitudes: London, New York, Paris, Berlin, Seattle, Toronto, Moscow, Montreal.

B. You can learn many things about geography by simply studying a map. Using Figures 2:1 and 2:2, find the correct name for each blank. Write the letter for each blank on your paper, followed by the correct name.

1. (*a*) ———, the capital of France, is on the (*b*) ——— River, which flows into the (*c*) ——— ———.
2. The northern parts of Norway, (*d*) ———, (*e*) ———, and Russia are within the Arctic Circle.
3. Copenhagen, the capital of (*f*) ———, sits on an island in a passage between two seas: the (*g*) ——— Sea to the west and the (*h*) ——— Sea to the east.
4. The Strait of (*i*) ——— is south of Spain. This strait separates the continents of Europe and (*j*) ———. It is the only direct link between the (*k*) ——— Sea and the (*l*) ——— Ocean.
5. The Caucasus Mountains reach from the (*m*) ——— Sea to the (*n*) ——— Sea.
6. (*o*) ———, the capital of Greece, borders the (*p*) ——— Sea, which has many small islands. This sea is part of the larger Mediterranean Sea.
7. (*q*) ——— is the capital of Austria. If you traveled down the (*r*) ——— River from this city, you would enter the country of Hungary and pass through its capital, (*s*) ———.
8. The Danube passes by Belgrade, the capital of (*t*) ———. After flowing between the countries of Bulgaria and (*u*) ———, it empties into the (*v*) ——— Sea.
9. (*w*) ——— is the capital of Spain, and (*x*) ——— is the capital of Portugal. Which of these two cities is a seaport? (*y*) ———
10. The country of (*z*) ——— lies between France and the Netherlands.

Further Study

1. Wars and treaties have frequently changed the boundaries of Europe. Use yearbooks, almanacs, or other up-to-date sources to learn whether the boundaries of Europe have been altered since this book was published. (See copyright date in the front of this book.) List any significant changes, and tell what caused them.
2. The text mentions several breeds of livestock that originated in Europe. Research the development of other breeds of domestic animals, and see how many you can find that originated in Europe.

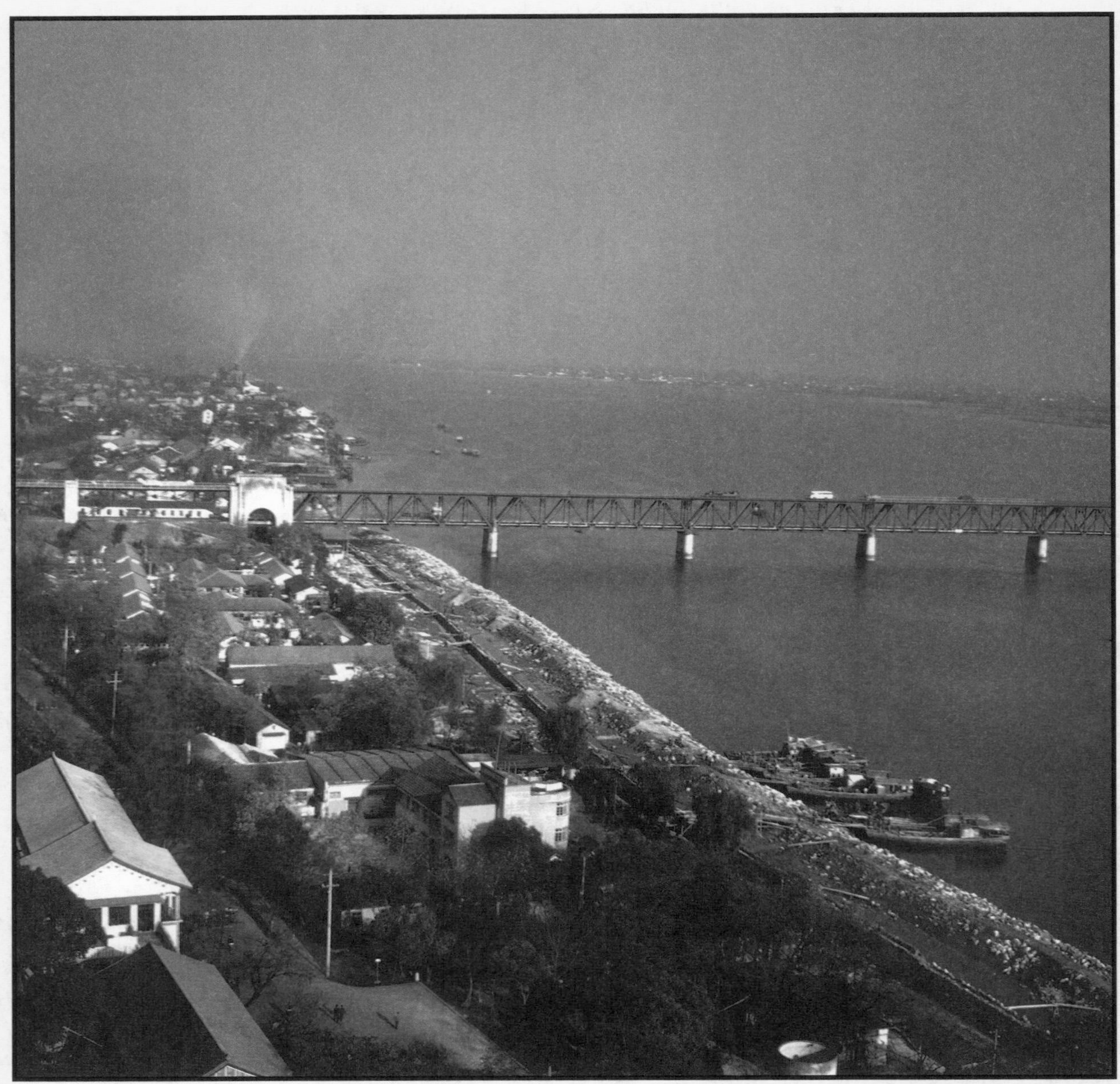

Asia's rivers are literally streams of life for millions of people. The rivers provide water for irrigation, transportation, and daily cleaning, and also provide harbors for exporting and importing. Shown here is the royal blue Ch'ien-t'ang River which flows toward the ocean through Hangzhou (Hangchow), China, a coastal city.

3 Asia

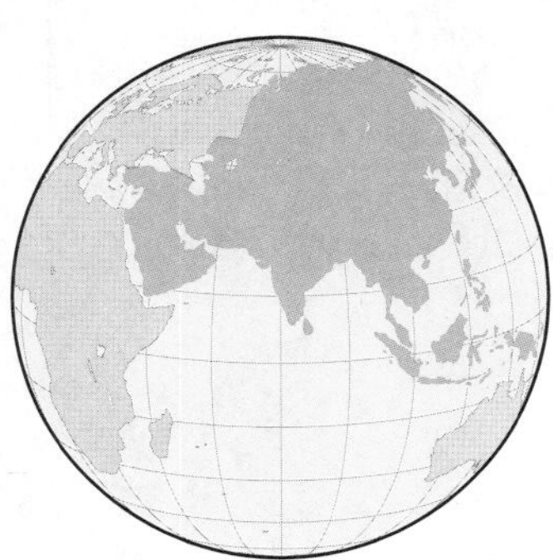

Afghanistan • Armenia • Azerbaijan • Bahrain • Bangladesh • Bhutan • Brunei • Cambodia • China • Cyprus • Georgia • India • Indonesia • Iran • Iraq • Israel • Japan • Jordan • Kazakhstan • Kuwait • Kyrgyzstan • Laos • Lebanon • Malaysia • Maldives • Mongolia • Myanmar • Nepal • North Korea • Oman • Pakistan • Philippines • Qatar • Russia • Saudi Arabia • Singapore • South Korea • Sri Lanka • Syria • Taiwan • Tajikistan • Thailand • Turkey • Turkmenistan • United Arab Emirates • Uzbekistan • Vietnam • Yemen

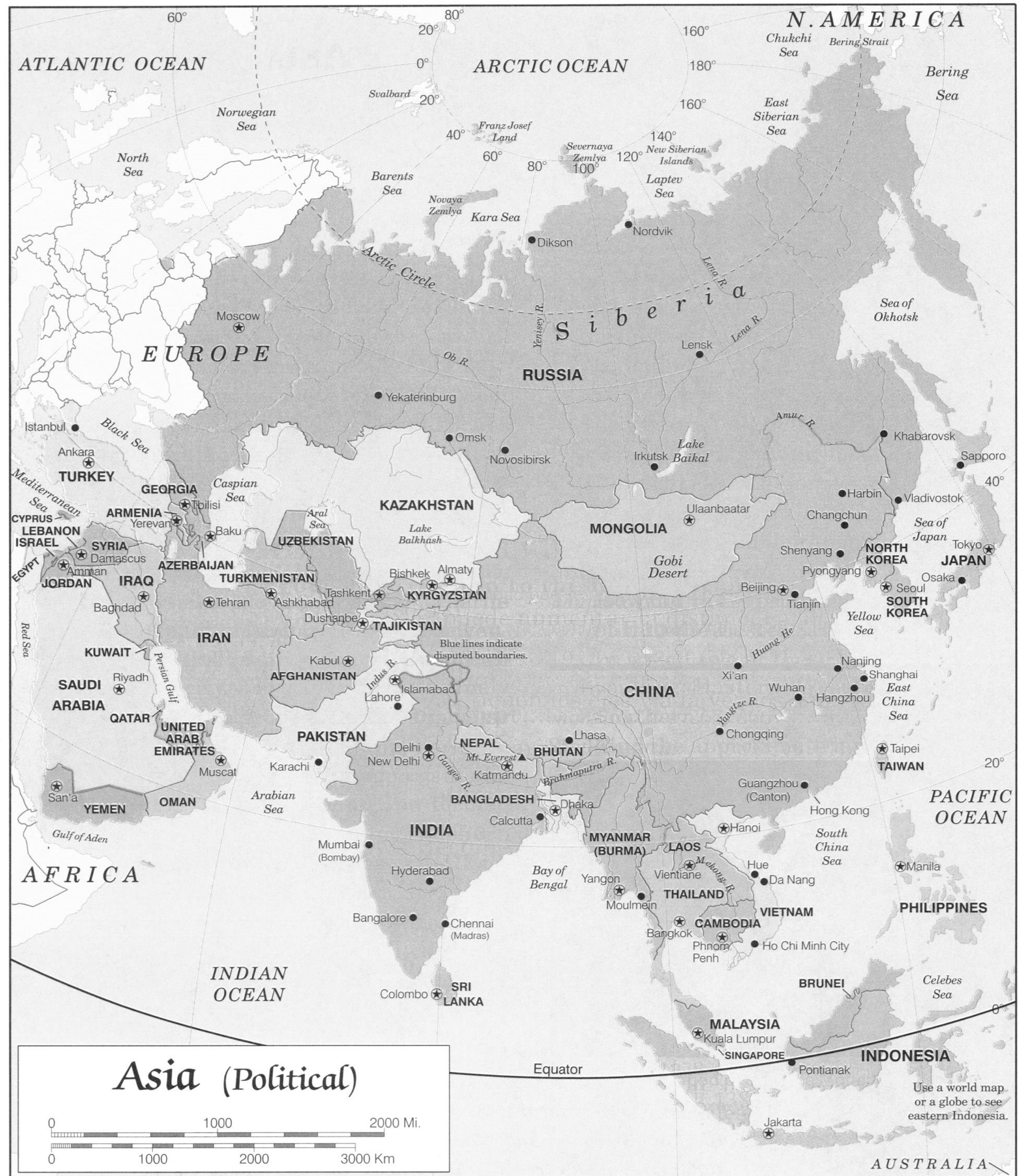
Asia (Political)
N. AMERICA
ATLANTIC OCEAN
ARCTIC OCEAN
Chukchi Sea
Bering Strait
Bering Sea
East Siberian Sea
Svalbard
Norwegian Sea
Franz Josef Land
Severnaya Zemlya
New Siberian Islands
North Sea
Barents Sea
Laptev Sea
Novaya Zemlya
Kara Sea
Dikson
Nordvik
Arctic Circle
Lena R.
Siberia
Sea of Okhotsk
Moscow
EUROPE
Yenisey R.
Lensk
Ob R.
RUSSIA
Yekaterinburg
Amur R.
Istanbul
Black Sea
Omsk
Khabarovsk
Ankara
Novosibirsk
Irkutsk
Lake Baikal
Sapporo
TURKEY
Mediterranean Sea
GEORGIA
Caspian Sea
Tbilisi
KAZAKHSTAN
Harbin
Vladivostok
CYPRUS
LEBANON
ISRAEL
ARMENIA
Yerevan
Aral Sea
Ulaanbaatar
Changchun
Sea of Japan
Baku
UZBEKISTAN
Lake Balkhash
MONGOLIA
SYRIA
Damascus
Shenyang
NORTH KOREA
Tokyo
JAPAN
EGYPT
Amman
JORDAN
AZERBAIJAN
Gobi Desert
IRAQ
TURKMENISTAN
Bishkek
Almaty
Pyongyang
Osaka
Tashkent
KYRGYZSTAN
Beijing
Seoul
Tehran
Ashkhabad
Tianjin
SOUTH KOREA
Baghdad
Dushanbe
TAJIKISTAN
Yellow Sea
Red Sea
IRAN
Blue lines indicate disputed boundaries.
Huang He
KUWAIT
Persian Gulf
Kabul
Nanjing
AFGHANISTAN
Xi'an
Shanghai
SAUDI ARABIA
Riyadh
Indus R.
Islamabad
Wuhan
East China Sea
Lahore
CHINA
Hangzhou
QATAR
Yangtze R.
UNITED ARAB EMIRATES
PAKISTAN
Chongqing
Lhasa
NEPAL
Delhi
New Delhi
BHUTAN
Taipei
Mt. Everest
Muscat
Karachi
Ganges R.
Katmandu
Brahmaputra R.
TAIWAN
20°
San'a
Guangzhou (Canton)
YEMEN
OMAN
Arabian Sea
BANGLADESH
Dhaka
PACIFIC OCEAN
Hong Kong
Calcutta
INDIA
Hanoi
Gulf of Aden
Mumbai (Bombay)
MYANMAR (BURMA)
LAOS
South China Sea
AFRICA
Hyderabad
Bay of Bengal
Vientiane
Mekong R.
Hue
Da Nang
Manila
Yangon
Moulmein
THAILAND
VIETNAM
PHILIPPINES
Bangalore
Chennai (Madras)
CAMBODIA
Bangkok
Phnom Penh
Ho Chi Minh City
INDIAN OCEAN
BRUNEI
Celebes Sea
Colombo
SRI LANKA
MALAYSIA
Kuala Lumpur
SINGAPORE
INDONESIA
Equator
Pontianak
Use a world map or a globe to see eastern Indonesia.
Jakarta
AUSTRALIA
0
1000
2000 Mi.
0
1000
2000
3000 Km

Figure 3:1

Asia (Physical Relief)
0
1000
2000 Mi.
0
1000
2000
3000 Km
ARCTIC OCEAN
North Pole
N. AMERICA
Chukchi Sea
Bering Strait
Bering Sea
East Siberian Sea
Laptev Sea
New Siberian Islands
Severnaya Zemlya
Franz Josef Land
Barents Sea
Novaya Zemlya
Kara Sea
Taymyr Peninsula
North Siberian Lowlands
Yamal Peninsula
Gyda Peninsula
Arctic Circle
Central Siberian Plateau
Verkhoyansk Range
Chersky Range
Kolyma Mountains
Kamchatka Peninsula
Sea of Okhotsk
Sakhalin Island
Kuril Islands
North Sea
EUROPE
Moscow
Volgograd
Istanbul
Ankara
TURKEY
Black Sea
Caspian Depression
Caucasus Mts.
Pontic Mts.
Mediterranean Sea
Cyprus
Suez Canal
Ural Mountains
West Siberian Plain
Siberia
RUSSIA
Omsk
Lake Baikal
Irkutsk
Stanovoy Range
Yablonovo Range
Greater Hinggan Range
Manchurian Plain
Hokkaido
Honshu
Sea of Japan
Tokyo
JAPAN
Osaka
Shikoku
Kyushu
NORTH KOREA
SOUTH KOREA
Seoul
Yellow Sea
Beijing
KAZAKHSTAN
Kazakh Upland
Lake Balkhash
Aral Sea
Ustyurt Plateau
Caspian Sea
Kyzyl Kum Desert
Tara Kum Desert
Sayan Mts.
Altai Mts.
MONGOLIA
Gobi Desert
SYRIA
Mesopotamia
Zagros Mountains
Elburz Mts.
IRAN
Plateau of Iran
AFGHANISTAN
Tien Shan
Pamirs
Tarim Basin
Hindu Kush
Khyber Pass
Kunlun Mountains
Plateau of Tibet
CHINA
Qin Ling
Huang He
Shanghai
East China Sea
Red Sea
SAUDI ARABIA
Arabia
Persian Gulf
Gulf of Oman
Rub'al-Khali
YEMEN
OMAN
Gulf of Aden
AFRICA
PAKISTAN
Lahore
Delhi
Himalayas
NEPAL
Mt. Everest
BHUTAN
Thar Desert
Ganges R.
Brahmaputra R.
Arabian Sea
INDIA
Calcutta
Mumbai (Bombay)
Deccan Plateau
Western Ghats
Eastern Ghats
Chennai (Madras)
Bay of Bengal
Sri Lanka
INDIAN OCEAN
Hanoi
Hainan
Nan Ling
Hong Kong
Taiwan
Formosa Strait
PACIFIC OCEAN
THAILAND
Andaman Sea
Gulf of Thailand
Malay Peninsula
Strait of Malacca
SINGAPORE
South China Sea
Luzon
Manila
Philippine Sea
PHILIPPINES
Palawan
Sulu Sea
Mindanao
BRUNEI
Celebes Sea
Celebes
Borneo
Banda Sea
Sumatra
Java Sea
Java
Timor
Timor Sea
Equator
Use a world map or a globe to see eastern Indonesia.
AUSTRALIA
Approximate Elevation
Sea Level
250 Ft.
1,500 Ft.
6,000 Ft.
24,000 Ft.

Figure 3:2

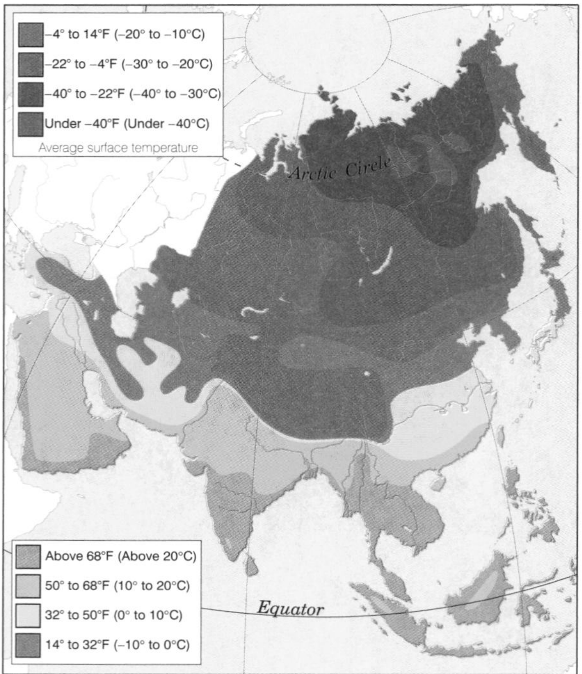

Figure 3:3. Average January Temperature

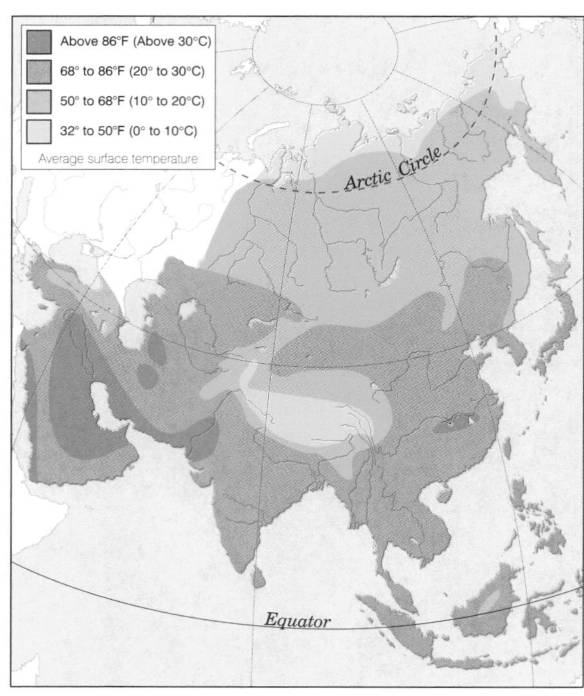

Figure 3:4. Average July Temperature

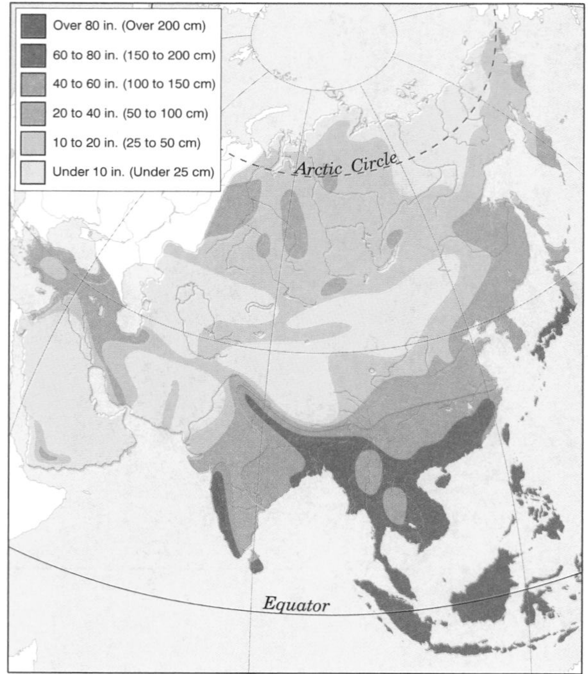

Figure 3:5. Average Annual Rainfall

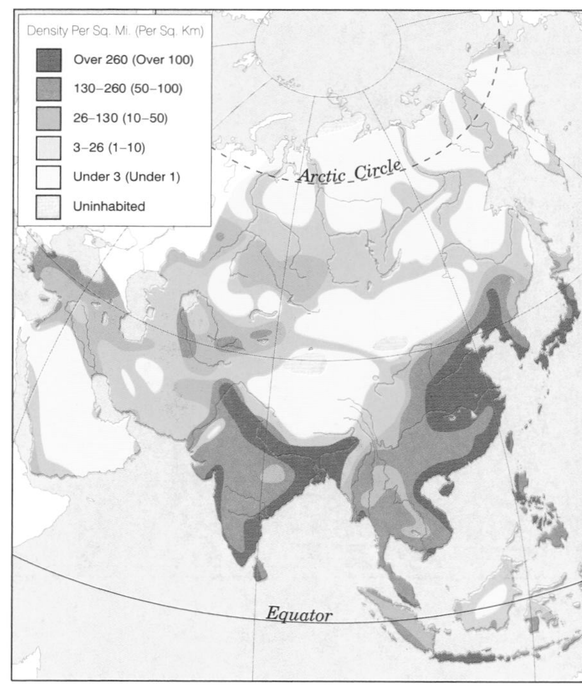

Figure 3:6. Population Distribution

Asia

The Size and Shape of Asia

Asia, the world's largest continent, is as large as North and South America combined. It reaches from the bleak, cold Arctic coast to the hot jungle islands of the Indian Ocean. It stretches eastward from Europe until it almost touches the outermost islands of Alaska.

Asia is sometimes called the ***Orient,*** or the East. It lies so far east in the Eastern Hemisphere that even its westernmost corner is called the *Middle East* or the *Near East.* Each day on the calendar comes first to the East; thus Asians enjoy their days before North Americans begin theirs. While students in Oregon are still in school on Friday afternoon, many people in Japan are eating breakfast on Saturday morning.

Asia has no particular shape, although you can see on a map that it has a narrow southwestern corner and a broad eastern edge along the Pacific Ocean. Notice the three large peninsulas along its southern edge: Southeast Asia, India, and Arabia (uh RAY bee uh).

The peninsula of Southeast Asia contains about half a dozen small countries. India forms so big and broad a peninsula that it is sometimes called a subcontinent. Arabia, farthest to the west, might be hard to recognize as a peninsula at first because of the land masses all around it.

Note also the important island groups, or ***archipelagos*** (ahr kuh PEHL uh gohz), that God placed near eastern and southeastern Asia. The islands of Japan, lying to the east of China, have developed into the most modern and prosperous country of Asia. These islands are close enough to China to have been influenced by China, yet far enough away from the mainland to be a separate country. Other important archipelago countries of Asia include the Philippines, with over 7,000 islands, and Indonesia (ihn duh NEE zhuh), with more than 13,600. Many of these islands are too small to be included on most maps, but other islands are of considerable size. New Guinea is the second largest island in the world, after Greenland. (Australia is too big to be called an island.)

Study Exercises

1. From Asia, in which direction is (*a*) Europe? (*b*) Alaska?
2. What three oceans wash the shores of Asia?
3. Which of the three large peninsulas of southern Asia lies between the other two? (See Figure 3:2.)
4. Of the three archipelago countries mentioned, which lies farthest south? (See Figure 3:1.)

Rivers

Southwestern Asia. The most important rivers of southwestern Asia are the Ganges (GAN jeez) and the Brahmaputra (brah muh POO truh) of India, and the Indus of Pakistan. You may need to look twice for the Brahmaputra. It flows through the easily forgotten northeastern corner of India, and through Bangladesh (bahng gluh DEHSH), where it joins the Ganges to form a broad ***delta.***

Followers of the Hindu (HIHN doo) religion believe the Ganges is the most sacred river of India. Every year they come by thousands to visit the cities along its banks. They bathe in the Ganges to purify themselves or to seek healing of some ailment. Some come there to die, for they believe that anyone who dies by the Ganges will go straight to a better life. Christians know that it is not where one dies that matters,

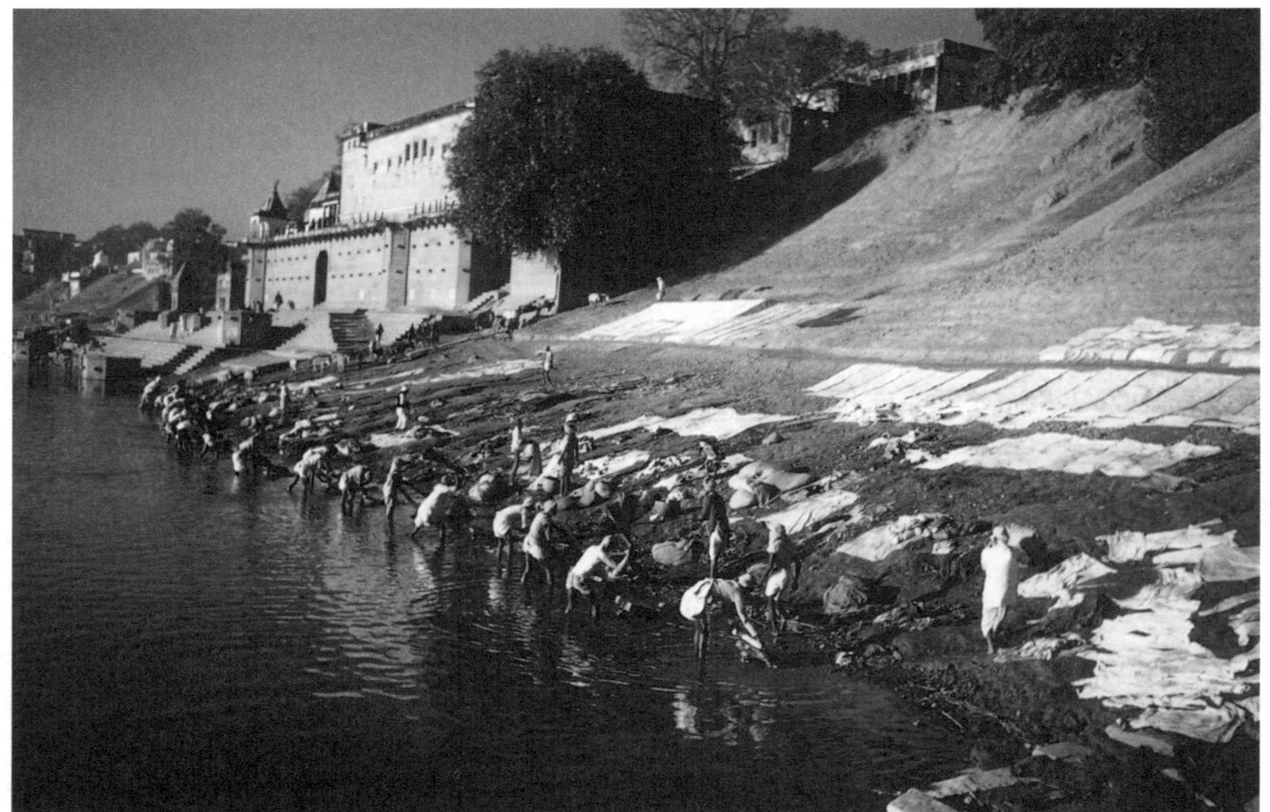

The Ganges River begins in the Himalaya Mountains, about 10,000 feet (3,048 m) above sea level. Fed by melting snow and glaciers, this great river winds its way through deep mountain gorges before reaching the level plains of India. Together with its tributaries, the Ganges drains approximately one-quarter of India and a large part of Bangladesh. The river is used extensively for irrigation.

but whether the blood of Jesus has cleansed him from sin.

In Pakistan, so much of the mighty Indus is used for irrigation that the water level has dropped greatly. Only small boats can use the river now. In Bangladesh, the Brahmaputra irrigates the countryside by flooding from time to time. Normal floods serve the rice farmers well, but severe floods cause much damage.

Southeastern Asia. Flowing through the mainland peninsula of Southeast Asia is the Mekong (MAY kahng), one of Asia's largest rivers. The Mekong River begins in China and flows south through Laos (LAH ohs), Cambodia (kam BOH dee uh), and Vietnam (vee eht NAHM). Myanmar (myan MAH), which was formerly called Burma, and Thailand (TY land) also lie along sections of the Mekong. During the rainy season, the Mekong floods large sections of the countries it passes through, especially Cambodia and Vietnam. Its flood plains are excellent for growing rice.

Eastern Asia. The earliest civilization of eastern Asia seems to have developed in the Huang He (HWAHNG HUH) river valley of northern China. The Huang He (Yellow River) has been nicknamed "China's Sorrow" because it has caused great floods. Thousands of people have drowned, and others have starved because of ruined crops.

One reason for the floods is that the river flows through a large region of ***loess*** (LOH uhs) soil, which contains much silt. Streams wash the silt into the river and it settles on

Flat-bottomed passenger boats, such as these on the Huang He, are a common sight on China's rivers.

the riverbed, causing it to rise higher and higher. To keep the rising river from flooding their land and from changing courses, the Chinese must build higher and higher dikes along the river. In some places the riverbed is higher than the surrounding countryside! No large boats sail on the Huang He.

The most important river in China is the Yangtze (YANG see). The Chinese people call it the "long river"; it is 3,915 miles (6,300 km) long. In its upper stretches it is very beautiful as it winds through deep gorges among the mountains. Farther downstream, thousands of people make their homes right on the river, living in boats called junks. Millions of others live along the shore. The Yangtze provides good transportation for large sea-going ships, which can travel nearly 700 miles (1,100 km) up the river. Smaller ships can go a 1,000 miles (1,600 km) farther.

Northern Asia. All the major rivers of northern Asia flow through Siberia, the vast eastern part of Russia. The Amur (ah MOOR) forms a long stretch of the boundary between China and Russia before it turns northeast and empties into the Pacific Ocean. Several other rivers, the Lena (LEE nuh), the Yenisey (yehn ih SAY), and the Ob, begin in central Asia and flow north into the Arctic Ocean. They are among the world's longest rivers. During the winter these frozen rivers serve as major highways in Siberia.

Because the rivers flow north, this part of Asia has a problem in the spring. The southern parts of the rivers thaw while the northern mouths are still frozen. This causes the water to back up and flood the countryside.

One branch of the Yenisey drains Lake Baikal (by KAHL), the deepest lake in the world. Lake Baikal contains about one-fifth of all the earth's fresh surface water. The lake is remarkable for its deep blue color.

Study Exercises

5. Are the Ganges and Brahmaputra Rivers in northern India or southern India? (See the map.)
6. Give two ways in which the Yangtze is a greater advantage to the Chinese than the Huang He is.
7. Why do the major rivers of Siberia flood in the spring?

Mount Everest juts nearly 5½ miles (8.9 km) above sea level. Since the first ascent in 1953, more than 700 mountain climbers have reached the top of the mountain. However, over 150 climbers have died on the frozen, rocky slopes. Christians ought to avoid such unnecessary risks. God owns our bodies, and we are to be good stewards of them.

Mountains

God formed more mountains in Asia than on any other continent. Afghanistan (af GAN ih stan), Nepal (nuh PAHL), and Tibet (tuh BEHT) are especially mountainous. Tibet, a region of China, is a high ***plateau,*** surrounded by still higher mountains. It has been called the "roof of the world."

To simplify the study of the mountains in Asia, notice that most of the mountain ranges fan out from a central point. Actually, this "point" is a large cluster of mountains known as the Pamir Knot (pah MEER). You can find it where China, India, Pakistan, and Afghanistan meet.

The Himalayas. The best-known of the mountain ranges are the Himalayas (hihm uh LAY uhs). These massive mountains stand in silent testimony to their mighty Creator, who speaks of weighing the mountains in scales (Isaiah 40:12). The Himalayas contain Mount Everest, the highest mountain in the world. It rises to 29,028 feet (8,848 m) on the border of Tibet and Nepal. (Many of the taller Rocky Mountains are only half that high!) It took the first climbers more than two months to reach the top.

Few people live in the high mountains of central Asia. As usual in mountains, the soil is poor and the climate is too cool for successful farming.

Transportation is difficult. Many of the ***passes*** through the mountains are higher than the highest peaks elsewhere in the world. The most famous pass in central Asia is the Khyber Pass (KY bur) between Pakistan and Afghanistan. Many invaders have entered India through the Khyber Pass. Military men learned to guard the pass, for it was the easiest way for an army to get through the mountains.

The Himalayas are the source of many of Asia's great rivers. Notice on a map how the Indus, the Ganges, the Brahmaputra, the Mekong, the Yangtze, the Huang He, and many other rivers all begin in the Himalayas or the Tibetan plateau. There the runoff from melting snow and glaciers begins its long journey to the sea.

The Himalayas benefit southern Asia by blocking icy winds from the north. But they also keep rain-bearing winds from the south out of central Asia, which explains why that part of Asia is so dry.

Other Mountain Ranges of Central Asia. Besides the Himalayas, other mountain ranges branch off the Pamir Knot. To the east are the Kunlun Mountains (KUN LUN) in western China, and the Tien Shan (TYEHN SHAHN) along the northwestern border of China. To the west, the majestic Hindu Kush (HIHN doo KOOSH) reach into Afghanistan.

Mount Fuji, Japan's highest mountain, rises to a height of 12,388 feet (3,776 m). This volcano has not erupted since 1708.

Mountainous Islands. Many of the archipelago countries of Asia are mountainous. Some of the mountains that make up the islands, such as Mount Fuji (FOO jee) in Japan, are famous and beautiful. But their rugged terrain reduces the amount of useful land on these islands. Besides, many of these mountains are volcanoes. Along with volcanic mountains go earthquakes. This is one reason the Japanese have traditionally built lightly framed houses. During an earthquake, such houses will not crash heavily on the people inside.

Study Exercises

8. At what central point do most Asian mountain ranges meet?
9. How do the Himalayas affect the climate north and south of them?
10. How are some mountains of Japan and other Southeast Asian islands different from the Himalaya Mountains?
11. Why does Japan have so little good farmland?

How the Climate Affects Life in Asia

Asia has practically every type of climate found in the world, since it reaches from the equator to Arctic regions.

Southern Asia. Much of southern Asia has a wet and a dry season. The length of the wet or dry season varies, depending on the ***monsoon*** (mahn SOON) winds. These steady winds change direction twice each year. In winter the land cools more rapidly than the sea. Warm air over the sea rises, and cooler air flows out from the interior of Asia, bringing cool, dry weather to southern Asia. In summer the land heats more rapidly than the sea. Warm air over the land rises and cooler air flows in from the sea, bringing moisture-laden air. It does not rain at first. The days are hot and the humidity is oppressive. But when the wet monsoon winds bring rain, it pours.

Monsoons can be unpredictable. In the past, if monsoon rains failed to come, millions of people had little or nothing to eat. Irrigation helps that problem somewhat, but many Asians still depend on monsoon weather for their food.

In Southeast Asia, the climate is mostly warm and moist. Areas near the sea receive moisture year round, although the wet monsoon season brings the most rain. Rice grows well in this climate. It is the most important crop in southern China, Thailand, and other nearby countries.

Bangladesh has a humid climate. Some parts of the country receive over 200 inches (500 cm) of rain per year. The climate stays warm year round, so farmers can often harvest three crops of rice a year. But the people of Bangladesh have suffered from many terrible floods. Sometimes during monsoon storms, high waves from the Bay of Bengal (behn GAWL) come crashing onto the low coastline, and sometimes the Brahmaputra and the Ganges Rivers overflow their banks.

Rice is not the only crop in southern and southeastern Asia. The people plant wheat, corn, and vegetables, just as farmers do in North America.

Rice

Rice is not mentioned in the Bible, but about half of the people in the world, mostly in Asia, depend upon rice as their chief food source.

Rice is a grass related to wheat, rye, and other grain crops, but it grows in many places too warm and wet for some of the other grains. There are thousands of varieties of rice; some varieties prefer lowlands, some prefer uplands, and other varieties are able to grow well in either place. Rice needs an average temperature of 75°F (24°C) during the growing season. Because it needs a constant supply of water, it is usually planted in flooded fields called paddies. Rice can be grown on land too hilly to be flooded if there is plentiful rainfall, but rice grown on paddies usually yields better than rice grown on hills.

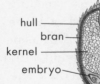

hull
bran
kernel
embryo

For years, many Southeast Asians have suffered from a disease called beriberi (BEHR ee BEHR ee). Symptoms include partial paralysis of the legs and arms, anemia, and emaciation. It was discovered that their main food, polished rice, was deficient in thiamine, an important vitamin. Rice bran contains thiamine, but the bran is removed during the process of polishing the rice to make it white. The bran and some starch that is rubbed off the grains are used as livestock feed and made into other products. More Southeast Asians are now eating brown rice, which has the bran layers left on it, or polished rice that has been enriched with vitamins and minerals. As a result, beriberi is less of a problem than it used to be.

A rice-straw floor mat

Growing 2 to 6 feet (.7 to 2 m) tall, the typical rice plant has several stalks, each ending in a head that bears from fifty to three hundred flowers. Many of these flowers are pollinated and later become the rice grains. Each starchy grain kernel is surrounded by some bran layers that contain most of the vitamins and minerals found in rice. A rough outer hull protects each grain. Some rice growers classify rice by grain length—short, medium, and long, because consumers often have a length or type they prefer.

A primitive way to hull rice

Rice hulls are used as a packing material, as burnable fuel, or for use in making adobe-type building bricks. Rice straw is used to make sandals and hats, to thatch roofs, and for other uses.

Asian farmers usually plant rice seeds in a small, well-fertilized patch of soil and then flood it. Then the farmers make or repair the short dirt walls of the large paddy, flood it, and plow the soil in preparation for receiving the young rice transplants. After carefully tending the small seedbed from thirty to forty days, the farmers neatly transplant bunches of one to six young rice plants into the flooded paddies to finish maturing. The water level is kept at 2 to 6 inches (5 to 15 cm) until the grain begins to ripen, and then the paddies are drained so that the soil can dry by harvesttime. Most rice is harvested by hand, using knives or sickles to cut the stalks. The stalks are tied into sheaves and allowed to dry in the sun. The sheaves are then threshed and the hulls removed by various means. Polishing is done by machines.

Transplanting young rice plants

Harvesting rice

Rice paddies near Guangzhou (Canton), China.

Threshing by machine

Ripening times for different types of rice vary. Some types of rice ripen in eighty days, and some types take over two hundred days! Work is being done to develop new varieties to help reduce food shortages. In the 1960s, a new type of rice was developed that was a cross between a high-producing dwarf variety and an ordinary tall variety. The result has been called "miracle rice" because the short, sturdy plant produces well and does not fall down and spoil as easily in wind and rain as the taller rice often does. Wild rice is used the same way as ordinary rice, although it is not a true rice plant.

China leads the world in producing rice, followed by India, Indonesia, and other Southeast Asian countries. Much of the rice produced in these countries is consumed by the people who raise it. Other countries also produce rice and export much of it to the Asian countries that do not produce enough to feed their own people.

Bangladesh is one of the poorest and most crowded countries of the world. Since much of the country is on the delta formed by the Ganges and Brahmaputra Rivers, it has very fertile land where tons of rice grow annually. Every year the small country suffers from floods, such as this one in 1988. In 1970, an estimated 500,000 people were drowned when a tropical storm called a cyclone struck the coastal areas.

Southeast Asians also raise warm-weather foods such as peanuts, sugar cane, bananas, and coconuts. There are crops less familiar to Americans too, such as millet and sesame (SEHS uh mee), and luxuries such as tea, pepper, and spices. Farmers also raise nonfood crops, such as cotton, rubber, and ***jute*** for making burlap and twine.

Since rivers abound in southern Asia, many people live along riverbanks. Some homes are even built on stilts in the water. In crowded areas such as central and southern China, people live in houseboats that may be no larger than your living room.

Southeastern China is the most densely populated part of Asia. The land can support many people because farmers usually raise two crops of rice each year.

The Chinese people maintain the fertility of their land very carefully. All plant and animal wastes go back into the fields. The ***terraces*** that farmers have built on their hillsides to make level rice fields also help to prevent erosion. The Chinese have kept the land in good condition for thousands of years.

Because much of China is so crowded, the Chinese need to make wise use of their land. They raise more crops than animals because they can get more food per acre from plants than from animals. But they do raise hogs, since hogs eat almost any kind of food and can be kept in pens rather than in pastures. China has more hogs than any other country. The Chinese also raise fish in ponds, where they harvest them periodically.

Built over water, this Filipino house frees valuable land for other uses. It is made from nipa palm leaves, which provide inexpensive building material.

This Tibetan nomad is one of several thousand who roam the northern Tibetan plateau with their herds of yaks, sheep, horses, and camels. They wear sheepskin clothing and live in tents made of yak hair.

Northern Asia. Farther north in China, the weather is cooler and drier. Rice does not grow there; in fact, millions of Chinese people do not eat rice at all. Their grain is wheat.

Across the border from China in southwestern Siberia, wheat is also the main crop. The rich, black soil of Siberia's steppes would produce a variety of crops, but the climate is too dry and cool for most crops other than wheat.

North and east of the steppes is the taiga, a vast wooded region of Siberia. The taiga is mostly evergreen forest, inhabited by wild animals and a few loggers and hunters. Here and there are new cities, recently populated by people who moved to Siberia to mine or make use of the abundant natural resources.

North of the taiga, the forest dwindles to shrubs and clumps of grass on a plain called the ***tundra.*** Here the topsoil thaws during the short summer, but the ***permafrost*** underneath is permanently frozen to a depth of 1,000 feet (300 m) or more. The low bushes and grass of the tundra provide food for herds of reindeer. Tribes of ***nomads*** follow the reindeer as the herds migrate north and south in search of sufficient grazing.

Central Asia. The high mountains of central Asia block moisture-bearing winds from the sea. As a result, northwestern China has a huge dry region. This is one way "the West" in China is much like "the West" in North America. The driest part of China's western region is the Gobi Desert (GOH bee). It is hot in summer but very cold in winter. The northern part of the Gobi Desert is in Mongolia (mahng GOH lee uh), a large, dry country between China and Russia.

Water is precious in central Asia. Most people live where they can irrigate their cropland from rivers fed by melting snow from the high mountain ranges. Some of the rivers that enter desert areas dry up before they reach the sea.

Sheep graze the sparse grass in the outlying areas of China, Afghanistan, and Pakistan. Wandering herdsmen follow their flocks, hunting the best pastures. In the high Tibetan plateau, nomads keep herds of yaks—ox-like animals that not only carry loads for them but also provide milk, meat, and skins to make tents. Yak dung is the only source of fuel on the treeless Tibetan highlands.

Study Exercises

12. What happens when warm summer air rises above southern Asia?
13. How can a farmer raise crops on steep hillsides without having his soil wash away?
14. The most important grain in southern Asia is rice. (*a*) What is the most important grain in northern Asia? (*b*) What causes this difference?
15. Why are more crops raised in Southeast Asia than in central Asia?

Bamboo

A giant of the grass family, bamboo may be the world's most useful plant. The uses of bamboo are almost endless. It is used for food for humans and animals (young shoots as a vegetable, seeds as grain), and is used to make sandals, houses, furniture, paper, tools, cooking utensils, candles, medicine, baskets, garden fences, fishing rods, walking sticks, scaffolding, bridges, cables, cages, rafts, sails, musical instruments, planters, dolls, boxes, gutters, weapons, and even a diesel-engine fuel! Bamboo is also the main food of the black and white giant panda of China.

Lightweight bamboo "carryall" transports pigs.

Culms of six different bamboo varieties

Bamboo grows in warm regions of temperate climates and in tropical climates, with many of the more than seven hundred kinds thriving in East and Southeast Asia and on islands of the Pacific and Indian Oceans. Depending on the variety, the hollow jointed stems called culms (KUHLMS) range in height from about 4 inches (10 cm) to about 130 feet (40 m). The largest kind may have culms about 12 inches (30 cm) in diameter. Sword-shaped leaves usually fall off when they mature, leaving the lower culms mostly bare. A full-grown culm may stand for years; it does not add a growth ring each year as trees do.

A bamboo plant forms a thick, underground root-like stem called a rhizome (RY zohm) that enriches the soil and helps to prevent erosion. Growing much the same way as asparagus spears grow, new culms grow each year from the rhizome; and the older and thicker the rhizome, the larger and taller the culms will be. The culms form a dense undergrowth that excludes other plants.

Bamboo shoots in a bamboo basket

The stiff, lightweight culms are the most valuable part of the bamboo plant. Left whole, the hollow, jointed culms are very strong. Culms can also be split into different widths to be woven into baskets, mats, and other useful and decorative articles. Bamboo is used in construction—layers of bamboo glued together have strength comparable to soft steel. It can be used as a reinforcement for concrete.

Tiny basket woven from finely-split bamboo is about the size of a nickel.

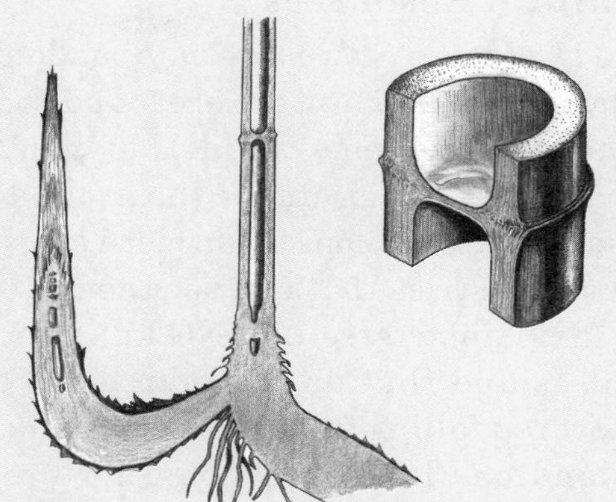

Cross section of bamboo rhizome and culm

Like asparagus spears, many newly sprouted and tender bamboo shoots are harvested and eaten, especially by the Chinese. The emerging bamboo shoot is already the same diameter as the full-grown culm will be. Depending on the kind, culms reach their full height in sixty to ninety days. One grew up to 3 feet (.9 m) in a day!

Black and white giant panda bear

God has designed that bamboo plants die after they flower and produce their rice-like seeds. However, most kinds of bamboo only flower once at intervals of from 30 to 120 years. And, no matter where they are in the world, all bamboo plants of the same type will burst into flower at the same time! Flowering time causes economic hardships for bamboo growers and harvesters because few rhizomes survive, and it takes from three to five years until new rhizomes grown from seeds can produce culms that are big enough to harvest. Culms must be 3 to 5 years old before cutting. Younger culms may look beautiful, but they contain much water and will shrink and crack when they are dried. However, all is not loss—the abundant bamboo seeds are edible!

Natural Resources

The Indian Subcontinent. Abundant supplies of coal and iron ore are found in India. The people do some mining, but many minerals are waiting under the ground until the country develops the modern equipment and industries that can use them.

Sri Lanka (sree LAHNG kuh) is a tropical island that on the map looks like a teardrop falling from southern India. This island has long been noted for precious stones and spices such as cinnamon. Perhaps this is what inspired a poet to write, "What though the spicy breezes blow soft o'er Ceylon's isle." (Sri Lanka was formerly called Ceylon.)

Southeast Asia. God provided some Southeast Asian countries with rich supplies of minerals. For example, Malaysia (muh LAY zhuh) produces more tin than any other country in the world. Indonesia is also a major producer of tin, and it has more oil reserves than any other country in Southeast Asia.

Much of Southeast Asia's natural wealth comes from trees. Malaysia, Thailand, and Indonesia produce most of the natural rubber used in the world. However, natural rubber is not used as much today as it once was. It has largely been replaced by ***synthetic*** rubber, which is made from petroleum and other raw materials.

Bamboo grows well in Southeast Asia. It is so strong and useful that a family's house, furniture, and fences (as well as other items) might all be made of bamboo.

In Myanmar and Thailand, elephants drag heavy teak logs through the forest to rivers, where the logs are floated to sawmills. Teak does not warp or rot easily, and it is used for ships and furniture. Even termites will not harm teak. Some temples in Myanmar have teak beams that are more than 1,000 years old. Beautiful black ebony wood also comes from Southeast Asia.

Teak

Teak is a hardwood tree native to India, Thailand, and Myanmar. Teak trees have a straight trunk that is often thicker at the base. The tree has four-sided branches. The gray or brownish gray bark is about 1 inch (2.5 cm) thick. Teak trees are leafless in the dry season. When the monsoon rains come, the tree produces leaves that grow 2 feet (61 cm) long, as well as flowers and seeds. The leaves are used for thatch and to make a purple dye.

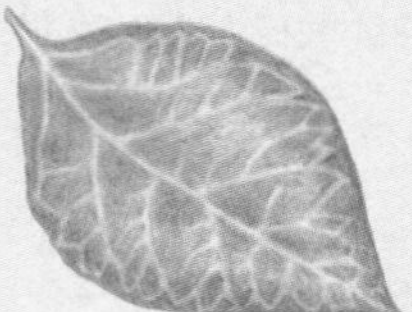

A teak leaf

Teakwood is one of the most valuable woods in the world because it is of medium weight, strong, and extremely durable. The sapwood is white, and the heartwood is a lovely golden yellow, which darkens to a beautiful brown with darker streaks when seasoned. The heartwood contains a long-lasting, fragrant oil that helps it resist termites and other insect pests. Teak is also water-resistant, so it is especially valuable in warm, humid countries. Teakwood takes a high polish, has a pleasant fragrance, and has beautiful grain patterns, which add to the value of furniture and hand-carved items made from it.

Groups of teak trees usually grow on low, forested hills up to an elevation of about 3,000 feet (914 m), but some are now grown on plantations. The trees grow about 145 feet (44 m) high, and produce logs about 60 feet (18 m) long. For the best lumber, the tree should reach a circumference of 6 feet (2 m) or more. To reach this size, teaks are seldom less than one hundred years old in a natural forest setting. However, in the good soils of the plantations, teak trees have reached a height of about 60 feet (18 m) in fifteen years, with a circumference of about 6½ feet (2 m).

Most of the world's supply of teak comes from Myanmar. The Myanmar government selects which teak trees will be cut. The trees are then killed by girdling them (removing a horizontal band of bark from around the tree). The girdling date is marked on the tree trunk. The tree usually dies in a few days, but it is left standing for two or three years because newly cut teak is so heavy it will not float. After the trees are dry, fellers skillfully cut them down, sometimes with only a saw and a small axe. Holes are drilled in the ends of heavy logs so that trained elephants can drag them over uneven ground. Smaller logs are pushed or lifted by the elephants. The logs are piled in streambeds that are mostly dry.

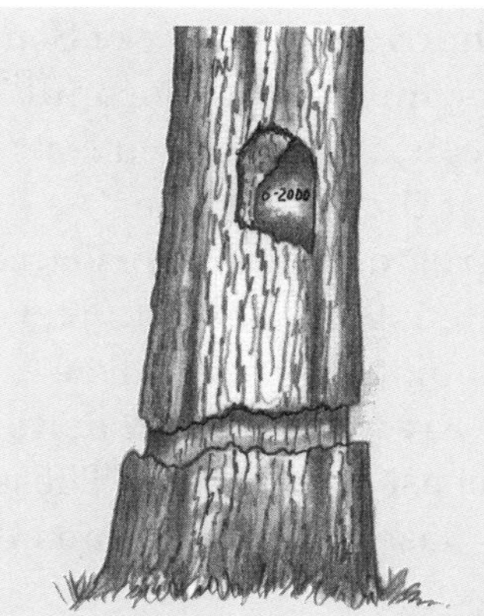

A girdled tree

Likely from Kuwait, this dhow (Arabian sailing ship) has a prow made of teak.

Heavy seasonal rains put an end to the fear of the logs catching fire. Swollen streams carry the logs to the rivers where they are caught and made into rafts of about 125 logs each, in the charge of four or five men.

The rafts drift down the big rivers, and then are guided by small boats through the shipping lanes to the waiting sawmills of Myanmar's capital, Yangon (formerly called Rangoon). From there, the lumber is distributed. Most of it is used locally for building houses and furniture, but the best lumber is exported, often for shipbuilding material.

Another valuable tree of Southeast Asia is the coconut palm. Coconut oil and the dried coconut meat called copra are major exports of the Philippines.

The greatest natural resources God gave to Southeast Asia are its fertile soil and warm, moist climate. Areas such as the Mekong River valley and delta have some of the richest land in Asia. These conditions make it possible for millions of people to live there.

China. China has awakened to its many untouched mineral riches. The country has much coal and petroleum besides iron ore and other minerals.

China has yet to develop many of its hydroelectric possibilities. In some places, the upper Yangtze River has mountains over a mile high on both sides of it. Imagine the mighty dams that could be built there! One resource the Chinese have been using well is the fishing grounds along their country's shores. The Chinese harvest fish not only from the ocean but also from rivers, lakes, and canals. They have one of the largest fishing industries in the world.

Siberia. Russia, with its great size, is the richest of all Asian countries in natural resources. It has abundant supplies of gold, diamonds, and coal. It also has a large portion of the world's oil and natural gas. Vast Siberian forests supply much of Russia's timber.

However, it is difficult to work in Siberia. Throughout much of the year the ground stays frozen solid. Winter temperatures below -90°F (-68°C) have been recorded in northern Siberia. Summer brings deep mud and swarms of mosquitoes. But with modern machinery moving in, Siberia will yield more of its treasures.

Japan. The islands of Japan do not have many mineral resources—at least, not much of each kind. Japan must import most of its raw materials: petroleum, coking coal, and iron ore. However, hydroelectric plants on mountain streams supply some of the energy the country needs. And Japan has a great resource in its workers. The Japanese people have become well known for producing much with few resources.

The Japanese also take advantage of the many fish in nearby waters, as well as those at fishing grounds around the world. Japan has one of the largest catches of fish of any country in the world, and they eat most of what they catch. They probably eat fish as often as you eat chicken or beef.

Study Exercises

16. What three large countries mentioned in the text have many untouched natural resources?
17. When mineral resources are mined, they are gone. But many of the natural resources in Southeast Asia are renewable. Explain why this is true.
18. Are the most mineral resources found in southern Asia or in northern Asia?
19. For meat, the Japanese and Chinese are both noted for eating much ———.

What Religions Do Asians Follow?

Most major world religions came from Asia. Christianity, Judaism, and Islam are three main religions that developed in southwestern Asia. These will be described in the chapter on the Middle East. This section describes the Eastern religions, which have been practiced for thousands of years by people in eastern and southern Asia.

Hinduism is the main religion of India. It developed over thousands of years as various people added their ideas to it. Hindus believe in many gods, with a main spirit-god known as Brahman (BRAH muhn). The belief in more than one god is ***polytheism*** (PAHL ee thee ihz uhm); the belief in one God is ***monotheism*** (MAHN uh thee ihz uhm).

Hindus also believe in reincarnation, the false idea that a person who dies is reborn as another person or perhaps as an animal. According to Hinduism, people who have lived good lives can be born into a higher level after they die. They hope that after they have died and been reborn a number of times, they can be reborn into such a high level that they become one with Brahman. That is what they look forward to instead of heaven.

This helps us to understand why Hindus consider animals sacred. They believe the animals have souls. They hold their cows to be especially sacred. For that reason India has more cattle than any other country—most Hindus would not think of killing one. Some Hindus are careful not to kill even the tiniest insect.

Hindus observe the ***caste*** (KAST) system. They class all people in four main categories: (1) the priests, which are the highest class, (2) the soldiers and rulers, (3) the merchants and landowners, and (4) the farmers and laborers. At one time there was a class of people below all castes called the untouchables, who did the lowliest work. But the government has ruled that no one shall be classed as an untouchable. The caste system is no longer quite as strong as it once was.

Out of Hinduism there developed a religion called Buddhism (BOO dihz uhm). Today millions of people worship in

The Pulguksa Buddhist temple is one of the oldest and best-known temples in Korea. Over 1400 years old, this temple is a masterpiece of ancient architecture. It shows the effort that men will put forth to worship and to satisfy their spiritual desires. However, fantastic buildings have failed to satisfy the deep needs of mankind. Millions of Asians need to hear the simple Gospel and see faithful Christians live it. "God that made the world and all things therein, seeing that he is Lord of heaven and earth, dwelleth not in temples made with hands" (Acts 17:24).

Some Asian religions and cultures have traditionally taught deep respect for older people. Here, Korean children bow before an older couple to show their honor.

Buddhist temples. Pagodas, elaborate towers with many stories, have also been built for worship. Buddhists who are especially devoted to their religion live in poverty and spend much time studying and meditating. You will read about the founder of Buddhism in Chapter 13.

There are still other religions. Shintoism (SHIHN toh ihz uhm) is the most important in Japan. Strangely, it does not emphasize life after death. It teaches that one should respect his ancestors, live a clean moral life, and keep various traditional ceremonies. Shintoists worship many gods.

One of the main religions in China was founded by Confucius (kuhn FYOO shuhs), who lived about five hundred years before Christ came to earth. This religion, called Confucianism, is really more of a philosophy than a religion. Confucius said that people should respect the gods but pay little attention to them. The most important things, he taught, were respect for ancestors, respect for scholars, and living together in peace. One of his famous sayings was, "Do not do to others what you would not want them to do to you."

Thousands of Asians observe a mixture of two or more religions. Many Buddhists in Southeast Asia also accept ideas from Hinduism. Buddhists in Japan and China usually follow Shintoism or Confucianism as well.

Communist governments have controlled China and several of her Southeast Asian neighbors, such as Vietnam, during part of the 1900s. The communists do not want people to practice religion, but some people hold on to their beliefs anyway. Often such people feel a greater need for God than those who are allowed to believe as they wish. Some people living under communist rule have turned to the Christian faith because of the hope it offers them.

Study Exercises

20. What seven major religions do Asians follow?
21. Why do Hindus consider cows sacred and avoid killing animals?
22. Galatians 3:28 says, "There is neither Jew nor Greek, there is neither bond nor free, there is neither male nor female: for ye are all one in Christ Jesus." What Hindu system is different from this?

In the city of Taipei, the capital of Taiwan, a modern factory produces cars. Taiwan is one of the most advanced industrial centers of Asia, exporting a wide range of goods. Taiwan also has improved its rice production to the point of producing more than its people use.

Where Multitudes Live

Asia has over half the world's population. About one out of every five persons in the world lives in China, the world's most populous country. India also has an enormous population—more than North and South America combined—and its population is steadily increasing.

Asia is extremely crowded in areas where people can make a living by farming or fishing, such as along rivers and seacoasts, or in fertile valleys and plains. Southeastern Asia includes some of the most densely populated regions of the world.

These overcrowded living conditions cause problems for many Asians. Having many people is in itself not a serious problem for a country—many small European countries also have millions of people. But the people must be able to earn enough money to buy food, since there is not enough land to raise their own. If most of the people are poor, they cannot afford to buy food from other countries. Sadly, the people who need food most are usually the first to do without, because they have no money and no land.

In Seoul, South Korea, like many Asian cities, gleaming new office buildings, hotels, and apartment houses rise next to palaces and temples that are many centuries old.

India contains over one-seventh of the world population, and Mumbai (formerly called Bombay) holds its fair share of that one-seventh. Mumbai, which originally was a small fishing village, is now India's major port on the west coast.

Some parts of Asia are very sparsely populated because the land is too cold, rugged, or dry to support many people. Still, in the 1990s Asia had an average of about 200 persons per square mile (77 per km^2). That is much more crowded than the United States, where the average was about 70 persons per square mile (27 per km^2). In Canada the average was only about 7 persons per square mile (3 per km^2)!

Asia has some of the largest cities in the world. See if you can find the following cities in Figure 3:1: Tokyo (TOH kee oh), the capital of Japan; Seoul (SOHL), the capital of South Korea; Shanghai (shahng HY), a Chinese port city; Mumbai, a crowded city in western India (Mumbai was formerly called Bombay); Calcutta, a port in eastern India; Beijing (BAY JIHNG), China's capital (Beijing was formerly called Peking); and Jakarta (juh KAHR tuh), the capital of Indonesia.

Several of these cities are very busy and modern. They are in countries such as Japan, which has quickly become one of the most modern nations in the world. The Japanese people work hard, and they are willing to learn and accept new ideas. Other countries along the Pacific that have grown amazingly in recent years are South Korea, Taiwan (ty WAHN), and Singapore. These countries and Hong Kong, a former British colony now under Chinese control, manufacture anything from cars to computers. They have been called "mini-Japans" because of how quickly they modernized their factories and cities. Along with modern development, however, come modern problems such as pollution and traffic jams.

In some cities of southern Asia the modern sections look as modern as any other city in the world. But conditions in the slums are terrible. People there are thankful if they can live in shanties made of tin or cloth. Many people have no shelter at all and sleep in the streets. Mumbai (Bombay) and Calcutta in India are two examples of cities that have both very rich and very poor people.

Asia's problems are increased by misunderstandings, hatred, and wars. In Vietnam, Cambodia, Afghanistan, and other countries, thousands of refugees have fled their homes because of warfare.

The many different religions, customs, and languages of Asian people make these situations worse. Not only do various countries have different languages, but one country may have many different groups of people speaking different languages. For example, in India people speak more than one hundred languages, plus hundreds of dialects. Misunderstandings because of different languages, customs, and religions are made much worse by the fact that people do not know and follow the Prince of Peace.

The people of Asia need to hear of Jesus Christ and how He can change their lives. Just having better living conditions is not enough. A young Chinese man who moved to Hong Kong remarked, "I saw people all about me working hard and making lots of money, but without any particular purpose. I wondered about the meaning of such lives, and what would happen after death."

Jesus Christ has the answer to such questions. Those who become His true, dedicated followers find purpose for this life and hope for the future. In spite of poverty, misunderstandings, and wars, they can live at peace with themselves, with their neighbors, and with God.

Study Exercises

23. What kind of regions are most densely populated in Asia?
24. In a densely populated area, what two problems do poor people have that the rich people there do not have?
25. Give two reasons for misunderstandings that cause suffering in Asia.

Clinching the Chapter

Use the text and maps to complete these exercises.

Multiple Choice

A. *Write the country* least *associated with the first item.*

1. Archipelagos: Bangladesh, Indonesia, Philippines, Japan
2. Pamir Knot: Afghanistan, Pakistan, Myanmar (Burma), China
3. Himalayas: Thailand, India, China, Nepal
4. Khyber Pass: Afghanistan, Sri Lanka, Pakistan, India
5. Rubber and tin: Malaysia, Thailand, Indonesia, Russia
6. Southeast Asia: Vietnam, Laos, Mongolia, Cambodia
7. Large cities: Afghanistan, China, Japan, India
8. New prosperity: Japan, Hong Kong, Vietnam, South Korea
9. Communism: Russia, China, Vietnam, Taiwan
10. Rice: Philippines, Russia, Thailand, India

B. *Write the correct words.*

1. The ocean to the south of most of Asia is the (Pacific, Atlantic, Arctic, Indian).
2. Asia is sometimes called the (Shinto, Orient, Himalaya, Baikal).
3. The river considered sacred by Hindus is the (Indus, Brahmaputra, Ganges, Huang He).
4. A river whose flooding helps farmers grow rice is the (Amur, Lena, Mekong, Yenisey).

5. "China's Sorrow" is the (Huang He, Yangtze, Brahmaputra, Indus).
6. The peninsula farthest to the southwest in Asia is (India, Arabia, Malaya, Scandinavia).
7. The time of summer monsoons is a period of (cool weather, rains, famine, drought).
8. The most popular meat in Japan is (beef, chicken, fish, pork).
9. A common religious philosophy in China is (Buddhism, Shintoism, Hinduism, Confucianism).
10. Belief in many gods is called (polytheism, monotheism, reincarnation, communism).

Matching

A. *For each clue, write the correct name from the right-hand column.*

1. Great fishing industry, Shintoism	China
2. Gobi Desert, Kunlun Mountains	India
3. Hinduism, caste system	Japan
4. 7,000 islands, copra, coconut oil	Pakistan
5. On peninsula of Southeast Asia	Philippines
6. Indus River, Khyber Pass	Siberia
7. A "mini-Japan"	Sri Lanka
8. Steppes, taiga, tundra	Taiwan
9. Yaks, "roof of the world"	Tibet
10. Formerly called Ceylon	Vietnam

B. *Match as in Part A.*

1. Dry climate, nomads, sheep	Bangladesh
2. Diamonds, gold, coal, oil, timber	central Asia
3. Humid climate, Ganges River delta	China
4. Seoul, east Asia peninsula	Hong Kong
5. Former British colony now under Chinese control	India
6. Off tip of Malay Peninsula	Indonesia
7. Tokyo, Mount Fuji	Japan
8. Most populous country in the world	Siberia
9. Over 13,600 islands	Singapore
10. Subcontinent, Ganges River, Hinduism	South Korea

Completion

1. Though ships can't sail the Huang He to the sea,
   Great freighters cruise far up the deep ————.
2. When Asians go to work on Monday,
   Americans still are having ———.
3. Of all great mountains east or west,
   The tallest is Mount ———.
4. Many travelers from Afghanistan
   Take the Khyber Pass to ———.
5. Volcanic mountains indicate,
   The lands around might have ———.

6. Every year, at least twice,
   Southeast Asians harvest ———.
7. Instead of rice, northern Chinese eat
   A dry-land grain that we call ———.

Thought Questions

1. The Pamir Knot has been compared to the center of an octopus. Why is this a good comparison?
2. What are two problems that the mountains of Asia cause for people?
3. In what two ways are the mountains beneficial to the Asians?
4. Southeast Asia has more natural resources than Japan, yet Japan is much more prosperous than Southeast Asia. What are some reasons for this?
5. What is one advantage and one disadvantage of living in regions of Asia where much rain falls?
6. Suppose you owned a small plot of farmland in Southeast Asia and had to feed as many people as possible. (*a*) Would you be more likely to raise crops or raise animals? (*b*) What would be the most promising crop? (*c*) What would be the most productive animal? (*d*) How could you farm steep hillsides? (You should be able to see that in many ways Asian people farm very wisely.)
7. Jesus said in John 14:6, "I am the way, the truth, and the life: no man cometh unto the Father, but by me." How is this statement different from the attitude that many Asians take toward religion?
8. How was the "golden rule" that Confucius taught not as good as the Golden Rule taught in the New Testament? (Consider its basis, as stated in Romans 13:9, 10.)
9. What is a good reason that so many of Asia's people live near rivers and seacoasts?
10. If Christianity would solve so many problems in Asia, why has it not solved more problems in North America, where many people claim to be Christians? (Carefully read the last paragraph in the text.)

Geographical Skills

1. Name the capital city found at each location. Also name the country of which it is the capital. (If Figure 3:1 does not show the exact latitude or longitude, you should be able to estimate correctly.)
   a. 39°55′N 116°26′E
   b. 14°37′N 120°58′E
   c. 6°08′S 106°45′E
   d. 35°40′N 139°45′E
   e. 1°17′N 103°51′E
   f. 28°37′N 77°13′E
2. Which of the capital cities named in number 1 is (*a*) farthest south? (*b*) farthest north? (*c*) farthest east? (*d*) farthest west?
3. Using a map scale, find the approximate distance between these cities.
   a. New Delhi—Calcutta
   b. Manila—Kabul
   c. Hanoi—Ho Chi Minh City
   d. Shanghai—Beijing
   e. Singapore—Jakarta
   f. Seoul—Tokyo
4. Population maps show where people live. Climate maps help explain why people live where they do, why they do the kind of work they do, and why they raise certain

crops. After studying the maps on pages 54–56, write *true* or *false* for each statement.

a. Most people in Asia live where the climate is cool.
b. The most heavily populated part of Asia has abundant rainfall.
c. Because dairy cows do best in a cool climate, the southern islands are the best part of Japan for dairying.
d. Sugar cane, a crop that grows best in warm weather, does better in India than in Siberia.
e. Wheat, a cool-weather crop, is more likely to grow well in Bangladesh than in Afghanistan.
f. There are more trappers of fur-bearing animals in Vietnam than in Siberia.
g. Rice, a crop that needs warmth and moisture, does better in Mongolia than in the Philippines.
h. A city is more likely to be located along a river or seacoast than away from it.

Further Study

1. What is the difference between a monsoon and a typhoon? Write one or two paragraphs describing how they each affect life in Asia.
2. Find the elevation of a site near your home, and compare it with the height of Mount Everest.
3. Copy and complete the following chart.

MAJOR RIVERS OF ASIA

Name (Country at Mouth)	Length	Ocean It Flows Into
Brahmaputra (Bangladesh)		
Ganges (Bangladesh)		
Indus (Pakistan)		
Mekong (Vietnam)		
Huang He (China)		
Yangtze (China)		
Amur (Russia)		
Lena (Russia)		
Ob (Russia)		
Yenisey (Russia)		

Be Sure You Know

Can you answer all these questions? If not, study Chapters 1–3 to find the answers.

A. Where are these items on a map?

1. the continents of Europe and Asia
2. the Alps, the Pyrenees, and the Himalayas
3. the Straits of Gibraltar, Bosporus, and Dardanelles
4. the Rhine, Danube, and Volga Rivers in Europe
5. the Ganges, Indus, Huang He, and Yangtze Rivers in Asia

B. What

6. people first realized that the earth is a sphere?
7. (*a*) are some advantages of globes? (*b*) of flat maps?
8. (*a*) is the starting point for latitude? (*b*) for longitude?
9. hemispheres are important in geography?
10. are the three geographical regions of Europe?
11. is the longest river in Europe?
12. is the highest mountain (*a*) in Europe? (*b*) in Asia?
13. river is considered sacred by Hindus?
14. seven major religions do Asians follow?
15. major mountain range helps to keep southern Asia warm and central Asia dry?

C. What do these words mean?

16. archipelago
17. caste
18. communist
19. continental shelf
20. culture
21. distortion
22. great-circle route
23. hemisphere
24. hydroelectricity
25. International Date Line
26. Iron Curtain
27. latitude
28. legend
29. loess
30. longitude
31. Mediterranean climate
32. meridian
33. monotheism
34. monsoon
35. North Atlantic Drift
36. Orient
37. parallel
38. permafrost
39. plateau
40. polytheism
41. prime meridian
42. sphere
43. steppe
44. strait
45. taiga
46. terrace
47. tundra

D. Why

48. does western Europe have a mild climate?
49. is the crooked coastline of Europe a benefit?
50. must Europeans be especially careful in using their resources?
51. are some west longitude areas usually considered part of the Eastern Hemisphere?
52. are Europe and Asia considered as two different continents?
53. have Asians not used more of their rich supply of minerals?

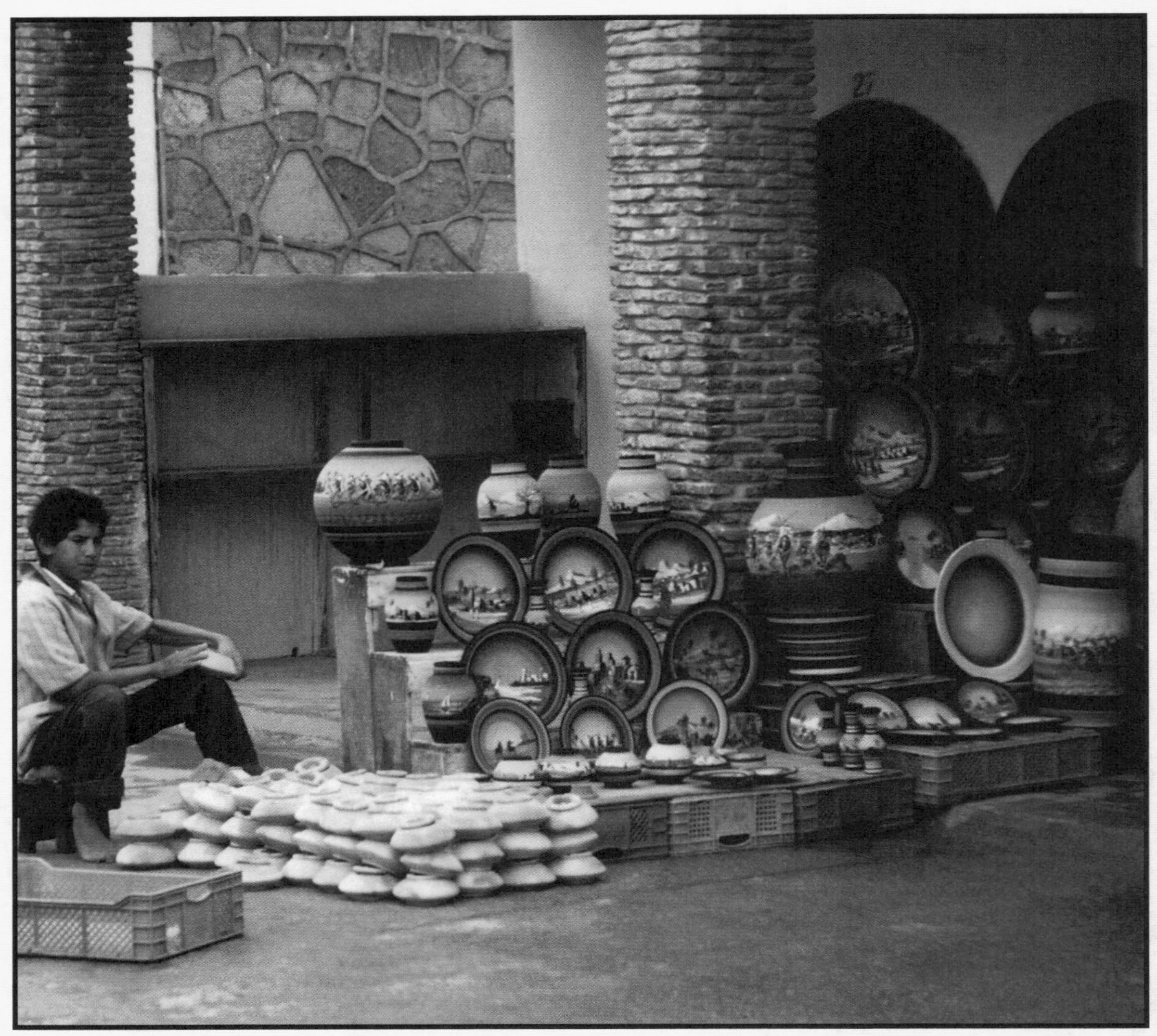

This lad sells some of Morocco's fine pottery to tourists. Interesting places, a moderate climate, and traditional handcrafts such as pottery bring many tourists to some parts of Africa.

4 Africa

Size and Location

Climate and Land Use

Rivers and Lakes

Cities

Farming in Africa

Trade and Industry

African Cultures—a Great Variety

African Nations Today

African Religions

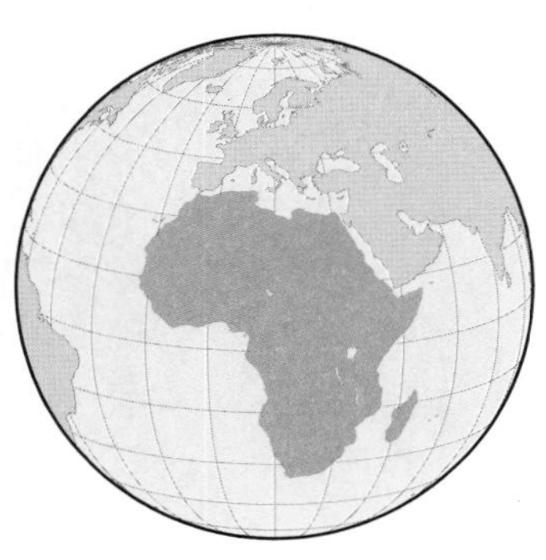

Algeria • Angola • Benin • Botswana • Burkina Faso • Burundi • Cameroon • Cape Verde • Central African Republic • Chad • Comoros • Congo • Congo (Dem. Rep.) • Djibouti • Egypt • Equatorial Guinea • Eritrea • Ethiopia • Gabon • Gambia • Ghana • Guinea • Guinea-Bissau • Ivory Coast • Kenya • Lesotho • Liberia • Libya • Madagascar • Malawi • Mali • Mauritania • Mauritius • Morocco • Mozambique • Namibia • Niger • Nigeria • Rwanda • São Tomé & Príncipe • Senegal • Seychelles • Sierra Leone • Somalia • South Africa • Sudan • Swaziland • Tanzania • Togo • Tunisia • Uganda • Western Sahara • Zambia • Zimbabwe

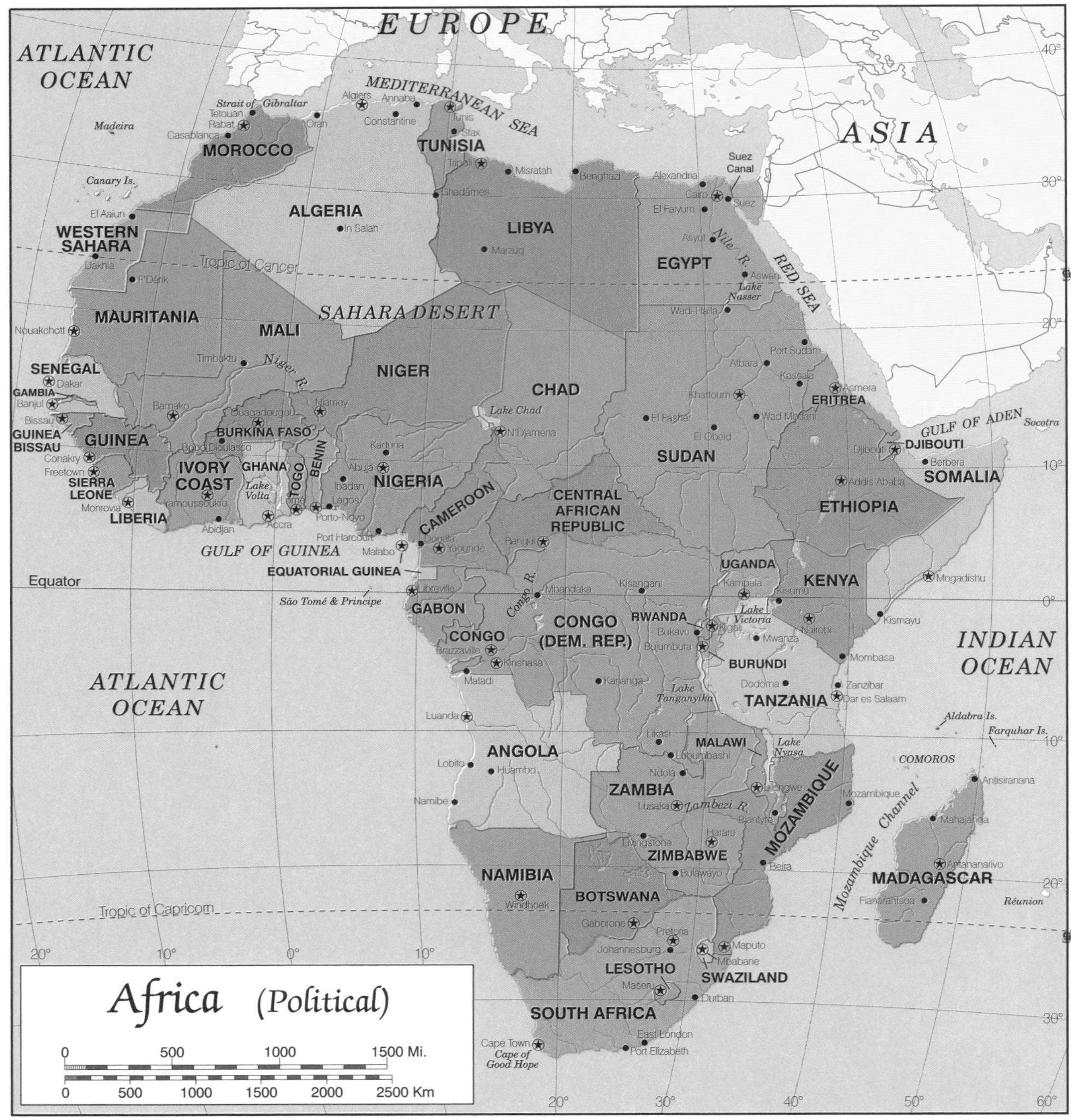

Africa (Political)
EUROPE
ASIA
ATLANTIC OCEAN
INDIAN OCEAN
MEDITERRANEAN SEA
RED SEA
GULF OF ADEN
GULF OF GUINEA
SAHARA DESERT
Tropic of Cancer
Tropic of Capricorn
Equator
MOROCCO
ALGERIA
TUNISIA
LIBYA
EGYPT
WESTERN SAHARA
MAURITANIA
MALI
NIGER
CHAD
SUDAN
ERITREA
DJIBOUTI
SOMALIA
ETHIOPIA
SENEGAL
GAMBIA
GUINEA BISSAU
GUINEA
SIERRA LEONE
LIBERIA
IVORY COAST
BURKINA FASO
GHANA
TOGO
BENIN
NIGERIA
CAMEROON
CENTRAL AFRICAN REPUBLIC
EQUATORIAL GUINEA
São Tomé & Príncipe
GABON
CONGO
CONGO (DEM. REP.)
UGANDA
KENYA
RWANDA
BURUNDI
TANZANIA
ANGOLA
ZAMBIA
MALAWI
MOZAMBIQUE
ZIMBABWE
NAMIBIA
BOTSWANA
SOUTH AFRICA
LESOTHO
SWAZILAND
MADAGASCAR
COMOROS
Mozambique Channel
Madeira
Canary Is.
Socotra
Aldabra Is.
Farquhar Is.
Réunion
Strait of Gibraltar
Suez Canal
Nile R.
Niger R.
Congo R.
Zambezi R.
Lake Chad
Lake Victoria
Lake Tanganyika
Lake Nyasa
Lake Nasser
Lake Volta
Cape of Good Hope
0 500 1000 1500 Mi.
0 500 1000 1500 2000 2500 Km

Figure 4:1

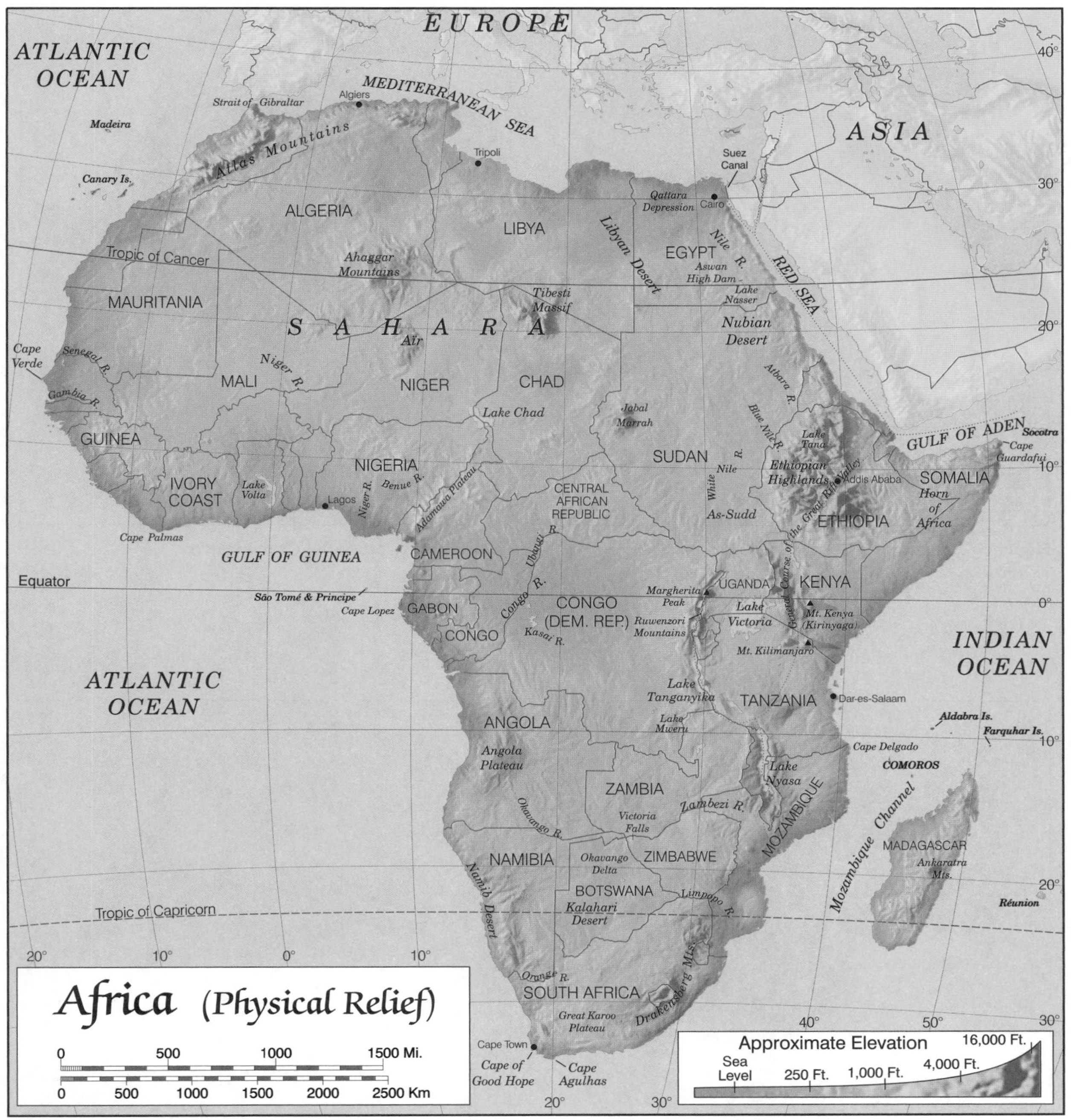
EUROPE
ATLANTIC OCEAN
MEDITERRANEAN SEA
Algiers
Strait of Gibraltar
Madeira
Atlas Mountains
Canary Is.
Tripoli
ASIA
Suez Canal
Qattara Depression
Cairo
ALGERIA
LIBYA
Libyan Desert
EGYPT
Nile R.
RED SEA
Aswan High Dam
Lake Nasser
Tropic of Cancer
Ahaggar Mountains
MAURITANIA
Tibesti Massif
SAHARA
Aïr
Nubian Desert
Cape Verde
Senegal R.
Niger R.
MALI
NIGER
CHAD
Atbara R.
Gambia R.
Lake Chad
Jabal Marrah
Blue Nile R.
Lake Tana
GULF OF ADEN
Socotra
Cape Guardafui
GUINEA
NIGERIA
SUDAN
Ethiopian Highlands
Addis Ababa
SOMALIA
IVORY COAST
Lake Volta
Benue R.
Adamawa Plateau
White Nile R.
Great Rift Valley
Horn of Africa
Lagos
Niger R.
CENTRAL AFRICAN REPUBLIC
As-Sudd
ETHIOPIA
Cape Palmas
Ubangi R.
GULF OF GUINEA
CAMEROON
Equator
São Tomé & Principe
Margherita Peak
UGANDA
KENYA
General Course of the Great Rift Valley
Cape Lopez
GABON
Congo R.
CONGO (DEM. REP.)
Ruwenzori Mountains
Lake Victoria
Mt. Kenya (Kirinyaga)
CONGO
Kasai R.
Mt. Kilimanjaro
INDIAN OCEAN
ATLANTIC OCEAN
Lake Tanganyika
TANZANIA
Dar-es-Salaam
Aldabra Is.
ANGOLA
Lake Mweru
Farquhar Is.
Cape Delgado
Angola Plateau
COMOROS
Lake Nyasa
ZAMBIA
Zambezi R.
Mozambique Channel
Okavango R.
Victoria Falls
MOZAMBIQUE
NAMIBIA
Okavango Delta
ZIMBABWE
MADAGASCAR
Ankaratra Mts.
Namib Desert
BOTSWANA
Limpopo R.
Kalahari Desert
Réunion
Tropic of Capricorn
20°
10°
0°
10°
Orange R.
SOUTH AFRICA
Drakensberg Mts.
Great Karoo Plateau
40°
50°
30°
20°
10°
0°
10°
20°
30°
40°
Africa (Physical Relief)
0 500 1000 1500 Mi.
0 500 1000 1500 2000 2500 Km
Cape Town
Cape of Good Hope
Cape Agulhas
20°
30°
Approximate Elevation
Sea Level
250 Ft.
1,000 Ft.
4,000 Ft.
16,000 Ft.

Figure 4:2

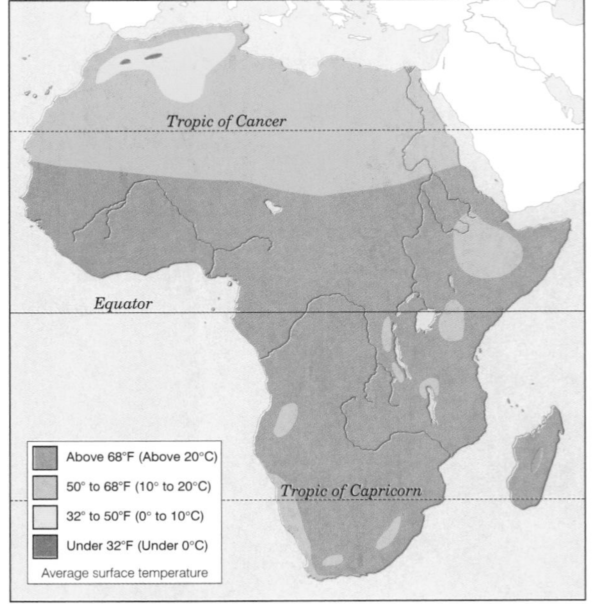

Figure 4:3. Average January Temperature

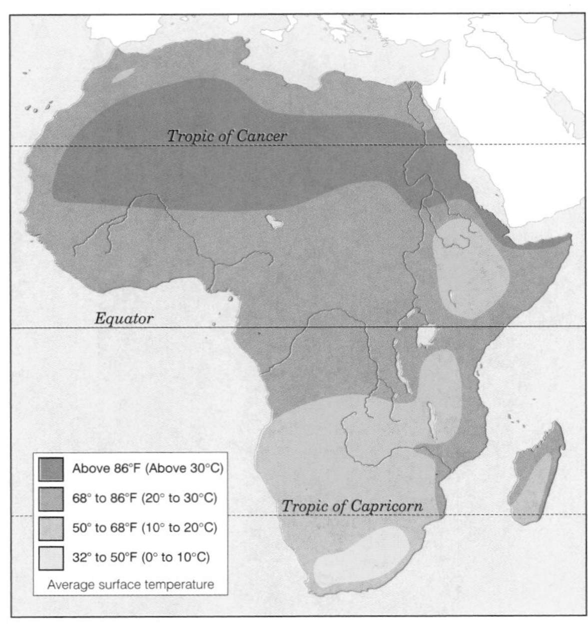

Figure 4:4. Average July Temperature

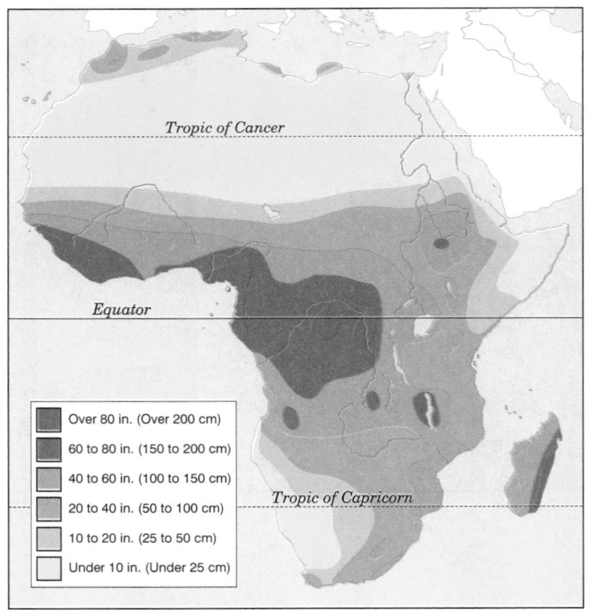

Figure 4:5. Average Annual Rainfall

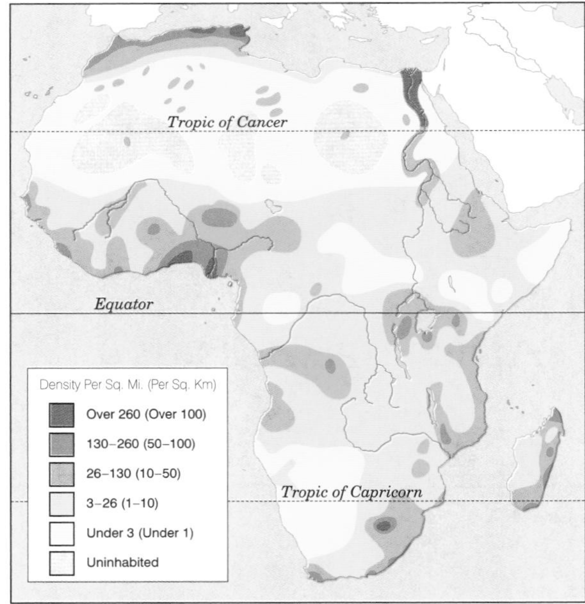

Figure 4:6. Population Distribution

Africa

Size and Location

"Dark Africa," Europeans used to call it. This may have been partly because the people were dark-skinned, and partly because the light of the Gospel had not yet reached much of Africa. But Africa was also dark to the Europeans because they did not know much about it.

What a large continent has been explored since then! Only Asia is larger than Africa. At its greatest breadth, Africa is about 4,600 miles (7,400 km) wide from the Atlantic Ocean to the Indian Ocean. North to south, it is about 5,000 miles (8,000 km) long.

On the map, notice that northern Africa nearly touches Europe at the western end of the Mediterranean Sea. The two continents are separated by the narrow Strait of Gibraltar. At one time the northeastern corner of Africa joined Asia north of the Red Sea. Now these two continents are separated by the Suez Canal (soo EHZ), which is a narrow separation indeed.

The Strait of Gibraltar and the Suez Canal mark the northwestern and northeastern corners of Africa. Three other main

The Suez Canal has had a turbulent history. According to some sources, Egyptians dug a canal connecting the Nile River with the Red Sea about 4,000 years ago. This early effort was rebuilt several times, but was finally abandoned in the A.D. 700s. After that, boat travelers going from Europe to Asia had to make the long, hazardous journey around the southern tip of Africa.

In the 1850s, a French engineer gained Egypt's permission to build the present canal, which is 107 miles (172 km) long. It opened in 1869. The Arab–Israeli conflict of recent years has caused it to be closed at times.

(Left) Rice, coffee, corn, and peanuts are some of the crops grown in Madagascar's attractive fields. Farming provides about 85 percent of the jobs in Madagascar. Coffee is the leading export. When you eat vanilla-flavored ice cream or pudding, you might be eating a product of this country—Madagascar produces about two-thirds of the world's vanilla. *(Right)* On the tiny island of Nosy Bé, near Madagascar, the crater of an extinct volcano forms a beautiful lake.

corners can be seen on a map. Locate Cape Verde (VURD) at the tip of the bulge of western Africa. Near the tip of the southern bulge, find the Cape of Good Hope. Also find what is called the Horn of Africa, the easternmost part that juts into the Indian Ocean south of the Red Sea and the Gulf of Aden.

Africa does not have hundreds of islands or many peninsulas. No arms of the sea reach into the continent, and the mouths of most African rivers do not form natural harbors. This means that Africa has fewer ports than other continents. Also, much of its area lies far inland from the ocean. This is one reason, among several others, that parts of Africa are dry.

Off the southeast coast of Africa lies Madagascar (mad uh GAS kur), the fourth largest island in the world. Madagascar is the only large island associated with the continent of Africa.

Study Exercises

1. Between what two oceans does Africa lie?
2. What two continents does Africa touch or nearly touch?
3. Name five corners on the outline shape of Africa.
4. Which includes more islands: Africa or Asia?

Climate and Land Use

Since the equator passes through Africa, most of the continent lies within the Tropics. The climate of Africa is often thought of as hot and humid, with rain forests and monkeys. Actually, the area of rain forest is relatively small; much of Africa is either hot desert or open grassland. God also gave Africa some pleasant highland regions where people live comfortably. There are even mountain peaks near the equator that are covered with ice!

To study African climate, you will start in northwestern Africa and move south. You should be able to see a pattern in the climate that will help you to understand and remember it.

Northwesternmost Africa: Mediterranean Climate. Along the Mediterranean coast of Morocco (muh RAHK oh), Algeria, and Tunisia (too NEE zhuh), you cross a narrow strip of land having a Mediterranean climate. This climate is similar to that in Bible lands. Rain falls in the winter, but the summers are very dry. Drought-resistant trees such as olive, fig, and date trees grow well. Grapes and grain also do well. Not far inland, the climate is more dry. The Atlas Mountains in northwest Africa receive some rainfall. Farmers there can grow crops and raise livestock. But farther south the land changes to desert.

South of the Mediterranean Climate: Desert. As you travel across the huge Sahara (Arabic for desert), you see some

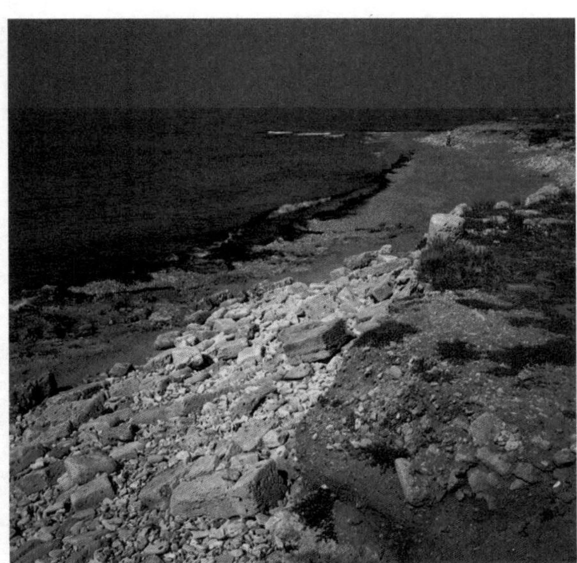

Libya, once called the Desert Kingdom of Africa, has over 1,000 miles (1,610 km) of coastline on the Mediterranean Sea. Most of the country is part of the Sahara, but the Libyans have coaxed a good living from the petroleum that lies beneath their sandy domain.

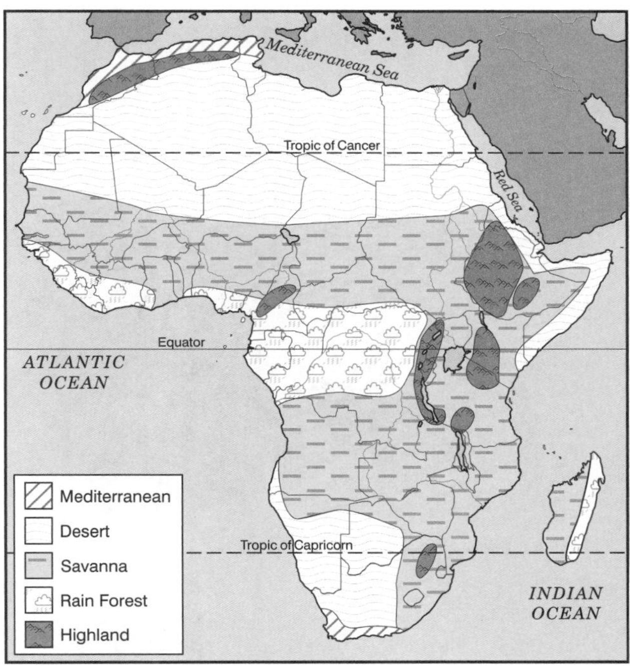

Figure 4:7. African Climate Zones

sand dunes—great heaps of sand that is blown by constant winds. However, you might be surprised to learn that rocks and gravel cover much of the Sahara. The strong winds constantly sweep the sand into dunes and leave the rest of the desert bare.

The Sahara is not flat everywhere. For example, the barren mountains in the deserts of Algeria are taller than most of the Atlas Mountains. The Sahara is hot—in the daytime. But when the sun goes down, the dry air cannot hold its heat. The desert becomes cold so fast that rocks sometimes crack from the sudden temperature change.

Here and there across the desert is an ***oasis*** with wells, date palm trees, gardens, and fields. These oases are often created by an ***artesian*** (ahr TEE zhuhn) well, where water rises to the surface without pumps. On the oases, desert dwellers raise crops such as figs and barley. Sometimes they stay at one oasis only for a while, and then they move on to another. The world's largest oasis lies far to the east along the Nile River in Egypt. Without this long strip of green,

DATES

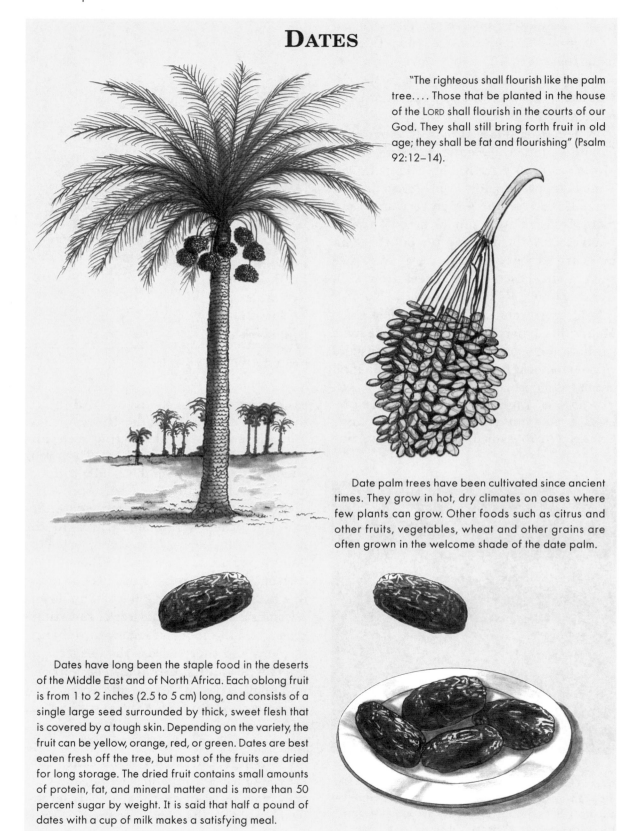

"The righteous shall flourish like the palm tree.... Those that be planted in the house of the LORD shall flourish in the courts of our God. They shall still bring forth fruit in old age; they shall be fat and flourishing" (Psalm 92:12–14).

Date palm trees have been cultivated since ancient times. They grow in hot, dry climates on oases where few plants can grow. Other foods such as citrus and other fruits, vegetables, wheat and other grains are often grown in the welcome shade of the date palm.

Dates have long been the staple food in the deserts of the Middle East and of North Africa. Each oblong fruit is from 1 to 2 inches (2.5 to 5 cm) long, and consists of a single large seed surrounded by thick, sweet flesh that is covered by a tough skin. Depending on the variety, the fruit can be yellow, orange, red, or green. Dates are best eaten fresh off the tree, but most of the fruits are dried for long storage. The dried fruit contains small amounts of protein, fat, and mineral matter and is more than 50 percent sugar by weight. It is said that half a pound of dates with a cup of milk makes a satisfying meal.

A date palm tree starts bearing fruit at about five years of age, and commonly produces at least 100 pounds (45 kg) of fruit each year for about sixty years. Clusters of dates grow at the end of stalks hanging high in the tree. Often a tree yields from eight to ten clusters of dates in a season, with each cluster weighing up to 25 pounds (11 kg) and containing a thousand or more individual fruits. A date palm may live to be 150 years old, but modern growers often replace the trees with younger trees at an earlier age to keep up the productivity. New trees are started from suckers that sprout near the base of the old tree. Flowers are artificially pollinated (often by hand) since the male and female flowers grow on different trees. To depend on wind pollination would be too risky, for dates are the main food for millions of people.

Date clusters grown close to the ground are easy to harvest.

All parts of the date palm tree are useful. Lumber is obtained from the trunk; baskets, mats, cordage, ropes, and packing material are made from the fibrous parts; fuel is obtained from the leaf bases; furniture and crates are made from the midribs of the leaves; a coffee substitute is made from roasted seeds, and animal feed is made from ground-up seeds. When a palm tree is cut down, the tender terminal bud is eaten.

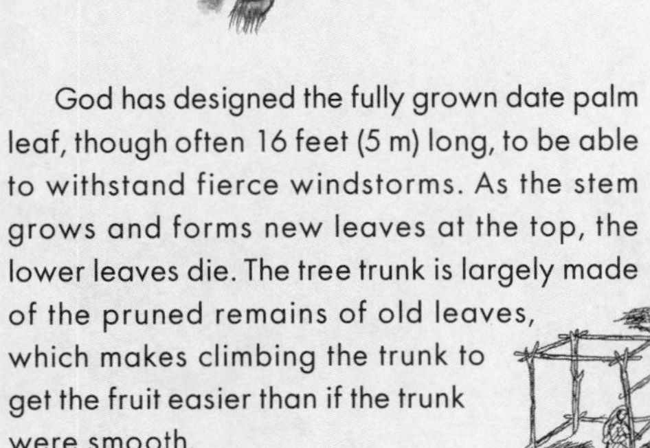

God has designed the fully grown date palm leaf, though often 16 feet (5 m) long, to be able to withstand fierce windstorms. As the stem grows and forms new leaves at the top, the lower leaves die. The tree trunk is largely made of the pruned remains of old leaves, which makes climbing the trunk to get the fruit easier than if the trunk were smooth.

Preparation for the annual Feast of Tabernacles. Read Leviticus 23:39–43.

In northern Africa, the date palms are so valuable that they pass from father to son as wealth and often form the dowry of a daughter. A man's position in society is governed largely by the number of date palm trees he owns.

Saudi Arabia, Egypt, Iran, and Iraq are world leaders in date production.

Egypt would be almost total desert.

After a long journey south across the desert, you finally begin to see tufts of grass, a few drought-resistant bushes, and then a few animals and people. You are coming to the Sahel (suh HAYL), the land on the southern edge of the desert. A short rainy season each year keeps the Sahel from turning completely into sand and dust. Nomads roam these almost-empty lands. During the long dry season, the nomads may suffer from thirst or even hunger while they constantly look for grass to keep their skinny cattle alive. Sometimes the rains fail and the Sahara extends its sands onto the Sahel, driving the cattle herders south in a desperate search for life-sustaining grass and water.

South of the Desert: Savanna. Farther south, the grass becomes thicker and taller. These grasslands of Africa are called ***savanna.*** Many herdsmen make a living in the savanna. More herds would graze there if it were not for the ***tsetse*** (TSEHT see) fly. This bite of this insect transmits a disease that can weaken and kill cattle. The tsetse fly also carries the African sleeping sickness, which is fatal to people.

The savanna supports many of Africa's best farms. Besides animals, savanna farmers raise warm-weather crops such as cotton, corn, and sweet potatoes. (Regular white potatoes do not grow well in too warm a climate.) They also raise millet, the tiny round grains that make good food for birds as well as for people. Millet matures in just ninety days, a fact that makes it possible for farmers to raise this grain where the rainy season is short.

People also eat the ***cassava*** (kuh SAH vuh) root. Cassava, or manioc, grows well even where the soil is poor and where hungry locusts abound. It is the same plant from which tapioca is made. Africans raise peanuts too, not only to eat but also for peanut oil, which is used in a variety of products.

Countries such as Mauritania (mor ih TAY nee uh), Mali (MAH lee), Niger (NY jur), and Chad have desert land in their northern parts and savanna in their southern parts. Comparing Figures 4:2 and 4:7 will help you see what kinds of climate each country of Africa has.

These agricultural plants are grown on Africa's savanna. Clockwise from the left, they are millet, cotton, sweet potatoes, cassava, peanuts, and corn.

Millet

In ancient times, millet was the most important crop of Europe and parts of Africa and Asia. Then wheat and other grains became more popular, and millet was not grown as much. It is listed among the bread ingredients in Ezekiel 4:9. Millet is a grass plant that usually grows from 1 to 4 feet (.3 to 1.2 m) high, depending on the variety, although one type grows up to 15 feet (4.6 m) tall. Many millet varieties can grow in less fertile soils and hotter, drier weather than most other grains can. Because the plant matures rapidly, it is sometimes planted as an emergency crop after a previous crop failure.

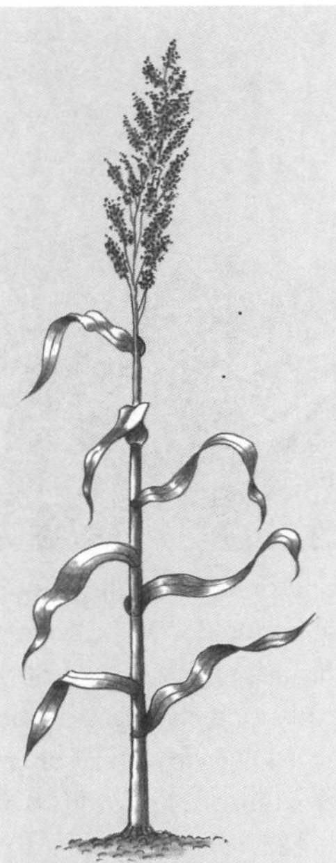

Millet flat bread

Millet produces small, edible seeds that are an important source of food for people in dry areas of Africa and Asia. The seeds form in a cluster at the top of the stem and remain in their hulls after threshing in all varieties except pearl millet. Hulled millet seeds are usually creamy white and have a high carbohydrate content and about 8 percent protein content. Somewhat strong in taste, they are used in porridges, cooked like rice, and are also ground into flour for flat breads and thin, fried cakes. Millet seeds, stems, and leaves are used to make feed for animals and birds in some parts of the world.

Main varieties include pearl millet, foxtail millet, and proso millet. Each of these is also known by various other common names. Pearl millet is grown mostly in Africa and India. Foxtail is grown as a food crop in China, Russia, and nearby countries. Proso is grown mostly in Asia and has such a hard seed that it must be ground if it is used to feed livestock. Many Americans are familiar with millet birdseed, but they may not be aware that after the seeds have been removed, the seed head of some proso varieties can be made into brooms.

Today, India, China, and Nigeria are leading millet producers.

The largest land animal, a full-grown African elephant can weigh up to 8 tons (7,500 kg) and stand 10–13 feet (3–4 m) at the shoulder. He can eat 500 pounds (225 kg) of vegetation daily and live to be about 60 years old. However, poachers kill many elephants for their valuable ivory tusks, which are about 6 feet (1.8 m) long and weigh about 50 pounds (23 kg) apiece.

The farther south you go across the savanna, the more rain falls during the rainy season and the taller the grass grows. Trees appear here and there. The animals for which Africa is famous—elephants, giraffes, lions, zebras, and hippopotamuses—roam this part of the savanna. (There are no tigers in Africa.) However, these animals are becoming fewer today, largely because people are crowding them out. Many animals are also killed by foreigners on hunting ***safaris*** (suh FAHR eez), and by ***poachers*** who hope to sell the skins and other parts of the animals.

Equatorial Africa: Rain Forest. The land continues to change. You see more trees and thickets until finally you are in thick forest. Now you are close to the equator, where every season is rainy season. Vines twist upward along tree trunks. Monkeys chatter overhead in trees that stand as much as 160 feet (48 m) tall. Snakes, brightly colored birds, and millions of insects live in the rain forest, along with gorillas, leopards, crocodiles, the brilliant Congo peacock, and other African animals.

The insects make life in the rain forest not only uncomfortable but also dangerous. Some of them carry diseases such as ***malaria.*** The hot, humid climate also saps people's strength. It is difficult to work hard in this climate. Still, God gave the rain forests some treasures of their own. Trees such as mahogany and ebony may someday be cut and dragged out of these forests to make fine furniture.

In the hottest, most humid areas, ordinary farming is difficult. Rain falls in torrents, washing the nutrients out of the soil. Sometimes tree crops are best. In areas that once were rain forest, people produce much ***cacao*** (kuh KAH oh) for chocolate; palm oil for soap, candles, and vegetable oil; and rubber. Rice and sugar cane are also raised in the tropical region.

Notice on the map that countries such as Ghana (GAH nuh), Nigeria (ny JEER ee uh), and Cameroon (kam uh ROON) have grasslands in the northern parts and forests in their southern parts. Sudan (soo DAN), farther east, has three of the climates you have studied: desert in the north, grasslands in the central region, and forests in the south. But the Democratic Republic of Congo (formerly Zaire) and the Republic of Congo, on the equator, have mostly rain forest.

South of the Rain Forest: Savanna. As you continue south through the rain forest, the trees thin out and you are back in familiar grassland country—savanna again! You are discovering that African climates south of the equator are in many ways a mirror image of Africa north of the equator.

South of the Savanna: Desert. Farther away from the equator, you again find deserts. Two deserts, the Kalahari (kah luh HAH ree) and the Namib (NAH mihb), are much smaller than the Sahara. Africa is narrower there, and winds bring rain from the Indian Ocean.

Southernmost Africa: Mediterranean Climate. Perhaps you predicted it: the southernmost tip of Africa has a Mediterranean climate like that of northernmost Africa.

Highland Areas: An Exception. Not all of Africa has as neat a pattern of climates as you have seen on this journey south. Highland areas, even though they are in the equatorial part of Africa, are not covered with tropical rain forests. Mount Kenya stands almost on the equator, yet its peak—17,058 feet (5,199 m) high—is always covered with snow and ice. The Ruwenzori Mountains (roo wuhn ZAWR ee), once called the Mountains of the Moon, have glaciers on their peaks. Extending east from these are the highland areas of Uganda (yoo GAN duh) and Kenya, which have a pleasant climate. The nearby countries of Ethiopia and Tanzania (tan zuh NEE uh) also have many mountains and plateaus with a cool, invigorating climate.

Africa's highest mountain, Mount Kilimanjaro (kihl uh muhn JAHR oh), stands in Tanzania near the border of Kenya. The landscape on Mount Kilimanjaro, from the base to its peak at 19,340 feet (5,895 m), illustrates how climate changes with altitude. At the base of the mountain is savanna. Higher up more rain falls, and forests cover the slopes. As the climate becomes colder, the forest ends and only shrubs and grasses grow. Still higher are moss and lichens, and above these you would find bare rock, ice, and glaciers.

Study Exercises

5. Going from north to south in Africa, a simplified climate pattern would be as follows: Mediterranean, desert, savanna, rain forest, ———, ———, ———.
6. What keeps some tropical regions from being uncomfortably warm?
7. Write the name of one of these climates for each item: Mediterranean, desert, savanna, rain forest.
   a. home of the tsetse fly
   b. grapes, grain, dates, olives
   c. elephants, zebras, giraffes, lions
   d. mahogany, rubber, cacao
   e. insects, heat, and high humidity
   f. hot days and cold nights

Soaring above the surrounding plain and clouds, snow-capped Mount Kilimanjaro rises 19,340 feet (5,895 m) above sea level. It is the highest point in Africa. This picture was taken from Kenya, but the mountain actually stands in Tanzania.

David Livingstone, a British missionary and explorer, first sighted Victoria Falls in 1855. He named it after Queen Victoria of Britain. Compared with Niagara Falls in North America, Victoria Falls is twice as wide and twice as high.

Rivers and Lakes

Rivers. Africa has only a few well-known rivers. One of these is the Nile. The Nile is well known not only because Egypt is so dependent on it but also because it is the longest river in the world. The Nile begins in central Africa, with Lake Victoria as one of its sources. The branch of the river that flows from Lake Victoria is called the White Nile. The branch called the Blue Nile is fed by rains in Ethiopia. After the White Nile and the Blue Nile meet in Sudan, the Nile flows through Egypt to the Mediterranean Sea.

The muddy Congo River carries even more water than the Nile. It flows through the rain forests of central Africa, where heavy rainfall gives it a flow of water second only to that of the mighty Amazon. Ships use the river for many miles, although ***rapids*** keep ships from traveling the whole length of the river. Railroads take goods around the rapids to other ships that travel farther inland.

The Niger River, in the southern part of Africa's western bulge, takes a rather strange course. Instead of flowing straight from its source to the ocean, it curves away and flows north, east, and then south before it finally empties into the Atlantic. Along its course of 2,600 miles (4,185 km), much of it through savanna and desert land, the Niger provides water to irrigate huge areas. Understandably, two of the countries it flows through are called Niger and Nigeria.

The Zambezi River (zam BEE zee) flows generally eastward through southern Africa. This river is not as famous as its great Victoria Falls, which David Livingstone discovered and named after Queen Victoria. There the water of the Zambezi River falls about 350 feet (100 m) into a canyon. The falls are more than 1 mile (1.6 km) wide. Victoria Falls sends up so much mist that the African people called it the "smoke that thunders."

Lakes and the Great Rift Valley. Looking carefully at a map of eastern Africa near Tanzania, you notice several long lakes that form a crooked chain. They include Lake Nyasa (ny AS uh), Lake Tanganyika (tan guhn YEE kuh), and several smaller ones. These lakes all lie in the Great Rift Valley, which begins in Bible lands and continues south from there. The Sea of Galilee, the Jordan River, the Dead Sea, and the Red Sea also lie in the Great Rift. A ***rift*** is a deep crack in the earth's surface, and this one is more than 3,000 miles (4,830 km) long.

Northeast of Lake Tanganyika, Lake Victoria lies in a plateau basin between two branches of the Great Rift Valley. In surface area, Lake Victoria is the second largest freshwater lake in the world. Only Lake Superior covers more square miles.

Cities

Most of Africa's great cities are located around the edge of Africa, near the sea. Notice this as you find these cities on a map: Algiers (al JEERZ), the capital of Algeria; Tripoli (TRIHP uh lee), the capital of Libya; Cairo (KY roh), the capital of Egypt; Dar es Salaam (DAHR ehs suh LAHM), the capital of Tanzania; Cape Town, one of the capitals of South Africa; Lagos (LAH gohs), the largest city of Nigeria; and the many other cities near the coast. One of Africa's large cities not near the coast is Addis Ababa (AD ihs AB uh buh), the capital of Ethiopia.

Various African cities have a similar problem—a problem often found in less-developed countries. While they have a modern section with wide streets, parks, colleges, hospitals, and libraries, they also have some very poor sections. For example, a large, dirty slum area full of mud huts surrounds the city of Addis Ababa. And the lower section of Algiers has tall, modern buildings, while its old part farther up the hill has narrow streets and crowded, rundown buildings.

One reason for the poor sections is that people from the countryside come to cities, looking for work. But they have no skills, so they find no job or else find a very poor one. Their only choice is to make huts for themselves and try to survive as best they can.

Study Exercises

8. (*a*) Which African river is the longest in the world? (*b*) Which carries more water than any other African river? (*c*) On which river is the famous Victoria Falls?
9. A chain of lakes is found along what natural feature in eastern Africa?
10. Where are most of the large African cities located?
11. Cities are a home for both the very rich and the very ———.

The building in the foreground is a hotel in Nairobi, the capital of Kenya. Nairobi is a favorite spot for tourists and the starting point for safaris, whether for hunting, wildlife watching, or photography. In Kenya the word *safari* means "a trip of any kind."

Barley

Barley is frequently mentioned in the Bible, and was one of the first cultivated crops. It is a very hardy plant, and thrives in cooler climates, at high altitudes, and in hot, dry places. In warmer climates, it is often planted in the fall as a winter crop and harvested the following summer. Barley has a shorter growing season than any other grain.

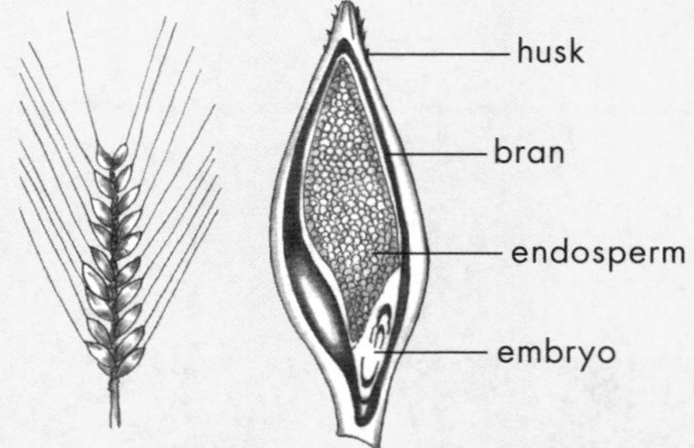

pearl barley

barley soup

Barley resembles wheat, with spikes at the top of the stems that contain the seeds. Many varieties have awns (beards) growing from the seed husks. The hulled grain, used for soups and gruels, is comparable to wheat in nourishment, but the popular pearl barley loses many of its nutrients through a process that grinds the kernel into a smooth, polished ball.

barley bread

Barley bread is dark in color, and rather heavy because the grain lacks gluten, which is needed to make a light loaf. Perhaps the heaviness was in focus in the following Bible passage: "Behold, I dreamed a dream, and, lo, a cake of barley bread tumbled into the host of Midian, and came unto a tent, and smote it that it fell, and overturned it, that the tent lay along" (Judges 7:13).

Most of the barley grown in the world is used for animal feed and for making malt, which is an ingredient in some baked goods, baby foods, malt vinegar, other malted foods, and for the detrimental use of making beer and other strong drinks. The leading Old World barley-producing areas are Russia, Germany, France, and Spain.

Farming in Africa

Most African workers are farmers—and poor. This is not because farming in itself makes people poor. But since Africa does not have many factories, farmers do not have the equipment they need. Since there are not many teachers, farmers cannot learn the best farming practices. Neither can they study ways to improve their farming, because they do not know how to read. Besides, many people find it difficult to give up their old ways of doing things, even if those methods are not as efficient as newer ways. Millions of African farmers barely raise enough food to feed their own families. They are called ***subsistence farmers.***

Much African topsoil is poor and thin. Farmers in some regions avoid plowing the soil to keep the nutrients in it from being washed out by rain. Many farmers have to shift their planting from one field to another when the soil wears out. Droughts cause widespread hunger.

The droughts are sometimes made worse by man's carelessness and covetousness. Some people cut down too many trees. Others allow cattle to overgraze, leaving some areas bare and good for nothing. Carelessness and greed help to hasten the expansion of desert lands, a process called ***desertification.***

But even more serious, wars interfere with farming and keep farmers in one part of Africa from feeding fellow Africans in another part. African soil could easily feed all the African people if the land produced its full potential and the food could be distributed freely. But as Solomon said in Proverbs 13:23, "Much food is in the tillage of the poor: but there is that is destroyed for want [lack] of judgment."

Trade and Industry

Africa does not have many great seaports. One reason for this is that the continent has few natural harbors. But a more important reason is that African countries do less trading than many countries on other continents. African countries have few large industries. There are a number of historical reasons for this.

Africa was explored and claimed by Europeans later than other continents. Europeans discovered that Africa's tropical diseases could quickly kill them. So they did not trade with Africa unless it was very profitable to do so, as was true of the slave trade. Merchants did not settle in Africa as they did in the New World, so they did not bring their European ways of manufacturing with them.

Africans who traded with Europeans found it easier to sell slaves for the goods they needed than to learn to make cloth, guns, and hatchets for themselves. Nor did European businessmen try to help the African people learn better ways of doing things. Most Europeans did not want Africans to take important, high-paying jobs.

Present-day problems still keep industry from advancing rapidly. Most African countries do not have enough ***capital*** to develop modern industries. It takes money to build dams for hydroelectric power, to set up factories, and to train people to work in them. Most African nations get help from non-African countries, but often they still do not have enough money.

In many places, African transportation is poor. Rivers are still the most important "roads" into the back country. Road builders find it difficult to cross deserts and slash through rain forests. The roads that do exist are often unpaved—dusty in dry weather and muddy during rainy seasons. Several countries are ***landlocked.***

Some African countries have few mineral resources, while others are blessed with rich supplies. Nigeria and the North African countries of Libya and Algeria have great deposits of petroleum. Nigeria also has

Scorching liquid gold is poured from a furnace in South Africa. South Africa produces nearly half of the world's gold supply. Over 400,000 people work at mining and processing this gold.

Gold refining has been done since ancient times. The writer of Proverbs 17:3 used gold as an object lesson: "The fining pot is for silver, and the furnace for gold: but the LORD trieth the hearts."

large amounts of iron ore, coal, and tin. Some of the world's richest copper mines are located in the Democratic Republic of Congo and Zambia (ZAM bee uh). South Africa is well known for its diamond and gold mines. South Africa also has vast coal deposits that are easy to mine, besides abundant supplies of other minerals such as iron ore, uranium, and phosphate.

Already various countries are developing industries in a small way, such as making bicycles and plastic items or assembling automobiles. South Africa is a highly industrialized country that manufactures everything from electrical appliances to jet planes.

For some countries, minerals make the difference between being rich and being poor. Libya was a poor nation until petroleum was discovered beneath its desert sands. Zambia would be poor if it were not for its copper and other minerals. Some African countries that lack mineral riches are among the poorest countries in the world.

Study Exercises

12. What is a subsistence farmer?
13. What problem does carelessness, overcrowding, and overgrazing help to cause in a dry area?
14. (*a*) What is capital? (*b*) How has insufficient capital contributed to Africa's problems?
15. (*a*) What is a landlocked country? (*b*) Name at least four landlocked African countries.
16. South Africa manufactures more goods than any other African country. One advantage South Africa has is its great amounts of mineral resources, such as iron ore. Read Judges 1:19 and tell how iron was an advantage to a Bible nation.
17. How has the discovery of mineral resources changed countries like Libya and the Democratic Republic of Congo?

African Cultures—a Great Variety

North Americans have one main culture. Most people are familiar with stoves and refrigerators, forks and spoons, cars and buses, books and newspapers, suits and shoes, and hamburgers and peanut butter.

Africans have little such unity. They have many cultures. It would be useless to ask, "How do you say 'Good morning' in the African language?" because there are over one thousand African languages. Some are widely understood, such as Swahili (swah HEE lee), Hausa (HOW suh), and Arabic (AIR uh bihk). Many Africans can speak English or French. But other languages are understood only by small tribes. Even people speaking the same language may have difficulty understanding each other because they speak different dialects.

Some Africans are seven feet tall; others are less than five feet tall. Some live in cool, breezy regions; others live in hot, barren deserts or in tropical rain forests. Many Africans are black, but not all. The San (Bushmen) of the Kalahari Desert have yellowish brown skin. Other Africans are white.

A missionary to Africa observed that even within each country, customs vary. For example, in Tanzania, where this missionary had lived for ten years, the women in one tribe always milked the cows; and in the next tribe, milking cows was men's work. Now if you were of the *Jita* tribe and married a girl or boy of the *Zanaki* tribe, who do you think would milk the cows? Or if you were from central Tanzania where the main food is bananas, could you get used to the thick, mush-like ugali [oo GAH lee] eaten in surrounding areas?

The varying cultures make it difficult for the people within a given country to work together and trust each other. Different tribes have heated disputes over who should control the government. Civil wars have flared up.

Still, many Africans probably understand neighbors who are different from themselves better than we would. Some African people know four, five, or even more languages.

Many Africans are changing. They are accepting the habits of Europeans and North Americans in their thinking, eating, and manner of dress. We say they are becoming more westernized.

African tribesmen sometimes go to towns to find work. When they come home, they bring new ways of raising crops or building houses. Many Africans still live in mud-walled huts with thatched roofs, but some of them try to save enough money for a house with concrete walls and a metal roof.

Learning Western ways can be both good and bad. Africans have some excellent customs that no European can improve upon.

These buildings are part of a small jungle village in Nigeria. Many Nigerians leave their home villages and go to the cities to find jobs.

For example, the African custom of respecting older people is good (except when it leads to ancestor worship). Also, some African foods are better than some Western-style foods. Many Africans faced less danger of appendicitis before they began eating European foods.

On the other hand, most Africans were ***illiterate*** before Europeans came. The Europeans not only taught Africans to read European languages, but they also developed alphabets for African languages and taught Africans to read in their own languages. Most of this work was done by missionaries who wanted to help Africans read the Bible for themselves.

African Nations Today

Most modern African nations are young. Although Africa has been settled for thousands of years, almost all the present governments have become independent only since World War II. Europeans gained control of most of Africa during the last half of the 1800s. But in the last half of the 1900s, Africa went from being ruled largely by Europeans to being ruled largely by native Africans.

Workers pack high-quality tomatoes—some of South Africa's produce. Most areas of the country need irrigation to produce quality vegetables.

Sometimes this transition worked smoothly, but at other times it did not. When the Europeans and the Africans cooperated well, the Europeans helped the Africans learn how to run their farms and factories and how to fill places of responsibility in government. Such countries have had strong, stable leadership. They have established schools, hospitals, and industries; and they have encouraged foreign investors to start businesses in their countries. But when the relationships were unfriendly, the Europeans sometimes left without properly preparing the Africans for self-government. Farms and factories closed down because not enough people knew how to operate them. Turmoil and fighting often broke out because of poor government.

The last nation to strongly hold out against native African rule was South Africa. Until the 1990s, white people of English and Dutch ancestry controlled the government, the mines, the farms, the factories, and the best jobs, even though they were far outnumbered by black people and other non-Europeans. Black people were required to live in separate areas. They could not enter a white community unless they carried a pass giving them permission to do so. This policy is called ***apartheid*** (uh PAHRT hyt), meaning "apartness." Many people of African ancestry resented this policy, and it caused much turmoil and violence in South Africa.

The New Testament teaches against favoring one class of people above another. "God is no respecter of persons: but in every nation he that feareth him, and worketh righteousness, is accepted with him" (Acts 10:34, 35).

African Religions

Many people in northern Africa are Muslims (also spelled *Moslems*), since they live close to the Middle East. Muslims follow

In Casablanca, a Moroccan city along the Atlantic Ocean, a huge new mosque was built on land gained from the sea. The mosque cost approximately 500 million dollars.

the Islam religion. Their influence in architecture is seen in the domes of the ***mosques*** (MAHSKS) and the slender towers called minarets. Muslim leaders call the people to prayer from the minarets. Women often veil their faces in public. Many Africans, not only in northern Africa but elsewhere, are becoming Muslims.

Other Africans still follow tribal religions. Although they claim to believe in one main god, they also believe in less important gods and spirits such as the spirits of ancestors. They believe that these spirits are very powerful, with the ability to make a person sick or well, to cause good crops or bad, or even to cause death. Some people believe that every object, even a clay pot or a stool, has a spirit. People with such beliefs fear that someone might cast an evil spell on them. They wear charms that they hope will protect them against spells.

Christian missionaries and native African Christians have tried to change these beliefs. Although Christians are in the minority, the teachings of the Bible have had a great effect, especially in areas that still follow tribal religions. Some Africans have gotten rid of their charms, have quit scarring their bodies to "beautify" them, and have stopped the practice of marrying more than one wife. Wherever people follow the teachings of the Bible, bad practices are changed to good practices and many problems are solved.

Study Exercises

18. What differences of culture hinder people in Africa from working together?
19. What are some reasons many African governments are not as stable as some other governments?
20. What two major religions besides tribal religions are found in Africa? (Name first the religion found mainly in northern Africa.)

Clinching the Chapter

Use the text and maps to complete these exercises.

Multiple Choice

A. *Write the country* least *associated with the first item.*

1. Mediterranean coast: Somalia, Libya, Algeria, Morocco
2. Sahara: Mali, Niger, Chad, Kenya
3. Highlands: Mali, Tanzania, Uganda, Ethiopia
4. Nile: Ethiopia, Sudan, Egypt, Angola
5. Savanna: Angola, Morocco, Ghana, Nigeria
6. Lake Victoria: Tanzania, Ethiopia, Kenya, Uganda
7. Niger River: Niger, Nigeria, Egypt, Mali
8. Landlocked: Zambia, Zimbabwe, Tunisia, Chad
9. Mineral riches: Libya, Chad, South Africa, Zambia
10. Islam: South Africa, Egypt, Libya, Algeria

B. *Write the correct words.*

1. Which body of water lies west of Africa? (Atlantic Ocean, Indian Ocean, Mediterranean Sea, Red Sea)
2. Which is a grain? (cacao, millet, tapioca, cassava)
3. Which name refers to a strait? (Gibraltar, Suez, Verde, Good Hope)
4. In a rain forest, which would be the least troublesome? (snakes, insects, lions, heat)
5. Which river drains the wettest part of Africa? (Nile, Congo, Niger, Zambezi)
6. Which river flows north through the Sahel before turning south toward the Atlantic Ocean? (Nile, Congo, Niger, Zambezi)
7. Which of these is not in the Great Rift? (Mediterranean Sea, Jordan River, Red Sea, Lake Nyasa)
8. Which is not a problem to the people of the Sahel? (desertification, overgrazing, tigers, drought)
9. Which is not a widely used African language? (Swahili, Arabic, Kalahari, Hausa)
10. What do African countries need from non-African countries? (capital, culture, natural resources, transportation)

Matching

A. *For each clue, write the correct name from the right-hand column.*

1. Strait of Gibraltar	Addis Ababa
2. Africa's largest island	Cameroon

3. Scattered oases	Chad
4. Desert in north, savanna in south	Kilimanjaro
5. Grasslands in north, forests in south	Libya
6. Congo River	Madagascar
7. Africa's highest mountain	Morocco
8. Large inland city	Sahara
9. Apartheid	South Africa
10. Petroleum	Congo (Dem. Rep.)

B. *Match as in Part A.*

1. Africa's southern tip	Atlas Mountains
2. Africa's western tip	San
3. North of Sahara	Cape of Good Hope
4. Threat to Africa's large animals	Cape Verde
5. Southern edge of Sahara	illiteracy
6. Named Victoria Falls	independence
7. A source of the Nile	Lake Victoria
8. Natives of Kalahari Desert	Livingstone
9. Inability to read	poachers and safaris
10. Young, unstable countries	Sahel

Completion

1. Some of Africa lies on a pleasant plateau;
   On the high mountain peaks you can even find ———.
2. In the grasslands, both cattle and people may die
   If infected by bites from the ——— ———.
3. On the Zambezi River, a mapmaker calls
   The great "smoke that thunders," ——— ———.
4. The mosquitoes that thrive in a tropical area
   May be carrying illnesses such as ———.
5. Northern lands are Islamic, one never forgets
   When he sees the round domes and the tall ———.
6. One's love for his native tongue nothing can quench,
   Yet some Africans also speak English and ———.

Thought Questions

1. Why does Africa have fewer ports than Europe?
2. In which kind of African climate described in this chapter would you most enjoy to live? Give one or two reasons for your choice.
3. Why can you not point to any one part of Africa and say, "This is typical of Africa"?
4. Why do African cities have many poor people?
5. (*a*) What problems have African farmers created for themselves? (*b*) What problems are not necessarily their fault?
6. African industry also faces problems. What is the problem for which people are least to blame?
7. Even if you could set up a factory in an underdeveloped area without high cost or

other difficulties, what problems would you face in trying to operate it?

8. What is something we can admire as we look at African cultures?
9. Why did most African nations object to the South African policy of apartheid, even though South Africa was a prosperous nation during that time?
10. (*a*) What are three reasons that Africa was once known as "Dark Africa"? (*b*) How can true Christianity deal with each of these reasons?

Geographical Skills

A. This chapter contains various kinds of maps. Use an appropriate map or maps to find the right answer. You may need to compare maps.

1. Which country has a coastline facing south? (*a*) Mauritania, (*b*) Ghana, (*c*) Algeria
2. Which capital city has the highest elevation? (*a*) Abuja, Nigeria; (*b*) Algiers, Algeria; (*c*) Addis Ababa, Ethiopia
3. Which city has the greatest change in average temperature between January and July? (*a*) Cairo, (*b*) Addis Ababa, (*c*) Cape Town
4. Where are Africa's coldest temperatures in July? (*a*) Algeria, (*b*) Ethiopia, (*c*) South Africa
5. Which country has the highest yearly rainfall? (*a*) Egypt, (*b*) Ethiopia, (*c*) South Africa
6. Near the equator in Africa, (*a*) rainfall is less, (*b*) temperatures are about the same year round, (*c*) there is more savanna.

B. Tell whether these statements are true or false. The lines of latitude and longitude on a map or globe may help you.

1. Africa extends farther south than South America.
2. Egypt is about the same latitude as Florida.
3. Nigeria is farther west than England.
4. The northern tip of Africa is about the same latitude as Norfolk, Virginia.
5. Africa has more land north of the equator than south of it.
6. Nigeria is farther north than the Philippines.

C. Find which African capital cities are at these locations.

1. 30°03′N 31°15′E
2. 14°38′N 17°27′W
3. 33°56′S 18°28′E
4. 1°17′S 36°50′E

Further Study

1. Write an account of Livingstone's exploratory journey across Africa, and the reason he made it. Describe the type of country and vegetation through which he passed.
2. Make a chart called "Raw Materials of Africa and Their Uses." List the major agricultural products and minerals produced in Africa. Then list finished products that are made from each one.
3. Trace a map of Africa, and show the different climate areas you studied in this chapter. Color the climate zones different colors, and make a key for the map. Mark the major cities on your map.

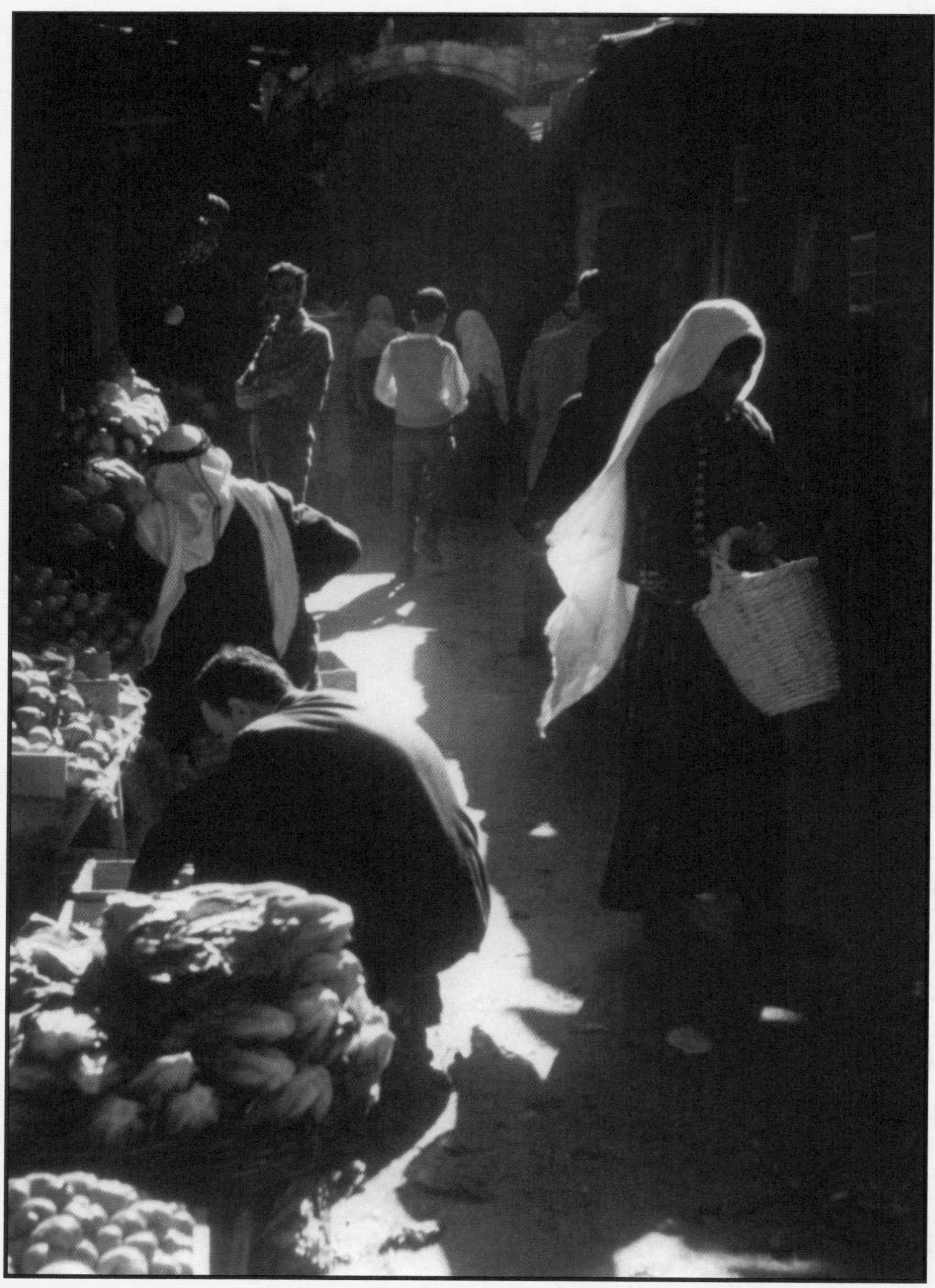

The morning sun lights a shaded alley in a Jerusalem market. In Jerusalem you will find people dressed in traditional Jewish and Muslim clothing, as well as Jews, Arabs, and tourists from around the world dressed in modern styles.

5 THE MIDDLE EAST

Where Is the Middle East?

Gulfs, Rivers, and Seas

Famous Mountains and Lowlands

A Sunny Climate

Oil, Water, and Other Resources

Cities

Tourism

Homeland of Three Major Religions

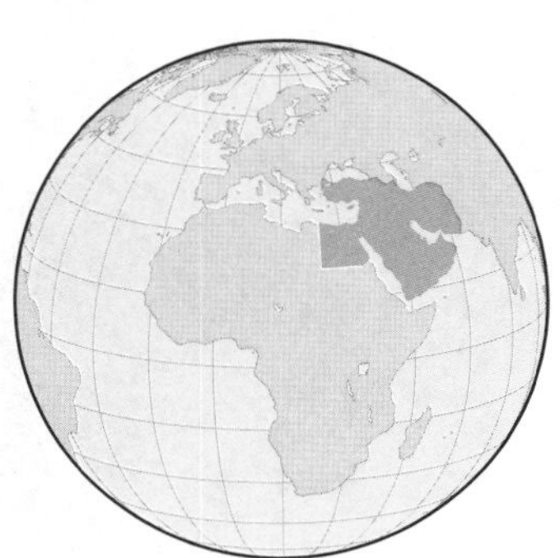

Bahrain • Cyprus • Egypt • Iran • Iraq • Israel • Jordan • Kuwait • Lebanon • Oman • Qatar • Saudi Arabia • Syria • Turkey • United Arab Emirates • Yemen

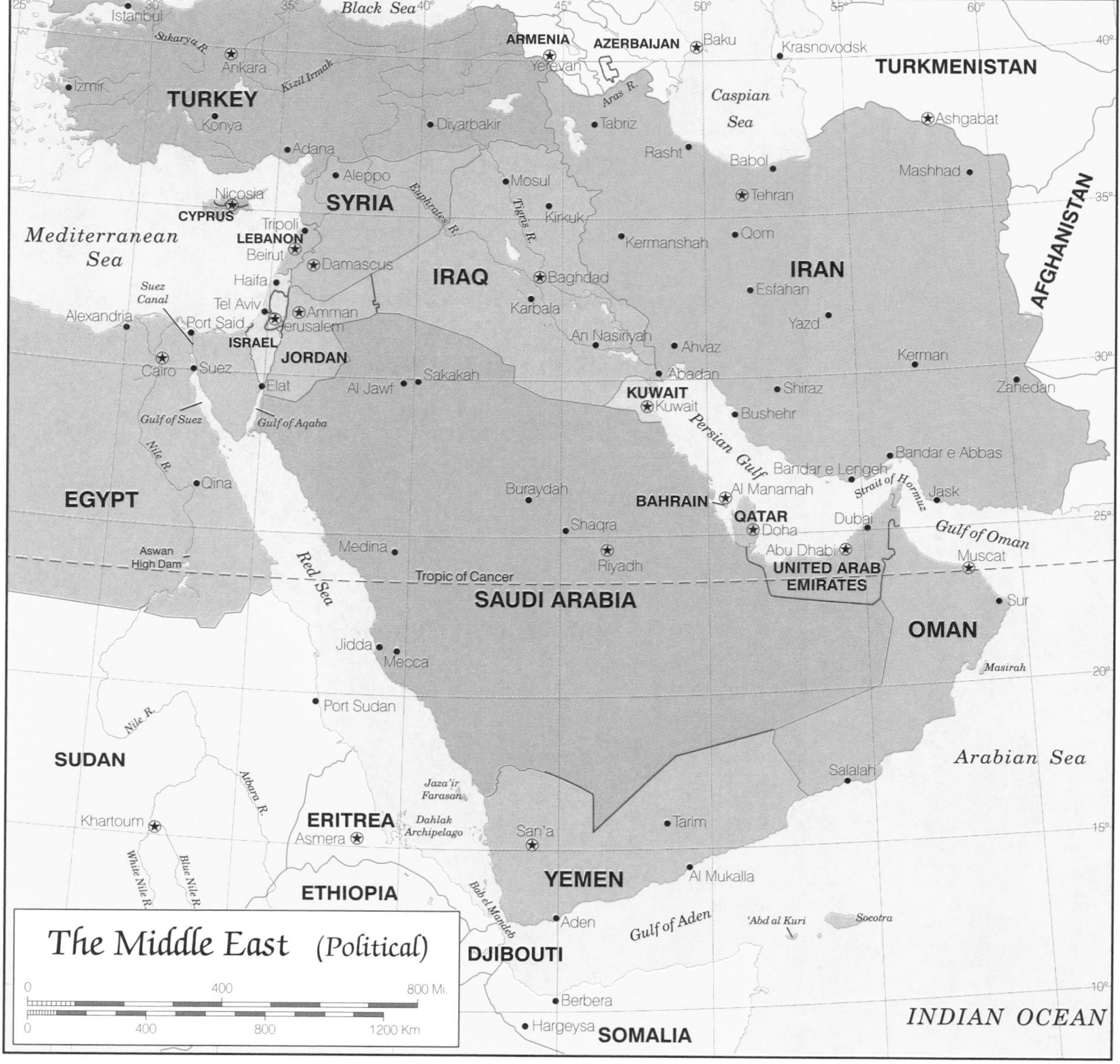

The Middle East (Political)
Black Sea
Istanbul
Sakarya R.
Ankara
Kizil Irmak
Izmir
TURKEY
Konya
Adana
ARMENIA
Yerevan
AZERBAIJAN
Baku
Aras R.
Krasnovodsk
TURKMENISTAN
Caspian Sea
Ashgabat
Diyarbakir
Tabriz
Rasht
Babol
Mashhad
Aleppo
SYRIA
Euphrates R.
Mosul
Tigris R.
Kirkuk
Tehran
Nicosia
CYPRUS
Tripoli
LEBANON
Beirut
Damascus
Mediterranean Sea
Qom
Kermanshah
AFGHANISTAN
IRAQ
Baghdad
IRAN
Esfahan
Haifa
Suez Canal
Tel Aviv
Amman
Jerusalem
Karbala
Yazd
Alexandria
Port Said
ISRAEL
JORDAN
An Nasiriyah
Ahvaz
Cairo
Suez
Elat
Sakakah
Al Jawf
Abadan
Kerman
Zahedan
KUWAIT
Kuwait
Shiraz
Gulf of Suez
Gulf of Aqaba
Persian Gulf
Bushehr
Nile R.
Bandar e Abbas
Bandar e Lengeh
Strait of Hormuz
Qina
EGYPT
Buraydah
Al Manamah
BAHRAIN
Jask
QATAR
Doha
Dubai
Shaqra
Gulf of Oman
Aswan High Dam
Medina
Riyadh
Abu Dhabi
Muscat
Red Sea
Tropic of Cancer
UNITED ARAB EMIRATES
SAUDI ARABIA
Sur
Jidda
Mecca
OMAN
Masirah
Port Sudan
Nile R.
SUDAN
Arabian Sea
Salalah
Atbara R.
Jaza'ir Farasan
Khartoum
ERITREA
Dahlak Archipelago
Tarim
Asmera
San'a
White Nile R.
Blue Nile R.
ETHIOPIA
YEMEN
Al Mukalla
Bab el Mandeb
Aden
Gulf of Aden
'Abd al Kuri
Socotra
DJIBOUTI
Berbera
Hargeysa
SOMALIA
INDIAN OCEAN
0 400 800 Mi.
0 400 800 1200 Km

Figure 5:1

The Middle East (Physical Relief)
0
400
800 Mi.
0
400
800
1200 Km
Approximate Elevation
Sea Level
250 Ft.
1,000 Ft.
4,000 Ft.
16,000 Ft.
Black Sea
Sea of Marmara
Bosporus
Dardanelles
Aegean Sea
Sakarya R.
Pontic Mountains
Central Anatolian Plateau
Kizil Irmak
Lake Tuz
TURKEY
Taurus Mountains
Mt. Ararat
Lake Van
AZERBAIJAN
Aras R.
Lake Urmia
TURKMENISTAN
Caspian Sea
Elburz Mts.
Tehran
ASIA
AFGHANISTAN
CYPRUS
SYRIA
IRAQ
Euphrates R.
Tigris R.
Mediterranean Sea
LEBANON
Mt. Hermon
Damascus
Mt. Carmel
Syrian Desert
Mesopotamia
Baghdad
Zagros Mountains
IRAN
Plateau of Iran
Suez Canal
Jordan R.
Jerusalem
Nile Delta
ISRAEL
Qattara Depression
Cairo
Sinai Peninsula
JORDAN
Shatt-al-Arab
KUWAIT
an Nafud (desert)
Gulf of Suez
Mt. Sinai
Gulf of Aqaba
Persian Gulf
Western Desert
Nile R.
Arabian Desert
Midian
ad Dahna (desert)
SAUDI ARABIA
Strait of Hormuz
EGYPT
Hejaz
BAHRAIN
QATAR
Arabian
Gulf of Oman
Aswan High Dam
Riyadh
Red Sea
Tropic of Cancer
UNITED ARAB EMIRATES
Lake Nasser
Peninsula
OMAN
AFRICA
Mecca
Masirah
Rub'al-Khali (The Empty Quarter)
Nile R.
Asir
Arabian Sea
SUDAN
Atbara R.
Jaza'ir Farasan
Khartoum
ERITREA
Dahlak Archipelago
YEMEN
White Nile R.
Blue Nile R.
ETHIOPIA
Bab el Mandeb
Gulf of Aden
'Abd al Kuri
Socotra
INDIAN OCEAN
SOMALIA
25°
30°
35°
40°
45°
50°
55°
60°
40°
35°
30°
25°
20°
15°

Figure 5:2

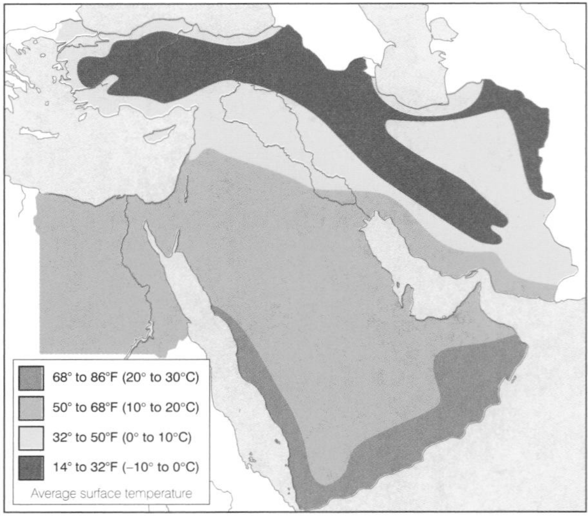

Figure 5:3. Average January Temperature

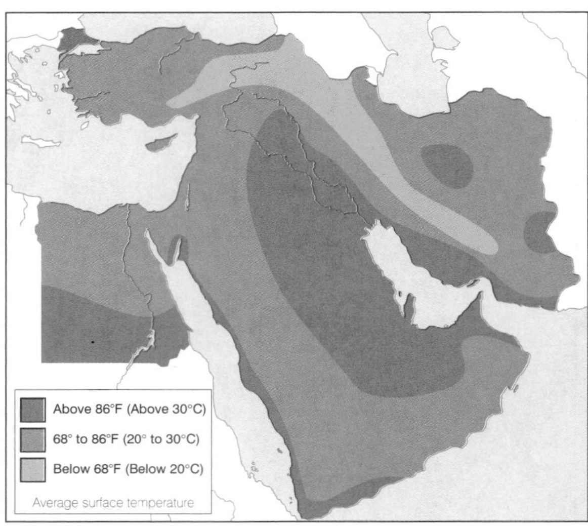

Figure 5:4. Average July Temperature

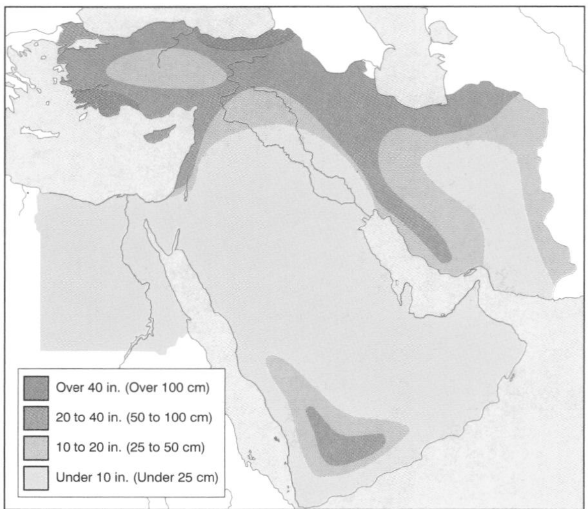

Figure 5:5. Average Annual Rainfall

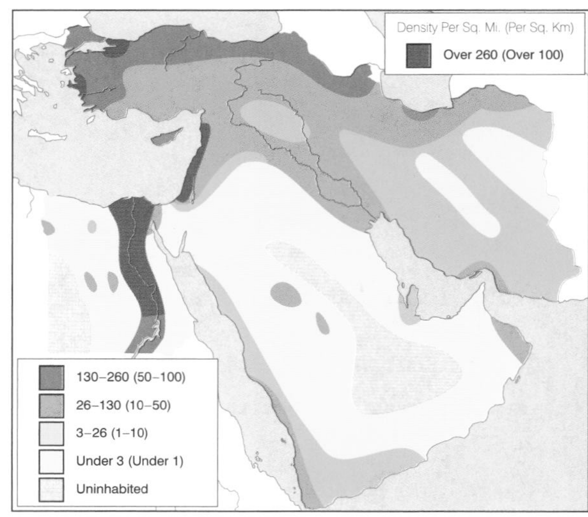

Figure 5:6. Population Distribution

The Middle East

Where Is the Middle East?

Although the Middle East is not a continent in itself, it is worth a separate study. Many important historical events, which you will study later, took place in the Middle East. Even today, much of the world's attention is focused on the Middle East because of its wars and unsettled political conditions.

The Middle East is sometimes called the Near East. The Europeans who first used that name did so because that region is nearer to them than countries in the Far East, such as India, China, and Japan. Actually, for many North Americans, the Near East is as far away as the Far East, depending on which way around the world they travel to get there.

The boundaries of the Middle East are hard to define. Most of the Middle East lies in the southwest corner of Asia. But one Middle East nation, Egypt, lies in Africa; and the corner of another nation, Turkey, is in Europe. Perhaps the Middle East could be considered the general region where most Bible history took place.

The Middle East lies at the junction of three continents. One old map places Jerusalem squarely in the center, with Europe, Asia, and Africa extending out from the center like the petals of a flower. (See Figure 5:7.) Of course an accurate map looks different from that. But it is true that anyone traveling by land from Africa to Asia or Europe must travel through the Middle East. Also, ships traveling from Europe to Asia usually pass through the Middle East by way of the Suez Canal. The Middle East is a crossroads for international traffic.

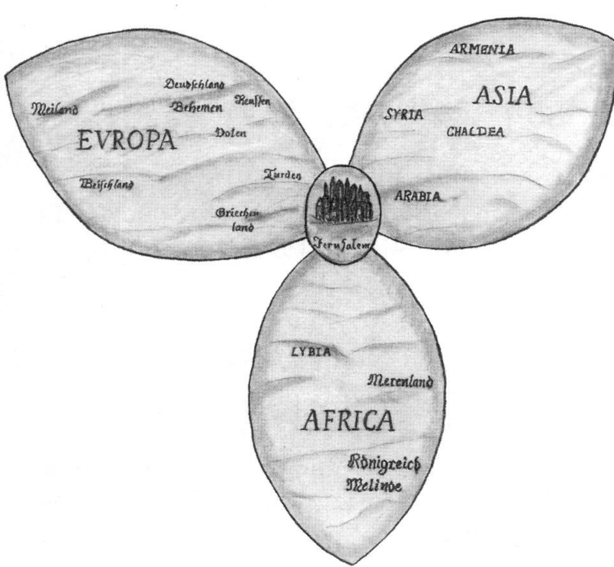

Figure 5:7. Because of Jerusalem's significance for the Christian and Jewish religions, a mapmaker in the late 1500s considered the city the center of the world. Extending out from Jerusalem like a three-leaf clover are the continents of Africa, Europe, and Asia. This map illustrates how ignorant many people were about accurate geography in medieval times.

Gulfs, Rivers, and Seas

Gulfs. Several important gulfs reach into the Middle East from the Indian Ocean. The Persian Gulf provides an important route for oil tankers. The tankers fill up at ports along the shores of Iraq (ih RAK), Iran (ih RAN), Saudi Arabia (SOW dee uh RAY bee uh), Kuwait (koo WAYT), and other oil-rich countries. When they leave, they pass through the narrow Strait of Hormuz (HOR muhz), where a horn of land from the Arabian peninsula nearly blocks their path. Since the Middle East is a tense area that is often threatened by war, various nations that depend on Middle East oil carefully watch the Persian Gulf and the Strait of Hormuz, to ensure that it remains a safe route for ships.

Near the northwestern corner of the Arabian peninsula, the Red Sea reaches one finger north along the coast of Egypt almost

Oil is loaded onto a tanker at a Saudi Arabian port. Saudi Arabia is the world's leading oil exporter and has more known oil resources than any other country. These resources have changed Saudi Arabia from a country of nomads herding sheep and camels to a country of oil derricks, petroleum refineries, and growing cities. There are few nomads left.

to the corner of the Mediterranean Sea. This finger is the Gulf of Suez. It is connected to the Mediterranean Sea by the Suez Canal, which allows ships from Europe or North America to sail to oil ports of the Persian Gulf without traveling thousands of extra miles around Africa. The Suez Canal is so important that nations have fought to control it. During one war, ships were sunk in it, and traffic was blocked for years.

The other finger of the Red Sea, called the Gulf of Aqaba (AH kuh buh), touches the southern tip of Israel. This gives Israel a sea outlet besides its ports on the Mediterranean Sea. It also gives Jordan its only seaport.

Rivers. The Nile River, which is about 4,145 miles long (6,670 km), is the longest river in the world. For thousands of years, the Nile has watered the desert land and made it possible for millions of people to live along its shores. Later you will see how the Egyptians have tried to make the Nile even more useful.

In Iraq, the Tigris and Euphrates Rivers run generally parallel and finally join to form a river called the Shatt-al-Arab. In Bible times, Babylon stood along the Euphrates and Nineveh along the Tigris. Today Baghdad (BAG dad), the capital of Iraq, stands beside the Tigris.

The winding Jordan River is short but well known. God parted its waters for Joshua, Elijah, and Elisha. Here Naaman was healed and Jesus was baptized. It has often served as an important border in Israel.

Lakes and Seas. Several small bodies of water have had great importance in Bible history. Jesus spent many hours beside the

Sea of Galilee. The Dead Sea, called the Salt Sea in the Bible, was part of the boundary between the tribe of Judah and the land of Moab. (These two "seas" are actually lakes.) The Dead Sea is unusual in several ways. It is the lowest body of water on earth, which is why no rivers flow out of it. Since the water can escape only by evaporation, the sea has become very salty.

The Mediterranean Sea has also been important in history. In the Bible it is called the Great Sea, and it has long been a main route of travel for Middle East countries. Near the eastern end of the Mediterranean lies the island of Cyprus. This island has beautiful mountains and seashores. Its climate is generally sunny and dry, but many farmers use irrigation to grow vegetables, citrus fruits, and grapes. Barnabas, a companion of the apostle Paul, was from Cyprus.

Study Exercises

1. Why is the Middle East also called the Near East?
2. Name the three continents whose corners touch in the Middle East.
3. Explain why the nations of the world are concerned about keeping the Persian Gulf open to shipping.
4. Name the two gulfs that open into the Red Sea.
5. What two great ancient cities were built in what is now Iraq?

Famous Mountains and Lowlands

The mountains of the Middle East have played an important part in the region's history. Mount Ararat, where Noah's ark landed, stands in eastern Turkey. Using Mount Ararat as a central point, notice how mountain ranges run westward through Turkey and southeastward through Iran.

Mountains also run from Turkey southward along the Mediterranean Sea. From the land of Israel, the snow-capped peak of Mount Hermon can be seen to the north, on the boundary between Lebanon and Syria. Far to the south stands Mount Sinai, the southernmost mountain peak named in the Bible. Between these two peaks are many other mountains with familiar Bible names.

God called the Promised Land "a land of hills and valleys" (Deuteronomy 11:11), and so it is. A backbone of hills and mountains runs north and south through Israel. You probably recall names like Mount Carmel, Mount Gilboa (gihl BOH uh), Mount Zion, and Mount of Olives. Jesus went to a mountain to be alone with God, and He preached His most famous sermon "on the mount." Jerusalem sits high in the mountains, which explains why people in the Bible went *up* to Jerusalem.

Lower land is found on both sides of this ridge of highlands. Along the Mediterranean Sea lie the Plain of Sharon and the Plain of Philistia, with their fields, orchards, and towns. East of the ridge of mountains is a long depression. This depression is the northern part of the Great Rift Valley that extends into Africa. Within the depression, the Sea of Galilee lies nearly 650 feet (200 m) below sea level, and the Dead Sea lies lower yet at 1,312 feet (400 m) below sea level. The Jordan River flows from one sea to the other.

A Sunny Climate

Most of the Middle East has a sunny, dry climate. Deserts cover large parts of Syria, Iraq, Iran, and neighboring countries. Saudi Arabia is nearly all desert. At some places in the Middle East, roadmen plow drifting sand off highways as if it were snow. If a vehicle gets off the highway and is stuck in the sand, the driver cannot simply put on chains and drive away, for there is always more sand below the surface sand.

Figs

Fig trees have been cultivated since early in man's existence. The first of many Bible references to figs is in Genesis and refers not to the famous fruit, but to the broad, rough, deeply lobed leaves. Adam and Eve vainly tried to sew themselves fig leaf aprons after they had sinned. God was not pleased with such flimsy clothing, nor with their disobedience.

The fig is a bush or small tree that grows to a height of 3 to 39 feet (1 to 12 m). The round or pear-shaped fig fruits grow by ones or twos just above leaves or leaf scars on the branches. These fruits may have yellow, green, purple, pink, brown, or black skins, depending on the variety. Technically, fig "fruits" are not really fruits at all, but the flowers of the tree! If you would carefully turn a fig inside out, you would see what looks somewhat like the top of a dandelion flower with its tiny petals. If these flowers (figs) are not pollinated, they will fall off the tree.

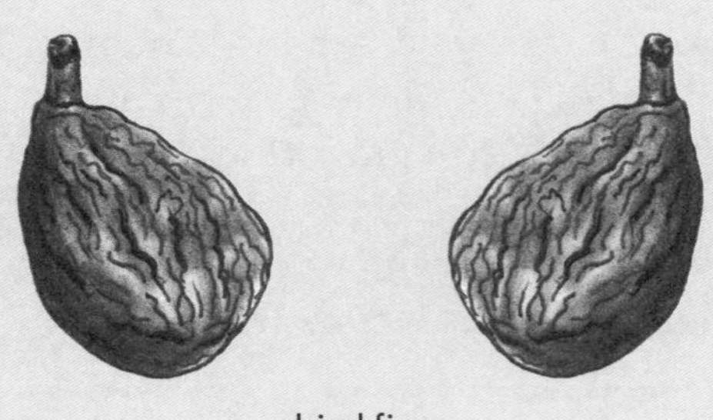

dried figs

fig bars

Among all the fruits, the fig stands out for its high food value. Dried figs are more nutritious than bread, if compared in equal weights. A one and one-half pound serving of figs supplies four-fifths of the daily nutrition needed by a man. Figs contain significant amounts of potassium, calcium, phosphorus, and iron. In some Mediterranean countries, both fresh and dried figs are so widely used that they are called "the poor man's food." Ripe figs cannot be shipped long distances because they spoil easily, therefore most growers dry their figs before shipping them. They can also be canned or preserved in sugar.

Four types of fig trees are commonly grown: caprifig, Smyrna figs, White San Pedro figs, and common figs. Growers in ancient times found out that the good-tasting Smyrna figs ripened properly only when the inedible caprifig (wild fig) was grown nearby. Why? The "secret" was discovered in the late 1800s: a little wasp pollinates both the Smyrna and the caprifig. These wasps live and grow inside a caprifig flower. Each female wasp wants to lay eggs in another flower before she dies, so she crawls out of a small opening at the end of the pollen-laden caprifig flower. In her search, she lands on and enters a Smyrna flower. She is unable to lay her eggs in the Smyrna flower because it is shaped a bit differently. So the wasp crawls out in search of another flower and repeats the process until she finds a caprifig flower, where she can lay her eggs. As she searches for the "right" flower, she pollinates the Smyrna flowers, and the good-tasting figs develop!

Fig branch with fruit

Cross section of a fig flower

Pollen-laden wasp entering fig flower

Leading Old World fig-growing countries are Italy, Turkey, Algeria, Greece, Portugal, and Spain. Colder European countries such as England have for years been raising potted fig trees in greenhouses.

The fig tree is used in the Bible to teach us some valuable truths. Luke 21:29–31 reminds readers that just as the familiar yearly cycle of figs and other trees helps us to know what time of year it is, so the coming to pass of prophesied events helps us to know how close to the end of time we are. We can also better picture the future event in Revelation 6:13 if we know about unpollinated fig flowers.

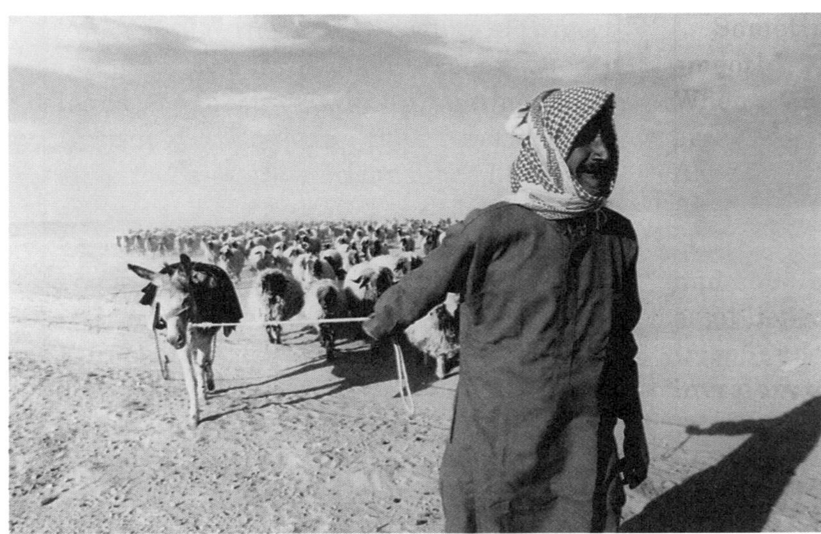

One of Saudi Arabia's few remaining Bedouins leads his donkey and sheep through blowing desert sands. Notice his desert clothing.

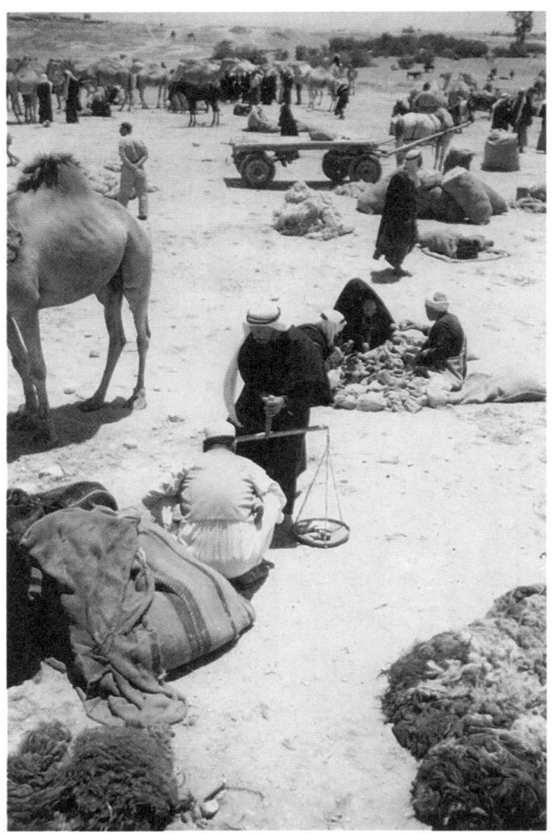

At a Bedouin camel market near Beersheba, Israel, vendors sit in the sand and trade their wares with the nomads. Notice the piles of hairy skins or wool in the foreground. Nomads probably traded them to the vendor for fruit, salt, or some other necessity they cannot provide for themselves.

Here and there, scattered across the broad, dry deserts, are oases with wells and palm trees. On these oases, people raise warmth-loving fruits such as dates, oranges, and grapes. They might also raise wheat and barley.

Across the sparsely populated deserts, nomads called ***Bedouins*** (BEHD oo ihnz) roam from oasis to oasis, seeking pasture for their sheep, goats, and cattle. The Bedouins wear flowing, light-colored, loosely woven robes. This kind of clothing keeps them cool during the hot days, in much the same way that a straw hat keeps a man's head cool in North America.

For the desert wanderers, home is a tent. Desert dwellers who live in one place build houses with thick earthen walls and narrow windows to keep out the heat. Houses often have flat roofs, since little rain falls. People sometimes sleep on the roofs to keep cool at night.

At one time, camels provided the best way to cross a desert. Camels are still important to desert people. They can withstand the driving winds. Their long eyelashes, hairy ears, and slit-like nostrils keep out the blowing sand. They store fat

A computerized sprinkler system brings life to the Negev, a desert in southern Israel.

in their humps, which enables them to make long journeys across the desert. They can go for several days without water; but when they are thirsty, they can each drink as much as twenty-five gallons in ten minutes.

Deserts vary; some are semideserts such as those found in southern Israel. The soil is fertile, but it lacks enough water to grow crops. It does grow enough grass and shrubs to provide some grazing for animals. Israel irrigates its southern semideserts by bringing water all the way from the Sea of Galilee. With water, the semidesert produces fine crops.

Many places in the Middle East enjoy a Mediterranean climate. The sky is often bright and clear. The growing season comes in the winter, when enough rain falls. The summers are too hot and dry for crops to grow. Many plants that grow in a Mediterranean climate have small, thick, waxy leaves to conserve what moisture their roots can find. One plant that does well in a Mediterranean climate is the date palm. More dates are raised in the Middle East than in any other region of the world. Olive and fig trees also grow well in this climate.

Study Exercises

6. What natural feature separates the lowlands of Galilee and Jordan from the lowlands of Sharon and Philistia?
7. What is the lowest body of water in the Middle East (and in the world)?
8. Why do desert dwellers prefer flowing robes in hot weather?
9. What advantage do thick-walled houses have in the desert?
10. What name is given to the type of climate with dry summers and rainy winters?

Oil, Water, and Other Resources

Petroleum is the most important export for many of the Middle East countries. Saudi Arabia is one of the world's leading oil producers. The Middle East countries, together with oil-producing countries in northern Africa, produce a large percentage of the world's petroleum. Over half of the world's proven reserves of underground oil are in the Middle East.

Until the 1940s and 1950s, most Middle East nations were poor. But with the discovery of oil, they began to prosper, especially in the 1970s when they raised oil prices.

Some ***Arabs*** became fabulously rich. The tiny nation of Kuwait, the world's greatest oil producer for its size, provides its people with free education and free medical services—all without any income tax! The wealth in the Middle East, however, is not shared evenly. Many Middle Eastern people are still very poor. And prosperity can bring its own problems. In 1990, Iraq invaded Kuwait and tried to seize its wealth. But other nations were concerned about the availability of oil, and they helped Kuwait to regain her land.

For oil-producing countries, petroleum brings both money and political power. Highly developed nations like the United States and Japan use much foreign oil. In 1973, Saudi Arabia and her allies cut oil shipments to the United States and other nations that supported Israel. This made people fearful about finding enough oil and gas for their cars, furnaces, and businesses. It was the oil-producing countries' way of putting pressure on other countries without fighting a war.

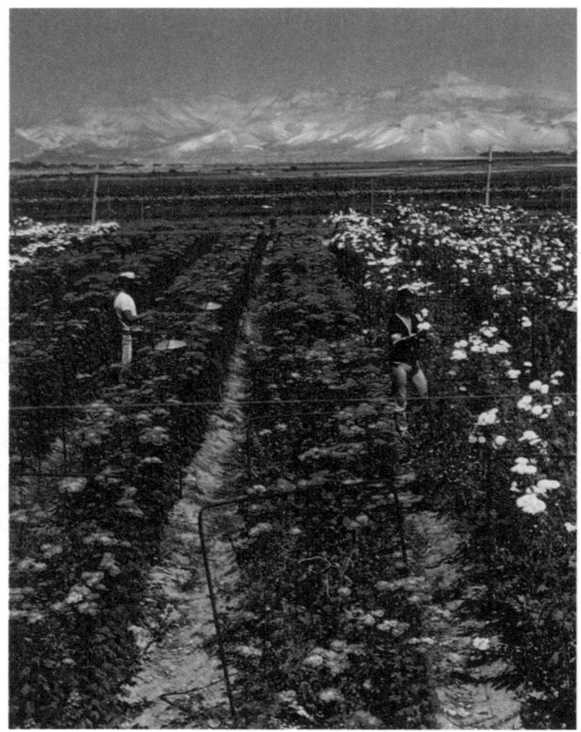

Flower fields adorn a valley in Jordan. Only about 6 percent of Jordan is suitable for farming. The rest of the country is too dry for crops, so the land is used to pasture sheep.

Several Middle Eastern nations have very little oil and earn their income in other ways. Jordan depends heavily on farming. Lebanon took in much income from trading and banking, before civil war ruined much of the country. But the most remarkable nation with little oil is Israel. This country has prospered not because of mineral riches but because of her energetic, knowledgeable people. They are her best resource.

Many of Israel's people are Jews who moved in from other parts of the world, bringing new ideas from the countries where they had lived. The land was poor and dry when Israel formed a nation in 1948. But the Israelis (ihs RAY leez) dug wells, built dams, and set up irrigation systems for their farms and orchards. They planted millions of trees on the hillsides to stop erosion. They established food processing plants and built factories to make machinery, to cut and polish diamonds, to produce electronic equipment, and to make many other things.

The Israelis draw from an unusual mineral resource—the Dead Sea. This sea is about nine times saltier than the ocean. Salt, potash, and other minerals are extracted at chemical plants in nearby Sedom (named after Sodom, which probably stood in that area). The Israelis have made dikes in the Dead Sea to trap water in shallow pools. When the great heat of the region evaporates the water, workmen remove the minerals that remain.

Archaeologists have discovered the remains of copper mines, from Old Testament times, in southern Israel. Encouraged by history, the Israelis are again mining copper in the same region today.

This is an aerial view of potash refining on the shores of the Dead Sea, likely at Sedom. Although potash is mainly used to make fertilizer, it is also used to make other products such as soaps, glass, textiles, and chemicals.

Leading Petroleum-Producing Countries

Country	Barrels
*Saudi Arabia	🛢🛢🛢🛢🛢🛢🛢🛢🛢🛢🛢🛢
Russia	🛢🛢🛢🛢🛢🛢🛢🛢🛢🛢🛢
United States	🛢🛢🛢🛢🛢🛢🛢🛢🛢🛢
*Iran	🛢🛢🛢🛢🛢½
China	🛢🛢🛢🛢½
Mexico	🛢🛢🛢🛢
Venezuela	🛢🛢🛢½
Norway	🛢🛢🛢½
*United Arab Emirates	🛢🛢🛢½
Nigeria	🛢🛢½
*Kuwait	🛢🛢½
United Kingdom	🛢🛢½
Canada	🛢🛢½
Libya	🛢🛢

(🛢 Each barrel represents 250 million barrels of crude petroleum produced in one year. Asterisks indicate Middle East nations.)

The Aswan Dam, on the Nile River, harnesses one of the most powerful flows of water in the world and helps to control flooding. It was completed in 1902.

Minerals bring income, but water supports life. In the dry Middle East, people count water extremely precious. Desert dwellers center their activities around oases, water holes, and wells. No country illustrates the importance of water better than Egypt. Without the Nile River, all Egypt would be a sandy wasteland. Egypt has been called "the gift of the Nile."

In past centuries, Egyptian farmers raised one crop a year in their fields because the Nile overflowed its banks once a year. The Nile water would spread across the land, bringing not only water but also fertile silt. When the water went down, farmers would plant their crops.

But the Egyptians wanted to farm more acres. So during the early 1900s they completed the Aswan Dam, and more recently, the Aswan High Dam. The High Dam holds back a lake about 300 miles long (500 km) that contains enough water to irrigate 2 million acres (800,000 hectares). Egyptian farmers can now irrigate during any season of the year. They can raise two or three crops in a year's time.

Below the dam, the Nile no longer floods as it once did. Farmers miss the fertile silt that the flood waters brought long ago. They need to use other fertilizers. Another problem is the buildup of salt in the soil, left there by irrigation water as it evaporates. Still, Egypt now has more food and more hydroelectricity than before the dams were built. The dam also has already saved Egypt from several floods and famines. Time will tell whether it does more good or more harm.

Study Exercises

11. What two things does petroleum provide for the Arabs?
12. From where did Israel get many of its ideas?
13. Why is water from the Dead Sea not used for irrigation?
14. Name three good and two bad effects of the Aswan High Dam.

Cities

Many cities in the Middle East have a new part and an old part. The new part looks much like modern cities around the world, with wide streets, tall buildings of steel and glass, parks, schools, and factories. The old part has narrow, winding streets, some of which are too narrow for any traffic except donkeys and camels.

The best-known old section is in Jerusalem. This part of Jerusalem contains places that people of Jewish, Muslim, and some Christian religions consider holy. For example, the Wailing Wall is there. This

Jerusalem is the capital of Israel and the home of about 662,700 people. The building with the gold dome is a mosque called the Dome of the Rock. The building is built at the site believed to be where Abraham prepared to sacrifice Isaac.

wall, which is part of a retaining wall that once surrounded the temple mount, is the Jews' closest link with Herod's temple. The temple itself was completely destroyed, fulfilling Jesus' prophecy that not one stone would be left standing upon another.

On the old temple mount itself stands the Dome of the Rock, a Muslim ***shrine.*** Muslims claim that it stands over the spot where their prophet Muhammad (also spelled *Mohammed*) ascended to heaven on a winged horse.

Middle Eastern cities are becoming more modernized all the time. For example, Tehran (teh RAHN) in Iran is very modern. But many people would be disappointed to see all the old sections of cities disappear. Tourists love to visit the ***bazaars*** (buh ZAHRZ) of Baghdad in Iraq and of Damascus in Syria. Bazaars are markets consisting of narrow streets lined with small shops. Also, the people who live there point out that narrow streets are shady. They appreciate this in a land where the sun shines bright and hot.

Tourism

Middle Eastern countries depend on tourists for millions of dollars of their income. Taking a trip to Palestine is a big investment. Many Christians think it better to use their money in other ways. Those who do visit the land where Jesus walked learn several important things.

Many scenes have changed since Bible times. The "little town of Bethlehem" has become a much bigger, more modern town, as Nazareth and many others also have. The city of Jerusalem has become a fair-sized ***metropolis*** (mih TRAHP uh lihs), although the old section where the Bible stories took place can still be toured.

Olives

The Bible contains many references to the olive tree, its fruit, and its oil. Genesis 8:11 reveals that the olive was known in pre-Flood days. Other references refer to olive oil as a food, an anointing oil, a lamp oil, and various uses in tabernacle worship. Olive wood was used in parts of Solomon's temple.

Olive trees have distinctively gnarled bark and live longer than most other fruit trees, for the wood resists decay. Palestine has some olive trees that probably date back to the time of Christ.

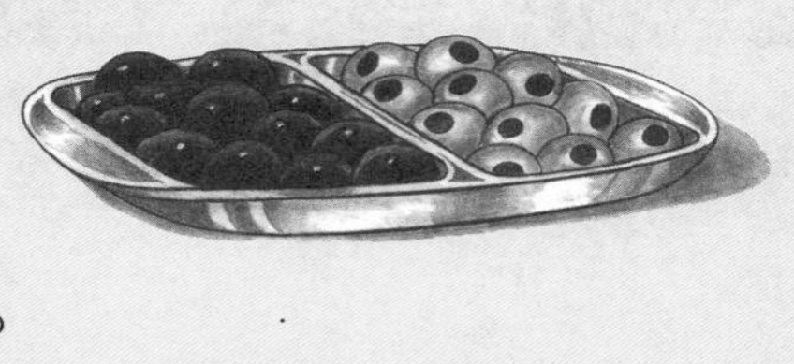

Olives are purplish black fruits similar in shape to plums or peaches, although smaller. Most of the world's olive crop goes for olive oil. If fruit production is desired, the fruits are picked at the green immature stage and are treated with lye and salt to remove a bitter substance that makes fresh, unprocessed olives unpleasant to eat. People eat the processed fruits two ways—as pickled, unripe, green, pitted olives, or as ripe, black, unpitted olives. These are processed by different methods.

An ancient olive press

When ripe, each fruit contains 20 to 30 percent oil. If the olives are wanted for their oil, the fruit is allowed to mature on the tree. The best oil comes from olives that are picked just after they ripen and before they turn black. The oil is bitter if the olives are picked too green and is rancid if the olives are picked too ripe. The oil-rich fruits are crushed under low pressure with hydraulic presses, which generates little heat. Therefore, the oil retains its flavor, color, and nutritional value without requiring further processing. It can be stored for months without refrigeration or danger of spoilage. This crushing is often done in several stages, with only some of the oil obtained each time. Each successive pressing yields a lower-quality oil than the previous one. The first pressing is usually called virgin olive oil, which is considered a gourmet item. The next pressing mixes other vegetable oils and water with the olive oil. The oil obtained by the last pressings is inedible and is used to make soaps, lamp oil, medicines, and textiles.

Spain, Italy, Greece, and Turkey are the leading four nations in olive production.

In Damascus, capital of Syria, natives and tourists buy produce and crafts at a bazaar. Some historians consider Damascus to be the oldest occupied city in the world. The Old Testament mentions Damascus many times, and it was here that a faithful Christian named Ananias helped lead Saul (later Apostle Paul) to Christ.

"And Jesus, walking by the sea of Galilee, saw two brethren, Simon called Peter, and Andrew his brother, casting a net into the sea: for they were fishers. And he saith unto them, Follow me, and I will make you fishers of men" (Matthew 4:18, 19). The Sea of Galilee still yields bountiful quantities of fish, nearly 2,000 years after Jesus stood on these banks.

Sheep graze on the picturesque Mount of Olives. The mount is a limestone ridge about 1 mile (1.61 km) long, basically extending all along the east side of Jerusalem. The mount itself has not changed much since Jesus' time, but a man from two thousand years ago would be bewildered by the highways and modern buildings of the city today.

It is difficult to pinpoint the exact location of many Bible events. Where was Jesus born? Where was He buried? Where was Calvary? Since those who try to answer these questions often disagree, some Bible characters may have two tombs—both of which might be wrong.

But one can see where prophecy has been fulfilled. For example, Jesus once said, "Woe unto thee, Chorazin! woe unto thee, Bethsaida! . . . And thou, Capernaum, which art exalted to heaven, shalt be thrust down to hell" (Luke 10:13,15). Today, Chorazin and Capernaum lie in ruins, and Bethsaida has completely disappeared.

Important landmarks can also be seen—the Mount of Olives, the mountain basin where Nazareth lies, the shores of Galilee. Loaded donkeys still plod past flat-roofed houses. Ancient olive trees still stand on the Mount of Olives, perhaps in the same spot where Jesus prayed in Gethsemane. And fishermen still catch fish on the Sea of Galilee.

Study Exercises

15. Name one delight and one disappointment experienced by visitors to the Middle East.
16. How does tourism help Middle Eastern countries?
17. Name one thing typical of old city sections and at least two things typical of new sections.

Homeland of Three Major Religions

Christianity, Judaism, and Islam began in the Middle East. All three religions trace their history back to Abraham.

Judaism. Judaism is the main religion of the Jews. Its followers teach that the Messiah has not yet come and that Jesus Christ was only a pretender. Many ***orthodox*** Jews observe Old Testament laws very strictly. Although they no longer make animal sacrifices, they eat only ***kosher*** (KOH shur) food, observe the Sabbath from sundown Friday night to sundown Saturday night, and keep various other rules. Most Jews are less strict, but many still observe the Jewish festivals, keep certain Jewish customs, and claim to worship the God of Abraham, Isaac, and Jacob.

Jews have ***synagogues*** that serve as

Jews gather in a synagogue in Israel. The buildings and furnishings have changed drastically since synagogues were first used, but the aim is still the same—to provide a place for Jewish religious exercises and study. Like churches, synagogues vary widely in architecture, but they usually are furnished with an ark containing scrolls of the Law and some special candles and candleholders.

The six-pointed star, called The Star of David, is formed by interlacing two triangles. It is a symbol of Judaism and is used on the national flag of Israel.

churches and schools. They look to their local ***rabbi*** as their spiritual leader, much as you look to your minister.

It is not simple to say exactly what is the holy book of Judaism. Of course, the followers of Judaism have the Old Testament. The first five books of the Bible, called the ***Pentateuch*** (PEHN tuh took), are further commented on and explained in another book, called the ***Talmud.*** The Talmud is no small book—it consists of sixty-three books bound in eighteen volumes!

Islam. This is the main religion of the Arabs. Muslims, the followers of Islam (ihs LAHM), believe that the last great prophet sent from God was Muhammad. This man was an Arab who began preaching a new religion in the A.D. 600s. Muhammad claimed that he had seen a vision in which the angel Gabriel appointed him a prophet and told him to go and preach.

One of the cities Muhammad lived in was Mecca (MEHK uh), which today is a holy city to Muslims. The Islamic religion says that every Muslim should visit Mecca at least one time if possible. So every year during the Muslim month of pilgrimage, "the world's biggest traffic jam" presses its way along the road to Mecca. Pilgrims crowd the city and worship at Islam's holiest shrine.

Muslims pray five times a day—at dawn, at noon, in the afternoon, in the evening, and at nightfall. Every mosque has a minaret, a tall, slender tower from which a leader calls the people to prayer. They wash their hands, faces, and feet, and bow down facing Mecca.

The Muslims' holy day is Friday. (Jerusalem, with its many Jews, Muslims, and Christians, has three holy days in a row—Friday, Saturday, and Sunday.) The Muslims also observe ***Ramadan*** (ram uh DAHN), a month for fasting. During Ramadan, the people may eat at night but not during the day.

The Muslims' holy book is the ***Koran*** (koh RAHN), a book about the size of the New Testament. Many young Muslims memorize all of it.

Muslims do some good things. They emphasize that there is only one God and

A highlight in a Muslim's life is saying prayers before the Kaaba in Mecca, Saudi Arabia. The Kaaba is a room containing a black stone that Muhammad supposedly valued. Christians remember what Jesus told the Samaritan woman at the well: "Woman, believe me, the hour cometh, when ye shall neither in this mountain, nor yet at Jerusalem, worship the Father." . . . The true worshippers shall worship the Father in spirit and in truth. . . . God is a Spirit: and they that worship him must worship him in spirit and in truth" (John 4:21, 23, 24).

that people must submit to Him. (They call God *Allah,* which means "the God" in Arabic.) The word *Islam* means "submission." Muslims teach kindness, courage, modesty in dress, avoidance of alcoholic drink, and many other virtues. They forbid anyone to draw pictures of people or animals, lest someone should be tempted to worship them. Islamic art emphasizes beautiful designs instead of pictures. Muslims even teach that Abraham, Moses, Jesus, and other Bible characters were good men.

However, Muslims do not teach that "ye must be born again." They reject Jesus as the Son of God and the only Saviour of the world. Their religion cannot save them, for Jesus said, "He that believeth not is condemned already, because he hath not believed in the name of the only begotten Son of God" (John 3:18).

Islam has spread out from Arabia and is now the main religion in most Middle Eastern countries.

Christianity. Jesus spent most of His earthly life in what is now the modern nation of Israel. Later the Holy Spirit empowered Jesus' disciples as they were assembled in Jerusalem. From there Christians have spread throughout the world. But even though Christianity began in the Middle East, real Christians are a minority there today.

The country of Lebanon has often been called "Christian" because many Lebanese consider themselves Christians rather than Muslims. However, there are also many Muslims in Lebanon. And many of those who consider themselves Christians think of Christianity more as a culture than as a personal relationship with God. In recent years, fighting among various groups of Muslims and so-called Christians has caused much destruction in Lebanon.

True Christians know that following Jesus means more than just identifying with a "Christian" culture. Jesus calls people to true repentance, holiness, and peace. He calls Jews to recognize Him as their Messiah, the one who fulfilled the Old Testament prophecies. To believing Arabs He offers spiritual blessings far greater than the material wealth Ishmael lost when he was cast out of Abraham's family. To all true believers, Jesus provides forgiveness

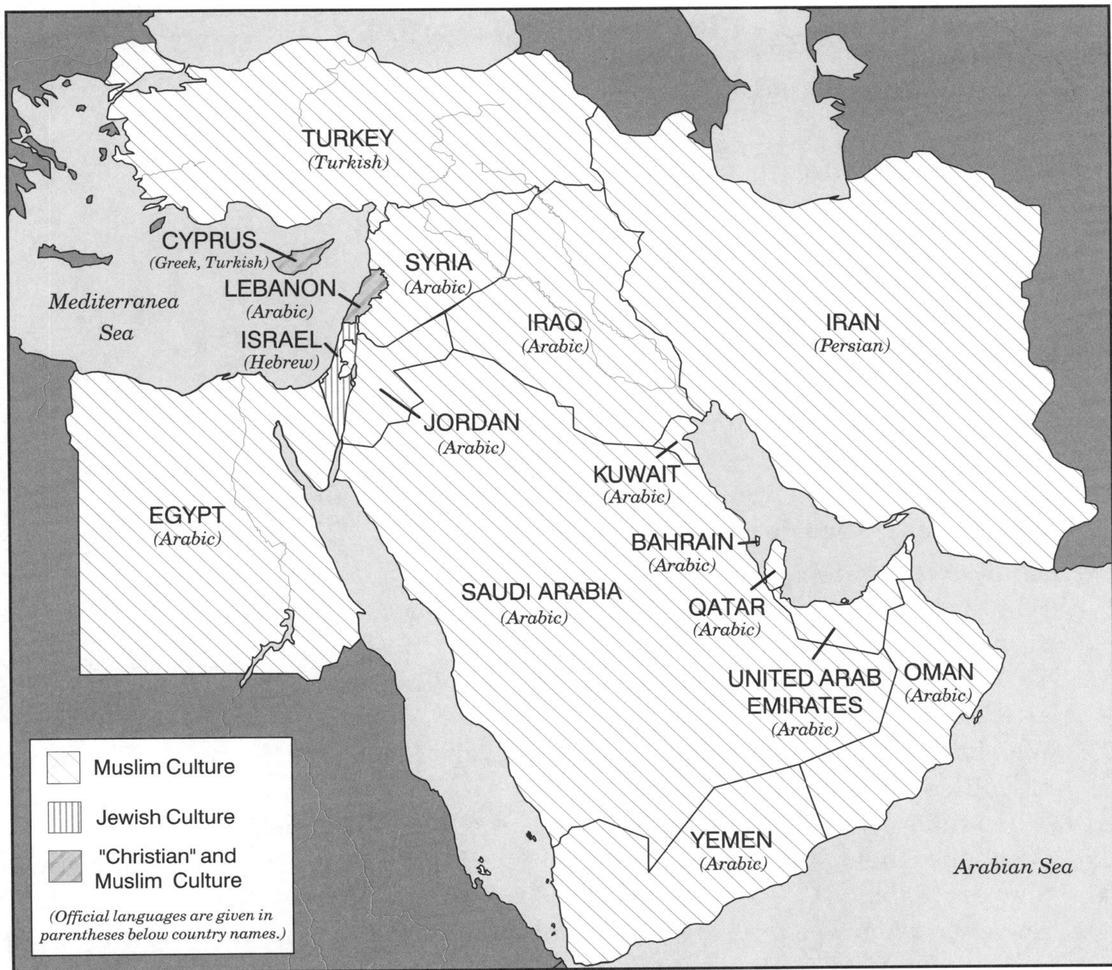

Figure 5:8. Middle East Religious Cultures and Official Languages

of sins, the grace to live godly lives in this present world, and the promise of eternal life. Jesus said, "I am the way, the truth, and the life: no man cometh unto the Father, but by me" (John 14:6).

Study Exercises

18. Which part of the Bible do followers of Judaism accept as Scripture?
19. (*a*) What serves the same purpose as a church building for followers of Judaism? (*b*) Who serves as a minister?
20. (*a*) What do Christianity, Judaism, and Islam have in common? (*b*) What do true Christians believe that Judaism and Islam reject?
21. What book do Muslims have as their holy book?
22. Use Figure 5:8 to answer these questions.
    a. What is the official language of Israel?
    b. In what way are Iran and Turkey different from most other Arab countries?
    c. In which country is Greek a main language?
    d. Are Jews or Muslims more numerous in the Middle East?
    e. In what way is Lebanon similar to other Middle East countries? In what way is it different?

Clinching the Chapter

Use the text and maps to complete these exercises.

Multiple Choice

A. *Write the word or phrase* least *associated with the first item.*

1. Asia: Egypt, Iran, Syria, Iraq
2. Persian Gulf: Iraq, Iran, Saudi Arabia, Cyprus
3. Red Sea: Egypt, Israel, Syria, Saudi Arabia
4. Euphrates: Lebanon, Turkey, Syria, Iraq
5. Mediterranean: Cyprus, Israel, Lebanon, Jordan
6. Far East: China, India, Turkey, Japan
7. Petroleum: Iran, Lebanon, Saudi Arabia, Kuwait
8. Arab: Egypt, Jordan, Syria, Israel
9. Great Rift Valley: Jordan River, Nile River, Sea of Galilee, Dead Sea
10. Desert: oases, Bedouins, camels, metropolis

B. *Write the correct words.*

1. What is one of the world's greatest shipping shortcuts? (Persian Gulf, Suez Canal, Jordan River, Gulf of Aqaba)
2. The Tigris and Euphrates unite to form the (Tehran, Hormuz, Ramadan, Shatt-al-Arab).
3. Which *two* bodies of water are below sea level? (Dead Sea, Mediterranean Sea, Sea of Galilee, Persian Gulf)
4. When did modern Israel become a nation? (1776, 1863, 1948, 1973)
5. Name the climate found in many parts of the Middle East. (tropical, Mediterranean, temperate, frigid)
6. Ancient Sodom was probably located in the area of the (Nile River, Dead Sea, Gulf of Suez, Shatt-al-Arab).
7. Archaeology has helped Israel to rediscover a source of (petroleum, copper, potash, gold).
8. The Dome of the Rock is a shrine of the (Christians, Jews, Muslims, Hindus).
9. Jews who observe Jewish laws very strictly are known as (rabbi, minaret, kosher, orthodox).
10. The name *Allah* is the Arabic word for (Abraham, Muhammad, Jesus, God).

Matching

A. *For each clue, write the correct name from the right-hand column.*

1. East of Iraq	Cyprus
2. No income tax	Egypt
3. Small peninsula in the Persian Gulf	Iran
4. Partly in Europe	Israel
5. One of the world's leading oil producers	Jordan
6. Aswan dams	Kuwait
7. Mount Hermon on its eastern boundary	Lebanon
8. Many immigrants	Qatar
9. Shares Dead Sea shore with Israel	Saudi Arabia
10. Island in the Mediterranean Sea	Turkey

B. *Match as in Part A.*

1. Persian, Suez, Aqaba	books
2. Nile, Jordan, Tigris, Euphrates, Shatt-al-Arab	capital cities
3. Red, Mediterranean, Dead, Galilee	foods
4. Ararat, Hermon, Gilboa, Sinai	gulfs
5. Sharon, Philistia	"holy" places
6. Baghdad, Damascus, Jerusalem	Middle East languages
7. Wailing Wall, Dome of the Rock, Mecca	mountains
8. Kosher requirements	plains
9. Talmud, Pentateuch, Koran	rivers
10. Arabic, Hebrew, Turkish, Persian	seas or lakes

Completion

1. Bedouins live on a nomadic basis;
   Often they move to another ———.
2. Now that the dams on the Nile have been built,
   Farmers are wishing for good, fertile ———.
3. Old crooked alleys, too narrow for cars,
   Offer a good, shady place for ———.
4. Under the barren, unpromising soil,
   Lies a great source of new riches called ———.
5. Dutiful Muslims observe Ramadan;
   Everyone fasts to obey the ———.

Thought Questions

1. Since God wanted to show His glory to the world through His people, why is it understandable that He placed Israel in the land where He did?
2. Nations with various sources of income have a more secure future than those whose only resource is petroleum. Why is this true?
3. How do you think wars in the Middle East affect the tourist industry?
4. Counterfeit money is made to resemble real money as closely as possible. How is Islam a counterfeit religion?
5. Would you be sorry to hear that all old sections of Middle Eastern cities had been made modern? Why or why not?

Geographical Skills

1. The Middle East countries include parts of which three continents?
2. What important degree of latitude passes through Saudi Arabia?
3. (*a*) Which Middle East country is nearest the North Pole? (*b*) Which is nearest the equator?
4. (*a*) Name the capitals of Iraq and Iran. (*b*) Which of these cities has a higher elevation? (See the physical relief map in this chapter.)
5. Use a map scale to find the approximate distances between Jerusalem and these capital cities.
   a. Cairo, Egypt
   b. Amman, Jordan
   c. Damascus, Syria
   d. Beirut, Lebanon
   e. Baghdad, Iraq
   f. Tehran, Iran
   g. Riyadh, Saudi Arabia
   h. Muscat, Oman

6. Name the body of water found at each of these locations.
   a. 20°N 40°E
   b. 35°N 20°E
   c. 28°N 50°E
   d. 15°N 60°E
7. Use a map to find which country in each pair extends farther south.
   a. Lebanon or Syria
   b. Israel or Jordan
   c. Israel or Syria
8. Use a globe to find which country in each pair extends farther south.
   a. the United States or Saudi Arabia
   b. the Philippines or Egypt
   c. Israel or the United States
9. Which is farther west: the capital of Israel or the capital of Ethiopia?
10. Name the Middle East nations crossed by longitude 40°E.

Further Study

1. Compare a map of Bible times with a modern map, and tell which modern country or countries occupy the area of the following Bible places.
   a. Babylon
   b. Syria
   c. Tarshish
   d. Moab
   e. Nineveh
   f. Shushan
   g. Mesopotamia
   h. Tyre and Sidon
   i. Asia (New Testament)
2. The countries of North America and Europe depend heavily on petroleum from the Middle East. If suddenly there were no petroleum available, how might your lifestyle be affected? What things might you have to do differently?

Be Sure You Know

Can you answer all these questions? If not, study Chapters 4 and 5 to find the answers.

A. Where are these items on a map?

1. the continent of Africa
2. the Nile, Congo, Niger, and Zambezi Rivers
3. the Middle East
4. the Tigris, Euphrates, and Jordan Rivers
5. the Mediterranean Sea, the Red Sea, and the Persian Gulf

B. What

6. climate pattern can be found in Africa?
7. is the highest mountain in Africa?
8. problems are faced by farmers in Africa?
9. are the main religions in Africa?
10. (*a*) two sections can be seen in many African cities? (*b*) two sections can be seen in many cities of the Middle East?
11. is the climate of lands around the Mediterranean Sea?
12. resource has brought great wealth to countries in the Middle East?
13. is a major shipping shortcut in the Middle East?
14. three major religions were founded in the Middle East?

C. What do these words mean?

15. apartheid
16. bazaar
17. Bedouin
18. cacao
19. capital
20. cassava
21. desertification
22. illiterate
23. Koran
24. metropolis
25. mosque
26. nomad
27. oasis
28. orthodox
29. Pentateuch
30. poacher
31. Ramadan
32. rift
33. savanna
34. subsistence farmer
35. Talmud
36. tsetse fly

D. Why

37. does much of Africa have a very warm climate?
38. do not all equatorial areas of Africa have a very warm climate?
39. have mining and manufacturing been slow to develop in Africa?
40. have young African nations gone through turbulent times?
41. has Africa been called the "dark continent"?
42. is the Middle East called by that name?
43. do many tourists come to the Middle East?

So Far This Year

See how many answers you can give from Chapters 1–5 without looking back.

A. *Match the letters on the map to the names below. You will not use all the letters.*

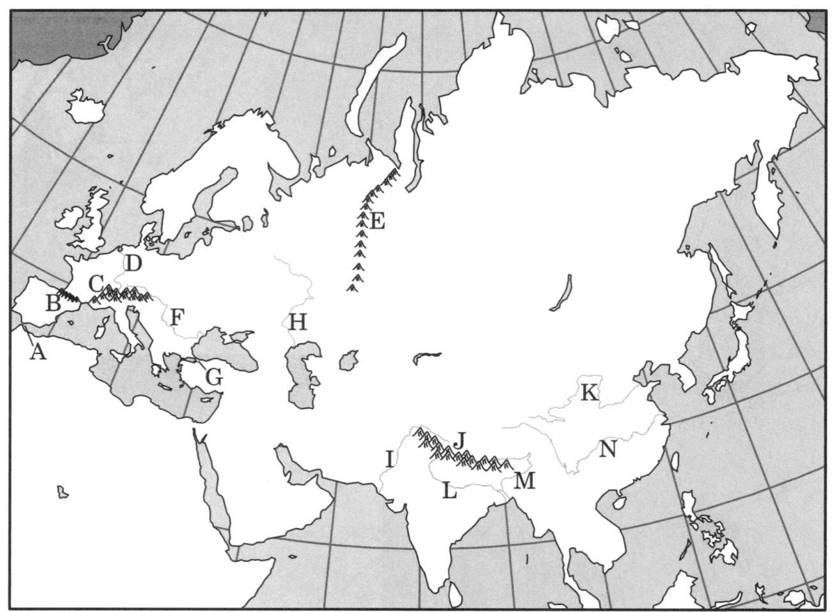

_____ 1. Alps
_____ 2. Himalayas
_____ 3. Pyrenees
_____ 4. Danube River
_____ 5. Ganges River
_____ 6. Huang He River
_____ 7. Indus River
_____ 8. Rhine River
_____ 9. Volga River
_____ 10. Yangtze River
_____ 11. Strait of Gibraltar

B. *Give the correct answers.*

12. Because of (disruption, distention, distortion), a flat map is not as accurate as a globe.
13. The geographical regions of Europe include all the following *except* (northern mountains, eastern plains, central plains, southern mountains).
14. The North Atlantic Drift causes a (dry, mild, cold) climate in Europe.
15. Trade is especially important to a country with (much, little) farmland and (many, few) natural resources.
16. Europe and Asia are considered two different continents because of their great difference in (climate, culture, landscape, history).
17. The climate regions of Africa include all the following *except* (arctic, desert, Mediterranean, savanna, rain forest).
18. Common problems for African farmers include all the following *except* (floods, poor soil, lack of education, overcrowding).
19. Major religions founded in the Middle East include all the following *except* (Buddhism, Christianity, Islam, Judaism).
20. The Middle East is the "middle point" in relation to all the following *except* (Asia, Africa, Australia, Europe).

Section 2

History of the Old World—From the Creation to the Reformation

Astronauts on the moon took this photograph of the earth. It reminds us that the earth and its inhabitants are a very small part of the universe. King David never saw this scene, but as he pondered on the Creation, he said, "When I consider thy heavens, the work of thy fingers, the moon and the stars, which thou hast ordained; what is man, that thou art mindful of him? and the son of man, that thou visitest him?" (Psalm 8:3, 4).

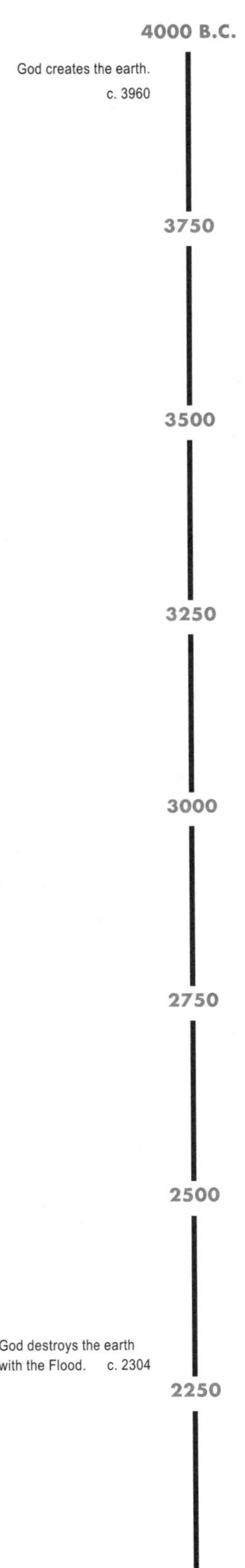
4000 B.C.
God creates the earth.
c. 3960
3750
3500
3250
3000
2750
2500
God destroys the earth
with the Flood. c. 2304
2250
2000 B.C.

6 The First World

"In the Beginning God Created the Heaven and the Earth"

How Was the First World Different From Ours?

How Did the First People Live?

How Did the Flood Affect the Earth?

Archaeology: Digging Into the Past

Time line note: Most ancient dates are approximate, as indicated by the label *c.* (*circa,* which means about). Dates marked with asterisks are especially uncertain.

"For this they willingly are ignorant of, that by the word of God the heavens were of old, and the earth standing out of the water and in the water: Whereby the world that then was, being overflowed with water, perished."
2 Peter 3:5, 6

The First World

"In the Beginning God Created the Heaven and the Earth"

"There must be a first time for everything." You have probably heard this before and may even have said it yourself. This is true of man and the things of this world, but not of God. God has always been, and always will be—unchanged and unchangeable! We can trace history back to God before Creation, but there we must stop, as if we have suddenly come out on an ocean too big to comprehend.

So there is no point in asking, "How did God begin?" Even if we try to answer simpler questions like "How did the world begin?" we soon discover how limited our knowledge is. The Bible tells us only that "God said, Let there be . . . and there was." God created things by commanding them to be, and that is all we need to know.

How Was the First World Different From Ours?

Regarding where mankind began, the Bible gives only a few indications. It does say that a river flowed from Eden and then formed four rivers. Of these four, we recognize the Euphrates (yoo FRAY teez) and possibly the Hiddekel (HIHD eh kehl), which is usually identified as the Tigris River. The Flood may have altered the courses of these two rivers; but from their general location, we conclude that the Garden of Eden was somewhere in the Middle East. Here God placed the man whom He had created.

Before humans fell away from God by sinning, they were perfect. Adam must have been very intelligent, for God gave him the task of naming all the animals. Man and nature worked in harmony. There was no disease, no killing, and no fear of death.

But life for man had barely begun when a disastrous event took place that changed the course of history more than all wars and all inventions since that time. We call this event simply the Fall. It was the result of Adam and Eve's disobedience to God's command.

Winding through countless palm trees, the Tigris flows through Iraq. The sandy areas near the river are probably flooded when the river is high.

The Fall was a spiritual fall away from God, but it affected men physically as well. From this point on, people began to experience pain and sickness, and everyone could expect to die eventually.

God also pronounced a curse that affected plants and animals. Now humans had to struggle against nature to make a living. Thorns and thistles crowded out man's crops. Animals and people sometimes competed with each other. (For example, rats eat foods that humans have gathered.) The apostle Paul wrote, "We know that the whole creation groaneth and travaileth in pain together until now" (Romans 8:22).

After the Fall, Adam lived in a world quite different from the one he had known before. But it was also different from the world we know now. The Bible indicates that before the Flood it never rained. Some people also think that the seasons as we know them began only after the Flood.

Fossils suggest that the climate of the first world was temperate all over the earth. Fossils of warmth-loving plants and animals such as lions and buttercups have been found in cold regions where such plants and animals could not live today.

"Wherefore, as by one man sin entered into the world, and death by sin; and so death passed upon all men, for that all have sinned" (Romans 5:12).

And people lived long—hundreds of years. What must it have been like to live 930 years, as Adam did? He lived long enough to see his great-great-great-great-great-great-grandson! However, people

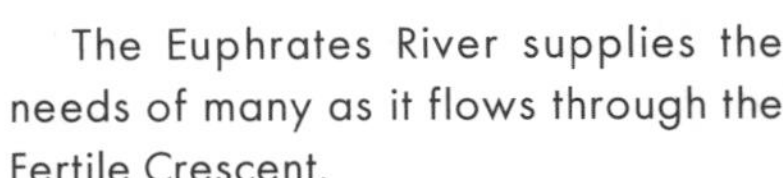

The Euphrates River supplies the needs of many as it flows through the Fertile Crescent.

were spiritually degenerating (losing quality) during Adam's time. Perhaps with their long earthly lives, it was easy to become careless about spiritual things.

Study Exercises

1. What words in Psalm 90:2 tell us that God has always been and always will be?
2. What does the Bible tell us about the method God used to make the universe?
3. According to Genesis 1, did it take God a short time or a long time to create the world?
4. In what general area of the world did mankind begin?
5. How did the Fall affect plant and animal life?

How Did the First People Live?

Many historians assume that the first humans wandered about gathering wild fruits and seeds, and that it took a long time to develop the idea of farming. This is not true. Adam and his sons were farmers from the first. God placed Adam in the Garden of Eden "to dress it and to keep it" (Genesis 2:15). Cain tilled the ground, and Abel raised sheep.

Before long, men were building cities. It seems too bad that Cain, the first murderer, has the credit for building the first city. But maybe there is a connection. Although cities in themselves are not evil, there is violence and immorality wherever crowds of ungodly people live together.

Early men were by no means ignorant. Among Cain's descendants were musicians and metalworkers. Seth's descendants kept

"Abel was a keeper of sheep, but Cain was a tiller of the ground. . . . And the LORD had respect unto Abel and to his offering: but unto Cain and to his offering he had not respect. . . . And Cain talked with Abel his brother: and it came to pass, when they were in the field, that Cain rose up against Abel his brother, and slew him" (Genesis 4:2–8).

accurate records of their long lives and their family history—using either an early writing system or careful memorization. Noah and his sons needed engineering skills to build the ark, which was probably the largest vessel ever made until recent times.

The ruins of people who lived soon after the Flood also give evidence that people before the Flood were highly civilized. Men marvel again and again at these ancient ruins. How did the Sumerians (soo MUR ee uhnz), one of the earliest known civilizations, develop such a high standard of living? How could ancient men have been organized and educated enough to make the Egyptian pyramids? No doubt Noah and his sons remembered well what had been before the Flood, and they likely passed some of this knowledge on to their descendants.

In spite of men's intelligence, the Bible tells us in Genesis 6:13 that before the Flood the earth was filled with violence. This is a point to remember in these modern days of violence. Man's wickedness indicates that God's judgment will soon fall upon the whole world again. "And as it was in the days of Noe, so shall it be also in the days of the Son of man" (Luke 17:26).

How Did the Flood Affect the Earth?

The Flood brought the second drastic change in the history of the world. It destroyed all civilization so completely that we say people who lived before it lived in "the world that then was" (2 Peter 3:6).

What we do not know about the Flood would fill more pages than what we do know. But obviously the Flood, being much more than a cloudburst, greatly changed the geography of this planet. Think of the terrific erosion along the sides of hills and mountains. Imagine streams raging where no streams had flowed before, cutting deep chasms. Think of sea animals carried in surging currents until they came to rest far from home. Fossils of sea life have been found in mountains, and sediments dropped by moving water have formed thick layers

This wreckage was left in the wake of the Johnstown flood, caused by a broken dam upstream from Johnstown, Pennsylvania. Over 2,200 people died in this flood. It is hard to imagine the power that the water had to so completely wreck the heavy steel locomotives and parts of the city.

Fossils of small marine animals are embedded in rock.

How Did Fossils Form in Rocks?

A fossil sometimes forms when an animal or a plant is buried very quickly in sand or mud. If conditions are right, the sediment around the plant or animal hardens into rock, and the shape of the remains is preserved as a fossil. Sometimes a fossil consists of original bone or shell, but often the original materials decay, and minerals fill the spaces they left in the rock. Such fossils still show the shape of the original plant or animal.

Very few fossils are being formed today. Under normal conditions, most animals and plants decay or are consumed long before sediment can bury them. But the Flood of Noah's time provided ideal conditions for fossils to form. Many plants and animals destroyed by the Flood were no doubt covered by thick layers of sediment. The sediment eventually hardened, and today these sedimentary rocks give evidence of God's great judgment that buried millions of living things.

of rocks far inland from any ocean.

Because many scientists "willingly are ignorant" of the changes God wrought through the Creation and the Flood, they argue that fossils and ***sedimentary*** rocks were deposited by slow processes that took millions of years. They try to explain the history of the earth as if "all things continue as they were from the beginning of the creation" (2 Peter 3:4–6). But Christians who accept the Bible as God's Word believe that many of the strange finds that fossil hunters use as "proof" of evolution can be used just as well—and often better—as evidence of a worldwide Flood.

Just remember that we do not need to explain everything we find in the earth as soon as we discover it. When you are putting together a jigsaw puzzle and find a piece that does not fit, you lay it aside, hoping to find a place for it later. We can do the same with some of the mysteries the Lord has placed in the earth, though we will never solve them all in this life. "For now we see through a glass, darkly; but then face to face: now I know in part; but then shall I know even as also I am known" (1 Corinthians 13:12).

Many different peoples from various places around the world tell old tales remarkably like the Bible account of the Flood. Most of the stories agree that there was a worldwide flood and that a few people were saved in an ark or a boat. Many stories also say the Flood came to punish men for their wickedness.

Study Exercises

6. During whose lifetime did farming begin?
7. Who built the first city?
8. List several evidences that the people who lived before the Flood were highly intelligent.
9. Fossils that unbelievers use to "prove" evolution might actually be proving what?
10. What should we do with fossils and other objects in the earth that we cannot explain?

Archaeology: Digging Into the Past

Have you ever found an old arrowhead, bottle, or buried tool that made you wonder about its history? That gives a simple illustration of how ***archaeology*** (ahr kee AHL uh jee) helps us learn about the past. Archaeologists look for ancient objects and try to form a better picture of historical civilizations. As they discover more and more ***artifacts*** (manmade objects), monuments, and written works of ancient times, they open a window into the life of ancient peoples.

Archaeology today is a highly refined science, quite different from the mere treasure seeking that it once was. Often a large museum, university, or branch of government directs and pays for an archaeological expedition.

First the scientists must choose a ***site*** to explore. They may choose a spot because they already know some history about it, or because someone has discovered a few artifacts there. They might also choose to explore a spot because they have noticed some unusual variation in the surface of the ground. An innocent-looking mound might prove to be a ***tell,*** which is a hill formed through the ages by men building on top of buried ruins left by past generations. Sometimes the archaeologists dig a vertical shaft into a site to see whether large-scale digging would be worthwhile.

These ancient objects were found in the Middle East. They all seem to be scribe's tools. Most of them are made of wood. The box with a hole in the top and the long black stone dish were probably inkwells. A stamp appears in the lower right corner.

Archaeologists dig around an ancient foundation in Beirut, Lebanon. Archaeology is hard work, especially under the Middle East's blazing sun.

These Egyptian hieroglyphics are the oldest hieroglyphics ever discovered. German archaeologists discovered them in an Egyptian tomb.

Once the directors of the expedition choose a site, many workers help with the actual digging. As they dig down through the tell, they may find various "layers" of civilization, caused by men building one city on top of another. The archaeologists keep a careful record of the precise location of each article they find. Later they try to fit all the facts together to determine how the site appeared as it passed into buried history.

Interpreting the different layers is not easy. The archaeologists have to ask questions like "Does this layer come immediately before the layer above it in time, or was the city deserted for a number of generations between layers?" After the archaeologists have carefully examined the records and various finds, they publish an account of them. People who have been working in other areas

We can learn about history from the Bible, other old books, artifacts like arrowheads and pottery, archaeological finds, and from stories passed by word of mouth.

can study the results and help to form an even broader picture.

Students of history must be careful not to assume too much from archaeology. Sometimes archaeologists form wrong conclusions because they already have their minds made up about what they want to prove. For example, those who accept the theory of evolution may try to use archaeological discoveries to discredit the Bible. In their eagerness to prove their point, they sometimes falsely interpret what they find.

In spite of its limitations, archaeology has been highly valuable in increasing our knowledge of history. Many artifacts that have been discovered make Bible history even clearer and more vivid. Much of what you will study in the next several lessons we know largely through the labors of archaeologists.

Study Exercises

11. Name one evidence that might help an archaeologist decide it is worthwhile to dig at a particular spot.
12. What is a tell?
13. Name one very important thing archaeologists do at a site besides supervising digging.
14. How do archaeologists working at separate sites benefit each other?
15. Why might men wrongly interpret an archaeological finding?

How Accurate Are Ancient Dates?

Several hundred years ago, most people living in Western cultures accepted the Bible's record of ancient events. By adding the number of years between generations, kings, or events, Bible scholars calculated that God created the world about four thousand years before Christ was born.

Then some men began to question whether the earth was older than the Bible indicated. They pointed out that a historian named Manetho (MAN uh thoh) had made lists of Egyptian kings going back more than five thousand years before Christ. Soon they convinced others that the early Bible records were not true.

Eventually historians realized that Manetho's records are not dependable. Manetho lived several centuries before Christ, long after most of the events that he recorded. Some of the pharaohs he listed must have reigned over different parts of Egypt at the same time, and others probably did not reign as long as he said. But by the time historians admitted that Manetho's records were not accurate, many of them had completely rejected the Bible. Today they admit that historical records go back only a few thousand years, yet they still insist that it took man thousands and even millions of years to develop modern civilizations.

Since many historians reject the accuracy of the Bible, they must look for other ways to date ancient events. They often base "prehistoric" dates on radiocarbon tests, which are based on the fact that living plants and animals contain carbon that slowly breaks down after death. Scientists try to determine the age of a bone, piece of wood, or other artifact that was once part of a living organism by measuring the amount of carbon left in it.

However, scientists admit that a number of factors can distort a carbon reading. The potential for error in this method is so great that historians disregard any radiocarbon date that seems too high or too low. Other scientific methods of dating early events are not much better. It is little wonder that many of these questionable dates are much older than the Bible record allows. Nevertheless, most modern reference books give these dates as facts.

Many people do not realize that the dates given for early events, such as the founding of Jericho or the building of the pyramids, are only educated guesses. Secular dates back to about 2000 B.C. are more reasonable, since they are based partly on historical records. However, some historians think that even dates between 1000 and 2000 B.C. might be several hundred years too old.

Christians should remember that any dates that cannot be proven by the Bible or reliable historical records are subject to error. The Bible gives the only dependable record of chronology before about 1000 B.C. Although we cannot determine the exact date of Creation, the Bible shows that 4000 B.C. is very nearly correct.

Clinching the Chapter

Multiple Choice

Write the word or phrase least *associated with the first item.*

1. The Fall: curse, death, pain, sleep
2. Cain: shepherd, farmer, builder, murderer
3. Pre-Flood men: intelligent, civilized, evolving, violent
4. Modern archaeology: science, artifacts, tells, treasure hunting
5. The Flood: fossils, sediments, peaceful, many accounts
6. Bible: facts, history, science, legends
7. Civilization: artifacts, climate, monuments, cities
8. After the Flood: rain, seasons, mild climate, pyramids
9. Tell: farm, layers, mound, shaft
10. Artifact: man-made, arrowhead, skeleton, Egyptian toy

Matching

A. *For each clue, write the correct term from the right-hand column.*

1. Was given task requiring intelligence	Abel
2. A shepherd	Adam
3. Four rivers	Creation
4. "Let there be . . ."	Eden
5. General area where man began	the Fall
6. Had no beginning	the Flood
7. Changed earth's geography	fossils
8. Found in unusual places	God
9. Material dropped by water	Middle East
10. The immediate result of sin	sediment

B. *Match each statement with the reference that supports it. You may use your Bible.*

1. God has always been and will always be.	Genesis 1:1
2. For man, "the beginning" starts with the creation	Genesis 1:3
of heaven and earth.	Genesis 6:13
3. God created by commanding things to be.	Exodus 20:11
4. God finished His Creation in six days.	Psalm 90:2
5. The Fall of Man affected the whole creation.	Luke 17:26
6. The pre-Flood world was full of violence.	Romans 8:22
7. "The world that then was" perished.	2 Peter 3:4
8. Some men are willingly ignorant of the Flood.	2 Peter 3:5
9. All things have not continued the same since the Creation.	2 Peter 3:6
10. The last days of this present world will be like the days of Noah.	

Completion

1. Where man began, we think at least,
   Was somewhere in the Middle ———.
2. The fossils found where once was mud
   May have been left there by the ———.

3. The Bible and the facts agree,
   As shown by ———.
4. An ancient town that rose and fell
   Might leave a mound we call a ———.
5. A dug-up object, old and cracked,
   Might be a priceless ———.

Thought Questions

1. Why is it unlikely that archaeologists will find much, if anything, from pre-Flood civilizations? (Genesis 6:13; 7:17–24; and 2 Peter 3:6 give clues.)
2. What do the days just before the Flood have in common with our days?
3. Since we already believe the Bible is true, what point is there in reading about artifacts from Bible times?
4. (*a*) What do you think would be the most pleasant part of an archaeologist's work? (*b*) What would be the least pleasant?
5. Tell the class, if you can, of a time when you guessed the history of some place or object near your home. Perhaps you observed a long ridge and guessed that a railroad had once been there. Perhaps you discovered an old foundation and speculated about what had been built on it. You may have noticed a building that evidently had had a piece added or torn away. Observations like these are a form of archaeology.

Geographical Skills

1. Since the Flood, the area around the equator generally has a warm and humid climate. On a globe or world map, follow the equator around the world. What present-day countries does it cross in the Eastern Hemisphere?
2. Give the location of Mount Ararat in latitude and longitude degrees.

Further Study

1. In various cultures, stories about the Flood have been handed down. Find out more about these stories in reference books such as *Halley's Bible Handbook,* and write a report.
2. According to the article "Archaeology" in *Unger's Bible Dictionary,* what is better proof than archaeology that the Bible is true?

A medieval painter's concept of the Tower of Babel. Notice that the top is in the clouds.

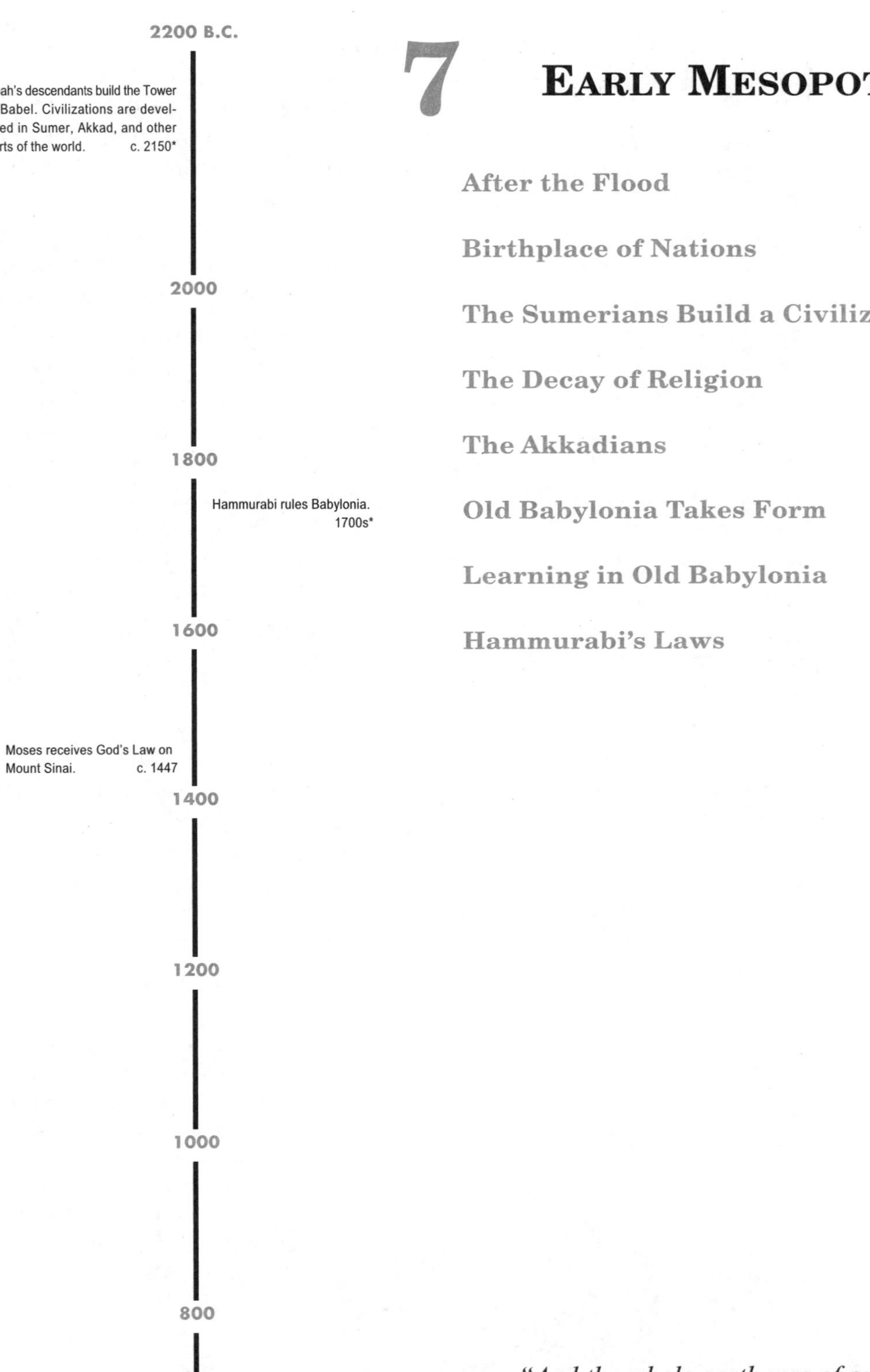
2200 B.C.
Noah's descendants build the Tower of Babel. Civilizations are developed in Sumer, Akkad, and other parts of the world. c. 2150*
2000
1800
Hammurabi rules Babylonia. 1700s*
1600
Moses receives God's Law on Mount Sinai. c. 1447
1400
1200
1000
800
Ashurbanipal, king of Assyria, collects documents from Old Babylonia. c. 650
600 B.C.

7 Early Mesopotamia

After the Flood

Birthplace of Nations

The Sumerians Build a Civilization

The Decay of Religion

The Akkadians

Old Babylonia Takes Form

Learning in Old Babylonia

Hammurabi's Laws

"And the whole earth was of one language, and of one speech. And it came to pass, as they journeyed from the east, that they found a plain in the land of Shinar; and they dwelt there."

Genesis 11:1, 2

Early Mesopotamia

After the Flood

When the ark finally settled, Noah and his family found themselves on one of the mountains of Ararat, north of the Tigris and Euphrates Rivers. The early descendants of Noah moved southward to the fertile land between these two rivers. This was the region of Mesopotamia (mehs uh puh TAY mee uh), a Greek name meaning "between the rivers." The Bible also uses the Hebrew name *Shinar* (SHY nahr), which means "country of two rivers."

Throughout history, whenever people moved into new lands, they settled first along rivers. The rivers served as highways for boats, and the fertile soil along the rivers made good farmland. The rivers also provided water for irrigation in dry areas such as Mesopotamia.

Mesopotamia became one of the world's ***cradles of civilization.*** In other words, an infant civilization started there and grew until it affected world history. Some of the world's most ancient ruins lie in southern Mesopotamia, or Shinar. It was here that the people began to build the Tower of Babel. Archaeologists working in Iraq have discovered one or two sites where the tower might have been.

Some people think that Nimrod, whom Genesis calls "a mighty hunter before the LORD," may have ruled the whole world of that time. According to ancient Jewish tradition, he directed the building of the Tower of Babel. One thing is clear: the ambitious people who attempted to make a name for themselves utterly failed. Their fear of being "scattered abroad upon the face of the whole earth" was realized. Had they continued to honor God, His blessing would have been upon them. But like the men before the Flood, they elevated their own abilities and forgot about God.

The word *babel* is now used to mean "a confusion of sounds and voices"—in reference to the confusion at the Tower of Babel when God confounded the languages of men. The city that was built at the site of the tower was later called Babylon.

This rock tower, called Birs Nimrud, is thought to be the remains of the Tower of Babel. It is located 10 miles (16.1 km) south of the ancient city of Babylon. The tower is made of bricks that were probably made from the soil of this region, which hardens to stone when mixed with water and exposed to heat.

Birthplace of Nations

Everyone born since the Flood descends from one or more of Noah's three sons: Shem, Ham, and Japheth. After the confusion at the Tower of Babel, the descendants of Japheth moved north into Asia and Europe. Most of Shem's children stayed in Mesopotamia and nearby areas such as Syria and Arabia. Later some settled in Canaan. The families of Ham who left Mesopotamia settled in parts of Arabia, Canaan, and northern Africa.

Study Exercises

1. How did Mesopotamia get its name?
2. Why did the earliest civilizations grow up along rivers? Give three reasons.
3. Who may have directed the building of the Tower of Babel?
4. From which son of Noah do most Europeans descend: Shem, Ham, or Japheth?

The Sumerians Build a Civilization

In southern Mesopotamia, even farther south than Babylon, a great civilization called Sumer (SOO mur) developed. Sumer is of special interest because one of its chief cities was the traditional "Ur of the Chaldees" where Abram grew up. Also, being one of the earliest known civilizations, Sumer helps to answer questions like these: "What is a civilization, and what makes it work?" "What were the first steps that brought about the highly developed civilization we have now?" "Is a high level of civilization always a good thing?"

A civilization is not simply a few million people living in a region, each man for himself. A civilization is a group of people cooperating closely with each other—so closely that they can live in communities and cities and work together smoothly.

Already in Chapter 6, you saw some elements of civilization. They include (1) raising crops, (2) raising ***domestic*** animals, (3) working with metals, and (4) pursuing arts such as music. Following are several more elements of civilization, which we find in Sumer.

A System of Transportation. Most modern countries have a network of paved highways, but the main highways of the Sumerians were their rivers and canals.

These Sumerian statues were found in an ancient temple. They may have been gods that were worshiped by the Sumerians. These statues likely indicate how the Sumerians dressed and what kind of hairstyles they had.

They probably used the Euphrates River more than the Tigris. The Euphrates flows more slowly, which made sailing easier. The Sumerians built many cities along this river.

Advanced Agriculture. Mesopotamia had hot, dry summers. Farmers depended on river water for irrigation. Probably their most common method of irrigation was to build systems of reservoirs and canals. In the spring the rivers overflowed their banks, filling the reservoirs with water. During the growing season, the farmers released the water into their fields through the canals. The Sumerians worked together to plan, dig, and manage their irrigation systems.

Money. The Sumerians used their crops not only for food but also for money. If you worked on a farmer's canal, he might pay you with two measures of barley, which you could use to buy something else. This way of doing business was better than the clumsy system known as ***barter.*** A fisherman bartering for a cow needs to find a farmer willing to trade a cow for fish. But in Sumer the fisherman sold his fish for grain, and then anyone selling a cow was willing to take the grain as payment because he could use it to buy something else.

Specialization. Not all Sumerian boys grew up to be farmers. Some became boat builders, potters, jewelers, or scribes. The practice of doing just one special thing well is called ***specialization.*** Today, people in advanced civilizations are specializing in very narrow skills. Some men specialize not just in masonry, but in brick masonry or stone masonry. Most people who help to make shoes specialize in only one part of a shoe.

Writing. No one knows who invented writing, but the Sumerians are the first people on record who used writing. Learning to write was a tremendous step. Without writing, there would be no books, and there would be no good way to preserve the learning of people who died long ago or who live far away. With writing, each succeeding generation can preserve facts and ideas from the past, and they can also add what they have learned to the store of knowledge.

Wealthy Sumerian boys went to school. They learned to write with a stylus, making wedge-shaped impressions on soft clay tablets. Wedge-shaped ***cuneiform*** (kyoo NEE uh form) writing was used for hundreds of years in Mesopotamia. Writers in the Sumerian language used hundreds of different symbols—a bit more complicated, of course, than our twenty-six letters.

What did Sumerian schoolboys read in reading class? Archaeologists have discovered thousands of clay tablets containing

Cuneiform writing was used most extensively in the Middle East. It is a combination of pictures, shapes, and symbols.

This Sumerian artwork was excavated from a tree trunk. It depicts various aspects of Sumerian life, such as leisure, farming, fishing, and transporting goods.

stories, proverbs, and laws that students probably read and memorized. In fact, many of the tablets were obviously written by students.

New Ideas. A civilization open to better ideas will prosper, and that was certainly true of the Sumerians. They must have had open, creative minds. We have already noticed some of their inventions, but two more are worth mentioning. As far as we know, the Sumerians were the first people to use wheels. A wheel looks simple enough, but it took someone with imagination to invent the first one. Today all our major factories depend on wheels—not to mention our transportation. Our whole way of life would grind to a stop without them.

The Sumerians also invented a number system based on sixties. We still use this idea some four thousand years later by dividing hours into sixty minutes and minutes into sixty seconds. We also divide circles into 360 degrees (six times sixty).

A System of Government. It appears that the earliest people of Sumer had a measure of self-rule. They chose a leader only for emergencies such as war. But soon each city had its own king. A city and the surrounding area that it governed is called a ***city-state.***

Sometimes fierce battles erupted as a city tried to gain additional land or conquer its neighboring city-states. At various times the ruler of one city-state grew strong enough to control several neighboring city-states.

Study Exercises

5. Give two reasons why Sumer is given special attention in this book.
6. Name two ways the Sumerians used the Tigris and the Euphrates.
7. What did the Sumerians often use for money?
8. Why is our system of writing simpler than cuneiform writing?
9. What did Sumerians use for writing instead of paper?
10. What invention that greatly improved transportation may have come from the Sumerians?

The Decay of Religion

Often as people become more civilized, they become more self-centered and proud of their human achievements. Maybe the confusion of languages at the Tower of Babel humbled people a little. It certainly gave civilization a jolt from which it has never recovered. But in spite of God's action, Noah's descendants quickly fell into idolatry. They "changed the truth of God into a lie, and worshipped and served the creature more than the Creator" (Romans 1:25). The Sumerians envisioned the gods that they worshiped to be just as wicked as themselves.

Each major city of Sumer had its own temple tower, called a ***ziggurat*** (ZIHG uh rat). Similar towers in other parts of the world suggest that they were all patterned after the original Tower of Babel. The ziggurat at Ur, which was about 70 feet (21 m) high, would not seem tall beside today's skyscrapers. But in Ur it towered over the rest

The photograph pictures the remains of an ancient ziggurat, and the drawing shows what many ziggurats probably looked like. A ziggurat was an artificial hill, erected in valleys where there were no high places, because people felt that they needed to conduct their idolatrous worship in a place of high elevation.

of the city. Baked mud bricks covered the walls, and three stairways led up to the top. Priests ascended the steps with offerings for their moon god. More temples were clustered around the base of the ziggurat, for the Sumerians worshiped hundreds of gods.

Stories about the Creation and the Flood became very distorted. So did people's ideas about life and death. Many of these myths were completely unrealistic, yet they still included fragments of truth. For example, one tale related how man was created from dust. Another story told of a king who sought immortality. After much effort and a long journey, he secured a plant that would give eternal life. On his way home, he stopped to rest. While he was sleeping, a serpent came and took the plant. This myth might have had its roots in the account of the tree of life and the serpent.

Most Sumerians had little hope of eternal life. They seem to have resigned themselves to whatever the gods willed for them in this life, whether it was good or evil. And they expected nothing better in the lower world, to which they supposed all the dead passed.

Apparently the Sumerians did not appreciate the truth that Noah had passed down to them. So they soon found falsehoods to replace the truth. The Bible warns that if people refuse God's truth, He allows them to be snared by lies. "They received not the love of the truth, that they might be saved. And for this cause God shall send them strong delusion, that they should believe a lie" (2 Thessalonians 2:10, 11).

The Akkadians

North of Sumer, but still in southern Mesopotamia, lay the land of Akkad (AK ad). The Akkadians (uh KAY dee uhnz) were ***Semites*** (SEH myts). They lived much like the Sumerians, but they spoke an unrelated language.

An Akkadian king named Sargon (SAHR gahn) built what might have been the first true ***empire*** in history. First he conquered the Akkadian and Sumerian city-states, and then he gained control over other lands. For perhaps one hundred years, Sargon and his successors ruled an empire that stretched from the Persian Gulf to the Mediterranean Sea. Then invaders from the north broke up Sargon's empire.

Since the invaders did not set up a strong empire of their own, the Sumerians began to assert themselves again. Their kings ruled both Sumer and Akkad. During this period, which might have been about the time of Abram, Ur was a flourishing city.

This Akkadian portrait is solid bronze (an alloy of copper and tin). It is supposed to be Sargon or his son. Originally, the eyes were made of precious stones, which is why they have been roughly hacked out by a looter or an enemy.

Study Exercises

11. A number of Sumerian myths are based on actual happenings. Where can we find an accurate record of those events?
12. Where did Sumerians expect to go when they died?
13. What important first is associated with Sargon?

Old Babylonia Takes Form

Much of the world's population at this time lived in the ***Fertile Crescent.*** This area of land extended from the Mediterranean Sea to Mesopotamia. It was crescent-shaped because it curved northward around the Syrian Desert.

Sometime after the fall of Sargon's empire, various groups invaded Mesopotamia. One of these groups, the Amorites, came from the area of Syria and Canaan in the western part of the Fertile Crescent. They gradually extended their power until they controlled much of the Fertile Crescent, including Sumer and Akkad. A number of Amorite kings ruled, sometimes cooperating with each other and sometimes fighting each other.

The most outstanding of these Amorite kings was Hammurabi (hah moo RAH bee). He ruled Babylon for about forty-three years, possibly in the 1700s B.C. During this time he conquered most of Mesopotamia. Hammurabi used cruelty and trickery, but he did some good things that governments still do today. He kept the irrigation systems in good repair, and he took great interest in the day-to-day affairs of his empire. Hammurabi's empire is called Old Babylonia.

Hammurabi's successors were not as

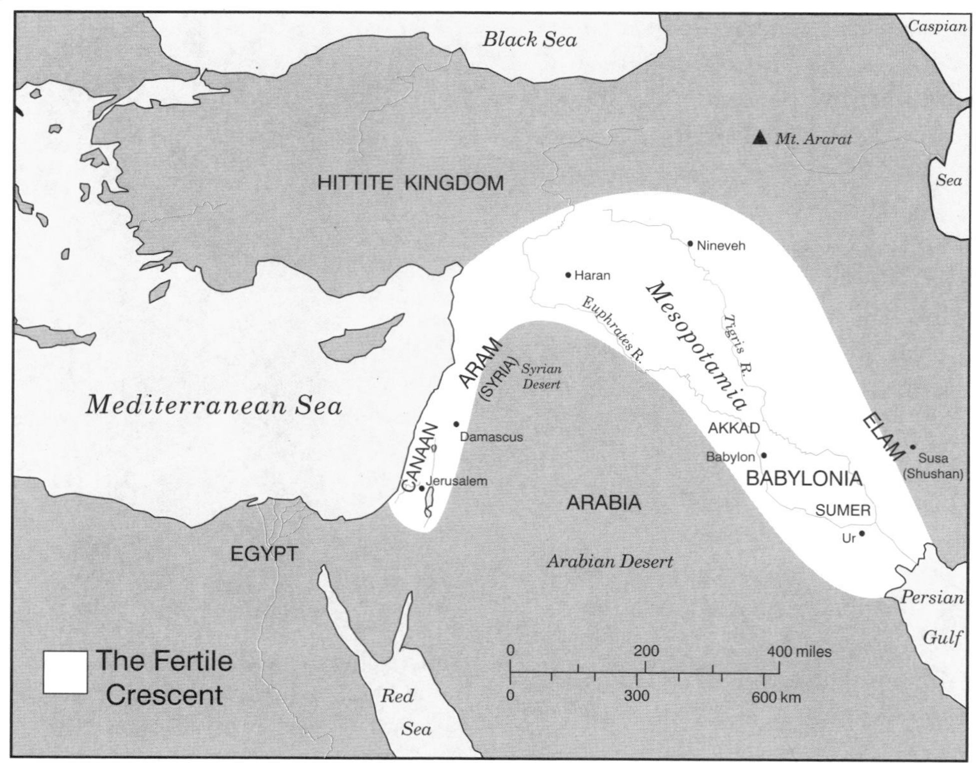

Figure 7:1. The Fertile Crescent

This art from Old Babylonia shows war chariots and horses. Violence and bloodshed have been a part of ungodly society ever since Cain killed Abel.

strong and capable as he, and they could not hold the empire together. However, Babylonian ways continued even after the empire fell. For over a thousand years, people patterned their lifestyles after the culture of Babylon.

Learning in Old Babylonia

Among the ruins of Nineveh, archaeologists have discovered a library of Ashurbanipal (ah shur BAH nuh pahl), an Assyrian king who lived about a thousand years after Hammurabi. This library of clay tablets included thousands of copies of documents and texts from Old Babylonia that reveal much about the life and learning of Hammurabi's time.

From the records found in Nineveh and other ancient sites, it appears that most Babylonians of Hammurabi's time knew how to speak Akkadian, though some spoke the language of the Amorites. Since Sumerian was also still used for some documents, a scribe had to be able to work in all three languages. Possibly he used a dictionary that listed words in one language along with their meanings in another.

Astronomy was an important study in Old Babylonia. The Babylonians used astronomy to maintain an accurate calendar. But they also had a second reason for studying the heavens. They thought that what happened on earth resulted from what happened in the sky, the realm

This is a view of what was once a part of ancient Nineveh, as seen from a platform that once bore a king's palace.

of the gods. By observing how the sun, moon, and stars were moving, they thought they could predict coming events on earth.

This study of the heavens is called ***astrology,*** and it has a direct connection to horoscopes and fortunetelling. It differs drastically from true astronomy! God warns that "astrologers . . . shall be as stubble; the fire shall burn them; they shall not deliver themselves from the power of the flame" (Isaiah 47:13, 14).

Study Exercises

14. Who was the first Amorite named in this lesson?
15. How much territory did Hammurabi conquer?
16. What is the difference between astronomers and astrologers?

This stele contains Hammurabi's law. Pictured at the top is a supposed god giving the law to Hammurabi. We are thankful that the one true God established order and appreciation for law among men.

Hammurabi's Laws

We have seen that Hammurabi understood what it took for a civilization to work well. The most important thing for which he is remembered is his system of laws. He updated the old laws and organized them into a ***code*** of several hundred laws. Fragments of clay tablets bearing sections of Hammurabi's law have been found scattered throughout his empire.

Hammurabi also wrote his laws on stone monuments called ***steles*** (STEE leez). Remarkably, in 1901, French archaeologists in Iran found one of these steles. It was at ancient Susa (called Shushan in the Book of Esther), where a conqueror had carried it.

Hammurabi's law has often been compared with the Law of Moses. It is true that in some ways they are similar, for both laws use the principle of "an eye for an eye, and a tooth for a tooth." But they have important differences too. For example, Hammurabi's law code prescribed a different penalty for a noble than for a common citizen or a slave, even if they committed the same crimes. God's Law meted out equal punishment to anyone who committed a particular crime, no matter who he was.

It is also worth noting that Moses gave the credit for his laws to God. Hammurabi claimed that he had received his laws from one of his gods, yet he also took much glory to himself. But the most important difference is that God's Law upheld a higher standard of purity and respect for human life. God said, "Ye shall be holy; for I am holy" (Leviticus 11:44).

Study Exercises

17. A systematic collection of laws is called a ———.
18. About how many years passed from the time of Hammurabi to the modern discovery of his famous stele?

19. How did the Law of Moses demonstrate that God is no respecter of persons?

20. Why can God require a higher standard of moral conduct than Hammurabi could?

Clinching the Chapter

Multiple Choice

A. *Write the word or phrase* least *associated with the first item.*

1. Babel: confusion, Sumer, Babylon, languages
2. Sons of Noah: Nimrod, Shem, Ham, Japheth
3. Civilization: money, transportation, specialization, astrology
4. Rivers: transportation, irrigation, domestication, floods
5. Sumerian developments: city-states, empire, wheels, number system
6. Sumerian writing: clay, stylus, cuneiform, paper
7. Rulers: Abram, Sargon, Hammurabi, Nimrod
8. Ziggurat: myths, religion, priests, eternal life
9. Hammurabi's empire: laws, irrigation, holy living, Mesopotamia
10. Fertile Crescent: Canaan, Akkad, Arabia, Babylonia

B. *Write the correct words.*

1. Which was farthest north? (Ararat, Sumer, Akkad, Ur)
2. As far as we know, Abram never lived in (Ur, Sumer, Babylon, Mesopotamia).
3. Trading goods for goods is called (specialization, barter, cuneiform, agriculture).
4. Cuneiform writing has (wedge-shaped, sixty, round, twenty-six) characters.
5. The Sumerians based their number system on (sevens, ones, sixties, hundreds).
6. In the name of religion, a Sumerian might build a (dam, reservoir, stele, ziggurat).
7. Sargon was (a Sumerian, an Akkadian, an Amorite, a Babylonian).
8. Hammurabi was (a Sumerian, an Akkadian, an Amorite, an Israelite).
9. The Fertile Crescent was shaped like the outline of (a ball, a barrel, a block, a banana).
10. Hammurabi's capital city was (Susa, Ur, Babylon, Euphrates).

Matching

A. *For each clue, write the correct term from the right-hand column.*

Clue	Term
1. City of Abram	Akkad
2. Continued long after Hammurabi died	Amorite
3. River of Mesopotamia	Babel
4. Invading group from the west	Babylonian culture
5. Means "between the rivers"	Hammurabi
6. Traditional builder of the Tower of Babel	Japheth
7. Early lawgiver	Mesopotamia
8. Early name for Babylon	Nimrod
9. World's first known empire	Tigris
10. Descendants in Asia and Europe	Ur

B. *Match as in Part A.*

1. Descendant of Shem	astrology
2. Stone monument	civilization
3. Where civilizations begin	cradle
4. Needed for crops in southern Mesopotamia	empire
5. Many people working smoothly together	irrigation
6. Associated with fortunetelling	Semite
7. Specific types of work	specialization
8. May have been invented by Sumerians	stele
9. Many lands under one government	wheel
10. Place of idol worship	ziggurat

Completion

1. Bible readers remember that
   Noah landed on Mount ———.
2. Of all great hunters known by God,
   Few reigned and built as did ———.
3. Waterways are used for transportation;
   Reservoirs hold water for ———.
4. Boys in Sumer wrote each day,
   Wedge-shaped marks on slabs of ———.
5. Trading fish for cows seems strange and funny;
   Grain would be a better kind of ———.
6. Abram worshiped God—but surely not
   At a temple called a ———.
7. Hammurabi's reign had many flaws,
   But he organized a code of ———.
8. Where different tasks are specialized,
   Countries are more ———.
9. No one knowing ancient laws supposes
   They were better than the Laws of ———.

Thought Questions

1. (*a*) What do you think may have been the greatest contribution the Sumerians made to civilization? (*b*) Why do you think this was the greatest contribution?
2. (*a*) What advantage would people have if they produced all their own food, clothing, and shelter instead of depending on others? (*b*) What is an advantage of specialization?
3. Historians who do not believe the Bible have difficulty explaining why the early Akkadians and Sumerians practiced similar customs, yet spoke unrelated languages. How can this unusual fact be explained in light of Bible truth?
4. The language barrier between peoples creates serious problems today. Yet God saw that it is better for mankind to have that problem than to not have it. Explain.
5. Jesus told the Jews, "Walk while ye have the light, lest darkness come upon you" (John 12:35). How do the descendants of Noah illustrate what Jesus was saying?

Geographical Skills

1. Trace the outline of Map A in the map section, and label it "The Ancient Middle East."
2. Mark Mount Ararat with a mountain symbol (▲) and label it. Using a blue colored pencil, trace the Tigris and Euphrates Rivers. Label them.
3. On your map, label the areas of Sumer and Akkad. Using larger letters, label this entire region Babylonia. Also label the cities of Ur and Nineveh.

Further Study

1. There is a remarkable similarity between the temple pyramids built by dwellers in Bible lands and those built by American Indians. There were also many similarities in their worship customs. Find information about this in an encyclopedia, and write a report about it. (Look under "American Indians," "Aztec," "Inca," or "Maya.")
2. Make a time line from Adam to Abraham, showing the birth and death of each man in this godly line. The time line will need to extend from the Creation (0 A.M.) to at least 2200 A.M. (The abbreviation A.M. means "in the year of the world.") Use Genesis 5:3–31 to determine the dates for each man from Adam to Lamech, and Genesis 11:10–25, 32 for each man from Shem to Terah.
   Special note concerning Noah: According to Genesis 7:11, God sent the Flood when Noah was 600 years old. Since Shem was 100 years old two years after the Flood (Genesis 11:10), Noah must have been 502 years old when Shem was born. (Genesis 5:32 might refer to Noah's age when his first son was born, or it might be an approximate figure.) Genesis 9:29 gives Noah's age when he died.
   Special note concerning Abraham: The year given in Genesis 11:26 also seems to refer to the birth of the oldest son rather than to all three. (Note that in both Genesis 5:32 and 11:26, the son through whom the godly line descends is named first, even though he might not have been the oldest.) Abram left Haran when he was 75 years old (Genesis 12:4), apparently soon after his father Terah died at the age 205 (Acts 7:4; Genesis 11:32). This means that Terah must have been 130 years old when Abram was born (205 - 75 = 130). Genesis 25:7 gives Abraham's age at his death.

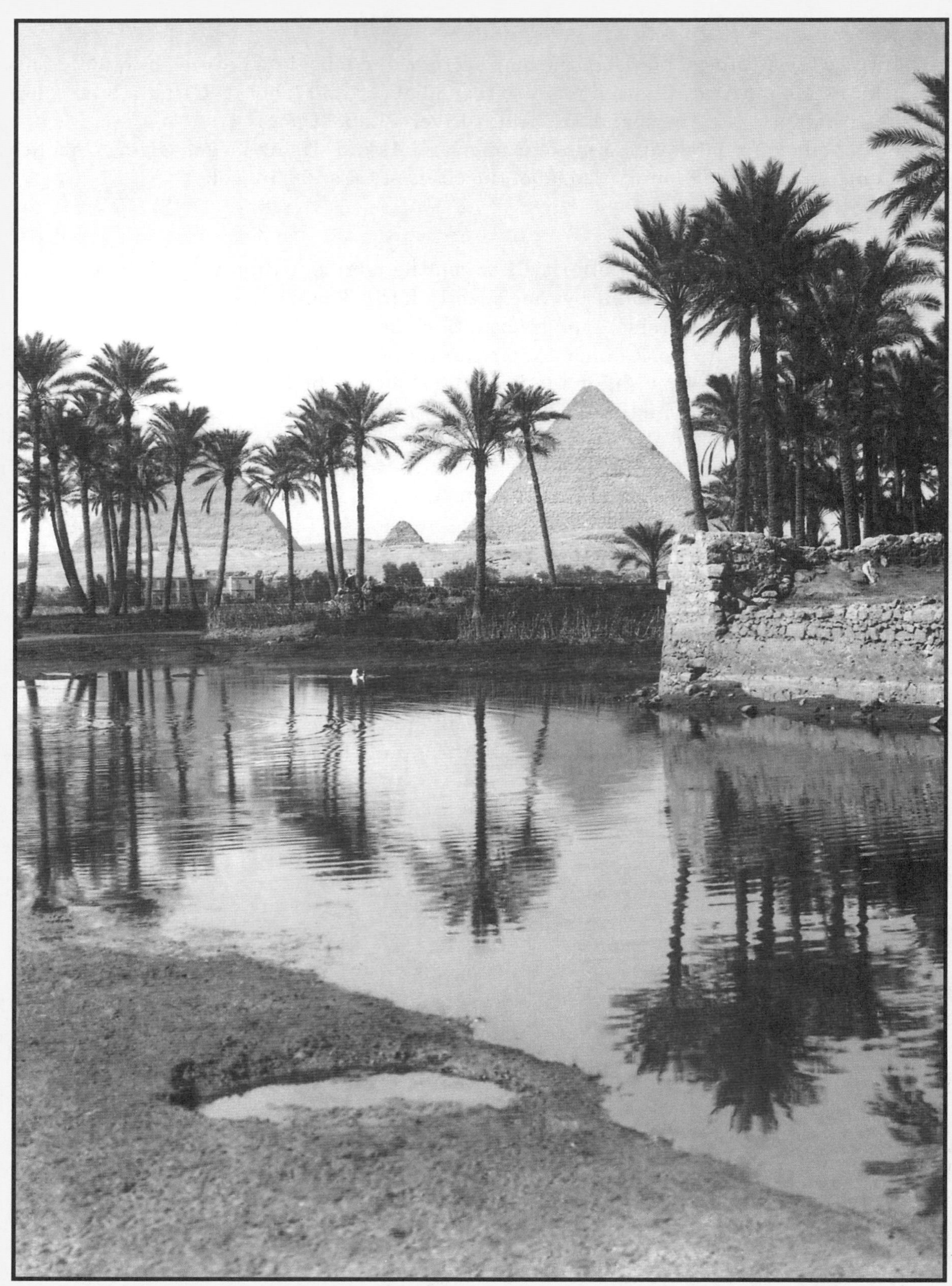

Three Egyptian pyramids in the distance dwarf a small village along the Nile River.

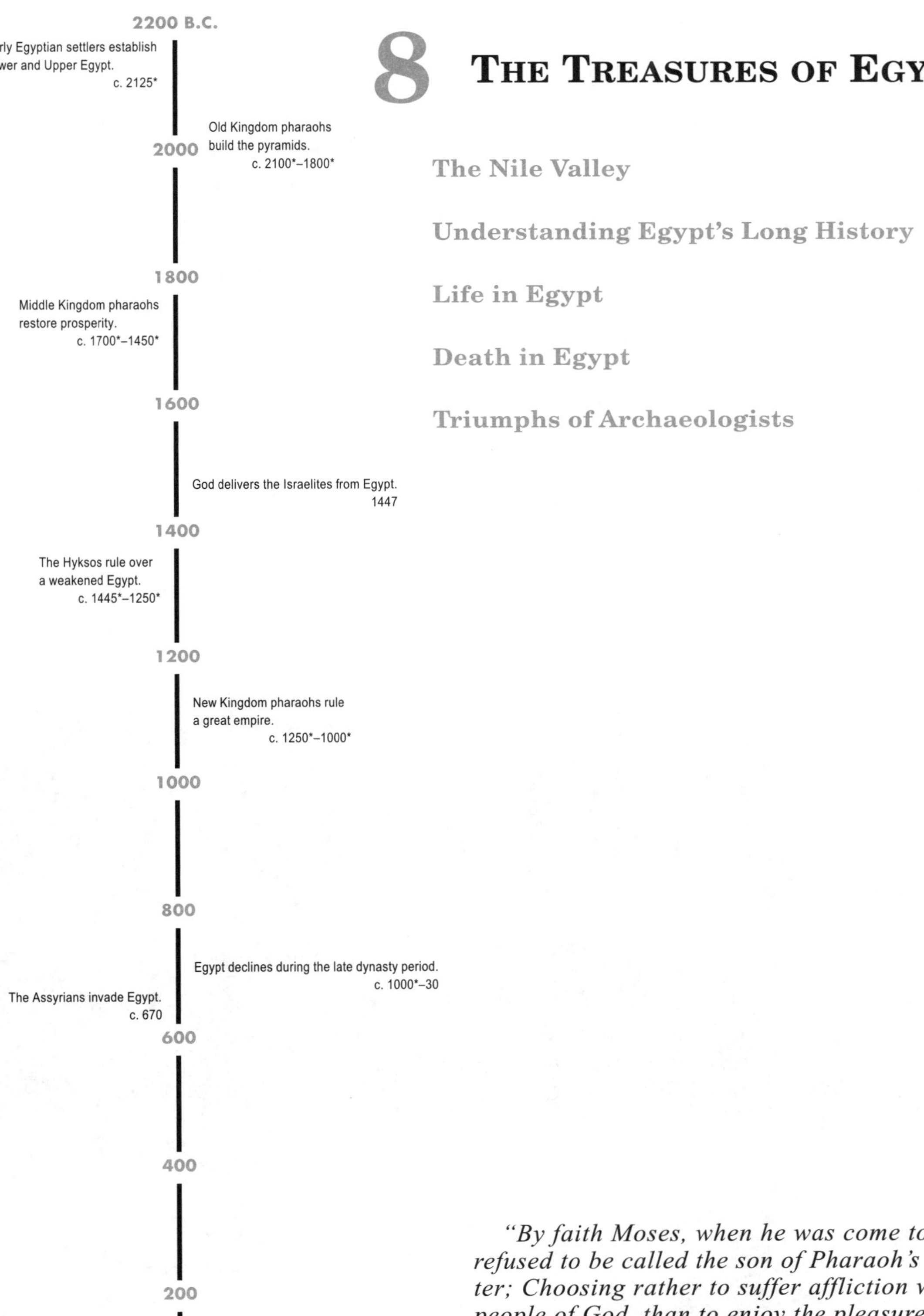
2200 B.C.
Early Egyptian settlers establish Lower and Upper Egypt. c. 2125*
2000
Old Kingdom pharaohs build the pyramids. c. 2100*–1800*
1800
Middle Kingdom pharaohs restore prosperity. c. 1700*–1450*
1600
God delivers the Israelites from Egypt. 1447
1400
The Hyksos rule over a weakened Egypt. c. 1445*–1250*
1200
New Kingdom pharaohs rule a great empire. c. 1250*–1000*
1000
800
Egypt declines during the late dynasty period. c. 1000*–30
The Assyrians invade Egypt. c. 670
600
400
200
The Romans make Egypt a Roman province. 30
0 B.C.

8 The Treasures of Egypt

The Nile Valley

Understanding Egypt's Long History

Life in Egypt

Death in Egypt

Triumphs of Archaeologists

"By faith Moses, when he was come to years, refused to be called the son of Pharaoh's daughter; Choosing rather to suffer affliction with the people of God, than to enjoy the pleasures of sin for a season; Esteeming the reproach of Christ greater riches than the treasures in Egypt: for he had respect unto the recompence of the reward."
Hebrews 11:24–26

The Treasures of Egypt

The Nile Valley

Egyptian history began long before the Israelites entered Egypt. The first Egyptians were descendants of Noah's son Ham—the Bible calls Egypt "the land of Ham" in Psalms 105 and 106. The people who first came to this sunny, dry land naturally settled along the Nile River. Egypt, like Mesopotamia, became a cradle of civilization.

The Nile is the longest river in the world, with its source in the African highlands thousands of miles south of Egypt. Yet Egyptian settlers moving up the river stopped soon after 700 miles (1,100 km). Their way was blocked by tumbling, foaming rapids, which are now called the First ***Cataract.***

As the Nile approaches the Mediterranean, it divides into several branches, forming a delta. Here the Nile waters slow down, dropping soil and sand. Over the years this process supplied the delta with the richest soil in Egypt. The land of Goshen, where the Israelites settled with their flocks and herds, was in the northeastern part of the delta.

The delta area received some rainfall, but south of the delta, Egypt was desert except for a narrow valley about 2 to 30 miles (3 to 50 km) wide along the Nile. Yearly floods left a layer of rich soil on this land; and even more important, the river provided irrigation water. In fact, Egypt was one long oasis. This is why Herodotus (hih RAHD uh tuhs), an ancient historian,

In the distance, the Nile rolls toward the Mediterranean Sea. The contrast between the irrigated valley and the barren hillside remind us that God gives "streams in the desert" (Isaiah 35:6). Cotton, corn, rice, wheat, and other crops are grown in the Nile Valley.

For thousands of years, the Nile River has been a main source of transportation for millions of Africans. Boats heading north are propelled by the current. Boats heading south need wind power to propel them. In which direction are these sailboats probably headed?

called Egypt "the gift of the Nile."

Early Egypt was nearly isolated from other countries. To the south was the First Cataract. To the north was the Mediterranean Sea. To the east and west were high cliffs and forbidding deserts. These natural features helped to keep invaders out.

Even though the boundaries of Egypt were eventually pushed east and west to include large areas of desert, the Nile Valley has always remained the heart of Egypt. The descendants of Ham who settled there did not know that God's chosen people, some of Shem's descendants, would live and multiply in their land for many years. They saw only that this rich valley was an excellent place to settle.

Study Exercises

1. Is the climate of Egypt cloudy, cool, and damp; or sunny, warm, and dry?
2. What is the one natural feature that saves Egypt from being almost solid desert?
3. What did the Nile provide for Egyptian farmers besides water?
4. How did the deserts on both sides of the Nile Valley help the Egyptians?

At the top of this photograph taken in northern Egypt, the solid gray area is the Mediterranean Sea. Notice the rough, broken country and the white salt marshes. Such inhospitable countryside was difficult to cross, especially for enemy armies who were unfamiliar with the land.

Understanding Egypt's Long History

The Egyptians did not number each passing year in order as we do. They counted years within each king's reign and then started over with the next king. This makes events in Egypt's history extremely hard to date. In many books, historians place a little *c* in front of their dates. It stands for the word *circa,* which means "about." Those who study Egyptian history sometimes differ with each other on their dates by hundreds or even thousands of years.

An Egyptian historian named Manetho, who lived several centuries before Christ, tried to give an orderly history of his country. But since he relied on old folk tales and stretched Egypt's history many thousands of years into the past, his work is not reliable. In spite of this fact, most historians follow at least some of Manetho's system. Manetho divided Egypt's history into periods, with each period consisting of

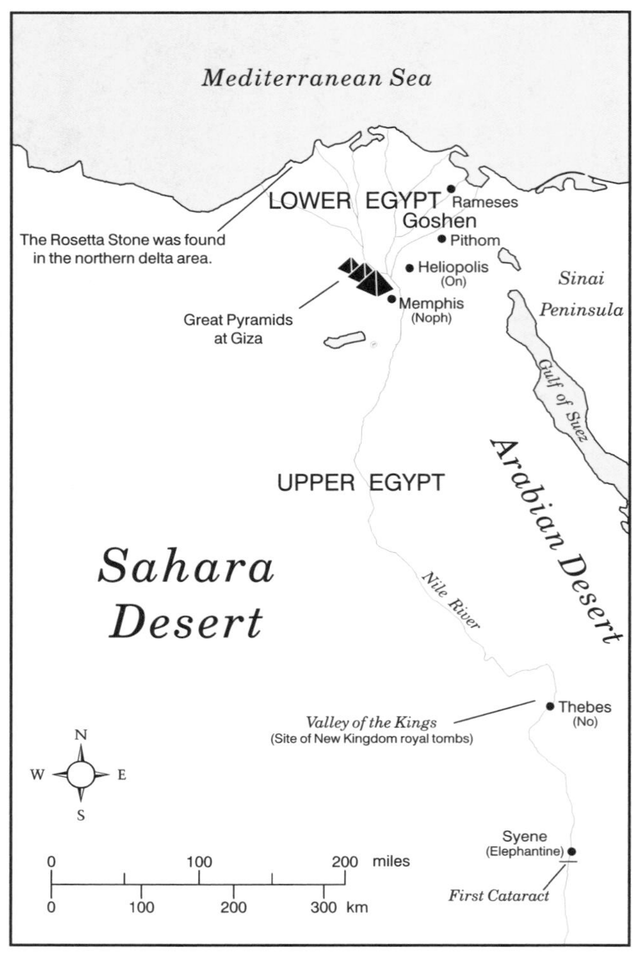

Figure 8:1. Ancient Egypt

a number of dynasties. A ***dynasty*** (DY nuh stee) is a line of kings all belonging to the same family. The following periods of Egyptian history are based partly on Manetho's arrangement of dynasties.

Lower and Upper Egypt. Early in Egypt's history, probably soon after God scattered men from Babel, the country was two large districts. The delta area was Lower Egypt, so called because it lay downstream. ("Up north" would not have applied to Egypt because Lower Egypt was north.) The rest of the valley, all the way south to the First Cataract, was called Upper Egypt.

Then a strong king named Menes (MEE neez) joined the two districts to form one kingdom. He and the kings after him wore a double crown to show that they ruled both lands. Egypt became known as the Kingdom of the Two Lands.

The Old Kingdom. Over a period of several hundred years, the kings increased their riches and power. They became interested in other lands besides Egypt, sending

During the Old Kingdom and the Middle Kingdom, some Egyptian kings built their tombs in the form of pyramids. They built step pyramids and true pyramids, both shown in the picture above.

men sometimes to trade, sometimes to work in distant mines, and sometimes to battle. These strong kings directed the building of the great pyramids. Sometimes the Old Kingdom is called the Age of the Pyramids.

The Middle Kingdom. After a period of confusion when the earlier kings lost their power, a new line of powerful kings took control. One of the strongest kings extended Egypt's influence as far as Syria. These kings ruled a prosperous country. Joseph and his family probably came to Egypt either before or during the Middle Kingdom.

In those days, the king (called Pharaoh) usually chose a wise, able man called the ***vizier*** (vih ZIHR) to help him rule the country. The vizier had more authority than anyone else except Pharaoh. Other men such as the governors, army captains, and priests also had much responsibility and honor, but they all gave account to the vizier.

The vizier had no easy job. He was Pharaoh's most trusted servant. He made sure the people paid their taxes, and he managed the wealth of Egypt. He was responsible to see that Pharaoh's commands were carried out. On top of all this, he was usually commander of the army.

Joseph—A Godly Vizier

"And there was no bread in all the land; for the famine was very sore.... And Joseph gathered up all the money that was found in the land of Egypt, and in the land of Canaan, for the corn which they bought: and Joseph brought the money into Pharaoh's house. And when money failed in the land of Egypt, and in the land of Canaan, all the Egyptians came unto Joseph, and said, Give us bread: for why should we die in thy presence? for the money faileth.

And Joseph said, Give your cattle; and I will give you for your cattle, if money fail. And they brought their cattle unto Joseph: and Joseph gave them bread in exchange for horses, and for the flocks, and for the cattle of the herds, and for the asses: and he fed them with bread for all their cattle for that year.

When that year was ended, they came unto him the second year, and said unto him, We will not hide it from my lord, how that our money is spent; my lord also hath our herds of cattle; there is not ought left in the sight of my lord, but our bodies, and our lands: wherefore shall we die before thine eyes, both we and our land? buy us and our land for bread, and we and our land will be servants unto Pharaoh: and give us seed, that we may live, and not die, that the land be not desolate. And Joseph bought all the land of Egypt for Pharaoh; for the Egyptians sold every man his field, because the famine prevailed over them: so the land became Pharaoh's....

Then Joseph said unto the people, Behold, I have bought you this day and your land for Pharaoh: lo, here is seed for you, and ye shall sow the land. And it shall come to pass in the increase, that ye shall give the fifth part unto Pharaoh, and four parts shall be your own, for seed of the field, and for your food, and for them of your households, and for food for your little ones" (Genesis 47:13–20, 23, 24).

While Joseph was the vizier of Egypt, he managed Pharaoh's business well. By the end of the seven years of famine, the Egyptians had given Pharaoh all their money, their livestock, their land, and finally even themselves as servants. All Egypt, except the land of the priests, ended up in Pharaoh's hand (Genesis 47:18–26).

The priests were powerful people in Egypt. Joseph's father-in-law was a priest, and Pharaoh himself was their chief. Pharaoh and the priests required the people to bring offerings of grain to their gods. They also required the people to donate labor to build the temples and tombs.

Foreigners Come—and Go. When the Middle Kingdom weakened, Egypt was invaded by foreigners from Syria and Palestine. These rulers are known as Hyksos (HIHK sahs), which literally means "rulers of foreign lands." The native Egyptians despised the Hyksos and their foreign ways. But the foreigners promoted many new ideas in Egypt, including the use of bronze and the horse and chariot in warfare.

The New Kingdom. Eventually the native Egyptians rose up and drove out the Hyksos. A new and different king on the throne brought new and different thinking into the government. This was the last great period of Egyptian history. Some people think it was during this time that the Israelites, who were also foreigners, fell from the government's favor. On the other hand, the "new king over Egypt, which knew not Joseph" (Exodus 1:8) could have risen to power during one of the many other changes in government. This new king oppressed the Israelites and forced them to build cities for his treasures.

The Late Dynasty Period. Egypt gradually declined after the New Kingdom pharaohs. Some notable pharaohs ruled, but they never attained as much power and glory as the earlier kings. About 670 B.C. the Assyrians invaded Egypt. The Egyptians rebelled against Assyria, but soon they had to contend with the Babylonians, the Persians, and the Greeks. The final breakdown of Egyptian self-rule came in 30 B.C. when the Romans made Egypt a Roman province. Not until modern times were the Egyptians able to govern themselves again.

Study Exercises

5. Why are events in early Egyptian history difficult to date?
6. Why did Menes and his successors wear a double crown?
7. During which kingdom were the largest pyramids built?
8. What position was Joseph given in Egypt?
9. Why would the New Kingdom pharaohs have disliked foreigners more than the Hyksos rulers did?

Life in Egypt

Families. Egyptian families were close-knit. Their paintings often show a family working or playing together. When a man died, he passed not only his belongings on to his children, but also his job or position in government.

Food. Most Egyptians had plenty to eat. Besides the usual vegetables, fish, and barley bread, the wealthy enjoyed other meats, baked goods, fruits, and sweets. After the Israelites left Egypt, they complained, "We remember the fish, which we did eat in Egypt freely; the cucumbers, and the melons, and the leeks, and the onions, and the garlick" (Numbers 11:5).

Houses. The ancient Egyptians lived in simple mud-brick houses. Stone probably cost too much and held in too much heat. Instead of windows, most Egyptian houses

Sesame

Sesame seeds are more than just a decorative addition adorning the top of some baked goods. They are extensively used as a food and a flavoring in Asia and the Middle East.

Sesame seeds on bun

Sesame flour

In use since ancient times, sesame seeds were ground into flour by the Egyptians before the time of Moses, and the Romans also used them for food in their time. The Chinese have made soot for the finest Chinese ink blocks by burning the oil pressed from the seeds.

Presently, whole sesame seeds are frequently used in Middle Eastern and Asian cooking. Tahini is a paste made from crushed seeds and is used to make different types of sauces. Halvah is a type of candy made from sesame seeds, honey, and other ingredients.

Halvah

Sesame plant and seed capsule

The small, flat seeds grow in seed capsules produced by the annual sesame plant, which is now cultivated in many of the warm regions of the world. Varieties can grow from about 2 to 9 feet tall (.5 to 2.5 m). Until the mid-1900s, when a nonscattering variety was developed, much of the harvesting had to be done by hand because the seed capsules opened when dry, and the seeds were scattered.

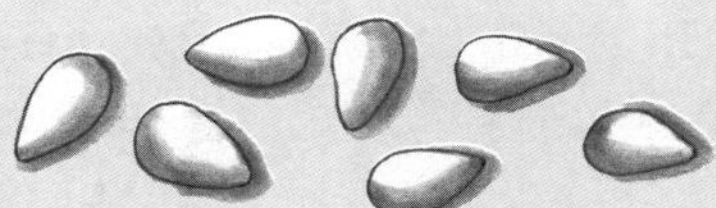

Sesame seeds

When ripe, each seed is composed of 44 to 60 percent oil. Much of the sesame seed crop is crushed to obtain this valuable oil, which is very resistant to turning rancid. The oil is used as a salad oil or a cooking oil, in shortening and margarine, and for making soap, skin lotions, and more. After the oil is pressed out, the remaining mass of crushed seeds is eaten. It is very nutritious.

Valuable sesame oil

Traditional Egyptian houses.

had small grilles set high in the walls to let out the heat and keep out the bright sun.

Farming. In Egypt, as in Mesopotamia, farmers looked for the overflowing of the river. The Nile flood came on a much more regular schedule than the floods of Mesopotamia. Each year in June, after the rains began to fall farther south in Africa, the river began to rise. Sometime in September it reached its highest level, flooding the farmland on both sides of the river.

In a good flood, the water rose as much as 40 feet (12 m) at the First Cataract. At the mouth of the river, it rose about 4 feet (1.2 m). The river returned to its bed during the next three months, leaving a layer of rich, black soil. As the water went down, the farmers planted their crops. Egyptians could plan their work around the flood because it was so regular.

Like the Sumerians, the Egyptians dug reservoirs to store flood water, and canals to direct the water to the fields during the growing season. The Nile usually rose high enough to supply plenty of moisture for Egypt's crops, even when Canaan and other lands were dry. But occasionally, as during the seven-year drought of Joseph's time, less rain fell in the highlands south of Egypt, and the river failed to flood sufficiently.

Learning. Few if any girls in ancient Egypt went to school. But the boys received a thorough education, especially the ones who would grow up to be scribes or nobles. Their training began in early childhood. After studying a number of years under strict discipline, they left the schoolroom and continued their learning by working with an experienced man. Moses, the Bible tells us, "was learned in all the wisdom of the Egyptians" (Acts 7:22).

Unlike the Sumerians, who wrote in clay,

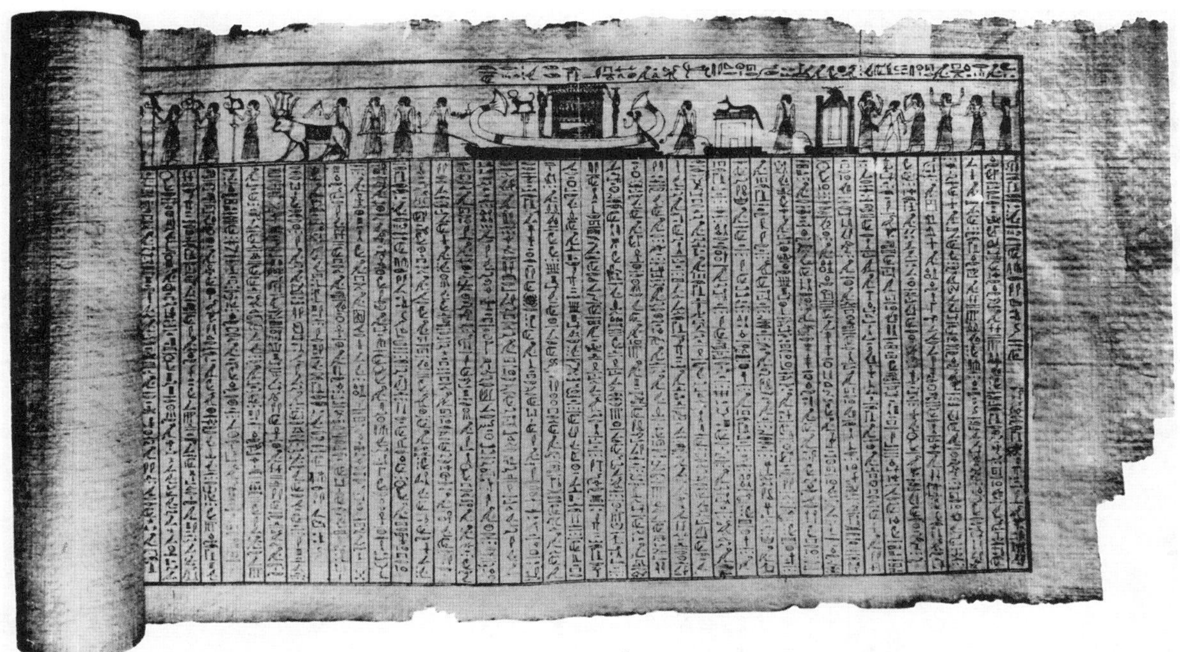

The dry climate of Egypt has preserved this papyrus for over 2,000 years. It is still in the form of a roll about 40 feet (12 m) long, and is part of the "Book of the Dead."

the Egyptians carved or painted their writings on pieces of pottery or rocks. They also discovered how to use a water plant called ***papyrus*** (puh PY ruhs) to make the world's first paper. Sheets of papyrus (from which paper got its name) soon became brown and brittle, and people eventually learned to make better kinds of paper. Still, the invention of even this poor-quality paper was a big step in civilization. Papyrus was cheaper and less bulky than other writing materials. Today we can estimate how developed a country is by how much paper it uses.

The Egyptians also studied arithmetic and ***geometry.*** They knew how to make pyramid foundations exactly square and level, and how to slant all sides of a pyramid the degree needed to meet perfectly at the peak. The Egyptians also used geometry to survey land. Each year the floods washed away boundary markers between fields. After the water went down, the Egyptians carefully measured the lands and replaced the missing markers.

Egyptian doctors knew more about medicine and how the body works than most other people of their time. They saw the close relationship between a person's heartbeat and his health. Sometimes they operated on their patients. Yet in spite of their knowledge, they still relied on many superstitious practices.

Egyptian scholars set up a calendar having twelve months of thirty days each. Because they found this was not accurate, they added five days after each year to give them 365 days. They spent these five days between one year and the next in feasting and worshiping their gods. Eventually the Egyptians learned that an additional day was needed every fourth year. Later the Romans borrowed the idea of a 365-day calendar with leap years, and from them it has been handed down to us.

Trade and Travel. Egyptians traded with many other countries. Timber was scarce in Egypt, so they imported logs.

This Egyptian wall painting comes from a tomb about 3,300 years old. It depicts foreign subjects bringing tribute to the Pharaoh. The Pharaoh is not pictured.

These Egyptian women are carrying sticks to burn for cooking fires.

Traders also brought gold, copper, and other ores, and they left with such things as grain and cloth.

In Egypt, the Nile was the most important trade route. Travelers could easily reach all of Egypt from the Nile. Traders heading north had the help of the river's current. Returning south, they hoisted their sails, and the prevailing winds usually sped them along.

Religion. The Egyptians worshiped many gods, including Pharaoh himself. Because they depended so much on the Nile River, they called it an important god. Did it not provide transportation, irrigation, fertile soil, fish, papyrus, and mud for brick? Egyptians also worshiped many animals—cats, crocodiles, frogs, and cows, to name a few. The pictures they drew of their gods sometimes showed them as human, sometimes as animals, and sometimes as part human and part animal. A human body might have an animal head, or the other way around.

The shadoof was invented in ancient times and is still used today in India, Egypt, and a few other countries. The weight on the end of the stick makes it easy to lift the heavy water bucket to a higher canal. The shadoof is usually used to lift water from a lake, stream, or river into a higher irrigation canal.

Although the Egyptians had many gods, Pharaoh in Moses' day refused to acknowledge the God of the Hebrews. He asked, "Who is the Lord, that I should obey his voice to let Israel go?" (Exodus 5:2). But Pharaoh and the Egyptians learned of the Lord's power when He sent the ten plagues upon them.

Perhaps one reason God chose the particular plagues He did was to confound the Egyptians concerning their gods. The Egyptians must have been sick of their frog gods after the plague of frogs. They must have taken a different view of the Nile god after the river turned to blood, and of the sun god after three days of darkness. Even their trust in Pharaoh as a god must have been shaken when Pharaoh's son died along with all the other firstborn of Egypt.

Study Exercises

10. Name two advantages of using mud bricks for houses.
11. How did Egyptian boys continue their education after leaving school?
12. What invention was probably Egypt's biggest contribution to world civilization?
13. (*a*) Name one way in which Egyptian doctors seemed advanced for their time. (*b*) What evidence of ignorance did they show?
14. Name two types of products Egypt needed to import.

Death in Egypt

The Egyptians thought much about death and the afterlife. They spent much time preparing for death. Not knowing the facts about life after death, they assumed that the soul could return to a well-preserved body. The nobles, and especially the pharaohs, built huge, elaborate tombs, often closely connected to a temple. The Egyptians thought of a tomb as the home of a person's soul. This explains why they devoted so much time and effort to their tombs and pyramids.

A pharaoh's servants would decorate the walls of his tomb with scenes from his life. They also placed furniture, models of buildings, and images of servants in his tomb. They provided food for him at his burial and brought fresh food regularly for him afterward.

Preserving a dead body took forty to seventy days. Physicians, who did the embalming, first removed all the internal organs except the heart. Then they treated the body with salts, spices, and pitch from plants. Next they stuffed the body with linen or sawdust; then they wrapped it in

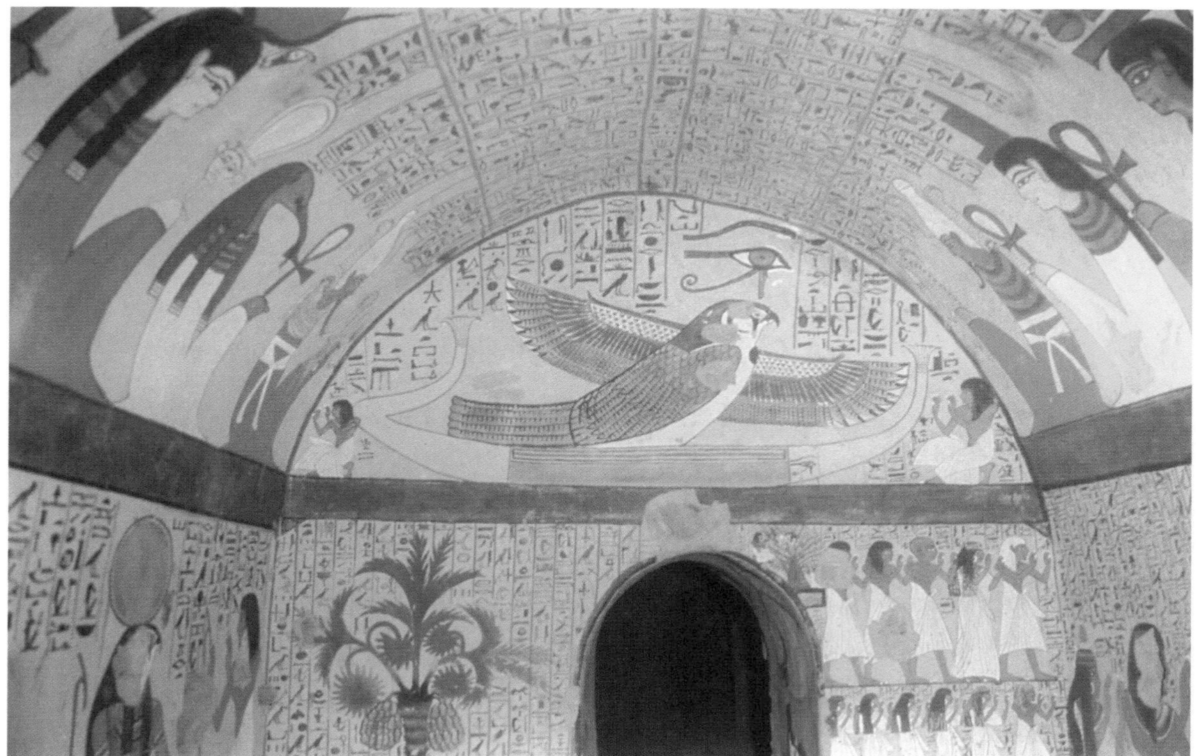

The paintings in Egyptian tombs revealed their wrong view of death. How can someone enjoy paintings and finery after his body has returned to dust and his spirit has returned to God, who gave it? (Genesis 3:19; Ecclesiastes 12:7).

long strips of linen—sometimes as much as 600 yards (550 m) or more. Finally they placed the ***mummy*** in a coffin. If the person had been a noble, his coffin might be made to resemble him.

Why did the physicians leave the heart in the body? Ancient paintings show the gods weighing the heart against a feather, the symbol of truth or righteousness. If it balanced, the person would be happy in the afterlife. If not, he would suffer misery.

What kind of heart did the Egyptians think would balance with the feather of truth? A righteous one? Not necessarily. They placed a papyrus roll, "The Book of the Dead," in the burial chamber. They thought that if the departed one used the lengthy formulas in the book and denied that he had done wrong, he would pass the test. These Egyptian beliefs illustrate that man by nature is conscious of his accountability to a Higher Being. Sinful man often rejects God's plan of salvation and foolishly attempts to appease or even deceive God his own way. "Because that, when they knew God, they glorified him not as God, neither were thankful; but became vain in their imaginations, and their foolish heart was darkened. Professing themselves to be wise, they became fools" (Romans 1:21, 22). It is little wonder that the Egyptians never became models of moral, upright living.

Pyramids, Tombs, and Temples. Judging from ancient ruins, Egyptians spent more time and effort in building pyramids, tombs, and temples than they spent in building houses. Some monument builders lived permanently in their own villages close to their work. Others were farmers who worked on the building projects while the Nile was flooding. The Egyptians also used forced laborers, such as the children of Israel, for their building projects.

The first Egyptian king to build a pyramid was Zoser (ZOH sur). Historians call his tomb a step pyramid because it has six big steps going up the outside. Later kings built the true pyramids. When a king died, he was laid to rest in a room inside his pyramid.

It is hard to imagine, even when looking at pictures, how big the pyramids are. When the largest one was new, it stood more than 480 feet high (146 m). Its base measures more than 750 feet (230 m) on each side, and it covers about 13 acres (5 ha). How does that area compare with the size of your school grounds?

How did the Egyptians manage to build such huge monuments without power equipment? Evidently all those stones, averaging about 2½ tons (2¼ m.t.) each, were pulled up long ramps of earth and brick—all by manpower! The builders made the ramps higher and longer as the pyramid became higher.

How long did it take to build a pyramid? Perhaps twenty years. And how many men worked on it? Thousands of them—probably hundreds of thousands. The Egyptians finished off the pyramids with white casing stones. From a distance, the pyramids looked like single white stones pointing upward. However, most of those outer stones have disappeared, so the pyramids look a bit ragged now.

Near the Great Pyramid lies the Great Sphinx (SFINGKS). This huge statue has a lion's body but a pharaoh's head in honor of one of the pharaohs. It stands some 66 feet (20 m) above the desert when no drifts of sand fill in around its base.

Besides being extremely costly to build, the huge pyramids had another serious drawback—they made it easy for grave robbers to find the royal tombs. By New Kingdom times, the pharaohs had stopped building pyramids. They built ***mortuary temples*** (MOR choo air ee) along the Nile Valley, but they tried to conceal their tombs in a secluded desert valley some distance away. They hoped to escape the thieves who broke into tombs and carried off the valuable treasures.

The Great Sphinx at Giza, Egypt, has a man's head and a lion's body. It was constructed during the Old Kingdom period.

But the grave robbers found and plundered almost all the New Kingdom royal tombs anyway, leaving only a fraction of the riches that had been placed in them. Even the royal mummies were in danger until priests loyal to the pharaohs secretly moved many of them to a concealed pit.

The Egyptian preparations for death were impressive but vain. Even the few treasures that thieves missed did not benefit the dead. The Bible says, "We brought nothing into this world, and it is certain we can carry nothing out" (1 Timothy 6:7). When the pharaohs stand before God on the Day of Judgment, the lengthy formulas from the Book of the Dead will not help them. God will spare only those people whose names are written in the Lamb's Book of Life (Revelation 21:27).

(*Above*) This carved wooden statue of Tutankhamen is over 3,300 years old. (*Below*) The golden statue (front and back views) is actually a miniature stone coffin overlaid with gold. Four of these were found in Tutankhamen's tomb.

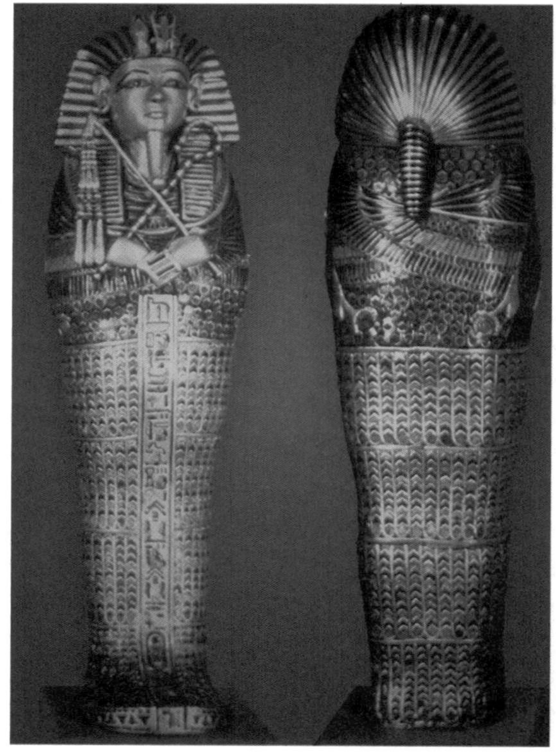

Study Exercises

15. Why did the Egyptians spend so much time and effort in building tombs and preserving dead bodies?
16. What source of power did the Egyptians use to build the pyramids?
17. Where did the New Kingdom pharaohs prepare their tombs?
18. Give two ways that the pharaohs' preparations for death were in vain.

Triumphs of Archaeologists

Archaeologists meet many frustrations in their work. People have often had little respect for things archaeologists call treasures. For example, a poor man who stumbles onto a grave might decide to sell its treasures for money rather than hand them over to a museum. Gunners have used the Great Sphinx for target practice. Builders have removed stones from pyramids and other great monuments, and used them in other buildings. Farmers have used crumbled mud bricks from ancient buildings for fertilizer.

Still, Egypt is an excellent place for archaeologists. Perishable items such as mummies, papyrus, wood, and cloth—which would decay quickly in most lands—have been preserved for thousands of years in Egypt's dry climate.

Archaeologists have studied many old Egyptian tombs, usually finding that grave robbers were there ahead of them. But in 1922, an English archaeologist discovered a New Kingdom pharaoh's tomb that still had many of its original contents. The pharaoh's mummy lay undisturbed in three coffins, one inside another. The innermost coffin was solid gold. The

The Rosetta Stone, a slab of black basalt, was found in the town of Rosetta, in northern Egypt. Egyptian hieroglyphics are on top, simplified hieroglyphics in the middle, and Greek on the bottom. Look at all the little figures in the top set of hieroglyphics. How difficult it must have been to learn to write this way!

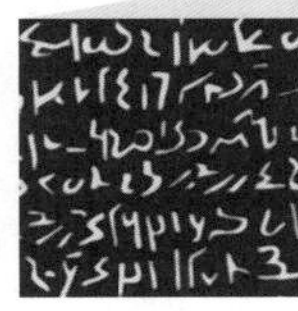

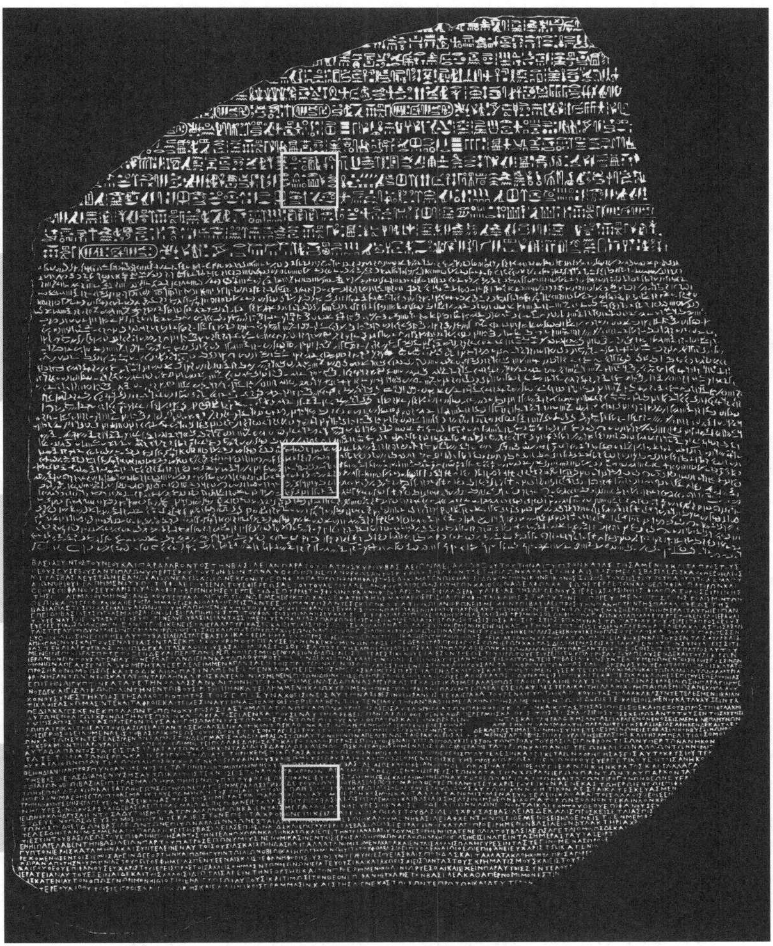

pharaoh's chariot, his throne, and priceless works of art glittered nearby. This pharaoh's name was Tutankhamen (toot angk AH muhn), but most people just call him King Tut. He had died when he was only about eighteen years old. King Tut's body now rests in his tomb again, but his treasures have been shown far and wide.

For many years, the strange Egyptian symbols called ***hieroglyphics*** (hy ur uh GLIHF ihks) were a puzzle to archaeologists. The experts were not even sure that hieroglyphics were a kind of writing. Did they have something to do with religious ceremonies?

Then in 1799, a French officer in Egypt discovered a stone, now called the Rosetta Stone, with three different kinds of writing carved on it. One writing was in hieroglyphics, another was in a simplified form of hieroglyphics, and the third was in Greek. Experts reasoned that the three writings all said the same thing. Since they could read the Greek, they tried to find words in the hieroglyphics that meant the same thing, starting with easy words like names.

No wonder the hieroglyphics were so puzzling! The Egyptians had learned to use letters representing sounds, as we do, but they did not write vowel sounds. Words like *taste* and *test* would have been written exactly the same. Furthermore, the Egyptians had not altogether given up their earlier practice of using pictures to stand for entire words. They mixed these word symbols with the sound symbols.

The puzzle was finally solved by a French scholar who patiently studied the strange symbols for years until he was able to read the hieroglyphics on the Rosetta Stone. Of course by then he could also read other hieroglyphic inscriptions, and he could teach the language to other scholars. Today scholars have a number of resources, including hieroglyphic dictionaries, to help them study the ancient Egyptian language.

Study Exercises

19. Name one advantage archaeologists have in Egypt that they do not have in most other parts of the world.
20. Why were hieroglyphics harder to learn to read than most other kinds of writing?

Clinching the Chapter

Multiple Choice

A. *Write the word or phrase* least *associated with the first item.*

1. Barriers around Egypt: cliffs, forests, deserts, seas
2. Nile: delta, floods, cataracts, ziggurats
3. Hyksos: despised by natives, pyramids, invaders, chariots
4. Physicians: operations, superstition, calendar, embalming
5. Egyptian history periods: Old Kingdom, New Kingdom, Double Kingdom, Middle Kingdom
6. Plagues: blood, frogs, darkness, floods
7. Pyramid: tomb, mummy, papyrus, ramp
8. Monument builders: forced workers, farmers, priests, permanent workers
9. Rosetta Stone: Greek, hieroglyphics, cuneiform, symbols
10. King Tut: young, rich, undisturbed, pyramid

B. *Write the correct words.*

1. The Egyptians were descendants of (Shem, Ham, Japheth, Cain).
2. A fertile deposit of earth at the mouth of a river is called (a delta, an oasis, a cataract, a source).
3. The best transportation in Egypt was provided by (chariots, good highways, camels, the Nile).
4. The New Kingdom pharaohs prepared their tombs in (pyramids, Nile cliffs, a secluded valley, grand temples).
5. Manetho was (a historian, a pharaoh, a doctor, an archaeologist).
6. Egypt imported (grain, papyrus, cloth, timber).
7. Papyrus was the world's first (pottery, paper, irrigation system, mummy).
8. The Sphinx is (a step pyramid, a statue, a tomb, a plague).
9. Most of the riches in the royal tombs were removed by (archaeologists, grave robbers, pyramid builders, modern men).
10. In 1922, an archaeologist discovered (King Tut's tomb, the Rosetta Stone, step pyramids, the Sphinx).

Matching

A. *For each clue, write the correct term from the right-hand column.*

1. Oppressed the Israelites
2. Region of the Nile Delta
3. First king of all Egypt
4. Supplied water during the growing season
5. Built first pyramid
6. More powerful than Pharaoh
7. Used to build pyramids
8. Disaster in Egypt
9. Godly vizier
10. Very regular in Egypt

"a new king over Egypt"
canals and reservoirs
floods
geometry
Goshen
Joseph
Menes
ten plagues
the LORD
Zoser

B. *Match as in Part A.*

1. A preserved body
2. God's record of true saints
3. Written partly in pictures
4. The Nile Delta area
5. Contained lengthy formulas
6. Handed down to us from Egyptians and Romans
7. Process of preserving a body
8. Term meaning "approximately"
9. Nile Valley south of the delta
10. Family line of kings

Lamb's Book of Life
Book of the Dead
365-day calendar
circa
dynasty
embalming
hieroglyphics
Lower Egypt
mummy
Upper Egypt

Completion

1. To the north lies the delta, the Nile River mouth,
   While the source of the river lies far to the ———.
2. The Egyptian physicians knew only in part,
   The connection between a man's health and his ———.
3. All the rulers but Pharaoh gave honor and fear
   To the one he appointed to be the ———.
4. Starting early each summer, the river would flood,
   Bringing with it a layer of fertile, black ———.
5. It is thought that Egyptian men possibly slid
   Heavy stones up long ramps to make each ———.
6. When Jehovah sent Moses, with only a rod,
   All the idols of Egypt were no match for ———.
7. How to read hieroglyphics was no longer known
   Until scholars discovered the ——— ———.

Thought Questions

1. Even though it rained very little in Egypt, the Egyptians still depended on rain. How?
2. What things are tragic about the pyramids and other tombs of the pharaohs?
3. How would life in Egypt have been affected if the flooding of the Nile had been less regular?

4. Do you think archaeologists should have removed King Tut's treasures to show them to the public, or do you think they should have allowed his tomb to remain undisturbed?
5. Why does the first section under "Death in Egypt" end by saying, "It is little wonder that the Egyptians never became models of moral, upright living"?

Geographical Skills

1. Trace the outline of Africa, the Nile River, and its main tributaries on Map B in the map section. (You do not need to trace the country borders.) The map title should read "Large Rivers of Africa." Also label the Egyptian cities of Alexandria and Cairo. (You will use this map again in Chapter 25.)
2. (*a*) How long is the Nile River? (Find the answer in Chapter 5 or in a reference book.) (*b*) Name the large lake that is an important source of the Nile. (*c*) Name the body of water at the mouth of the Nile. (*d*) What general direction does the water flow?
3. From its farthest source in the African highlands, the Nile drops to sea level at the delta. Does the river course gradually lower in altitude, or are there some abrupt drops in altitude along it?

Further Study

Study an encyclopedia or another book on the Egyptian pyramids and find answers to these questions. Write your answers in form of an essay.

1. Where are the largest pyramids in Egypt?
2. How many are there?
3. For which pharaohs were these pyramids built?
4. About how many stone blocks are in the largest pyramid? How much did each block weigh?
5. How did the workers cut the pyramid stones? From where did they mine the stones?
6. How did they place the stones in the pyramids?
7. Why did the Egyptians build the pyramids?

Be Sure You Know

Can you answer all these questions? If not, study Chapters 6–8 to find the answers.

A. What

1. was the prevailing climate of the earth before the Flood?
2. kinds of work did the earliest people do?
3. is the purpose of archaeology?
4. three early civilizations began in southern Mesopotamia?
5. form of government did the earliest civilizations have?
6. king built the first true empire?
7. early Babylonian emperor is famous for his code of laws?
8. natural barriers helped to keep invaders out of Egypt?
9. is meant by *Upper Egypt* and *Lower Egypt*?
10. was the name of the first king to rule over both Upper and Lower Egypt?
11. are the three periods of ancient Egyptian history?
12. important product did Egyptians learn to make from the papyrus plant?
13. discovery provided a key to deciphering ancient hieroglyphic writing?

B. What do these words mean?

14. archaeology
15. artifact
16. astrology
17. barter
18. cataract
19. city-state
20. code
21. cradle of civilization
22. cuneiform
23. domestic
24. dynasty
25. empire
26. Fertile Crescent
27. fossil
28. geometry
29. hieroglyphics
30. mortuary temple
31. papyrus
32. sedimentary
33. Semite
34. site
35. specialization
36. stele
37. tell
38. vizier
39. ziggurat

C. Where

40. do people think the Garden of Eden was located?
41. did early civilizations generally begin whenever people moved into new lands?

D. How

42. did the Fall affect creation?
43. did the Flood affect the earth?
44. is our number system based on the system developed by the Sumerians?
45. was the Law of Moses better than Hammurabi's code?
46. was the study of geometry helpful to the Egyptians?

E. Why

47. do people depart from the truth and accept myths instead?
48. is the Nile such an important river to Egyptians? (Give two reasons.)
49. does a delta sometimes form at the mouth of a river?
50. is it hard to date Egyptian history?
51. did the Egyptians go to great efforts to preserve dead bodies?
52. is Egypt an excellent place for archaeology?

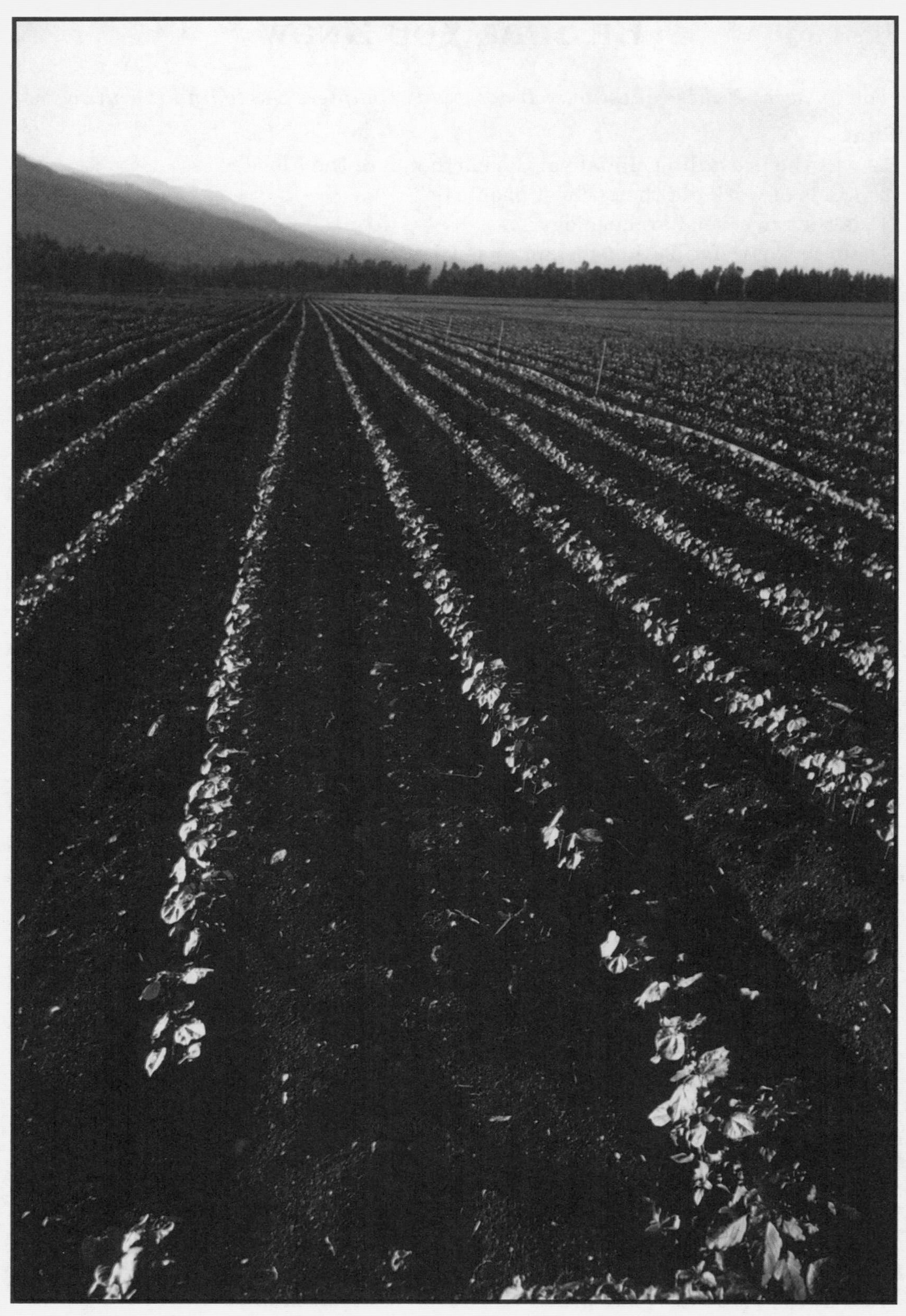

A rich field in Galilee produces a fine crop of beans. The land of Canaan was much more fertile in ancient times than it is today. With careful management, however, bountiful crops are still produced there.

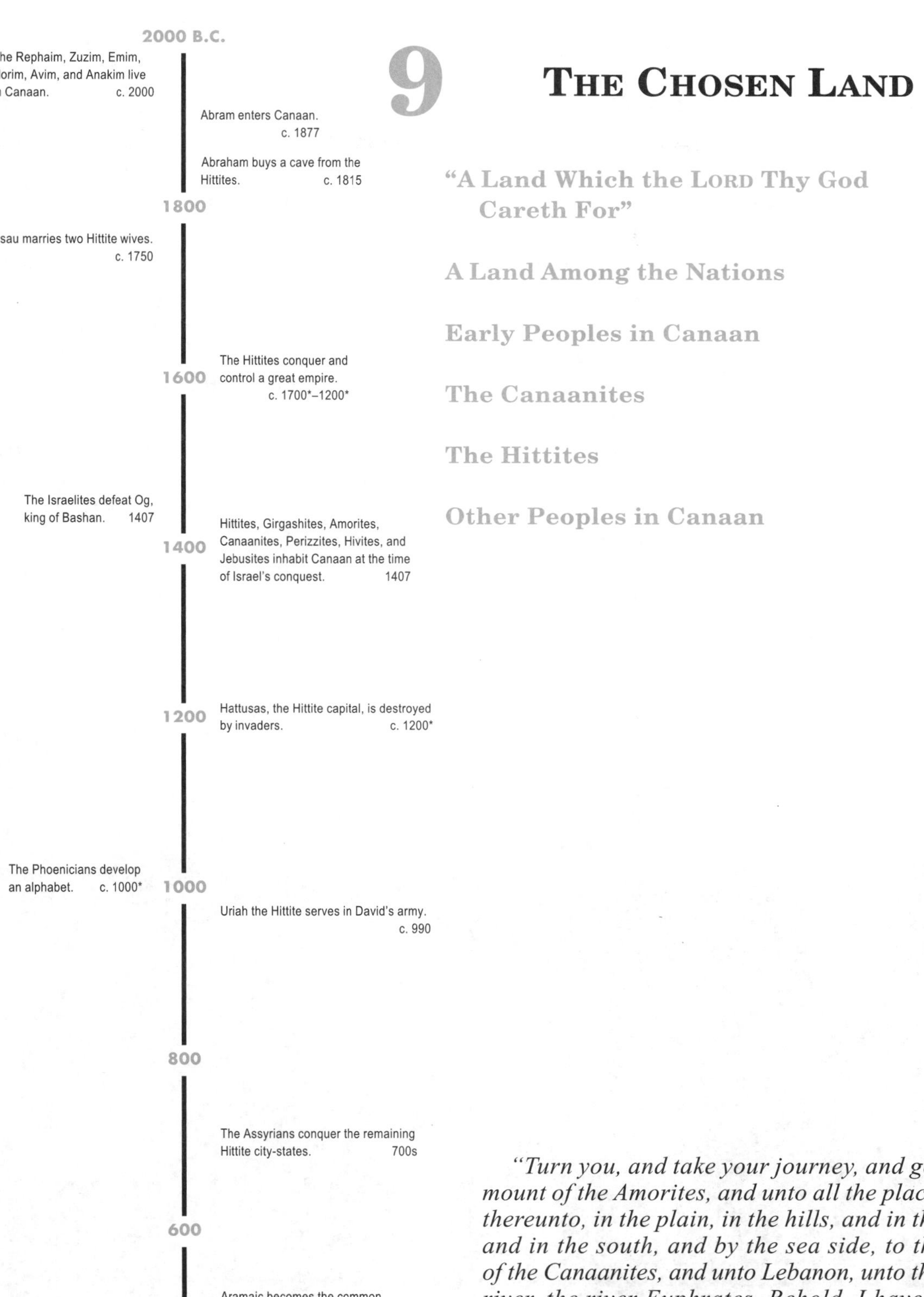
2000 B.C.
The Rephaim, Zuzim, Emim, Horim, Avim, and Anakim live in Canaan. c. 2000
Abram enters Canaan. c. 1877
Abraham buys a cave from the Hittites. c. 1815
1800
Esau marries two Hittite wives. c. 1750
The Hittites conquer and control a great empire. c. 1700*–1200*
1600
The Israelites defeat Og, king of Bashan. 1407
Hittites, Girgashites, Amorites, Canaanites, Perizzites, Hivites, and Jebusites inhabit Canaan at the time of Israel's conquest. 1407
1400
Hattusas, the Hittite capital, is destroyed by invaders. c. 1200*
1200
The Phoenicians develop an alphabet. c. 1000*
1000
Uriah the Hittite serves in David's army. c. 990
800
The Assyrians conquer the remaining Hittite city-states. 700s
600
Aramaic becomes the common language of the Fertile Crescent. c. 500
400 B.C.

9 The Chosen Land

"A Land Which the LORD Thy God Careth For"

A Land Among the Nations

Early Peoples in Canaan

The Canaanites

The Hittites

Other Peoples in Canaan

"Turn you, and take your journey, and go to the mount of the Amorites, and unto all the places nigh thereunto, in the plain, in the hills, and in the vale, and in the south, and by the sea side, to the land of the Canaanites, and unto Lebanon, unto the great river, the river Euphrates. Behold, I have set the land before you: go in and possess the land which the LORD sware unto your fathers, Abraham, Isaac, and Jacob, to give unto them and to their seed after them." *Deuteronomy 1:7, 8*

THE CHOSEN LAND

"A Land Which the LORD Thy God Careth For"

"The LORD made a covenant with Abram, saying, Unto thy seed have I given this land, from the river of Egypt unto the great river, the river Euphrates" (Genesis 15:18).

Canaan can mean different things to different people. Often the name is used for the small area called Palestine. But in this chapter, *Canaan* will include all the land God promised to Israel. The southern border of this land is the River of Egypt (a stream southwest of Philistia), and its northern border is the big bend of the Euphrates River (Genesis 15:18). The Mediterranean Sea forms the western border, and the Syrian and Arabian deserts form the eastern border.

The name *Canaanite* can also be confusing. It refers specifically to the descendants of Ham's son Canaan, but in this chapter it will mean the people in general who lived in the land of Canaan.

Canaan was a rich land that God Himself chose for His people. He described it to them before they crossed the Jordan River: "The land, whither ye go to possess it, is a land of hills and valleys, and drinketh water of the rain of heaven: a land which the LORD thy God careth for: the eyes of the LORD thy God are always upon it, from the beginning of the year even unto the end of the year" (Deuteronomy 11:11, 12).

Unlike Egypt and much of Mesopotamia, the land of Canaan did not depend upon irrigation. Some parts of Canaan were dry,

Fertile valleys and barren, rocky hillsides are typical of Palestine. This is the Valley of Lebon, the border between Judah and Samaria, in present-day Jordan.

The Jordan River meanders through the Great Rift Valley on its way to the Dead Sea, which is the lowest spot on earth at 1,312 feet (400 m) below sea level. If you look closely at this aerial photograph, you will notice how the hills are much drier than the darker, lush valley.

but most of it received enough rainfall for crops to grow. Besides, most of Canaan would have been difficult to irrigate. Many brooks in Canaan dried up during the dry season, and the Sea of Galilee and the Jordan River lay in the Great Rift Valley—far below most of the farmland. Ancient civilizations had no good method of lifting irrigation water to elevations high above its source.

The lack of good irrigation systems made the Israelites more dependent on God. God promised them that "if ye shall hearken diligently unto my commandments, . . . I will give you the rain of your land in his due season" (Deuteronomy 11:13, 14). When they disobeyed, God withheld the rain to remind them that they needed Him.

Nomads wandering through the land usually found water and good grazing for their flocks and herds. Farmers found fertile soil for grain fields, vineyards, and orchards. Woodsmen in the forests of the north shipped lumber to Egypt and other places.

Study Exercises

1. (*a*) What two rivers were on the borders of the land God promised to Abraham? (*b*) What formed its eastern and western borders?
2. What natural blessing did Canaan receive that Egypt and most of Mesopotamia did not receive?
3. Why would it have been difficult to irrigate the farmland of Canaan during Bible times?

A Land Among the Nations

The most important feature of Canaan was probably not its rainfall or fertile soil, but its location. Figure 9:1 shows that Canaan was the center of the known world in Bible times. Here Israel would be able to show God's might and glory to all nations.

Canaan was not only well situated among the nations; it was also well placed between deserts and the sea. With the deserts of Syria and Arabia on the east and the Mediterranean Sea to the west, Canaan

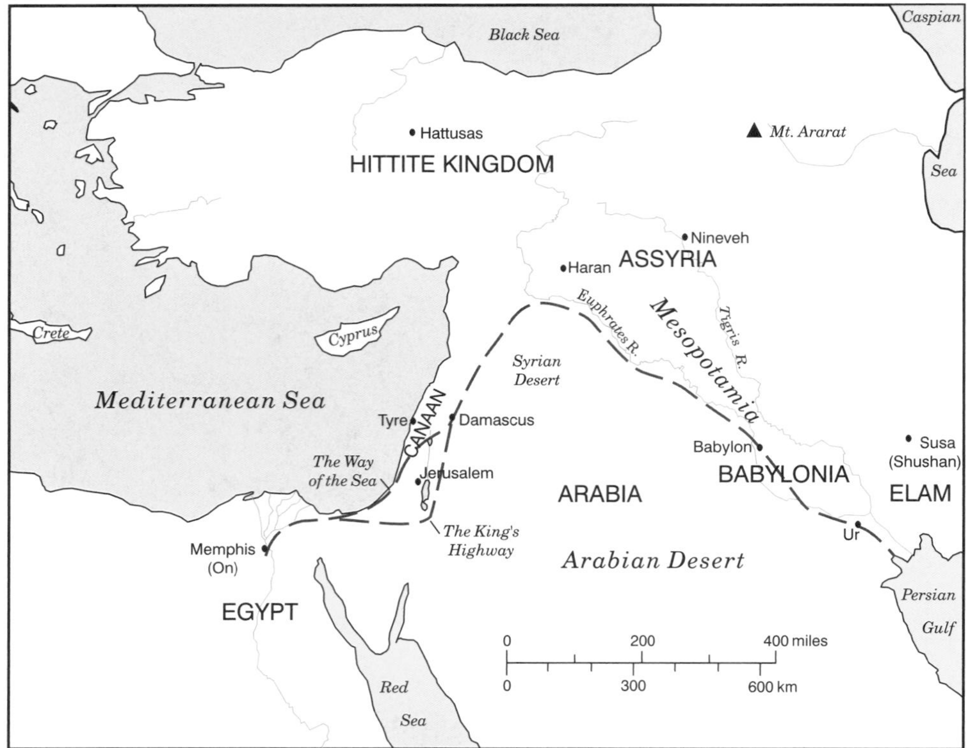

Figure 9:1. Canaan Among the Nations

became a land bridge between Egypt and the kingdoms to the north and east.

Important trade routes ran through Canaan. The two routes that traders used most were the Way of the Sea and the King's Highway. Many Egyptian records tell of Pharaoh or his servants traveling on the Way of the Sea. This route followed the Mediterranean coast through southern Canaan. Near Megiddo (mih GIHD oh) it turned northeast, passed by the Sea of Galilee and through Damascus, and then stretched on toward Mesopotamia.

The King's Highway ran east from Egypt across the Sinai Peninsula and the land of the Edomites. East of the Dead Sea, it turned north and passed through the lands of the Moabites and the Ammonites, and the regions of Gilead and Bashan. At Damascus it joined the Way of the Sea.

Some rulers of Canaan benefited from their favored position by taxing the ***caravans*** that traveled through their land. They also enjoyed the benefits of trading with people of other nations. But these local kings were not the only ones who were concerned about the trade routes. The great

The mound on this picture is the remains of Megiddo. This site was probably occupied in the early centuries after the Flood. The Way of the Sea ran near here.

Haifa is located partly on the slopes of Mount Carmel. This modern port in Israel allows the import of raw materials for the city's steel industry. Small ships and fishing vessels are also built there.

empires nearby also kept an eye on them.

Traders traveled by sea as well. Even before Abraham's time, ships were coming and going on the Mediterranean. However, there were few good harbors on the southern coast of Canaan. Palestine in ancient times had only one or two main ports—one at Joppa and (later) one at Caesarea (sehs uh REE uh). Most of the sea trade went through ports in a northern region of Canaan that was later known as Phoenicia (fih NEE shuh).

The trade routes in Canaan were probably more important to Egypt than to any other nation. The Hittites, Babylonians, and Assyrians could trade among themselves without going through Canaan, but the Egyptians had less choice. Much of Egypt's trade passed over the sea and through the northern ports of Canaan. Some also moved on pack animals through Canaan. Because the Egyptians depended so much on this flow of trade, the early pharaohs soon gained control of the routes through Canaan. Egypt established stopping places and cities along the Way of the Sea and kept soldiers stationed there.

Some pharaohs claimed to have much control over Canaan, almost as if it were part of their kingdom. However, historians

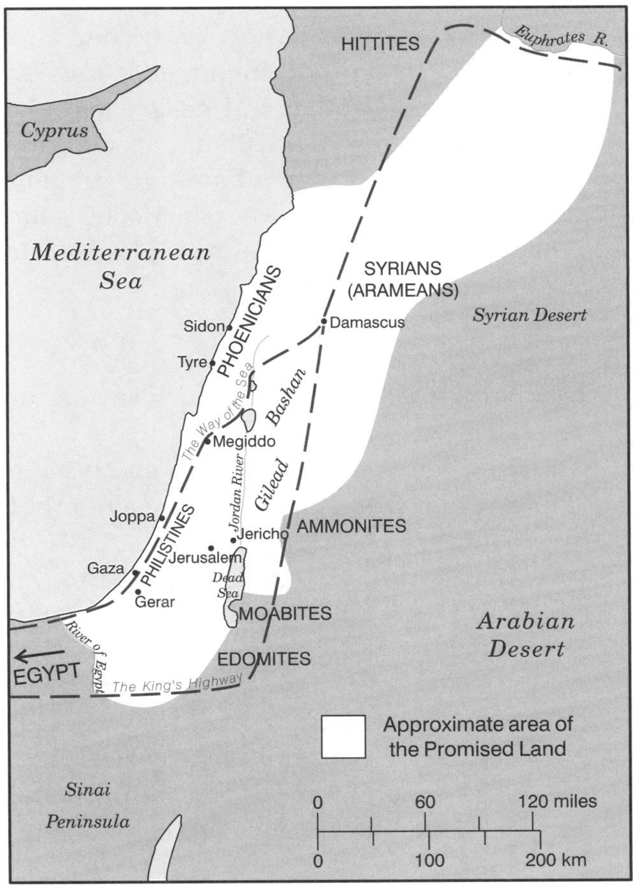

Figure 9:2. Canaan

have found little evidence to support these claims. Probably the pharaohs had only enough power in Canaan to make sure their traders could easily travel back and forth. Usually the Egyptians permitted the Canaanites to rule themselves and to live as they wanted.

Canaan became a meeting place—in fact, a battlefield—for the great empires. The Canaanites often watched as armies of one kingdom went to war against another. Situated in the middle, Canaan acted as a ***buffer*** between Egypt to the south and the Hittites, Babylonians, and Assyrians to the north. In Canaan, these empires could battle and even be defeated sometimes without losing any home territory. The fact that Canaan put some space between the empires may have helped to discourage fighting among them.

It is interesting to note that when God led Israel to Canaan, no strong, unified empire was controlling it. Had God kept the Canaanite power divided for a special reason? Of course we do not know for sure, but we do know that God's way is perfect (Psalm 18:30). When the time was right, He led His people into the Promised Land.

Study Exercises

4. Why was Canaan a good location for God's chosen people?
5. How might a trade route going through a country be a source of money to that country?
6. Why did more sea trade go through ports on the northern coast of Canaan than through ports on the southern coast?
7. How did Canaan serve as a buffer between Egypt and the great empires of Mesopotamia? Use the definition of *buffer* (in the glossary) for help to write your answer.

Early Peoples in Canaan

People began living in Canaan shortly after the Flood. Some of them built a few large towns such as Jericho and Megiddo, but most of the earliest Canaanites probably lived in small villages or wandered from place to place as nomads.

Since many people living in Canaan belonged to small, wandering tribes, we have almost no records of Canaan's earliest history. The Bible mentions a few of the tribes: the Rephaim (REHF ah ihm), the Zuzim (ZOO zihm), the Emim (EE mihm), the Horim (HOR ihm), the Avim (AY vihm), and the Anakim (AN uh kihm). Some—if not all—of these tribes were giants (Genesis 14:5–7; Deuteronomy 2:20–23).

By the time of Abraham, some of these tall, strong men had already been defeated and had lost their towns. Others were driven out later by the Amorites, Edomites, Moabites, and Ammonites. When the Israelites moved into Canaan about 1400 B.C., they destroyed the last king of the giants—Og, king of Bashan. Some descendants of the giants, including Goliath, remained in Canaan until the time of King David.

The Canaanites

The Bible often refers to "the Hittites, and the Girgashites [GUR guh shyts], and the Amorites, and the Canaanites, and the Perizzites [PEHR ih zyts], and the Hivites, and the Jebusites [JEHB yoo syts]" who were living in Canaan in Joshua's time. God said that these seven nations were mightier than Israel, but He promised to deliver them into Israel's hands (Deuteronomy 7:1, 2).

The Amorites were among the most powerful Canaanites. In fact, some people of that time called Canaan "the land of the Amorites." You may recall that after the time of the Sumerians and Akkadians,

Amorites conquered much of the Fertile Crescent. Hammurabi was an Amorite king who ruled at Babylon.

Many Jebusites lived in Jebus (JEE buhs), a city that Israel later captured and named Jerusalem. The Hivites who lived in Gibeon and the nearby towns were the ones who tricked Israel into promising never to destroy them. (You probably remember these Hivites better as Gibeonites.)

The Canaanites had many gods. One they greatly glorified was Baal, whom they considered lord of the earth. His wife was Ashtoreth (ASH tuh rehth), goddess of fertility. During religious ceremonies, the people performed many immoral acts in her honor. The Canaanites also sacrificed their children to these gods. Near the ruins of heathen temples, archaeologists have found whole cemeteries of babies who had been sacrificed to Baal and Ashtoreth. People who fall into such terrible sins are ripe for God's judgment. These horrible religious practices were part of the reason God commanded the Israelites to utterly destroy the Canaanites.

The Canaanites considered Baal the lord of the earth. When some Israelites worshiped him, Gideon threw the idol down at the Lord's command. When the idolaters wanted to kill Gideon for his deed, Gideon's father said, "Will ye plead for Baal? will ye save him? . . . if he be a god, let him plead for himself, because one hath cast down his altar" (Judges 6:31). This corroded and broken statuette of Baal shows the power of this manmade god. He had none.

Study Exercises

8. The Bible briefly mentions some tribes of giants who settled in or near Canaan after the Flood. (*a*) Which tribe of giants lived in the land later occupied by the Moabites (Deuteronomy 2:9–11)? (*b*) Which tribe was conquered by the Edomites (2:12)? (*c*) Which tribe was conquered by the Ammonites (2:20, 21)?
9. Give an early name for Jerusalem.
10. Which chapter of Joshua tells how the Hivites of Gibeon deceived the Israelites? (Use a Bible concordance if you need help.)
11. What powerful group of Canaanites conquered much of the Fertile Crescent?
12. What did Baal worshipers do that helps us understand why the Lord's servants such as Elijah so ruthlessly destroyed them?

The Hittites

Hittite History. The Hittites are of special interest to us, partly because Israel encountered the Hittites many times. They were descendants of Heth, a son of Canaan and grandson of Ham. Esau took two Hittite wives. They were a poor choice, and his

A close-up look at a face on some Hittite pottery.

mother said, "I am weary of my life because of the daughters of Heth" (Genesis 27:46).

The Bible mentions that the Hittites lived in the mountains (Numbers 13:29). Many Hittites lived in the rugged mountains of Asia Minor, the land of modern Turkey. Some Hittites also lived in the mountains of Canaan, especially in the northern part that later became known as Syria.

The story of the Hittites begins about the time of Abraham. Some of the small Hittite villages grew and developed into city-states. In time, the Hittites developed into a great empire, sometimes by threatening, sometimes by making treaties, and more often by battle. Since the people taken into the kingdom continued living much as they had before, the Hittite Empire soon had many different peoples, practices, and gods. The Hittites were generally more merciful to defeated foes than were many ancient conquerors. They did not usually torture and abuse their enemies as other conquerors often boasted of doing.

The empire expanded until the Hittites had brought some of the northern parts of Canaan under their rule. This helps to explain why the Bible mentions the Hittites so many times.

Hattusas (HAT uh sas), the capital of the mighty Hittite Empire, was one of the most strongly protected cities of its time. The Hittites built Hattusas on the highest land in the area, about 3,000 feet (900 m) above sea level. At its greatest, it covered about 400 acres (160 ha) and was enclosed by a wall almost 4 miles (6.4 km) long. The Hittites laid the wall over ridges, through valleys, and across rushing streams. In one place they bridged a chasm 28 feet (9 m) wide. A solid foundation of huge stones supported the wall and towers of mud bricks.

For nearly five hundred years, this fortress served as the religious and governmental center of the Hittites. Then suddenly, perhaps about 1200 B.C., invading tribes destroyed Hattusas. Today we marvel at its destruction as much as we marvel at its greatness. Archaeologists point out that the invaders set fire to everything that they could burn. The intense heat turned the mud bricks into ceramics, as in a giant kiln. Now only the foundations are left to tell of its one-time grandeur.

But the end of the empire was not the end of the Hittites. A few scattered city-states remained, each having its own king. Much of what we know about the Hittites comes from ruins of these smaller Hittite centers.

God directed Israel to conquer the Hittites in Canaan. But some Hittites continued to live among the Israelites. Uriah the Hittite was one of the mightiest men in David's army (2 Samuel 11:6; 23:8, 39).

To the people of Canaan, the nearby Hittite city-states were a fearsome power. Even as late as the ninth century B.C., people feared the Hittite kings. On one occasion God frightened the Syrians away from besieging an Israelite city by causing them to think the Hittites and the Egyptians were coming (2 Kings 7). Finally, in the eighth century B.C., Assyrian kings conquered all the remaining Hittite city-states. (The eighth century B.C. was from 701 to 800 B.C.)

Daily Life of the Hittites. We have seen that the Hittites readily mixed with the many different peoples in their empire. Records in at least eight different languages have been found in the capital city. Because of this mixture of cultures, it is difficult to know how typical Hittites lived and acted.

The Hittites did have a typical manner of dress. The men usually wore knee-length garments that resembled long shirts, while the women wore long, full cloaks. Hittites often wore boots with turned-up, pointed toes.

As the Hittites took in various peoples, they also took in their gods—hundreds of them. In fact, they often sealed treaties with other kingdoms by calling "the thousand gods" to witness.

The laws of the Hittites also show the influence of many different people. The Babylonian law code seems to have influenced them most. The Hittite laws usually had milder punishments than most other laws of the time.

Very few of the Hittites lived in great cities. Most of them lived in small farming villages and tilled the nearby fields. Today small farming villages are still found in Turkey, similar in many ways to the old Hittite villages.

The Hittites had interesting ways of buying and selling. Do you remember the Bible story of Abraham buying a cave from the Hittites to use for burials? They carefully described exactly what they were selling: "the field, and the cave which was therein, and all the trees that were in the field" (Genesis 23:17). After the sale was properly witnessed, no one could come back to Abraham and say, "Yes, we sold you the field, but not the trees."

The Hittites Produced Iron. Moses, the Israelite leader, described the Promised Land as a land whose stones are iron (Deuteronomy 8:9). Why was this so important? Today we seldom think of iron as a precious metal. If we bend a nail badly, we throw it away and reach for another. This was not always so. As recently as two hundred years ago, iron was valued highly. People reused nails and other iron products if they could. In ancient history, iron was worth more than silver and sometimes even more than gold!

According to Genesis 4:22, men learned to use iron before the Flood. But iron is a very hard metal and was difficult for ancient men to ***smelt.*** For tools and weapons they often used ***bronze*** (called brass in the Bible), which is an ***alloy*** of copper and tin. However, bronze is not as

This Hittite warrior carries a shield, a spear, and a sword sheathed in his belt.

strong and durable as iron. When Israel entered Canaan, iron was still uncommon, but some of the Canaanites had chariots of iron that helped them resist the Israelites.

For many years, the Hittites led out in the production and use of iron. Then a tribe subject to the Hittites discovered an easier and better way to refine iron. Eventually the use of iron spread, and it began to replace bronze.

The Forgotten Nation. For hundreds of years the Hittites held a place among the great nations of the East. Could such a nation disappear from recorded history? ***Skeptics*** of the 1700s and 1800s said that was impossible. They had no records of the Hittites other than the Bible. They pointed fingers of scorn at the more than forty Bible verses that mention Hittites. "Myths," they said.

Then in the early 1800s, a French explorer discovered the ruins of a great city in the central plateau of Turkey. His findings did not attract much attention at the time. Only after several other men had made related discoveries did the history of the Hittites begin to emerge. About 1880, an authority confidently declared that the ruins belonged to the Hittites. The French explorer's city turned out to be Hattusas, the Hittite capital itself. And the Hittites of Canaan, instead of being a myth, turned out to be only a small part of a once-mighty empire.

Such discoveries do not surprise Christians. They know that all of God's Word is true, even if some Bible facts have not been proven by archaeology. "Thy word is true from the beginning: and every one of thy righteous judgments endureth for ever" (Psalm 119:160).

Study Exercises

13. Name at least three Bible men who had dealings with the Hittites of Canaan. Do not include Heth, Canaan, or Ham.
14. (*a*) What factors made Hattusas impressive? (*b*) In what way was its destruction also impressive?
15. What empire finally conquered the last Hittite city-states?
16. Why do students of history have trouble knowing what practices were distinctly Hittite?
17. Why did early men not use iron much, even though they knew about it?
18. How were the Hittites a surprise to archaeologists?

Other Peoples in Canaan

The Philistines. One group of people whom the Israelites did not drive out of their land was the Philistines. They lived in southern Canaan along the Mediterranean coast.

The Philistines may have come from the island of Crete. Perhaps their first settlers in Canaan came to establish a trade colony there. During the days of Abraham, Isaac, and Jacob, their most important town was Gerar (GEE rahr). Historians think a busy trade route ran through it. Abraham and Isaac both spent many years in this area. Most of the time they lived in peace with the king of Gerar.

Later, some Philistines tried to invade Egypt. When the Egyptians fought them off, they settled in southern Canaan, along the Mediterranean coast. Have you read in your Bible about Gath, Ekron, Ashdod, Gaza, and Ashkelon? These were the five Philistine cities, each ruled by a lord or king. After Israel entered Canaan, the Israelites and their Philistine neighbors seldom had peace with each other.

The Phoenicians. Another group of people, the Phoenicians, lived along the Mediterranean coast north of the Philistines. The Phoenicians make a surprising contrast to most peoples. They never bothered about conquering other countries and building an

The Phoenicians probably sailed farther from their homeland than anyone else of their time. This Phoenician galley, powered by sails and muscular oarsmen, glides by the Rock of Gibraltar.

empire. They were interested only in trading with anyone who cared to buy or sell. Many Phoenicians were sailors. They must have been daring ones, for according to an ancient historian, they sailed around Africa long before the Portuguese did in the late A.D. 1400s.

The Phoenicians were famous also because they produced "royal" dye from shellfish. They used the dye to produce various shades of color from red to purple. The finest of this Phoenician purple was in great demand throughout the ancient world—and was very expensive. Anyone "clothed in purple and fine linen" had to be rich. Interestingly, the Phoenician city of Tyre was famous not only for its dye but also for its bad smell, which came from the dye-making process.

Perhaps the biggest mark the Phoenicians made on world history was to develop a short alphabet. Other cultures had hundreds of symbols that a reader had to memorize. Egyptians had a kind of alphabet, but they mixed picture words along with the other symbols. But the Phoenicians helped to establish a simple alphabet with

A lavishly decorated Phoenician court.

These Tyrians are dyeing their cloth a rich purple. The shellfish from which the purple dye was made abounded on the eastern shores of the Mediterranean. For some reason, even though other countries had access to this shellfish too, the Phoenician city of Tyre always maintained pre-eminence over all other producers of purple cloth. Possibly they knew the techniques of production better than anyone else.

only about as many letters as ours.

The Syrians. The Syrians, who were also called Arameans (ar uh MEE uhnz), were descendants of Shem's son Aram. In Abraham's time they lived around Haran in northern Mesopotamia. From there they spread out and established states as far south as northern Canaan. Damascus was the capital of one of their chief states.

The Arameans were apparently as eager to trade by land as the Phoenicians were to trade by sea. We get a glimpse of this in the Bible story of Ahab defeating the Syrian king Ben-hadad. To make peace, Ben-hadad offered Ahab the right to "make streets" (set up markets) in Damascus (1 Kings 20:34).

The Syrians adopted many customs of the people around them, but they kept their own language. By about 500 B.C., the Aramaic (ar uh MAY ihk) language had spread throughout the Fertile Crescent, much as English has spread throughout the world today. It was the common language of the people, as well as the official language of the Persian Empire. Long after the Aramean kingdom was gone, people were still using the Aramaic language, which is similar to Hebrew. Jesus spoke it every day.

Study Exercises

19. In whose time did the Hebrews have a peaceful relationship with the Philistines?
20. Was the Phoenician alphabet short or long compared to the number of symbols in other writing systems?
21. Who were the Arameans?

Clinching the Chapter

Multiple Choice

A. *Write the word or phrase* least *associated with the first item.*

1. Canaan: hills, fertile soil, rain, irrigation
2. Bordering the Promised Land: deserts, Nile, Mediterranean, Euphrates

3. Canaan: isolated, buffer, battlefield, land bridge
4. Trade routes: Mediterranean, King's Highway, Dead Sea, Way of the Sea
5. Sea trade: Joppa, Caesarea, Euphrates, Phoenicia
6. Giants: Emim, Edomites, Horim, Anakim
7. Asia Minor: Turkey, Hattusas, Gibeonites, Hittites
8. Great empires: Canaan, Babylon, Egypt, Assyria
9. Philistines: Crete, Tyre, Gerar, Gath
10. Phoenicians: dye, shellfish, alphabet, iron

B. *Write the correct words.*

1. Who depended most on trade routes through Canaan? (Babylon, Egypt, Assyria, Hittites)
2. The god that Canaanites called "lord of the earth" was (Og, Goliath, Baal, Ashtoreth).
3. Which group was the most centrally located? (Babylonians, Assyrians, Egyptians, Canaanites)
4. The descendants of Heth were (Hittites, Amorites, Hivites, Israelites).
5. Which group conquered much of the Fertile Crescent? (Perizzites, Amorites, Anakim, Israelites)
6. Who was a notable Hittite warrior in David's army? (Heth, Jephthah, Abner, Uriah)
7. The Hittite capital was (Jericho, Caesarea, Hattusas, Megiddo).
8. Jerusalem was once called (Gibeon, Jebus, Hattusas, Joppa).
9. Which of these did the Hittites have? (distinctive lifestyle, many gods, harsh laws, unfortified capital city)
10. Which group disappeared from secular history until the 1800s? (Egyptians, Babylonians, Amorites, Hittites)

Matching

A. *Match each clue with the correct name from the right-hand column.*

1. Early port in southern Canaan	Arabia
2. Home of Og	Aramaic
3. Widely used ancient language	Assyria
4. Conquered the last Hittite city-states	Bashan
5. Land from River of Egypt to Euphrates	Ben-hadad
6. Desert region east of Canaan	Canaan
7. Leader in early production of iron	Damascus
8. King of Syria	Hittites
9. Capital of important Syrian state	Joppa
10. Modern nation of Asia Minor	Turkey

B. *Match as in Part A.*

1. Not usually needed in Canaan	alloy
2. Group of travelers	alphabet
3. Watched over by neighboring empires	bronze
4. Doubted Biblical mention of Hittites	buffer
5. Separates enemy nations	caravan

6. Once worth as much as silver	iron
7. Example of an alloy	irrigation
8. Process of obtaining metal from ore	skeptics
9. Easier to use than hieroglyphics	smelting
10. Any mixture of metals	trade routes

Completion

1. Canaan was blessed with rich soil and with rain;
   Farmers in Canaan raised grapes, figs, and ———.
2. God gave His people a heavenly mission;
   Therefore He gave them a central ———.
3. On the King's Highway men rode for a fee,
   Or they could follow the ——— ——— ——— ———.
4. Israel destroyed all who rose in defiance—
   Yes, even Og, the last king of the ———.
5. Those who tricked Israel were known as Hivites,
   But they could also be called ———.
6. Doubters of Scripture no longer make light
   Of Biblical reference to ancient ———.
7. Books about Hittites can mention at last
   The greatness and downfall of old ———.
8. People in Canaan put children to death,
   All to please Baal and his wife ———.
9. Of all inventions, don't forget
   The short Phoenician ———.
10. Bronze against iron would surely not win;
    Bronze is an alloy of copper and ———.

Thought Questions

1. Why was it good for the Israelites to depend on God for rain rather than to depend on irrigation?
2. What connection do wars have with trade?
3. (*a*) How was the central position of Canaan an advantage to Canaanites? (*b*) When was it a disadvantage?
4. Not everything religious is good. How can you prove that from this chapter?
5. The Hittites have been called inveterate synthesizers. (*a*) What does this mean? (*b*) How is it a fitting description of the Hittites?

Geographical Skills

1. Trace Map C in the map section, and label it "Neighbors of Israel."
2. Use colors to show the approximate areas occupied by the Philistines, the Phoenicians, and the Syrians (Arameans). Label the colored areas.
3. What is the elevation of the Dead Sea?
4. In Bible times, the Dead Sea was called the Salt Sea. What is the relationship between the elevation of the Dead Sea and the names men have given it?

Further Study

1. God called Canaan “a land flowing with milk and honey.” This does not mean that every acre was a lush paradise. Relatively dry areas can support milk-producing goats, and bees can make honey from desert flowers. However, the Bible does indicate that Canaan was a rich, fruitful land. Read Deuteronomy 8:7–9; 11:9–12; and Joshua 17:15, 18. Then briefly describe the climate and vegetation of Canaan in early Bible times. How does the Bible description of Canaan compare with its climate today?
2. Find maps that will help you tell whether these sentences about Canaan are true or false.
   a. The Jordan River flows north, like the Nile.
   b. Mount Lebanon is a mountain range.
   c. Tyre and Sidon are west of Mount Hermon.
   d. Mount Carmel is near the Dead Sea.
   e. Megiddo is near the Plain of Esdraelon (Valley of Jezreel).
   f. Gilead is west of the Jordan River.
   g. Mount Gerizim and Mount Ebal stand close together.
   h. Traveling west from the Dead Sea, you would go up to Jerusalem and then down to the Mediterranean Sea.
   i. The northern part of Canaan received more rainfall than the southern part.
   j. Canaan has about the same latitude as the state of Georgia.

The Israelites cross the Jordan River.

2000 B.C.
Abram enters Canaan. c. 1877
1800
Jacob and his family move to Egypt. c. 1662
1600
Moses is born. 1527
God delivers the Israelites from Egypt. 1447
The Israelites wander in the wilderness. 1447–1407
Joshua leads the Isrealites into Canaan. 1407
1400
Judges rule Israel. c. 1375–1051
1200
Saul is crowned king of Israel. c. 1051
David becomes king of Israel. 1011
1000
Solomon begins to build the temple 480 years after Israel left Canaan (1 Kings 6:1). 967
The kingdom is divided after Solomon's death. 931
Elijah and Elisha remind Israel of the true God. c. 870–800
800 B.C.

10 The Hebrews Become a Nation

God's Special People

The Call of Abraham

The Patriarchs

Israel in Egypt

Israel in the Wilderness

Early Years in Canaan

Israel's First King

The House of David

The Divided Kingdom

"And what one nation in the earth is like thy people, even like Israel, whom God went to redeem for a people to himself, and to make him a name, and to do for you great things and terrible, for thy land, before thy people, which thou redeemedst to thee from Egypt, from the nations and their gods?"
2 Samuel 7:23

The Hebrews Become a Nation

God's Special People

"The LORD thy God hath chosen thee to be a special people unto himself, above all people that are upon the face of the earth" (Deuteronomy 7:6). The Hebrews are not usually considered a great nation in comparison to other ancient civilizations. Abraham, Isaac, and Jacob wandered from place to place with their flocks and herds. Jacob's descendants served as bondmen in Egypt. God Himself said that they were "the fewest of all people" (Deuteronomy 7:7). Yet He loved them and called them to be His own people.

We owe a special debt of gratitude to the Hebrews. It was through them that God gave us the Old Testament—in fact, the whole Bible. The Hebrews also helped the world to remember that there is one God.

Some people think that monotheism, the belief in one God, was a new idea that the Israelites introduced. Actually, mankind knew the one true God at first and later degenerated into polytheism. The Hebrews continued to believe in the one true God, which everyone else should have done too.

"When the fulness of the time was come," God sent Jesus to earth through the Hebrews (Galatians 4:4). Although many of the Jews rejected Him, those who believed in Him became the first Christians, and through them the Gospel has been passed on to us.

The Call of Abraham

The history of God's chosen people begins with Abram. God called Abram to leave his country, his people, and his father's idols. Because Abram believed God and obeyed His command, God promised to bless him and to make his name great.

After Abram moved to Canaan, God changed his name to Abraham, which means "father of many nations." Abraham became the earthly father of both the Jews and the Arabs. (Many Arabs descend from Ishmael, Esau, or the sons of Abraham's wife Keturah.) But Abraham became the spiritual father only of those who have faith in God—first to the faithful Jews in the Old Testament and now to all who believe and obey the Gospel. "If ye be Christ's, then are ye Abraham's seed, and heirs according to the promise" (Galatians 3:29).

From before Abram's day to the present, camels have served desert peoples. They are sometimes called "ships of the desert" because they can carry heavy loads about 25 miles (40.25 km) a day, and can go up to four days without drinking. There are several million camels in the world, and almost all of them are domesticated.

Abraham and his clan probably lived in shelters much like these Bedouin tents. The tents generally have sides which can be raised for ventilation.

The Patriarchs

A ***patriarch*** is the leader of a family or tribe. Abraham, Isaac, and Jacob each served as early Hebrew patriarchs.

When God called Abram, his father Terah was still the family patriarch. Terah led the family from Ur to Haran. After Terah died, Abram traveled on through the Fertile Crescent and finally reached Canaan.

Abram's own caravan was no small one. He likely received a share of the flocks, herds, and servants his father had gathered. When Lot was carried captive by foreign kings, Abram rescued him with 318 men who had been born as servants in the family clan.

The patriarchs never settled permanently, although they sometimes stayed at one place long enough to dig wells and to plant and harvest crops. Once during a famine, Abram led his family as far south as Egypt. It was common for nomads to go to Egypt when their usual roaming grounds suffered from drought. Later Jacob and his sons moved to Egypt, where they lived and multiplied for a number of generations.

Archaeologists have discovered the word *Habiru* on some old clay tablets found in the Middle East. *Habiru* closely resembles the word *Hebrew,* and it referred to groups of people who lived as semi-nomads. The Habiru sometimes camped close to or even within a city. Townspeople probably used the word as a term of contempt.

Was Abraham the Hebrew one of the Habiru? We do not know the exact meaning of *Habiru* well enough to answer the question for sure. We do know that the Hebrews lived the same kind of life as the Habiru.

We can learn some facts about the Hebrews from archaeology, but we can learn much more from the Bible. Because the Bible is God's Word, all its accounts are true, even those that archaeology has not proved.

Study Exercises

1. What are two gifts that God gave the world through the Hebrews?
2. (*a*) What man led Abram's family out of Ur? (*b*) What man led them into Canaan?
3. Write a sentence describing the life of nomads.
4. What ancient term resembles the word *Hebrew*?

Israel in Egypt

In Egypt, Jacob's little nomad family grew to hundreds of thousands. They became known as Israelites because God had changed Jacob's name to Israel. Exodus 12:40 states that they sojourned for 430 years, but from Galatians 3:17 it appears that those years might have included the 215 years that Abraham, Isaac, and Jacob sojourned in Canaan. If this is correct, they lived in Egypt for 215 years.

Exodus 1:11 records that the Israelites helped to build Pithom (PY thuhm) and Rameses (RAM eh seez). At Pithom, archaeologists have uncovered walls that were made partly of bricks without straw. Perhaps Israelite workers made these bricks after the Egyptians stopped supplying straw. (See Exodus 5:10–19.)

Another interesting find is an Egyptian document that tells of some workers who carved royal tombs out of the cliffs. It kept track of their "days worked" and "days idle." Among the reasons for "days idle" may be found "his wife is ill," "stung by a scorpion," and "offering to his god." Sometimes an entire crew was excused for a day or more to keep a religious feast. So it is not surprising that Moses asked Pharaoh to excuse his Hebrew workers so that they could go and sacrifice in the wilderness (Exodus 5:3).

At first Pharaoh was not ready to release the Israelites, for they were valuable workers. He did not care what the God of the Hebrews said. But Pharaoh soon learned

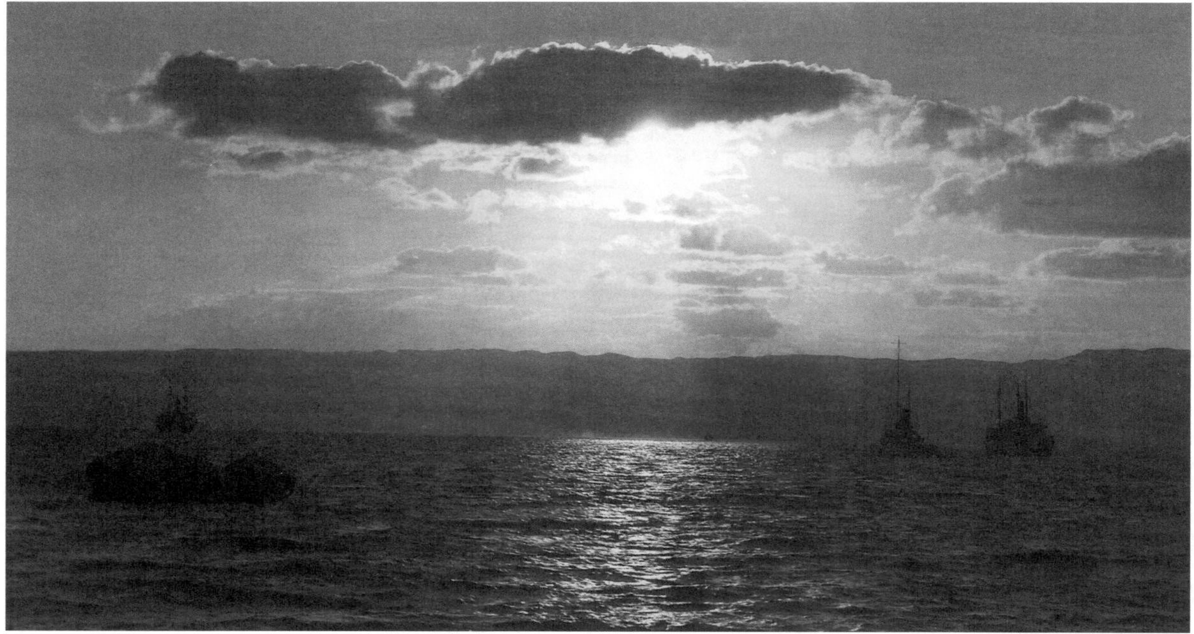

Many ships use the Red Sea. God divided the waters of this sea to allow the children of Israel to pass over on dry ground during their escape from Egypt. The Red Sea in the area of the Exodus is about 200 feet (61 m) deep. Exodus 14:22 says that "the waters were a wall unto them on their right hand, and on their left."

The Israelites reached the wilderness and Mount Sinai about three months after leaving Egypt. God supplied the needs of His people in this dry land for 40 years.

that his own power and even the power of his many gods was no match for Israel's God. The Lord delivered His people from their bondage, just as He had promised Abraham.

Israel in the Wilderness

When the Hebrews finally left Egypt, the whole group included women, children, and a "mixed multitude"—probably people whose parents were not both Israelites. The crowd must have numbered two or three million. There were over 600,000 men, besides women and children (Numbers 1:46).

The Israelites gather manna. "And when the children of Israel saw it, they said one to another, It is manna. . . . And Moses said unto them, This is the bread which the LORD hath given you to eat. . . . Gather of it every man according to his eating, an omer for every man, according to the number of your persons; take ye every man for them which are in his tents" (Exodus 16:15, 16).

Out among the bare rocks and mountains of Sinai, the people began to face problems. Remember, the Israelites were not accustomed to the freedoms they now had. They had no experience in governing themselves as a nation. Moses tried to govern the nation by himself until his father-in-law told him he would wear himself out. Then Moses set up helpers so that he could concentrate on the most important matters (Exodus 18:13–26).

While the Israelites were in the wilderness, God gave Moses His Law for them. Other nations had laws too, but God's Law was better. For example, both Israel and other nations had laws that forbade stealing, but God's Law went a step further. It also said, "Thou shalt not covet"; in other words, do not even want to steal. The laws of other nations tried to help people treat their neighbors fairly, but God's Law was much nobler. It said, "Thou shalt love thy neighbour as thyself." God's Law also placed great value on human life, whereas some lawgivers did not consider human lives especially important.

The wilderness journey was a time of testing for the Israelites, and most of them failed miserably. Because of their rebellion, almost all the men and women who left Egypt died before reaching Canaan. Their children had to wander in the desert for forty years.

You might think that Israel fought all the nations they met as they traveled to Canaan. This is not true. On the border of Edom, Israel politely asked if they might go through the country on the King's Highway. When the Edomites said no, Israel made a long detour around their land (Numbers 20:14–21). God specifically commanded Israel to avoid conflicts with the Edomites, Moabites, and Ammonites. The Edomites were descendants of Esau, and the Moabites and Ammonites were descendants of Lot.

But when Sihon, king of the Amorites, came out to fight against the Israelites, "Israel smote him with the edge of the sword, and possessed his land" (Numbers 21:24). The Israelites also defeated Og king of Bashan. Then they moved across the Jordan into the Promised Land to destroy the tribes and nations there.

Study Exercises

5. In what country were the cities of Pithom and Rameses?
6. Give at least two ways that God's Law was better than the laws of other nations.
7. Name three peoples with whom Israel avoided fighting while traveling to Canaan.

Early Years in Canaan

Archaeologists say they have found evidence that Jericho was destroyed in ancient times. Some say an earthquake

Instead of walls, fertile fields and date palm trees surround modern Jericho.

shook the city and then a fire broke out, causing more destruction. Actually, they may have found the ruins left when God caused the walls to collapse and Israel burned the city.

The Israelites won many great battles under Joshua's leadership. They lost only when they sinned or when they failed to ask counsel of the Lord. The Bible says that the Lord fought for Israel. He caused the walls of Jericho to fall down, He stopped the sun when Joshua needed a longer day, and He sent great hailstorms against Israel's enemies. The heathen feared and trembled before the mighty God of the Hebrews.

In spite of their great victories, the Israelites were slow to possess all of their land. When Joshua died, no great Canaanite army could oppose Israel, but groups of Canaanites still lived in some regions. Not until the time of David did the Israelites completely subdue their enemies.

After Joshua's death, the Israelites quickly turned away from God. They began to worship the gods of the people whom they had not destroyed. For several hundred years, they went through cycles of sin and repentance. When they sinned, God delivered them into the hands of their enemies. Then they cried to the Lord in their trouble, and He sent a judge to deliver them. Usually they had peace as long as the judge lived; but afterward they fell into sin again, and the cycle would be repeated.

During the time of the Israelite judges, it appears that the Philistines had a ***monopoly*** on iron in Canaan. That means they kept the iron they wanted for themselves and kept other people from having too much. This prevented others, such as Israel, from having a good supply of weapons.

Shamgar, Samson, Eli's sons, Samuel, and Saul all fought against the Philistines.

This Philistine warrior wears a feathered headdress.

Finally David subdued them, and they were no longer able to threaten Israel. But they continued as a distinct people until about the fourth century B.C.

Israel's First King

Samuel was the last judge of Israel. When his sons failed to follow his good example, the people requested a king. They wanted a strong earthly leader like the kings of the nations around them.

God had called Moses and Joshua to lead His people out of Egypt and into Canaan. Later He had chosen judges to lead the Israelites in battle and to help the people follow His laws. But God was always the supreme ruler over Israel. When He appointed leaders, He expected them to lead the nation according to His will. A country that is ruled by God is called a ***theocracy.***

God was displeased with the people's request for a king. He knew that a king would bring them trouble. If they had wholly followed God as their king, they would not have desired a strong earthly ruler. God told Samuel to anoint Saul as king of Israel, but He sent a great thunderstorm to warn the Israelites not to forsake Him. Even though

He chose a king for them, God wanted Israel to remain a theocracy. The kings were subject to God's Law; and when they sinned, God sent prophets to rebuke them.

Though Saul began well, he soon became proud and rebellious. God rejected him and sent Samuel to anoint David as the next king. Saul, the tallest man in Israel, ended his life in calamity and defeat.

The House of David

When God sent Samuel to anoint a second king, He told Samuel not to look at the outward appearance or the height of a man. God chose David and called him a man after His own heart (1 Samuel 13:14). Even though David committed some terrible sins, through repentance he was one of Israel's best leaders.

Under God's blessing, David enlarged the borders of Israel to their greatest extent. Besides defeating the Philistines, he subdued the Amalekites, the Jebusites, the Moabites, the Syrians, the Ammonites, and the Edomites.

David also established Jerusalem as a center of true worship. He moved the ark of the covenant there, and he made plans to build a temple. God told him that Solomon would build the temple instead, but He promised to establish David's kingdom forever (2 Samuel 7:16). David's descendants sat on his throne until the Babylonians burned Jerusalem in 586 B.C. The promise of an everlasting reign was eventually fulfilled in Jesus.

Unlike most of Israel's neighbors, the Phoenicians made friends with David. Hiram, king of Tyre, sent wood from the cedars of Lebanon for David's house. He also sent cedar wood to Solomon for the temple. Not everything the Phoenicians exported to the Israelites was a blessing, however. Years later King Ahab's wife Jezebel, a Phoenician, helped to establish Baal worship in Israel. God pronounced

Most of the references to cedar in the Bible refer to the cedars of Lebanon. Their strong wood was used for beams in buildings and ships, and was also useful for carving. Much of Solomon's temple was built of this cedar. These trees have sturdy trunks up to 40 feet (12 m) in circumference. The cedars of Lebanon are very rare today.

judgment on the Phoenician cities of Tyre and Sidon.

Israel prospered tremendously under King Solomon. He joined the Phoenicians in shipbuilding and trading ventures. He traded in horses and chariots with Egypt and Asia Minor. Besides, he controlled and taxed traders who passed through Israel. He made silver and cedar trees as common in Jerusalem as stones and sycamore trees.

In spite of all this revenue, Solomon needed more money for his luxurious living and his great building projects. So he divided Israel into twelve districts and began a system of taxation. The result was a growing discontentment among his own people.

Study Exercises

8. Describe the cycles the Israelites experienced during the time of the judges.
9. What is a monopoly?
10. What is a theocracy?
11. (*a*) What physical characteristic set Saul apart from the rest of the Israelites? (*b*) How was David better suited for leadership?
12. How did God fulfill His promise to establish David's kingdom forever?
13. How was David's relationship with the Phoenicians different from his contacts with the other nations around Israel?
14. How did Solomon bring discontentment to his own people?

The Divided Kingdom

Solomon overburdened the Israelites with his taxing. His son Rehoboam, the next king, declared that he would increase the tax burden instead of reducing it. Ten tribes could not bear this and ***seceded.*** Now there were two kingdoms. The ten tribes in the

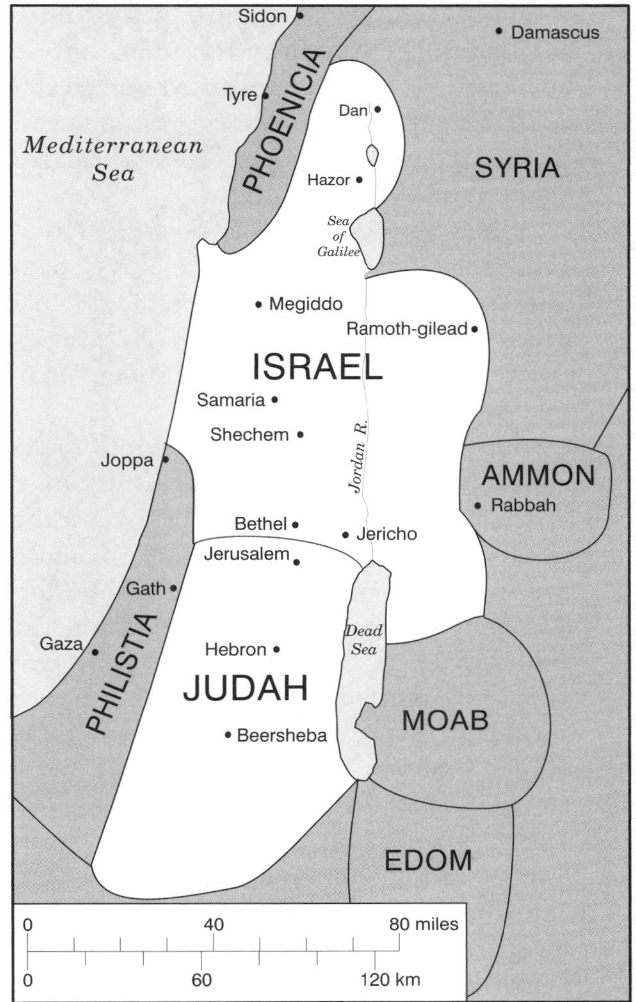

Figure 10:1. The Divided Kingdom

north were called Israel, and the two tribes in the south were called Judah.

Jeroboam was the first king over the separate Northern Kingdom. God promised Jeroboam that if he was faithful, He would establish his dynasty in the Northern Kingdom as He had established David's dynasty in Judah. Instead, Jeroboam built centers of idol worship and earned the reputation as the one "who made Israel to sin."

Two years after Jeroboam's death, God sent Baasha to destroy Jeroboam's family as punishment for his sin. But Baasha also did evil in God's sight, and soon God cut off

Baasha's family too. Family after family reigned in the Northern Kingdom, only to be overthrown by the next ***usurper.*** In contrast, David's family ruled over Judah continuously except for the seven-year reign of the wicked queen Athaliah.

The two kingdoms were never as strong separately as they would have been together. Sometimes they even fought each other. This made them easy victims for neighboring countries such as Edom, Moab, and Egypt.

Syria also caused much trouble to the two Hebrew kingdoms. Under King David, Israel had conquered much of Syria's territory; but during the last part of Solomon's reign, a Syrian named Rezon rebelled. Sometime later the Syrians gained full independence. This led to a three-way power struggle among Syria, Judah, and Israel. At some times Israel and Judah made an ***alliance*** against Syria. At other times Israel and Syria united against Judah or Judah and Syria against Israel. For example, you may recall the time Jehoshaphat, king of Judah, helped Ahab, king of Israel, to fight against the Syrian army. Ahab was struck by an arrow during that battle, and he died soon afterward (1 Kings 22:29–37).

Some of David's descendants served God and brought revival to Judah, but others lived carelessly or worshiped idols. The Northern Kingdom, which had no righteous kings, fared even worse spiritually. Ahab and his wife Jezebel led Israel deep into Baal worship. Even Jehu, the best of the northern kings, "departed not from the sins of Jeroboam" (2 Kings 10:31).

During the reign of Ahab and his descendants, the prophets Elijah and Elisha worked mighty miracles to remind the Israelites of the true God. Many other prophets also warned the people to repent. Sometimes the king and the people paid attention, but often they rejected God's messengers. Sometimes they even killed the prophets.

Meanwhile, God was preparing two heathen nations, Assyria and Babylonia, to bring judgment on the Israelites. By allowing His sinful people to go into captivity, He would preserve a faithful remnant of Jews. And after Assyria and Babylon had fulfilled His will, God would bring judgment on their lands as well.

Study Exercises

15. Why did the northern tribes secede?
16. Who was the only usurper in Judah?
17. What three kingdoms were often in conflict during this time?
18. How did God warn His people when they fell into sin?

Clinching the Chapter

Multiple Choice

A. *Write the word or phrase* least *associated with the first item.*

1. Hebrews: Bible, Christ, monopoly, monotheism
2. Patriarch: Jesus, Abraham, Isaac, Jacob
3. Israelites in Egypt: Rameses, Sihon, bondage, growing population
4. Name for Hebrews: Habiru, Israelites, Jews, Ammonites
5. Israel in the wilderness: theocracy, dynasties, laws, rebellion
6. Joshua: Jericho, Canaan, Assyria, long day
7. Samuel: Saul, David, Phoenicians, Philistines

8. David's dynasty: Solomon, Rehoboam, Jesus, temporary
9. Kingdom of Judah: alliances, usurpers, some righteous kings, several revivals
10. Northern Kingdom: alliances, usurpers, some righteous kings, secession

B. *Write the correct words.*

1. Abram's father was (Terah, Hammurabi, Isaac, Japheth).
2. A roaming herdsman was a (patriarch, slave, Philistine, nomad).
3. The first time the Israelites had to govern themselves as a nation was in (Canaan, Egypt, the wilderness, Bashan).
4. Moses received good advice from (the mixed multitude, his father-in-law, the Edomites).
5. God's Law placed the highest value on (animals, possessions, humans, trade).
6. The Israelites went through many cycles of sin, oppression, repentance, and deliverance during the period of the (judges, kings, prophets, priests).
7. Exclusive control over a certain product is (an empire, a monopoly, a symbol, a hieroglyphic).
8. King Saul was known for being above average in (fairness, height, godliness, wisdom).
9. A country ruled by God is called (an alliance, a dynasty, a theocracy, a monotheism).
10. David conquered all of the following except the (Phoenicians, Jebusites, Moabites, Syrians).

Matching

A. *For each clue, write the correct name from the right-hand column.*

1. City Abram left	Edom
2. Country where Abram went during a famine	Egypt
3. City in Egypt	Israel
4. Land Israel detoured	Jerusalem
5. Had a monopoly of iron in Canaan	Judah
6. David's city of true worship	Philistia
7. City of David's friend Hiram	Pithom
8. Southern Hebrew kingdom	Syria
9. Northern Hebrew kingdom	Tyre
10. Made alliances with Judah and Israel	Ur

B. *Match as in Part A.*

1. Father of many nations	Abraham
2. Traveled with Abram from Ur to Haran	Ammonites and Moabites
3. History's greatest lawgiver	David
4. Descendants of Esau	Edomites
5. Descendants of Lot	Hiram
6. Helped to spread Baal worship	Jezebel
7. Israel's first king	Moses
8. Subdued the Philistines	Rehoboam
9. Lost part of his kingdom	Saul
10. Supplied wood for the temple	Terah

Completion

1. Abraham was father to Arab and Jew,
   But his spiritual sons can include me and ———.
2. The Hebrews looked for straw to mix
   With clay. It gave them better ———.
3. Though Israel bypassed Edomites,
   They battled with the ———.
4. The crumbled walls near Jordan's flow
   Had once surrounded ———.
5. For tax relief ten tribes did plead;
   When answered, "No," they did ———.

Thought Questions

1. Why did God choose a special people from among the nations of the world?
2. God told Abram, "Walk through the land in the length of it and in the breadth of it" (Genesis 13:17). Why would it have been natural for Abram to do this?
3. How was Athaliah's usurpation of the throne of Judah different from the frequent changes of royal families in the Northern Kingdom?
4. Aside from taxing the Israelites, where did Solomon get many of his riches?
5. How did the Hebrews illustrate the saying "United we stand; divided we fall"?

Geographical Skills

1. (*a*) Give the latitude and longitude of Jerusalem. (*b*) Which one of the following American cities is at about the same latitude as Jerusalem: Atlanta, Georgia; El Paso, Texas; Miami, Florida?
2. (*a*) What is the approximate distance between the Sea of Galilee and the Mediterranean Sea? (*b*) What is the approximate distance between the northern point of the Sea of Galilee and the southern point of the Dead Sea?
3. Which two of the following cities were located on a mountain ridge: Jerusalem, Jericho, Caesarea, Capernaum, Hebron, Tyre?

Further Study

1. What are some contributions the Hebrews have made to the world besides the ones mentioned in this chapter?
2. Do some research on monopolies. When might a monopoly be a good thing? When might it be bad?

Be Sure You Know

Can you answer all these questions? If not, study Chapters 9 and 10 to find the answers.

A. What

1. was ideal about the location of Canaan?
2. two important trade routes passed through Canaan?
3. country was especially dependent on the trade routes in Canaan?
4. seven tribes inhabited Canaan in Joshua's time?
5. three Bible characters are known to have dealt with the Hittites?
6. important gift did the Phoenicians give to the world?
7. are two gifts that God gave through the Hebrew nation?
8. men are known as the patriarchs of Israel?
9. kind of life did the Israelites have in Egypt?
10. are three tribes of giants that settled in or near Canaan after the Flood?
11. important promise did God make to David?
12. kind of kings ruled in the north after Israel was divided?
13. three nations competed for power while the kingdom of Israel stood?

B. What do these words mean?

14. alliance
15. alloy
16. bronze
17. buffer
18. caravan
19. monopoly
20. patriarch
21. secede
22. skeptic
23. smelt
24. theocracy
25. usurper

C. Where

26. was the capital of the Hittite Empire? (Give the name of the city.)
27. did the Philistines live?
28. did the Phoenicians live?

D. How

29. might a trade route be a source of money to a ruler?
30. did the Hittites deal with people whom they conquered?
31. did the Hittites help to confirm that the Bible is true?
32. is the Law of God better than the laws of other nations?
33. did God try to bring the straying Israelites back to Himself?

E. Why

34. was little irrigation used in Canaan?
35. did kings of other nations often fight battles in Canaan?
36. did God command Israel to utterly destroy the Canaanites?
37. was David better suited for leading God's people than Saul was?
38. did ten tribes break away from the rule of David's family?

So Far This Year

See how many answers you can give from Chapters 1–10 without looking back.

A. *Match the letters on the map to the names below. You will not use all the letters.*

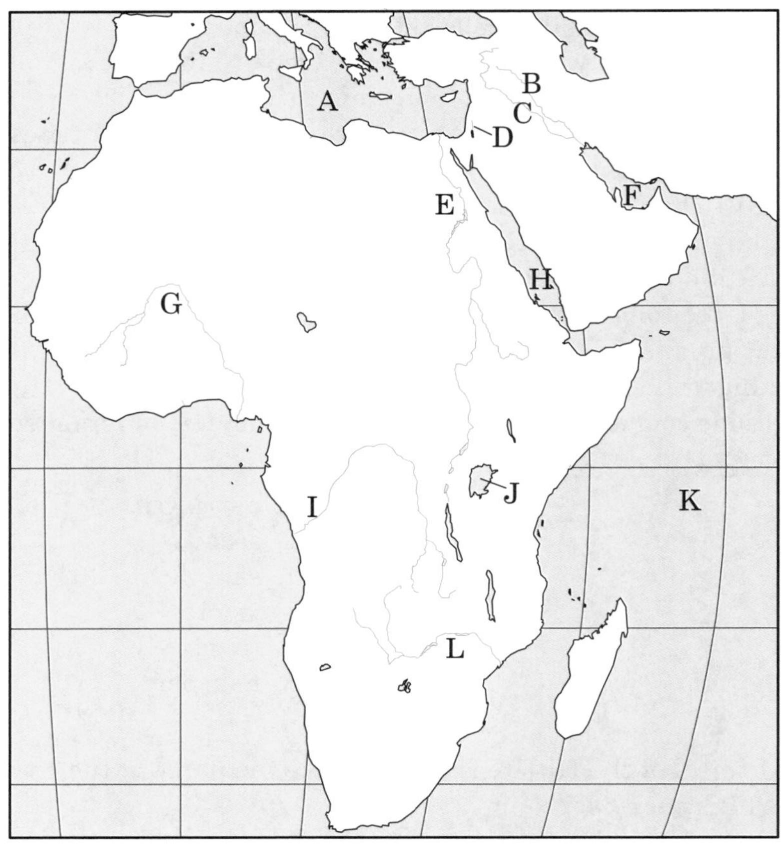

_____ 1. Congo River
_____ 2. Euphrates River
_____ 3. Jordan River
_____ 4. Nile River
_____ 5. Niger River
_____ 6. Zambezi River
_____ 7. Lake Victoria
_____ 8. Mediterranean Sea
_____ 9. Red Sea
_____10. Persian Gulf

B. *Give the correct answers.*

11. The beginning point for measuring degrees of longitude is the (equator, prime meridian, North Pole, International Date Line).
12. The geographical regions of Europe include all the following *except* (northern mountains, central plains, southern mountains, western plains).
13. Japan is a land of all the following *except* (limited farmland, few natural resources, little manufacturing).
14. True or False: Most of Africa has a warm, rainy climate.
15. Government of the earliest civilizations was in the form of (city-states, kingdoms, republics, empires).

16. Evidences of the Flood include all the following *except* (fossils, canyons, layers of sedimentary rock, remains of ancient civilizations).
17. An important Egyptian contribution to writing was (alphabetic symbols, cuneiform, papyrus, parchment).
18. Contributions of the Hebrew nation include all the following *except* (the Bible, the concept of one God, Christianity, Islam).
19. The Hittites' way of dealing with conquered people was (deporting them, enslaving them, allowing them to continue living much as before).
20. In Bible times, Canaan was watered mostly by (irrigation, rainfall).

This well-preserved prism details the war campaigns and building activities of Sennacherib, an Assyrian king. It was found in 1830 and is now in a British museum. The prism is 14½ inches (36.8 cm) high and is covered on all six sides with fine Assyrian script.

11 THE ASSYRIAN EMPIRE AND THE HEBREWS

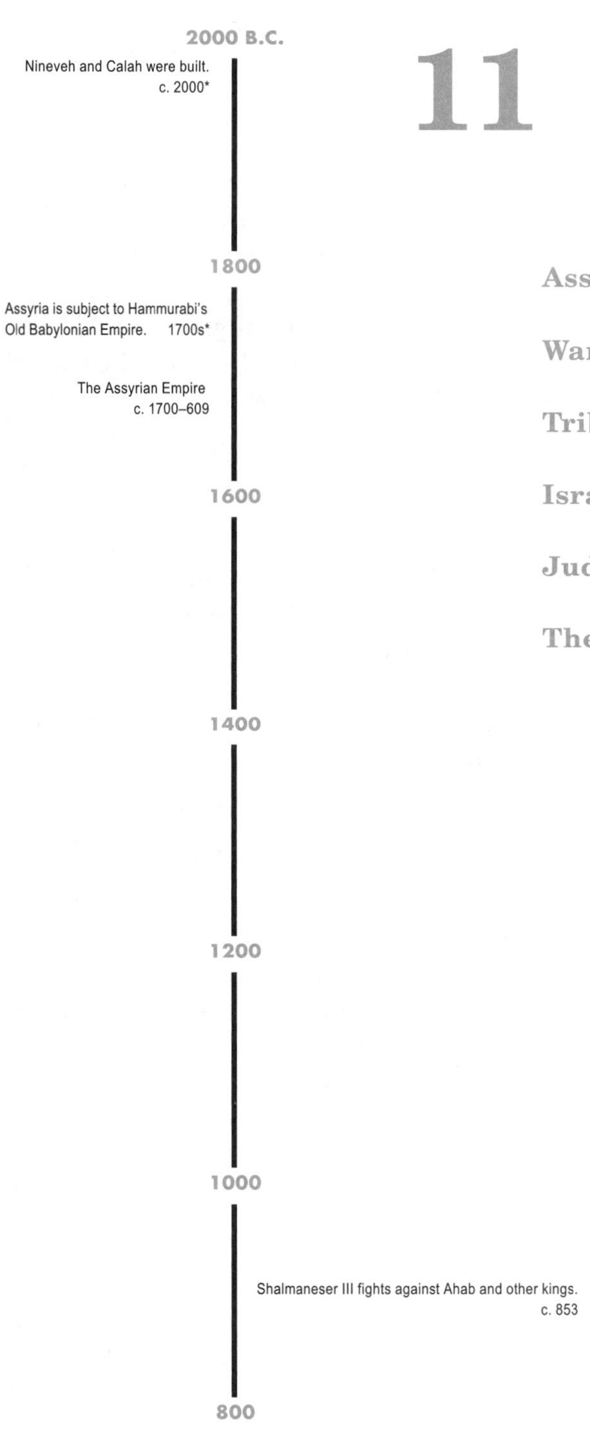
2000 B.C.
Nineveh and Calah were built. c. 2000*
1800
Assyria is subject to Hammurabi's Old Babylonian Empire. 1700s*
The Assyrian Empire c. 1700–609
1600
1400
1200
1000
Shalmaneser III fights against Ahab and other kings. c. 853
800
Jonah preaches at Nineveh. c. 775*
Tiglath-pileser III (Pul) rules Assyria. c. 745–727
Samaria falls to the Assyrians. c. 722
Sennacherib attacks Judah. c. 701
Nineveh is destroyed by the Babylonians and the Medes. 612
Ashurbanipal collects a large library of cuneiform tablets. c. 668–627
The last Assyrian army is defeated. 609
600 B.C.

Assyria's Beginnings

War Tactics and Their Effects

Tribute Riches

Israel and Judah Face Assyria

Judah Faces Assyria

The Fall of Assyria

"And it came to pass that night, that the angel of the LORD went out, and smote in the camp of the Assyrians an hundred fourscore and five thousand: and when they arose early in the morning, behold, they were all dead corpses."

2 Kings 19:35

The Assyrian Empire and the Hebrews

Assyria's Beginnings

Assyria began in the rolling farm country along part of the Tigris River. This area is now in northern Iraq. Peaceful though their homeland looked, the Assyrians became some of the world's most feared warriors. The Bible tells how they threatened Judah and conquered ten tribes of Israel.

Genesis 10:11, 12 mentions a few early Assyrian cities, including Nineveh and Calah (KAY luh); but we know little about these first Assyrians. Although several ancient Assyrian cities were quite strong, they sometimes had to submit to other peoples such as the Amorites and the Babylonians. Assyria was part of the Old Babylonian Empire ruled by Hammurabi.

The Assyrians controlled the major trade routes that passed through their homeland. But as they grew stronger, they looked wistfully farther west along the trade routes that ran toward the Mediterranean Sea and Asia Minor. They wanted these routes to belong to people friendly to the Assyrians. Better yet, why should the Assyrians not possess both the trade routes and the lands through which they passed? Whenever the Assyrians were strong enough, they conquered and controlled additional lands.

During the reigns of David and Solomon in Israel, the Assyrians lost power. However, by the end of the 900s B.C., Assyria was beginning to grow mighty again. Strong Assyrian kings regained control of areas to the northwest. They also pushed the Assyrian border south, taking land that had belonged to Babylonia.

Study Exercises

1. Name a river and a country that you could find on a modern map to help you locate the area of Assyria.
2. How did the Assyrians' interest in trade lead to war?
3. Name an empire that competed with Assyrian power.

War Tactics and Their Effects

The Assyrians were any nation's worst nightmare. They fought fiercely, and after they had defeated their enemies, they burned their cities and fields. They seemed to enjoy torturing their prisoners. Sometimes they blinded them, skinned them, or burned them alive.

Countryside in northern Iraq, the area where the Assyrian nation began.

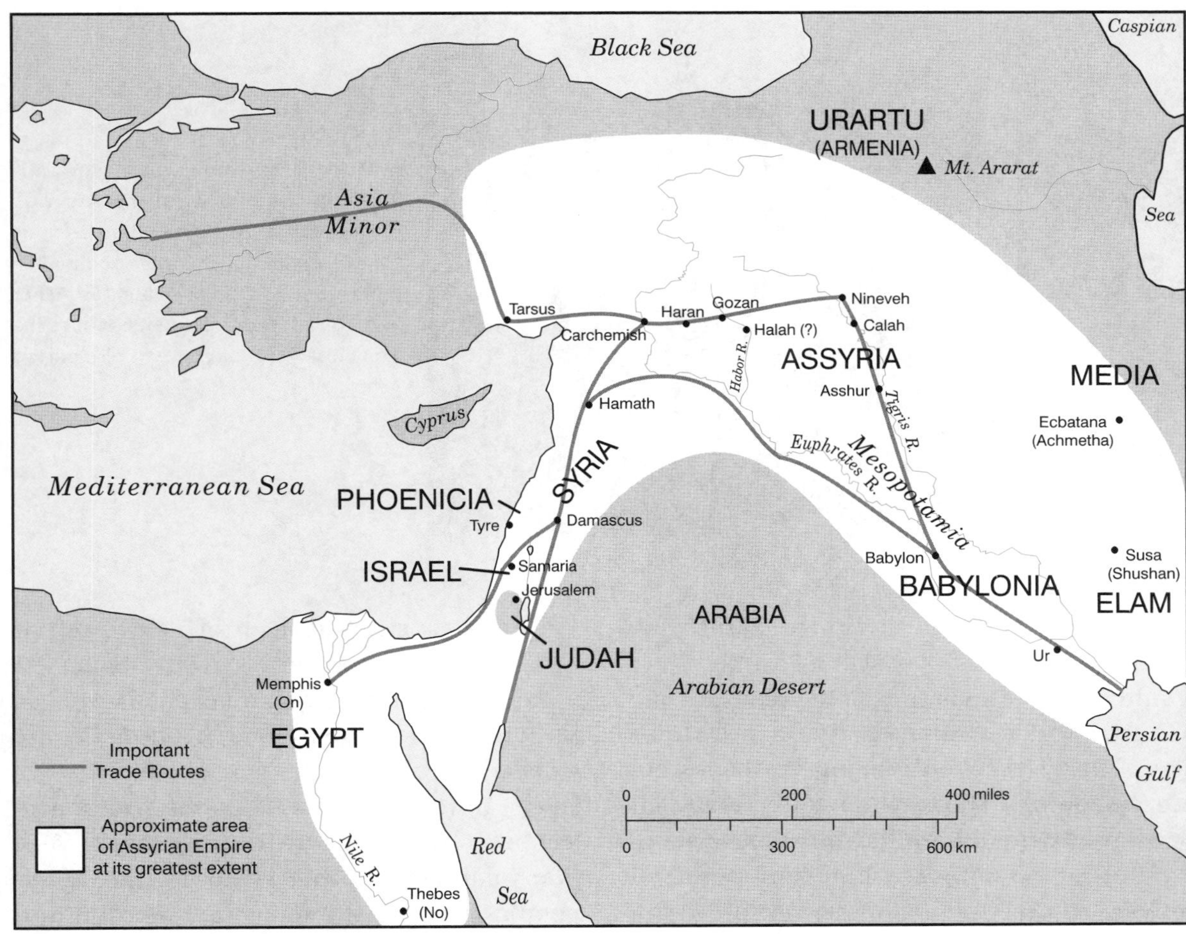

Figure 11:1. The Assyrian Empire

The Assyrians used terror as a tool to help them conquer a country. People who heard how savage they were often surrendered to them rather than risk being tortured. And if conquered people later rebelled, the Assyrians made a special point of using terror as a warning to keep others from rebelling. Some historians suspect that they kept people frightened by boasting of being even more brutal than they actually were. When the Assyrian army was on the march, many kings in their path brought gifts to avoid further trouble with them.

Isaiah 10:14 tells us that the Assyrian king thought, "My hand hath found as a nest the riches of the people: and as one gathereth eggs that are left, have I gathered all the earth; and there was none that moved the wing, or opened the mouth, or peeped." Later in this lesson you will see how God felt about the Assyrians' pride.

Why did the Assyrians want to control so much? First, like most humans, they wanted more resources and products than they already had. Second, they may have felt insecure. Unlike countries such as the United States and Canada, which have large oceans forming part of their borders, the Assyrians did not have many natural barriers that offered protection. Rather than worrying that enemies might attack, Assyria attacked the enemies.

The Assyrians tried to destroy people's

Ashur, now lying in ruins, was once the religious capital of the Assyrian Empire. Other Assyrian cities, such as Nineveh, were much larger and built in better locations than Ashur, but Ashur was considered important because the main false Assyrian god was also named Ashur.

sense of belonging to their own country by scattering them to distant lands. They would ***deport*** thousands of people from one locality and make them live somewhere else. Then they would bring in other people to replace those they had deported. Scattered people had difficulty organizing a rebellion. During the last four hundred to five hundred years of the empire, the Assyrians deported thousands and possibly millions of people.

This Assyrian artwork shows three Assyrian soldiers leading a walking prisoner, while another prisoner is seated on the oxcart.

The Assyrians did an effective job of mixing many national groups. Since so many people had neighbors from elsewhere, the empire became a ***melting pot.*** People worked together and grew accustomed to their neighbors' strange customs and accents. In the Assyrian army itself were many soldiers of other nationalities. Many people adopted the Assyrian religion and accepted Ashur, the chief Assyrian god, as their own.

While the conquered people in the empire were becoming like Assyrians, the Assyrians were becoming like the people they had conquered. For example, they started using the Aramean (Syrian) method of writing in addition to their own cuneiform writing. They borrowed Babylonian styles of art and ***architecture.***

The Assyrians set up offices in the provinces to govern them efficiently. They helped farmers by supplying them with plows. They required the conquered cities and countries to pay ***tribute.***

Tribute Riches

The conquered nations had to send almost more tribute than they could afford to the Assyrian kings. Assyria became very

On the left is a small round stone seal with figures carved into it. It is an Assyrian cylinder seal from about 1300 B.C. If an Assyrian scribe wrote in a soft clay tablet and wanted to "sign" the tablet, he would roll his cylinder seal across the soft clay. When the tablet hardened, it was permanently inscribed, like the clay shown to the right of the seal.

rich as she received great herds of cattle, flocks of sheep and goats, and long camel caravans carrying gold and silver. One Assyrian king received horses by the thousands as tribute from regions to the north. The Assyrians used many of these horses in warfare.

Did the Assyrians do much trading after they gained control over other lands? In early times, Assyrian merchants traded with countries to the west. For example, they imported precious metals from the mines of Asia Minor. Later, however, Assyrian trade appears to have dwindled away. Perhaps they thought, "Why trade for riches when wealth can be obtained more easily by fighting?" Assyrian records from this period always speak of war—not trade. It seems that for a time the king counted it a religious duty to go on a war campaign almost every year.

Some tribute that Assyria received was what other countries had obtained through trade. For example, the Arameans paid tribute in gold, silver, bronze, tin, myrrh, dromedaries (DRAHM ih dair eez), ivory, inlaid furniture, textiles, iron, cattle, sheep, donkeys, ducks, and grain. Not all of these could have been produced in Aram (Syria). Some of them may have come from Arabia, Phoenicia, and other places.

The Assyrians used much of their incoming wealth to support the army, the government, and government projects. They built palaces and temples. They repaired old cities and built new ones. Sennacherib (sih NAK ur ihb), for example, rebuilt Nineveh, surrounding it with massive walls, and made it the capital. To

An Assyrian king had this sculpture of a bull with wings and a man's head mounted as a "guardian" at his palace gate. The winged bulls were supposed to ward off evil. Prominent in Assyrian art, winged bulls show the Assyrian's excellent sculpting talent as well as the strange beliefs people concoct when they do not trust God.

Assyrian kings often hunted lions and other big game when they were not on the warpath. The top picture on the left side is probably an exaggeration to impress people with the great abilities of their king.

bring water to Nineveh from mountain streams, he built a water system about 30 miles (48 km) long. Part of it was an ***aqueduct*** (AK wih duhkt) more than 300 yards long (275 m), where the water was brought across a river.

Many kings had zoos with foreign animals such as apes, crocodiles, and two-humped camels. Some kings laid out parks where they planted trees and plants from faraway lands. Sennacherib even had some "wool-bearing trees" (cotton plants) in his park at Nineveh. It was reported that people "plucked the wool-bearing trees and wove it into cloth." Today, of course, cotton is no longer strange to us.

The Assyrians set up a postal system using horses or mules. Messages were carried by relay, much as the American pony express did thousands of years later. From most places in the empire, an official could send a message to the capital and get an answer in about a week.

Study Exercises

4. What did the Assyrians want to accomplish by torturing people?
5. What did they want to accomplish by deporting people?
6. Name one thing the Assyrians learned from people they conquered.
7. Where did the Assyrians get money to finance their building of cities, canals, roads, parks, and zoos?

Israel and Judah Face Assyria

By the 800s B.C., the Assyrian kings deliberately set out to form a larger empire, rather than just collecting tribute. First they established a ring of fortifications and soldiers around their homeland. Then they marched westward through Syria and conquered lands all the way to the Mediterranean Sea. Tyre, a trading city on the Mediterranean, became an Assyrian prize. The Assyrians took control of the coveted trade routes through the area.

During this period, Assyrian history touches Bible history. Shalmaneser III (shal man EE zur) must have fought against Ahab, king of Israel, about 853 B.C. The Assyrian record mentions "2,000 chariots and 10,000 soldiers of Akhabbu of Sin'ala." (Historians understand *Akhabbu* to be Ahab and *Sin'ala* to be Israel.) Another Assyrian monument shows Jehu paying tribute to Assyria about twelve years later.

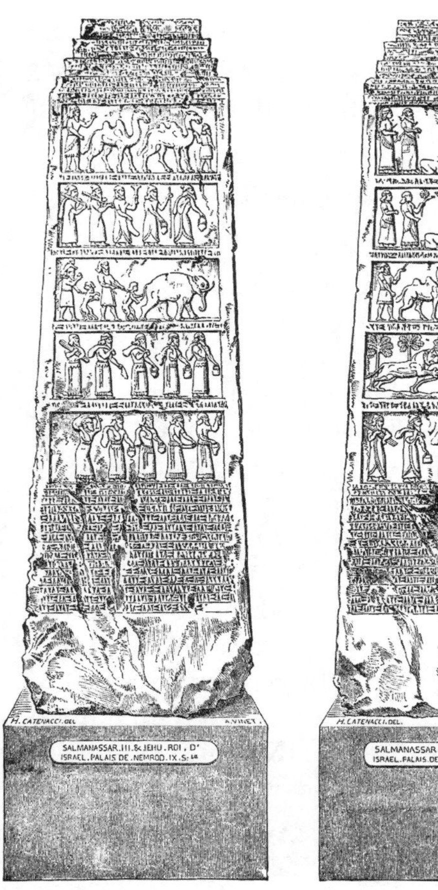

At the top of the right Assyrian monument, Jehu is shown bowing to the Assyrian king. Most of the other pictures appear to be people bringing tribute in various forms to the king. Perhaps some or all of them are Israelites.

The Assyrians usually had little regard for Israel and Israel's God. But one day a prophet from Israel walked into Nineveh and began crying, "Yet forty days, and Nineveh shall be overthrown" (Jonah 3:4). Surprisingly, the Ninevites believed Jonah and repented in sackcloth and ashes. It was one of the world's most sudden and sweeping revivals.

Why was Jonah so reluctant to preach a warning to the Ninevites? The Assyrians were his people's deadly enemies. He would have been happy to see them destroyed. He had been afraid his preaching might spark a revival and that God would spare the Ninevites if they repented (Jonah 3:10; 4:1, 2). That is exactly what happened, and God withheld judgment for a time.

About 745 b.c., the empire was taken over by an ambitious man who was eager for expansion. He is called Pul, or Tiglath-pileser III (TIHG lath puh LEE zur). To keep all areas firmly in his control, he set up a well-organized communication system. Officials in various parts of the empire sent prompt, regular reports to the capital.

Yet this king allowed some areas to keep their local rulers. He gave them a fair amount of independence—even protection—if they paid their tribute and submitted to the Assyrians. An example of such a ruler is King Ahaz of Judah, as mentioned in 2 Kings 16:7–9.

The ten tribes of Israel were ripe for God's judgment. These tribes had had only two kinds of kings: the bad and the worse. Ahab and his two sons, who worshiped Baal, were among the worst of all. The closest Israel had come to true revival was when Elijah called fire from heaven and then destroyed the prophets of Baal. Jehu later finished purging Israel of Baal worship; yet in spite of all his "zeal for the Lord," he still worshiped the golden calves set up by Jeroboam (2 Kings 10:16–31).

In addition to their trouble with idolatry and wicked kings, Israel was becoming a land of the very rich and the very poor. The prophet Amos declared that the rich were buying "the poor for silver, and the needy for a pair of shoes" (Amos 8:6). The poor could not take the rich to court for cheating them because judges took bribes and ignored the rich people's dishonest dealings.

Tiglath-pileser threatened to conquer Israel until Israel's king Menahem (MEHN uh hehm) agreed to pay a thousand talents of silver. But soon afterward, a man named Pekah (PEE kah) took the throne of Israel. Unwilling to pay the heavy tribute, he

An Assyrian man on a horse.

joined forces with Rezin (REE zihn), king of Syria, to rebel against Assyria. These two also attacked Ahaz, king of Judah.

They must have regretted their attack on Judah, however. Ahaz sent a large present to the king of Assyria, saying, "I am thy servant and thy son: come up, and save me out of the hand of the king of Syria, and out of the hand of the king of Israel" (2 Kings 16:7). Seizing the opportunity to expand his empire, Tiglath-pileser attacked the capital of Syria and killed the Syrian king. But he also took Ahaz at his word and made Judah a tributary of Assyria. The Bible says that Tiglath-pileser, king of Assyria, "came unto him, and distressed him, but strengthened him not" (2 Chronicles 28:20).

Hoshea, the king after Pekah, cooperated with the Assyrians for a time. But later he thought he saw a chance to throw off Assyrian rule by turning to Egypt for help. In the end, the Egyptians let Hoshea down; and he found himself without help, facing angry king Shalmaneser V, the next Assyrian king. The Assyrians besieged Samaria, the capital city of Israel; and it fell three years later, about 722 B.C.

According to Assyrian records, 27,290 Israelite captives were carried away by Sargon II, Shalmaneser's successor. He also brought thousands of people from other lands into Israel. The Bible tells the story in 2 Kings 17. It also gives an interesting account of what happened to the people who moved into the area.

God's Judgment on Sin

> "In the ninth year of Hoshea the king of Assyria took Samaria, and carried Israel away into Assyria, and placed them in Halah and in Habor by the river of Gozan, and in the cities of the Medes. For so it was, that the children of Israel had sinned against the LORD their God, . . . and had feared other gods, and walked in the statutes of the heathen. . . . Yet the LORD testified against Israel, and against Judah, by all the prophets, and by all the seers, saying, Turn ye from your evil ways, and keep my commandments and my statutes. . . . Notwithstanding they would not hear, but hardened their necks, like to the neck of their fathers, that did not believe in the LORD their God. . . . Therefore the LORD was very angry with Israel, and removed them out of his sight: there was none left but the tribe of Judah only" (2 Kings 17:6–8, 13, 14, 18).

The Assyrian policy of moving and mixing the people worked as they had planned in this case. The ten tribes of Israel never regrouped and formed a kingdom again.

The Assyrians were proud of their conquering ability. They thought that the God of the Hebrews was no stronger than the gods of other nations that they had conquered. But in Isaiah 10:5, God called Assyria "the rod of mine anger." Although the Assyrians did not realize it, God was using them as an instrument to punish wicked nations and His own disobedient people.

God knew that the proud Assyrian king was thinking, "By the strength of my hand I have done it, and by my wisdom." But God asked, "Shall the axe boast itself against him that heweth therewith?" He declared, "It shall come to pass, that when the Lord hath performed his whole work upon mount Zion and on Jerusalem, I will punish the fruit of the stout heart of the king of Assyria, and the glory of his high looks." (See Isaiah 10:12, 13, 15.)

Study Exercises

8. Name in order the last two kings of Israel.
9. Name in order the four Assyrian kings mentioned in this section.
10. Which prophet had a more responsive audience—Jonah or Amos?
11. Which nation did God compare to a rod and an axe?

This limestone monument shows an Assyrian priest with a knotted whip. He used the whip to chase away evil spirits. We are thankful that we can rely on Christ to deliver us from evil, who through His death destroyed "him that had the power of death, that is, the devil" (Hebrews 2:14).

Judah Faces Assyria

At the time of Israel's final collapse, Judah was still surviving. Judah had her spiritual low times too. But occasionally God used righteous kings such as Hezekiah and Josiah to bring revival. As a result, Judah lasted almost a century and a half longer than Israel.

You have already learned how Ahaz was forced to accept Assyrian control over Judah. In the process, he gave the gold of the temple to the king of Assyria and gave up the independence of his people. Ahaz also brought foreign idols to Judah, which became "the ruin of him, and of all Israel" (2 Chronicles 28:23).

During Ahaz's miserable reign, the prophets Isaiah and Micah called the people to return to the Lord, trust and obey Him, and practice fairness and mercy again. But since Ahaz refused to listen, most of the people would not listen either.

But the next king was Hezekiah, and he started a great revival. Once again God's people gathered for a Passover. It was a month late that year, but they still observed it.

When a new Assyrian king, Sennacherib, came to the throne, Hezekiah rebelled against the Assyrians, making secret treaties with Babylon and Egypt. He felt he could do this because the rebellious Babylonians were keeping the Assyrians busy in another part of the empire, and because Egypt offered him some support.

When the Assyrian army finally approached the land of Judah, Hezekiah and the people stopped the springs around Jerusalem, saying, "Why should the kings of Assyria come, and find much water?" (2 Chronicles 32:4). He also stopped the spring Gihon (GY hahn) outside the wall of Jerusalem. His workmen cut a tunnel more than 1,700 feet long (518 m) under the city wall to bring its water to the pool of Siloam

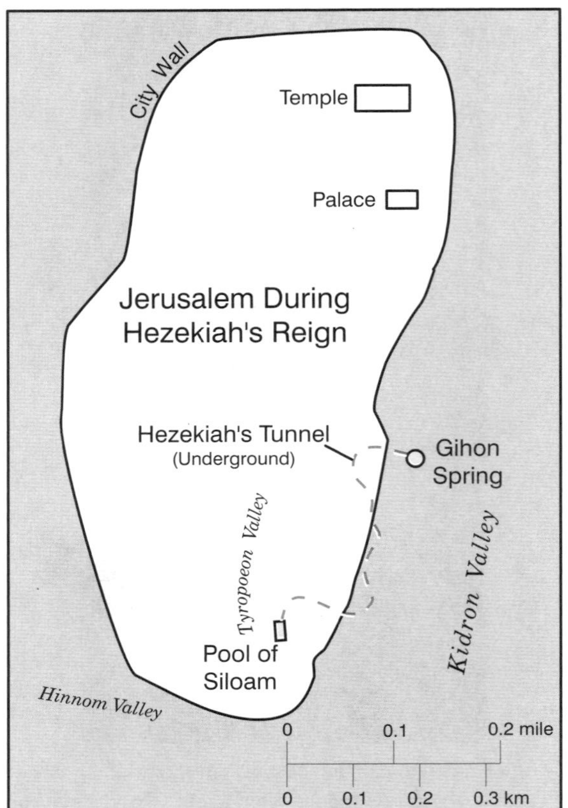

Figure 11:2. Hezekiah's Tunnel

(sy LOH uhm) inside the city. That tunnel was discovered by accident in A.D. 1880 and may still be seen today, for it was cut through solid rock.

Investigators discovered in the tunnel an inscription written in ancient Hebrew characters. Following is a translation.

> The boring through is completed, and this was the story of the boring through. While the workmen were cutting their way from opposite ends, and while there were still three cubits to be bored through, they heard voices calling from each side, for there was a crevice in the rock. And on the day when the boring was completed, the stone cutters hacked their way toward each other until they met. Then the water flowed from the spring to the pool twelve hundred cubits, and the height of the rock above the heads of the stone cutters was a hundred cubits.

Hezekiah needed the tunnel soon after his workmen finished it. Around 701 B.C., Sennacherib attacked Judah and captured forty-six towns. Perhaps Hezekiah had second thoughts about his rebellion, for he sent word to the Assyrians, "I have offended; return from me: that which thou puttest on me will I bear" (2 Kings 18:14).

According to the Jewish historian Josephus (joh SEE fuhs), the Assyrians promised to leave him in peace if he paid three hundred talents of silver and thirty talents of gold. Hezekiah paid the price, removing gold and silver from the temple for part of it. But Sennacherib was still determined to capture Jerusalem.

As usual, the Assyrians tried to terrorize the people they wanted to conquer. An Assyrian officer came and shouted to the people on the city wall, trying to frighten them into surrender. The Assyrians had beaten every other city, he boasted, and Jerusalem did not have a chance. He said that starving in Jerusalem was much worse than being deported "to a land like your own land, a land of corn and wine, a land of bread and vineyards" (2 Kings 18:32).

But Hezekiah and his men of war knew that they would get no corn and wine. Once in the hands of the Assyrians, they might be torn apart. No wonder Hezekiah prayed earnestly to the Lord. At that moment of helplessness, God gave Hezekiah an amazing deliverance. During the night, the angel of the Lord killed 185,000 Assyrian soldiers. A famous poem called "The Destruction of Sennacherib" describes that fateful night.

And what do the records of the proud Assyrians say about such a crushing defeat? Sennacherib recorded that he captured forty-six of Hezekiah's cities and shut up Hezekiah in Jerusalem "like a bird in a cage." It is

The Tigris flows on, but Sennacherib's boasting has crumbled in the dust. Here, the remains of his once-grand castle lie in ruins. The scene reminds us of Solomon's words: "What profit hath a man of all his labour which he taketh under the sun? One generation passeth away, and another generation cometh: but the earth abideth for ever. . . . There is no remembrance of former things; neither shall there be any remembrance of things that are to come with those that shall come after" (Ecclesiastes 1:3, 4, 11).

interesting, though, that he did not claim to have conquered Jerusalem. If he had taken the city, he certainly would have boasted about it. Sennacherib said nothing concerning the thousands of soldiers he lost. No Assyrian king would have admitted that such a thing could happen to him.

Sennacherib was killed shortly afterward, and Esarhaddon (ehz ur HAD uhn) took the Assyrian throne.

God Delivers Judah

> "And it came to pass that night, that the angel of the LORD went out, and smote in the camp of the Assyrians an hundred fourscore and five thousand: and when they arose early in the morning, behold, they were all dead corpses. So Sennacherib king of Assyria departed, and went and returned, and dwelt at Nineveh. And it came to pass, as he was worshipping in the house of Nisroch his god, that Adrammelech and Sharezer his sons smote him with the sword: and they escaped into the land of Armenia. And Esarhaddon his son reigned in his stead" (2 Kings 19:35–37).

When Hezekiah died, twelve-year-old Manasseh became king. He submitted to the Assyrians, and for a time they left him in peace. However, he was one of Judah's most wicked and idolatrous kings. Ancient Jewish writers say that Isaiah was "sawn asunder" at Manasseh's command. (If this tradition is true, Hebrews 11:37 includes Isaiah.)

God warned Manasseh of His judgment on sin, but Manasseh would not listen. So once again God used the Assyrians to accomplish His purpose. Esarhaddon made war with Manasseh, captured him, and carried him off to Babylon. Finding himself a prisoner, Manasseh humbled himself and turned to the Lord. Amazingly, in spite of all his former wickedness, the Lord restored him to his kingdom. Manasseh genuinely repented, but his sin had been so great that he has always been remembered more for his wickedness than for his repentance.

Manasseh's Captivity and Repentance

> "And the LORD spake to Manasseh, and to his people: but they would not hearken. Wherefore the LORD brought upon them the captains of the host of

> the king of Assyria, which took Manasseh among the thorns, and bound him with fetters, and carried him to Babylon. And when he was in affliction, he besought the LORD his God, and humbled himself greatly before the God of his fathers, and prayed unto him: and he was intreated of him, and heard his supplication, and brought him again to Jerusalem into his kingdom. Then Manasseh knew that the LORD he was God" (2 Chronicles 33:10–13).

Assyria reached its greatest strength during Manasseh's reign. Esarhaddon was killed during his campaign against Egypt, but his son Ashurbanipal (ah shur BAH nuh pahl) destroyed Thebes (THEEBZ), the capital of upper Egypt. (Thebes is called No in the Bible.) But Ashurbanipal could not completely subdue the Egyptians. Perhaps it was a sign that Assyria would not always prevail.

Ashurbanipal was the last great king of Assyria. During his reign, Nineveh was still enjoying its peak of glory. Ashurbanipal is remembered for his love of collecting old records. He gathered thousands of cuneiform clay tablets into a large library, which archaeologists discovered in the 1800s. The documents, old letters, and history have taught us much about Assyrian culture.

Study Exercises

12. Which king started a revival in Judah after the wicked reign of Ahaz?
13. Why did Hezekiah have a tunnel dug under the wall of Jerusalem?
14. How did Manasseh manage to keep peace with the Assyrians for a time?
15. Name in order the three Assyrian kings mentioned in this section.
16. How did Ashurbanipal contribute to our knowledge of Assyrian history?

The Fall of Assyria

Constant warfare weakens a nation. The Assyrians did not pay enough attention to farming and business. Many of their strong men were too busy fighting, or had been killed in battle.

Jonah's revival had long since faded, and now the prophets Zephaniah and Nahum were predicting that Nineveh would be destroyed. This time the Ninevites did not repent. Their walls were as much as a 100 feet high (30 m), and so thick that three or four chariots could ride abreast on the top. A ***moat*** full of water lay just outside the wall. Who or what could harm them?

In 612 B.C., an army of Babylonians and Medes besieged Nineveh. At first the Ninevites were not too alarmed. They had plenty of food in the city and could wait. But then a flood caused part of the walls around Nineveh to collapse, and the besieging army marched right in.

When the king of Nineveh saw what was happening, he burned his palace down over his wealth, his wives, and himself. Nineveh was completely overthrown. For centuries, all that remained of the city was a mound. Archaeologists have now dug up some of its ruins.

Zephaniah Foretells the Destruction of Nineveh

> "And he [the Lord] will stretch out his hand against the north, and destroy Assyria; and will make Nineveh a desolation, and dry like a wilderness. And flocks shall lie down in the midst of her, all the beasts of the nations: both the cormorant and the bittern shall lodge in the upper lintels of it; their voice shall sing in the windows; desolation shall be in the thresholds: for he shall uncover the cedar work. This is the rejoicing city that dwelt carelessly, that said

The mound in the background is all that remains of Nineveh.

in her heart, I am, and there is none beside me: how is she become a desolation, a place for beasts to lie down in! every one that passeth by her shall hiss, and wag his hand" (Zephaniah 2:13–15).

Assyrian power crumbled quickly after the destruction of Nineveh. Other powers—Babylonia and Egypt—were rising. About 609 B.C., Pharaoh Necho (NEE koh) of Egypt marched north through Canaan to try to help the remaining Assyrians defeat the Babylonians. When King Josiah of Judah tried to block his path, Necho killed him and went on.

The Jews anointed Jehoahaz, a son of Josiah, as the next king. But three months later, Necho replaced him with his brother Jehoiakim, a king of his own choosing. (Jehoiakim was the infamous bookburner of Jeremiah 36.) Jehoiakim taxed the land to raise tribute for Necho (2 Kings 23:30–35).

Several years later, the armies of the Egyptians and the Babylonians clashed at the great battle of Carchemish (KAHR kuh mihsh). The Babylonians defeated the Egyptians, as described in Jeremiah 46. They took "from the river of Egypt unto the river Euphrates all that pertained to the king of Egypt" (2 Kings 24:7). Meanwhile, the once-mighty Assyrian Empire toppled completely—only about twenty years after Ashurbanipal's death.

Now the people of Judah had to deal with the Babylonians instead of the Assyrians or the Egyptians. When the Babylonians challenged Judah, King Jehoiakim became their servant. God was showing that He "is the judge: he putteth down one, and setteth up another" (Psalm 75:7).

Study Exercises

17. How does warfare weaken a nation?
18. How did a flood help to defeat the Assyrians?
19. Name in order the three kings of Judah mentioned in this section.
20. Which king of Judah lost his life while trying to stop the Egyptian army?
21. At the battle of Carchemish, what power emerged as the winner?

Clinching the Chapter

Multiple Choice

A. *Write the word or phrase* least *associated with the first item.*

1. Assyria: Tigris, Iraq, Jordan, Calah
2. Adopted by Assyrians: writing, true worship, art, architecture
3. Assyrian methods of control: terror, deportation, tribute, trade
4. Assyrians noted for: mail, aqueducts, warfare, manufacturing
5. Lived at same time: Manasseh, Pekah, Rezin, Ahaz
6. Idol worshipers: Sennacherib, Hezekiah, Jehu, Ahaz
7. Jerusalem: Gihon, Siloam, zoo, temple
8. Hezekiah: revival, Passover, treaties, deportation
9. Fall of Nineveh: flood, fire, fighting, famine
10. Spoke against Nineveh: Jonah, Nahum, Jeremiah, Zephaniah

B. *Write the correct words.*

1. The Assyrians terrorized their neighbors in order to (make them give up more easily, reduce their population, get more of their riches, frighten them away).
2. The last king of Israel was (Pekah, Menahem, Hoshea, Rezin).
3. The Assyrian king who besieged Samaria about 725 B.C. was (Shalmaneser III, Tiglath-pileser III, Shalmaneser V, Sennacherib).
4. What has provided the most information about Assyria? (Pul's mail system, Ashurbanipal's library, Sennacherib's park, Sennacherib's aqueduct)
5. A "melting pot" as used in this chapter is (a very warm climate, a mixing of peoples, a postal system, tribute gathered from many lands).
6. Judah lasted longer than Israel because it had (some righteous kings, a more defensible position, a submissive attitude, better ties with Egypt).
7. What did the Assyrians want most from lands they had conquered? (loyalty, tribute, deportation, communication)
8. Hezekiah provided Jerusalem with (a reliable source of water, a reliable source of food, places of idol worship, a moat around its wall).
9. In this chapter, Judah had to submit to all but (Syria, Egypt, Assyria, Babylonia).
10. Which king died a natural death? (Sennacherib, Hezekiah, Esarhaddon, Josiah)

Matching

A. *For each clue, write the correct name from the right-hand column.*

1. A spring	Babylon
2. Where Egypt was defeated	Carchemish
3. Was carried captive by Sargon	Egypt
4. Where Manasseh was taken as a captive	Gihon
5. Modern name for where Assyria began	Iraq
6. Offered help but did not give it	Israel
7. Capital of upper Egypt	Judah
8. Capital of Assyria	Nineveh
9. Kings included Ahaz, Hezekiah, Manasseh, Josiah	Samaria
10. Capital of Israel	Thebes

B. *Match as in Part A.*

1. Joined Rezin in rebellion against Assyria	Ahab
2. Lived in the time of Shalmaneser	Ashur
3. Was taken captive by Esarhaddon	Ashurbanipal
4. Name for one of the pharaohs	God
5. Planned a water tunnel for Jerusalem	Hezekiah
6. Used Assyria for his "axe"	Isaiah
7. Collected cuneiform tablets	Manasseh
8. Assyrian god	Menahem
9. Paid tribute to Tiglath-pileser	Necho
10. Was martyred during Manasseh's reign	Pekah

Completion

1. Ancient armies building up their forces
Quickly saw the worth of using ———.
2. Ahab and his sons did worse than fail;
They encouraged worshipers of ———.
3. Stone was used in order to construct
A waterway we call an ———.
4. Great Nineveh seemed very safe and sound,
Yet in the end was nothing but a ———.
5. Once a bold Assyrian message bearer
Tried to scare the Jews by using ———.
6. Faithful kings were few—but good Josiah
Followed in the steps of ———.

Thought Questions

1. The Assyrians used a relay system to carry messages. How does such a system work?
2. What happened to the strangers who were moved into the land of Israel after the Israelites were deported? Answer with several sentences, using information from 2 Kings 17:24–41.
3. What the Assyrian records do not say is as important as what they do say. How is this illustrated by the story of Sennacherib's defeat?
4. In this chapter, what are two examples of God's great mercy to repentant sinners?
5. (*a*) What three cities named in this chapter were besieged? (*b*) How did attacking armies hope to conquer a city by besieging it?

Geographical Skills

1. About how far was Tyre from Nineveh?
2. Challenge Question: Jonah tried to flee from delivering God's message to Nineveh by boarding a ship that was bound for Tarshish. If he had made it to Tarshish, about how far would he have been from Nineveh? (It is thought that Tarshish was located near the Strait of Gibraltar, in what is now southern Spain.)

Further Study

1. The Assyrians were by no means the last people to use terrorism. Study about terrorist groups of recent history, and write a short description of their methods and the results of them.
2. Describe aqueducts used today.

The Jews hang their harps on the willows in Babylon.

12 Judah Under the Neo-Babylonians and Persians

650 B.C.

Nabopolassar throws off Assyrian rule and reigns in Babylon. 626–605

Daniel and other Jewish captives are taken to Babylon. 605

Nebuchadnezzar extends the Neo-Babylonian Empire. 605–561

600

Jehoiachin, Ezekiel, and other captives are taken to Babylon. 597

Jerusalem falls to the Babylonians. 586

Evil-merodach reigns in Babylon and frees Jehoiachin. 561–560

Cyrus rules the Persian Empire. 559–530

550

Nabonidus and Belshazzar rule Babylonia. 555–539

Babylon falls to the Medes and the Persians. 539

Cyrus allows the Jews to return to Jerusalem. 537

Darius the Great rules the Persian Empire. 522–486

500

The Greeks win the battle at Marathon. 490

The Greeks defeat the Persians at Salamis. 480

Ezra leads a large group of Jews to Jerusalem. 458

450

Nehemiah rebuilds the walls of Jerusalem. 444

400

350

The Persian Empire falls to Alexander the Great. 334–323

300 B.C.

"By the rivers of Babylon, there we sat down, yea, we wept, when we remembered Zion."
Psalm 137:1

Judah Under the Neo-Babylonians and Persians

Neo-Babylonia Arises

You learned about Hammurabi and the Old Babylonian Empire in Chapter 7. In this chapter, you will study the Neo-Babylonian Empire that arose hundreds of years later in the same area of southern Mesopotamia. (*Neo-* means "new.") This new empire had kings such as Nebuchadnezzar (nehb uh kuhd NEHZ ur) and Belshazzar (behl SHAZ ur). What happened between the times of those two great empires?

When the strength of the first Babylonian Empire declined, the Hittites ***plundered*** and destroyed much of Babylon. Various powers ruled Babylon after this. When the Assyrians grew strong, they took control of the region.

The Babylonians revolted against the Assyrians several times. The most notable of these revolts were led by the Chaldeans, a group of tribes who had settled in southern Babylonia. You read about one such revolt in Chapter 11, when Hezekiah joined in their uprising. That time the rebel Chaldean king of Babylon was Merodach-baladan (meh ROH dak BAL uh dan), from whom Hezekiah received a present after he had been sick. The rebellion was crushed, however, and the Chaldeans had to flee.

Later the picture changed. You may recall that when the Assyrian king Ashurbanipal died, Assyria was at the point of collapse. A Chaldean named Nabopolassar (nab oh poh LAY sur) took advantage of this and set up his own kingdom. He joined his Babylonian army with the Medes and others, and together they destroyed Nineveh.

Nebuchadnezzar Appears

At the historic battle of Carchemish a few years later, Nabopolassar's son Nebuchadnezzar commanded the Babylonian army. The Babylonians defeated the

This is an artist's idea of the royal palaces at Nineveh. Notice the Assyrian-style relief artwork on some of the buildings.

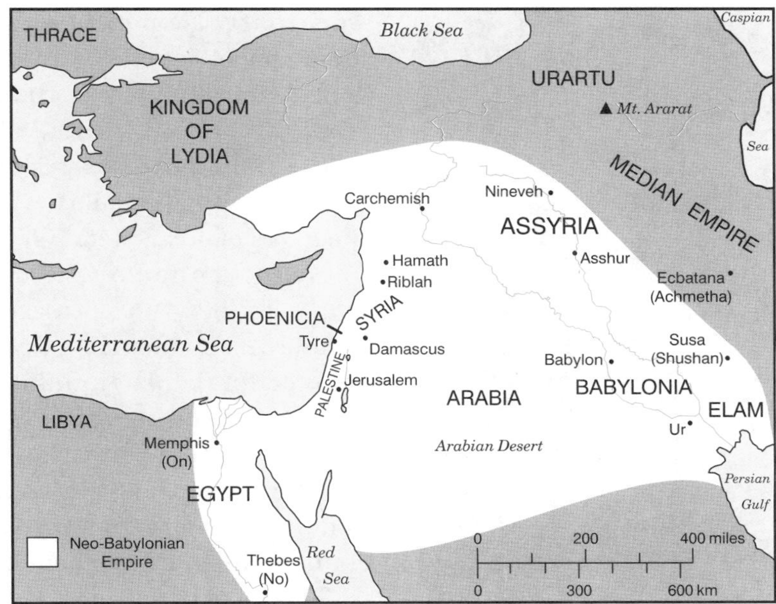

Figure 12:1. The Neo-Babylonian Empire

Egyptians and the remaining Assyrians. Soon afterward, hearing that his father had died, Nebuchadnezzar hurried back to Babylon to claim the throne for himself. He would reign as the second king of Neo-Babylonia for forty-three years.

It was a turbulent world. Now that Assyria had collapsed, nations that had been subject to Assyria were quick to say, "We are free!" But Nebuchadnezzar made sure that those countries, such as Syria and Phoenicia, soon came under the iron hand of Babylon. He strengthened Babylonia and expanded it all the way to the border of Egypt.

God Raises Up Babylon

"I [the Lord] have made the earth, the man and the beast that are upon the ground, by my great power and by my outstretched arm, and have given it unto whom it seemed meet unto me. And now have I given all these lands into the hand of Nebuchadnezzar the king of Babylon, my servant; and the beasts of the field have I given him also to serve him. And all nations shall serve him, and his son, and his son's son, until the very time of his land come: and then many nations and great kings shall serve themselves of him" (Jeremiah 27:5–7).

Study Exercises

1. What empire kept Neo-Babylonia from rising to power sooner than it did?
2. Who was the famous son of Nabopolassar?
3. How was the battle of Carchemish important to the Babylonians?

Jerusalem Falls

Nebuchadnezzar took captives from Jerusalem three times. The first time was in the third year of King Jehoiakim, about 605 B.C. Nebuchadnezzar took Daniel and other Hebrews to Babylon, along with some vessels from the temple. This was probably the time when he "bound [Jehoiakim] in fetters, to carry him to Babylon" (2 Chronicles 36:6).

An artist's idea of Babylon at the height of its power. It was the greatest city of the world in its day. But when Nebuchadnezzar began to think he was the greatest man in the world, God made him realize that He was Ruler of the world. "There fell a voice from heaven, saying, O king Nebuchadnezzar, to thee it is spoken; The kingdom is departed from thee. And they shall drive thee from men, and thy dwelling shall be with the beasts of the field... until thou know that the most High ruleth in the kingdom of men, and giveth it to whomsoever he will" (Daniel 4:31, 32).

Apparently Nebuchadnezzar changed his mind and let Jehoiakim return to his throne. Jehoiakim submitted to the Babylonians for several years but then rebelled. Because of Jehoiakim's wickedness, Jeremiah prophesied that his body would be "cast forth beyond the gates of Jerusalem" (Jeremiah 22:19).

Nebuchadnezzar subdued Jerusalem again in 597 B.C., three months after Jehoiakim's death. Jehoiakim's son Jehoiachin (jeh HOI uh kihn) surrendered and was taken to Babylon. Another well-known captive in this group was the prophet Ezekiel. Nebuchadnezzar set Jehoiakim's brother on the throne and changed his name to Zedekiah.

The third incident was the hardest, both for the Jews and for the Babylonians. King Zedekiah had promised loyalty to Babylon, but later he rebelled. While Nebuchadnezzar's army besieged Jerusalem, Zedekiah kept hoping that the Egyptians would come and help him. He refused to surrender, even though the prophet Jeremiah urged him to do so.

Finally, when the people in Jerusalem were starving, the Babylonians forced their way into the city. Zedekiah fled, but Nebuchadnezzar's army caught him near Jericho. They killed his sons in front of his eyes. Then they put out his eyes and took

On the left side of the picture, a Babylonian king stands while a servant fans him. A subject shows respect by bowing in front of him while another prepares to shake his hand.

A glazed brick lion from ancient Babylon.

him in chains to Babylon in 586 B.C. The Babylonians plundered and burned Jerusalem.

Nebuchadnezzar set up a governor over the few poor people he left in the land. But if he thought that everyone in Judah had learned to submit to him, he was mistaken. A rebel band soon killed the governor he had appointed. Then fearing Nebuchadnezzar's revenge for the ***assassination,*** the people fled to Egypt, taking Jeremiah with them. However, this was direct disobedience to God, for Jeremiah had told them to remain in the land. They soon found that Egypt was no safe refuge. Nebuchadnezzar invaded it less than twenty years later.

Jeremiah had prophesied that the Jews would be captives for seventy years (Jeremiah 25:11). The seventy-year captivity began in several stages, as you have seen. It also ended over a period of time, as you will see later.

Study Exercises

4. Name two famous Jewish prophets who were taken to Babylon.
5. To what vain hope did Zedekiah cling?
6. How did the Jews resist Babylonian government even after the fall of Jerusalem?
7. How did the remaining Jews show their rebellion against God?

The Hanging Gardens of Babylon were irrigated with water from the Euphrates River. The gardens were elevated, but they did not actually hang. Many people think that the ziggurat in the background is the Tower of Babel.

Life in Babylon

Jeremiah advised the Jews in Babylon that since their captivity would be long, they should build houses, plant gardens, and plan to stay in Babylon for many years (Jeremiah 29:4–7). The Babylonians did not scatter the Jews as the Assyrians might have done, so they were able to live together in communities. They began working as farmers and businessmen, and some of them became wealthy and influential.

The Jews in Babylon often thought of their temple in Jerusalem. But now they could not go there for worship; and besides, Nebuchadnezzar's army had destroyed the temple. So they established ***synagogues*** in various communities. There they could pray, study the Word of God, and receive teaching from their leaders. Synagogues were so common among the Jews that they became the centers of Jewish life.

Nebuchadnezzar was a mighty conqueror, but he took his greatest delight in building Babylon. His palace was large and beautiful. He built what is called the Hanging Gardens to please his wife, who was homesick for the mountains of her native country. (The area around Babylon is flat.) The Hanging Gardens were made of huge columns and great arches that supported terraces filled with flowers and trees. The Hanging Gardens became known as one of the Seven Wonders of the Ancient World.

The exact size of Babylon is not known, but the double walls seem to have been about 11 miles (18 km) around. They were at least 50 feet high (15 m), and they were wide enough on top for two chariots to pass. The outer wall had more than 150 watchtowers spaced at regular intervals. Outside the walls, a deep moat surrounded the city.

All this made Babylon the most magnificent city in the world. But God, who lives in a truly glorious city, was not impressed. When Nebuchadnezzar boasted of how great and powerful he was, God smote him with insanity for a time. This was God's way of showing him "that the most High ruleth in the kingdom of men, and giveth it to whomsoever he will" (Daniel 4:25).

Nebuchadnezzar's successor, Evil-merodach (EE vihl meh ROH dak), was the king who took Jehoiachin out of the dungeon and treated him kindly (Jeremiah 52:31–34). After several other men reigned for a short time, Nabonidus (nab uh NY dus) came to the throne. He was an intelligent man who loved to study old writings and archaeology, and he spent some of his time traveling. He also tried to change some of Babylon's religious practices, which angered many Babylonians. Nabonidus set up his son Belshazzar as king in Babylon while he went elsewhere. One record says that he remarked, "But I kept myself afar from my city of Babylon . . . ten years to my city Babylon I went not in."

Since Babylon already had two kings, it is understandable why Belshazzar later proclaimed Daniel the *third* ruler in the kingdom rather than the second (Daniel 5:29).

Many Babylonians did not like either Nabonidus or Belshazzar. The Neo-Babylonian Empire had been a world power for less than one hundred years, but its end was drawing near.

Study Exercises

8. What Jewish institution was begun during the seventy-year captivity?
9. What chapter in the Bible records the story of Nebuchadnezzar's insanity?
10. According to what you have read here, which came first—the event of Jeremiah 52:31–34 or of Daniel 4:31–34?
11. What king had authority over King Belshazzar?

One of the gates of ancient Babylon, called the Ishtar gate, was partially preserved amid the rubble of the fallen city.

Babylon Falls to the Medes and Persians

Trouble was brewing in the mountains to the east. The Medes had once been friendly toward the Babylonians, but that good feeling had disappeared. About 559 B.C., a Persian named Cyrus revolted against his Median masters and made himself king. While Nabonidus and Belshazzar ruled over the Babylonian Empire, Cyrus was strengthening and expanding the empire of the Medes and Persians.

Capturing Babylon appeared difficult at first for Cyrus. Babylon's high double walls and deep moat provided a good defense against invading armies. But Cyrus eyed the Euphrates River that flowed under the city walls and through Babylon. If a river could get into the city and out again, why not an army?

Cyrus's men built an earthen dam; and when all was ready, they diverted the flow of the river. Soon the riverbed was a broad path that allowed Cyrus's army to walk right under the wall. That very night Daniel read the inscription that a hand had mysteriously written on the palace wall during Belshazzar's wild party (Daniel 5). By morning, Belshazzar was dead—slain by Cyrus's invading army. The year was 539 B.C., and the Medes and Persians now ruled Babylon.

What about Darius (duh RY uhs) the Mede, of whom the Bible speaks in Daniel 6? It appears that Cyrus set up Darius as the king, or governor, of Babylon. Cyrus, who had taken the city, was the supreme ruler over the whole empire, and Darius served as a local king under his authority.

The Jews Return to Jerusalem

Cyrus was careful to treat his subjects well. He did not accept the Assyrian idea that people had to be crushed in order to keep them down. He allowed local officials to keep their positions, and he respected the religions of the peoples he had conquered. He believed that if he respected people's gods, the people would respect him in turn.

But he may have had more than the usual amount of respect for the God of the Jews. No one knows how much contact the Jews had with Cyrus as a new king. It is possible that he had an interview with Daniel, who by then would have been an old man. If

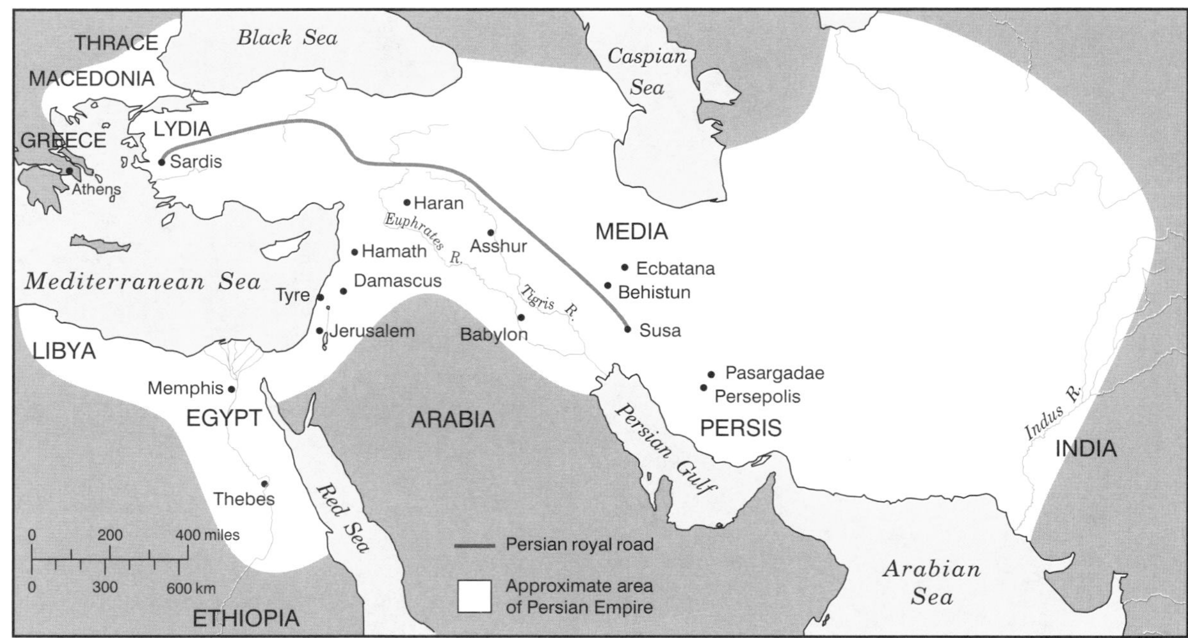

Figure 12:2. The Persian Empire

Daniel showed him the Scriptures, Cyrus must have been astounded to see his own name in a book written 150 years before.

God Calls Cyrus by Name

> "Thus saith the LORD, . . . I am the LORD that maketh all things; . . . that saith of Cyrus, He is my shepherd, and shall perform all my pleasure: even saying to Jerusalem, Thou shalt be built; and to the temple, Thy foundation shall be laid.
>
> Thus saith the LORD to his anointed, to Cyrus, whose right hand I have holden, to subdue nations before him; and I will loose the loins of kings, to open before him the two leaved gates; and the gates shall not be shut; I will go before thee, and make the crooked places straight: I will break in pieces the gates of brass, and cut in sunder the bars of iron: and I will give thee the treasures of darkness, and hidden riches of secret places, that thou mayest know that I, the LORD, which call thee by thy name, am the God of Israel. For Jacob my servant's sake, and Israel mine elect, I have even called thee by thy name: I have surnamed thee, though thou hast not known me.
>
> I am the LORD, and there is none else, there is no God beside me: I girded thee, though thou hast not known me: that they may know from the rising of the sun, and from the west, that there is none beside me. I am the LORD, and there is none else" (Isaiah 44:24, 28; 45:1–6).

Hearing that God promised, "I will go before thee, and . . . break in pieces the gates of brass," perhaps Cyrus thought of the brass gates of Babylon that he had conquered. Of course no one can be sure of Cyrus's thoughts at this time. But it is certain that he made the proclamation recorded in 2 Chronicles 36:23: "All the kingdoms of the earth hath the LORD God of heaven given me; and he hath charged me to build him an house in Jerusalem, which is in Judah. Who is there among you of all his people? The LORD his God be with him, and let him go up."

More than forty thousand Jews answered the call and returned to Jerusalem. Cyrus even allowed them to carry along gold, silver, and the temple vessels that the Babylonians had removed. God used Cyrus to free the repentant Jews from their captivity in Babylon and to reestablish them in their homeland. The Book of Ezra tells the story.

The Persian Empire continued to expand until it was greater than the former Assyrian and Babylonian empires. It stretched from India to Ethiopia, and it included areas as far away as Libya and part of modern Greece.

When Cyrus was killed, he was succeeded by his son Cambyses (kam BY seez), who is remembered today for his hot temper. Cambyses defeated Egypt after a long struggle, but he died before he got back to Persia. In the later years of Cyrus's reign, and during Cambyses' reign, the work on the temple at Jerusalem came to a halt. Cambyses did not support the work, and the Israelites became more concerned about their own fields and houses than about God's house.

Cambyses was succeeded by Darius—not the Mede this time, but Darius the Great. This king made it clear that he was returning to Cyrus's policy of friendliness toward the Jews. Darius even commanded that the taxes paid by the people of Palestine should go toward building the temple (Ezra 6:6–12).

And so the seventy-year captivity came to an end. From the time the first captives left Jerusalem to the time the first captives returned was seventy years. And from the time the temple was destroyed to the time it was rebuilt was also seventy years.

This ancient Babylonian brick tower was probably a place of religious worship. It is 100 feet high (30.5 m) and is located at Baghdad, Iraq.

What was the religion of Darius? It may have been Zoroastrianism (zor oh AS tree uhn ihzm), which was introduced around 600 B.C. by a man named Zoroaster (ZOR oh as tur). This man taught that the world is a battleground between good and evil, and between light and darkness. People should fight for the light, he said, for that side will finally win. Some of Zoroaster's teachings were similar to Bible truths, but his teaching also included errors. We must reject anything that does not agree with God's Word, for "all scripture is given by inspiration of God" (2 Timothy 3:16).

Study Exercises

12. What difficulties did Cyrus face in his effort to conquer Babylon?
13. Darius the Mede was an important character in what famous Bible story?

14. How was Cyrus's way of treating his subjects different from the Assyrians' way?
15. How was Darius the Great like Cyrus in his attitude toward the Jews?

Ups and Downs of the Persian Kings

Darius set up a systematic method of taxing people. He established standard measures, weights, and money. (We follow the same principle today: everyone's yardstick is the same length.) One of his great achievements was to dig a canal between the Nile River and the Red Sea. This was a forerunner of the Suez Canal.

Darius had workmen climb high up on a cliff, now called the Behistun Rock (bay hihs TOON), to write some records of his reign. They recorded the same story in three languages. One was in cuneiform, the wedge-shaped writing you read about before.

In 1835, a British army officer noticed the Behistun inscription and guessed correctly that the cuneiform said the same thing as the other two records. For many centuries before this, no one had been able to read cuneiform writing. But after archaeologists read one of the other languages, they could decipher what the cuneiform writing said. Just as scholars had learned to read hieroglyphics from the Rosetta Stone, they learned to read cuneiform writing from the Behistun Rock. The rock gives valuable information about the Persian Empire.

Darius the Great is also remembered for one of his defeats. In 490 B.C., his great Persian army attacked Greece to punish the Greeks for helping some cities near them to rebel against Persia. Darius wanted to add the small Greek states to the Persian Empire. The Greeks and Persians met on the plains of Marathon (MAR uh thahn) along the shores of Greece. (See map in Chapter 14.)

A view of Darius the Great's tomb, carved into a mountainside near Persepolis, Iran. Archaeologists work nearby.

The Greeks were badly outnumbered, but they finally decided to charge. They outfought the Persians, and the Persians had to retreat to their ships. The next day at Athens, the Greeks defeated the Persians again. Darius had to temporarily give up his plans to conquer Greece. He died before he could invade Greece again.

Darius's son Xerxes (ZURK seez) was another famous king. Some historians say he is the Ahasuerus (uh haz yoo EE rus) who married Esther (Esther 2:17). Xerxes ruled from Susa, or Shushan (SHOO shan), the capital. He did not need to make hanging gardens for his queen, for the countryside around Shushan had many mountains.

Xerxes invaded Greece as Darius had done. At first he seemed to be more successful than his father. His army even burned the main buildings in Athens. Then at the nearby bay of Salamis (SAL uh mihs), his Persian navy set out to defeat the Greek navy. Xerxes sat on a nearby hilltop to watch.

But the small Greek ships could move more quickly than the larger Persian vessels. The Greeks lured the Persians into fighting inside the bay, where their ships were so crowded together that they got in each other's way. Xerxes watched in helpless fury as the Greeks rammed and sank many of the Persian ships. The rest sailed away in disorder.

The defeat at Salamis in 480 B.C. dealt a heavy blow to the king's ambition of conquering the Greeks. Xerxes was disheartened and went back home.

The Persian kings were wise leaders in many ways. They borrowed ideas from their neighbors, such as the idea of minting metal coins. They built on what previous empires had done. The Assyrians had already built many roads; the Persians kept them up and built more. The Assyrians had developed a postal system; the Persians perfected it. Day and night, horsemen carried messages from one point to another in their relay system.

Persian kings could not change a law once they had made it. This prevented them from changing their minds repeatedly, but it sometimes caused serious trouble when a king made a mistake. Because Darius the Mede could not change his law against worshiping anyone but himself, Daniel had to spend a night in the lions' den. This custom continued in the time of Esther. After King Ahasuerus gave Haman the right to destroy the Jews, he could not change the decree. But he changed the effect of his mistake by allowing the Jews to stand together and resist their enemies. He even gave them some help.

Later Xerxes was assassinated, and his son Artaxerxes (ahr tuh ZURK seez) took the throne. He is called Artaxerxes Longimanus because his arms were unusually long. *Longimanus* means "the long-handed."

Under this king, Ezra led another large group of Jews to Jerusalem. But Ezra had a problem. During the seventy years of captivity, the Jews had begun using the language of the people around them. Many of them did not fully understand the Hebrew language anymore. So when Ezra read the law to them, he also "gave the sense, and caused them to understand the reading" (Nehemiah 8:8).

About thirteen years after Ezra went to Judah, Nehemiah received permission from Artaxerxes to return to Jerusalem and

These Persian spearmen are preserved on a wall in Iran. The Persians fought many enemies in establishing their empire, but they did not gain a reputation for cruelty such as the Assyrians had.

rebuild its walls. Apparently the king also appointed him as governor of Jerusalem. For a time he and Ezra worked together, helping to bring the people back to godly living and true worship.

The later Persian kings were weaker, and the Persian Empire began sliding downhill like the previous empires. Soon a young warrior from Macedonia, a land just north of Greece, would rise to conquer the world.

The Persians had done their part in preserving God's people. They had made an imprint on the world's history. Today, people in Iran claim the Persians as their ancestors.

Study Exercises

16. How is the Behistun Rock similar to the Rosetta Stone?
17. What country did Persia attack repeatedly but fail to crush?
18. Who is thought to have been a wife of Xerxes?
19. What two Jewish leaders were authorized by Artaxerxes to go to Palestine?
20. Ancient Persia was the forerunner of what modern country?

Clinching the Chapter

Multiple Choice

A. *Write the word or phrase* least *associated with the first item.*

1. Babylon: Nabopolassar, Nabonidus, Evil-merodach, Xerxes
2. Jews: Darius, Daniel, Ezekiel, Zedekiah
3. Kings: Jehoiakim, Jehoiachin, Ashurbanipal, Nehemiah
4. Empires: Assyria, Behistun, Babylon, Persia
5. Jewish captivity: seventy years, synagogue, Carchemish, Babylon
6. Babylon: Belshazzar, Esther, Hanging Gardens, Euphrates
7. Persians: Cyrus, Cambyses, Xerxes, Nabopolassar
8. Darius the Great: taxing, standard measures, synagogue, Behistun Rock
9. Return to Jerusalem: Belshazzar, Ezra, Nehemiah, Artaxerxes
10. Greeks: Marathon, Salamis, Athens, Euphrates

B. *Write the correct words.*

1. Of the following empires, the first to fall was (Persia, Neo-Babylonia, Assyria, Greece).
2. Zedekiah broke the promise of loyalty he had made to the (Assyrians, Babylonians, Egyptians, Jews).
3. Jeremiah told the Jews that their stay in Babylon would be (short, long, full of disturbances, prosperous).
4. God punished Nebuchadnezzar because of his (pride, violence, injustice, carelessness).
5. Just before Babylon was destroyed, Daniel became the "third ruler" under (Jehoiakim and Jehoiachin, Hezekiah and Zedekiah, Nebuchadnezzar and Darius, Nabonidus and Belshazzar).
6. The Medes and Persians defeated Babylon by diverting (an army, a river, a riot, food supplies).

7. Which of these kings came last? (Darius the Mede, Darius the Great, Xerxes, Cyrus)
8. It is an established fact that (Xerxes married Esther, God named Cyrus before he was born, Artaxerxes Longimanus's hands reached to his knees, Darius believed in Zoroastrianism).
9. Archaeologists learned to read cuneiform by (studying the Rosetta Stone, studying the Behistun Rock, discovering ancient clay tablets, researching modern libraries).
10. Two kings who regretted their own decrees were (Nebuchadnezzar and Nabonidus, Darius the Mede and Ahasuerus, Ezra and Nehemiah, Cyrus and Cambyses).

Matching

A. *For each clue, write the correct term from the right-hand column.*

Clue	Term
1. Key to cuneiform writing	Babylon
2. Where Babylon crushed Egypt	Babylonia
3. Site of Persian defeat on land	Behistun Rock
4. Both an old and a new empire	Carchemish
5. Site of Persian defeat on sea	Ethiopia
6. Distant corner of Persian Empire	Euphrates
7. One of the Seven Wonders of the Ancient World	Hanging Gardens
8. City of Nebuchadnezzar	Marathon
9. Jewish meetinghouse	Salamis
10. Was blocked during attack on Babylon	synagogue

B. *Match as in Part A.*

Clue	Term
1. King who preferred to study rather than rule	Cyrus
2. Was taken to Babylon with the first Jewish captives	Daniel
3. Sent Jews back to Jerusalem	Darius the Great
4. Was defeated at Salamis	Ezekiel
5. Greatest king of Neo-Babylonia	Jeremiah
6. Father of Nebuchadnezzar	Nabonidus
7. Last king of Judah	Nabopolassar
8. Prophesied a seventy-year captivity	Nebuchadnezzar
9. Encouraged renewed temple building	Xerxes
10. Was taken captive with Jehoiachin	Zedekiah

Who Are We?

1. When you look at my name, do not think of a chin,
   For the syllable last in my name is called "kin."
   Who am I?
2. Jeremiah once told us we should not refuse
   To be settled in Babylon. We are the ———.
3. Even I had to learn that to boast does not pay,
   And I lived in insanity many a day.
   Who am I?
4. With the Persians we marched, doing valorous deeds.
   Even Babylon fell to us. We are the ———.

5. Though my trusted man Daniel was faithful and pious,
   I ordered his death. I'm a Mede named ———.
6. Though Darius and Xerxes crossed mountains and creeks
   To defeat us, they never could. We are the ———.
7. Zoroastrianism says light will be master
   Over darkness. I taught this, for I'm ———.
8. To speak of my life, you must say that "God blessed her!"
   I was married to Xerxes. My name is called ———.

Thought Questions

1. Some captives are as important in history as kings are. What examples from this chapter can you give to illustrate this?
2. How could Nebuchadnezzar's insanity help him to see the truth?
3. In Daniel 8, verses 3 and 20, the ram representing the Medes and Persians had two horns, one longer than the other, with the longer horn coming up last. What is the meaning of this?
4. Why can no exact dates be given for the beginning and end of the seventy-year captivity?
5. Daniel may have been in his teens when Nebuchadnezzar took him captive. If this is correct, about how old was he when Darius the Mede had him thrown into the lions' den? (Clue: Daniel was thrown to the lions soon after Babylon fell.)

Geographical Skills

1. Trace Map A again, and label it "The Return Route of the Jewish Exiles."
2. Show the average annual precipitation on the map by using colors that are coded with a legend. (See Figure 5:5.)
3. Draw a line showing the route that the Jewish captives would likely have taken to and from Babylon. (They probably followed the important trade routes. See Figure 11:1.) Why would they not have taken the most direct route?
4. The Euphrates River flowed through the city of Babylon. Which was Babylon located closer to, the source of the river or the mouth of the river?

Further Study

1. What three books of the Bible are named after prophets living in the days of Ezra and Nehemiah?
2. How has Isaiah 13:17–22 been fulfilled?

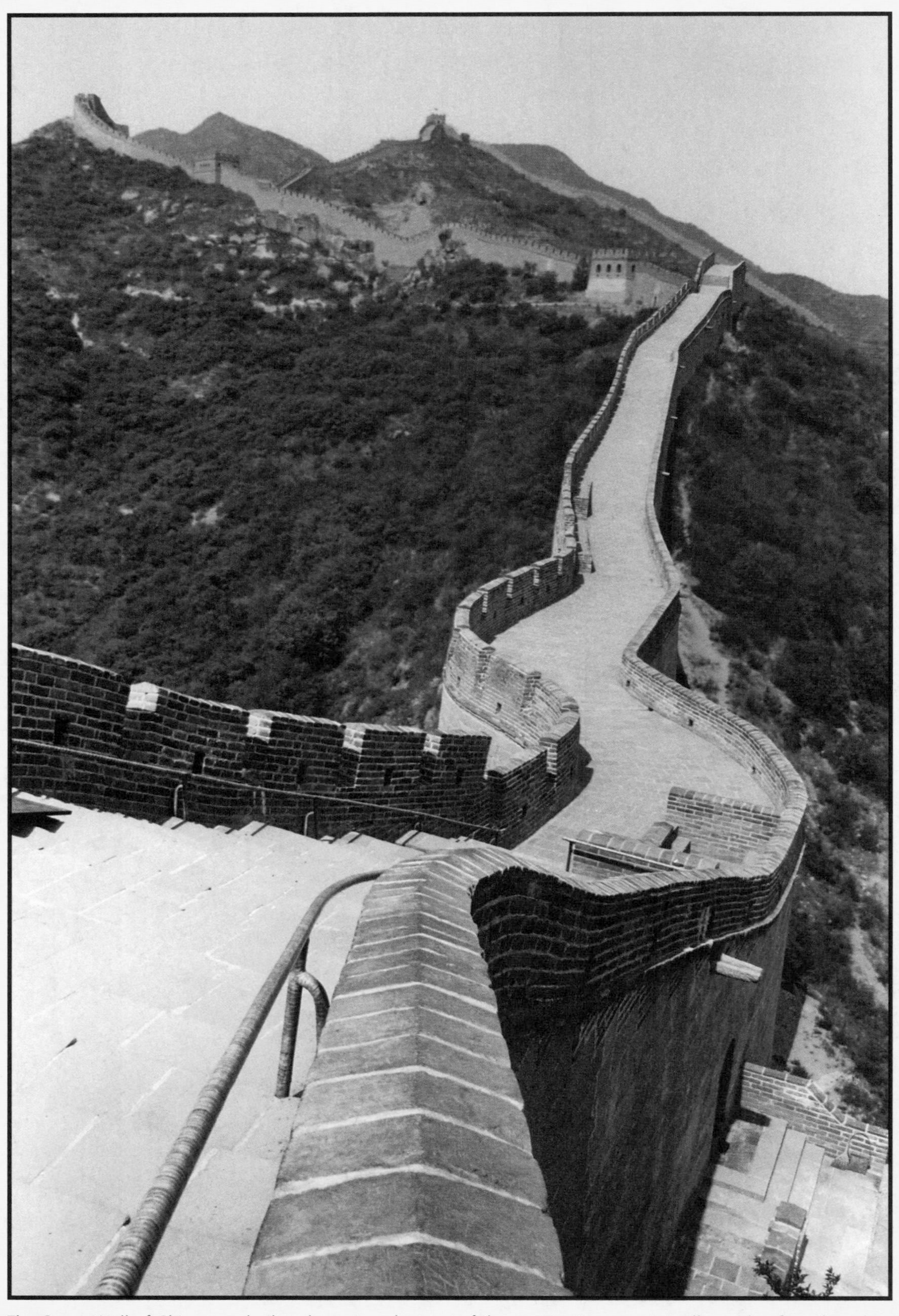

The Great Wall of China was built to keep invaders out of the country. It was originally made of earth and stone. Some parts, as the section shown in this picture, have been rebuilt and maintained as tourist attractions.

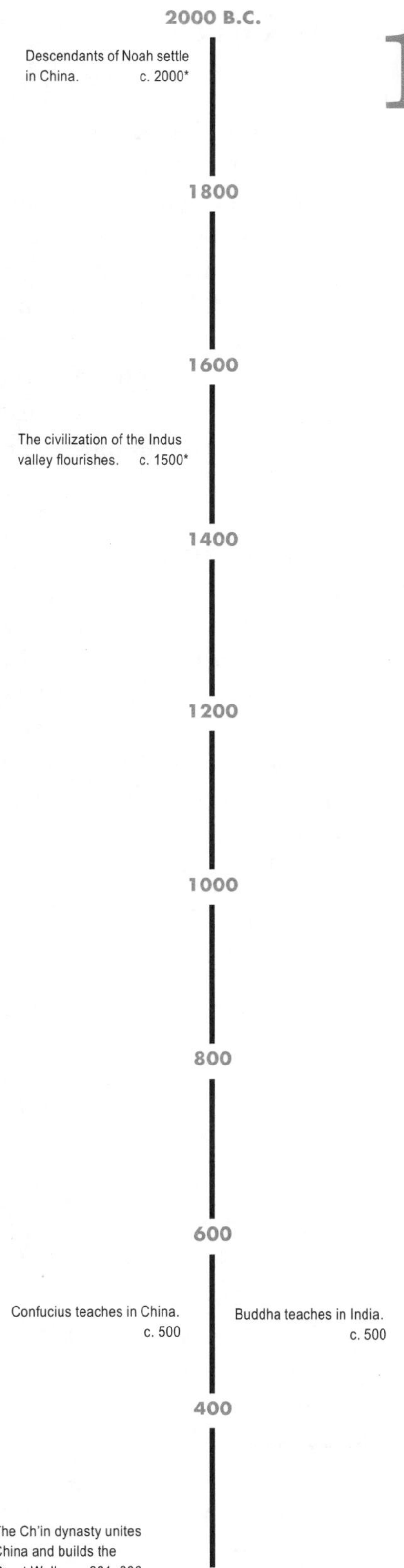
2000 B.C.
Descendants of Noah settle in China. c. 2000*
1800
1600
The civilization of the Indus valley flourishes. c. 1500*
1400
1200
1000
800
600
Confucius teaches in China. c. 500
Buddha teaches in India. c. 500
400
The Ch'in dynasty unites China and builds the Great Wall. 221–206
200 B.C.

13 Ancient History of India and China

Why Study the History of India and China?

Ancient History of India

The Caste System Develops

How Religion Grew in India

Ancient Culture of China

The Influence of Confucius

The Ch'in Dynasty and the Great Wall

And [God] hath made of one blood all nations of men for to dwell on all the face of the earth, and hath determined the times before appointed, and the bounds of their habitation.

Acts 17:26

Ancient History of India and China

Why Study the History of India and China?

You have already studied two cradles of civilization, as historians call them. One of them was along the Tigris and Euphrates Rivers. The other was in Egypt along the banks of the Nile. These early civilizations are important because many of their inventions and customs have come down to modern civilization.

In this chapter you will study two other ancient cradles of world civilization. They developed in southern and eastern Asia. Like the first two, they began along rivers.

The civilizations of ancient India and China do not affect most North Americans and Europeans as much as the other civilizations you have studied. Yet some of the ancient Asians might be influencing you more than you realize.

For example, the people of ancient India helped to develop the number system most commonly used today. Our Arabic numerals—1, 2, 3, and so on—may also be called Hindu-Arabic numerals. The ancient Hindus invented place value for numerals. In other words, they decided that a 7 in the tens' place should be worth ten times as much as a 7 in the ones' place. The Hindus also invented the zero to show when a place value is empty. The Arabs learned this numeral system from the Hindus and spread its use into Europe.

Studying the ancient history of Asia helps us to understand the people who live there today. It shows why their thinking and habits are so different from (or similar to) our own.

Ancient History of India

Historians have found it difficult to learn much about the ancient history of India. The ancient Indians did not build stone pyramids, as the Egyptians did, to last for thousands of years. Many of their buildings were made of wood that finally collapsed and rotted away. Only a few of their writings have been found, and they are written in a long-forgotten language. They have puzzled everyone who tries to read them.

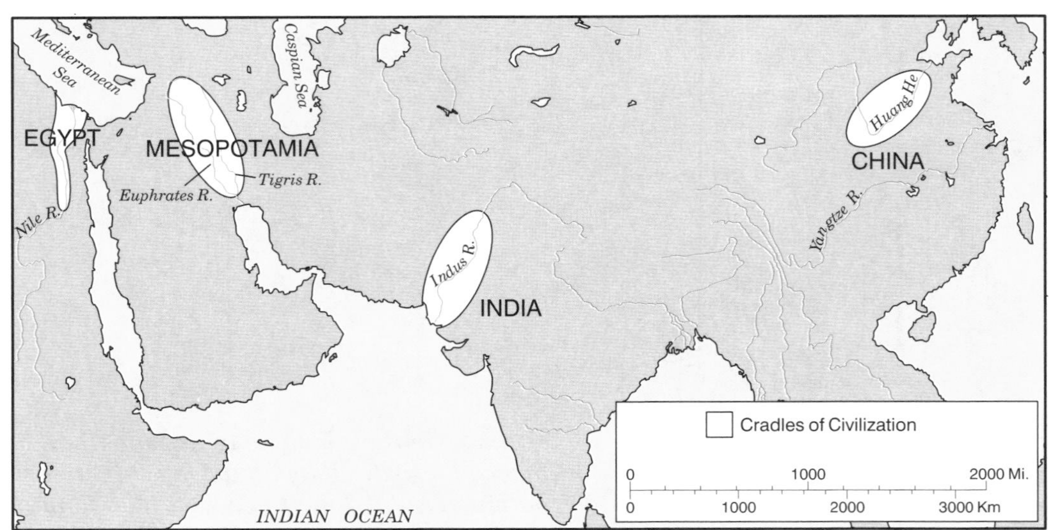

Figure 13:1. Cradles of Civilization

This mound on the bank of the Indus River is the remains of one of the earliest Indian civilizations. It is called Mohenjo-Daro, meaning "the mound of the dead." The name probably comes from the fact that a catastrophe seems to have devastated Mohenjo-Daro, in which many people were killed.

During the 1920s archaeologists discovered fascinating ruins along the Indus River, in what is now Pakistan. They dug up bricks that once were used for buildings. These were bricks that had been baked in a kiln—not the crumbly, sun-dried kind the Sumerians had used. Among the bricks they found little statues, carved signature seals, jewelry, beads, and other items. As they cleared away the rubble and dirt, they discovered old brick foundations. Here must have been a house . . . over there a large warehouse . . . over there part of the city wall. They found a large building that may have been a king's palace.

The ancient people along the Indus River were surprisingly modern in some ways.

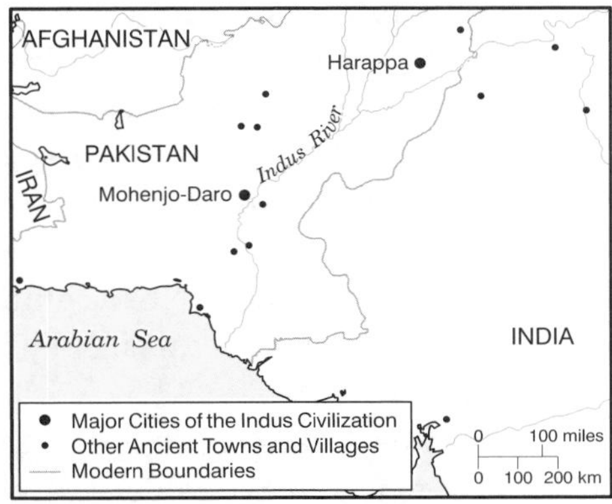

Figure 13:2. The Indus Valley Civilization

They had well-planned cities with wide, straight streets that formed regular blocks. Many of the people lived in two-story brick houses complete with bathrooms. They used the same type of items that are common today—toys, razors, fishhooks, and so on.

The ancient Indians did much buying and selling. They traded with faraway places such as Sumer and even Egypt. One of the most important products they sold was cotton cloth. Some historians think they were the ones who showed other people in the world how to make it. Yet this civilization came to an end in ancient times—possibly by the time of Moses.

What brought the civilization of the Indus Valley to ruin? No one knows for sure. Archaeologists have noticed that some people apparently left their houses in haste. They also found skeletons of people who had not been buried, but left in the wreckage. Was there an earthquake? Did the Indus River flood? Did sudden disease overcome people? Or were there several reasons? Perhaps a disaster weakened the people and then an invasion of enemies finished the destruction.

It is known that in ancient times, invaders came to this general area east of the Indus River. These Aryans (AIR ee uhnz), as they are called, settled in what is

Many Mohenjo-Daro buildings and streets have been excavated and found in good condition. It is thought that this building may have been a public restaurant. The food was likely cooked over fires in the pits on the floor.

now northern India. This may have happened about the same time Israel moved into the Promised Land.

Study Exercises

1. Name one of the greatest gifts of the Hindu civilization.
2. Why have archaeologists not found many remains from ancient civilizations of India?
3. What building material was used by ancient Indians, which shows a fairly advanced level of civilization?
4. Along what river did the ancient Indian civilization arise?
5. Who were the Aryans?

The Caste System Develops

As the light-skinned Aryans moved into India, they met darker-skinned people who had been living there. They thought the dark-skinned people were not as good as they were, and they treated them accordingly. Many of the people they looked down upon moved farther south. Today the people of southern India are generally darker than those who live farther north. They also speak completely different languages.

Gradually the different peoples of India grew accustomed to each other. But they continued to think that some classes of people are better than others. Even today, many Indians believe this very strongly.

When people in India first began to think that some people are better than others, they were not strict about it. Anyone who wanted to belong to a different class could join it if he followed its rules. But later this changed. Anyone born into a certain class, called a caste, stayed in it for his whole life. He usually could not marry someone of a different caste, nor could he eat with such persons.

There are many hundreds of castes in India, but they are divided into four main groups. The people belonging to the most honored class are the Brahmans. This class includes priests and scholars. Next are the Kshatriyas (kuh SHAT ree uhz), which includes the rulers and soldiers. Below them are the Vaisyas (VY shuhz): farmers, merchants, and craftsmen. Next come the Sudras (SOO druhz): servants, laborers, and wage earners.

There once was a class of people called the untouchables, who were considered too low for any caste. They did work that none of the other classes would do. The untouchables included the street sweepers, fishermen, hunters, butchers, undertakers, and grave diggers.

The caste system has been harmful to India. In North America, anyone is welcome to choose any job he wants, as long as the job is available and he is able to do the work. But in India, a man whose father was a farmer could not decide to be a carpenter, and a carpenter's son could not decide to be a farmer. No one encouraged young people to find a job where they could best use their abilities.

Today the caste system has lost some of its effect. The government of India has made it illegal to treat any person as an untouchable. But the caste system still has a strong influence on people's thinking.

An Indian woman draws water from a well. Indian villages usually have several wells that provide water for drinking and washing, if there are no rivers nearby. The women usually fetch the water and exchange news with their friends, and they pass on the news to the men in the evening. Since less than half of the rural people can read or write, these channels help to keep them informed of the activities of their neighbors and the government.

How Religion Grew in India

The language of the Aryans was called Sanskrit. The people who spoke Sanskrit brought their own stories, poems, and religious sayings to India. At first they did not write them down but simply passed them orally from generation to generation. After hundreds of years, these traditions were set down in writing. A number of religious books, called the Vedas (VAY duhz), give an idea of how people lived in early India.

The Vedas show that the people believed in many gods (polytheism), especially nature gods. The people believed that the gods behaved like humans. They also thought that the gods could take the form of animals.

Later, long poems known as ***epics*** were written. One of them, called the *Ramayana* (rah MAH yuh nuh), tells of a prince named Rama whose wife was kidnapped by a wicked king. He rescued her and proved that good can triumph over evil.

People admired and tried to be like the heroes described in the epics. They thought the epics could guide them in deciding what is right and wrong. Followers of the Hindu religion today use the Vedas, the epics, and other ancient literature as their sacred writings. You studied some teachings of Hinduism in Chapter 3.

Several hundred years before Christ, Buddhism was founded in India by a man named Buddha. This man is said to have grown up as a prince in a beautiful palace. But in the world around him he noticed people who were sick, suffering, and dying. This made him think seriously. Although he enjoyed many luxuries, they did not satisfy him. He had not found meaning in life.

This drawing is of a statue called *Standing Buddha*. Most statues of Buddha show him meditating while sitting with his legs crossed. Christians can be thankful that the One they worship is living today, and not just a cold statue.

Buddha left his wife and baby son and began to wander across the countryside. He suffered by living in rags and dirt. Often he ate very little food each day. Finally he decided that making himself suffer did not answer his questions either. He still had not found peace and satisfaction in life.

One day, as he sat under a tree thinking, a light seemed to dawn in his mind. He decided that no one can completely escape suffering in this life. But if a person is loving and truthful and can keep himself from desiring earthly things, he can be born into a better person after he dies. If he pursues these goals through a number of lives, he will finally be perfect and find happiness.

People began to call this man Buddha, which means "enlightened one." After he died, they thought of him as a god and made statues of him. You may have seen pictures of such statues, showing Buddha sitting cross-legged and meditating. Today Buddhism has largely died out in India, but it is popular in some parts of Southeast Asia and the nearby regions.

Christians know that peace and satisfaction come only by receiving Christ as

This ornate Indian temple, built about A.D. 700, could not help the worshipers find peace and joy in their hearts. Only Jesus can—and He dwells in men's hearts, not in fancy buildings.

their Lord and Saviour and walking in daily obedience to His Word. Jesus said, "Peace I leave with you, my peace I give unto you: not as the world giveth, give I unto you" (John 14:27). He also said, "I am come that they might have life, and that they might have it more abundantly" (John 10:10).

Study Exercises

6. In what part of India would you expect to find the greatest population of dark-skinned people?
7. Has the caste system of India become stronger or weaker in recent years?
8. How has the caste system been harmful to India?
9. What early Indians spoke Sanskrit?
10. What writings do the Hindus regard in the same way that Christians regard the Bible?
11. In what country was Buddhism founded?

Ancient Culture of China

Little is known about ancient China. Its history has not been studied as thoroughly as the ancient history of some other parts of the world. Besides, the ancient Chinese often wrote on wooden tablets that decayed long before modern archaeologists were interested in them.

Many historians believe that by the time of Abraham, a well-developed civilization had grown up along the Huang He (Yellow River) in northern China. This river flowed through yellow soils and carried yellow mud. Remains of early civilizations have also been found south of the Huang He along an even greater river—the Yangtze.

For many years, the Chinese lived almost in a world of their own. Anyone trying to visit China found his way barred by deserts, mountains, and jungles. Since not many people traveled back and forth, the Chinese lived by their own ideas. Outsiders did not disturb them, but neither did they benefit from new ideas. The Chinese thought of their country as the "Middle Kingdom." People from other countries were considered ***barbarians.***

The early Chinese were intelligent people. They farmed well and knew how to use irrigation canals and ditches. They built dikes to keep the Huang He from flooding the countryside. They also dug canals for

In this ancient Chinese library, many books were written on strips of bamboo fastened together. A single book could be quite heavy. The ancient Chinese wrote books on science, philosophy, arithmetic, medicine, and war, and books of poetry.

The man in the foreground is Confucius, mentioned later in this chapter.

In 1974, Chinese farmers who were digging a well found an underground passageway. Inside were huge statues made of hard, waterproof ceramic clay. The farmers had stumbled across the tomb of Shih Huang-ti, the first Chinese emperor. When archaeologists unearthed more of the tomb, they found about 6,000 statues of ancient Chinese soldiers. No two statues are alike. In the tomb there were also clay horses and chariots, and a replica of the Chinese empire complete with rivers and seas of mercury that actually flowed by mechanical means. It took nearly a million laborers about 36 years to construct this tomb.

travel by boat. Other countries may have learned the value of canals from the Chinese.

The Chinese were probably the first to produce tea. They noticed that people who drank tea were more likely to stay healthy than people who drank ordinary water. (Boiling the tea killed the germs in the water.) Today tea is a favorite drink in many countries.

The Chinese were also the first to produce silk. They discovered that silkworm caterpillars like mulberry leaves best. When the caterpillars spun cocoons, the Chinese unwound the long fibers and wove them into cloth. Woven silk makes a strong, beautiful fabric. The Chinese people kept the secret of how to make it for almost three thousand years.

The early Chinese are remembered for their beautiful art. They carved ***jade*** and worked with bronze. Some rich Chinese built beautiful houses and palaces. Of course there were also many common people during this time. Most of them lived by farming.

The Chinese raised soybeans long before the time of Christ. They used this high-protein crop not only for food but also to make medicine. Soybeans are still one of China's greatest crops. The soybeans grown around the world today are from ancient Chinese varieties. Soybean ingredients are used in many modern foods, paints, adhesives, and other products.

The Chinese never thought of certain other inventions. One of these was the alphabet. Other people learned to simplify their writing by using symbols that represent sounds rather than words. As a result, today we have an alphabet of twenty-six letters.

But the Chinese use separate symbols to represent whole words. To read a newspaper, they must know more than two thousand symbols, rather than just twenty-six letters as in English. To read a story written by a famous Chinese author of the past, they might need to know ten thousand or more symbols.

Almost all Chinese words have just one syllable. But only a limited number of one-syllable words is possible; after a certain point there are no new ways to put sounds together. So the Chinese people say words in different tones to mean different things. For example, the syllable *ma* in Chinese can mean "mother," "hemp," "horse," or "scold." It all depends on which tone the speaker uses.

In one way the Chinese language is simpler than ours. In English, we use *go, went, gone,* and *going* as different forms of the same word. If we followed Chinese language rules, we would simply say *go* each time. (The context would indicate the tense.)

Study Exercises

12. Along what two rivers did the Chinese civilization begin?
13. Name a food, a drink, a fabric, and a valuable stone that are associated with Chinese culture.
14. In what way is the Chinese language simpler than ours?

The Influence of Confucius

During much of China's long history, it was ruled by dynasties. The first known dynasty was the Shang (SHAHNG) dynasty, which lasted from 1766 B.C. to 1122 B.C. Power was passed from father to son generation after generation. However, no single ruler controlled all of China, especially during the early years. Various men ruled in different areas. Sometimes they cooperated, and sometimes they fought. The Chou (JOH) dynasty was one of the most important early Chinese dynasties.

During these unsettled times, one young man looked with concern at his country. This man, who came to be called Confucius (kuhn FYOO shuhs), was born about 550 B.C. He could have been a soldier, but he thought there must be a better way to serve his fellow men. He thought that if only the government leaders were wise, good examples to the people, the country would be a better place to live. But when he tried to

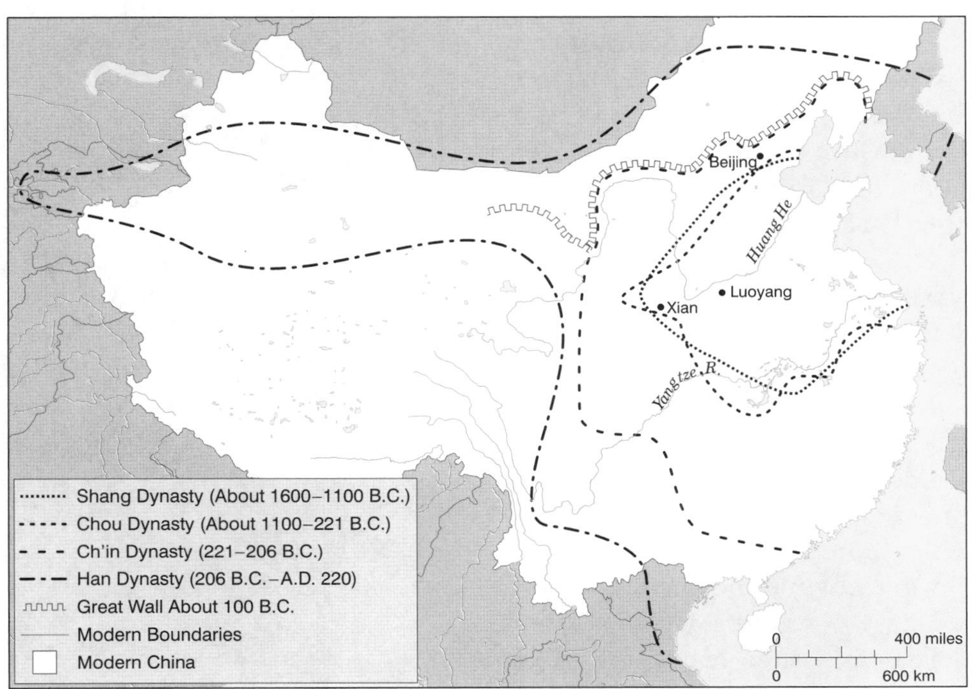

Figure 13:3. Ancient China

Confucius instructs his disciples.

give advice to government officials, he was not well accepted.

So he turned to the common people. Confucius walked the roads from village to village, teaching the people to be good, kind, and fair. He learned from other men who did much thinking. It was not long until people thought him very wise. When he died as an old man, he had a number of followers.

After Confucius's death, many people respected him and his writings even more. They did not worship him, but they believed that his writings were sacred. Later an emperor of the Chou dynasty declared that Confucius's writings should be the main philosophy of China. For many centuries, the writings of Confucius were used as Chinese textbooks and were memorized in school.

The writings of Confucius both helped and hindered the Chinese people. The writings encouraged people to be thoughtful and polite and to respect their parents. But Confucius so strongly encouraged the respect of elders that people worshiped their ancestors.

Besides, people began to think that the old ways were always the best. They did not seek for ways to improve their lives. For this reason, other countries made much more progress in learning than the Chinese did. After the Chou dynasty ended, China remained basically unchanged for two thousand years.

The Ch'in Dynasty and the Great Wall

During the long period when the Chinese followed the philosophy of Confucius, a new

Shih Huang-ti's servants sadly burn their books.

Royal travelers in carriages journey along the Great Wall of China.

conqueror arose and established the Ch'in (CHIHN) dynasty. This dynasty lasted only fifteen years (from about 221 B.C. until 206 B.C.), but it marked the first time that all China was united under one strong ruler. The name China probably comes from the Ch'in dynasty.

The first Ch'in emperor, named Shih Huang-ti (SHIHR HWAHNG DEE), was an aggressive, strong-willed man. One of his strangest commands was to destroy almost all the books that had been written up to that time. He did not want people to read other ideas about government and become dissatisfied with his reign. But because of Shih Huang-ti's harshness, people became dissatisfied anyway.

But what Shih Huang-ti is most remembered for is his biggest project—building the Great Wall of China. Other rulers had built short walls to keep out invaders. Shih Huang-ti drafted thousands of Chinese men to build a wall that would link the short walls into one extremely long wall in northern China. Many Chinese men lost their lives building the wall, and the Chinese people were charged high taxes to pay for it. But the wall was built, and it did keep out Mongol invaders for many years.

Later emperors added to the Great Wall until it included a total of about 4,000 miles (6,400 km), counting all its branches. From start to finish, the wall took hundreds of years to build. Much of it is still standing, with a height of 20 to 30 feet (6 to 9 m) and enough room at the top for a road 10 feet wide (3 m). A watchtower stands every few hundred yards; there are over twenty thousand of them in all!

Study Exercises

15. Who developed the philosophy that influenced the Chinese throughout much of their history?
16. Where did China probably get its name?
17. Why did the Chinese build the Great Wall of China?

Clinching the Chapter

Multiple Choice

A. *Write the word or phrase* least *associated with the first item.*

1. Gifts from India: cotton cloth, silk, zero, number system
2. Ancient Indus civilization: fired bricks, wooden buildings, cotton cloth, caste system
3. Caste system: Kshatriyas, Vaisyas, Confucius, Sudras
4. Vedas: Sanskrit, polytheism, Aryans, jade
5. Buddhism: India, Chou, Southeast Asia, meditation
6. Early Chinese: open-minded, inventive, intelligent, artistic
7. Silk: caterpillars, mulberries, fragile, beautiful
8. Dynasty: Chou, Ch'in, sacred, generations
9. Great Wall: taxes, death, towers, Vedas
10. Ch'in dynasty: Wall, Shih Huang-ti, unified China, Confucius

B. *Write the correct answers.*

1. You are studying the ancient history of India and China because (choose two answers)
   a. it has influenced your own culture.
   b. it has influenced the culture of present-day India and China.
   c. it is helpful for understanding Christianity.
   d. it helps to explain the 26-letter alphabet.
2. Most honored in the caste system are the
   a. rich. c. priests.
   b. rulers. d. craftsmen.
3. The caste system has been harmful to India because
   a. it confuses people seeking for an occupation.
   b. it prevents India from having enough farmers.
   c. it keeps people from making the best use of their abilities.
   d. it teaches people to worship Confucius.
4. The ancient ruins along the Indus River are in present-day
   a. China. c. India.
   b. Russia. d. Pakistan.
5. The Aryans spoke
   a. Sanskrit. c. Hindi.
   b. Chinese. d. Aramaic.
6. According to the meaning of *Buddha,* the founder of Buddhism was supposed to have been
   a. wealthy. c. divorced.
   b. lonely. d. enlightened.
7. The Chinese have long been noted for all the following *except*
   a. tea. c. simple alphabet.
   b. soybeans. d. jade.
8. The usual number of syllables in a Chinese word is
   a. one. c. three.
   b. two. d. four.

9. Confucius is remembered for being
   a. a soldier.
   b. a philosopher.
   c. a father.
   d. an emperor.
10. Shih Huang-ti was
   a. a Mongol.
   b. a Ch'in emperor.
   c. an early dynasty.
   d. a Buddhist.

India, China, or Both?

For each item below, write **I** *for* India, **C** *for* China, *or* **B** *for* both.

1. cradle of civilization
2. Indus River
3. Huang He River
4. invention of the zero
5. Aryans
6. caste system
7. Confucius
8. Brahmans
9. Sanskrit
10. Shih Huang-ti
11. dynasties
12. first tea producers
13. cotton cloth
14. first silk producers
15. Buddha
16. Great Wall
17. Mongols
18. Vedas
19. *Ramayana*
20. untouchables

Completion

1. Customs are hard to leave back in the past.
   Indians still classify people by ———.
2. How many old Indian gifts have we gotten?
   One is the weaving of cloth out of ———.
3. If you will follow the Saviour of Judah,
   He will enlighten you much more than ———.
4. Silk caterpillars are easy to please.
   Feed them with leaves from the ——— ———.
5. Ornaments, statues, and carvings are made
   Out of a beautiful stone we call ———.
6. Ancient it is, but it's sturdy and tall.
   Tourists come to see it—it's China's ——— ———.

Thought Questions

1. What is one difficulty that a person might have if he tried to spread the Gospel in India?
2. How does this chapter show that a wrong philosophy can hinder the progress and prosperity of a nation?
3. Can you think of any good points that might be found in the caste system?
4. We often think of the Chinese language as difficult to learn. Does this chapter support that idea? Explain.
5. What disadvantages do archaeologists face in India and China that they do not face in Egypt?

Geographical Skills

1. Trace Map D, and label it *"India and Its Neighbors."*
2. Mark the Khyber Pass with a mountain pass symbol ()() and Mount Everest with a mountain symbol (▲) and label them.
3. Label the present-day countries that appear on this map, and their capitals. Also label the cities of Mumbai (Bombay) and Calcutta. Color each country a different color.
4. Trace Map E, and label it "China and Some of Its Neighbors."
5. Trace and label the Huang He and Yangtze Rivers.
6. Label Mongolia, Taiwan, North Korea, South Korea, the island of Hainan, and the Gobi Desert. Label the Chinese cities of Beijing (Peking), Shanghai, Hangzhou (Hangchow), Guangzhou (Canton), and Victoria (former capital of Hong Kong). Also label the cities of Ulaanbaatar, Mongolia; and Taipei, Taiwan.
7. The Grand Canal is a series of canals that is more than 1,000 miles long. Part of it may have been dug as early as several hundred years before Christ. The Chinese extended it several times until it reached its present length around A.D. 1300. On your map of China, use special symbols to show the routes of the Grand Canal and the Great Wall of China. Make a legend for your map.

Further Study

1. For thousands of years, certain people in China were highly honored. Of what occupation were they?
2. Find several more interesting facts about the production of silk.

Be Sure You Know

Can you answer all these questions? If not, study Chapters 11–13 to find the answers.

A. What

1. was the Assyrians' main way of getting wealth?
2. was God's part and what was man's part in delivering Judah from the Assyrians?
3. Assyrian king is remembered for his great library?
4. were the two Babylonian empires?
5. two kings first ruled Neo-Babylonia?
6. great calamity took place while Zedekiah was king?
7. became the center of Jewish life after the temple was destroyed?
8. were the Hanging Gardens?
9. two kings were ruling Babylon when it was destroyed?
10. is notable about the laws made by Persian kings?
11. important inscription was made by Darius the Great?
12. was developed by the Hindus, which we use every day?
13. three major religions developed in India and China?
14. four products are the Chinese known for?
15. are two ways that the Chinese language is different from English and related languages?

B. What do these words mean?

16. aqueduct
17. architecture
18. assassination
19. barbarian
20. deport
21. epic
22. jade
23. melting pot
24. moat
25. plunder
26. tribute

C. Where

27. (*a*) was Assyria located? (*b*) was Babylon located?
28. did the Greeks defeat (*a*) Darius the Great (*b*) Xerxes?

D. How

29. was Nineveh overthrown?
30. did Persian attackers gain entrance into Babylon?
31. did Cyrus deal with the Jews?
32. has the caste system been harmful to India?

E. Why

33. did the Assyrians try to terrorize people?
34. did the Assyrians scatter the people they conquered?
35. are there few records of ancient people who lived in India and China?
36. did Chinese rulers build the Great Wall of China?

Greece has a long coastline on the Aegean, Ionian, and Mediterranean Seas. Fishing and shipping are a major part of the country's economy. Besides small fishing boats, Greek sailors own large fleets of ships that sail all over the world.

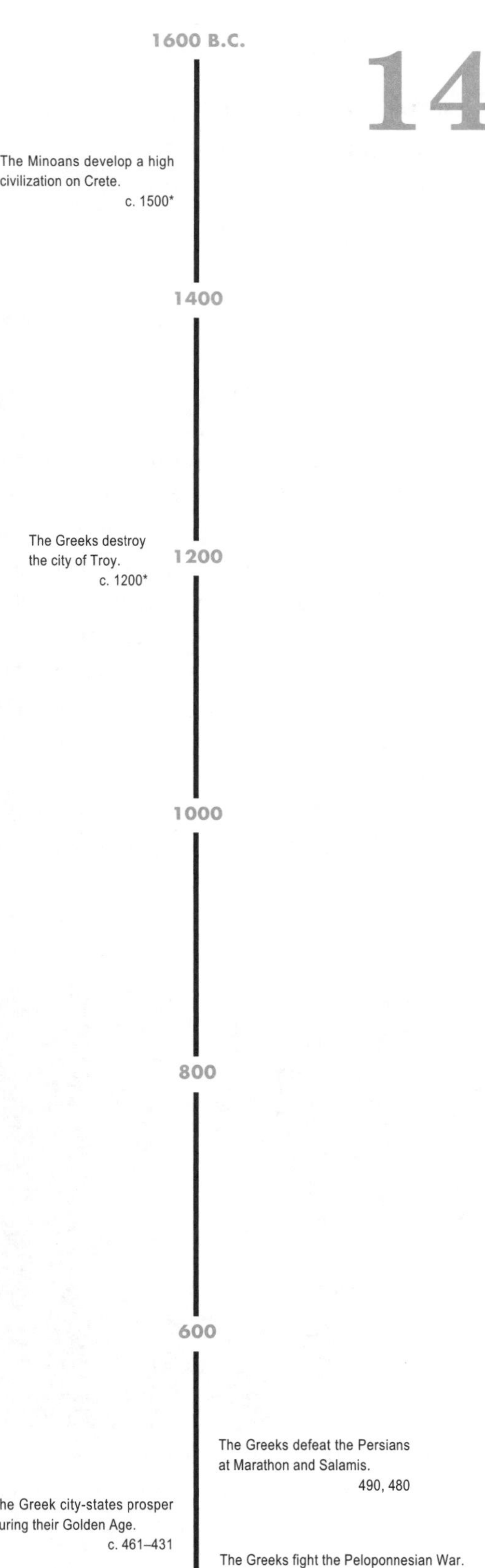
1600 B.C.
The Minoans develop a high civilization on Crete.
c. 1500*
1400
The Greeks destroy the city of Troy.
c. 1200*
1200
1000
800
600
The Greeks defeat the Persians at Marathon and Salamis.
490, 480
The Greek city-states prosper during their Golden Age.
c. 461–431
The Greeks fight the Peloponnesian War.
431–404
400 B.C.

14 The Ancient Greeks

Early History

Similarities Among the Greeks

Everyday Life in Ancient Greece

Differences Among the Greeks

Our Greek Heritage

Socrates, the Philosopher

Hippocrates, the Doctor

Greek Values

Athens and the Gospel

Greece After the Golden Age

"For after that in the wisdom of God the world by wisdom knew not God, it pleased God by the foolishness of preaching to save them that believe. For the Jews require a sign, and the Greeks seek after wisdom."

1 Corinthians 1:21, 22

The Ancient Greeks

Greece is a beautiful country. The sky is usually blue, and every object casts vivid shadows in the bright sunshine. Stony hills and mountains stand along the rugged shores of the blue-green Mediterranean Sea. Vineyards, fields of grain, and thousand-year-old olive trees add to the picture.

But the bright blue skies never bring much rain. The rocky mountains are hard to cross. Much of the land is not suited for crops, and natural resources are few. For these reasons, Greece is not a rich nation today.

At one time, however, the Greeks were the most modern people in the world. "Future ages will wonder at us," said one of their leaders. Their progressive schools, great buildings, and rich trade were the envy of other countries. More important, Greek ***philosophers*** produced ideas about nature, life, and healing. Some of these concepts still influence people's thinking today.

In this chapter you will see how the Greeks became great in the eyes of the world, and also how they began to fall from their earthly glory.

Early History

The first known civilization in the region of Greece was that of the Minoans (mih NOH uhnz). These people lived southeast of the Grecian peninsula on the island of Crete. Archaeologists have dug up ruins showing that the Minoans had many modern conveniences, perhaps as long ago as the time of Moses. They had paved streets and roads. They made paintings and worked with precious metals and stones. They made fine pottery and sold it to people around the Mediterranean Sea. Later, people on the mainland of Greece also developed more advanced ways of living.

One of the most famous ancient wars was fought during the early years of Greece.

A lone road cuts through mountainous terrain, which is typical of much of Greece. In the northern part of the country, winter may bring heavy snowfall. Most of the rain comes in the spring, and summer and fall are usually extremely dry.

The beauty of Greece attracts many foreign tourists. Some of the seaside villages look spick-and-span in their coats of whitewash.

According to an old story, the Greeks sailed across the Aegean Sea (ih JEE uhn) and besieged the city of Troy for ten years. When they could not defeat the city, the soldiers built a huge wooden horse near the city walls. Then they returned to their ships and sailed away.

The people of Troy, called Trojans (TROH juhnz), were delighted. They thought that the attackers had given up and had even left a gift. They pulled the wooden horse inside the city and celebrated their victory.

Unknown to the Trojans, the wooden horse was hollow and contained Greek soldiers. When darkness fell, the soldiers slipped out of the horse and opened the gates of Troy. The Greek ships returned (they had only gone to a nearby island), and together the soldiers captured and burned the city.

Many people have supposed this story is only a legend. But archaeologists have proved that the city of Troy did exist. It was about 20 miles (32 km) north of Troas, a city mentioned several times in the Book of Acts.

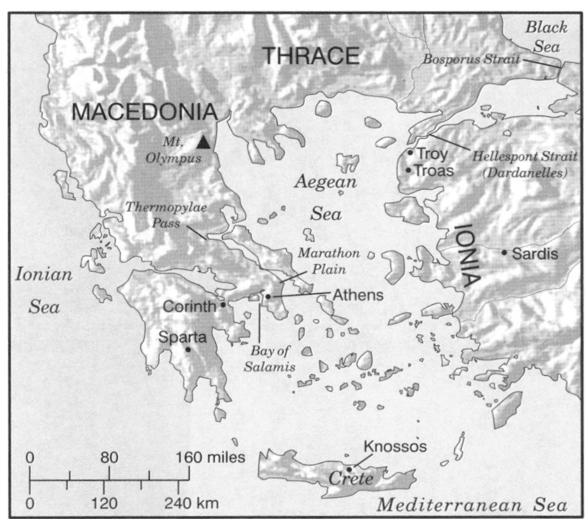

Figure 14:1. Greek Cities and Neighboring Regions

For a time in the early history of Greece, people became less civilized rather than more so. Rough, uncivilized invaders from the north pushed into Greece. The invaders cared little for fine and beautiful things. They made slaves of many people that they conquered, and they did little trading with

An artist's idea of Greek soldiers emerging from inside the Trojan horse, intent on conquering the city of Troy.

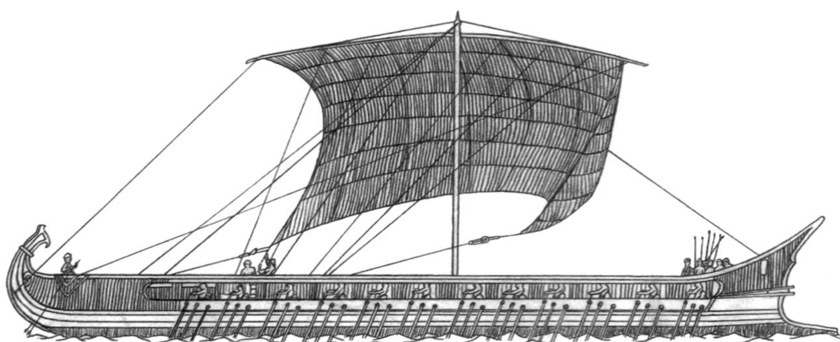

An ancient Greek ship, called a trireme, carried 170 rowers, 30 crewmen, and 10 to 18 soldiers. The pointed front end of the ship had metal-tipped rams that the Greeks used to puncture and sink enemy ships.

other countries. The writings left by earlier Greeks were neglected and forgotten. These "dark ages" of Greece apparently started before King David's time, and continued for several hundred years.

But gradually the Greeks relearned the things they had lost. They borrowed ideas from visiting traders and used them to improve their lives. For example, they made ships like the Phoenician ships that brought goods to their ports, and eventually they learned to build even better ships of their own. They sent out their ships and established trading posts around the Mediterranean and the Black Sea.

The Greeks learned to read and write again—but not with the same writing system the Minoans and others in their land had used long before. This time they learned to use the Phoenician alphabet. They also made some improvements on it. This is important to us because the Greek alphabet is an ancestor of the English alphabet. In fact, the word *alphabet* comes from *alpha* and *beta,* the names of the first two letters in the Greek alphabet.

Over the years, the Greeks also developed their own special way of governing themselves. You may recall that the Egyptians were linked together by the Nile River. But the Greeks had no natural feature that unified them; instead, they were separated by high mountains. It was easy for them to stay in their own valleys, clustered around their own cities, and think of other Greeks living just 20 miles (32 km) away as foreigners.

The little clusters they lived in were called city-states, and these were independent of each other. Some neighboring city-states got along peaceably, but others did not. Sometimes a strong city-state would bring neighboring city-states under its own rule. The fact that the Greeks never learned to work together well finally led to their downfall, as you will see later.

In Chapter 12 you saw how Greece was invaded by the Persians under Darius and Xerxes. Do you remember the names *Marathon* and *Salamis*? Although the Persians advanced so far into Greece that they were able to burn Athens, they never completely conquered the Greeks. The Persians finally had to withdraw.

The Greeks soon rebuilt Athens and made it even more beautiful than before. Because the fleet of Athens had defeated the Persians at Salamis, Athens took the lead among the Greek city-states for about thirty years. This time of peace and prosperity is called the Golden Age of Greece. Not only did the Greeks prosper in building, but they also produced many artists, sculptors, and philosophers during this time.

Study Exercises

1. Name three foods that farmers in Greece can grow.
2. Greek civilization began with what people and what place?
3. Where was the ancient city of Troy?
4. What visitors to Greek shores brought the alphabet?
5. How was the geography of Greece a hindrance to transportation and communication?

Similarities Among the Greeks

Although the Greeks generally failed to work together, several things gave them at least a little unity.

Language. People throughout Greece spoke the same basic language, although different dialects were used in different parts of the country. When the Greeks later conquered other nations, they took their language with them. The Greek language became common in Palestine; the New Testament was written in Greek. Many English words come from Greek, such as *automatic, microphone, philosophy,* and *hippopotamus.*

Olympic Games. Another thing that partly united the Greeks was the Olympic games they played. Every four years, athletes from various city-states would gather for races and other contests. The Greeks even stopped fighting wars when it was time to play their games.

Winners received great honors. The trophy they seemed to prize most was a crown of leaves from a wild olive tree that was considered sacred. Perhaps the apostle Paul had this crown in mind when he wrote, "Every man that striveth for the mastery is temperate in all things. Now they do it to obtain a corruptible crown; but we an incorruptible" (1 Corinthians 9:25).

The time came when the Greeks no longer played Olympic games. But in the late 1800s, Olympic games were started again, named after the old Greek contests. It was thought that if athletes from different nations played games together, it would promote peace among the nations. To this day, athletes from all over the world gather from time to time for racing, jumping, throwing, swimming, skiing, and other contests.

Religion. The Greeks offered prayers and sacrifices to many gods. They thought the

This ancient stadium was probably used for foot races. Spectators may have sat on the grassy, sloping area.

Historians think that 12,000 to 14,000 people sat in this ancient Greek stadium to watch athletes perform in the level area below the seats.

chief god was Zeus (ZOOS), who was supposed to live on Mount Olympus with other gods. Unlike the true God who is and always was, Zeus became king of the gods by overthrowing his father. Athena, the goddess of wisdom, supposedly sprang from the forehead of Zeus. There were gods for every part of life—gods of battle, of sunlight and music, of love and beauty, and so on.

The Greeks believed that the gods were superhuman but not all-powerful. In fact, the gods were supposed to have the same problems, faults, and quarrels that humans had. Many of the Greeks' ideas about their gods came from two long story poems known as the *Iliad* (IHL ee uhd) and the *Odyssey* (AHD uh see). These epics were said to have been composed by a blind man named Homer, who may have lived about a hundred years after Solomon. Homer spoke of the gods a number of times in his poems.

The *Iliad* is a story based on the Trojan War. The *Odyssey* describes the adventures of Odysseus (oh DIHS ee uhs), a Greek commander returning from the conquest of Troy. The god of the sea had a grudge against Odysseus. He sent storms and so many troubles that Odysseus did not get home for ten years. (The English word *odyssey,* meaning "long, wandering trip," comes from the name of this poem.)

Greek ***mythology*** (mih THAHL uh jee) did not teach a resurrection after death. Perhaps the story that came closest to hinting at a resurrection was the story of Orpheus (OR fee uhs). According to the Greek myths, he went to Hades (HAY deez), the place of the dead, to find his wife who had died. He was instructed not to look behind him as he led his wife back to the land of the living. But when he looked back too soon to see if she was following, she vanished.

It may seem strange, but the very poems that taught the Greeks about the gods also caused some thinking Greeks to begin questioning the gods. Somehow the stories seemed more like childish fairy tales than accounts of true miracles.

Many Greeks turned to philosophy, the human search for wisdom, to try to answer their questions about life. They did not understand that "the wisdom of this world is foolishness with God" (1 Corinthians 3:19). Others searched for a better religion. Some of them finally heard of Jesus Christ and found the truth and satisfaction they were seeking.

Everyday Life in Ancient Greece

Food, clothing, and shelter in Greece were simple. Most of the people were poor. They lived in small houses of brick or stone, for stone was a very common material. They dressed in simple clothes somewhat like those of people in Palestine. They went barefoot at home and wore sandals outside.

The Greeks enjoyed the same foods as other people who lived around the Mediterranean. Wheat or barley bread, vegetables, and figs were common foods. Grapes and olives were pressed to make wine and olive oil. The Greeks used olive oil in much the same way that North Americans use butter.

The rocky hillsides could not produce enough food for everyone in Greece. The Greeks had to import grain and meat from other countries. In turn they exported some of their surplus products such as wine and olive oil.

The Greeks also traded things that they had made, such as pottery and jewelry. But their trade depended somewhat on the weather. Shipping was practically impossible in winter. You may recall that the apostle Paul once traveled on a ship whose master counted on sailing during the last few days of mild weather before winter. But a sudden wind caught the ship, and it was tossed on the waves for two weeks before finally being wrecked (Acts 27:9–44).

Very few girls in Greece went to school. Most girls stayed at home and learned from their mothers how to manage a household. Boys went to school accompanied by a trusted slave, who served as a guardian or tutor. Such a slave was what the apostle Paul had in mind when he wrote, "The law was our schoolmaster to bring us unto Christ" (Galatians 3:24).

Study Exercises

6. Name three things that united the Greeks.
7. Name two of the Greek gods or goddesses.
8. Briefly describe the character of the Greek gods.
9. (*a*) How were the stones of Greece useful? (*b*) How were they troublesome?
10. Name at least three things the Greeks produced for export.

Differences Among the Greeks

You have seen some ways in which the various Greek city-states were similar. In some other ways, the Greeks were far apart in their thinking. The most famous city-states, Sparta and Athens, illustrate these differences.

Life in Sparta. Life was rough for the Spartans. That was the way they wanted it to be. They thought that a rough life would train them to be strong soldiers, which they thought was the only worthwhile occupation. Farming, carpentry, road building, and other work could be done by the many lower-class people or slaves who lived among them. And they saw no need for fine pottery, beautiful poetry, and eloquent speeches.

At age seven, all boys had to begin living in army barracks. They were given no shoes and only one simple garment, which they had to wear in the warm summer as well as the chilly winter. They were not given much food. If they wanted more, they had to steal it. But if they were caught stealing, they were punished—not for doing wrong, but for not being clever enough to avoid being caught. Occasionally the boys were given severe beatings to toughen them. They were taught that it was a shame to cry out.

Girls, too, were trained to be tough and strong. The Spartans believed that strong women would have strong babies. Strong babies would grow to be strong warriors.

Did the Spartans succeed in building a powerful army? Yes, they did, for their homes were well protected. But many people who have studied the Spartans wonder if their kind of life was worth protecting. Other Greeks talked about how strong the Spartans were, but they did not want to live like them.

Life in Athens. Boys and girls in Athens grew up much more comfortably than children in Sparta. There were many other differences too. People's whole way of thinking was different in Athens (and in most other parts of Greece).

The people of Athens wanted a well-rounded life. Although they also had an army, they wanted to take time for education, for beauty, for games, and for talking. In school the boys learned to appreciate poetry and music as well as physical education. The people believed that the ideal man had a sound mind in a sound body.

In many ways the Greeks lived a simple life, but they also built some grand marble temples. The most famous Greek temple is probably the Parthenon (PAHR thuh nahn), built on top of a high hill in Athens. Its many pillars with their simple, stately lines have inspired modern architects. The Lincoln Memorial in Washington, D.C., is one example of a building that resembles the Parthenon.

The Parthenon *(left)* was the chief temple of the false Greek goddess Athena. It took about nine years to complete the basic construction. The ancient building remained in fairly good condition until 1687 when gunpowder stored in it exploded. The Lincoln Memorial *(right)*, dedicated to the memory of U.S. President Abraham Lincoln (1809–1865), was completed in about seven years.

Study Exercises

11. In Sparta, what occupation was thought to be suitable for upper-class people?
12. What belief of the Athenians carried the concept that an ideal man lives a balanced life?
13. Give at least two adjectives describing Greek architecture, of which the Parthenon is an example.

Our Greek Heritage

Although the ancient Greeks lived over two thousand years ago, they still influence people's ideas and attitudes today.

The Greeks liked to think. They asked hard questions about simple things. They believed that to understand life, they needed to understand its simplest parts, just as a child must learn the alphabet before he can write sentences. "What is everything made of?" they wondered. "What is the smallest possible particle of anything?"

They also raised the same kind of questions about more serious matters. "How do we know what is real?" they asked. "How do we decide that one thing is good and another thing is bad?" "What is truth?"

In Greek academies, professors and their students discussed arithmetic, philosophy, literature, history, and law. The students did not need to pay to attend, but most of them came from upper-class families who made substantial donations to the school.

In their eagerness to explain things, some Greeks jumped to conclusions. They invented stories instead of continuing to seek for the truth. For example, to explain why the world has troubles, they told about a woman named Pandora (pan DOR uh) who was given a box and told not to open it. Curiosity finally overcame her, and she opened it. Instantly all kinds of troubles flew out of the box, and there have been troubles ever since.

But other Greeks were not satisfied with story explanations. They wanted to find out the facts.

Plato (427?–348 B.C.) was a student of Socrates.

Socrates, the Philosopher

Men who spend much time discussing life's deep questions are called philosophers. Perhaps the most famous philosopher of Athens was Socrates (SAHK ruh teez), who lived from about 470 B.C. to 399 B.C. He believed that the most important question anyone can ask is, "What is the best way to live?" He did not know the answer himself, but he looked for an answer by asking other people similar questions. Often the people he talked to discovered that they did not know the answer either.

Socrates, Greek philosopher

Some Greeks argued that truth can never be found, but Socrates did not agree with them. Still, he realized that there were many great truths he simply did not know. He sometimes said, "One thing only I know, and that is that I know nothing."

One of Socrates's students was Plato (PLAY toh), who was born about 427 B.C., just after the Golden Age. This man wrote, "We must lay hold of the best human opinion in order that, borne by it as on a raft, we may sail over the dangerous sea of life, unless we can find a stronger boat, or some word of God, which will more surely and safely carry us." It is too bad Plato did not know about the Holy Scriptures.

One of Plato's students was a scientist and teacher named Aristotle (AR ihs taht uhl). He observed many patterns in nature, just as we can find them in flowers, spider webs, and snowflakes. He saw over and over that the universe is orderly. Aristotle concluded that there must be a mind behind the design—a God who gave order to it. But he did not know the Lord as the Bible reveals Him.

Hippocrates (460?–377? B. C.) helps the sick in a marketplace.

Hippocrates, the Doctor

Hippocrates (hih PAHK ruh teez), who lived about the same time as Socrates, was another man who wanted facts and did not just make guesses. In those days, people knew very little about what causes disease. Many people thought their diseases could be cured by using charms, performing ceremonies, and offering sacrifices to the gods.

Hippocrates, however, kept careful records of the symptoms and course of a disease. "To know is science," he said, "but merely to believe one knows is ignorance." If a medicine worked well on a patient, he made a note of that and tried it on the next patient with the same illness. He tried to teach young doctors to be good observers like himself.

Hippocrates also taught that a doctor should love people. He said that when a physician examines a patient, he should be well dressed, give the patient his full attention, answer objections patiently, be calm in the presence of difficulties that arise, and give his directions in a friendly, quiet manner.

Hippocrates is called the "Father of Medicine." He helped many patients, but the most important thing he did was to direct people's thinking away from superstition.

Greek Values

Today many people value the same things that the Greeks valued. Following are some of the most important ones.

Freedom. The people of Athens believed that all citizens should be free—free to speak out for what they believe is right, free to ask questions, and free to search for the best way to live. It is true that many Greeks had slaves in those days, but a few people of Athens even spoke out against slavery. It is also true that some philosophers, such as Socrates, were exiled or condemned to die by rulers who thought they were stirring up trouble. But in comparison to other ancient nations and even some modern countries, the Athenians had much freedom.

Justice. The Athenians believed that when someone was accused of a crime, he should be treated fairly. A group of his fellow citizens, called a ***jury,*** would be called to hear the accusations and decide if he really was guilty. Today the courts in many countries still use juries.

Democracy. Many governments through the centuries have oppressed the people. But the Athenians believed that the people themselves should rule. That is what ***democracy*** means—rule by the people. They believed that the government should serve the people and that the people should accept a reasonable government.

New Ideas. Although the Spartans did

not like new ideas, the Athenians were always ready to hear them. The Athenians did not believe everything they heard; but if they thought a new idea was sensible, they often accepted it. Even today, countries that are quick to accept helpful new ideas tend to prosper, while countries that cling to old, unproductive ways remain poor and undeveloped.

Study Exercises

14. What are people tempted to do when they want quick answers to their questions?
15. What was the most important question Socrates thought he could ask?
16. Finish this statement: "Merely to believe one knows . . ."
17. What title of honor has been given to Hippocrates?
18. Name four values of the ancient Greeks that are still considered important today.

Athens and the Gospel

How do you suppose the people of Athens accepted Christianity many years later, when the first Christian missionaries came? Acts 17 tells us that the apostle Paul visited Athens and preached to the philosophers. Some of them made fun of him. Others said, "We will hear thee again of this matter." Only a few became true believers.

But why? One would expect that such thinking people would have been eager to hear the Gospel.

Probably the main reason the Greeks rejected the Gospel is that when people consider themselves wise, they often become blind to God's simple truths. When Paul later wrote to the Christians in Corinth, near Athens, he asked, "Where is the wise? where is the scribe? where is the disputer of this world? hath not God made foolish the wisdom of this world?" (1 Corinthians 1:20). This verse does not mean it is wrong to learn about the things around us. But God knows that people's own minds can easily become their idols. It is foolish to esteem our own "wisdom" more highly than God's message to us.

Greece After the Golden Age

The Golden Age lasted only about thirty years, from about 461 B.C. to 431 B.C. During this time, Athens became more and more powerful. Other city-states came under the rule of Athens. The Spartans feared that it would be only a matter of time until that also happened to them. In 431 B.C., the tension between these two powers finally flamed into the Peloponnesian War (pehl uh puh NEE shuhn).

At first Athens seemed to be winning. A year after the fighting began, Pericles (PEHR ih kleez), the leader of Athens, made a famous funeral speech praising the soldiers who had died for Athens. He said that the whole world would remember them as great men. But he did not know that the war would last another twenty-six years,

Pericles (495?–429 B.C.) worked to make Athens a center of art, literature, and architecture.

robbing Athens, Sparta, and other city-states of many fine young men.

The Athenians could have "quit while they were ahead." Instead, they chose to keep on fighting—and they began to lose. In the end, Sparta won the war and became the most powerful city-state in Greece. But Athens remained an important center of learning, art, and thought.

The 27-year war weakened the Greeks. To the north of them in Macedonia, a strong leader named Philip saw his opportunity. In a short time his army would sweep down and conquer Greece.

Study Exercises

19. What does 1 Corinthians 3:19 say about the wisdom of this world?
20. What apparently helped to bring the Golden Age to a close?
21. For what did Athens remain famous even after it lost power?

Clinching the Chapter

Multiple Choice

A. *Write the word or phrase* least *associated with the first item.*

1. Greek unity: language, attitudes, religion, games
2. Early Greek history: Trojan War, "dark ages," Aristotle, Minoans
3. Persian invasions: Marathon, Salamis, Athens, Troy
4. Minoans: Crete, Italy, paintings, pottery
5. Philosophers: Socrates, Pandora, Plato, Aristotle
6. Trojan War: Troy, Greeks, wooden horse, Phoenicians
7. Greek values: democracy, monotheism, freedom, new ideas
8. Sparta: poetry, soldiers, barracks, stealing
9. Hippocrates: superstition, facts, calmness, science
10. Golden Age: artists, sculptors, thinkers, 100 years

B. *Write the correct words.*

1. Ancient Greece influenced modern society most by its (trade, pottery, thinkers, Trojan horse).
2. The most famous example of ancient Greek architecture is probably the (Lincoln Memorial, Great Pyramid, Parthenon, Salamis).
3. The Golden Age of Greece came after (Plato, Aristotle, the Peloponnesian War, the battle at Salamis).
4. The scientist who believed that nature reveals God was (Odysseus, Aristotle, Homer, Philip).
5. The English alphabet came from the Phoenicians by way of the (Greeks, Minoans, Persians, Olympics).
6. Socrates said, "One thing only I know, and that is that I know (something, nothing, everything, enough)."
7. Who is called the "Father of Medicine"? (Socrates, Plato, Aristotle, Hippocrates)
8. Superstition is based on (facts, science, democracy, ignorance).
9. Which man had the answer to the question "What is truth?" (Paul, Socrates, Plato, Aristotle).
10. The Peloponnesian War was fought between the (Greeks and Minoans, Greeks and Persians, Spartans and Athenians, Greeks and Trojans).

Matching

A. *For each clue, write the correct name from the right-hand column.*

1. Recommended following the best human opinion unless a better way or a word from God could be found
2. King of the mythical Greek gods
3. Provided basis of Greek alphabet
4. Led Athenians against Sparta
5. Conquered Greece
6. Failed in his attempt to bring his wife back from Hades
7. Civilized in the days of Moses
8. Took ten years to get home
9. Presented Jesus Christ to Greek philosophers
10. Goddess of wisdom

Athena
Minoans
Odysseus
Orpheus
Paul
Pericles
Philip
Phoenicians
Plato
Zeus

B. *Match as in Part A.*

1. City near Athens
2. Home of Minoans
3. scene of battle with Persians
4. Home of Philip
5. Center of Greek culture
6. Home of gods
7. Was destroyed by trick with wooden horse
8. Greek trading posts
9. Glorified a soldier's life
10. Place of the dead

Athens
Black Sea
Corinth
Crete
Hades
Macedonia
Marathon
Mount Olympus
Sparta
Troy

Completion

1. Minoans paved both road and street
   Upon the ancient isle of ———.
2. Since mountains had no easy gates,
   The Greeks had separate ——— ———.
3. The different peoples learned to speak
   A common language known as ———.
4. The morals of Greek gods were loose.
   The chief of all the gods was ———.
5. In any good democracy,
   The people rule, and they are ———.
6. The best of men the Greeks could find
   Were sound in body, sound in ———.
7. A thinking man was Socrates;
   A doctor was ———.
8. Not even lofty lords and ladies
   Escaped the gloomy realm of ———.

Thought Questions

1. What did Pilate say in his conversation with Jesus that suggests the influence of Greek thought? (See John 18:33–40.)
2. What doctrine did the apostle Paul teach on Mars Hill that was ridiculed by some of the Athenians? (See Acts 17.)
3. What did Paul say in Acts 17 that shows he knew something about Greek literature?
4. Socrates asked many people what is the best way to live. What is *your* answer?
5. To be saved, what must a person do besides recognizing that there is a God?

Geographical Skills

1. (*a*) How wide is the Bosporus Strait at its narrowest point? (*b*) the Dardanelles Strait?
2. What is the approximate distance between Athens and Sparta?

Further Study

1. See if you can find out how Greek democracy was different from democracy in a modern country like the United States. Why would Greek ways of doing things not work in a large city?
2. One of the Greek thinkers was Democritus (dih MAHK rih tuhs), who proposed an idea that scientists today still use in a modified form. See if you can learn what it is.

Alexander the Great conquered Darius III and the Persian Empire. Here, Darius's family kneels before Alexander, their new lord.

15 A Hellenized World

350 B.C.

Alexander the Great becomes king of Macedonia. 336

Alexander conquers the Persian Empire. 334–323

Alexander dies at Babylon. 323

300

250

200

The Seleucids defeat the Ptolemies and gain control of Palestine. 198

Antiochus Epiphanes defiles the temple and forbids Jewish worship. 168

Mattathias and his sons fight the Seleucids. 167–135

Judas the Maccabee purifies the temple. 165

150

100 B.C.

"And as I was considering, behold, an he goat came from the west on the face of the whole earth, and touched not the ground: and the goat had a notable horn between his eyes. . . . And the rough goat is the king of Grecia: and the great horn that is between his eyes is the first king."

Daniel 8:5, 21

A Hellenized World

Early Days of Alexander the Great

God showed the prophet Daniel a vision about Alexander the Great long before Alexander was born. Can you identify Alexander in this prophecy from Daniel?

> I saw in a vision . . . a ram which had two horns. . . . I saw the ram pushing westward, and northward, and southward; so that no beasts might stand before him. . . . And as I was considering, behold, an he goat came from the west . . . and touched not the ground: and the goat had a notable horn between his eyes. . . . And the rough goat is the king of Grecia: and the great horn that is between his eyes is the first king (Daniel 8:2–5, 21).

Aristotle teaches young Alexander. Before Alexander was king, he said that he preferred to surpass others in knowledge, not in power. However, after he reached the throne, war and power absorbed him. He led thousands of soldiers, and conquered and controlled millions of subjects, yet he could not control his own spirit. The Bible says, "He that is slow to anger is better than the mighty; and he that ruleth his spirit than he that taketh a city" (Proverbs 16:32).

The first king of Greece who had much contact with the Hebrews was Alexander the Great. He grew up in Macedonia, a region north of Greece. As a boy, Alexander was bright and energetic. He loved to study the *Iliad,* Homer's long story-poem about how the Greeks conquered Troy. The story excited him. He wanted to conquer other lands too.

Alexander's father, Philip of Macedonia, was already conquering the Greeks to the south. When Alexander was about thirteen years old, he became a pupil of Aristotle, one of the best-known Greeks. Aristotle taught Alexander to love the Greek way of life, called ***Hellenism*** (HEHL uh nihz uhm). (According to Greek mythology, Hellen was the founder of the Greek race.) In later years, Alexander would spread Hellenism to every land he conquered.

When Philip was killed in 336 B.C., Alexander became king at the age of twenty. Now he could do all he had dreamed of doing. Alexander and his army marched east, crossed the strait of Hellespont (HEHL ihs pahnt), now called Dardanelles, and entered Asia Minor. After defeating the Persians there and in Syria, he marched south toward Palestine.

Conquering the city of Tyre posed a special challenge for Alexander. Part of Tyre was on an island half a mile (1 km) away from the Mediterranean shore. When Alexander's army approached, the people of Tyre made themselves secure on the island, where they thought the Greek soldiers could not reach them.

How could Alexander get his army to the island? It was tantalizingly close.

Alexander decided to build a ***causeway***

out to the island. Taking fill from the coast and dumping it into the water, his soldiers made a peninsula that extended farther and farther into the sea. Finally the causeway reached all the way to Tyre. With the help of warships, Alexander's men conquered the city. The peninsula they built is still there today.

Study Exercises

1. What is the name for the ancient Greek way of life?
2. Who brought Alexander in contact with Greek thinking and values?
3. Give the ancient and modern names of the strait Alexander crossed to enter Asia Minor.
4. At the site of Tyre, what would you find instead of what was formerly an island?

An artist's idea of Alexander's siege of Tyre.

Alexander leads his soldiers on horseback. In their 11 years of travel and conquest, Alexander and his men ranged nearly 3,000 miles (4,830 km) from their homeland.

Alexander's Later Adventures

The Jewish historian Josephus says that while Alexander was besieging Tyre, he sent messengers to Jerusalem, asking the high priest for help. But the high priest had already promised loyalty to the king of Persia, and he replied that he did not see how he could break his promise.

Hearing this, Alexander angrily declared that he would soon visit Jerusalem and punish the high priest so that everyone would know to whom they should make promises. When the high priest heard that Alexander and his army were coming, he was frightened. He and his people prayed earnestly, and soon the high priest received a vision in which he was told to dress in his high priestly robes and go out to meet Alexander.

The high priest and a number of others went out together. To everyone's amazement, when Alexander saw the high priest, he walked up to him and reverenced him.

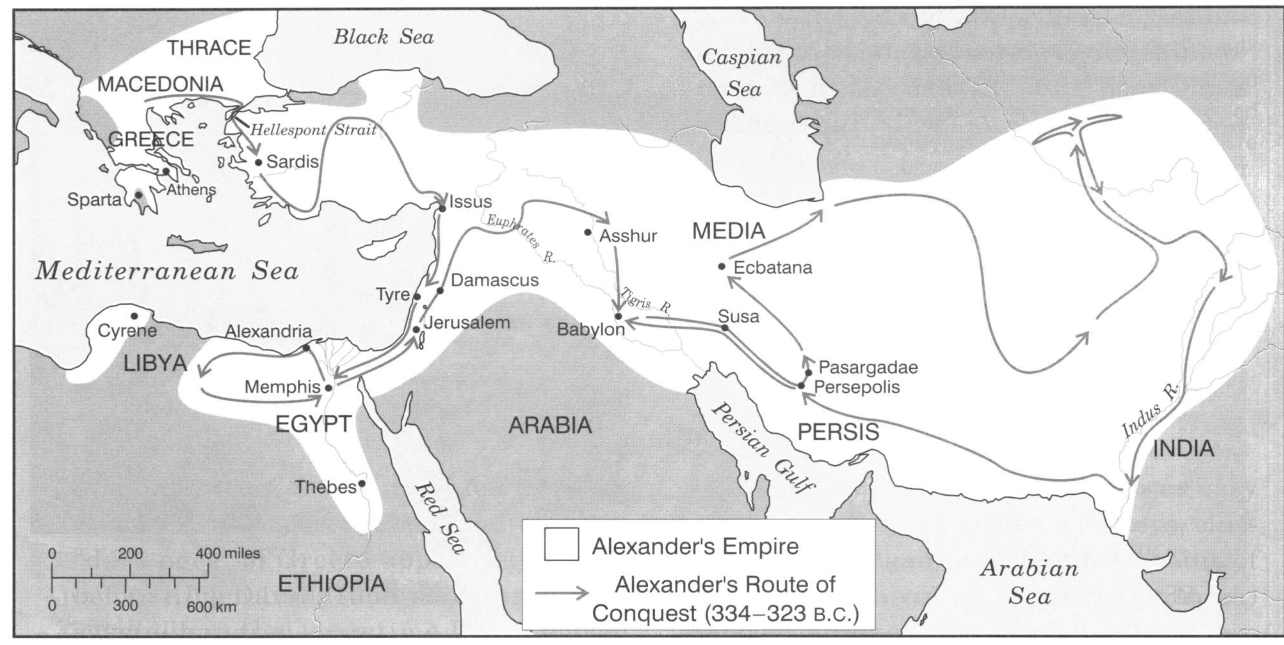

Figure 15:1. Alexander's Greek Empire

He explained that some time before, he had received advice in a dream from a man who was dressed just like this high priest. Alexander then entered the city, and the Jews showed him the prophecies about himself in the Book of Daniel. According to this story by Josephus, the Greeks left Jerusalem on friendly terms with the Jews. History tells us that the Greeks did not destroy Jerusalem.

After conquering Egypt, Alexander again marched eastward. Within eight years after he became king, he had conquered the mighty Persian Empire. Here and there he built cities named after himself. Alexandria (al ihg ZAN dree uh) in Egypt is still a well-known city today.

Where did Alexander get his astounding energy and understanding that enabled him to master so much so quickly? He may have thought it came from within himself, for he began requiring people to treat him as a god. He did not seem to understand that the prophecies spoken by Daniel were God's plan and not his own.

Alexander's hot temper and love for sinful pleasure caused him to do some foolish things. Once in a drunken quarrel, he

Alexander founded Alexandria, Egypt, in 332 B.C. Since then it has grown to over 3,431,000 inhabitants. Most of Egypt's imports and exports pass through Alexandria's harbor.

killed one of his close friends. After that, his soldiers were not as loyal to him as they had been.

Alexander and his army pressed on until they conquered the Indus River valley in what is now Pakistan. Alexander would have gone farther, but his weary men refused. He believed he had conquered practically all the known world. An old story says he sat down and wept because there were no more empires to conquer.

Alexander returned to Babylon, looking forward to ruling the huge empire he had conquered. But shortly afterward he became seriously ill. He died in 323 B.C., when he was almost thirty-three years old. Only 11 years had passed since he had led his Macedonian soldiers into Asia Minor.

Study Exercises

5. What great empire did Alexander overthrow as he expanded the Greek Empire?
6. What city did Alexander plan to overthrow but decide to spare?
7. Alexander conquered many lands, but he did not rule them very long. Why not?
8. Alexander called many cities after his own name. What city in Egypt is named for him?

The Greek Empire Falls Apart

Now that Alexander was dead, who would rule his empire? Four of his main generals claimed various parts of it. They began fighting each other, and in less than fifteen years the empire was in pieces.

The most important concern to the Jews was who would rule Palestine. This territory came under the control of the general who had seized Egypt. His name was Ptolemy (TAHL uh mee), a name that his sons carried on.

Life Under the Ptolemies

The Ptolemies learned to trust the Jews. The second Ptolemy set free more than a hundred thousand Jewish slaves in Egypt, and paid their masters for them.

Ptolemy II also asked the Jews to translate the Old Testament from Hebrew into Greek so that he could have their Scriptures in his library. According to tradition, seventy-two Jews went from Jerusalem to Alexandria, the capital of Egypt, to begin the translation. Their translation is called the ***Septuagint*** (SEHP too uh jihnt), a name that refers to the number seventy. Since Greek was the everyday language of most people at the time—including many Jews—the Septuagint became a source of new light and understanding for thousands. This knowledge of God's Word helped prepare the world for the Gospel message that the early Christians would preach.

The Ptolemies ruled the Jews for more than a hundred years. But in 198 B.C. Egypt lost an important battle to Syria, and Syria took over Palestine.

Times Change Under the Seleucids

The Syrians who ruled the Jews were called Seleucids (sih LOO sihdz). They were named after Seleucus (sih LOO kuhs), the general who claimed Syria and surrounding lands. The Seleucids, like Alexander, wanted to spread Hellenism, the Greek way of thinking and living. It was not long before they tried to force Hellenism on the Jews, whether they liked it or not.

Some Jews liked Hellenism. The philosophies of Socrates, Plato, Aristotle, and other Greeks excited them. They enjoyed the challenge of Greek athletic games.

Other Jews thought differently. They loved the old Jewish laws that God had given to them. They treasured the Ten Commandments, the temple worship, the

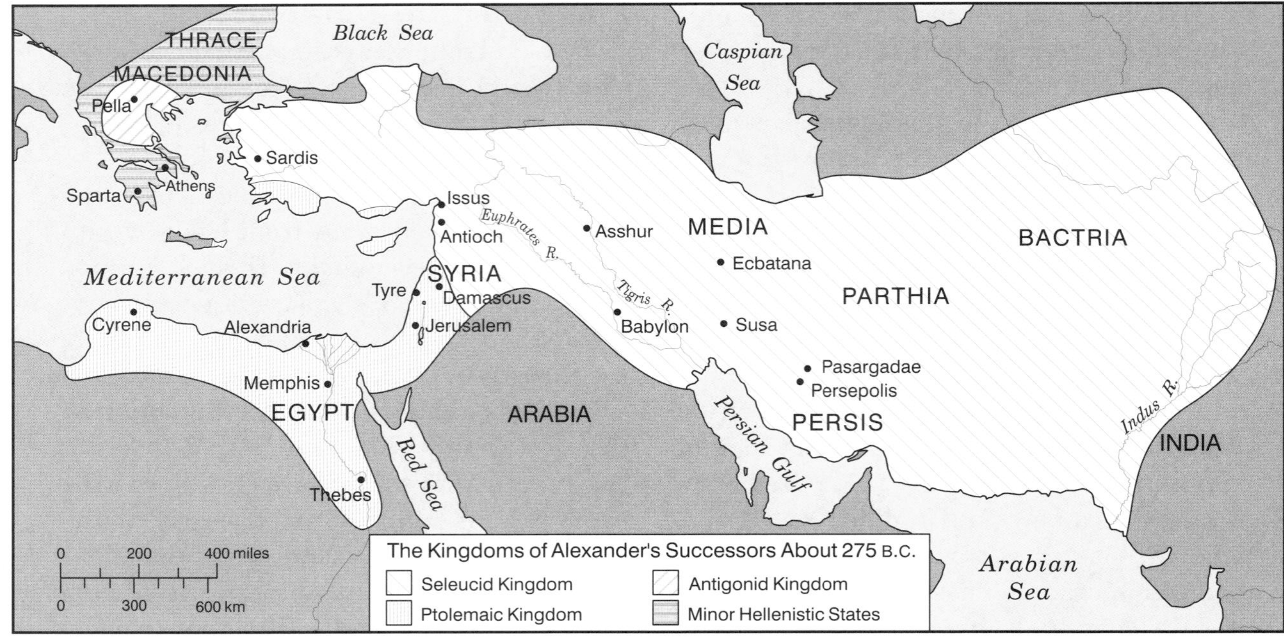

Figure 15:2. The Kingdoms of Alexander's Successors

sacrifices, the Bible stories, and the prophecies of great men like Isaiah and Jeremiah.

Furthermore, they realized that the worldly attitudes of the Greeks were not good. The Greek philosophers gave too much glory to man and nature and none to God. They tried to reason everything for themselves, never thinking that only God could reveal life's deepest mysteries. And godly Jews were shocked at the immodesty of the athletes who played at Greek games. They refused to have any part in such activities.

When the Syrian king Antiochus Epiphanes (an TY uh kuhs ih PIHF uh neez) came to power, he was determined to stamp out all resistance to Hellenism. He forbade the Jews to worship according to their faith. He even offered a pig on the temple altar and set up an image of a heathen god. His men killed anyone they found who possessed the Scriptures. Jews who tried to keep God's Law were beaten, burned, strangled, and sold as slaves.

Study Exercises

9. Name the series of rulers that governed Egypt and Palestine after Alexander's death.
10. (*a*) What is the Septuagint? (*b*) Why was it given this name?
11. From what country did the Seleucids rule?
12. Who was the worst of the Seleucids?

Antiochus Epiphanes, 215?–164 B.C.

The Maccabees Revolt

One day a Syrian officer ordered an elderly priest named Mattathias (mat uh THY uhs) to offer a heathen sacrifice as an example to the other Jews of his town. Mattathias refused, but to his shock, another Jew agreed to offer the sacrifice. Mattathias and his sons killed both the Jew and Antiochus's officer, along with several other soldiers; then they fled to the wilds. Other faithful Jews soon joined them. Revolt had begun.

Mattathias died soon afterward, but his sons carried on the struggle. One son, Judas the Maccabee (MAK uh bee), led his poorly equipped soldiers against armies larger than his own—and he won time after time.

Judas's secret was simple. He trusted in the Lord and told his men to do the same. Often he and his men prayed that God would give them victory in their battles. One time Syrian officers planned to trick the Jews by a surprise attack at night, but Judas learned about their scheme. He knew that only part of the Syrian army would attack, so that night he moved his men to the camp where most of the enemy army was stationed. Taking the Syrians by surprise, he beat them and burned their camp. When the would-be attackers returned and saw what had happened, they fled.

This plaque was placed at the temple entrance, warning Gentiles against entering sacred Jewish areas. But the Syrians entered anyway and desecrated God's house by offering unclean animals and setting up false gods. Perhaps God allowed these things to happen to help prepare the Jews for the change to the New Testament—when God would dwell in godly hearts instead of temples made with hands, and when His people would offer spiritual sacrifices of submission and praise instead of animal sacrifices on stone altars.

After defeating the Syrians several more times, Judas and his men entered Jerusalem and purified the temple in 165 B.C. Three long years had passed since Antiochus had stopped the temple worship. Finally the Jews could again worship God according to the Law. In memory of that happy day, the Jews still celebrate the Feast of Lights, which they often call ***Hanukkah*** (HAH nuh kuh), meaning "dedication." The New Testament also calls it the Feast of Dedication (John 10:22).

But Judas and his men had to fight more battles. Finally a huge Syrian army came upon Judas when he had only three thousand men with him. Most of his men fled,

The Maccabees knew the scrubby hills and dry washes of their homeland far better than the Syrians did. In the area of Beth-horon (pictured above), northwest of Jerusalem, the Maccabees won several important victories.

and only eight hundred remained. They urged him to back off for the time, gather an army, and then fight.

Judas replied, "Let not the sun ever see such a thing, that I should show my back to the enemy." During the battle, he and his best soldiers attacked the strongest part of the enemy army and even chased it. But the rest of the Syrian army surrounded him, and in this way Judas met his death.

After Judas's death, his brothers took turns ruling the Jews. The family, known as the Maccabees in memory of Judas, gradually gained control of the Jewish homeland. The last brother to rule was Simon. When he died, his sons took the leadership.

But Simon's sons were ungodly men. The story of them and their descendants is quite different from the noble story of Judas the Maccabee. After studying the Roman Empire, you will learn in Chapter 17 how the Jewish rulers in Palestine lost their power.

Study Exercises

13. Name the Jewish family who led the struggle against the Syrians.
14. Give two other names for the Feast of Lights.

Clinching the Chapter

Multiple Choice

A. *Write the word or phrase* least *associated with the first item.*

1. Alexander: ram, goat, horn, bull
2. Book: Septuagint, Iliad, Epiphanes, Daniel
3. Tyre: mountain, island, peninsula, causeway
4. High priest: vision, promise, Jerusalem, empire
5. Hellenism: Greeks, Syrians, Medes, Epiphanes
6. Septuagint: seventy, Ptolemy, Jews, Persia
7. Hanukkah: Judas, Feast of Lights, Passover, Feast of Dedication
8. Epiphanes: pig, translation, persecution, image
9. Egypt: Ptolemies, Alexandria, Hellespont, Septuagint
10. Maccabees: Socrates, Mattathias, Judas, Simon

B. *Choose the correct answers.*

1. The goat in Daniel's vision "touched not the ground" because
   a. he was traveling fast.
   b. he came by way of the sea.
   c. he never had to fight battles.
   d. he was frightened.
2. The Bible calls Alexander the first king of the Greeks because
   a. his father Philip was only a pretender.
   b. he was the first Greek king to have much contact with the Jews.
   c. he was crowned by Homer.
   d. he lived in the days of the first Greeks.
3. Asia Minor is
   a. south of Palestine.
   b. east of Egypt.
   c. north of Spain.
   d. east of Greece.

4. During the siege of Tyre, Alexander asked for help from
   a. Ptolemy II.
   b. Philip of Macedonia.
   c. the Jewish high priest.
   d. Aristotle.
5. According to Josephus, Alexander left Jerusalem in peace, partly because of
   a. a defeat.
   b. a victory.
   c. an apology.
   d. a dream.
6. The main direction Alexander moved in his conquests was
   a. north.
   b. south.
   c. east.
   d. west.
7. Ptolemy II did all the following *except*
   a. free some Jews from slavery.
   b. ask for a Greek translation of the Scriptures.
   c. trust the Jews.
   d. reverence the high priest.
8. Devout Jews considered Hellenism to be
   a. opposed to godly values.
   b. exciting and stimulating.
   c. mostly appealing to old people.
   d. better than what Moses taught.
9. Judas the Maccabee was
   a. a traitor.
   b. a disciple of Jesus.
   c. a leader against Syrian persecution.
   d. a Seleucid.
10. The Jewish celebration of the time when Judas cleansed the temple has been called all the following *except*
    a. Purim.
    b. Hanukkah.
    c. the Feast of Lights.
    d. the Feast of Dedication.

Matching

A. *For each clue, write the correct name from the right-hand column.*

1. Source of Hellenism	Alexandria
2. Birthplace of Alexander	Asia Minor
3. Where Alexander died	Babylon
4. Where Judas entered and cleansed the temple	Egypt
5. City where the Septuagint was translated	Greece
6. Easternmost extent of Alexander's conquests	Jerusalem
7. Empire crushed by Greeks	Macedonia
8. Land between Greece and Palestine	Pakistan
9. Where much persecution came from	Persia
10. Home of Ptolemies	Syria

B. *Match as in Part A.*

1. Worst persecutor of the Jews	Alexander
2. Greatest of the Maccabees	Antiochus Epiphanes
3. Egyptian ruler	Aristotle

4. Treated the Jewish leader with respect
5. Family who led Jews to victory
6. Alexander's father
7. Prophesied of Alexander's conquests
8. Met Alexander peacefully
9. General who took part of Alexander's empire
10. Alexander's teacher

Daniel
high priest
Judas
Maccabees
Philip
Ptolemy II
Seleucus

Completion

1. Long before the Grecian king was born,
   Daniel saw him as a broken ———.
2. Alexander, lord of land and sea,
   Died when he was only ——— ———.
3. Alexander's men did not require
   Boats to reach the island home of ———.
4. Many people could no longer speak
   Hebrew, so the scholars wrote in ———.
5. Syrians did their best to kill or seize
   Judas and his fellow ———.
6. Ever since they won those bitter fights,
   Jews still celebrate the Feast of ———.

Thought Questions

1. In Ezekiel 26, God foretold that He would bring many nations against Tyre. Nebuchadnezzar of Babylon was specifically named as one of these oppressors. What did Alexander do that also helped to fulfill the destruction foretold in verses 4 and 12?
2. "The great horn [Alexander] was broken; and for it came up four notable ones toward the four winds of heaven" (Daniel 8:8). How was this prophecy fulfilled?
3. Josephus's story about Alexander's visit to Jerusalem is probably true in general, but it is hard to prove. What expressions are used in this chapter to indicate a cautious viewpoint?
4. What was Antiochus Epiphanes trying to do by offering a pig on the temple altar?
5. How did Judas the Maccabee show that he believed in intelligent planning as well as trusting the Lord?

Geographical Skills

1. What is the approximate distance between Macedonia (located in what is now northern Greece) and the Indus River (in modern Pakistan)?

Further Study

1. The Septuagint included some Jewish writings that were not part of the Hebrew Scriptures. This section, called the Apocrypha, is not considered part of the inspired Word of God. The Apocrypha is divided into books just as the Bible is. Use a Bible dictionary to learn which books in the Apocrypha would give much of the information that you have read in this chapter.
2. How do Jews celebrate Hanukkah in modern times?

Be Sure You Know

Can you answer all these questions? If not, study Chapters 14 and 15 to find the answers.

A. What

1. kind of civilization did the ancient Greeks have?
2. contributions did the Greeks make to the English language?
3. was the Golden Age of Greece?
4. bay near Athens was the site of an important Greek victory?
5. were some similarities among the Greeks?
6. is Hippocrates sometimes called?
7. ideals did the Greeks value highly?
8. prophet foretold the coming of Alexander?
9. way of life was Alexander eager to spread?
10. empire did Alexander conquer?
11. did Josephus write about Alexander's visit to Jerusalem?
12. happened after Alexander's conquests were finished?
13. rulers governed Palestine after Alexander's death?

B. What do these words mean?

14. causeway
15. democracy
16. Hanukkah
17. Hellenism
18. jury
19. mythology
20. philosopher
21. Septuagint

C. How

22. did the Greeks conquer the city of Troy?
23. were the Spartans different from the Athenians?
24. did the Golden Age come to an end?
25. did Alexander conquer the city of Tyre?
26. did the Seleucid rulers treat the Jews?

D. Why

27. did the Greeks not work together as one united nation?
28. did the Greeks need to trade for some of their food?
29. did the Athenian philosophers reject the Gospel?
30. did the Maccabees go to war?

So Far This Year

See how many answers you can give from Chapters 1–15 without looking back.

A. *Match the letters on the map to the names below. You will not use all the letters.*

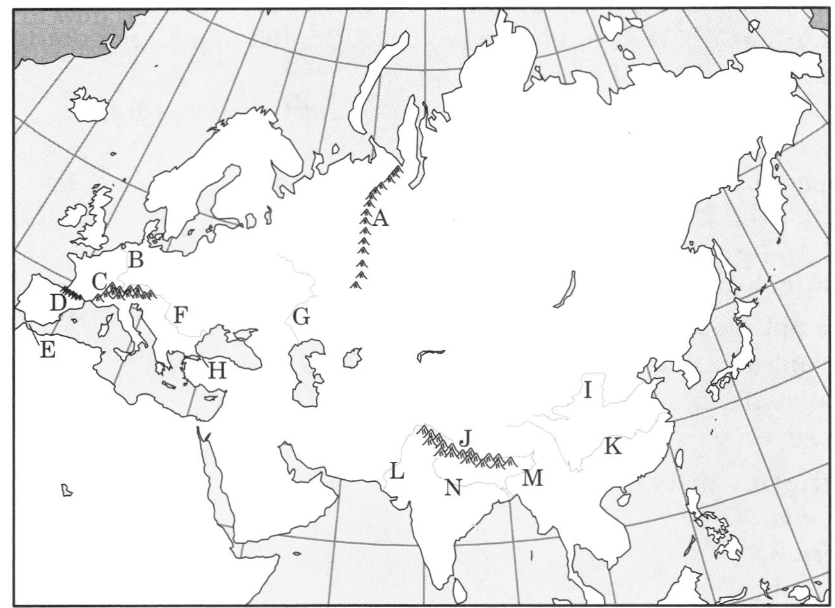

_____ 1. Brahmaputra River
_____ 2. Ganges River
_____ 3. Huang He River
_____ 4. Indus River
_____ 5. Rhine River
_____ 6. Volga River
_____ 7. Yangtze River
_____ 8. Alps
_____ 9. Himalayas
_____ 10. Ural Mountains
_____ 11. Bosporus Strait

B. *Give the correct answers.*

12. The North Atlantic Drift causes a (dry, mild, cold) climate in Europe.
13. Major religions that developed in India and China include all the following *except* (Hinduism, Islam, Buddhism, Confucianism).
14. Common problems for African farmers include all the following *except* (floods, poor soil, lack of education, overcrowding).
15. The earliest civilizations began (along seacoasts, along rivers, on broad plains).
16. Upper Egypt was the (northern, southern) part of the country, and Lower Egypt was the (northern, southern) part.
17. An important Phoenician contribution to writing was (alphabetic symbols, cuneiform, papyrus, parchment).
18. The land of (Assyria, Babylon, Egypt) was especially dependent on the trade routes in Canaan.
19. The Assyrians' main way of getting wealth was by (manufacturing, trading, warfare).
20. The Assyrians deported conquered people so that those people (could be governed

more efficiently, would find it harder to organize a rebellion, would learn to get along with people of other nations).

21. Of the kings named below, which one is associated with (*a*) the first Babylonian Empire? (*b*) the Neo-Babylonian Empire?
    Ashurbanipal, Hammurabi, Nebuchadnezzar, Sargon, Xerxes
22. The (Aryan, Brahman, caste, commercial) system of India has been harmful by keeping people from making the best use of their abilities.
23. Well-known products of China include all the following *except* (tea, silk, sugar, jade, soybeans).
24. (Alexander, Cyrus, Darius) was eager to spread Hellenism throughout his empire.
25. Hippocrates was a famous Greek (god, physician, warrior).

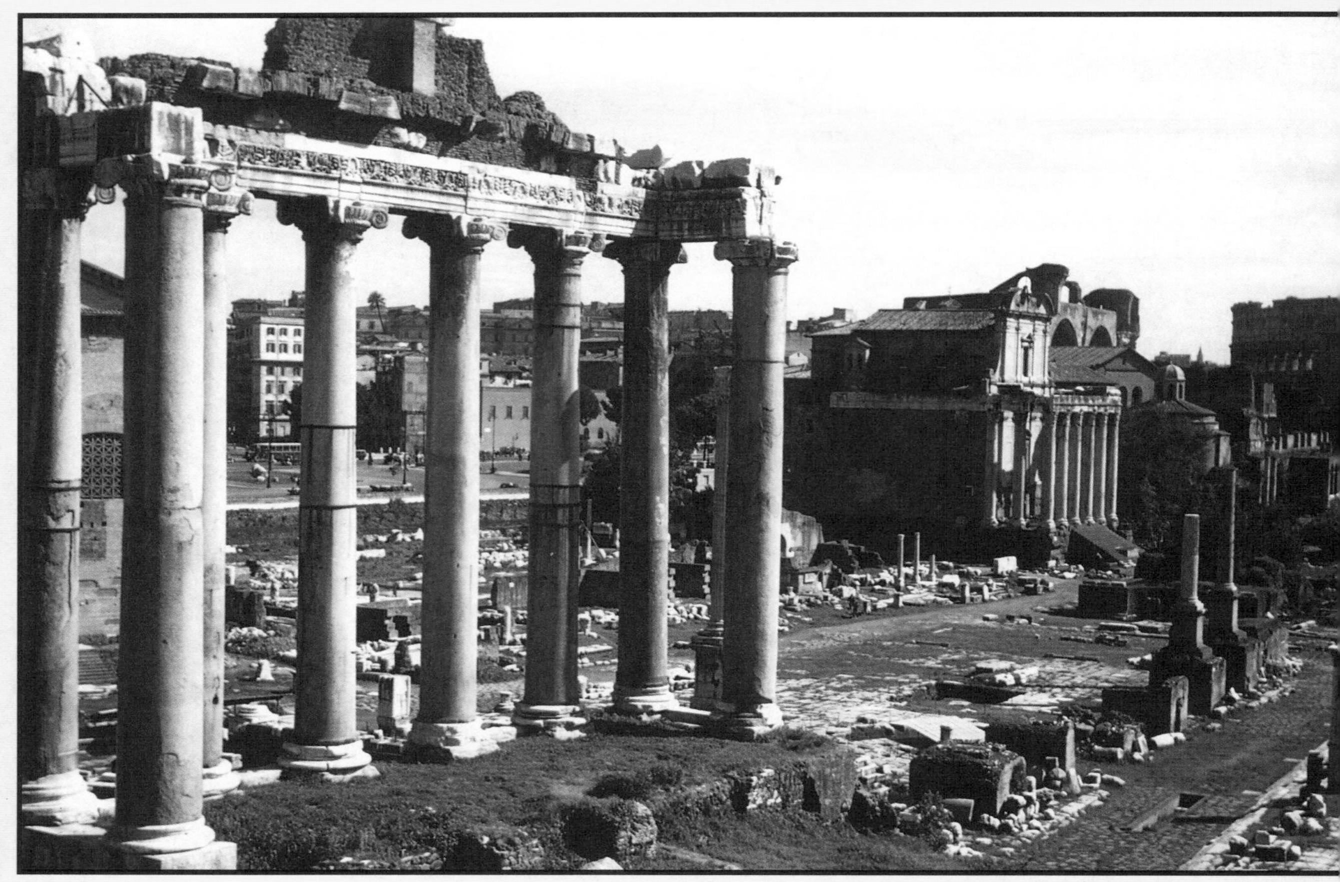

In Rome, ruins of an ancient temple and government buildings brood quietly amid the bustle of the twenty-first century.

16 Mighty Rome

First Settlements Along the Tiber

The Roman Republic Arises

The Struggle With Carthage

Daily Life Under the Romans

Greek Influence

Society Slides Downhill

A Strong Man Rises

Emperors Take Charge

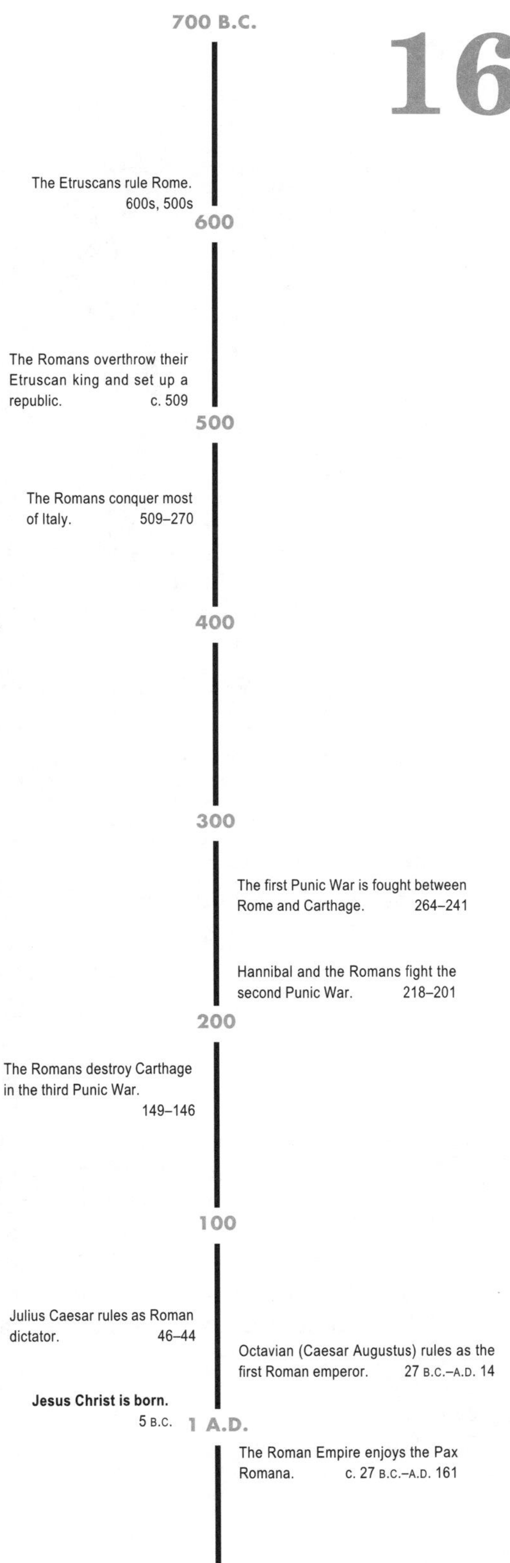

700 B.C.
The Etruscans rule Rome. 600s, 500s
600
The Romans overthrow their Etruscan king and set up a republic. c. 509
500
The Romans conquer most of Italy. 509–270
400
300
The first Punic War is fought between Rome and Carthage. 264–241
Hannibal and the Romans fight the second Punic War. 218–201
200
The Romans destroy Carthage in the third Punic War. 149–146
100
Julius Caesar rules as Roman dictator. 46–44
Octavian (Caesar Augustus) rules as the first Roman emperor. 27 B.C.–A.D. 14
Jesus Christ is born. 5 B.C.
1 A.D.
The Roman Empire enjoys the Pax Romana. c. 27 B.C.–A.D. 161
200 A.D.

"And the fourth kingdom shall be strong as iron: forasmuch as iron breaketh in pieces and subdueth all things: and as iron that breaketh all these, shall it break in pieces and bruise."

Daniel 2:40

Mighty Rome

First Settlements Along the Tiber

What surprises history reveals as it unfolds from one generation to the next! The ancient Greeks worried that they might be conquered by Persians from the east. They did not know they would finally come under the power of Romans from the west.

The Romans lived on a peninsula in the Mediterranean, as the Greeks did. On Figure 16:2, find the boot-shaped peninsula west of Greece called Italy. Like Greece, it has hot, dry summers and mild, rainy winters. Wheat, olives, and grapes grow well there. But Italy has fewer mountains and more good farmland than Greece has.

The first houses in the Rome area were little huts made of wood and grass. Compared to the pictures of later Rome, these huts remind us that "Rome was not built in a day."

While the Greeks were building their renowned civilization, the ancestors of the Romans were still common farmers. These people spoke Latin. They settled in a region of seven hills along the Tiber River. Later, Rome was called the city of seven hills.

Eventually these Latin-speaking people were conquered by neighbors from the north, across the Tiber River. The conquerors, called Etruscans (ih TRUHS kuhnz), must have had much energy and many ideas. They built roads and bridges, and they drained low-lying, marshy areas near the river. The Romans learned much from the Etruscans.

The Roman Republic Arises

About five hundred years before Christ, the Romans decided that their Etruscan king was too harsh. They rose up and overthrew him, and then they declared themselves a

The Tiber River was an important sea connection for ancient Rome. Wheat, oil, and wine from other Mediterranean countries came up the Tiber to Rome. Down the Tiber from Rome went fleets of ships that helped the Romans control their huge empire.

republic instead of a kingdom. In a republic, the people elect government officials to represent them and to rule the country. The people are not governed by a ruler who holds absolute power.

In the new Roman republic, as in Greece, there were many common people who received no right to vote or have any influence in government affairs. That right belonged only to people of the upper class, called ***patricians*** (puh TRIHSH uhnz). The common people were called ***plebeians*** (plih BEE uhnz).

The main rulers of the Romans were the Senate and two ***consuls.*** The Senate was a group of wealthy and powerful men, and the consuls were the heads of government. But the consuls were elected for one-year terms only, and they had to share their power between themselves. They were expected to consult with the Senate when they made important decisions. This kept any one man from gaining too much power.

The Romans knew that in an emergency such as war, it might not work to have two men trying to rule. What if they disagreed when a decision had to be made quickly? So the Romans decided that at such a time, they could choose a ***dictator*** to rule them for six months. Even then they were glad when the dictator gave up his powers.

To illustrate their idea that a dictator should rule only temporarily, the Romans liked to tell the old story of Cincinnatus (sihn suh NAY tuhs), who was chosen to be dictator when an enemy army threatened them. Cincinnatus was out in his field plowing when he heard the news. He left his farm and led the Roman army to a brilliant victory. When some people asked him to stay on as dictator, he refused. Back he went to his farm, just sixteen days after he had taken command of the Roman army.

As time went on, the suppressed plebeians demanded that the patricians treat them more fairly. They believed that the common people were important to Rome too. Gradually the plebeians gained more influence in the government. Eventually they had some powers that were greater than those of the patricians.

Early Rome had many enemies around her. Once enemies even invaded Rome,

These Roman soldiers are crossing a river on a bridge of boats. Notice that each man is carrying provisions bound up on a stick.

The Romans constructed the first sophisticated roads. They made their best roads in layers, as described in the text. The road in this picture is probably about 2,000 years old. It is worn from centuries of use, but its base still endures. At the peak of their empire, the Romans had approximately 50,000 miles (80,000 km) of road.

burned it, and ruled the Romans for more than half a year. For protection, the Romans and other Latin-speaking tribes formed a ***league*** to fight their enemies in Italy.

However, when others in the league saw that Rome was becoming their leader, they became fearful and fought against Rome. Rome fought back against her former allies and won. Then she was the unquestioned leader of the Latin tribes.

Slowly the Romans expanded their territory. They conquered neighboring peoples in the north, tribes in the mountains, and then some cities that the Greeks had built in southern Italy. By about 270 B.C., they ruled all Italy except the Po River valley far to the north.

The Romans could be cruel in warfare, but they treated most of the conquered people fairly. They granted many of them Roman citizenship.

To keep firm control of all their conquered territory, the Romans knew they needed good roads. They built their roads with care. After digging a deep trench, they filled the lower part with loose stones and then added more stones mixed with concrete. On the top they laid flat stones to make a smooth surface. Some parts of the old Roman roads still exist today.

Study Exercises

1. (*a*) How is farming in Italy similar to that in Greece? (*b*) In what way is Italy better suited for farming?
2. How did the Etruscans help to advance Roman civilization?
3. What is a republic?
4. Describe three ways the consuls were kept from gaining too much power.
5. Why did the early Romans admire Cincinnatus?

The Struggle With Carthage

Now that the Romans controlled the peninsula of Italy, they began to look for other lands to conquer. But one great enemy stood in the way. This was Carthage (KAHR thihj), a rich city-state just across the Mediterranean on the northern shore of Africa. Carthage wanted to expand too.

The people of Carthage already controlled part of Sicily (SIHS uh lee), the large island just off the "toe" of Italy. They wanted to take control of the whole island. If they

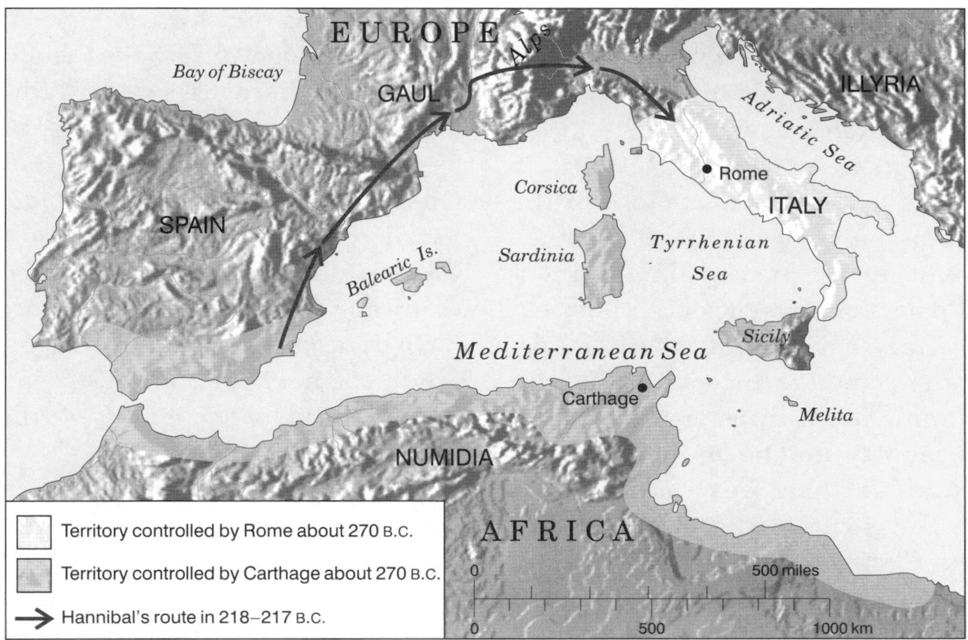

Figure 16:1. The Roman Republic and the Carthage Empire

succeeded, they could also control the strait between Sicily and Italy and could keep Roman trading ships from passing through. A war was fought over the matter, and Rome won. Carthage had to give up Sicily.

Later Carthage and Rome fought a second war. This time the army of Carthage was led by a brilliant general named Hannibal (HAN uh buhl). It is said that when Hannibal was nine years old, he had vowed that he would hate Rome forever. He led men, horses, and elephants through Spain, across the Alps, and into Italy. The Alps were so cold and dangerous that

Hannibal and his men were hindered by drifts and blowing snow as they crossed the Alps to fight the Romans.

Hannibal lost most of his elephants and over a third of his men. But when he began to fight, he beat the Romans badly. About fifty thousand Roman soldiers were killed in one battle alone.

The Romans learned to avoid fighting against Hannibal in open battles, but they resisted him enough to keep him from conquering Rome. For sixteen years, Hannibal stayed in Italy, threatening the Romans. But then the Romans attacked Carthage in Africa. Hannibal was called back to defend his home country, and he lost the war.

After that, Carthage was less of a threat to Rome. But some of the Romans were afraid that Carthage would grow powerful again. So Rome and Carthage went to war once again. The Carthaginians fought desperately to save their homes, but they were crushed. Fire raged across the city for days; and in the end, the Romans plowed the area and sowed it with salt. The struggle with Carthage had lasted for over one hundred years and ended less than 150 years before Christ. These wars are known as the three Punic (PYOO nihk) Wars.

It may seem unfair that the people of Carthage suffered so severely. But historians tell us that Carthage had been a wicked city, perhaps even worse than Rome itself. One of the great sins of Carthage was the sacrifice of little children to idols. If Carthage had conquered and ruled a world empire instead of Rome, the world might have been worse off than it was. As you will see in the next chapters, God was preparing the world for the coming of His Son and for the spread of the Gospel.

While the Punic Wars were going on, Rome was also expanding east into Greece. Sometimes the Romans used friendliness to win their way. Sometimes they used war. However it happened, one by one the Greek city-states came under the power of the Romans.

Daily Life Under the Romans

Life in Rome was good in many ways. For example, Roman law was fair. The Romans set up twelve tables of bronze, on

Roman forums were centrally located open areas in ancient Roman cities. The forums were surrounded by temples and other public buildings. In the forum, crowds would gather for entertainment and public ceremonies. Food and clothing shops were sometimes located around the edges of a forum.

Wealthy Romans lived in large houses built with small, mostly windowless rooms that opened onto a spacious courtyard called an atrium. An atrium had a roof opening to let in air and light. Often a second open courtyard called a peristyle was planted with trees, shrubs, and flowers; and sometimes even had a fishpond or fountain. A small walled-in fruit and vegetable garden at the rear of the house supplied food. In some homes, small shops faced the street.

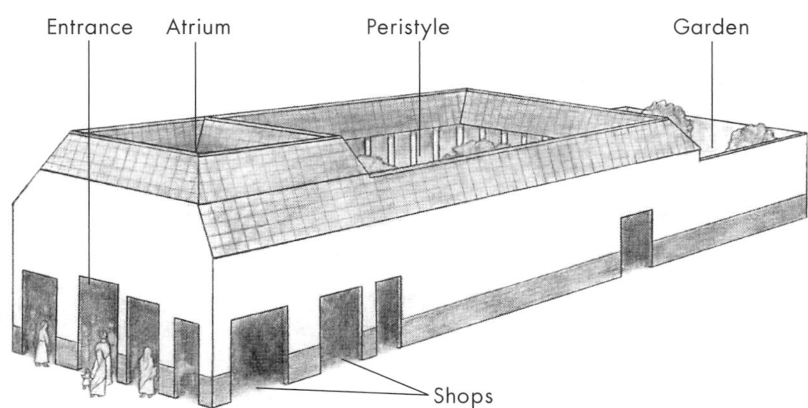

which laws were written so that everyone could see them. In this way even the poor people knew their rights, and upper-class people could not claim that the law was on their side when it was not. Roman schoolboys studied the twelve tables thoroughly. The Romans had great respect for the law.

The Romans tried to keep their laws consistent everywhere in their far-flung country. But they also made exceptions to be fair to people in special cases.

The early Romans tried to live by important ideals such as seriousness, simplicity, discipline, and dignity. They believed that farming is one of the most dignified occupations. That is noteworthy, since so many people today envy white-collar workers, who are employed in offices.

Roman farmers used wise farming methods. They knew how to rotate crops and how to irrigate their fields. They also learned that allowing land to lie ***fallow*** made the soil more fertile. Roman farmers who had enough land usually planted only half their land each year.

Most Romans lived simply. Their food, clothing, and housing were not greatly different from that of the Greeks, whom you studied earlier. In Rome's better days, not many people were extremely rich, and not many were extremely poor. That changed later, as you will see.

The Romans made some advances in building. They were the first to use concrete for bridges, houses, and pavement. Although they did not invent the arch, they developed new uses for it. Their bridges and their aqueducts, which brought water into the city of Rome, had many arches.

As you study the Roman way of life, keep in mind that Rome spread far. Many different kinds of people called themselves Romans—tribesmen from the mountains,

The Romans designed miles of sloping aqueducts to carry water from rivers and mountain springs to large cities. This aqueduct, called Pont du Gard, was built in 19 B.C. near Nîmes, France. It stands 160 feet (49 m) above the valley floor. When in operation, water flowed 25.5 miles (41 km) into a reservoir from the aqueduct, with most of the water channel being underground.

Pont du Gard was damaged by barbarians in the fifth century A.D., but it was repaired in 1743.

scholars in Athens, and captains on warships, to name a few. As time went on, it became increasingly difficult to describe a "typical" Roman.

Study Exercises

6. Where was Carthage located?
7. Who was the Carthaginian hero of the Second Punic War?
8. How did the Romans acquaint the common people with the Roman laws?
9. Give three good farming methods that Roman farmers practiced.
10. The Romans were the first people to use what building material?

Greek Influence

The Romans spread until they had taken in lands all around the Mediterranean Sea. They called it "Our Sea."

Romans borrowed from other cultures to enrich their own lives. They borrowed from the Greeks especially, for they had found much to admire in the Greek way of life. Educated Romans learned to speak and read Greek, and they had Greeks teach their sons.

Roman writers, artists, and architects copied Greek styles in their own writings, paintings, and buildings. Romans even began to worship Greek gods, though they called them by different names. The Roman god Jupiter, for example, was the equivalent of the Greek god Zeus.

The Romans spread Greek ideas far into Europe, just as Alexander had spread Greek ideas far into Asia. This explains why Greek ideas have filtered down to people in many areas of the world today—including those in North America.

When the Romans borrowed ideas, they made changes to suit themselves. For example, the Greeks thought it was important to make a building beautiful, but the Romans thought it was more important to make it useful. The Greeks enjoyed long discussions about abstract ideas, but the Romans wanted their discussions to lead to action.

The Romans also valued what they could learn from people who were not Greeks, such as the Hebrews and the Egyptians.

Society Slides Downhill

As time passed, the Romans gradually lost their high ideals. Their religion had

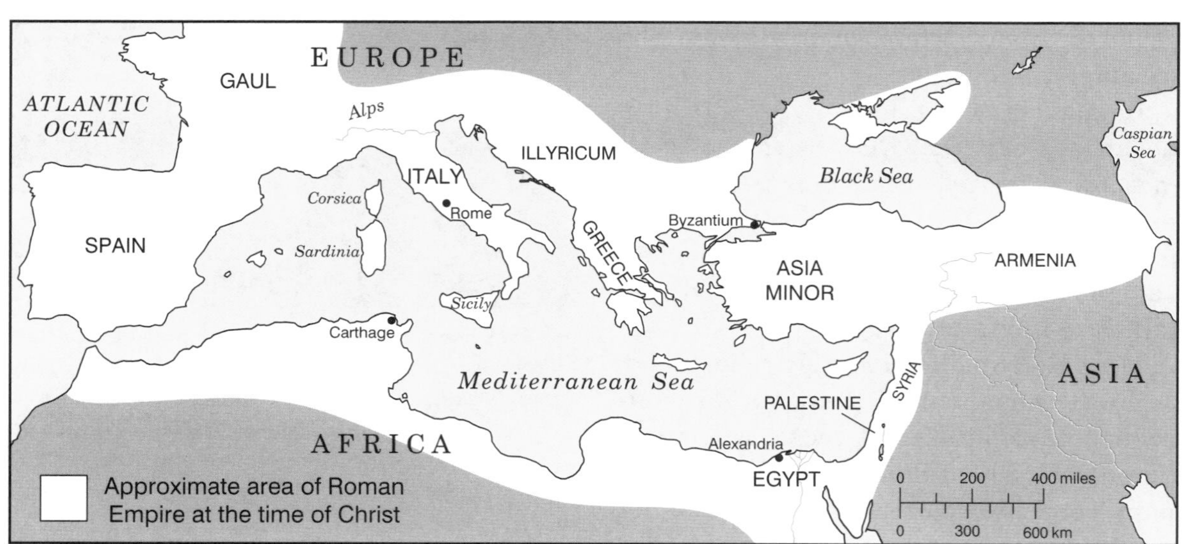

Figure 16:2. The Roman Empire

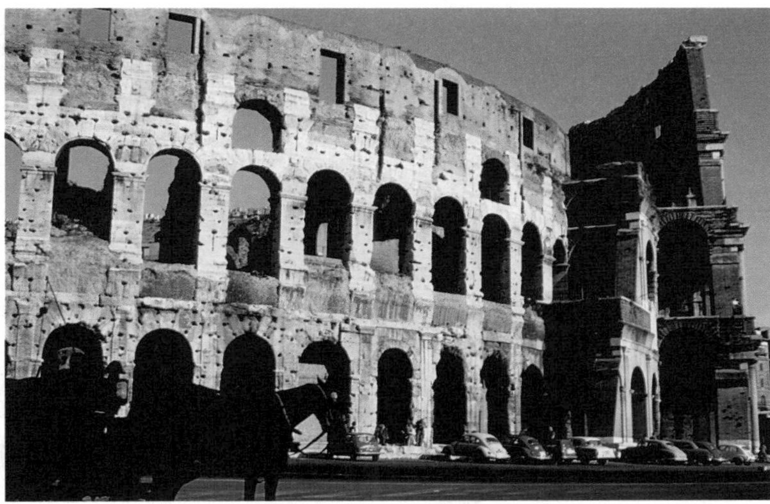

The circular Roman Colosseum could seat 50,000 spectators. The degenerate Romans loved to watch bloody fights, and the Colosseum became the scene of thousands of hand-to-hand combats between gladiators, of fights between men and animals, and of the killing of defenseless Christians.

much to do with this. If they failed to be serious and responsible, what did it matter? They were not sure whether the Roman gods would punish them or not. Many Romans did not think seriously about their spiritual needs. Since they did not seek after the true God, their idea of right and wrong was uncertain.

Slavery also caused Roman society to slide downhill. The Romans brought in slaves from the many countries they had conquered. These slaves did more and more of the work. Rich men could buy slaves and force them to work for no pay. This made them even richer. Poor farmers were often forced to sell their properties to rich men. This made them even poorer.

Many poor people went to the cities to look for work. But most of the work in the cities was also done by slaves. The poor people found little to do besides walking the streets.

To keep the poor people content, the government offered them free grain. To give them something to do, they provided circuses for them to watch. Bread and circuses! This was quite different from the past, when Romans had enjoyed making their own living from their own land. Perhaps worst of all, the poor became content to live on bread and circuses. No doubt they were still proud in some ways, but they had lost their self-respect.

When common citizens lose their high standards, the government also loses its high standards. Roman government leaders no longer thought of their high positions as a way to serve the people. They simply wanted power and money. Often they took ***bribes,*** and they stole government money that was set aside to help the people. They used the money to buy luxuries for themselves.

Wars began—this time within the Roman nation itself. Besides the soldiers who died in battle, government leaders and thousands of innocent citizens were killed. With so many violent, selfish people in power, the government could hardly function. A new kind of government was coming—the kind many Romans did not want.

Study Exercises

11. Give at least two ways that the Greeks influenced the Romans.
12. Describe one way that Roman thinking was different from Greek thinking.
13. Give at least two reasons for the decay of Roman morals.

14. When most of the citizens in a country lose a strong sense of right and wrong, what happens in the government?

A Strong Man Rises

During the turmoil in Rome, two important army generals became famous. One was Pompey (PAHM pee), a rich, ambitious man. Pompey won a name for himself when he and his army marched east and won Asia Minor, Syria, and Palestine for Rome. You will meet Pompey again when you read how the Romans first conquered Jerusalem.

The other general was tall Julius Caesar, another highly ambitious man. He had himself made governor of Gaul, a region north of Italy that is now called France. But he had to conquer Gaul before he could govern it. After his victory, he became a hero to the people of Rome.

Soon Caesar was so powerful and popular that Pompey and the Senate became worried. What would Caesar do with his power? Caesar was ordered to give up his army and come back to Rome.

Julius Caesar lived from 100–44 B.C.

Pompey flees in defeat from a battle.

Julius Caesar came back, but he brought his army along. This made him a lawbreaker in the eyes of Pompey. But Pompey also saw that he and the few soldiers he had in Italy were no match for Caesar. He and many senators fled.

Later Caesar's army defeated Pompey's army in Greece. Pompey fled again, this time to Egypt. Caesar followed him to Egypt, only to find that his enemy had already been killed. Pompey's followers fought on for a time, but Caesar eventually won.

Back in Rome, Julius Caesar began an ambitious program to improve the government. He removed dishonest officials and replaced them with honest men. He tried to win friends among those who had opposed him, by giving them positions in the government. He tried to give free grain to only the people who really needed it.

One of the most important things Caesar did was to improve the Roman calendar. Because the Romans had not computed the length of their year properly, spring was coming in what formerly had been winter months. Caesar consulted with an astronomer who understood that the year consists of about 365¼ days. Under Caesar's authority, the Romans established a calendar with a leap year to add an extra day every fourth year.

In spite of the good things Julius Caesar did, he had enemies. They resented his power, especially after he was made dictator for life. In 44 B.C., a number of senators conspired against him and stabbed him to death. Some of the murderers were men whom Caesar thought were his friends.

But Julius Caesar had probably understood one thing that the senators had not. Rome now needed a strong man to rule it. In the early days of Rome, a group of honorable men had been able to rule an honorable country. But now that many senators and other citizens were selfish and dishonest, the Senate could no longer rule Rome as it had done before.

This is a statue of Octavian (Caesar Augustus) when he was about 43 years old. He lived from 63 B.C. to A.D. 14.

Emperors Take Charge

Once again, men who wanted to rule began fighting each other. Those who had remained loyal to Julius Caesar battled the men who had conspired to kill him. The murderers lost, and two of their important leaders killed themselves.

One of the winners was a young relative of Julius Caesar named Octavian (ahk TAY vee uhn), whom Caesar had adopted as his son. Octavian shared power for a time with Mark Antony (AN tuh nee), who had helped to defeat the enemies of Caesar. Octavian took Italy and the western provinces of Rome, and Antony took the eastern provinces. But later, Octavian turned against Antony. After losing a sea battle, Antony fled and committed suicide. Octavian became emperor of all the Roman lands.

Mark Antony lived from 81–30 B.C.

Historians often divide the history of Rome into two parts. Up to this time, Rome had been a republic ruled by the Senate. From this point on, emperors would rule what became known as an empire. In a sense, however, Rome had been an empire long before this time, for it had controlled a vast territory.

Besides, Rome was still a republic in some ways. The new emperor did not like to say things were different now. He knew many people longed for the "good old days," and perhaps he himself wished things were as they had been long before. He treated the Senate with respect, as leaders of Rome had done in the past.

But it is still a fact that the emperor largely controlled the Senate. The Senate could discuss issues, but the emperor made the final decisions. Octavian began to be called Caesar Augustus. *Augustus* means "the exalted." His people regarded him almost as highly as a god.

Caesar Augustus did much good. His navy kept the Mediterranean free of pirates. He developed an efficient postal system, and he kept up the building program. In fact, he boasted that he had found Rome a city of brick and had left it a city of marble.

Perhaps most important, Augustus preferred peace rather than war. In his days the Roman Peace began. This period, called the Pax Romana (PAKS roh MAH nah) in Latin, would last for almost two hundred years.

Caesar Augustus probably did not realize that God was using him to prepare the world for the coming of His Son. The good roads, the well-policed sea, and the widespread peace all prepared the way for the Christian faith to spread. "And it came to pass in those days, that there went out a decree from Caesar Augustus, that all the world should be taxed" (Luke 2:1). By issuing that decree, Caesar Augustus helped to fulfill a prophecy regarding the birthplace of a King far greater than he.

Study Exercises

15. (*a*) How did Pompey become famous among the Romans? (*b*) How did Julius Caesar become famous?
16. What improvement in the calendar was introduced by Julius Caesar?
17. Julius Caesar was to Pompey much as Octavian was to ———.
18. During the rule of Caesar Augustus, did the Senate have more power or less power than it had during earlier days of the republic?

Clinching the Chapter

Multiple Choice

A. *Write the word or phrase* least *associated with the first item.*

1. Early Rome: Julius Caesar, Etruscans, Tiber, Latin
2. Roman roads: loose stones, flat stones, asphalt, concrete
3. Roman rulers: Senate, Carthaginians, consuls, dictators
4. Punic Wars: Sicily, Carthage, Hannibal, Pompey
5. Roman ideals: simplicity, discipline, beauty, dignity
6. Borrowed from Greeks: language, gods, architecture, Christianity
7. Roman corruption: drugs, slavery, violence, entertainment
8. Conquered by Pompey: Asia Minor, Carthage, Syria, Palestine
9. Calendar: leap year, astronomer, Julius Caesar, Pompey
10. Spread of Gospel: patricians, peace, police, roads

B. *Write the correct words.*

1. If the people have a voice in governing a country, it is called (a kingdom, a republic, an empire, a realm).
2. The common people of early Rome were the (Carthaginians, senators, patricians, plebeians).
3. The first Romans spoke (Greek, Latin, Etruscan, Aramaic).
4. The three wars between Rome and Carthage are called the (Civil, Etruscan, Punic, Alpine) Wars.
5. The Romans were the first to use (fired bricks, aqueducts, pavement, concrete).
6. The twelve tables represented Roman (law, agriculture, art, architecture).
7. The Romans tried to keep the poor people content with (slaves and money, bread and circuses, employment, self-respect).
8. If government officials are dishonest, they may do special favors for people who offer them (consuls, slaves, grain, bribes).
9. The use of the word *Pax* in the text shows that it means (Rome, police, pirates, peace).
10. An emperor rules (a city-state, a democracy, an empire, a republic).

Matching

A. *For each clue, write the correct term from the right-hand column.*

1. Upper class of citizens	Augustus
2. Foreigners brought in to work	consul
3. Ruler when Pax Romana began	Etruscans
4. Was defeated by Julius Caesar	Hannibal
5. Taught skills to early Romans	Julius Caesar
6. One of two heads of government	Jupiter
7. Strong man who became dictator for life	patricians
8. Roman god	Pompey
9. Carthaginian general	Senate
10. Group of men who governed Rome	slaves

B. *Match as in Part A. (If you need help with number 10, see a map or review Chapter 2.)*

1. Land conquered by Julius Caesar	Alps
2. Sea surrounded by Roman lands	Apennines
3. River flowing through Rome	Carthage
4. Mountains where Hannibal lost men	Cincinnatus
5. Peninsula where story of Rome begins	Gaul
6. Refused to be dictator very long	Greece
7. Land on peninsula east of Rome	Italy
8. Island close to Italy	Mediterranean
9. Trading city-state in northern Africa	Sicily
10. Mountain chain running through Italy	Tiber

Completion

1. On a boot-shaped peninsula making their home,
   The Latins once founded the city of ———.
2. The Etruscans taught Romans one long-lasting thing:
   They would have a republic, but not a strong ———.
3. After digging a trench, men would dump in great loads
   Of the stone that was needed to make solid ———.
4. There was no need to argue; the citizens saw
   On display on twelve tables the great Roman ———.
5. It was dignified, simple, and couldn't do harm
   For a Roman young man to grow up on a ———.
6. It's apparent a strong one can learn from a weak;
   Any Roman could learn from a widely read ———.
7. If a nation grows careless, then sooner or later,
   They may find themselves serving a selfish ———.
8. Unemployment was serious. The poor farmers fled
   To the city and lived on free handouts of ———.
9. He promoted stability, peacefulness, justice;
   He was called "the exalted," or Caesar ———.

Thought Questions

1. What is the connection between peace and the spread of the Gospel?
2. Why did the Romans so much dislike having a dictator longer than necessary?
3. Even though reinforced concrete is used to build modern roads, they do not last as long as Roman roads did. What is the reason?
4. How can we decide what is a worthwhile occupation?
5. It is not good for people to be proud, but neither should they lose their self-respect. Why not?

Geographical Skills

1. Tunis, the capital of Tunisia, is located near the site of ancient Carthage. Give the latitude and longitude of Tunis. (Be as precise as possible.)
2. About how far did Hannibal travel with his army and his elephants to fight the Romans? Use Figure 16:1 to find the approximate distance.

Further Study

1. Some people make a difference between a democracy and a republic. Others think of them as much the same thing. What can you learn about the difference in meaning that some people see in the two?
2. The United States and Canada do not use the two-consul system; only one man fills the highest office of the nation. How is he kept from gaining too much power?

Masada is a flat-topped mountain with steep slopes on all sides. After the Romans destroyed Jerusalem, it took them three more years to conquer the Jews in the fortress on Masada. Note the Dead Sea in the background.

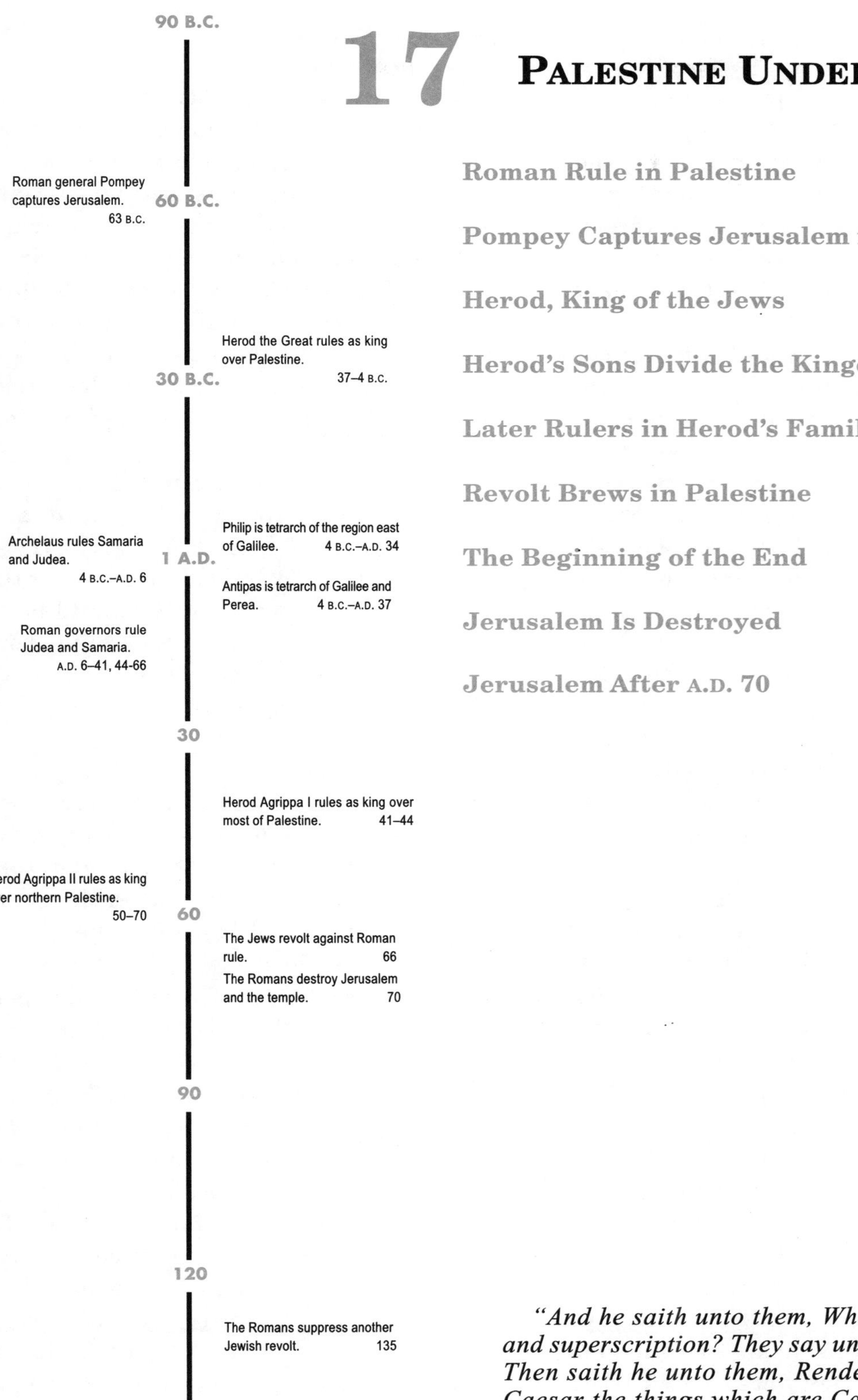
90 B.C.
Roman general Pompey captures Jerusalem. 63 B.C.
60 B.C.
Herod the Great rules as king over Palestine. 37–4 B.C.
30 B.C.
Archelaus rules Samaria and Judea. 4 B.C.–A.D. 6
Philip is tetrarch of the region east of Galilee. 4 B.C.–A.D. 34
1 A.D.
Antipas is tetrarch of Galilee and Perea. 4 B.C.–A.D. 37
Roman governors rule Judea and Samaria. A.D. 6–41, 44-66
30
Herod Agrippa I rules as king over most of Palestine. 41–44
Herod Agrippa II rules as king over northern Palestine. 50–70
60
The Jews revolt against Roman rule. 66
The Romans destroy Jerusalem and the temple. 70
90
120
The Romans suppress another Jewish revolt. 135
150 A.D.

17 Palestine Under Rome

Roman Rule in Palestine

Pompey Captures Jerusalem for Rome

Herod, King of the Jews

Herod's Sons Divide the Kingdom

Later Rulers in Herod's Family

Revolt Brews in Palestine

The Beginning of the End

Jerusalem Is Destroyed

Jerusalem After A.D. 70

"And he saith unto them, Whose is this image and superscription? They say unto him, Caesar's. Then saith he unto them, Render therefore unto Caesar the things which are Caesar's; and unto God the things that are God's."

Matthew 22:20, 21

Palestine Under Rome

The Roman Empire kept spreading. Palestine itself, with its many Jews, eventually came under the iron grip of Rome. To understand how strong the Romans were, read this part of a speech that King Agrippa once made to the Jews. He was trying to persuade them not to fight the Romans.

> Will you not carefully reflect upon the Roman Empire? The power of the Romans is invincible in all parts of the habitable earth. All Euphrates is not a sufficient boundary for them on the east side, nor the Danube [River] on the north, and for their southern limit, Libya has been searched over by them. They have carried their arms as far as such British islands as were never known before. Nay, the Romans have extended their arms beyond the pillars of Hercules [Strait of Gibraltar], and have walked among the clouds, upon the Pyrenean mountains, and have subdued these nations.
>
> Who among you hath not heard of the great number of the Germans? You have yourselves seen them to be strong and tall; yet these Germans, who dwell in an immense country, who have minds greater than their bodies, and a soul that despises death, and who are in rage more fierce than wild beasts, have the Rhine [River] for the boundary and are tamed by eight Roman legions.
>
> Do you also, who depend on the walls of Jerusalem, consider what a wall the Britons had: for the Romans sailed away to them, and subdued them while they were encompassed by the ocean. (Adapted from *Josephus*, "The Jewish War," 2:16:4.)

Roman Rule in Palestine

The Jews, sensitive and proud, resented Roman rule. Their merchants had to stop at bridges, along roadsides, and at city gates to let tax collectors rummage through their goods and decide how much tax to charge. The Jews knew that tax collectors, called ***publicans,*** charged extra to line their own pockets. It made them feel even worse that some of their fellow Jews took jobs as publicans, collecting taxes for a foreign government.

Once some Jews tried to trap Jesus by asking, "Is it lawful to give tribute unto Caesar, or not?" (Matthew 22:17). They thought if He said yes, He would anger the Jews, and if He said no, He would be in trouble with the Romans. Jesus pointed out that they were using Caesar's money, so by their actions they were admitting that Caesar was their ruler.

When Palestine was under Roman rule, soldiers were a common sight there. They served as policemen. An officer in charge of a hundred men was called a ***centurion.*** Groups of four thousand to six thousand soldiers were called ***legions.*** When Jesus was arrested, He said that God could easily send more than twelve legions of angels to help Him (Matthew 26:53).

Roman law said that a soldier could make anyone carry his pack for a mile. Jesus had something to say about that: "Whosoever shall compel thee to go a mile, go with him twain" (Matthew 5:41). With Roman soldiers so common, Jesus may have followed His own instruction a number of times.

Roman law and justice were usually fair, but some of their punishments, like crucifixion, were very harsh. Being nailed or tied to a cross was an excruciating way to die. Sometimes a man hung on a cross for several days before he finally died. Today,

An angry Jewish merchant pays the tax collector.

cruel punishments are against the law in many nations.

A soldier or jailer who let a prisoner escape was required to take the prisoner's punishment himself. This explains why the Philippian jailer drew a sword to kill himself when he supposed that his prisoners had fled (Acts 16:27). It also explains why the soldiers on the sinking ship with Paul wanted to kill the prisoners on board before they swam away and escaped (Acts 27:42).

Roman rulers were sometimes very cruel, slaughtering hundreds of citizens if they chose to do so. Sometimes the emperor rebuked or punished the rulers under him for such cruelty, but at other times the emperor might overlook or support their wrongdoing.

On the other hand, the Romans allowed the Jews many privileges, including some that they did not give to other conquered countries. For example, the Jews were not required to serve in the Roman army. They were also allowed a certain amount of self-government. The ***Sanhedrin*** (san HEE drihn), a council of Jewish leaders, could bring people to trial and mete out some punishments. But the Jews were not allowed to put anyone to death. That is why they went to the Roman governor Pilate when they wanted to have Jesus executed.

It was possible for a Jew to become a Roman ***citizen.*** At Philippi, Paul and Silas were beaten and jailed without a trial, even though they were Roman citizens. The authorities were frightened when they realized this, for they had violated the Roman law (Acts 16:38).

Different groups of Jews had different attitudes toward the Romans. The Pharisees definitely disliked Roman rule. The Sadducees were more worldly, and many of them worked along with the Romans. Some Jews hid out in the mountains and fought the Romans from time to time.

Jesus felt the distress of His people under Roman rule. When Satan offered Him all the kingdoms of the world, it was no small temptation. But Jesus came to bring something far more important than political freedom. His death and resurrection bring spiritual freedom to all who accept

God's redemption plan. He told the Jews, "If the Son therefore shall make you free, ye shall be free indeed" (John 8:36).

Study Exercises

1. Rome had extended far enough into Europe to subdue what two groups of people?
2. Why did the Jews feel especially resentful toward Jewish publicans?
3. How were the Jews admitting that the Romans ruled over them?
4. Name the power that the Roman government kept from the Sanhedrin.
5. Which group was more opposed to Roman rule: the Pharisees or the Sadducees?

Pompey Captures Jerusalem for Rome

How did the Romans first gain control over the Jews in Jerusalem? The story begins with a quarrel between two brothers. Hyrcanus (hur KAY nuhs) and Aristobulus (ar ihs tuh BYOO luhs), descendants of the Maccabees, both wanted to rule in Jerusalem. When the Roman general Pompey appeared in Palestine with his army, the two brothers asked him to decide who should rule. Hyrcanus argued, "I am older." Aristobulus argued, "I am more able."

Pompey did not trust Aristobulus, so he took him prisoner and invaded Jerusalem. Some of the Jews allowed him to enter the city. But others shut themselves up in the temple, which was surrounded by strong walls. The Roman army began pounding at the wall with their heavy machines.

Finally the biggest tower along the wall toppled, breaking down part of the wall as it fell, and the Roman soldiers poured in. Thousands of Jews were killed in the fighting and confusion that followed. In this way, Jerusalem fell to the Romans in 63 B.C.

Pompey and some of his soldiers horrified the Jews by entering the holy places of the temple, where God had said only the priests should go, and looking around as if they were tourists. But Pompey did no further harm to the temple. He left its treasures there and told the priests to cleanse the temple and continue offering their sacrifices to God. He also approved Hyrcanus to be the high priest and the ruler of Jerusalem and the surrounding areas.

Hyrcanus had a friend named Antipater (an TIHP uh tur). Antipater knew Hyrcanus was not really an able ruler, so he managed many of Hyrcanus's affairs for him. Antipater's two oldest sons were also appointed to government positions. Herod, Antipater's second son, was energetic, intelligent, athletic—and quite ambitious.

Herod, King of the Jews

Antipater and Herod were friends with Mark Antony, who was fighting to be the Roman emperor. Antony had Herod crowned king of the Jews. But Antony lost in the struggle to win control of the Roman Empire and committed suicide.

What was Herod to do now? He went to the winner, Octavian, and admitted freely that he had been a loyal supporter of Mark Antony. Then he said, "Consider how faithful a friend, and not whose friend, I have been." Octavian was so impressed that he again crowned Herod king of the Jews.

Later Herod became known as "Herod the Great." He was the tyrant who attempted to kill Jesus by ordering that all the baby boys of Bethlehem be slaughtered. But not everything Herod did was bad. Although at one point he conquered Jerusalem by force, he paid his soldiers to stop the destruction and killing once they had gained control of the city. King Herod tried to please the Jews by rebuilding the temple at Jerusalem, making it much bigger and grander.

This model shows the temple in Jerusalem after Herod the Great enlarged it and made it much more magnificent than the previous one. The Romans later destroyed it, just as Jesus had foretold.

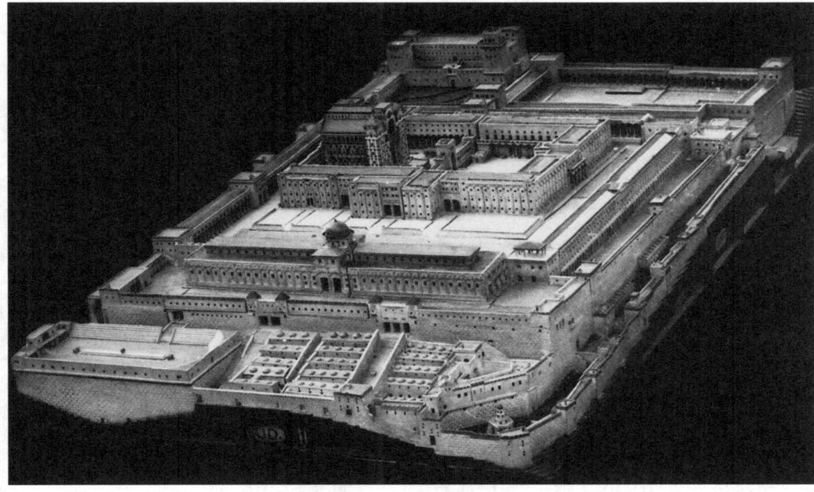

Herod had never learned to control his passions, and many people were victims of his hot temper and extreme selfishness. His favorite wife hated him because he had ordered her grandfather and brother killed. It was a stormy marriage, and Herod finally had her put to death.

As soon as his anger had cooled, Herod grieved over her death as deeply as he once had loved her. Later he ordered her two sons killed—and he was sorry for that too. He said, with tears in his eyes, that he had been a poor father and hoped he would be a better grandfather. However, just five days before he died, he had still another son killed. Octavian (Caesar Augustus) once remarked, "It is better to be Herod's hog than to be his son."

Herod knew that many Jews would rejoice when he died. He resented this and thought of a scheme to keep them from celebrating. He held a number of Jewish men prisoners and gave orders that when he died, these men should be killed. Then the Jews would be grieving at the time of his death.

But Herod's power ended as soon as he died, and the prisoners were released. The madness of Herod the Great had gone on long enough.

Study Exercises

6. When the Romans invaded Jerusalem, why did some Jews shut themselves up in the temple?
7. What did Pompey do that shocked the Jews?
8. Who was the famous son of Antipater?

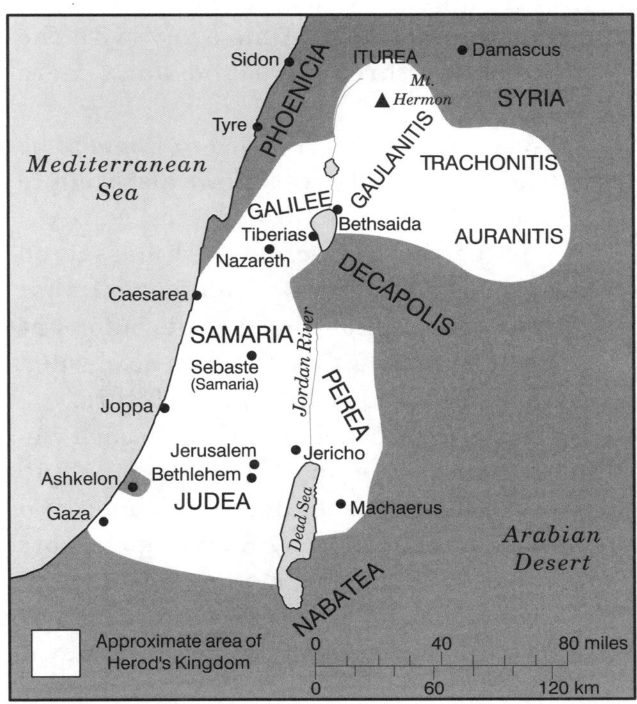

Figure 17:1. Herod's Kingdom

9. What great building did Herod build to please the Jews?
10. What evidence given in this section indicates that Octavian might have regretted his decision to crown Herod king?

Herod's Sons Divide the Kingdom

In his will, Herod had stated that several of his sons should divide his kingdom among themselves. Antipas and Philip each received a fourth of the kingdom. For this reason, they were called ***tetrarchs*** (TEHT rahrks); the prefix *tetra-* refers to the number four. Archelaus (AHR kee LAY uhs) was to rule the other half of Herod's kingdom, which included Judea and Samaria.

Archelaus began his rule with a generous speech to the Jews, trying to win their good will. But not long after, a large number of Jews wanted Archelaus to lighten their taxes and to correct some wrongs that Herod had done to them. When the Jews started a disturbance, Archelaus became excited and called out his army, with the result that three thousand Jews were slaughtered.

When Archelaus traveled to Rome to be made king officially, fifty Jews also went to Rome. They complained to emperor Augustus that Archelaus had massacred many Jews. Augustus finally said that Archelaus could continue to rule, but not as king. If he proved that he was a good ruler, perhaps he could be king in the future.

However, Archelaus ruled with such violence that he was finally banished to Gaul. For the next several decades, Judea and Samaria were ruled by Roman governors instead of by members of Herod's family. The best remembered of these governors is Pontius Pilate, who gave in to the Jews' demands to crucify Jesus.

Archelaus's brother Antipas ruled Galilee and part of the region east of the Jordan River. He was a capable ruler, but he was a selfish man like his father Herod the Great. The Bible says that Antipas "feared John [the Baptist], knowing that he was a just man and an holy, . . . and heard him gladly" (Mark 6:20). But later he had John put to death.

"Then the soldiers of the governor took Jesus.... And when they had platted a crown of thorns, they put it upon his head, ... and mocked him, saying, Hail, King of the Jews!... And after that they had mocked him, they ... led him away to crucify him" (Matthew 27:27–31).

Jesus once referred to Herod Antipas as "that fox" (Luke 13:32). When Pilate sent Jesus to Antipas for trial before Jesus' crucifixion, Herod "questioned with him in many words; but he answered him nothing" (Luke 23:9). Herod Antipas was also banished in the end, and he died in Spain.

The most respectable of all the Herods was Philip, the tetrarch who ruled northeastern Palestine. He governed his territory peacefully.

Later Rulers in Herod's Family

After Philip died, the Roman emperor gave his territory to a young relative who is known today as Herod Agrippa I. Soon afterward the emperor gave him Antipas's territory as well; and a few years later, the Romans also gave him the region that Archelaus had ruled. Suddenly Herod Agrippa I, grandson of Herod the Great, was king of almost all that his grandfather had ruled!

In many ways, this Herod was a better ruler than his grandfather had been. But his desire to please the Jews caused him to persecute the early church, and it eventually led to his death. Herod Agrippa I is the Herod who had the apostle James killed with the sword and who tried to kill Peter. Later when he allowed the people to honor him as a god, the angel of God smote him, and he was "eaten of worms" (Acts 12:23). He had ruled all of Palestine for only about three years.

The son of Herod Agrippa I is the one called Agrippa in Acts 25 and 26; today he is known as Herod Agrippa II. Because he was only about sixteen years old when his father died, the Roman government did not think he was old enough to be king. Later he received part of the kingdom that his father had ruled.

Herod Agrippa II listened to Paul's defense and made a statement people have never forgotten: "Almost thou persuadest me to be a Christian" (Acts 26:28). Was Agrippa mocking Paul, as some people have guessed? Probably not altogether. Probably, like many others who have heard the Gospel, Agrippa felt torn between right and wrong. Tragically, he chose wrong.

Study Exercises

11. What was a Roman tetrarch?
12. Who is the best remembered of the men that took Archelaus's office?
13. How was Herod Antipas related to Herod the Great?
14. What name do modern historians give (*a*) to the Herod who had the apostle James put to death? (*b*) to the Agrippa who listened to Paul's defense?

Revolt Brews in Palestine

While Herod Agrippa II reigned in parts of northern Palestine, Roman governors again ruled the territory that Pilate had once governed. You may remember Felix, who trembled when Paul spoke to him (Acts 24:25). Festus, who ruled after Felix, listened as Paul made his defense before King Agrippa (Acts 25:24–27).

The next two governors were careless, wicked rulers. The second one, named Florus, allowed robbers to continue their crimes as long as they gave him part of the stolen goods. Many citizens fled the country. It seemed that Florus did things deliberately to provoke a Jewish rebellion against the Romans. On at least one occasion he commanded his soldiers to plunder the people of Jerusalem. While greedily seizing goods for themselves, the soldiers killed thousands of men, women, and children.

Finally, about A.D. 66, the Jews revolted. But not all the Jews supported the rebellion. Many of them realized that if war broke out against the powerful Romans, Jerusalem might be destroyed.

News of the rebellion in Jerusalem reached the countryside and other towns. Many people took up arms, some on the side of the rebels and some against them. Towns and villages were burned, and scores of people were slaughtered.

To bring order back to Jerusalem, the governor of Syria marched his army to the city and attacked it. But after a while, he suddenly withdrew his troops and left. It seemed very strange, for he had suffered no

Nero was the cruel Roman emperor from A.D. 54 to 68.

defeat. Josephus says he left "without any reason in the world."

The Beginning of the End

Now people left the city by the hundreds, "as from a ship when it was going to sink." Many of them were Christians. They were heeding Jesus' warning: "When ye shall see Jerusalem compassed with armies, then know that the desolation thereof is nigh. Then let them which are in Judaea flee to the mountains" (Luke 21:20, 21). God had given the Jews about forty years to accept Jesus as their Messiah. But because the nation as a whole had rejected Jesus, the unbelieving Jews would soon face "the days of vengeance" (Luke 21:22).

In A.D. 67, the emperor Nero sent the Roman general Vespasian (vehs PAY zhuhn) with a large army to subdue the Jews. Vespasian conquered one city after another in Palestine. The Jews were discovering how difficult it was to fight against a well-trained army. Josephus wrote about one occasion as follows:

> Now the Jews were unskilful in war, but were to fight with those who were skilful therein; they were footmen to fight with horsemen; they were in disorder, to fight with those that were united together; they were poorly armed, to fight those that were completely so; they were to fight more by their rage than by sober counsel, and were exposed to soldiers that were exactly obedient, and did everything they were bidden upon the least intimation. So they were easily beaten.

While Vespasian was preparing to march against Jerusalem, he received news that Nero was dead. Soon after this, Vespasian departed for Rome to claim the emperorship, leaving his son Titus to besiege Jerusalem.

Meanwhile, the Jews in Jerusalem were trying to prepare for the Roman attack. But in some ways they were becoming less prepared rather than more so. Bands of robbers slipped into Jerusalem. They joined the rebels who were already there and took over the city, robbing and murdering as they pleased.

Vespasian, Roman emperor from A.D. 69 to 79, began constructing the Colosseum during his reign.

The more respectable people, shocked at all that these ruffians were doing, fought them and penned them in the temple. But later the rebels overwhelmed the city again. The robbers were so bold and killed so freely that those who had lost loved ones were afraid to mourn openly for fear that they too would be killed.

No doubt many people would have left the city at this point. But now another rebel army was outside the city walls, robbing and tormenting those who tried to flee.

It is hard to believe, but the people of Jerusalem, so oppressed by the rebels inside the city, finally called in the robbers from outside the wall to fight those inside. The two bands of robbers did fight each other. They also burned food storehouses so that their enemies in the city would run short. This soon brought severe famine to the whole city. But both bands of robbers agreed on one thing—that no one should leave the city to escape. They declared that anyone who opposed them or tried to leave was a traitor.

When Titus's army arrived at Jerusalem, the rebels in the city became a little more sober. Holding off their quarrels with each other, they rushed out and attacked the Romans before they could set up camp. But later they fought among themselves again, "and did everything that the besiegers could desire them to do; for they never suffered anything that was worse from the Romans than they made each other suffer."

Study Exercises

15. How did the withdrawal of the Syrian governor's army from Jerusalem help the Christians in the city?
16. Why did God allow the Romans to come against Jerusalem and bring great suffering to the Jews?
17. What army was said to be obedient and very well organized?
18. (*a*) Who invited the second group of robbers to come into the city? (*b*) Why?
19. What enemies were worse to the Jews than the Romans?

Jerusalem Is Destroyed

Shielding themselves from darts and stones that the Jews threw from the wall, the Romans began trying to break into Jerusalem. They used battering rams—heavy beams with iron heads—to pound repeatedly against a gate or the wall. They

This picture shows several methods the Romans used to conquer cities. To the left, several wind-up devices hurl stones. In the center, the soldiers prop ladders against the walls and storm to the top. On the right, a long, low shed protects a battering ram from the debris raining on it. On the far right, the soldiers have rolled a high tower up to the walls and are attempting to enter the city.

also used devices that hurled stones and darts at the defenders of the city.

After a hard struggle, the Romans conquered part of Jerusalem. The Jews in the part that remained faced worse and worse misery. People paid outrageous prices for small amounts of grain. They ate it secretly, sometimes raw, sometimes half-baked. Josephus reports that the robbers watched for houses closed up tight, suspecting that food could be found there. Even though the robbers themselves had enough to eat at that point, they seized all they could for future use. They broke doors open, snatched food out of people's hands, beat people, tore their hair, and shook children for the morsels they were holding.

The men of the city were in a terrible trap. They knew that if they gave themselves up freely to the Romans, they might receive mercy. But it was almost impossible to get their whole families out of the city. If they left by themselves, their families back in the city would probably be tormented by the rebels.

Some people were so hungry that they slipped out of the city at night to gather wild plants for food. But the Romans caught some of them and crucified them in sight of the city wall.

To make matters worse, Titus ordered a wall of his own to be built around Jerusalem. The Roman army had so many men that the wall, which normally would have taken months to build, was finished in just three days. This kept the people of the city from slipping out.

Now whole families of Jews began to starve. Rather than burying the many dead bodies, the living dropped the dead over the wall. When Titus saw the piles of corpses, he groaned and spread his hands to heaven, calling God to witness that all this was not his fault. Many times during the siege he had offered pardon to the Jews if they would surrender, but the rebel Jews had always refused to let anyone leave.

Titus was proclaimed emperor of the Romans in A.D. 79. Perhaps the man in the foreground is a Jewish priest who was forced to be at the celebration to show that his people had been conquered by Titus.

Finally the Romans attacked the massive walls of the temple, which the Jews were using as a fortress. To get in, Titus ordered that the gates of the temple be burned. He wanted to preserve the temple itself, but a vengeful Roman soldier set fire to it. While it was burning, the Roman soldiers killed about ten thousand people—men and women, young and old.

In the days following, the Romans captured and destroyed the rest of the city. The worst of the robbers were finally caught. The Romans killed the old and the sick, but they sold many as slaves, and they kept some to be killed for amusement in Roman games.

This detail from the Arch of Titus shows the Romans carrying away temple treasures, including the seven-branched candlestick.

Jesus Foretells the Destruction of Jerusalem

"And when he was come near, he beheld the city, and wept over it, saying, If thou hadst known, even thou, at least in this thy day, the things which belong unto thy peace! but now they are hid from thine eyes.

For the days shall come upon thee, that thine enemies shall cast a trench about thee, and compass thee round, and keep thee in on every side, and shall lay thee even with the ground, and thy children within thee; and they shall not leave in thee one stone upon another; because thou knewest not the time of thy visitation" (Luke 19:41–44).

The Arch of Titus was erected 11 years after the fall of Jerusalem. Its sculpture commemorates Roman military victories, including the victory over the Jews.

Jerusalem After A.D. 70

People often speak of the destruction of Jerusalem in A.D. 70 as if that were the end of the city. In many important ways, it was the end. The temple was destroyed, as Jesus had foretold. Temple sacrifices stopped. The glory had departed.

Yet, however painfully, history moves on. Many Jews lingered in and around Jerusalem. They again gathered strength; and amazingly, about sixty years after the temple was destroyed, they staged another major revolt. They even achieved a shaky independence for a while.

This time, when the Romans defeated the Jews in A.D. 135, they built another town on the site of Jerusalem and called it Aelia Capitolina (EE lee uh kahp uh tah LY nuh). No Jews were allowed to live in the new city or the surrounding area. Jews were restricted from even visiting the city, but

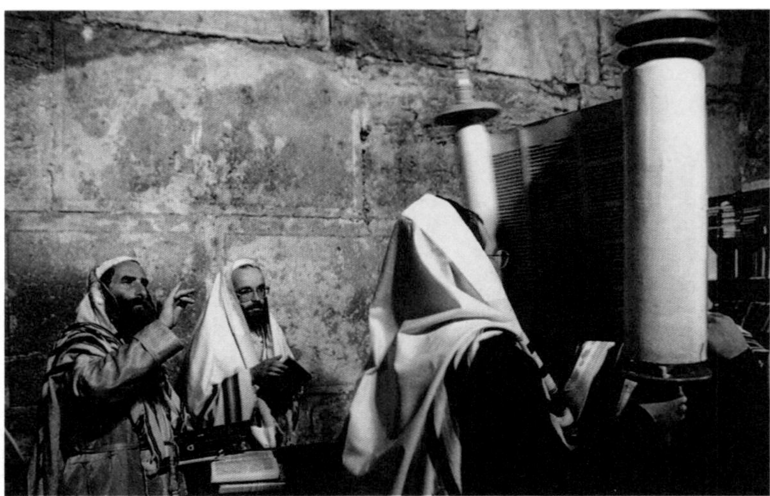

In a cave inside the Wailing Wall, ultra-orthodox Jews pray and read the Torah. The Torah contains Old Testament Scripture passages as well as other Jewish religious writings.

on one day each year some gathered to lament Jerusalem's fate. It was many years before the restrictions on Jews entering the city were relaxed.

Many Jews had already been scattered and were living in various countries. Following the destruction of Jerusalem, more Jews moved away from their homeland. This scattering of the Jews is called the Dispersion, and the scattered Jews became known as the ***Diaspora*** (dy AS pur uh). The result is that Jews have brought their religion, their knowledge, and their talents to almost every country in the world.

Study Exercises

20. Why did few of the starving Jews in Jerusalem flee to the Romans?
21. What did the Romans do that caused a great increase of starvation in the city?
22. About how old would Jesus have been if He had still lived on earth during the destruction of Jerusalem?

The Romans did not destroy quite everything in Jerusalem. In the center of the picture, part of the original wall still stands. This photograph was taken after a snowstorm on January 2, 1992, dropped 16 inches (40.6 cm) of snow on the city, the most in 42 years.

Pompeii was a rich and wicked Roman city in Jesus' time. In A.D. 79, nine years after the destruction of Jerusalem, God judged the people of Pompeii by allowing a violent eruption of Mt. Vesuvius, which rained ashes and debris on the city. When the eruption was over, Pompeii was covered with 19 to 23 feet (5.8 to 7 m) of volcanic material, and the city lay buried and mostly undisturbed for 1,700 years.

Above left: An artist's idea of what the eruption looked like. Notice the burning ships and the people jumping into the water to escape the terrible heat. *Above right:* Since 1709, archaeologists have uncovered much of Pompeii, including these remains of government buildings. Mount Vesuvius is in the background.

Clinching the Chapter

Multiple Choice

A. *Write the word or phrase* least *associated with the first item.*

1. Antipas: Herod, centurion, fox, banished
2. Jews: revolt, taxation, Rhine, Judea
3. After Archelaus: Pilate, Felix, Festus, Herod the Great
4. Book of Acts: Archelaus, Agrippa, Felix, Festus
5. Jewish defeat: 63 B.C., 4 B.C., A.D. 70, A.D. 135
6. Edge of Roman Empire: Palestine, Britain, Libya, Rhine
7. Roman army: legion, centurion, battering ram, publican
8. Archelaus: Judea, Samaria, Libya, Jerusalem
9. Conquered Jerusalem: Herod, Pompey, Josephus, Titus
10. Another name for Herod: Agrippa, Philip, Antipas, Pompey

B. *Write the correct words.*

1. Judea, Samaria, and Galilee were ruled by sons of (Herod the Great, Pompey, Titus, Josephus).
2. The most respectable of the Herods was (Philip, Antipas, Archelaus, Agrippa).
3. During the siege of Jerusalem, the city was crowded full of (Christians, Romans, Greeks, Jews).
4. What was another name for Octavian? (Mark Antony, Caesar Augustus, Antipater, Hyrcanus)

5. The Roman general who conquered Jerusalem in A.D. 70 was (Pompey, Titus, Herod, Octavian).
6. The Rhine and the Danube are both (rivers, provinces, empires, famous walls).
7. A Roman officer in charge of a hundred men was called a (publican, centurion, legion, tetrarch).
8. The apostle Paul had special Roman protection because he was (a soldier, a publican, a citizen, an apostle).
9. Who may have been the first to carry a soldier's pack a second mile? (Jesus, Aristobulus, Felix, Festus)
10. The Dispersion was a (rebellion, war, tax, scattering).

Matching

A. *For each clue, write the correct term from the right-hand column.*

1. Ruled where Archelaus had ruled	Agrippa
2. Tax collectors	Antipater
3. "Almost thou persuadest me . . ."	Germans
4. Incapable ruler	Herod
5. Father of Herod the Great	Hyrcanus
6. A strong people living beyond the Rhine River	Josephus
7. Name of several rulers in one family	Pharisees
8. Opposed Roman rule in Palestine	Pilate
9. Led first Roman invasion of Jerusalem	Pompey
10. Jewish historian	publicans

B. *Match as in Part A.*

1. General term for homeland of Jews	Danube
2. Conquered several times in this chapter	Galilee
3. Ruled by Archelaus	Jerusalem
4. Ruled by Antipas	Judea and Samaria
5. Border between Romans and Germans	Libya
6. African country ruled by Romans	Palestine
7. Rome ruled beyond this	Philippi
8. Area ruled by the governor who suddenly withdrew from an attack on Jerusalem	Rhine Rome
9. Where jailer intended to kill himself	Syria
10. Home of Augustus	

Completion

1. Traveling traders with camels and sacks
Had to let publicans charge them a ———.
2. Not many walls could stand up to the slams
Given by soldiers with ——— ———.
3. Jewish protesters declared, "He will slay us—
Thousands have died under cruel ———!"
4. Christ could call angels from heavenly regions
Who were much stronger than twelve Roman ———.

5. "At my convenience I'll give you a call,"
   Felix said, trembling, when talking with ———.
6. Jews in Jerusalem were shocked to see
   Temple walls topple in front of ———.
7. Herod was ruled by suspicion and hate.
   Strange that we label him "Herod the ———."
8. Much of his life was a blot and a stain;
   Antipas, exiled, departed to ———.

Thought Questions

1. (*a*) If a government like Rome's existed today, would it be considered a fairly good or a rather bad government? (*b*) Why?
2. How did Roman taxing help to determine the place where Jesus would be born? See Luke 2.
3. How did some Jews inside Jerusalem actually reduce the possibility of victory over the Romans?
4. How could such a terrible calamity as the destruction of Jerusalem happen to the Jews, whom God had chosen long before to honor in a special way?
5. What is one way that the Jewish Dispersion turned out to be good for the world?

Further Study

1. How does the Bible indicate that Archelaus was a cruel man?
2. Octavian may have said "It is better to be Herod's hog than to be his son" because he knew Herod was not likely to eat pork. Try to find out why Herod did not eat pork.

Many spectators watch as a hungry lion eyes a praying group of Christians that will soon be food for him and the other animals entering the arena of the Circus Maximus. Other Christians have been smeared with pitch and made into human torches.

18 The Church Is Born

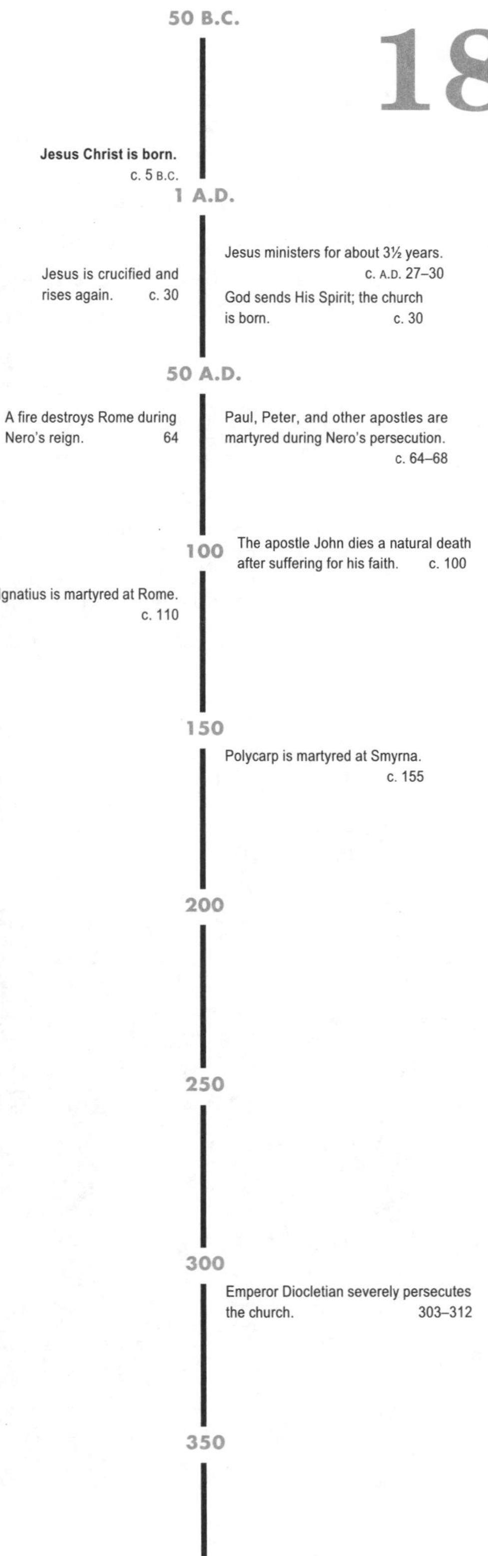

50 B.C.
Jesus Christ is born. c. 5 B.C.
1 A.D.
Jesus ministers for about 3½ years. c. A.D. 27–30
Jesus is crucified and rises again. c. 30
God sends His Spirit; the church is born. c. 30
50 A.D.
A fire destroys Rome during Nero's reign. 64
Paul, Peter, and other apostles are martyred during Nero's persecution. c. 64–68
100
The apostle John dies a natural death after suffering for his faith. c. 100
Ignatius is martyred at Rome. c. 110
150
Polycarp is martyred at Smyrna. c. 155
200
250
300
Emperor Diocletian severely persecutes the church. 303–312
350
The Council of Carthage issues an official list of the 27 New Testament books. 397
400 A.D.

In the Fullness of Time

Power From Within

How the Apostles Died

How the New Testament Came to Be

Church Leaders After the Apostles

Persecution of the Early Church

"But ye shall receive power, after that the Holy Ghost is come upon you: and ye shall be witnesses unto me both in Jerusalem, and in all Judaea, and in Samaria, and unto the uttermost part of the earth." *Acts 1:8*

THE CHURCH IS BORN

In the Fullness of Time

Old Testament saints must have thought it was taking a long time for the Messiah to come. But the Bible says God sent Jesus "when the fulness of the time was come" (Galatians 4:4). When we look back to the time of Jesus, we begin to understand what the Bible means by this.

God was preparing the world to receive the Gospel. Many Gentiles had become dissatisfied with their heathen gods and were ready to hear about the true God. The Jews were discontent with Roman rule and were looking for the promised Messiah. Poor people and slaves were eager to hear of a better life in the world to come. Not everyone searching for a better life received Jesus as Lord, but many honest seekers did.

The Roman Empire controlled much of the known world. Roman soldiers helped to keep roads safe from robbers and seas safe from pirates. Well-paved Roman roads ran between the large cities. Christians could travel freely through the empire, carrying the Gospel.

The Romans were enjoying the Pax Romana. No wars interfered with Christians' travel. In addition, most people spoke either Greek or Latin. The early Christians did not have to translate the Word of God into many different languages.

An overall view of Rome circa the A.D. 200s.

Power From Within

The fact that the world was ready for Christianity is only part of the reason that it spread so fast. God was not only preparing the way for His people; He was also impelling them from within. Following are some of the ways He did this.

The Life of Jesus. God sent His only Son, Jesus Christ, into the world to provide salvation for man and to begin the New Testament church. Jesus began His ministry when He was about thirty years old. He traveled about, healing the sick, blind, deaf, and lame. He also preached many sermons, calling on people to repent and to love God with their whole hearts.

Jesus called twelve disciples, who traveled about with Him. He taught them many things to prepare them for the work that He would give them.

But many Jewish leaders hated Jesus because He was more popular than they were. After several years of ministry, these leaders caught Jesus and accused Him of blasphemy against God. They condemned Him to death and persuaded Pilate to crucify Him. Christ's enemies thought they had won a great victory, but three days later God raised Him from the dead. Christ's death provides the perfect sacrifice for sins, and His resurrection gives assurance of eternal life for all true believers.

After appearing to His twelve disciples and about five hundred other followers, Jesus returned to heaven. He told His disciples that He would send another Comforter to them.

The Holy Spirit. Ten days after Jesus left the earth, 120 of His faithful followers waited at Jerusalem in an upper room. Suddenly, with the sound of a rushing wind, the Holy Spirit came upon each of them. With the Holy Spirit dwelling in their hearts, the apostles and other believers had a new power to live for the Lord and to testify of His death and resurrection. They began to preach to the crowds who had gathered in Jerusalem for Pentecost, and soon thousands of people repented and were baptized. The church was born on that day.

Persecution Spreads the Church. No one likes to be persecuted. But Jesus knew that His followers would face opposition and that God could use the persecution for a good purpose. He had told His disciples, "When they persecute you in this city, flee ye into another" (Matthew 10:23). When persecution began, they obeyed Him. Acts 8:4 tells us, "Therefore they that were scattered abroad went every where preaching the word." Persecution, like water thrown on a gasoline fire, only hastened the spread of Christianity.

Opening the Church to the Gentiles. Shortly before Jesus left the earth, He had said, "Ye shall be witnesses unto me both in Jerusalem, and in all Judaea, and in Samaria, and unto the uttermost part of the earth" (Acts 1:8). At first the disciples did not seem to understand that this included the Gentiles. As they traveled from place to place, the Christians preached mainly to Jews. Some of them, such as Philip, preached to the half-Jewish Samaritans.

But then the Lord instructed Peter to lead Cornelius, a Gentile centurion, to faith in Jesus. Later, missionaries to Antioch won many Gentile believers. This was a strange new step for the Jewish Christians. But the population of the church grew rapidly because of it.

The Conversion of Paul. At first Paul was a fierce persecutor of the Christians. But after he met Jesus, he became a zealous missionary to the Gentiles. At his conversion Jesus told him, "I will send thee far hence unto the Gentiles." One of Paul's important steps was actually a rather short voyage across the Aegean Sea. It was great

This mosaic shows a ship from about the time of Christ. Paul probably traveled on ships like this. A mosaic is artwork made by arranging small colored pieces of tile.

because it is the first record of the Gospel being carried to Europe. Macedonia was Paul's first stop there. Today many North Americans have ancestors who came from Europe. They can be thankful that Paul obeyed the "Macedonian call."

In later years Paul went farther, and finally he arrived at Rome. He even talked about taking a journey to Spain (Romans 15:24, 28).

Determined Missionary Efforts. Other apostles and believers spread the Gospel in all directions. Some preached in Egypt, especially at Alexandria, and that city became a great center of Christianity. Philip, you recall, preached about Jesus to a eunuch who then went rejoicing to spread the news in Ethiopia. According to tradition, Thomas traveled to India and was finally martyred there.

Study Exercises

1. Why were many pagan people eager to hear the Gospel?
2. Describe three ways in which the Roman Empire helped to prepare the world for the spread of the Gospel.
3. How many believers received the Holy Spirit when He was first given at Pentecost?
4. How did persecution help to spread the Gospel?
5. The first Christians gradually understood that faith in Jesus was not only for them but also for what other large group of people?

How the Apostles Died

The Christian missionaries knew that they might be killed for the sake of the Gospel. Peter, Andrew, and at least one other apostle were crucified. Others were stoned, beaten, beheaded, and burned. In fact, all the apostles except John died as martyrs.

Even though John died naturally, he lived a martyr's life. Once his persecutors tried to cook him in a vat of boiling oil. Another time they banished him to the lonely island of Patmos, where he wrote the Book of Revelation.

The large book called the ***Martyrs Mirror*** gives a more detailed account of how the apostles and many other early Christians died. Did you know, for example, that it tells how Peter asked to be crucified upside down because he felt unworthy to die as his Lord had died? Or that Andrew used his cross for a pulpit, preaching to the people as he hung there?

The Romans used the island of Patmos as a prison for exiles. Here, soldiers expel John the evangelist onto the rocky island.

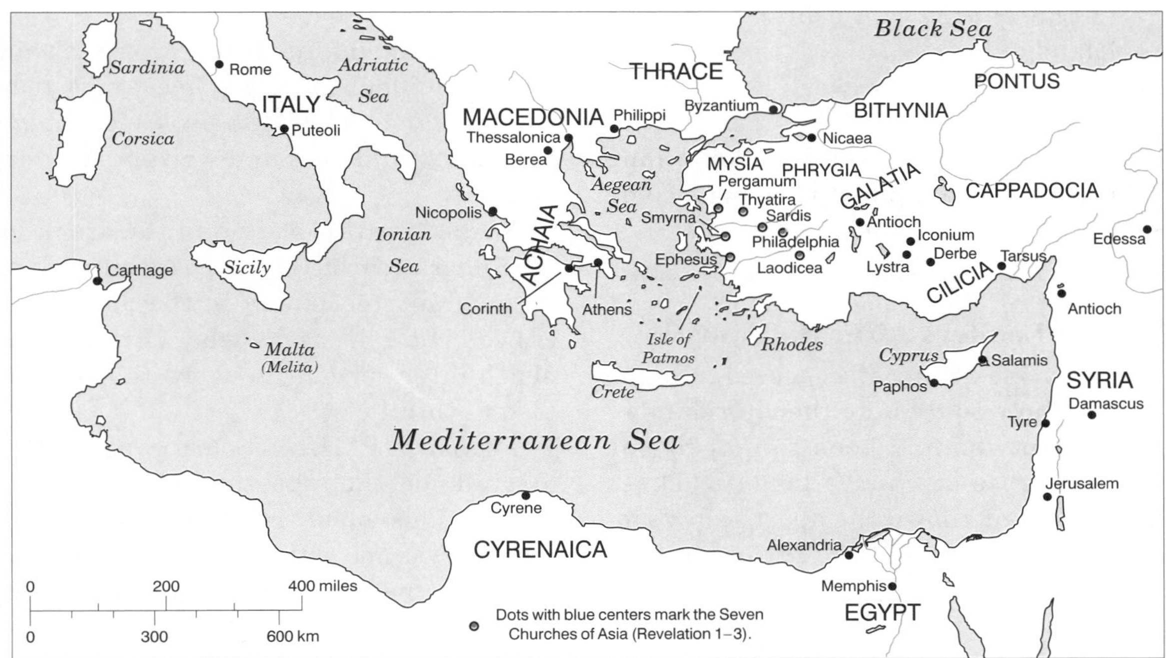

Figure 18:1. The Early Church Reaches Out

How the New Testament Came to Be

The apostles not only preached; they also wrote letters. The epistles that they wrote to one congregation were often shared with other congregations. Paul wrote most of the epistles in the New Testament.

Other men besides the apostles were also writing. Some writers were faithful Christians. Their writings had value, just as the writings of faithful Christians today can be helpful. However, not everything written by Christians was inspired by God as part of His Holy Word. Still other writers were ***heretics.***

The early Christians had to carefully evaluate the writings available to them. They asked questions such as the following to decide which writings were inspired by God: "Which writings teach the doctrines that we know Jesus taught?" "Which writings were written or authorized by the apostles?" "Which writings have our churches accepted to read at worship services?"

With these test questions to help them and the Spirit of God to guide them, the Christians came to agree more and more on what is God-inspired Scripture and what is not. This process took a long time because travel between churches was slow, and church leaders could not easily come together to discuss these matters. The leaders also wanted to be sure they did not accept false doctrine. It is a blessing to know that "all scripture is given by inspiration of God, and is profitable for doctrine, for reproof, for correction, for instruction in righteousness" (2 Timothy 3:16).

Much later, at the Council of Carthage in 397, the church made an official list of the twenty-seven New Testament books that are in the Bible. By this time, most churches were already using this group of books. The Council simply recognized and officially approved the books that the churches had already agreed upon.

Study Exercises

6. Name two apostles who were crucified.

7. What great contribution did John make to the church while he was on the island of Patmos?
8. What is another word for a false teacher?
9. Give two reasons why it took a long time to decide what writings to include in the New Testament.

Church Leaders After the Apostles

One by one the apostles passed from the scene. Who would guide the church now? Other men who had been taught by the apostles arose as church leaders. These men, who had known the apostles personally, were called ***apostolic fathers*** (ap uh STAHL ihk).

One of the apostolic fathers was Ignatius (ihg NAY shuhs), who had been a disciple of the apostle John. He served as a leader at Antioch in Syria, where the believers were first called Christians.

When the emperor Trajan (TRAY juhn) visited Antioch and sacrificed to the gods there, Ignatius openly reproved him. Furious at this rebuke, the emperor sent Ignatius to Rome to be torn to pieces by wild beasts.

Starved lions tore Christians to pieces almost instantly. Here, Ignatius awaits his death with calmness and a sure hope of eternal life in heaven.

On the day of his death, Ignatius said, "I feel confident that if my heart were to be cut open and chopped to pieces, the name of Jesus would be found written on every piece."

While Ignatius waited in the arena for the hungry, roaring lions to be set upon him, he gave his testimony to the assembled crowd. The Christians who witnessed his death later spread the word that he had died faithfully.

Polycarp (PAHL ee kahrp) was another disciple of the apostle John. He was ordained bishop of the church at Smyrna. Smyrna was one of the seven churches mentioned in the first chapters of Revelation. To this church the Lord had said, "Be thou faithful unto death, and I will give thee a crown of life" (Revelation 2:10).

When one of the authorities threatened to burn him, Polycarp replied, "Thou threatenest me with a fire, which will perhaps burn for an hour, and then soon go out; but thou knowest not the fire of the future judgment of God, which is prepared for the everlasting punishment and torment of the ungodly." Strangely, when the executioners lit the fire and the flames rose high, Polycarp did not seem to be hurt. Someone finally had to put him to death with a sword. Apparently God wanted the heathen to realize that they could do nothing to His saints unless He allowed it.

There were many other leaders and teachers in those early days. They were not all apostolic fathers, but each one who was faithful filled an important place in the Christian church.

Study Exercises

10. Name the emperor who had Ignatius put to death for personal reasons.

11. Where was the local congregation (*a*) of Ignatius? (*b*) of Polycarp?
12. Both Ignatius and Polycarp had been taught by which apostle?

Persecution of the Early Church

Persecution is so intertwined with the story of the early church that you have already read much about it in this chapter. Now you will go back to the first days of the church and study the history of persecution in more detail.

At first it was unbelieving Jews such as Saul who persecuted Christians. These Jews had been looking for a Messiah who would come in power and earthly glory, help them overthrow the Romans, and set up an Israelite kingdom. The meek, crucified Jesus was not at all what they had expected of the Messiah.

Besides, Jesus and His followers made them feel guilty. When Stephen preached to the Jews at Jerusalem, pointing out their part in murdering Jesus, they "were cut to the heart" (Acts 7:54). Stephen became the first Christian martyr, and many more would soon follow.

Later the Romans began to persecute Christians. The first Roman emperor to do so was Nero. During his rule, a six-day fire destroyed much of Rome. A legend says that Nero played music while Rome burned. Whether or not that is true, people suspected that Nero had started the fire. To turn away the accusations, Nero blamed the Christians.

During Nero's persecution, Christians in the city of Rome suffered many torments. Some were crucified. Others were sewn in the skins of wild animals, and then dogs were allowed to attack and kill them. Some were smeared with pitch, tied to stakes, and burned at night to light Nero's gardens. Paul was beheaded during Nero's reign.

For the next century and a half, persecutions came and went. Sometimes Christians suffered very little persecution; sometimes they were persecuted only by local rulers; and sometimes they were persecuted throughout the empire. The *Martyrs Mirror* lists ten general persecutions of the Christians, which began during the time that Nero ruled.

Why did the Romans persecute Christians? One reason was that the emperor wanted to be worshiped as a god. This strengthened his power in the empire. The Roman government had little sympathy for people who refused to honor the emperor so highly or to fight in his army.

This drawing depicts what some Romans thought—that Nero sang and played music while watching Rome burn. Actually, Nero was at his home about 35 miles (56 km) away from Rome at the time of the fire. The Romans suspected that Nero started the destructive fire so that he could build new, magnificent buildings to glorify himself. To divert the rage of the citizens, Nero blamed the Christians for starting the fire. Christians suffered horribly because of this.

Roman Christians had to disobey the Roman law which stated that no one may worship in secret. The Roman Empire allowed various religions, but all religions were supposed to be registered with the government. No religion could be considered greater than others, and all religion had to be practiced in public, never in private homes. Of course, Christians never ask governments for permission to worship God, for they know their religion is the only true one.

The common people also supported the persecution of Christians, especially at first. The Christians were different. They did not share the same interests that most people had, and they did not freely take part in their neighbors' social activities. It is easy for people to be suspicious of those who are different from themselves.

Besides, when troubles come, humans are quick to look around for someone to blame. If there was a flood, a drought, an earthquake, or a famine, people said it was the Christians' fault. Christians were easy to persecute, for they did not fight back.

The Christians of Rome had an excellent hiding place that helped them escape some persecution. Around Rome is an area of soft stone called tufa (TOO fuh). The Christians and others cut many tunnels into this stone for use as underground cemeteries. Graves were dug into the sides of the tunnels, and most of them were closed with marble or other stone. These manmade passages and caves are called ***catacombs*** (KAT uh kohmz).

In the catacombs, the Christians were able to hide from their persecutors and to hold worship services. Since the miles of winding, intersecting passageways were confusing to strangers, the Christians were fairly safe. Besides, most Romans did not care to invade the catacombs because they considered burying places to be sacred.

Notice the graves dug into the catacomb walls. It is not clear what the men in the picture are doing. Perhaps they are writing on the stone or reading something engraved there.

Although the Roman soldiers did not like to invade the catacombs, occasionally they found their way in and arrested Christians.

The tenth persecution, which began under the emperor Diocletian (dy uh KLEE shuhn), was the severest of all. In describing this persecution, the *Martyrs Mirror* (page 173) quotes an ancient writer:

> There was scarcely a large city in the empire, in which not daily a hundred Christians, or thereabouts, were slain. It is also recorded that in one month seventeen thousand Christians were put to death in different parts of the empire, so that the blood which was shed colored red many rivers. Some were hanged, others beheaded, some burned, and some sunk by whole shiploads in the depths of the sea.

Some Roman persecutors physically forced Christians to go through the motions of sacrificing to the gods. Then they announced that the Christians had sacrificed to the gods, even though they actually had not.

Some Christians had their noses, ears, or hands cut off; and then they were set free for everyone to see. The Romans hoped this would terrify weak Christians.

The persecutions did frighten some people away from Christianity. But many Christians counted it an honor to suffer for their Master, just as the apostles had rejoiced that they were counted worthy to suffer shame for His Name. What is more, many people were attracted to this religion that could give such faith and calmness in spite of torture and death. A leader in the early church once said, "The blood of the martyrs is the seed of the church."

Study Exercises

13. How many persecutions did Christians suffer from the Romans?
14. Why did Nero blame the Christians for setting fire to Rome?
15. Give at least three reasons why the Romans in general often persecuted Christians.
16. Give two reasons why Christians were fairly safe in the catacombs.
17. Which emperor began the last major persecution of the early Christians?

Clinching the Chapter

Multiple Choice

A. *Write the word or phrase* least *associated with the first item.*

1. Spread of Gospel: peace, persecution, paved roads, pirates
2. Paul's travels: Spain, India, Macedonia, Rome
3. Gentile converts: Ethiopians, Paul, Macedonians, Cornelius
4. Persecutors: Nero, Saul, Diocletian, Peter
5. Martyrs' deaths: John, Peter, Andrew, Paul
6. Crucifixion: Peter, Ignatius, Andrew, Jesus
7. Catacombs: passageways, tufa, cemeteries, arena
8. Missionaries: Trajan, Philip, Thomas, Peter
9. Church builders: apostles, apostolic fathers, heretics, martyrs
10. Known as martyrs: Ignatius, Stephen, Polycarp, Cornelius

B. *Write the correct words.*

1. Who was sent "when the fulness of the time was come"? (Jesus, Paul, Ignatius, Diocletian)
2. The first Europeans known to receive Christian missionaries were (Ethiopians, Egyptians, Macedonians, Romans).
3. Jesus said that if persecution arose, His followers should (flee, fight, protest, preach).
4. The first Gentile to become a Christian was (Nero, Diocletian, Cornelius, Polycarp).
5. While Rome burned, Nero is said to have (prayed, attended races, hid in catacombs, played music).
6. Paul was (crucified, drowned, beheaded, burned).
7. Thomas traveled to (Spain, India, Italy, Carthage).
8. The missionary whom God sent primarily to the Gentiles was (Paul, Peter, Philip, James).
9. Church leaders who had known the apostles were called (heretics, emperors, apostolic fathers, disciples).
10. John wrote the Revelation (on the island of Patmos, in the catacombs, in prison, at home).

Matching

A. *For each clue, write the correct name from the right-hand column.*

1. Persecuted Ignatius	Andrew
2. Helped the Ethiopian eunuch	Diocletian
3. Blamed Christians for a fire	Ignatius
4. Was banished	John
5. Began the tenth persecution	Nero
6. Carried Gospel to India	Peter
7. Was torn by wild beasts	Philip
8. Was crucified upside down	Polycarp
9. Bishop of Smyrna	Thomas
10. Preached from his cross	Trajan

B. *Match as in Part A.*

1. One of "the seven churches"	Aegean Sea
2. Where Ignatius gave his last testimony	Antioch
3. Continent that needed the Gospel	Egypt
4. Was evangelized through Philip's ministry	Ethiopia
5. Where Ignatius was church leader	Europe
6. Where John was banished	Macedonia
7. Country Alexandria was in	Patmos
8. To be evangelized after Judea	Rome
9. First area in Europe to receive the Gospel	Samaria
10. Was crossed by Paul on his way to Europe	Smyrna

Completion

1. When people heard that Jesus saves,
   The poor were glad. So were the ———.
2. Most people in the world could speak
   The Latin tongue, or else the ———.
3. A power nothing could exhaust
   Came to the church at ———.
4. Brave Andrew, dying, felt no loss;
   He preached the Gospel from his ———.
5. No earthly flame or weapon sharp
   Could frighten Bishop ———.
6. The first to trust in God's Good News
   Were persecuted by the ———.
7. Some Christians, fleeing from their homes,
   Hid underground in ———.
8. Since truth and error must not mix,
   Take heed; beware of ———.

Thought Questions

1. How does this study on the early church illustrate the truth of the lines below?
   "Life doesn't always bring to us the things we wish it would,
   But God can take the things it does, and bless them to our good."
2. What was one step the Jewish Christians took toward preaching to the Gentiles before Peter preached to Cornelius?
3. How was it an advantage to the early church to have at least one old apostle (John) still living after the other apostles had died?
4. How did New Testament writers make a greater contribution to the Christian faith by their letters than by their sermons?
5. Many martyrs took advantage of their deaths to give a ringing testimony. What three men did this, who are mentioned in this chapter?

Geographical Skills

1. Trace Map F, and label it "Where the Apostles Suffered."
2. Challenge Question: In the *Martyrs Mirror,* find the accounts of the suffering or death

of the twelve apostles: James the son of Zebedee, Philip, James the son of Alphaeus, Simon Peter, Andrew, Bartholomew, Thomas, Matthew, Simon Zelotes, Judas Thaddaeus, Matthias, and John. On your map, label the city or area where each account took place, and write in parenthesis the name(s) of the apostle(s) who suffered or died there.

Notes:

1. *Not all ancient sources that refer to the apostles' deaths agree in every detail. However, these accounts do show that the apostles spread the Gospel to many lands.*
2. *The* Martyr's Mirror *states that Thomas died as a martyr in the East Indies. Formerly* East Indies *applied to all Southeast Asia, including India. Other sources give Madras (now called Chennai), India, as the place of Thomas' death. On your map, label Chennai, and write* Thomas *nearby.*
3. *The* Martyr's Mirror *does not tell where Matthias was martyred, but the account states that he was condemned by the Jews. Write his name near Jerusalem.*

Further Study

1. Study a map showing Paul's missionary travels. (Such a map may be found in the back of some Bibles.) (*a*) During which two journeys did he cover much the same territory? (*b*) During which journey did he visit Cyprus? (*c*) What city was the starting point for his journeys?
2. Try to find out from an encyclopedia, commentary, or Bible dictionary some details about Paul's life after what is recorded in the last chapter of Acts.

Be Sure You Know

Can you answer all these questions? If not, study Chapters 16–18 to find the answers.

A. What

1. people conquered the early Romans and taught them useful things?
2. two kinds of government did the Romans have?
3. were the Punic Wars?
4. ideals were upheld by the early Romans?
5. ideas did the Romans borrow from the Greeks?
6. Roman ruler became dictator for life after defeating Pompey?
7. Roman emperor was reigning when Christ was born?
8. kind of ruler was Herod the Great?
9. five rulers governed the Jews after Herod's death?
10. Roman general destroyed Jerusalem?
11. two leaders in the early church were disciples of the apostle John?
12. people persecuted the early Christians?

B. What do these words mean?

13. apostolic father
14. catacombs
15. centurion
16. citizen
17. consul
18. Diaspora
19. dictator
20. fallow
21. heretic
22. league
23. legion
24. patrician
25. plebeian
26. publican
27. republic
28. Sanhedrin
29. tetrarch

C. How

30. did the Caesars come into power?
31. did Julius Caesar improve the Roman calendar?
32. did the Romans deal with the Jews?
33. did some Jews inside Jerusalem actually reduce the possibility of victory over the Romans?
34. did the Romans help to prepare the world for Christianity?
35. did the twelve apostles die?
36. did the persecution of Christians affect other people?

D. Why

37. did the Romans build many good roads?
38. did the Romans eventually lose their high ideals?
39. did the Christians leave Jerusalem before it was destroyed?
40. did God allow the Romans to destroy Jerusalem in A.D. 70?
41. were other people suspicious of the early Christians?

The Roman emperor Constantine took part at a gathering of church leaders called the Council of Nicaea in 325. Constantine was not even a member of the church, yet the decaying church was following his lead. Other signs of decay we see in this picture are the fine clothing, luxurious furnishings, and special religious headdresses.

19 Christianity Decays

300 A.D.

Constantine legalizes Christianity. 313

The Council of Nicaea states that Jesus is "very God of very God." 325

Constantine moves his capital to Byzantium (Constantinople). 330

A council at Constantinople issues a statement concerning the Holy Spirit. 381

Theodosius issues decrees making Christianity the state religion. 391, 392

400

The Roman Empire is permanently divided after Theodosius's death. 395

Jerome translates the Bible into Latin. The Vulgate becomes the standard Bible in Western Europe for over 1,000 years. c. 382–405

Ambrose (340?–397), Jerome (340?–420), and Augustine (354–430) are outstanding leaders in the Catholic Church. 300s, 400s

The (western) Roman Empire comes to an end. 476

500

600

700

800

900

1000

Roman Catholic and Eastern Orthodox church leaders excommunicate each other, causing a schism. 1054

1100 A.D.

"For I know this, that after my departing shall grievous wolves enter in among you, not sparing the flock. Also of your own selves shall men arise, speaking perverse things, to draw away disciples after them."

Acts 20:29, 30

Christianity Decays

Reviewing the First Three Hundred Years

Ever since the Christian church began, faithful leaders have needed to use strong effort to keep the church pure. Already in the time of the apostles, false teachers had begun to deceive people. Paul warned the elders of Ephesus, "Of your own selves shall men arise, speaking perverse things, to draw away disciples after them" (Acts 20:30). Jude wrote his short epistle to warn believers about false teachers.

Many teachings in John's first epistle helped to strengthen the Christians against the errors of ***Gnosticism*** (NAHS tih sihz uhm). Gnostics taught that spiritual things have value but physical things do not. Some Gnostics believed this so strongly that they said Jesus never lived, died, and rose again in a physical body. John wrote, "Every spirit that confesseth not that Jesus Christ is come in the flesh is not of God" (1 John 4:3).

The Roman emperor Diocletian ruled from A.D. 284–305. The leaders of pagan religions saw that Rome was declining in power, and they blamed the growth of Christianity for this decline. Under this pressure, Diocletian consented to persecute Christians harshly. Christian churches were destroyed, Bibles burnt, and many Christians lost all normal Roman citizenship rights.

Although the church had struggles, persecution had a refining effect on the Christians. Sincere, earnest people joined the church in spite of persecution, but those who were not willing to forsake all for Christ stayed away. Although some errors did creep into the church during these times of persecution, the church faced less false doctrine from within than it did in times of freedom.

The Church Becomes Romanized

Soon after the emperor Diocletian died, persecution stopped. The new Roman emperor, Galerius (guh LEER ee uhs), oppressed the Christians during most of his short rule, but he changed his mind after he began to suffer a serious illness. He believed that God was punishing him for persecuting the Christians. On his deathbed, he proclaimed that Christians should be given freedom of religion.

Some time later, a man named Constantine (KAHN stuhn teen) was struggling against several others to become the new Roman emperor. One night he had a vision that he thought was from God. He saw a cross in the sky, along with the words "In this sign conquer." Constantine went on to win the struggle and become the emperor. He was so impressed by his victory that he declared Christianity to be legal and even favored. Constantine's decree, issued in 313, is called the Edict of Milan (mih LAN). Except for a few brief persecutions, this marked the beginning of much freedom for Christians.

However, Constantine did not understand true Christianity. Even though he favored the Christians, he was tolerant

This is an artist's idea of Constantine's vision from heaven. We know that God does not tell men to fight and kill in the Name of Christ. The apostle Paul wrote, "But though we, or an angel from heaven, preach any other gospel unto you than that which we have preached unto you, let him be accursed" (Galatians 1:8).

toward those who continued to practice Rome's pagan religion. In fact, Constantine was not baptized until he lay on his deathbed. That delay was possibly due to the false idea that baptism itself washes away sin. Constantine may have wanted to be sure he did not sin after baptism.

Theodosius (thee uh DOH shuhs), a later emperor, took Constantine's reforms a step further. He forbade idol worship and declared Christianity to be the state religion. This meant that Christianity would be the religion of all the people.

But so-called Christianity had seriously decayed by this time. People who are forced to become "Christians" are really not Christians in their hearts. It is true that some groups of genuine Christians existed here and there. But most of the people had little idea what it meant to be a disciple of Jesus.

As you study history, remember that the terms *Christian* and *Christianity* are often used in a very broad sense to include all professing Christians. Also remember that Jesus said, "Not every one that saith unto me, Lord, Lord, shall enter into the kingdom of heaven; but he that doeth the will of my Father which is in heaven" (Matthew 7:21).

Study Exercises

1. Name three New Testament teachers who warned against false doctrine.
2. What book of the Bible helped the Christians to withstand Gnosticism?
3. Name the decree that offered religious freedom to Christians. In what year was it issued?
4. Why is it impossible to force people to become genuine Christians?

Councils and Creeds

Although the church had many ignorant and even heathen members, many church members had not lost sight of all truth. A number of times leaders came together to state exactly what they believed about important doctrines. Some of their conclusions were correct, even though the church was wrong in working closely with the government.

In one case, a church leader named Arius (uh RY uhs) was teaching that Jesus Christ is not God, as the Father is. But at the Council of Nicaea (ny SEE uh), in A.D. 325, other leaders pointed out that only God can save man from sin. If Jesus Christ is not God, He cannot save us. The Council drew up the Nicene Creed (NY seen), which

The Council of Chalcedonia (A.D. 451) pronounced that Christ is both true God and true man. Christian church leaders have always gathered together to discuss issues affecting the church. Although the Catholic councils decided some things correctly, they also decided many things contrary to God's Word. Their churches depended on these councils to decide things instead of simply accepting the clear Word of God. This made weak churches and gave too much power to a few men, who took the church into apostasy.

states that Jesus is "very God of very God." Thus the Nicene Creed reaffirms the ***deity*** of Jesus Christ.

Another time, in 381, a council came together at Constantinople (kahn stan tuh NOH puhl) to clarify what Christians believe about the Holy Spirit. The leaders stated the Bible doctrine that the Holy Spirit also is God. Although the word *Trinity* is not found in the Bible, it is a useful word to describe what the Bible teaches—that the Father, Son, and Holy Spirit together make up the Godhead.

To state in clear, simple form exactly what Christians believe, the church wrote out what is known as the Apostles' Creed. This creed is still used regularly in some Catholic and Protestant church services. Here is one form of it. (*Hell* in this statement refers to the grave, and *catholic* means "universal.")

> I believe in God the Father Almighty, Maker of heaven and earth; and in Jesus Christ His only Son our Lord; who was conceived by the Holy Ghost, born of the Virgin Mary, suffered under Pontius Pilate, was crucified, dead, and buried; He descended into hell; the third day He rose again from the dead; He ascended into heaven, and sitteth on the right hand of God the Father Almighty; from thence He shall come to judge the quick and the dead. I believe in the Holy Ghost; the holy catholic church; the communion of saints; the forgiveness of sins; the resurrection of the body; and the life everlasting.

Patriarchs and Popes

The church was becoming a large organization. From the beginning, the elders of the churches in various cities had looked to one man among them to lead them and help them work together. This man was called a bishop. Timothy had been a bishop in Ephesus, as Titus had been in Crete. As the bishops worked together in later years, they began looking to certain ones among themselves as leaders. The five most important bishops were called ***patriarchs.***

But as time went on, many church leaders no longer saw themselves as servants. They ignored Peter's warning that leaders should "feed the flock" and not become "lords over God's heritage" (1 Peter 5:2, 3). Instead, they became more and more interested in money, honors, elaborate robes, and costly buildings.

Eventually the church considered the patriarch of Rome as the most important of all. He was called the ***pope*** (meaning "father"), and he received high honor. The church began to teach that the pope held an office begun by the apostle Peter, and that Peter was the first pope.

This teaching was far different from the words of Jesus: "One is your Master, even Christ; and all ye are brethren. And call no man your father upon the earth: for one is your Father, which is in heaven" (Matthew 23:8, 9). The Bible does teach that churches should have leaders and that those leaders are to be honored, but it does not teach that one leader should rule all the churches.

Study Exercises

5. What is one important reason to believe that Jesus is God?
6. What is the word that refers to God in three persons?
7. What does *catholic* mean in the phrase "the holy catholic church"?
8. What did Peter say church leaders must not be?

Hermits and Monks

Serious-minded men observed the behavior of many church members, and they did not like what they saw. A number of them withdrew from society and lived alone. They thought that living with other people made it harder for them to live close to God.

One man, named Anthony, lived by himself in a cave along the Nile. He saw few people and lived very simply, spending much time in prayer, fasting, and meditation. He and other men who followed his example were called ***hermits.*** Such men certainly did much praying, but they did little to feed the hungry or win souls for the Lord.

This hermit lives in a hollow tree.

Another man in Syria, named Simeon, tried to get close to God by building a pillar and living on top of it. He kept building his pillar higher until it was about 60 feet tall (18 m). He taught those who came to see him, and a number of men followed his poor example by living on pillars themselves.

Other men who wanted to get away from the evil world thought it was best to live in groups. They were called ***monks,*** and they lived in ***monasteries.*** Each monastery kept a strict schedule. A typical monk might work seven hours in a day, pray seven hours, and sleep seven hours. He could use the remaining three hours for meals and studying.

Some monks were interested not only in trying to be holy but also in serving others. They did an important work in preserving old writings. Before the printing press was invented in the 1400s, all written material

These monks are praying. Probably their books are prayer books. Sometimes they recited prayers from such books for hours. It is good to spend much time in prayer, but we should think about what we are saying and pray from our hearts.

had to be produced by hand. The monks spent long hours copying the Scriptures and other books, and they took pleasure in a job well done. They wrote neatly and decorated the books with beautiful art.

Many monks supported themselves by farming. They also took in travelers, gave food and clothing to the poor, gave medicine to sick people, and did various other good deeds.

Hermits and earlier monks were ***ascetics*** (uh SEHT ihks). They knew that self-denial is good, but they carried the idea too far. They denied themselves of all pleasant things instead of remembering that God "giveth us richly all things to enjoy" (1 Timothy 6:17). Sometimes ascetics went hungry or stayed away from people when they could have served the Lord better in other ways.

Some monks spent tedious years copying books. They filled an important role in preserving the Scriptures.

On the other hand, they could not completely escape temptations to indulge in worldly things. The Bible says, "But every man is tempted, when he is drawn away of his own lust, and enticed" (James 1:14). This means that our sinful nature tends to draw us away from God—we cannot remove all temptation by living in seclusion. Some monks slipped into a less disciplined way of life. They ate better foods than ordinary people did, and dressed in better clothes. This made monasteries attractive for people who liked good food, fine clothes, and a roof over their heads without working too hard to get them.

Did Hermits and Monks Follow the Bible?

Some hermits and monks might have been honest seekers who loved the Lord and trusted in Him for salvation. However, it appears that most ascetics tried to find peace and salvation through their own works

These monks are hard at work making hay to help support themselves. Some monks worked hard, while others lived off taxes or begged for food.

and obedience to rules. They tried to overcome sin in their own strength, believing that this would bring them into communion with God. The Bible says, "For by grace are ye saved through faith; and that not of yourselves: it is the gift of God: not of works, lest any man should boast" (Ephesians 2:8, 9).

Ascetic ideas come from pagan religions rather than being based on God's Word. The Bible commands us to "come out from among them [unbelievers], and be ye separate" (2 Corinthians 6:17), but this means that we should live holy lives and avoid close fellowship with sinners. Christians are to "shine as lights in the world" as they live "in the midst of a crooked and perverse nation" (Philippians 2:15).

Hermits could not follow the Bible teaching on the need for fellowship with other believers, nor could they keep all the church ordinances. Most monks followed strict rules that forbade marriage and required fasting at certain times. The Bible expressly warns against those who teach that such practices bring a person closer to God. Read 1 Timothy 4:1, 3.

Ambrose, Jerome, and Augustine

During the 300s and 400s, three influential men arose to lead the church. They were Ambrose (AM brohz), Jerome (juh ROHM), and Augustine (AW guh steen). These leaders influenced the church partly for good and partly for bad.

Ambrose helped the church by defending the doctrine of the deity of Christ. However, he was quite involved in the politics of his day. Ambrose himself was a governor when he was chosen by the people to be bishop, and he was baptized just a few days before his ordination. When the emperor Theodosius slaughtered seven thousand of his subjects to punish them for a murder, Ambrose refused to let him take part in Communion until he repented and made public confession. This illustrates the unscriptural confusion that arises when the church receives the rulers of this world within its own ranks.

The most important work of Jerome was to translate the Bible into Latin, which was still spoken in his time. His translation was called the Latin Vulgate. Like Ambrose and Augustine, he encouraged men to enter monasteries.

Ambrose was baptized only about a week before he became a bishop of the Catholic Church in A.D. 374.

Augustine (A.D. 354–430) was probably the most influential so-called Christian that ever lived. Many false ideas that he taught are accepted even today by Catholic and Protestant churches.

Augustine taught against the false idea that people are basically good and do not need God to save them. However, he made the mistake of going to the other extreme. He taught that people by nature are so evil that they cannot even choose to become saved; God must do everything to save them. Many people still believe this false doctrine today.

Augustine also reacted strongly against people who formed church groups separate from his own. He insisted that there is only one true church—the Catholic Church. He said that anyone outside that church was lost.

Augustine encouraged the use of force to bring everyone into the church and keep them there. He based his belief on a statement in one of Jesus' parables: "Compel them to come in." In the years to come, many people would suffer torture and death because of what Augustine had taught.

Study Exercises

9. When a man lived as a hermit, what important things did he usually neglect to do?
10. What is the difference between a hermit and a monk?
11. What was probably Jerome's greatest contribution to the church?
12. What are two extremes to which some people go in their belief about salvation?

The Roman Empire Breaks Up

A nation or empire decays when the character of its people decays. The Roman Empire contained more so-called Christians than ever before. But the morals of its people continued to decline. Many of them wanted an easy life of pleasure. Paul warned Timothy to turn away from those who are "lovers of pleasures more than lovers of God" (2 Timothy 3:4).

The empire was in disorder. Men who wanted to become the emperor fought against each other. Sometimes several emperors tried to rule at the same time. Many struggles also took place between the popes and the emperors. Both the church and the state wanted to be the highest authority.

The Emperor Theodosius stated in his will that one of his sons should have the eastern part of the empire and the other son should have the western part. When Theodosius died in A.D. 395, the empire was permanently divided.

In A.D. 330, Constantine had moved the capital of the empire from Rome to Byzantium (bih ZAN tee uhm), a city in what is now Turkey. People called it Constantinople, after Constantine. When the empire split, Constantinople became the capital of the eastern empire. Rome was capital of the western part.

The eastern empire became known as the Byzantine Empire (BIHZ uhn teen). It lasted a thousand years longer than the Roman Empire in the west.

Even before the empire split, barbarians from the north were invading it. They were trying to get away from other barbarians, the Huns, who were even fiercer than themselves. The Romans did not have the strength to fight off the many invaders that poured in. Hordes of Goths and Vandals plundered the Roman lands. They had no love for Roman art, literature, or learning. They destroyed much of what they found.

The government of the Roman Empire broke down completely in A.D. 476. Many scholars fled eastward to the Byzantine Empire, taking books and manuscripts with them. For the next thousand years, Constantinople was the center of learning. If the scholars had not saved and carefully copied many writings, much knowledge would have needed to be discovered all over again.

Constantinople is now known as Istanbul, Turkey. Most of Istanbul is in the European part of Turkey. Across the Sea of Marmara, you see the other part of Istanbul, which is in Asia. The large buildings are mosques. Beneath the close-set roofs in the foreground are the bazaars of old Istanbul.

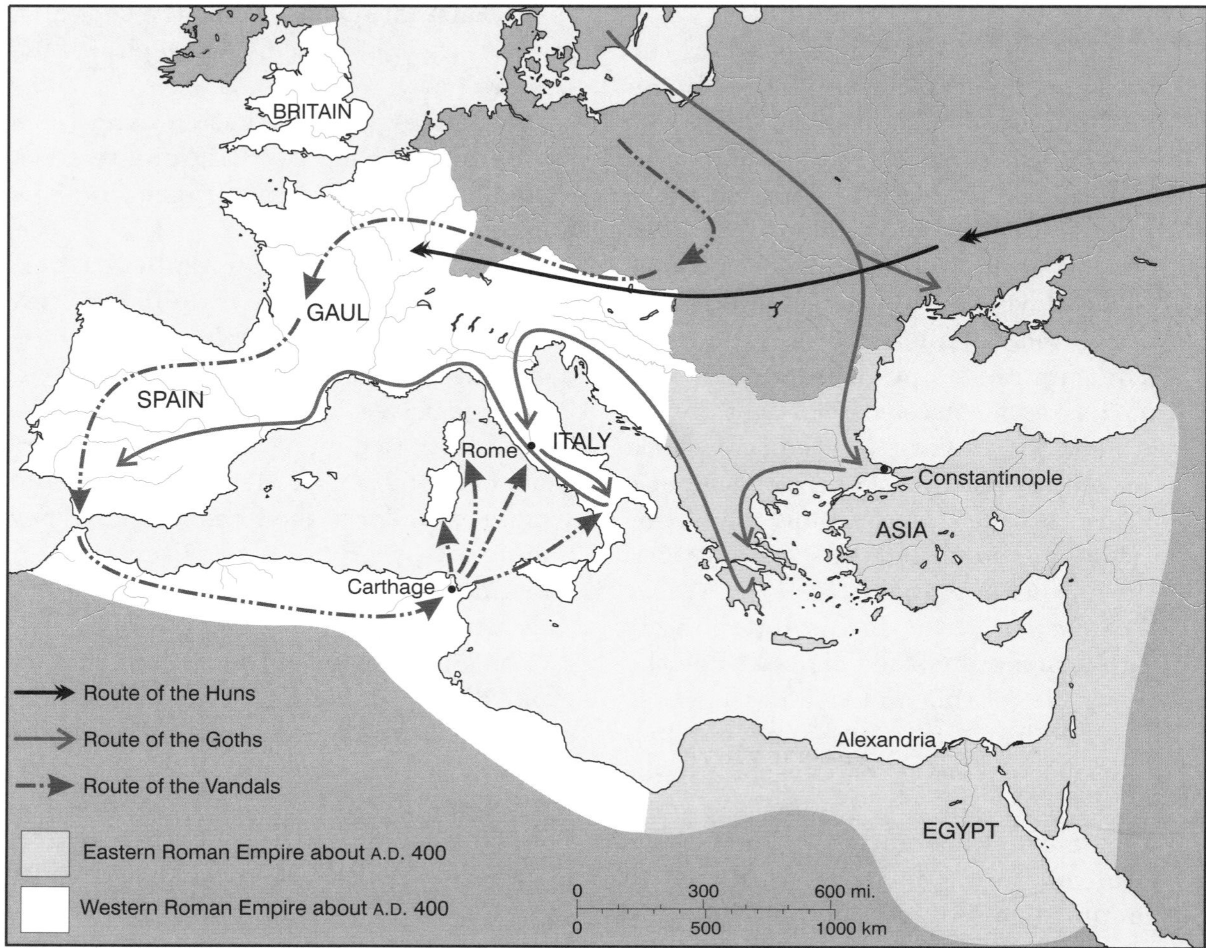

Figure 19:1. Barbarians Invade the Roman Empire

The Greek Orthodox Church Is Formed

Although the Roman government fell, the church kept its center at Rome. But since the empire had split in two, the churches in the two empires slowly drifted apart. The people belonging to the western church commonly spoke Latin. Many of them were barbarians or the descendants of barbarians. The people of the eastern part spoke Greek. They had not fallen to the barbarians, and they did not face the same kind of problems as people in the west.

The eastern and western churches disagreed over more and more issues. Finally, in 1054, the pope (leader of the western church) and the metropolitan (leader of the eastern church) excommunicated each other. Historians call this event a ***schism*** (SIHZ uhm). Today the western church is known as the Roman Catholic Church, and the eastern church is called the Greek (or Eastern) Orthodox Church. Many beliefs and practices of the two churches are similar.

Ignorance Reigns

After Rome fell, Europe entered a time of ignorance in both knowledge and religion. Why did this happen?

Europe was controlled largely by barbarians who cared little for education. Most people were ***illiterate.*** Even the few who

The Hagia Sophia, a Greek Orthodox church, was built in the A.D. 530s. After the Muslims conquered Constantinople in 1453, they used the building as a Muslim mosque. Today the Hagia Sophia serves as a museum. It is an example of the finery and show of the Greek Orthodox religion.

could read did not have a wealth of reading material such as we have today. Copies of the Bible were so scarce that very few people had an opportunity to read it.

People were content to copy and learn what teachers of the past had said. They were not interested in learning new facts themselves or in testing old ideas to see if they were correct. This led them to believe many false ideas and superstitions that had been handed down to them.

All these things kept Europeans ignorant for the first centuries after the fall of Rome. This was the beginning of a period of history known as the ***Middle Ages,*** which lasted about a thousand years. Because of the widespread ignorance after the fall of Rome, the first part of the Middle Ages is called the ***Dark Ages.***

Study Exercises

13. At whose death was the Roman Empire permanently divided?
14. How did Constantinople get its name?
15. Rome fell in the mid-400s. When did Constantinople fall?
16. What name was given to the church of the Byzantine Empire?
17. What was the most important information that people lacked in the Dark Ages?

Clinching the Chapter

Multiple Choice

A. *Write the word or phrase* least *associated with the first item.*

1. Emperor: Diocletian, Constantine, Theodosius, Augustine
2. Catholic: western, Greek Orthodox, Roman, Latin
3. Church leader: hermit, patriarch, pope, metropolitan
4. Hermit: soul winning, prayer, meditation, fasting

5. Schism: Roman Catholic Church, Greek Orthodox Church, pope, Constantine
6. Byzantine: Constantinople, learning, western, Orthodox
7. Barbarians: Huns, Romans, Goths, Vandals
8. Ascetic: hermit, monk, apostle John, Anthony
9. Middle Ages: illiteracy, truth, Dark Ages, fall of Rome
10. Dates to remember: 476, 1054, 298, 313

B. *Write the correct words.*

1. What place is associated with Constantine's announcement of toleration for Christians? (Constantinople, Nicaea, Milan, Rome)
2. Who is falsely said to have been the first pope? (Jesus, Paul, Peter, Arius)
3. What emperor made Christianity the state religion? (Theodosius, Constantine, Diocletian, Augustine)
4. What term refers to God? (deity, patriarch, creed, ignorance)
5. Constantinople was formerly called (Rome, Nicaea, Antioch, Byzantium).
6. One man who contradicted the teaching of Arius was (Constantine, Ambrose, Theodosius, Diocletian).
7. Which came last? (Edict of Milan, schism, fall of Rome, Nicene Creed)
8. What term means "father"? (monk, lord, elder, pope)
9. What was likely the most important factor in the downfall of the Roman Empire? (moral decay, Theodosius, Byzantine Empire, Huns)
10. Who was never a monk or a hermit? (Anthony, Simeon, Jerome, Constantine)

Matching

A. *For each clue, write the correct name from the right-hand column.*

1. Lived atop a pillar	Ambrose
2. Divided the empire	Anthony
3. Translated Bible into Latin	Arius
4. Said Jesus was not God	Augustine
5. Edict of Milan	Constantine
6. Apostle	Gnostics
7. Said that man is too evil to choose to be saved	Jerome
8. Disciplined an emperor	Peter
9. Taught Jesus had no physical body	Simeon (in Syria)
10. Hermit along the Nile	Theodosius

B. *Match as in Part A.*

1. Center of Catholic Church	Byzantium
2. Capital of eastern empire	catholic
3. Old name for Constantinople	Constantinople
4. Where Paul warned against false teachers	Council of Constantinople
5. Reaffirmed the deity of Christ	Council of Nicaea
6. Can mean "universal"	creed
7. Statement of beliefs	Ephesus
8. Means "father"	hell
9. Reaffirmed that the Holy Spirit is God	pope
10. "The grave" in the Apostles' Creed	Rome

Completion

1. Basic doctrines we should heed
   Are found in the ——— ———.
2. Freedom came with Constantine
   After A.D. ———.
3. Leaders judged a false idea
   At the Council of ———.
4. Peter preached a living hope,
   But he never was a ———.
5. Hermit life was solitary;
   Monks lived in a ———.
6. Anthony lived hermit-style
   In his cave along the ———.
7. Darkness reigned in early stages
   Of the lengthy ——— ———.
8. Catholics no doubt deplore
   The schism in ———.

Thought Questions

1. Some people point out that when the councils of Nicaea and Constantinople were held, the church had already drifted into apostasy. On this basis, they say that what these councils stated is not reliable. Why do we believe in the deity of Christ and of the Holy Spirit in spite of this argument?
2. When the church left the teachings of the Bible, the leaders began seeking worldly honors such as riches, fine robes, and palaces. What is the Biblical way of honoring church leaders?
3. What false doctrine taught that Jesus did not "come in the flesh"?
4. How is the present time similar to the times immediately following the reign of Constantine?
5. What connection do you see between what the Vandals did to the Romans and what vandals do today? A dictionary may help you.

Geographical Skills

1. Trace Map G, and label it "The Divided Roman Empire."
2. Draw the boundaries of the western Roman Empire, which fell to the barbarians; and the eastern Roman Empire, which became known as the Byzantine Empire. Color each empire a different color.
3. Label the two empires and their capital cities of Rome and Constantinople.

Further Study

1. Find references in the Bible that speak of Jesus as God, or of people worshiping Him.
2. Many hermits and monks had the idea that only spiritual things are good. They thought of things that can be seen, heard, touched, and tasted as basically evil. The very first chapter of the Bible contradicts this idea. What does it say over and over to show that the things in the world around us are not evil in themselves?

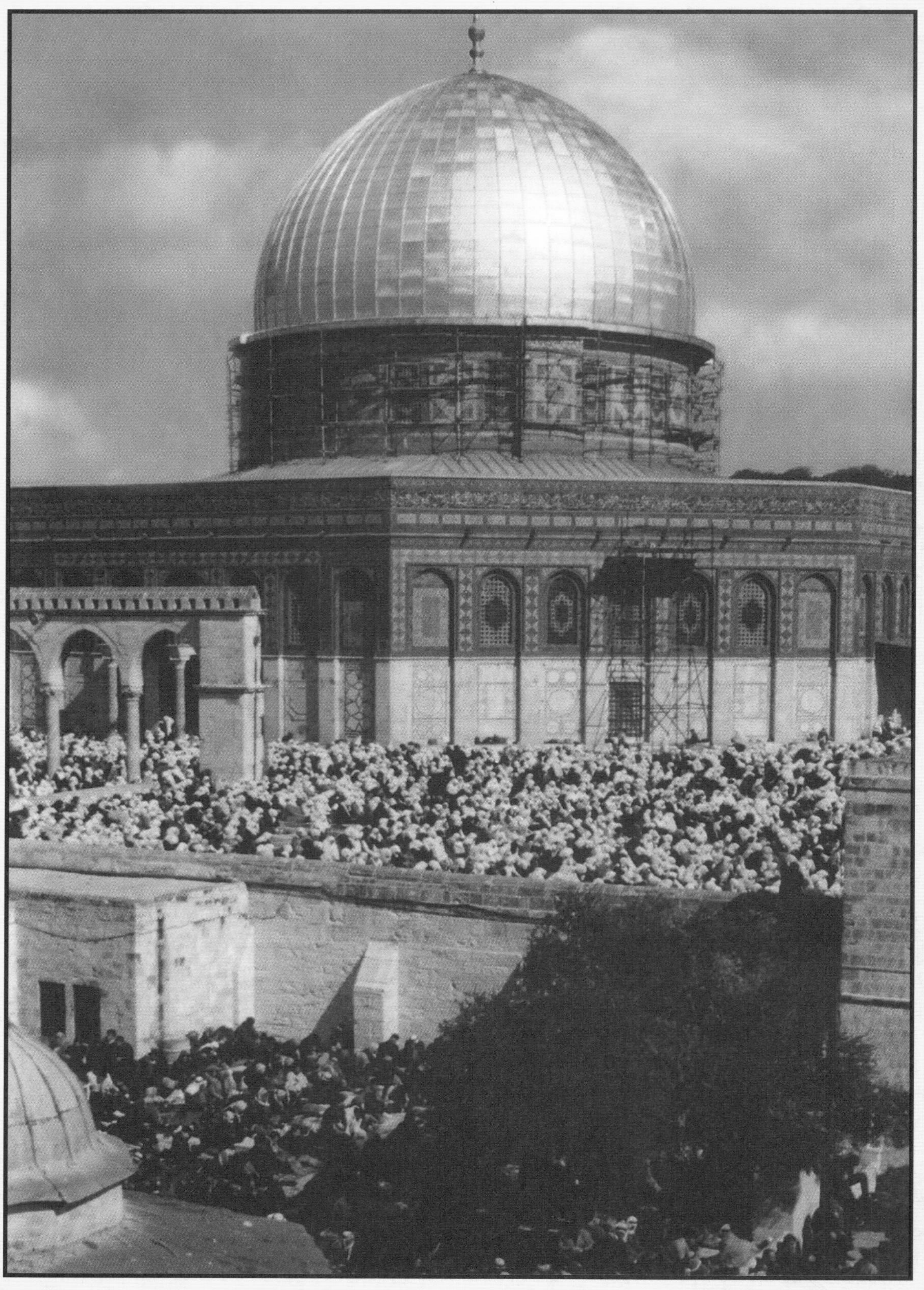

Muslims pray during Ramadan at a mosque (Islam place of worship) in Jerusalem. Many Muslims are fervent in their religion. Their zeal should challenge many casual, careless so-called Christians. But fervency alone does not make us right with God. We must be fervent, but we must also be wholly devoted to truth.

600 A.D.

Muhammad flees to Mecca. (the Hegira) 622

Islam spreads from Arabia to Persia, India, North Africa, and Spain. 600s, 700s

700

800

900

1000

1100

1200

1300

1400

1500

1600

The Taj Mahal is built in India. 1632–1643

1700 A.D.

20 The Muslims

How Islam Began

What Islam Teaches

How Islam Spread

What Happened to Conquered Peoples?

Muslim Education

Muslim Trade

"Beloved, believe not every spirit, but try the spirits whether they are of God: because many false prophets are gone out into the world."

1 John 4:1

The Muslims

How Islam Began

If you were to visit the deserts of the Middle East today, you could find a few people who still live as their ancestors did in Bible times. Dwelling in tents of camels' hair or black goats' hair and roaming in search of grass and water for their animals, their way of life is quite different from ours. But if you learned to speak the Arabic language, you might be surprised at how many friendly people you would meet.

However, these people's ancestors long ago accepted a religion called Islam, which is opposed to Christianity. It first began to spread among the Arab tribesmen who lived much as the desert nomads do today. The religion spread from land to land, and today many kinds of people in many countries are followers of Islam—businessmen, scientists, teachers, rich people, and poor people. Believers in Islam are called Muslims. This is the story of their religion and how it began.

Almost six hundred years after Christ, a boy named Muhammad grew up in the hot desert town of Mecca, in Arabia. His parents had both died when he was small, so his grandfather and his uncle raised him. As a young man, Muhammad became a trader and often traveled with camel caravans. He met many Christians and Jews, and through talking with them, he learned much about their religions. He decided that idol worship is wrong and that there is only one God.

But many of the Christians he met were Christians in name only. They were not converted in their hearts or godly in their behavior. Muhammad was not impressed. He did much thinking about religion, but he did not learn to believe in Jesus Christ as Saviour.

When Muhammad was forty years old, he claimed that the angel Gabriel had appeared to him in a vision. He thought Gabriel had told him that he was a prophet. At first Muhammad doubted whether his visions were real. But when he told his wife about them, she believed he was truly a prophet. Later he declared himself to be a prophet and tried to spread his beliefs.

Muhammad claimed to receive his teachings in a vision while he was in a cave. We know that all visions from God line up completely with His Word. Muhammad's "vision" had many teachings that erred from truth.

The people of Mecca persecuted Muhammad and his followers, so he fled. The followers of Muhammad still date their calendars from the year he fled from Mecca (A.D. 622). His famous flight away from Mecca is called the ***Hegira*** (hih JY ruh).

Muhammad arrived in Medina (mih DEE nuh), a town about 200 miles (325 km) north of Mecca. Many people at Medina accepted Muhammad as their spiritual leader. Soon he became their political leader as well. Later, Muhammad and his followers returned to Mecca and took control of it. He destroyed the many idols in it and gave Islam a strong foothold there.

Muhammad's religion kept on spreading. Many Arabs in the surrounding areas became his followers. In times past, they had often fought among themselves. Now they had one main religion, one that encouraged them to work together. They were ready to conquer other territories.

Thousands of Muslims from all over the world gather at the great mosque in Mecca every year. Mecca is considered the most sacred Muslim city. The building in the center of the picture contains a large black stone that is sacred to Muslims. The Muslims kiss and circle the stone a number of times in their rituals.

Study Exercises

1. True or false: Islam is mainly a religion for desert dwellers. Give a reason for your answer.
2. Why was Muhammad not impressed with the "Christians" that he met?
3. The Hegira was Muhammad's journey between what two cities?
4. Did the Islamic faith serve to unite the desert tribesmen or to divide them?

What Islam Teaches

What are some of the important differences between Islam and Christianity? You will see first what Muslims teach and then what they do not teach.

The five most important teachings that Muslims must observe are these: (1) Believe that there is only one God (whom the Muslims call *Allah*) and that Muhammad is his prophet. (2) Pray five times a day, facing toward Mecca. (3) Take a pilgrimage to Mecca if possible. (4) Give alms to the poor. (5) Fast during the month of Ramadan. During this month, Muslims are not allowed to eat or drink from dawn to sunset. But they may do so after sunset. These five teachings are called the five pillars of Islam.

And what truths do Muslims not teach? They reject the Bible as the Word of God and instead follow the doctrines of Muhammad as taught in the Koran, the holy book of Islam. Muslims do not believe that Jesus Christ is the Son of God and the Saviour of the world. They put Jesus on the same level with other prophets. The Koran calls Jesus the "son of Mary," but it denies that He is the Son of God.

The Koran includes some of Jesus' teachings. However, Muslims do not believe

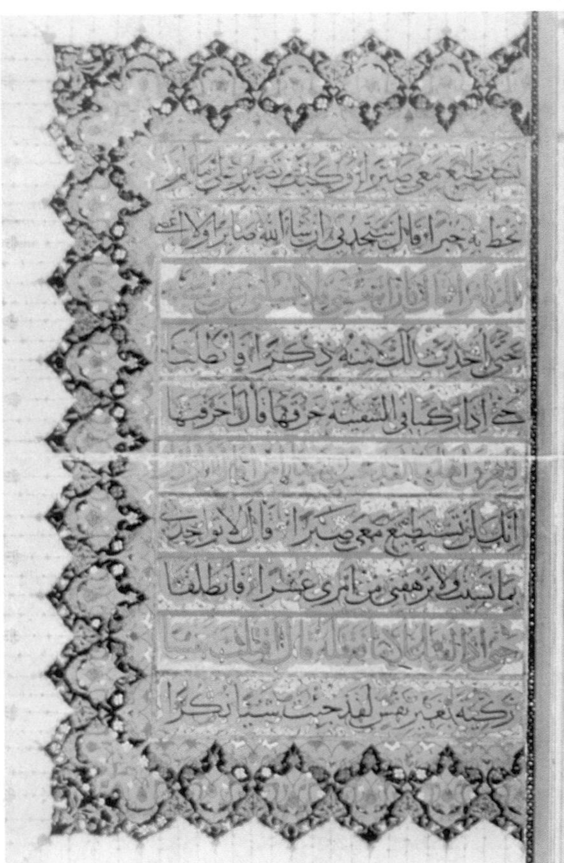

This decorated page spread is from a 1500s copy of the Koran.

many Bible truths, such as ***nonresistance.*** They have often spread their religion by force. In some cases, opposing groups of Muslims have fought each other.

Muslims do not view God as the Bible reveals Him. Muslim prayers are the same prayers recited time after time—not the kind of prayer in which true children of God have heart-to-heart communication with their heavenly Father.

Muslims do not believe they must be holy, even though they do perform certain religious duties. The Koran teaches them to be kind, fair, and good, but it does not set as high a standard as the New Testament does.

Islam does not deal with the sinful nature. It tries to keep people from sinning, but it does not reach deep into people's hearts and make them new creatures. It cannot give inner strength to overcome sin.

The Muslim idea of salvation is not according to the Bible. Instead of God reaching down to man by sending a Saviour, Muslims try to reach God by doing good works. They attempt to save themselves. This makes Islam look appealing to some, for many people do not like to admit that they cannot save themselves. But by trying to save themselves, they are trying to climb up some other way (John 10:1). Islam is a false religion that has deceived millions of people.

Study Exercises

5. Choose from the following list the practices that both Christians and Muslims observe. (*a*) Fast for religious reasons. (*b*) Pray frequently. (*c*) Make a pilgrimage to Mecca. (*d*) Give to the poor.
6. Choose the one doctrine that both Christians and Muslims believe. (*a*) God exists in three persons. (*b*) There is only one true God. (*c*) Muhammad was the last great prophet. (*d*) Christ is the only way of salvation.
7. What name do Muslims use for God?
8. What "Bible" do the Muslims have?

How Islam Spread

Muhammad lived just ten years after his flight from Mecca. But by the end of those ten years, nearly all Arabia had become Islamic. Within the next twenty years, the Muslims conquered Syria, Palestine, Persia, and Egypt. In another eighty years, they had expanded eastward to western India and westward across northern Africa into Spain.

Why did Islam spread so fast? It was partly because Muslim warriors helped to

This temple in Jerusalem, called the Dome of the Rock, houses a large limestone rock that Muslims consider sacred. Muslims built the temple over 1,300 years ago. This temple is supposed to be on the same location as Solomon's temple once stood. The Muslims say that Noah sailed around this rock seven times, that Abraham nearly offered up Isaac on this rock, and that on the last day, an angel will sound a trumpet from this rock.

Christians need no special stones and temples. The Rock Christ Jesus dwells in their hearts, no matter where they are. The Holy Spirit within them is incomparable to stones that will simply perish (1 Peter 1:7).

spread it. They fought fiercely because they thought they were fighting "holy wars." They thought they would benefit whether they overcame the enemy or were killed in battle. If they won, they could capture the enemy's goods for themselves. If they were killed, they thought they would immediately go to heaven.

Perhaps it was also because the people around them were ungodly—even many professing Christians. Although the Muslims themselves were far from holy, God may have used them to bring judgment on idol worshipers and on professing Christians who had turned from the truth.

In addition, the Muslims were united and strong while other empires around them had become weak. The Muslims fought for their religious beliefs, whereas many of the people around them had no specific cause for which to fight.

Although the Muslims took great sections of land from the Byzantine Empire, they did not overrun all of it. Constantinople, the Byzantine capital, did not fall until hundreds of years later.

Muhammad holds two symbols of his faith—the sword and the book of Koran. The sword and war always accompany the Islam religion. In contrast to this, God's true children are peaceful and often suffer persecution.

What Happened to Conquered Peoples?

When people heard that Muslim warriors were coming their way, they often decided the best thing to do was surrender. If they fought, they might be defeated and

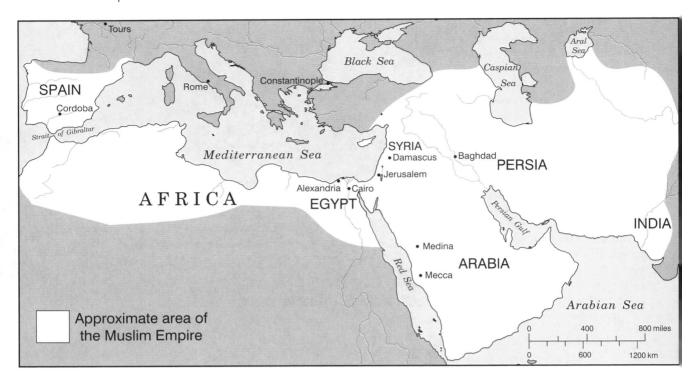

Figure 20:1. The Muslim Conquests

have their lands taken away. If they did not fight, they would have to pay taxes to the Muslims, but they would not lose everything.

How did the Muslims treat Christians in the lands they conquered? Christians were often persecuted and killed if they refused to give up their faith and accept Islam. Some Muslim rulers were more tolerant, but the Christians never knew when the next oppression would begin.

The *Martyrs Mirror* (page 242) records a period of persecution by a Muslim ruler in Spain. The Muslims told Christians that they would not be hurt as long as they did not say anything evil about Muhammad, did not go to church, and paid their taxes. They thought that in this way they would gradually win the Christians to Islam. But the true disciples of Jesus knew that they could not keep their faith secret. They spoke out against the evils they saw, even though they knew they might be beheaded for it.

A Muslim preaches the Koran to a crowd of fellow Muslims.

This drawing shows the Muslim temple at Medina, Spain. The Muslims controlled Spain for a few centuries before they were finally driven out in 1492.

Strangely, many professing Christians in Spain sided with the Muslims against faithful Christians. Even some church leaders declared that those who were killed for their steadfastness were not really martyrs. This of course encouraged the Muslims and made things worse for those who were truly serving God.

For an inspiring story of one who gave his life for Jesus, read the story of Pelagius on page 256 of the *Martyrs Mirror.* This boy was martyred in Spain when he was just thirteen years old. The Muslim king promised to raise him in his court if he would renounce Christ. But when Pelagius declared that he would remain a Christian, the king became very angry and ordered his guards to cut Pelagius in pieces and throw him into the river. Pelagius remained faithful unto death.

God allowed the Muslims to kill some Christians, but He did not allow them to destroy the Christian church. Although the number of genuine Christians must have been very small at times, God has always preserved a faithful remnant of believers.

Study Exercises

9. What was the first region to embrace Islam?
10. What empire lost land to the Muslims but did not totally collapse?
11. What punishment did the Muslims often use against active Christians?
12. How did some professing Christians make it especially difficult for true Christians to stand for the Lord?

Muslim Education

The Muslims were interested in education, and they learned many things from the people they conquered. Not satisfied with studying only what people were teaching in their day, they translated old Greek and Latin books into their own Arabic language. They studied astronomy, chemistry, and algebra. Long before the days of Columbus, they knew that the world is round. Their doctors performed some types of surgery.

Muslim mathematicians borrowed the numeration system of India. They saw that the simple numerals of the Hindus were much easier to add, subtract, multiply, and divide than Roman numerals were. Because Arabs introduced these numerals to Europe, we call the digits from 0 to 9 Hindu-Arabic numerals, or just Arabic numerals. If you doubt that they are simple, try multiplying two Roman numerals—such as LXIV times MCMLXXIII!

Muslim architects designed many beautiful buildings, especially ***mosques*** for worship. They avoided statues and pictures, since

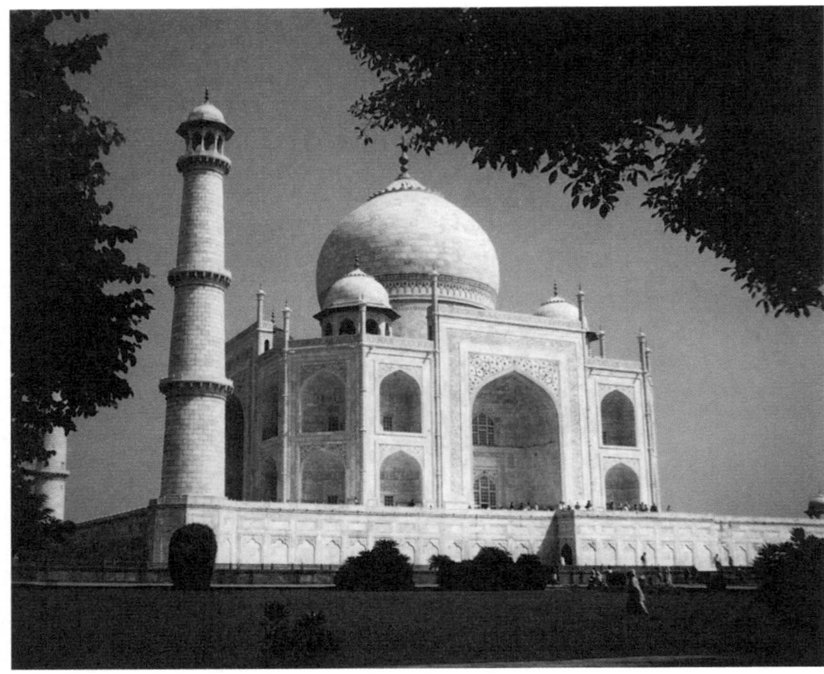

Over 20,000 workmen labored on the Taj Mahal for over 20 years.

Muhammad had commanded his followers not to make any likeness of people or animals. Instead, artists made beautiful leafy designs or geometric patterns.

Probably the most famous example of Muslim architecture is the Taj Mahal (TAHJ muh HAHL) in India. A ruler had it built as a tomb in memory of his wife, whom he had adored. In pictures of the Taj Mahal, you can see the Islamic dome and slender pillars.

During this part of the Middle Ages, Muslims possessed more knowledge than the Europeans who called themselves Christians. But Muslim learning did not stay only with the Muslims. Jews, Christians, and others came in contact with the Muslims and learned what they had learned. One example is the Arabic numeration system, as you have already seen. In later chapters you will read about more ways in which Muslims influenced other people.

Muslim Trade

Perhaps you have noticed that businessmen locate their stores and offices in towns or along highways. More customers will come to them if they build a store where many people pass by than if they try to sell their goods in a farmhouse at the end of a long lane.

Arab traders had a good location in the Middle East, the center of the then-known world. They could easily trade with countries east of them and west of them. Baghdad, the capital of the Muslim Empire, became a great trading city. From Baghdad, ships could sail down the Tigris River on their way to India, China, or eastern Africa. Ships also sailed from the Middle East westward to Europe.

Muslim traders traveled by land as well. Caravans of camels, horses, and donkeys plodded from the Middle East along the trade routes west through northern Africa, north through Russia, and east

An ancient Muslim trading ship.

along the Great Silk Road to China. The traders also sold goods they brought from their own land. Damascus did not have a seaport as Baghdad did, but it too was a great trading city.

When people trade goods, they also trade ideas. The Muslims learned from the people they met, and other people learned from the Muslims. In later chapters, you will read how the Muslims influenced the outside world and how this affects lives in many lands today.

Study Exercises

13. What language did most Muslims speak?
14. What other languages did many Muslim scholars know?
15. Why are the numerals 1, 2, 3, and so on called Arabic numerals?
16. Name the buildings that Muslim architects made especially beautiful, and describe their use.
17. Why are there no statues in mosques?
18. What city was the capital of the Muslim Empire?
19. In what direction from the Middle East are the following lands:
    (*a*) China (*b*) Russia (*c*) Northern Africa?

Clinching the Chapter

Multiple Choice

A. *Write the word or phrase* least *associated with the first item.*

1. Islam: Muhammad, Allah, Muslim, Pelagius
2. Arabia: desert, Mecca, Baghdad, Medina
3. Muhammad: Constantinople, Hegira, Mecca, Medina
4. Bible: Ramadan, Jesus, Gabriel, Christianity
5. Spread of Islam: "holy wars," corrupt "Christians," united cause, love of truth
6. A.D. 622: Hegira, Muhammad, Taj Mahal, Medina
7. Muslim trade: Damascus, Baghdad, Hegira, China
8. Baghdad: Tigris, harbor, capital, Pelagius
9. Koran: Arabic, Islamic, New Testament, "holy" book
10. Damascus: trade, ships, Syria, caravans

B. *Write the word or phrase* least *associated with the first item.*

1. Muslim studies: Greek, Latin, Hebrew, algebra, astronomy, chemistry, medicine
2. Constantinople: Byzantine, capital, weak, soon destroyed
3. Easy numerals: India, Rome, Hindus, Arabs
4. Middle East: central location, trade routes, Muslim influence, silk
5. Five pillars of Islam: prayer, fasting, holiness, giving, pilgrimage, belief in Allah
6. Ramadan: month, fasting, sunset, Gabriel
7. Muslim architecture: mosque, dome, minaret, church, Taj Mahal
8. Desert: Constantinople, nomads, tents, Arabs
9. Muslim art: pictures, leafy designs, geometric patterns, beauty
10. Pelagius: martyr, Spain, Damascus, young

Matching

A. *For each clue, write the correct name from the right-hand column.*

1. Founder of Islam	Allah
2. Town where Islam first became strong	Arabia
3. Holiest city of Islam	Arabic
4. Rejected by Muslims	Hegira
5. Region where Islam was born	Islam
6. Worshiper of Allah	Jesus
7. Language of most Muslims	Mecca
8. Worshiped by Muslims	Medina
9. Flight from Mecca	Muhammad
10. Non-Christian religion	Muslim

B. *Match as in Part A.*

1. Country of Damascus	Baghdad
2. Supposedly called Muhammad a prophet	Bible
3. Famous Muslim tomb	Egypt
4. European country to which Muslims spread	Gabriel
5. Weak empire east of Muslim capital	India
6. African country conquered by Muslims	Persia
7. The fasting month	Ramadan
8. Contradicts Muhammad's claims	Spain
9. True source of Arabic numerals	Syria
10. Capital of Muslim Empire	Taj Mahal

Completion

1. As the Muslims expanded, they came to obtain
   All the land from the East to the country of ———.
2. Every Muslim supposes his faithfulness pleases
   The God he calls Allah, who has no son ———.
3. We would know, if a diligent teacher should ask us,
   The center of Syria's trade is ———.
4. Several times in a day, after washing with care,
   Men will kneel, facing Mecca in reverent ———.

5. When the heavens have vanished, God's Word will live on.
   It is found in the Bible, not in the ———.
6. For the stories of Christians whose Saviour was dearer
   Than life, read accounts in the old ——— ———.
7. In working with math, if you want some frustration,
   Compute with the Romans' complex ———.

Thought Questions

1. Depending on what kind of Christians Muhammad had met as a young man, the world might never have known Islam. Why?
2. What statement of Jesus in John 14 shows that Muslims cannot gain salvation by their religion? (Peter made a similar statement in Acts 4:12.)
3. What is there about human nature that influences people to prefer Islam over Christianity?
4. How many times a day should a Christian pray?
5. During this period, it seems that many Muslims worked harder at their studies than did others who called themselves Christians. How can this be?

Geographical Skills

1. Trace Map A again, and label it "Islam Starts and Spreads."
2. Draw the route of the Hegira. Label the two cities involved, and Baghdad, the capital of the Muslim religion. Also label the present-day countries on your map.
3. How far apart are Mecca and Baghdad?

Further Study

1. See what other interesting facts you can learn about the Taj Mahal, especially those that indicate Islamic influence.
2. Think of some prosperous businesses in your local community. Why are many of these located in a town or city, or along a busy highway?

Be Sure You Know

Can you answer all these questions? If not, study Chapters 19 and 20 to find the answers.

A. What

1. edict made Christianity legal in the Roman Empire?
2. Roman emperor made Christianity the state religion?
3. (*a*) council reaffirmed that Jesus is God? (*b*) council reaffirmed that the Holy Spirit is God?
4. statement summarizes the basic doctrines of Christianity?
5. did Simeon do to get close to God?
6. are each the leaders Ambrose, Jerome, and Augustine remembered for?
7. part of the Roman Empire lasted a thousand years after the fall of Rome?
8. was the old name for Constantinople?
9. were the names of three barbarian tribes that helped to overthrow the Roman Empire?
10. was the result of the schism of 1054?
11. are the five pillars of Islam?
12. does Islam teach about Jesus?
13. (*a*) was the Muslims' attitude toward education? (*b*) was the Muslims' attitude toward art?
14. is probably the most famous example of Muslim architecture?

B. What do these words mean?

15. ascetic
16. Dark Ages
17. Gnosticism
18. Hegira
19. hermit
20. illiterate
21. *Martyrs Mirror*
22. Middle Ages
23. monastery
24. monk
25. mosque
26. nonresistance
27. patriarch
28. pope
29. schism

C. How

30. did the pope come to be considered the head of the church?
31. (*a*) was Islam established? (*b*) Give the approximate date it was established.
32. did the Muslims treat the people they conquered?

D. Why

33. did Christianity decay after the time of the apostles?
34. did the Roman Empire break apart?
35. do the Dark Ages have that name?
36. did Islam spread rapidly?
37. did the Muslims become especially involved in trading?

So Far This Year

See how many answers you can give from Chapters 1–20 without looking back.

A. *Match the letters on the map to the names below. You will not use all the letters.*

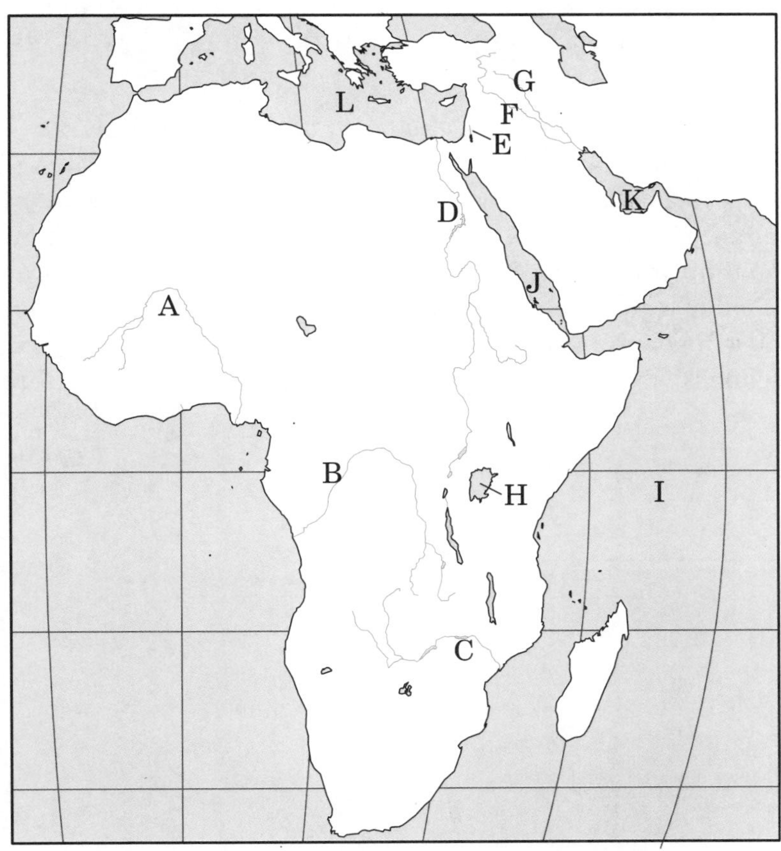

_____ 1. Euphrates River

_____ 2. Indian Ocean

_____ 3. Jordan River

_____ 4. Mediterranean Sea

_____ 5. Niger River

_____ 6. Nile River

_____ 7. Persian Gulf

_____ 8. Red Sea

_____ 9. Tigris River

_____10. Zambezi River

B. *Give the correct answers.*

11. Europe and Asia are considered two different continents because of their great difference in (climate, culture, landscape, history).
12. Government of the earliest civilizations was in the form of (city-states, kingdoms, republics, empires).
13. An important Egyptian contribution to writing was (alphabetic symbols, cuneiform, papyrus, parchment).
14. Many battles were fought in Canaan because (the inhabitants were unusually warlike, Canaan was a buffer between strong nations, the landscape of Canaan made it an excellent battlefield).

15. The Assyrians' way of dealing with conquered people was (deporting them, enslaving them, allowing them to continue living much as before).
16. The Behistun Rock is important because it provided the key to ancient (hieroglyphic, cuneiform, Phoenician) writing.
17. The Great Wall of China was built (as a monument, as a hard-labor project for criminals, to keep out invaders, to mark the boundary of China).
18. Famous Greek philosophers include all the following *except* (Socrates, Plato, Hippocrates, Aristotle).

C. *Write the correct name for each clue. You will not use all the names.*

19. Roman ruler who became dictator for life
20. Roman emperor when Christ was born
21. Roman emperor who first persecuted the Christians
22. Ruler who rebuilt the temple for the Jews
23. Herodian ruler who heard Paul's defense
24. Ruler who killed John the Baptist
25. Church leaders who were disciples of the apostle John (two)

Agrippa
Antipas
Antony
Caesar Augustus
Herod the Great
Ignatius
Julius Caesar
Nero
Polycarp

Vikings land on the coast of France during one of their many raids on continental Europe.

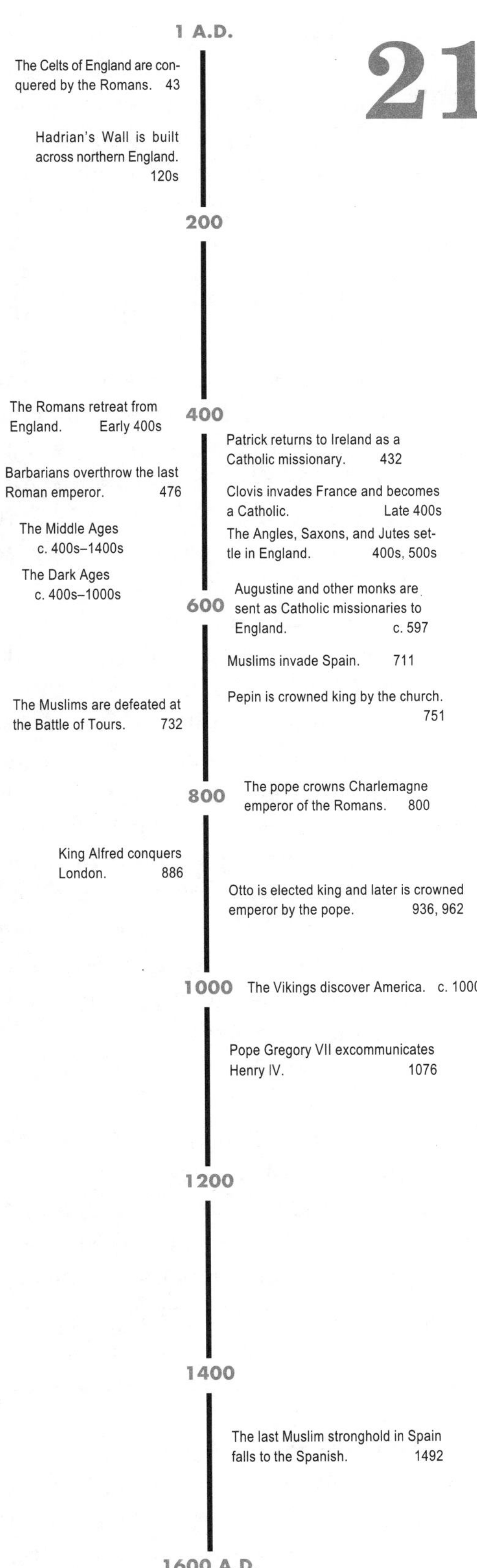
1 A.D.
The Celts of England are conquered by the Romans. 43
Hadrian's Wall is built across northern England. 120s
200
The Romans retreat from England. Early 400s
400
Patrick returns to Ireland as a Catholic missionary. 432
Barbarians overthrow the last Roman emperor. 476
Clovis invades France and becomes a Catholic. Late 400s
The Middle Ages c. 400s–1400s
The Angles, Saxons, and Jutes settle in England. 400s, 500s
The Dark Ages c. 400s–1000s
600
Augustine and other monks are sent as Catholic missionaries to England. c. 597
Muslims invade Spain. 711
The Muslims are defeated at the Battle of Tours. 732
Pepin is crowned king by the church. 751
800
The pope crowns Charlemagne emperor of the Romans. 800
King Alfred conquers London. 886
Otto is elected king and later is crowned emperor by the pope. 936, 962
1000
The Vikings discover America. c. 1000
Pope Gregory VII excommunicates Henry IV. 1076
1200
1400
The last Muslim stronghold in Spain falls to the Spanish. 1492
1600 A.D.

21 The Early Middle Ages

The Breakup of Government

The British Isles

The Angles, Saxons, and Jutes

The Moors in Spain

The Franks in France

The Vikings Invade Europe

The "Holy" Roman Empire

The Church in Politics

"This matter is by the decree of the watchers, and the demand by the word of the holy ones: to the intent that the living may know that the most High ruleth in the kingdom of men, and giveth it to whomsoever he will, and setteth up over it the basest of men." — *Daniel 4:17*

The Early Middle Ages

The Middle Ages started in the 400s and lasted about a thousand years. Sometimes the Middle Ages are called ***medieval*** (mee dee EE vuhl) times.

Some historians give the label "Dark Ages" to the first part of the Middle Ages—from the late 400s to perhaps 1000 or 1100. Maybe it is not quite fair to label one period of time as "Dark Ages" when much darkness persisted throughout the Middle Ages. In some ways, our modern world suffers under spiritual darkness as it never did before. But in many ways, the first part of the Middle Ages was a period of darkness.

What was especially dark about the Dark Ages?

In Chapter 19, you learned about the decay of Christianity and the fall of Rome. Spiritual decay, widespread ignorance, and the lack of strong government brought primitive conditions to Europe for hundreds of years. Most Europeans lived in mental darkness—without money, good transportation, trade, imported goods, books, and education.

The Breakup of Government

Modern nations such as the United States and Canada have a strong government system that controls many square miles of territory. The government directs military and police forces that protect the country.

Can you imagine a world with a totally different system? After the Roman Empire fell, government in Europe certainly was different. In fact, for a time there was hardly any system of government at all.

You have already learned that barbarians invaded Europe. In this chapter you will learn more about the Franks who moved into France and about the Angles, Saxons, and Jutes who settled in England. There were other barbarians—the Goths, the Huns, and the Vandals. They robbed the local people, and they fought each other. Barbarians who settled down to farm were themselves robbed by other barbarians. After the Roman Empire fell, there was no central government to maintain law and order.

Here and there, groups of people found protection under a local leader who commanded a number of armed men. He may have been a former noble of the Roman Empire or the chief of a barbarian tribe. In return for his protection, the people agreed to be loyal to him.

Europe no longer was controlled by one world empire, nor was it divided into medium-sized nations as Europe is today. Instead, Europe was controlled by hundreds of tiny governments during the Dark Ages. The territories of many rulers were no bigger than a county in the United States. Occasionally a strong ruler would gain control of a large area. You will learn about some of these men in this chapter. But keep in mind that even during the reigns of strong kings, the rulers of small, local territories were quite powerful.

Study Exercises

1. What period of European history is often called the Dark Ages?
2. What was the last central government in Europe before lawlessness took over?
3. Who gave the common people some protection after the central government fell?

The British Isles

While some barbarian tribes were invading the Roman Empire, other tribes from northern Europe were invading the British

Figure 21:1. The British Isles

Isles. Before studying this invasion, you should learn a few geographical terms and some earlier history of these islands.

The British Isles include two large islands—Ireland and Great Britain. The island of Great Britain has three parts—Scotland in the north, Wales in the southwest, and England in the center and southeast.

About the time Jesus lived on the earth, tribes of people called Celts lived in the British Isles. The Celts of England were conquered by the Romans in A.D. 43. This was during the reign of the emperor Claudius, whom the Bible mentions in Acts 11:28 and 18:2. Within several years, the Romans controlled what is now England, Wales, and part of Scotland.

The Romans never completely conquered Scotland, in northern Great Britain. An old story says that a Roman army once sneaked up on a band of exhausted Scottish soldiers, who were sleeping. A mysterious scream woke the Scottish soldiers. They jumped up, seized their weapons, fought the Romans, and won. After the battle, a captured Roman soldier admitted that he had screamed after stepping on a thistle with his bare foot. In gratitude to the thistle, the people of Scotland named it their official flower.

Although England was made a Roman province, the Romans were constantly troubled by Scottish invaders. Finally the emperor Hadrian had a long stone wall built across northern England to keep enemies out. The wall was guarded by forts, towers, and thousands of soldiers. Some parts of Hadrian's Wall are still standing today.

The Romans controlled England for about four hundred years. The people enjoyed law and order, good stone roads, and other advantages that came with being part of the Roman Empire. By the end of this period, Christianity had been brought to the island.

Only short sections of Hadrian's Wall across England still stand today. Originally, the wall was over 70 miles (112.7 km) long.

The Angles, Saxons, and Jutes

Gradually the Romans became weaker. They could no longer defend Hadrian's Wall. In the early 400s, they had to leave England to defend Rome itself against barbarians. This left the Celtic people without strong protection from enemies.

Soon England was overrun by many invaders. Some came from Scotland and others from Ireland. But the most important invaders were Germanic tribes from mainland Europe—the blond, blue-eyed Angles, Saxons, and Jutes who settled in England during the 400s and 500s. Because these people were less advanced than the Romans, England lost many Roman improvements, such as their methods of governing and their road-building skills.

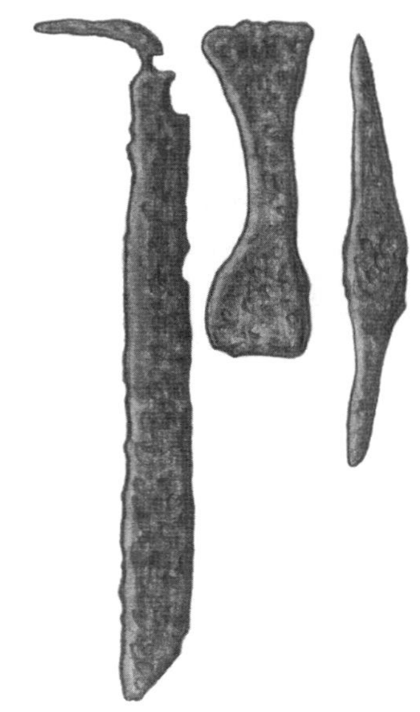

Anglo-Saxon farmers used iron and wooden tools to work land and harvest crops. The long knife was used as a sickle for harvesting grass and grain. The other two tools were used for chopping wood and cultivating soil. These tools were found in England.

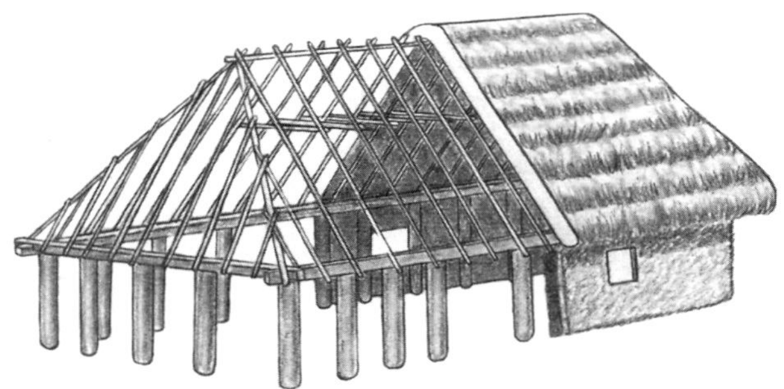

Early Anglo-Saxon dwellings were built with strong wall posts that supported the weight of the roof. This left the interior free of encumbering posts.

The invaders conquered all the Celtic tribes except the Britons. Most of the Britons fled to the hills and mountains of Wales. The Welsh people of today are descended from them. They still speak their ancient language, which has words that seem quite difficult to English-speaking people. How would you like to live at a place named Llwchwr or Mynyddislwyn?

The language of the Angles and Saxons was a form of German, and it included many short, strong words. The words *short* and *strong* themselves come from their language, which is called Anglo-Saxon, or Old English. It was the forerunner of our modern English. In fact, the name *England* means "Angle-land," the land named after the Angles.

Several days of the week are named after Anglo-Saxon gods, such as Tiu, Woden, Thor, and Frigg. Do you see which days these names resemble?

In Ireland, a different kind of "invasion" was taking place. When a youth named Patrick was brought from Great Britain as a slave, no one realized how important he would become to Ireland. Patrick served as a slave for six years, and then he escaped and eventually returned to his Catholic parents. But he could not forget the Irish people, so he returned to Ireland as a Catholic missionary about 432. Under Patrick's teaching, thousands of Irish people were baptized, and several hundred Catholic churches were established.

Today many people observe St. Patrick's Day on March 17. Most of them know very

This ancient Catholic church in England stands on the seashore at Dover. Ruins of a Roman lighthouse stand by the church.

The bearded man in the front is Patrick, a Catholic missionary to the Irish. Such missionary efforts had a significant impact on the history of the British Isles, even though the Catholic Church of Patrick's time had departed from the simple faith of the early church.

little about the Catholic priest who became known as the Apostle to the Irish.

The Angles and Saxons who invaded England were pagans. After their conquest, Christianity survived only in small areas of Great Britain. But one day in far-off Italy, a monk named Gregory took notice of some slaves who had been brought from England. Observing their fair skin and blond hair, he asked, "Who are these people?"

"They are Angles," came the reply.

"Not Angles, but angels!" exclaimed Gregory. "They should belong to the church. I will go and save them."

But Gregory was chosen to be pope soon afterward. So about 597, he sent a monk named Augustine and forty other monks to spread the Catholic faith in England. Thousands of Angles and Saxons became Catholics, and hundreds of churches sprang up.

Study Exercises

4. The ——— of England were defeated by the ——— in A.D. 43. The main groups who invaded England during the 400s and 500s were the ———, ———, and Jutes.

5. What is another name for the Anglo-Saxon language?
6. Which days of the week are named after gods worshiped in early England?
7. Who was the best-known Catholic missionary (*a*) to the Irish? (*b*) to the English?

The Moors in Spain

You have already learned how the Muslims spread to many countries in the Middle East and in northern Africa. There was also a Muslim country in Europe for a while, as you may remember reading in the previous chapter. Muslims from Africa, called Moors, invaded Spain in 711; and they ruled it for several hundred years. But the Moors never conquered a small area in northern Spain, and eventually the Catholic rulers of this region began to drive out the Muslims. However, the last Moorish stronghold in Spain held out until 1492—almost eight hundred years after the Muslim invasion.

Muslim rule in Spain sometimes meant persecution for Christians who lived there. However, the Moors taught the people of Europe some very useful things. During the Dark Ages, Spain under the Moors was one of the most advanced civilizations in Europe.

The Moors knew how to irrigate their crops—something worthwhile to know in sunny Spain. They introduced new crops to Europe. Can you imagine seeing a European eat his first strawberry? Not only strawberries, but also bananas, oranges, dates, sugar cane, and rice were new to the people of Europe.

Besides being the best farmers in Europe, the Moors knew how to make paper, raise silkworms for cloth, and produce steel and leather. Europeans bought the Moors' products and borrowed their ideas.

The Moors had their own ways of designing buildings and churches. Often they were decorated with designs made of many pieces of colored glass or stone. Such designs are called mosaics. Visitors to Spain today can still see the Muslim influence in the way old buildings are constructed.

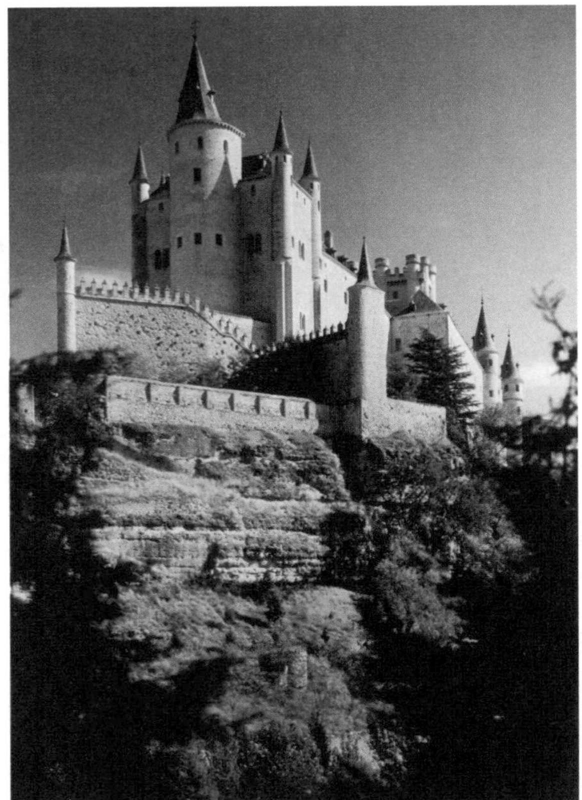

This Spanish castle was built by the Muslims. The pointed roofs and round towers are earmarks of Muslim architecture. The crosses on the tops of spires are likely a Catholic addition.

The Franks in France

From Spain the Moors pushed across the Pyrenees Mountains and into France, the next country to the northeast. To understand the people they met there, one must go back several hundred years.

The land today called France had once belonged to the Roman Empire. When that empire crumbled in the 400s, barbarians from other parts of Europe flooded into this region. One group of invaders was called Franks. Part of the land they settled became known as France, after the Franks.

The first powerful king of the Franks, who led their invasion in the late 400s, was named Clovis. Perhaps the most far-reaching decision he made was to become a Catholic. He and three thousand of his warriors were baptized. Clovis did not really understand what it meant to be a Christian, but his decision did pave the way for other people to learn more about God. Had it not been for Clovis's decision, many people in his kingdom may never have heard the Word of God at all.

The next kings were weak rulers whose reigns were plagued by immorality and domestic strife. Because of their carelessness, the chief palace officials, called the mayors of the palace, began to assume leadership of the country. One of these palace mayors was named Charles. He is remembered for his battles against the Muslims, especially the battle at Tours.

The Moors had already conquered most of Spain and had made their way far into France. Would they conquer all of Europe, as they had conquered the Middle East and northern Africa? Charles was determined to keep that from happening. He and his Catholic soldiers met the Muslim army near Tours, in France. A great battle was fought there, and the Moors retreated.

Very few other battles have been as important as this Battle of Tours in 732. It was a turning point in history. If the Muslims had won, they would have moved on through Europe and perhaps conquered all of it. Then Christianity might have been completely snuffed out in Europe. But there is no "might have been" with God. He made sure this did not happen.

Charles went on to defeat the Muslims in several more battles. For this he earned the name Charles Martel (mahr TEHL), which means "Charles the Hammer."

Charles's son Pepin the Short (PEHP ihn) was the next ruler. He decided to ask the pope to crown him king. As mayor of the palace, he had been ruling already; and he felt that being crowned king by the pope would win more respect for his authority. The pope consented to his request, and thus the church became involved in European politics. This involvement of the Catholic Church in government affairs would continue for many years.

Charles Martel (688–741) fought the Muslims. He was the grandfather of Charlemagne.

Jesus taught that His kingdom is not of this world (John 18:36). A true Christian is an ambassador for Christ who calls men to repentance (2 Corinthians 5:20, 21), while a government leader is "a revenger to execute wrath upon him that doeth evil"

Pepin kills a lion and a bull while the lords of his court look on.

(Romans 13:4). The church and the government can function according to God's plan only when they work separately. This principle is called the separation of church and state.

But Pepin's government worked hand in hand with the church. This kind of arrangement had already caused trouble for the church in the days of the Roman Empire. It would cause more problems in the future, as you will see in later chapters.

The greatest of all the early Frankish kings was Pepin's son Charlemagne (SHAHR luh mayn). His name means "Charles the Great." Big, strong, and energetic, Charlemagne fought other tribes around him and made his kingdom even larger.

In the year 800, the pope crowned Charlemagne emperor of the Romans. Charlemagne liked to think of himself as

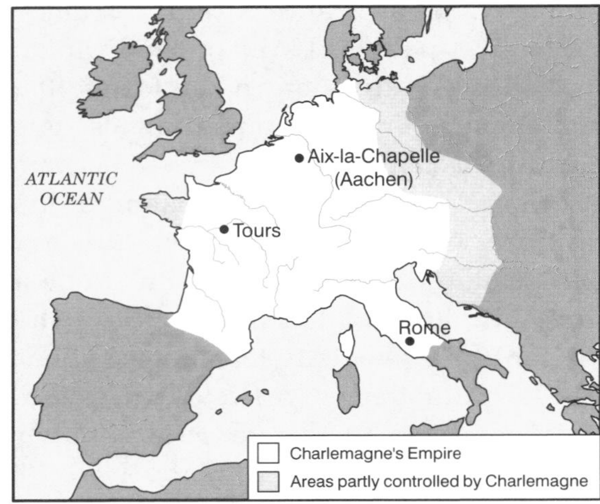

Figure 21:2. Charlemagne's Empire

ruler of a renewed Roman empire. But although his empire was enormous, it did not contain nearly all the land that the old Roman Empire had.

Charlemagne is remembered for his interest in schools and education. Although he never had much success in learning to write, he did learn to read. He studied

This drawing shows a cross section of part of Charlemagne's palace. Around the year 800, Charlemagne built an elaborate palace to serve as the center of his kingdom. The buildings were modeled along Roman lines—the brick arches are an example of this. Much of the stone for Charlemagne's buildings was scavenged from Roman ruins.

much, and he encouraged the organization of many schools. One of Charlemagne's main educational interests was to teach church leaders to read and write better. Many of them were so illiterate that he feared they could not properly understand and teach the Scriptures.

In spite of the good that Charlemagne did, his personal life was marred by much sin. Like Clovis and his soldiers, Charlemagne thought he was a Christian, but he did not obey all the New Testament teachings. The church leaders of his time were partly to blame for this. They did not teach all of God's truth, and they tolerated things that the Bible calls sin. Jesus said: "Not every one that saith unto me, Lord, Lord, shall enter into the kingdom of heaven; but he that doeth the will of my Father which is in heaven" (Matthew 7:21).

Study Exercises

8. (*a*) In what year did the Muslim Moors invade Spain? (*b*) When did the Catholics drive them from their last stronghold?
9. List several ways that the Moors in Spain were more advanced than most Europeans of the time.
10. France is named after what group of barbarians?
11. Who was the first ruler of the Franks to become a Catholic?
12. How was Charles Martel like a king, even though he was not called a king?
13. What Bible principle did Pepin violate?
14. What may have been Charlemagne's greatest contribution to his people?

The Vikings Invade Europe

During the last part of Charlemagne's rule, strange, swift boats began to appear along the seacoasts of Europe. The boats were long and narrow, often with dragon heads carved onto their high ends. Big, blond warriors rowed the boats.

These warriors were called Northmen, or Vikings. They had come from Scandinavia in the far northern part of Europe, where Norway, Sweden, and Denmark are today. Bold lovers of adventure, some of them eventually sailed far to the west—to Iceland, Greenland, and even farther. According to old legends, the Vikings landed in North America about five hundred years before Columbus made his discovery. Remains of an old Viking settlement in Newfoundland prove that they actually did reach North America.

In Europe, the Vikings sailed not only along the coasts but also up the rivers.

A Viking ship of the 700s.

Most Viking villages were small farming communities built near a river or fiord. Besides their skills at sea navigation, the Vikings were gifted metal workers and woodworkers. They made silver jewelry and fine carvings to decorate their homes and ships.

They traveled as far south as the Mediterranean Sea.

Some Vikings came to trade. But the Vikings that people remembered most were the fierce raiders. They would quietly approach a village and then make a surprise attack on it. They would rob houses and barns, burn buildings, and kill men, women, and children. Big towns, too, were sometimes attacked. The Vikings raided Paris twice, and they even attacked Constantinople.

It is interesting that in the land where the Vikings came from, many Norwegians still make their living today by shipping. They have a huge fleet and sail to ports around the world. Scandinavian people are still known for being tall, blond, and blue-eyed. But their raiding days are long past.

People were terrified at the stories they heard about the big Northmen. Many a priest would finish his prayers with the words, "God, deliver us from the fury of the Northmen." The invasion of the Vikings from the north and other invaders from the east helped keep Europe in the Dark Ages for two hundred or three hundred more years. Travel was dangerous, trade was limited, and kings found it difficult to rule large areas. For a time no strong leader arose in Europe after Charlemagne, so people looked to local

During the time of the Viking raids, the people of Ireland built tall, slender towers next to churches and monasteries to protect themselves and church valuables. The doors were well off the ground and could be reached only by a ladder, which was pulled up after the people were safely in the tower. These towers were about 100 feet (30.5 m) high.

leaders for protection and leadership.

In England, the people suffered greatly as Vikings overran much of the country. Finally a strong leader named Alfred gathered an army to fight the invaders. At first he was beaten. He had to disguise himself to avoid being caught. An old story says that once as he hid in the home of a herdsman, he was asked to watch some bread that was baking at the fireplace. The bread burned; and when the housewife saw it, she scolded, "Man, why did you not turn over the bread when you saw that it was burning?" The woman did not realize she was talking to King Alfred.

The struggle finally ended when Alfred and his men conquered London in 886. After that, the Vikings generally stayed out of Wessex, the part of England that Alfred ruled. Alfred made Wessex strong by fortifying many coastal towns and by building a fleet of ships.

Alfred was also interested in learning. The centers of education in those days were churches, but churches were favorite targets for Vikings to attack. Therefore, education had suffered greatly. Many of the priests could not even read or write.

Alfred started a school in his palace and encouraged scholars and teachers to come from other parts of Great Britain and from Europe. He was so interested in having books translated into English that he helped to translate some of them himself. Because of what Alfred did for England during this dark period of history, he became known as Alfred the Great.

Study Exercises

15. Why were towns along rivers and seacoasts in more danger from Viking attacks than those at inland locations?
16. In what direction did the Vikings sail to explore lands unknown to other Europeans of that time?
17. What important interest did Alfred the Great have that Charlemagne had had before him?

The "Holy" Roman Empire

When Charlemagne died, his empire fell apart. The western part eventually became France, and the eastern part was roughly what is now Germany. Most of the power was in the hands of local military leaders called ***dukes,*** who ruled small regions. The dukes elected a king, but usually the king had little power. However, several ambitious men were still excited by the word *empire.* They dreamed of reviving an empire in Europe.

In the year 936, the German dukes elected a man named Otto as king. Like Charlemagne, Otto became a strong leader. He defeated the Vikings and other invaders that were still threatening his country and gained control of a large region. In 962, Otto was crowned by the pope as emperor of a large region that included Germany and northern Italy. Later this empire became known as the ***Holy Roman Empire.***

The Holy Roman Empire of 962 included the eastern part of Charlemagne's empire.

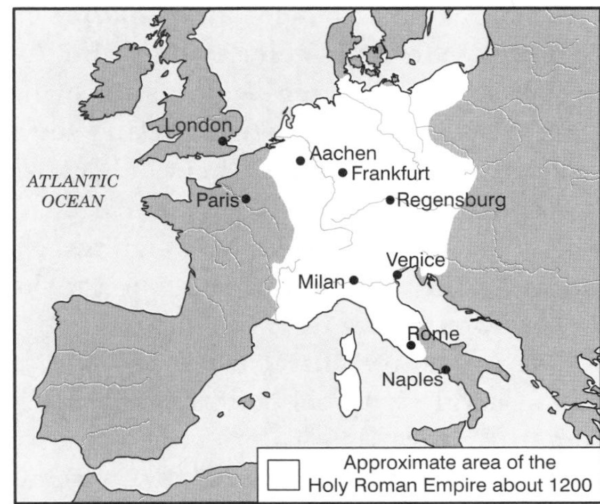

Figure 21:3. The Holy Roman Empire

However, it did not include France, and it contained other territories farther east that Charlemagne had never ruled. It was called holy because the pope crowned the emperor, but it was no holier than the corrupt Catholic Church. As to its being Roman, it was actually ruled by Germans who usually had little or no control over Rome.

Some historians date the beginning of the Holy Roman Empire from the year 800, when Charlemagne was crowned. By this reckoning, it had lasted a thousand years by the time it ended in 1806.

The countenance of Pope Gregory VII (1020?–1085) shows the stress and turmoil of a man trying to be a church leader without following God's will.

The Church in Politics

Among the most powerful men of medieval Europe were the leaders in the Roman Catholic Church. Although the church was called Roman, it did not lose power when the Roman Empire fell. In fact, it gained influence. During those dark days of fighting and disorder, people looked to the church for comfort and stability.

The pope had enormous powers. He considered himself under no one but God Himself. Some popes used their power to ***excommunicate*** kings to gain power over a country. Since people thought that only members of the Catholic Church could enter heaven, even kings were frightened at the thought of being excommunicated.

A pope could also place an ***interdict*** on a country to force its ruler to obey him. An interdict was the pope's command to the religious leaders to stop conducting services, baptizing, and so on. This would cause the people of the country to become frantic. What! No babies baptized! No weddings! No Christian burials! And so the ruler of the country would give in to the pope.

The Catholic Church went through a long struggle with the rulers of the Holy Roman Empire. The rulers of the empire wanted to control their own affairs without interference from church leaders. They also wanted some power to control the church. Popes wanted to control their own affairs without interference, and they also wanted some power in the government.

Matters became serious in 1076 when Henry IV, a strong-minded emperor, quarreled with Gregory VII, a strong-minded pope. Pope Gregory was determined to clean up some of the disgraces in the church. He wanted to stop the practice of letting the emperor appoint the bishops. That was quite understandable.

But Henry pointed out that church leaders were governing large territories in the empire. Should not the emperor decide who governed those territories? That was a good point too. If the church is involved in government, it is hard to keep the government from being involved in the church. When Gregory VII insisted on his way, Henry declared that Gregory was no longer pope.

For three cold winter days, Henry IV pleaded for forgiveness outside the castle door at Canossa, hoping the pope would restore his church membership.

In turn, Gregory excommunicated Henry and declared that he was no longer emperor.

Since many people respected the pope highly but disliked Henry, Henry knew that he was beaten. The only thing he could do to regain his position was to ask the pope's forgiveness. At the time, Gregory was staying at the castle Canossa (kuh NAHSS uh) in Italy. When Henry first arrived at the castle, Gregory refused to let him in. It was winter, and snow was on the ground. For three days Henry stood barefoot outside, knocking and asking for permission to enter. The pope finally pardoned him, but he had made it clear that he thought he should have authority over kings.

Pope Innocent III claimed power even more boldly than Gregory VII had. He claimed to be the supreme ruler over the church, and in many ways he acted as the supreme ruler of the world as well. Kings submitted to him. One of them was the English king John, who humbled himself after Innocent placed an interdict on England.

Pope Innocent III (1161–1216) brought papal power to its highest point. He was once described as the successor of Constantine, not of Apostle Peter as the Catholics taught. This meant that he acted like an emperor rather than a church leader. His name did not seem to fit his deeds.

As the contest went on, some popes proved to be stronger than kings and nobles. Some rulers were stronger than popes. Once a king of France even sent soldiers to arrest the pope! This kind of conflict did not end until centuries later, when leaders finally understood that the church and the state should be separate.

Study Exercises

18. Why does neither *holy* nor *Roman* accurately describe the Holy Roman Empire?
19. What part of Charlemagne's empire was included in the Holy Roman Empire?
20. What two powers did popes sometimes exercise over kings?
21. What problem arises when the church becomes involved in civil government?
22. What fact gave Pope Gregory VII an advantage over Emperor Henry IV?

Clinching the Chapter

Multiple Choice

A. *Write the word or phrase* least *associated with the first item.*

1. Great Britain: Ireland, England, Scotland, Wales
2. Middle Ages: medieval times, Dark Ages, Emperor Claudius, mental and spiritual darkness
3. Barbarians: Franks, Romans, Goths, Vandals
4. Moors: Africa, Europe, Spain, England
5. Invaders of Great Britain: Welsh, Angles, Saxons, Jutes
6. Frankish ruler: the Hammer, the Northman, the Short, the Great
7. Vikings: tall, thin, blond, blue-eyed
8. Scandinavia: Denmark, Wales, Sweden, Norway
9. Holy Roman Empire: holy, German, empire, long-lasting
10. Charlemagne: education, empire, Wessex, Catholic

B. *Write the correct words.*

1. During the Dark Ages, the strongest leaders in Europe were usually (kings, local rulers, world emperors, Muslims).
2. Augustine was sent as a missionary to (Rome, England, Constantinople, Spain).
3. The Viking invasion of England was stopped by (Charles Martel, Alfred the Great, Charlemagne, Otto).
4. Anglo-Saxon is also called (Welsh, Old English, Celtic, Scottish).
5. The Moors pushed into Europe as far as Tours in (Spain, France, Germany, England).
6. Twice the Vikings raided (Hastings, Paris, Rome, Constantinople).
7. In their westward explorations, the Vikings visited all the following places *except* (Asia, Iceland, Greenland, America).
8. Henry IV claimed the right to appoint church leaders because they were governing (large territories in his empire, the church affairs, the pope, the barbarians).
9. A weapon sometimes used by a pope was the (Hegira, interdict, dukes, illiterate).
10. To find the pope, Henry went to (England, Italy, Jerusalem, northern Africa).

Matching

A. *For each clue, write the correct name from the right-hand column.*

1. Had a wall built in northern England	Alfred
2. Was emperor when Rome conquered England	Charlemagne
3. Is remembered on March 17	Charles Martel
4. Defeated the Moors	Claudius
5. Was the first powerful king of the Franks	Clovis
6. Was called Charles the Great	Gregory VII
7. Asked the pope to crown him king	Hadrian
8. Ruled eastern part of what had been Charlemagne's empire	Otto
9. Helped to translate writings into English	Patrick
10. Excommunicated Henry IV	Pepin the Short

B. *Match as in Part A.*

1. Include Ireland and Great Britain	British Isles
2. Best farmers in Europe during early Middle Ages	Germany
3. Original home of Angles, Saxons, and Jutes	Holy Roman Empire
4. Mountains between France and Spain	Innocent III
5. Prize won by Alfred in 886	London
6. Provided leadership during reigns of weak Frankish kings	mayors of the palace
	Mediterranean
7. Lasted about a thousand years	Moors
8. Vikings explored as far south as this	Otto
9. Claimed much power as a pope	Pyrenees
10. was elected king by German dukes	

Completion

1. Southwestern Britain has mountains and dales.
   Britons once fled there; today it's called ———.
2. Gregory said, "It's not Angles I've seen,
   But angels!" To win them, he sent ———.
3. When France was invaded by Islamic Moors,
   The French turned them back at the battle of ———.
4. Pepin the Short, had his doctrine been straight,
   Would not have mingled the church and the ———.
5. Alfred helped teachers and served in translation,
   For he believed in a good ———.
6. Bold Viking men, who brought dread and dismay,
   Were Swedish or Danish or else from ———.

Thought Questions

1. Why are the first centuries of the Middle Ages sometimes called the Dark Ages?
2. You read in this chapter that failure to keep church and state separate had already caused trouble for the church in the days of the Roman Empire. (Review the story of Constantine and Theodosius in Chapter 19.) What trouble did it cause?
3. (*a*) Would you expect words like *man, sun, house, land, cow, fear,* and *love* to be Anglo-Saxon or French in origin? (*b*) Why?

4. Invasions are nearly always bad news to the people in the land being invaded. Can you think of any benefit that a country receives from being invaded?
5. Why could Vikings reach most cities of Europe by boat?
6. (*a*) Which power of a pope—excommunication or the interdict—would have been more effective against a king who had no respect for the pope? (*b*) Why?

Geographical Skills

1. Is the following a true statement? No one in the British Isles lives farther than 85 miles (137 km) from salt water.
2. What is the distance between London and each of the capitals of these countries?
   a. France
   b. Norway
   c. Denmark
   d. Austria

Further Study

1. Read *Mary Jones and Her Bible* if you have a copy. In what part of the British Isles did Mary live? What geographical information have you read in this chapter that the book confirms?
2. Learn what you can about Leif Ericson and his father. What did each one discover? What did Leif Ericson call the land he discovered?

Time Line

Copy the list of dates, and write the correct event after each. The text does not give all the dates listed, but some comparing should help you put events in the correct order.

1. 43	Alfred triumphs over Vikings.
2. 120s	Anglo-Saxons invade England.
3. about 432	Augustine arrives in England.
4. early 400s	Battle of Tours is fought.
5. late 400s	Charlemagne is crowned emperor.
6. 400s, 500s	Franks invade western Europe.
7. about 597	Hadrian's Wall is built.
8. 711	Moors invade Spain.
9. 732	Otto I is crowned.
10. 751	Patrick returns to Ireland.
11. 800	Pepin is crowned by pope.
12. about 800	Romans conquer England.
13. 886	Romans retreat from England.
14. 962	Vikings begin invasions.
15. 1000	Vikings discover America.

This mural, drawn around 1480, shows the medieval classes of society. At the top, a decorated knight rides on horseback. In the center, peasants shoot at a target and hunt with dogs and a falcon. On the bottom left side, monks are reading; and on the bottom right side, peasants speak to their seated lord.

400 A.D.

A monk named Benedict lays down rules for monasteries. c. 525

600

800

1000

Europeans begin building Gothic-style cathedrals. c. 1150

1200

Francis of Assisi founded a Catholic order of friars. c. 1209

1400 A.D.

22 Life in Europe During the Middle Ages

The Feudal System Develops

The Power Structure of the Church

Knights and Castles

Daily Life

A Self-sufficient Lifestyle

Darkness in the Church

Other Disorders in the Church

Monasteries and Convents

"This I say therefore, and testify in the Lord, that ye henceforth walk not as other Gentiles walk, in the vanity of their mind, Having the understanding darkened, being alienated from the life of God through the ignorance that is in them, because of the blindness of their heart."

Ephesians 4:17, 18

Life in Europe During the Middle Ages

The Feudal System Develops

You have learned that local military leaders gained power after the fall of Rome. Gradually a number of changes took place in European government. When one noble (person from a prominent family) defeated another in battle, the weaker one had to cooperate with the stronger one. Sometimes nobles made friendships and combined their small armies to make a stronger force.

By the days following Charlemagne, a system called ***feudalism*** began to take form. The key to this system of government was land. The king, at least in theory, was the head of a country. He had authority over all the land. He gave control of large sections to powerful nobles, such as the dukes of Germany. In return, they promised to be loyal to him and lend ***knights*** when he needed them. Knights were nobles who were trained as soldiers.

The nobles directly under the king gave sections of their land to other less-powerful nobles. In return, the lesser nobles promised to be loyal to and fight for the nobles who had given them land.

The lesser nobles did the same to nobles still lower in rank. Of course the chain had to end at some point. The lowest nobles owned just enough land to support themselves.

Who actually farmed the land? Not the landholding nobles! They thought such work was beneath their dignity. Ruling and fighting, they believed, were more honorable. They left the actual tilling of the land to very poor people called ***serfs,*** who were lower in rank than the lowest nobles.

This gives a simple picture of how feudalism worked. Each piece of land held by a knight or noble was called a feud or ***fief*** (FEEF). Each landholder who promised loyalty to a more powerful man was called a ***vassal,*** and each landholder who received a promise of loyalty from another man was called a ***lord.*** So a man near the top of the power pyramid could be the lord of a lord of a lord, and a man near the bottom could be the vassal of a vassal of a vassal.

Serfs were not vassals, nor did they take part in the feudal system of government. As far as the lord was concerned, the serfs were property—valuable, yes, but still property. The serfs were bound to the land. Whoever owned the land owned the serfs.

The feudal system did not always work as neatly as it may sound. With the system described here, you might think that the king was extremely powerful. Actually, the

A king distributes charters to the lords who have agreed to serve him.

nobles kept most of the power in their own hands. The nobles, or lords, were the real rulers in feudal Europe. Even strong kings depended on them. The strongest kings were those who won the support of many local rulers. With strong backing from many loyal nobles, a king could defeat an individual noble who rebelled. Then the king would give the rebellious noble's fief to a man who was faithful to him, and thus he became even stronger. But many kings failed to gain wide support, and the nobles did much as they pleased in spite of the king's wishes.

Many of the popes surrounded themselves with finery at the expense of the peasants. This is Pope Leo X with two of his nephews, about the year 1518.

The Power Structure of the Church

The Catholic Church had her own kind of power pyramid. At the top stood the pope, who held authority over the whole church and who sometimes was stronger than kings and emperors. Under him were archbishops, who had power over the bishops. The bishops had authority over the priests, and the priests were leaders in local churches.

Though the priests were not high on the ladder of power, they were greatly respected by their people. The priests administered the ***sacraments*** (ceremonies such as Baptism and Communion), which Catholic people depended on for salvation. Woe to anyone if the priest chose not to give him the sacraments!

Besides, the priest was often the only person in the neighborhood with at least some education. People looked up to him as a wise man.

Being so religious, many people did not think much of the fact that they were Europeans (or Germans or Spaniards). Their primary consideration was to be called Christians. Since Europe was controlled by people professing Christianity, Europe was called Christendom.

Europe, then, had several classes of people who supplied each other's needs. The nobles and knights fought for all the people. The church leaders prayed for all the people. The serfs worked for all the people.

Tragically, too many people expected the church to specialize in praying and in other spiritual activities for them. The common people helped to erect the local church building, paid a part of their goods to the church, and respected things that the church called holy. But they had no idea of how to draw near to God themselves. They assumed that the church would somehow get them to heaven.

Because the common people could not read the Bible, most of them did not know that many Catholic teachings were unsound. Many of the priests did not even read the Bible themselves. Much sin and deception were practiced in the Catholic Church during the Middle Ages.

Study Exercises

1. What did a king supposedly own that gave him power over his country?
2. What did a king give nobles in return for their loyalty to him?
3. If a man was the vassal of a vassal who served another vassal, did he have much power or little power?
4. Who was like a king in the power structure of the church?
5. Name the three different classes of people in Europe, and tell what each did for all the people.
6. Why did practically all of Europe fit under the term *Christendom*?

Knights and Castles

The Middle Ages were violent times. Many of the European people had descended from fierce barbarians. They seemed to enjoy fighting, and the nobles and kings used war to gain more land, wealth, and power. Although medieval Europeans considered themselves Christians, they did not follow Jesus' command to "love your enemies, bless them that curse you, do good to them that hate you, and pray for them which despitefully use you, and persecute you" (Matthew 5:44).

Knights, the soldiers of medieval times, wore heavy armor and fought on horseback. At first knights wore suits of mail, which consisted of metal rings linked together. Later they wore armor made of iron or steel plates that covered them from head to foot. They put armor on their horses too. A suit of armor was heavy, clumsy, and expensive.

When the knights closed their helmets, leaving only a narrow slit to see through, no one could tell who they were. So each knight had a design painted on his shield, indicating the family to which he belonged. This design was called a ***coat of arms.***

Gaily dressed knights ride on decorated horses.

In battle, opposing knights with long lances would charge toward one another. Each tried to pierce his enemy's armor or at least to knock him off his horse; for if a knight fell off, he usually could not get back on in his heavy armor. Knights also used weapons such as swords and battle axes.

To keep in practice, knights under different lords would sometimes hold mock battles. These were called ***tournaments*** (TUR nuh muhnts) and were watched by lords and ladies for entertainment. But the tournaments were so rough that they hardly deserve to be called games. Often there was little difference between a tournament and a real battle. Many knights were killed or crippled for life. Some became bitter enemies.

Castles were the strongholds of medieval times. Nobles usually built them on places easy to defend, such as on top of a cliff or a steep hill. Early castles were wooden structures on top of a mound, surrounded by a ditch or hills of dirt. Later, castles were made of stone and had thick stone walls surrounding them.

Often a castle was further protected by a moat outside the wall. The moat was spanned by a drawbridge, which could be raised when enemy soldiers approached. Enemies had a very difficult time getting into castles. Some castles built during the Middle Ages are still standing today.

Daily Life

The countryside in Europe had a patchwork of large farms called ***manors*** (MAN urz). Each manor was ruled by a lord, who lived in a large manor house or a castle. Powerful lords might have many manors in their fiefs, while less powerful lords controlled only the manor on which they lived. There were few towns in the early Middle Ages, and most people lived on manors.

Perhaps you think it would be exciting to live in a castle as a lord, lady, or knight. Actually, castle life was dreary. The stone walls were cool and damp, the fireplaces gave poor heat, and the grand rooms were drafty. Windows seldom had glass, so they were made small to keep out storms. But small windows also kept out the summer sunshine.

Compared to modern North Americans, even the upper-class people were crude and unrefined in their manners. They thought nothing of eating with their fingers and throwing leftover bones and bread to dogs under the table.

What about the common people? The serfs lived in a village close to the castle or manor house. Their homes were usually simple huts with thatched roofs. The floor was the bare earth. A hole in the roof served

In this room of a medieval castle, almost all family and official activities took place. Notice the throne-like chair, the height-adjustable lamp, and the bed with curtains for privacy. The fireplace is behind the men playing a game.

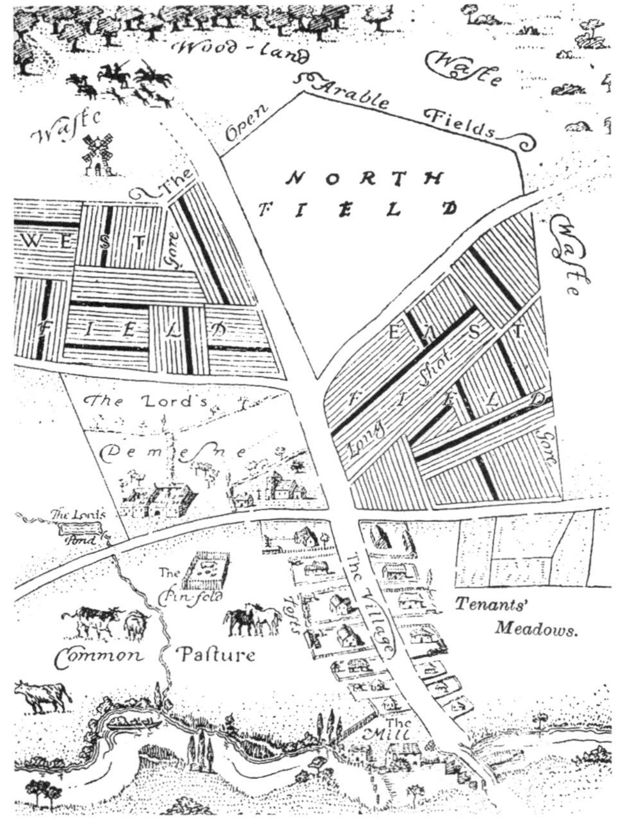

The layout of a typical medieval peasant village and lord's castle.

German serfs prepare the ground of a manor for planting.

as a chimney. Close to each hut, serf families kept a garden and a few animals.

A few serfs were craftsmen, but most of them worked on the broad fields of the manor. The crops on part of the land went to the lord of the manor. The other part provided food for the serfs.

Life was painfully hard for the serfs. Two or three days a week they had to work on their lord's land, raising his crops. Besides that, they also had to pay taxes to the lord out of the crops they raised for themselves. Few people seemed to know how to make the land produce well, so they could not build up a surplus of food. The threat of starvation was never far away.

A Self-sufficient Lifestyle

Most manors in Europe were self-sufficient; that is, the people who lived on them made practically everything they needed for themselves. They raised their own food. They made their own clothes and shoes from the plants and animals they raised on the manor. They made and repaired many of their own tools. They built their own houses and sheds.

Self-sufficiency has some advantages. For example, if a blizzard were to cut off your family from the outside world for a few days, you would be glad if you had your own food and water supply and had a way to heat your house that did not depend on anyone else.

But self-sufficiency has serious disadvantages. If you insisted on growing and making everything you ate and used, you would miss many interesting varieties of food from other places. Your clothes would be much more crude. Remember, you would have to make the cloth too, with a machine that you would also have to make. You would need to do without many useful tools and gadgets, and you would likely have few if any books at your house.

Peasants are planting grain by a medieval town in the late fifteenth century. Two people appear to be washing cloth near the town entrance. Two men are pulling long ropes that disappear down the channel; perhaps they are pulling a raft or boat.

Your life would probably be much less interesting.

During the Middle Ages, both lords and peasants lived in their own small world. Little news arrived from other countries. Hardly any products came from far away. Many people never ventured beyond the boundaries of the manor. Even in a typical lord's family, probably no one ever curled up with a book and sailed off in his mind to China. Books were scarce, and most people could not read.

Was there a middle class of people—neither very rich nor very poor—as in many modern countries? Not really, although there were some freemen. If a serf fled to a town and escaped being caught for at least one year and one day, his lord could no longer claim him. If a lord needed money, he sometimes let a few of his serfs buy their freedom. Free people could own land for themselves. Under certain conditions, they could sell it and move away if they pleased. But most of them had to pay goods to the lord of the local manor and help in his fields during the busy season. When fighting broke out, they would be drafted to help win the conflict. The rights and duties of freemen varied in different areas.

Study Exercises

7. Why did a knight need a coat of arms on his shield?
8. Why did tournaments hardly deserve to be called games?
9. What was uncomfortable about living in a castle?
10. What did most serfs do to earn a living?
11. Why would self-sufficient people have few books?
12. Name a food you enjoy that you would not have if you were totally self-sufficient.

Darkness in the Church

Some historians praise the Roman Catholic Church for being the light of the Dark Ages. That is true in some ways. The church helped the poor and the sick, taught the few who were educated, told people what little they knew about the Bible, and kept libraries of old and valuable books.

In many ways, however, the church itself was a cause of darkness. It had conquered the barbarians—often by force. Many people were in the church because they were required to be. They were still barbarians at heart. Now that they were members, they influenced the church from the inside. Many errors in the Catholic Church can be traced to pagan ideas.

The false teachings listed below would not have been accepted if the church had been faithful in obeying God's Word. Many church leaders of that time seemed to have no concern for truth. They pretended to serve God, but they also practiced secret or open sin. God says, "No man can serve two masters: for either he will hate the one, and love the other; or else he will hold to the one, and despise the other" (Matthew 6:24).

Vain Repetitions. Church leaders prayed much, but their prayers did not follow the Bible pattern. They prayed the same memorized prayers over and over again. Perhaps, as the scribes of that time copied Jesus' words in the Sermon on the Mount, some of them wondered if they were praying the best way. Jesus had said, "When ye pray, use not vain repetitions, as the heathen do: for they think that they shall be heard for their much speaking (Matthew 6:7).

The *Martyrs Mirror* (page 314) quotes a Christian who said, "They pray to, and call upon God, without considering their need, and without thinking why they call upon Him; they give Him their prayers by the number, as apples are bought."

Earning Salvation. The spiritual darkness of the Middle Ages was not due to people neglecting religion. Most people of

One of the reasons the Catholic Church grew so corrupt in the Middle Ages was because it became involved in political affairs. Everyone was required to be in the church; therefore the church contained thousands of sinners. In this illustration, a pope crowns a king in the 1200s.

those days were very religious. They gave money to the church, attended services, and paid their respects to the church leaders. Priests and monks were not allowed to marry; they were to give their whole attention to the church. Some of them went without food and sleep to discipline themselves.

However, the people were wrong in thinking that by doing so many "good" works, they could earn their salvation. The Bible teaches that good works in themselves cannot save. "For by grace are ye saved through faith; and that not of yourselves: it is the gift of God: not of works, lest any man should boast" (Ephesians 2:8, 9).

A true Christian will do good deeds after he is saved. But God does not accept those who reject His salvation and try to work their own way into His favor. The Bible warns against false teachings such as "forbidding to marry, and commanding to abstain from meats, which God hath created to be received with thanksgiving" (1 Timothy 4:3).

Adoration of Saints. In New Testament times, believers had all called each other saints—even the new Christians. The Bible teaches that all true Christians are saints (Romans 1:7). But the church in the Middle Ages called people saints only if they had done a remarkable amount of good or had died as a martyr. Often someone was called a saint only after he or she had been dead a long time.

In addition, the Catholics taught that a person could pray to the saints. They believed that the saints would intercede for the people before God. They thought that each saint specialized in a certain type of request—if someone had boils, he would pray to one saint; if he had pests in his crops, he would pray to another. That is not according to the Bible way of praying to God through Jesus. "For there is one God, and one mediator between God and men, the man Christ Jesus" (1 Timothy 2:5).

Not everyone agreed with the falsehood and sin in the Catholic Church. Here, Pope Innocent III issues a writing condemning heretics. In the Middle Ages, a heretic was usually closer to Bible truth than the Catholic Church was. All through these dark years, the Catholics issued warning upon warning against heretics, proof that remnants of true believers existed all through those years.

Priesthood and Sacrifices. The church set up men as priests to stand between God and men. Church members confessed their sins to the priests instead of to God. But the Bible teaches that God has made all true Christians "kings and priests unto God" (Revelation 1:6), and that we need no other priest. We can come directly to God ourselves by the blood of Jesus (Hebrews 10:19).

Along with priesthood, the church set up altars where they offered sacrifices. No, they did not burn animals on stone altars.

But they taught that when they held Communion, which Catholics call ***mass,*** the bread and wine changed by a miracle into the actual body and blood of Christ. This was their offering to God.

Jesus taught that Communion is only a memorial service. He said, "This do in remembrance of me" (Luke 22:19). The New Testament teaches that "by one offering he hath perfected for ever them that are sanctified" (Hebrews 10:14).

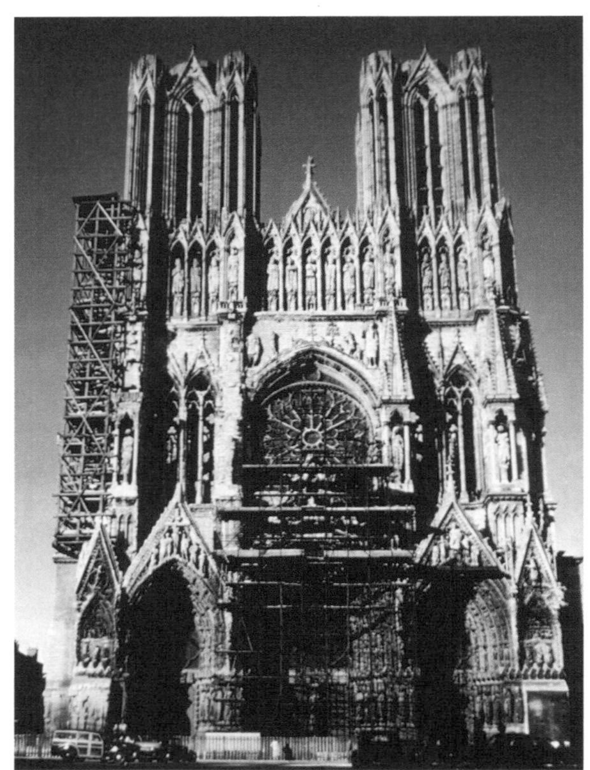

Rheims Cathedral in France is a stone cathedral built during the Middle Ages.

Study Exercises

13. Give one reason the Catholic Church of the Middle Ages was overtaken by darkness.
14. Does the Bible teach that salvation results from good works or that good works result from salvation?
15. What is wrong with praying to a saint?
16. Rather than being an actual sacrifice, what is Communion?

Other Disorders in the Church

Hiding the Light Under a Bushel. The Catholic Church of the Middle Ages never made a translation of the Bible in the language of the common people. In fact, church leaders of the later Middle Ages discouraged ordinary church members from reading the Bible. They were afraid people might get ideas from the Bible that differed from what the Catholic Church taught. (Of course that is exactly what would have happened.) The only Bible translation they approved was Jerome's Latin Vulgate, and very few people who were not church leaders could read Latin.

But did the people learn nothing from listening to the preaching in church? The fact is, many priests did not preach. They went through the usual ceremonies that were a part of mass, but much of what they said was in Latin. The people went home afterward without learning more about God's Word.

Glorying in Cathedrals. The people were fascinated by big, elaborate church buildings called ***cathedrals.*** During the earlier Middle Ages, cathedrals were built with heavy stone walls to hold up the arched stone ceilings. Windows in the walls had to be small, so cathedrals were rather dark. Then architects learned to build in a different style, known as Gothic. They used stone props called flying buttresses to hold up church walls from the outside. In this way they could have thinner walls and much larger windows.

Inside a cathedral, it was awe-inspiring to stand in the colored light of the stained-glass windows and look up to where the ceiling soared to a pointed arch at the top. Outside, towers and pinnacles reached heavenward. Most cathedrals were built with a floor plan in the shape of a cross. Cathedrals built hundreds of years ago still stand in Europe today.

It seems odd, but these fantastically beautiful church buildings suggest what was wrong with the church of that time. Outwardly, the worship was beautiful. Inwardly, much of it was empty. The corrupted church of that day was like the Pharisees whom Jesus rebuked. "Woe unto you, scribes and Pharisees, hypocrites! for ye are like unto whited sepulchres, which indeed appear beautiful outward, but are within full of dead men's bones, and of all uncleanness" (Matthew 23:27).

The building of huge cathedrals drained away large amounts of materials, labor, and talents that could have been used in better ways.

Moral Corruption in Church Leaders. Throughout the Middle Ages, there were some wise, kind, and upright church leaders. But many wicked men held church offices too. They committed fornication. They got drunk. Some were accepted as priests even though they had never been ordained.

Often men practiced ***simony*** (SY muh nee), buying or selling the office of bishop or priest. (This practice was named after the Simon mentioned in Acts 8:18–20, who tried to buy spiritual power from Peter.) Highest bidders became bishops. To those people, becoming a church leader had nothing to do with how righteous a man was. All they wanted was a high-paying position and a life of luxury.

During the worst of these times, popes themselves lived in gross sin, and men were no holier inside monasteries than outside. Reformers tried hard to rid the Catholic Church of these evils. But some of the reformers tried to grasp power for themselves. Truly it was a dark day for the Catholic Church.

Study Exercises

17. Why did Catholic church leaders disapprove of Bible reading by the common people?
18. Why did churchgoers learn little from what the priests said during services?
19. How did flying buttresses make thin cathedral walls possible?
20. How did the beautiful cathedrals illustrate what was wrong with much of the worship?
21. What is simony?

Monasteries and Convents

During these times, some men and women wanted to get away from the wickedness and turbulence they saw around them. No doubt many also wished to escape from the grinding poverty they endured. To do this, a man could join a monastery and become a monk, or a woman could join a convent and become a nun.

A monastery or convent looked like a tiny village, sometimes surrounded by a wall. It had a dormitory, a church, a kitchen and dining room, a library, and other useful build-

When this fortified convent in Italy was built, it was needed as a place of protection from roving bandits and foreign armies. That is one reason medieval buildings had tall, thick, stone walls.

ings. Nearby were its orchards and fields. It was a quiet place where people tried to get closer to God and become more holy.

One of the best-known monks, named Benedict, laid down rules that guided most monasteries for hundreds of years. He said that a monk should give all his property to the church and remain poor, should promise never to marry, and should always obey the ***abbot*** in charge of the monastery. There were other strict rules such as these.

This monk concentrates carefully on making a good manuscript.

Monasteries kept learning alive during a time when most people were uneducated. Monks spent many years copying Scriptures and other important writings by hand. They knew good farming methods and shared them with their neighbors.

But monasteries had several serious flaws. Some of them were mentioned already in this chapter. Many monks thought they had to earn their salvation by being good, rather than accepting salvation as a gift and living holy lives as a result.

Another error was the idea that one had to get away from ordinary life to be very good. You can see why people felt this way, with so little spiritual life all around. But Jesus did not put His followers in monasteries. He said, "Ye are the salt [preserving influence] of the earth" (Matthew 5:13)—and sent His disciples to preach.

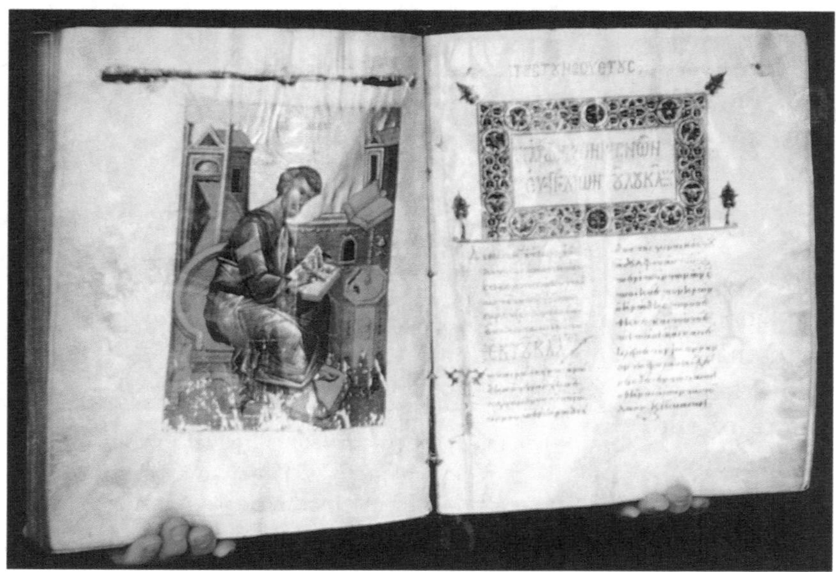

This is a colorful page spread from an illuminated Bible made by hand in the 1100s. An illuminated manuscript had ornamental designs, borders, and letters.

During the late Middle Ages, some men did take up the challenge to spread the teachings of the church to people outside monastery walls. These men were known as ***friars.*** The best-known of them was called Saint Francis of Assisi (uh SEE zee). These men lived simply and tried to help those in need. However, they remained in the Catholic Church, and they continued to follow and teach many false Catholic doctrines rather than only the pure Word of God.

Study Exercises

22. What is the difference between a monastery and a convent?
23. What is an abbot?
24. What did friars do that monks generally did not?

Clinching the Chapter

Multiple Choice

A. *Write the word or phrase* least *associated with the first item.*

1. Feudalism: lord, middle class, vassal, king
2. Catholic Church: sacraments, education, priests, tournaments
3. Knight: farm, mail, lance, coat of arms
4. Castle: moat, drawbridge, defensible, comfortable
5. Manor: archbishop, castle, farm, peasants
6. Mass: priest, marriage, altar, sacrifice
7. Self-sufficiency: independence, variety, few books, crude lifestyle
8. Cathedral: arch, flying buttress, pinnacle, simony
9. Monastery: Benedict, abbot, nun, monk
10. Forbidden: mass, marriage, meats, personal riches

B. *Write the correct words.*

1. A feud could also be called (a fief, an archbishop, a lord, a vassal).
2. A term describing the political structure of Europe is (sacrament, feudalism, Gothic, tournament).
3. Catholics believed that salvation was found in partaking of (fiefs, surpluses, tournaments, sacraments).
4. The serfs were (priests, soldiers, peasants, nobles).
5. A knight in armor could be identified by his (helmet, battle axe, coat of arms, lance).
6. At one time, mail was used to make (books, flying buttresses, castle walls, armor).
7. Who warned against vain repetitions in prayer? (the Pharisees, Benedict, Francis, Jesus)
8. Communion should be considered a (sacrifice, remembrance, mass, translation).
9. The practice of buying or selling positions in the church is called (simony, adoration, Vulgate, ordination).
10. The head of a monastery is called (a monk, a nun, an abbot, an archbishop).

Matching

A. *For each clue, write the correct term from the right-hand column.*

	Clue	Term
1.	Religion of the Middle Ages	Benedict
2.	Depended on help from powerful nobles	Calvary
3.	Area controlled by professing Christians	Catholic
4.	Place where sacrifice was made for mankind once for all	Christendom
5.	Considered rare in Middle Age church	Francis
6.	Established rules for monasteries	friar
7.	Traveling Catholic teacher	Jerome
8.	Lived in convent	king
9.	Translated Bible into Latin	nun
10.	Well-known friar	saint

B. *Match as in Part A.*

	Clue	Term
1.	Man who rules a manor or has vassals	cathedral
2.	Churchman closest to common people	freeman
3.	Poor farmer	highest nobles
4.	Held much power in government	intercessor
5.	No longer under a lord	knight
6.	What a saint was thought to be	lord
7.	Promised loyalty to a lord	priest
8.	Elaborate symbol of empty worship	salvation
9.	Medieval soldier	serf
10.	What people tried to earn by good works	vassal

Completion

1. A noble, in his drafty castle,
   Was probably both lord and ———.
2. The roofs of peasants' huts might catch
   On fire, for they were made of ———.
3. A king, perhaps in gratitude,
   Might give a lord a fief, or ———.
4. The base where feudal systems stand
   Is on control and use of ———.
5. Not even high archbishops hope
   To disobey their honored ———.
6. Being holy is not quaint;
   Each true Christian is a ———.
7. God delights in our petitions,
   But He hates ——— ———.
8. Monastery rules were strict.
   They were made by ———.
9. Services the people sat in
   Taught them little. Priests spoke ———.

Thought Questions

1. This chapter uses the term *power pyramid.* How does the power structure of feudalism resemble the structure of a pyramid?
2. Although serfs were needed to make the feudal system work, they were not actually a part of it. Why not?
3. Why did the king need the support of powerful nobles?
4. The text quotes a Christian who said, "They pray to, and call upon God, without considering their need, and without thinking why they call upon Him." Considering that, how *should* we pray?
5. According to the Bible, who is really a saint?
6. Why did most medieval people fail to realize that many Catholic teachings were false?

Further Study

1. (*a*) Who is the pope today? (*b*) From what country does he come?
2. Study the nobility (class of nobles) in modern times. How has the power of nobles (lords) been limited since medieval times? Give an example of how nobles still have an official role in government.

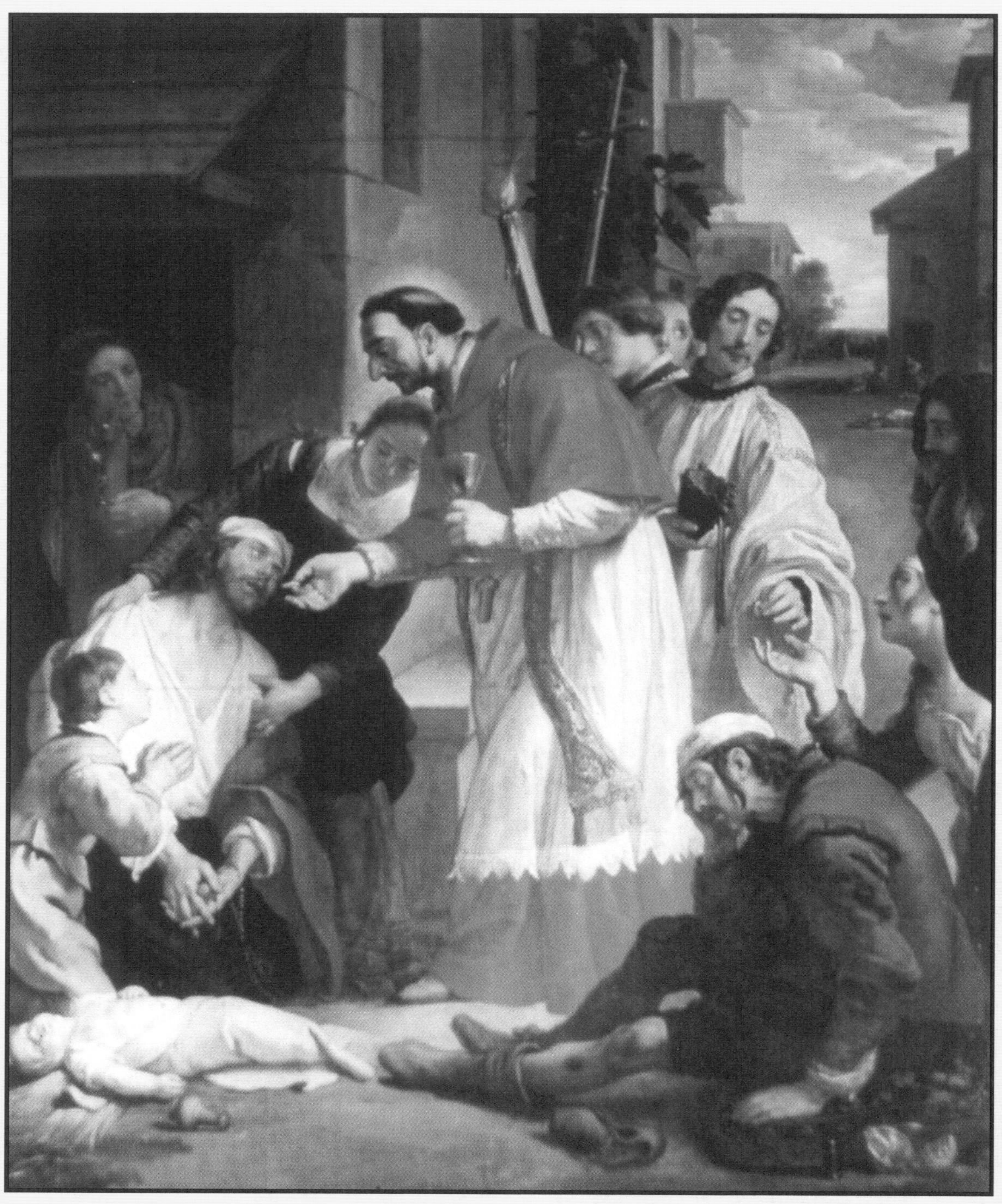

Plagues often broke out in medieval towns because of the poor sanitation and lack of advanced medication. Here, a priest "comforts" the stricken in Milan, Italy, by giving them the Catholic communion.

23 The Late Middle Ages

1000 A.D.

William the Conqueror wins the Battle of Hastings and is crowned king of England. 1066

Turks from central Asia take Palestine from Arab Muslims. 1071

Pope Urban II urges European Catholics to fight against the Muslims. 1095

The First Crusade 1095–1099

1100

Catholics capture Jerusalem from the Turks. 1099

The Second Crusade 1145–1147

The Muslims regain Jerusalem after the Second Crusade fails. 1187

The Third Crusade 1187–1192

Richard the Lion-Hearted is captured on his return home. 1192

1200

Thousands of children in the Children's Crusade are lost or sold into slavery. 1212

King John of England signs the Magna Carta. 1215

The popes organize the Inquisition. Early 1200s

1300

At least one-fourth of the Europeans die from Black Death. Middle 1300s

The Hundred Years' War c. 1337–1453

1400

Joan of Arc leads a French army to victory. 1429

1500 A.D.

The Normans Invade England

The Crusades

The Inquisition

Growth of Towns

Englishmen Win New Freedoms

The Hundred Years' War

"Beloved, follow not that which is evil, but that which is good. He that doeth good is of God: but he that doeth evil hath not seen God."

3 John 11

The Late Middle Ages

The Normans Invade England

While Alfred the Great was busy fighting the Vikings in England, other Vikings were invading France. Many of them settled in a section of northwestern France. This region of France became known as Normandy, after the Normans (Norsemen) who settled there. The Normans learned the French language and customs.

About two hundred years later, Normandy was ruled by a noble named William, who became known as the Conqueror. He believed he had a right to the English throne. So when the English king died in 1066 with no son to succeed him, he gathered an army to invade England.

But the English nobles had elected another ruler named Harold to be their king. The new king was watching the coast for William's invasion from Normandy.

Figure 23:1. France and England

Harold might have won the battle on the seashore, except that suddenly he received frightening news from northern England. The king of Norway was invading! While Harold's army was gone, fighting off the other invaders, William's forces landed with no one to oppose them.

King Harold and his soldiers defeated the king of Norway and rapidly returned south to fight William's army. They joined battle near the town of Hastings, in southern England. During the Battle of Hastings, the Norman army defeated the weary English soldiers, and King Harold himself was killed. On Christmas Day of 1066, William the Conqueror was crowned king of England.

The Battle of Hastings was a turning point in history. England had been a rather undeveloped country before, but William brought many new ideas. He set up a well-organized central government, introduced

William the Conqueror (1028?–1087)

Wearing his armor, a Norman knight at the time of William the Conqueror kneels by a cross with his weapons of war. Many medieval battles were fought "in the Name of Christ," but in Gethsemane, Christ told Peter to put his sword away. Christ's kingdom is not of this world, and men cannot receive God's blessing on wars simply by saying they are fighting in His Name.

a new style of building, and established trade with other countries. He made England much stronger than it had been under the Anglo-Saxons. During the years since, a strong England has influenced many parts of the world.

Before William's arrival, the English people spoke Anglo-Saxon (Old English). But for some time after this, French was the language of the ruling class in England, while the common people continued to speak English. Gradually the English and French languages blended into what is now called Middle English.

Middle English was different from Old English, largely because of all the French words that had been added to it. This helps to explain why many English words came from French, as the etymologies in a dictionary will show.

The following sample of Old English will help you to see how greatly the English language has changed.

> Sum monn him plantode wingeard and betynde hine ond dealf anne seath and getimbrode anne stiepel and gesette hine mid eorthtilium and ferde on eltheodignesse.
>
> —*American Heritage Dictionary*

You can probably guess some of the words by comparing this passage with Mark 12:1. Do you see the word that means "vineyard"? Instead of *tower,* do you see a word that looks like *steeple*? Instead of *husbandmen,* do you see a word that looks like *earth-tillers*?

Below is Psalm 1:1 in Middle English. The words still look strange, but this verse is definitely easier to read than the one in Old English.

> Blesced be the man that ghede nought in the counseil of wicked, ne stode nought in the waie of singheres, ne sat naught in fals jugement.
>
> —*A Structural History of English, p. 205*

Study Exercises

1. A Norseman may also be called a Northman, a ———, or a ———.
2. (*a*) In what year did the Normans invade England? (*b*) Where did they win a battle that changed the course of English history?
3. Middle English was largely a combination of Anglo-Saxon and ———.

The Crusades

During the Middle Ages, the Muslims controlled the Middle East. That included

Palestine, which Europeans called the Holy Land because Jesus had lived there.

The Catholic Church taught that one way to please God was to make a pilgrimage to the Holy Land. Those who went thought of themselves as pilgrims more than as tourists. The pilgrims would visit the places where Jesus lived and taught. Most important, they wanted to visit the sepulcher where He had been buried and had risen again.

In Old Testament times, the Israelites traveled to the tabernacle or temple to offer sacrifices and to attend certain worship ceremonies. Since God's presence and blessing were present there in a special way, the place could be called holy. But in the New Testament, Jesus taught that God no longer requires a special place of worship. God seeks those who worship Him "in spirit and in truth," wherever they are (John 4:20–24). Traveling to Palestine might help people learn about Bible lands, but it does not help them gain favor with God.

For several centuries, the Arab Muslims had let European pilgrims visit religious places in Palestine without causing them trouble. But about 1071, ***Turks*** from central Asia conquered Palestine. Although they were also Muslims, they were more aggressive than the Arab Muslims of that time. From then on, when pilgrims came to Palestine, the Turkish Muslim caused troubles. Shocking stories came back to Europe about pilgrims who had been hurt, robbed, or even killed.

In the year 1095, Pope Urban II made a fiery speech before a large audience. He said it was time Christians in Europe took the sacred places out of the heathen Turks' hands. The crowd was stirred and excited.

An army of European crusaders, on the right, meets an army of Muslims. This picture shows us the horrors and wickedness of war. Did these "Christian" crusaders love their enemies as Jesus teaches His followers to do in the New Testament?

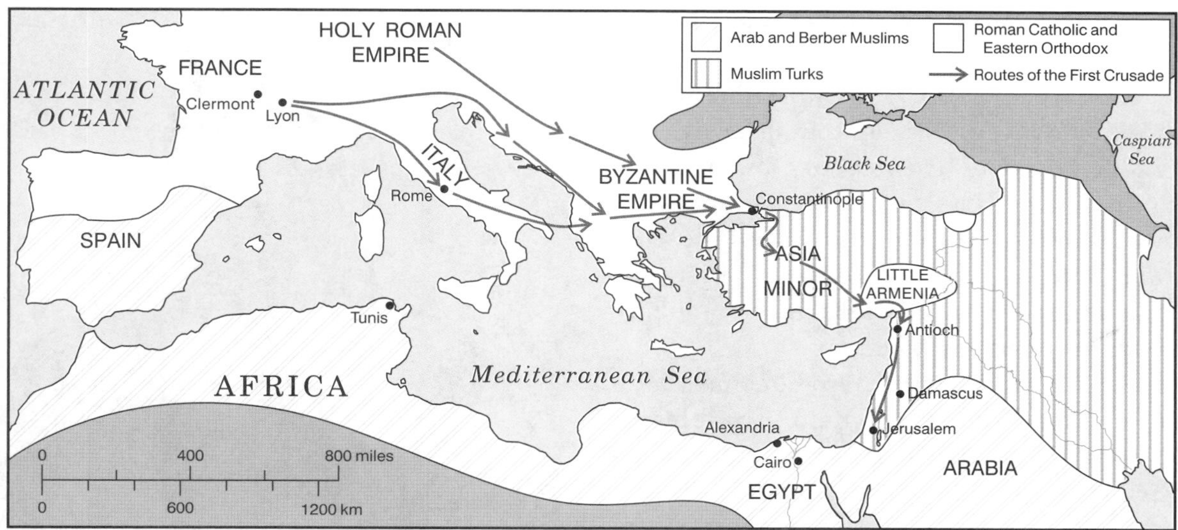

Figure 23:2. Mediterranean Lands About 1097

They were Middle Age Europeans who loved to fight. And this time they thought it would be a "good" fight—a "holy war"—because they were being called to fight Muslims. "God wills it!" they shouted. They sewed red crosses to their clothes, thinking they would be soldiers of the cross. The wars they undertook are called ***Crusades,*** from the Latin word for *cross.*

Some men hurried off to fight without making good plans or finding capable leaders. Several large groups of men, poorly trained and armed, headed for Palestine, only to meet well-trained warriors. Most of these crusaders were killed.

The first real Crusade was led by four experienced knights. This so-called Christian army reconquered Asia Minor, which had also been invaded by the Turks. Then they moved into Palestine and finally, after hard fighting, captured Jerusalem itself in 1099.

What did these so-called Christians do when Jerusalem was in their hands? Strangely, they seemed to lose all sense of right and wrong. They dashed here and there, killing everyone in sight—even women, children, and grandparents. Most of the people in Jerusalem lost their lives.

After witnessing such cruelty and bloodshed done in the Name of Christ, it is little wonder that Muslims continued to oppose Christianity. How much better it might have been had a true church sent peaceful, God-fearing Christians with the message of salvation to the Muslims. The Europeans had been alarmed at the fierceness of the Turks, but now they were being just as cruel. Jesus said, "And as ye would that men should do to you, do ye also to them likewise" (Luke 6:31).

Europe rejoiced when news came that Jerusalem was safely in the hands of "Christians." But after a time, they heard that the Muslims were starting to win back the land they had lost. The Second Crusade headed for the Holy Land, but these armies met defeat. By 1187, the Muslims had regained Jerusalem.

The Third Crusade took place after the fall of Jerusalem to the Muslims. A French, a German, and an English king led their armies toward Palestine. The German king drowned on the way, and most of his men went home again. The French king led his army back home after one victory in the

Holy Land. But the English king, Richard the Lion-Hearted, fought on.

Richard's enemy was Saladin (SAL uh dihn), the leader of the Muslim army. The two armies fought furiously, but neither could win a lasting victory. The hot summers and cool, muddy winters of Palestine made life hard for the crusaders. Diseases took many lives. Richard and his army never reached Jerusalem.

Back in England, Richard's enemies were trying to seize his kingdom. Troubles in Palestine and turmoil at home finally forced Richard to give up his Crusade. Before he left Palestine, he made a temporary agreement with Saladin that would allow Christians to visit Jerusalem unmolested. But as he traveled home, enemies captured him and put him in prison for over a year. England had to pay a staggering ransom to gain his release.

Saladin (1137–1193) was the Muslim leader of Egypt and Syria who fought against Richard the Lion-Hearted.

Richard the Lion-Hearted bids farewell to Palestine as he prepares to return to England.

Richard was called "the Lion-Hearted" because of his courageous fighting in Palestine. Actually, his battles there brought few results. He taxed the English people heavily to pay for the crusade and his ransom from prison. When all facts are considered, his Crusade was a failure.

There were more Crusades. One of the most tragic was the Children's Crusade. About 1212, a young French peasant boy began telling others that Christ had appeared to him and had told him to lead an army to Palestine. Today such a boy would not have a very large following. But the Middle Age Europeans were fervently religious, and they did not understand true Christianity.

Some people thought that earlier Crusades had failed because of sin in the crusaders' lives. They reasoned that surely God would deliver Jerusalem into the hands of innocent children. So thousands of

French children started for Palestine. Soon afterward, thousands of German children also formed a crusade. Historians estimate that over fifty thousand children left their homes in this way.

The French children arrived at the southern shore of France, along the Mediterranean Sea. They expected God to divide the waters as He had done for Moses at the Red Sea. The waters did not divide, and many disappointed children turned back. Later, some seamen offered to take the remaining children across the sea in their ships. Many children trusted them and went aboard.

But several of the ships wrecked, and some of the young crusaders drowned. The remaining children found out too late that the sailors had no intention of helping them reach Palestine. Instead, the sailors took them to Muslims in northern Africa and sold them as slaves. Years later, a priest who had traveled with the group escaped and made his way back to Europe to tell the fate of these children.

The last Crusade took place almost two hundred years after the first one. Finally the Europeans grew weary of paying for the expensive and fruitless Crusades. They could not understand why God did not give them victory, for they did not realize that "the weapons of our warfare are not carnal" (2 Corinthians 10:4).

Study Exercises

4. Why did people take trips to Palestine during the Middle Ages?
5. Which Muslims caused trouble for the travelers?
6. Which crusader fought with Saladin?

The Inquisition

In the early 1200s, Pope Innocent III became disturbed about several groups whom he called heretics—people who disagreed with what the Catholic Church taught. Some of these groups were indeed in error, but others taught Bible truths that the Catholic Church no longer kept. Innocent III sent out a crusade against those whom he considered heretics in southern France.

About fifteen years after Pope Innocent III died, Pope Gregory IX organized the ***Inquisition*** to continue what Innocent III had started. A special group of churchmen, called inquisitors, kept an eye open for those they considered heretics. Inquisitors encouraged people to inform them if they thought anyone believed doctrines different from church doctrines. If a neighbor reported a man, church officers might arrest the suspected heretic secretly. An inquisitor would ask him many questions.

Inquisitors read a paper to one of their victims, telling him the accusations against him and the torture that awaits him.

The inquisitors had many ways to force a man to agree with the church. He could be pinched, scorched, or stretched. One instrument of torture they used was the rack. A so-called heretic placed on it could be stretched until his bones were pulled from their sockets.

The dungeon itself, often dark, damp, chilly, and unventilated, wore down a person. After weeks, months, even years of silence with little to eat and nothing to do, the prisoner was sometimes more ready to cooperate with the inquisitors. If they decided he was hopelessly stubborn, they could turn him over to the authorities to be burned at the stake.

Studying the persecutions of those days can be gruesome, but the bright side is that many godly people endured all this and never gave up the true faith. They were ordinary people like faithful Christians of today, but they learned as they suffered that God's strength is more than ordinary.

Study Exercises

7. How did Pope Innocent III try to stop those whom he considered heretics?
8. What did inquisitors do, which gave them their name? (If you need help, check the meaning of *inquisitor* in a dictionary.)

Growth of Towns

What were towns like during the Middle Ages?

During the Dark Ages there were not many towns. To prosper and grow, towns need to trade with other towns. To trade, they need good roads from place to place. They need a money system used over a wide area so that people in various towns are able to buy and sell goods among themselves. When the Roman Empire collapsed, there was no money that people could use everywhere in Europe. Roads were not repaired or policed. So trade collapsed.

People left the towns and cities to make whatever living they could by farming on manors. Cities shrank. Some towns emptied completely. Big cities were still found in the Byzantine Empire and in the Muslim territories, but not many prospered in western Europe.

This medieval town in Italy has changed little since the Middle Ages. In the background to the right, two modern apartment buildings rise amid their drab, ancient neighbors.

Serfs who scratched a living from the soil had no extra food or other goods to trade. A man with no surpluses will not sell anything because he needs all he has for himself. He will not buy anything either, because he has no money or extra goods with which to buy things.

But slowly the times changed. As the Middle Ages progressed, farmers learned more efficient farming methods, and they began to produce a surplus of food. Tradesmen also became more efficient. Instead of wandering from manor to manor, serving as blacksmiths or carpenters, they found that they could do a better job if they stayed at one place. Often they settled near a castle or manor. As a result, towns began to develop near castles and manor houses.

The farmers near a town had extra food, and the townsmen had extra goods. So they traded with each other. They were learning that people are usually better off when they are ***interdependent.***

Another word closely related to *interdependency* is ***specialization.*** You might never have thought of an ordinary factory worker or tradesman as a specialist, but he is. When one man spends all his time making shoes, he makes better shoes than a man who occasionally makes a pair for his own family. That is also true of carpenters, weavers, smiths, and other tradesmen. People found that they could make more money specializing in just one product. They could then use that money to buy high-quality products from other craftsmen. They helped raise the quality of goods and the lifestyle for many people.

Craftsmen at various trades set up a system for training young people and keeping their products high in quality. A young man who wanted to learn a craft such as shoemaking would start out as an ***apprentice.*** He worked under a craftsman who gave him his clothes and food, but no pay. If the apprentice learned the trade fairly well, he became a ***journeyman*** after three to seven years. A journeyman received wages. He could continue working for the same craftsman, or he could work for others and learn from them.

When a journeyman wanted to set up a business of his own, he would produce a good example of his work, called a ***masterpiece,***

A nobleman (clothed in a red robe) comes to buy bread from a baker and his wife in the 1400s. This is an example of specialization. All the baker did was make baked goods. With the profit, he bought things he needed from other craftsmen who specialized in their trades.

to show to the other craftsmen of his trade. If they approved his work, the journeyman became a ***master*** like the others.

Usually the lord of the manor ruled the town, and the townspeople paid him taxes. During the late Middle Ages, the towns sought independence from the manor. Some towns paid a lord to give them their freedom. Some towns fought for freedom. Others simply had their freedom given to them. Free towns were responsible only to the king.

Life in town was more convenient for some people than life in the country, but it offered few comforts. A medieval town was crowded into a small area, and it was walled to protect it from raiders. To save space, buildings might be five, six, or seven stories high. The streets were narrow, crooked, and unpaved. The residents threw their garbage out the windows into the streets. Roaming pigs, dogs, and rats ate the litter and helped spread diseases. The lack of clean water also caused much sickness.

A doctor points to a jar in an apothecary shop in the 1500s. An apothecary was a man who prepared drugs and medicines, like a pharmacist does today. In medieval times, some useful medicines had been discovered, but much superstition and lack of research also surrounded this trade. The jars of medicine were marked by symbols instead of words.

With so many people using candles and fireplaces, fires could easily break out—and they often did. Most buildings were made of wood and were huddled close together, which allowed flames to race from one building to the next. A medieval town had no fire department. Fire could destroy a whole town in a single night. Some towns burned down several times.

During the 1300s, a terrible illness swept over Europe. We call it the ***bubonic plague*** (boo BAHN ihk), or Black Death. The Europeans did not know why so many people became sick. To us the answer is simple: the people were not careful to keep their towns clean. Often they threw garbage out into the street. Rats thrived on the garbage and multiplied quickly.

Rats carry fleas. Fleas carry germs. Germs can kill. When the Black Death struck Europe, whole families died. During a short period in the mid-1300s, at least a fourth of the people of Europe lost their lives. Some historians believe that figure could be as large as one-half.

But Europe was changing—indeed, it had already changed greatly. The Crusades had given these changes an enormous boost. European soldiers who visited the Middle East had made a startling discovery. The Muslim culture was more advanced than their own! These men saw things that many of them had never even heard of before.

The crusaders gazed at big cities and

beautiful buildings. They toured the marketplaces, ran fine silk cloth through their fingers, tasted apricots and oranges, and discovered pepper and cinnamon. They examined china cups and plates. They saw dozens of luxuries such as jewels, perfumes, and tapestries. The Europeans took home many of the wares they saw. Most of these items were not available in Europe or were luxuries for only the rich.

The crusaders had discovered the world "out there." As a result, European trade with Eastern countries increased greatly, and European towns and cities grew. Because the Europeans came in contact with new ideas, they even began to think differently. A new day was dawning.

Study Exercises

9. What do towns depend on in order to exist?
10. Where did medieval towns often develop?
11. What were some advantages of interdependence and specialization that self-sufficient manors did not enjoy?
12. What disease was the result of a failure to properly dispose of wastes?
13. From what culture did the crusaders get many useful ideas that contributed to the growth of European towns?

Englishmen Win New Freedoms

People of medieval Europe had fewer opportunities to improve their way of living than we have today. They made slow progress in developing better lives. But we can appreciate them for laying the foundation for freedoms we enjoy today.

The English people took a major step in the year 1215. Their king, John, was a very inconsiderate ruler. Other kings before him had considered the rights of their people. If they wanted to raise taxes or change laws, they would first call a council of nobles and churchmen to discuss the matter. John abolished the council and raised taxes whenever he pleased. He threatened to put people in prison if they did not cooperate with him.

The powerful nobles and church leaders in England became angry with John. They drew up a long list of demands. They wanted to have more rights and to place limits on the king's power.

King John was furious. But he knew that the nobles and churchmen, working together, were more powerful than he. In a meadow near London, he met with them and agreed to what they asked, making it

Forced by his insubordinate nobles, King John unhappily agrees to give up some of his power by signing the Magna Carta in 1215. Some Catholic church leaders are also present.

the law of the land. This agreement was known as the ***Magna Carta,*** which means "Great Charter."

The English people call the Magna Carta the "cornerstone of English liberty." English kings and queens since 1215 have been more careful to respect the rights of the people.

Although the Magna Carta gave rights to the ruling class in England, it said nothing about more rights for the common people. Ordinary citizens could not help to make laws. When lawmakers met, they included only the highest officials of the government and the church.

But soon the council of lawmakers began to include men who knew what the ordinary citizens thought and who could speak for them. Such men are called representatives because they represent other people. In England, a meeting of such a council was called a ***parliament*** (PAHR luh muhnt).

The English Parliament still meets in London today. Canada and other countries have a Parliament of their own. The United States has a lawmaking group patterned after Parliament, called Congress.

Another idea was growing in England. In the Middle Ages, persons accused of crimes were not always treated fairly. Sometimes authorities threw them into prison without giving them a trial to see if they really were guilty. At other times they gave accused persons unfair trials by making them go through ordeals.

For example, a man accused of teaching a false doctrine might be forced to carry a red-hot piece of iron. If the wound healed within a certain time, he was considered innocent. If not, he was counted guilty and was punished.

An accused criminal might be thrown into water that had been "blessed" by a priest. If he floated, he was considered guilty because the "holy" water rejected him. If he sank, he was considered innocent and was rescued—hopefully in time to save his life! People thought that even if an innocent person drowned, he would gain an entrance into heaven.

During the Middle Ages, a person being tried for an alleged crime might have to endure a trial by ordeal. This man had to pick a stone out of a pot of boiling water. If his hand blistered, he was guilty; if it did not, he was innocent.

Sometimes a fight was arranged between the accused man and his accuser. Whoever won the fight was thought to be right! People thought that God would help the innocent man win.

The English people believed there was a better way. They wanted to find out the facts of a matter. If a man was accused of a crime, they called together the people who knew something about it and questioned them. Out of this custom grew the practice of having trials by jury. In the United States, a person accused of a crime has the privilege to have a number of ordinary citizens (often twelve) listen to the facts and decide whether he is guilty.

Really, the idea of giving people fair trials is very old. Juries were also used by the ancient Greeks. But during the Dark Ages, superstition and guesswork often ruled people's thinking. In an age of ignorance, the English people reawakened an interest in justice for accused persons.

Study Exercises

14. In what year did King John consent to the Magna Carta?
15. What important group of rights were omitted from the Magna Carta, which have been granted in many countries since then?
16. Which group of people makes laws—a parliament or a jury?
17. Describe several ordeals that were used during the Middle Ages to try persons accused of crimes.

The Hundred Years' War

For over a century after the Battle of Hastings, the Norman rulers in England controlled both England and Normandy. But later they lost control of Normandy, and then they began to think of themselves as Englishmen.

Sword aloft, Joan of Arc leads the French soldiers to a victory over the English. She claimed to be led by voices from heaven. Do you think she was listening to Jesus, the Prince of Peace?

Still, various English kings would have liked to rule France. These descendants of the Normans tried to conquer France in the early 1300s. Of course the French resisted, and so the Hundred Years' War began. Really it was a series of wars that lasted more than a hundred years.

During the early 1400s, a peasant girl about seventeen years old came to the king of France. She said she had heard voices from heaven telling her to save France from her enemies. The girl, Joan of Arc, led the French army against the English and won a surprise victory. Soon other victories followed.

At last the English captured Joan, accused her of witchcraft, and burned her at the stake. But the French fought on and finally drove the English out of their country.

When the war ended in 1453, the English lost all their claims to land in France. The French gained nothing in England. Perhaps the most lasting result of the Hundred Years' War was the bitter feeling that had grown between England and France. A number of other wars would follow in years to come.

Study Exercises

18. (*a*) When did the Hundred Years' War begin? (*b*) When did it end?
19. Why is the name "Hundred Years' War" not completely accurate, aside from the fact that the fighting lasted more than a hundred years?

Clinching the Chapter

Multiple Choice

A. *Write the word or phrase* least *associated with the first item.*

1. Muslim: Middle East, Arabs, Canossa, Turk
2. First Crusade: children, knights, violence, cross
3. Third Crusade: Richard, Saladin, ransom, Inquisition
4. Inquisition: torture, interdict, rack, secret
5. Medieval town: trade, wide streets, fires, protective walls
6. Representative: Christendom, Parliament, Congress, freedom
7. Interdependence: specialization, self-sufficiency, quality, towns
8. Specialization: surplus, efficiency, trade, feudalism
9. Plague: garbage, rats, slaves, bubonic
10. Superstition: ignorance, guesswork, juries, unfair trials

B. *Write the correct words.*

1. Normandy is a region of (Spain, Italy, France, England).
2. The king killed at the Battle of Hastings was (Harold, Richard, William, John).
3. The language that developed in England after the Battle of Hastings is now called (Old English, Middle English, Norman French, French English).
4. A high standard of living is usually found in a community of (specialists, knights, serfs, inquisitors).
5. What did the crusading children hope would divide for them on their journey? (Red Sea, Mediterranean Sea, Asia Minor, Bosporus Strait)
6. One result of the Crusades was (increased trade, more pilgrimages, the Inquisition, more heretics).
7. The Turks were (Muslim, Christian, Catholic, French).
8. All of the following are examples of trial by ordeal *except* (burning with hot iron, throwing into water, burning at the stake, fighting with accuser).
9. The popes organized the Inquisition to suppress those who disagreed with (Jesus' words, Catholic teachings, jury decisions, heretic doctrines).
10. The Hundred Years' War was fought between the English Normans and the (Vikings, Muslims, Germans, French).

Matching

A. *For each clue, write the correct term from the right-hand column.*

1. Was called "Lion-Hearted"	Asia Minor
2. Advanced culture that crusaders discovered	Congress
3. Region crusaders reconquered on their way to Palestine	Jerusalem
4. City where so-called Christians slaughtered Muslims	Joan of Arc
5. Place where children were sold as slaves	Magna Carta
6. Region where crusaders were sent against so-called heretics	Muslim
7. Great Charter	northern Africa
8. Meeting of English representatives	Parliament
9. Leader in struggle for French independence	Richard
10. United States form of Parliament	southern France

B. *Match as in Part A.*

1. Year when William was crowned king	apprentice
2. Traveled to visit holy places	Greeks
3. Heretic hunter	inquisitor
4. Crusade warrior	journeyman
5. Expert tradesman	knight
6. Beginner at a trade	master
7. Wage-earning tradesman who worked for a master	pilgrim
8. Speaker for a group of people	representative
9. Year when Magna Carta was signed	1066
10. Had juries before England did	1215

Completion

1. What were only foolish raids,
   Many say were great ———.
2. William's brave Normans, like translated plants,
   Settled in England, though they were from ———.
3. Heretics faced forced submission
   By the dreaded ———.
4. Where roads are mud, and robbers raid,
   The towns grow small, for there's no ———.
5. The nobles, with their patience gone,
   Secured their rights from proud King ———.
6. The journeyman who labors faster
   Will likely soon become a ———.
7. English and French men, who both wanted more,
   Fought in the long-drawn-out ——— ——— ———.
8. Where quality in goods exists,
   The craftsmen all are ———.

Thought Questions

1. How might modern England be different if Harold had defeated William at the Battle of Hastings?
2. Why did God not honor the faith of the children in their Crusade?
3. During a time of war and disturbances, would it be an advantage to become more self-sufficient or more interdependent with other people? Explain.
4. Why were the crusaders surprised to learn that the Muslim culture was more advanced than their own?
5. Why is a trial by jury often considered more fair than a trial by a single judge?

Geographical Skills

1. The narrow waterway at the eastern end of the English Channel is called the Strait of Dover. How far is England from France at the narrowest point of the strait?
2. Pope Urban II gave his stirring speech in Clermont, France, which is near Lyon. If crusaders started from Lyon and traveled to Jerusalem mainly by land, about how far would they have needed to travel?

Further Study

1. Which two leaders mentioned in this chapter were brothers?
2. Sometimes a city, a state or province, or even a country is known for specializing in one kind of product or service (though it also produces other things). See if you can give several examples of such places.
3. Find information about the guilds that existed during the Middle Ages.

Time Line

Copy the list of dates, and write the correct event after each.

1. 1066	Black Death kills millions of Europeans.
2. 1071	French boy starts Children's Crusade.
3. 1095	Hundred Years' War begins.
4. 1212	Hundred Years' War ends.
5. 1215	Joan of Arc fights the English.
6. early 1200s	John signs Magna Carta.
7. early 1300s	Pope Urban II urges First Crusade.
8. middle 1300s	Popes organize Inquisition.
9. early 1400s	Turks capture Palestine from Arabs.
10. 1453	William wins the Battle of Hastings.

Be Sure You Know

Can you answer all these questions? If not, study Chapters 21–23 to find the answers.

A. What

1. (*a*) are the two main islands of the British Isles? (*b*) are the three parts of Great Britain?
2. three groups conquered most of the Celtic people in England?
3. (*a*) noted Catholic missionary worked among the Irish? (*b*) among the English?
4. Muslims invaded Spain in the A.D. 700s?
5. barbarian king of the Franks became a Catholic?
6. kind of men were the Vikings?
7. king was a great help to England during the 800s?
8. two weapons could a pope use against uncooperative European kings?
9. king was excommunicated by Pope Gregory VII?
10. pope was especially bold in asserting his power?
11. things in the Catholic Church helped to cause darkness during the Middle Ages? (Name at least six.)
12. (*a*) king was forced to approve the Magna Carta? (*b*) Give the year when this happened.
13. were some problems of town life in the Middle Ages?
14. girl helped the French to gain freedom from the English in the Hundred Years' War?

B. What do these words mean?

15. abbot
16. apprentice
17. bubonic plague
18. cathedral
19. coat of arms
20. Crusade
21. duke
22. excommunicate
23. feudalism
24. fief
25. friar
26. Holy Roman Empire
27. Inquisition
28. interdependent
29. interdict
30. journeyman
31. lord
32. Magna Carta
33. manor
34. mass
35. master
36. masterpiece
37. medieval
38. parliament
39. sacrament
40. serf
41. simony
42. specialization
43. tournament
44. Turk
45. vassal

C. How

46. did the Catholic Church gain power over the kings of Europe?
47. were Europeans motivated to start going on Crusades?

D. Why

48. did Hadrian build a wall across northern England?
49. was the Battle of Tours a major turning point in history?
50. (*a*) was the Battle of Hastings a turning point in the history of England? (*b*) Give the year when this battle was fought.

The Catholics often seized and burned the books of "heretics." Some of their victims probably were heretics, but some of them were true believers, whose books were simply the Bible translated from Latin into the languages of the common people. The Catholics did not want people to read the Bible, because it exposed how far their church was from truth.

Notice the flat circle behind the head of one man on the left. This man had been declared a saint by the Catholic Church. Medieval artists often portrayed Catholic saints, angels, and Bible characters with a halo (also called a nimbus) around their head to show that they were considered holier than other men. Some halos look like a simple ring floating above the head; others are a bright area surrounding the head. Halos are of pagan origin.

1 A.D.
The Montanists separate from the main church. Late 100s
200
The Novatians teach their beliefs regarding church purity. 200s
The Donatists separate from the main church. 300s
Priscillian is accused of heresy and beheaded. 385
400
600
800
1000
Berengarius teaches against infant baptism and transubstantiation. c. 1040
Peter de Bruys is martyred for his teachings. 1126
Peter Waldo is converted and becomes a leader of the Waldenses. 1160
1200
The pope sends out armies against Waldenses and other dissenters. Early 1200s
1400
The Waldenses join the Protestant churches. 1500s
1600 A.D.

24 The Faithful Church: A Light in the Dark

Those Who Desired a Pure Church

Through the Dark Ages

The Waldenses

What Happened to the Dissenters

"That ye may be blameless and harmless, the sons of God, without rebuke, in the midst of a crooked and perverse nation, among whom ye shine as lights in the world."

Philippians 2:15

The Faithful Church: A Light in the Dark

Those Who Desired a Pure Church

The church—what is it? Most people in western Europe during the Middle Ages would have said, "The Roman Catholic Church is *the* church. Doesn't *Catholic* mean 'universal'? Any other religious groups are only pretenders." They never considered that anyone outside their group could be a true Christian.

But others said, "No! The true church is everyone who loves and obeys Jesus Christ. No one needs to be baptized into the Roman Catholic Church to be saved. Besides, anyone in the Catholic Church who does not love and obey Jesus Christ is not saved."

Already in the late 100s, a group called Montanists (MAHN tuh nihsts) broke away from the established church because they were not satisfied with the lack of holiness they saw in church members.

Some beliefs and practices of the Montanists were good. They loved the Lord and were looking for Him to come at any time. They disciplined wayward members—something that the main church was neglecting to do. They did not stop testifying when persecution threatened them.

But they were wrong on other points. For example, some Montanists were more concerned about showing emotional fervor than about carefully following God's Word. They seemed to feel that some things they spoke had as much authority as the Bible. They also thought that it was not good to marry.

In the 200s, another group arose, called the Novatians (noh VAY shuhnz). The Novatians also wanted to keep the church pure. They felt that the church should be more careful in how it dealt with people who had left the church during persecution but later wanted to return. The Bible teaches that a person must show evidence of genuine repentance and faithfulness before the church accepts him as a member. But the Novatians went beyond the Bible; they said that some sins committed after Baptism could not be forgiven.

It is worth noting that Constantine later persecuted the Novatians. Do you remember his Edict of Milan in the year 313? Constantine was not supposed to persecute Christians!

In the 300s, yet another group, the Donatists (DAHN uh tihsts), separated from the main church. This group was especially concerned that church leaders remain pure, for they believed that ceremonies such as Baptism and Communion were not valid unless the one who administered them was holy. However, they failed to reject some of the false ideas they had learned in the Catholic Church.

Within the Catholic Church, some people were thinking deeply. One of them was a man in Spain named Priscillian (pruh SIHL yuhn). He had grown up wealthy and was well educated. Unhappy with pagan religion, he had searched for something better and had finally decided to become a Christian.

Priscillian eagerly studied the Bible and taught others what he had learned. He had such talent that he was finally made a bishop. But some church leaders disliked him because he was so popular. Besides, he based his teachings on the Word of God rather than on the doctrines of the Catholic Church.

The envious men accused Priscillian of heresy and of serious sins. He and six of his followers were finally beheaded in 385. But Priscillian's influence encouraged other people to go to the Bible alone to find a rock foundation for their faith.

Study Exercises

1. Name in order the three groups of Christians who broke away from the Catholic Church.
2. Which of the three groups believed that ceremonies such as Baptism and Communion had no value unless the leader was pure?
3. What did other church leaders dislike about Priscillian besides the fact that he was popular?

Through the Dark Ages

Reading church history, we can get the feeling that throughout the Middle Ages, the Roman Catholic Church covered most of Europe like a blanket. Of course there were important exceptions such as the Muslim and Viking invaders. But we might feel that true believers disappeared until the religious awakening in the 1500s that is called the Reformation.

However, through the centuries there were always some people who disagreed with the Catholic Church. Some had never been Catholics. Others were not brave enough to leave the church, but they raised serious questions.

One such man was Berengarius (behr uhn GAIR ee uhs), who was born about the year 1000. He taught that the bread and wine of the mass were not really the body and blood of Jesus, but a "shadow and figure" of it. He also taught that baptizing babies, as the Catholic Church was doing, is wrong.

However, under pressure from the church, Berengarius denied his beliefs several times. This cast a shadow on his testimony, though he repented and sought the Lord again.

This aerial view shows the imposing size of Saint Peter's Basilica, an ancient cathedral in Rome, Italy. This basilica and the surrounding area is called the Vatican. The Vatican is considered the center of the Roman Catholic Church. All through medieval times to the early 1800s, warnings and punishments were meted out against true believers by this powerful, apostate church.

Another such man was Peter de Bruys. He taught against infant baptism, religious superstitions, and praying to saints. His followers were called Petrobrusians (peht roh BROO zhuhnz). Peter de Bruys was burned to death in 1126.

Many Catholics were frustrated at sins they saw in the church, but too often they did not know where to turn. Sometimes those who rejected certain false teachings of the church added other false teachings of their own. For example, some of them taught that it was a sin to marry. Some believed it was wrong to eat meat or other animal products. Some believed it was honorable for a person to starve himself to death. A sect called Flagellants (fluh JEHL uhnts) beat each other, thinking this would remove the guilt of their sins.

It is hard to know exactly what some of these groups believed. Most of the historical records at the time they lived were written by their enemies. Often Catholics accused them of ***dualism.*** Dualism is similar to Gnosticism, the old idea that spirit is good and matter is bad. Dualists believed that Jesus Christ never had a human body. They believed their own bodies, made of matter, should be treated severely with hunger and hardships. Loyal Catholics knew the word *dualism* meant something bad. So the monks who wrote about people who disagreed with the church were inclined to call them dualists, whether or not they really were.

All the while, some saints were quietly serving the Lord. Various families lived in remote valleys and on mountain slopes, practicing a faith their fathers and grandfathers taught them. They believed their faith had been handed down from the times of the apostles.

Perhaps these quiet country people did not challenge the Roman Catholic Church enough. They were soon to receive a powerful new leader.

Study Exercises

4. This section mentions one thing that both Berengarius and Peter de Bruys taught against. What is it?
5. How did Petrobrusians get their name?
6. Why were some people called dualists even though they did not believe in dualism?
7. If a person believes that spirit is good and matter is bad, how will he treat his body?

The Waldenses

One day, about the year 1160, a young man named Peter Waldo (WAWL doh) was talking with a few other men in Lyon (lee OHN), France. Suddenly one of the men in the group slumped down and died.

Peter Waldo was frightened. He began to think seriously. He pondered the words

Peter Waldo of the twelfth century.

of Jesus in Matthew 19:21, "If thou wilt be perfect, go and sell that thou hast, and give to the poor, and thou shalt have treasure in heaven: and come and follow me." Those words impressed Peter, for he was wealthy.

Peter began to give his goods to the poor and to share what he knew of the Bible with others. He read, in Luke 10, how Jesus sent out disciples two by two as missionaries without money, trusting in God to supply their needs. He decided to let that be his pattern. He and other men who were attracted to his way of life traveled here and there, preaching.

At this point, Peter Waldo was still a Catholic. But the time came when the Catholic Church refused permission to let him preach. Peter believed he had to preach anyway, so the church excommunicated him.

Peter and his fellow preachers became known as the "Poor Men of Lyon." Like the apostle Peter, they could say, "Silver and gold have I none" (Acts 3:6). Some of them traveled here and there as peddlers. Stopping at various homes, they would quote the Scriptures. If the listeners seemed open to the Gospel, they would add a short sermon.

The missionaries showed much dedication. According to one story, a man swam a river one winter night to bring the Gospel to a seeker.

Of course not everyone who believed as Peter did became a traveling preacher. Many lived like other common people, but they were careful not to display wealth. They became known as Waldenses (wawl DEHN seez), after their widely known leader Peter Waldo. The Waldenses spread through parts of France and Italy and later throughout western Europe. Most Waldenses practiced nonresistance. They did not attend dances or wear jewelry. Someone described them as follows:

> In moral behavior they are composed and modest. They take no pride in their clothing, which is neither too rich nor too abject [very poor]. . . . They often make their living by the work of their hands, as craftsmen; their learned men are weavers and textile workers. They do not increase their riches, but are satisfied with necessities. They go neither to taverns, nor to shows, nor to any such vanities. They avoid anger. They are always working, teaching, or learning. . . . They may also be recognized by their words, which are precise and modest. They avoid . . . lying and taking oaths.

Some Waldenses traveled around the countryside, selling books and cloth. They used these contacts with people to spread Bible truth.

The Catholic church leaders tried to stamp out Waldensian teachings. But Waldensian missionaries were hard to catch. They would stop at an area, preach, and leave as quietly as they had come. They

A Waldensian church in the Alps of northwestern Italy.

seldom told their names. One enemy of the Waldenses had his own idea about the way they gathered for meetings.

> When the Waldenses wish to go to their conventicle [secret worship service], they first rub an ointment . . . on a stick, an ointment supplied to them by the devil. Then they straddle this stick and fly to whatever place they wish to go, over cities and forests and lakes.

Those were the days when many could not read. Besides, people found little to read. The printing press had not yet been invented, and everything had to be copied by hand. What is more, it was dangerous to possess copies of the Scriptures. People caught with them could be severely punished.

The Waldenses did copy and pass out portions of the Scriptures. But they found a perfect way around the danger of being caught with copies in their possession. They hid the Scriptures in their hearts. How they memorized! One monk said this:

> They learn by heart the Gospels and the New Testament, in the vernacular [language of the common people] and repeat them aloud to one another. . . . I have seen some lay-folk [those not ordained] so steeped in their doctrine that they could repeat by heart great portions of the Evangelists, such as Matthew and Luke, especially all that is said in them of Christ's teaching and sayings, so that they could repeat them without a halt and with hardly a word wrong here or there.

Studying the Waldenses can be confusing. Some people were called Waldenses who did not have the faith described here. Others who were not called Waldenses believed much as the Waldenses. Some Albigenses (al buh JEHN seez) did, for example. (But many other Albigenses taught false doctrines.)

Then too, Waldenses were called by various names in different places. Besides "Poor Men of Lyon," they were called "Little Brothers" because they treated each other like brothers. They were called "Travelers"; for besides taking missionary trips, they sometimes had to flee from country to country. They were called "Cave Dwellers" and

"Dwellers With Wolves" because they lived and met in out-of-the-way places. Some people simply called them "Sufferers"—or "Dogs."

Study Exercises

8. Where did Peter Waldo get ideas that were different from the ones he had grown up with?
9. How did some Waldensian missionaries make contacts with people?
10. The people named after Peter Waldo spread out from what country?
11. Which group was more consistently correct in doctrine—the Waldenses or the Albigenses?
12. Who are lay members of a church?

What Happened to the Dissenters

Pope Innocent III did all he could to root out the ***dissenters*** (dih SEHN turz). Whether they followed true Bible teachings or not, all those who disagreed with the Catholic Church were heretics as far as he was concerned. Southern France was so thick with so-called heretics that the Inquisition could not deal with them one by one. In the early 1200s, the pope sent armies (wearing crosses and sometimes called crusaders) marching to France. Over a period of twenty years, they slaughtered thousands of people and ruined the rich country.

Some Waldenses are still living today. However, they have lost much that their forefathers stood for. During the 1500s, they were happy to see a strong non-Catholic church arising. They let down their guard and consulted freely with the leaders of this church. But the new church leaders were Protestants (PRAHT ih stuhnts), who did not make a complete break with all false Catholic teachings. The Waldenses trusted them too much instead of testing the Protestant beliefs with the Word of God.

This is a Waldensian village high in the Italian Alps. When they were not driven off by persecution, the Waldenses had little farms in these valleys. They cultivated grain crops and orchards. The high pastures also supported a few animals for meat. Note the people walking along the narrow pathway on the hillside.

Since then, the Waldenses do not have the pure Gospel testimony they once had.

But God made sure He had a group of people who would be faithful to Him. As the Waldenses lost some of their beliefs, there arose a group called ***Anabaptists*** (an uh BAP tihsts), who would be a light to Europe.

Study Exercises

13. A heretic is usually one who teaches false doctrine. Why do we not call everyone a heretic that the Catholics called a heretic?

14. The Waldenses were not defeated by persecution. How did they lose some of their Biblical beliefs?

15. Why does it seem strange that the armies who invaded France were wearing crosses?

Clinching the Chapter

Multiple Choice

A. *Write the word or phrase* least *associated with the first item.*
1. Dissenters: Catholics, Montanists, Novatians, Donatists
2. France: Constantine, Lyon, Albigenses, Waldo
3. Taught false doctrine: Flagellants, Albigenses, Waldenses, dualists
4. False doctrine: mass, infant baptism, dualism, memorization
5. Remained Catholic: Berengarius, Priscillian, Innocent III, Waldo
6. Non-Catholic: crusader, Muslim, Viking, pagan
7. Shunned by certain heretics: marriage, meat, comfort, suffering
8. Waldo: illiterate, poor, excommunicated, missionary
9. Waldenses: weavers, monks, missionaries, memorizers
10. The Scriptures: memorization, handwriting, superstition, true doctrine

B. *Write the correct words.*
1. Which group called themselves the universal church? (Catholics, Waldenses, Flagellants, Petrobrusians)
2. Which group was persecuted by Constantine? (Albigenses, Waldenses, Novatians, Catholics)
3. Which man became a Christian after growing dissatisfied with pagan religion? (Berengarius, Peter Waldo, Peter de Bruys, Priscillian)
4. Which was a great problem among loyal Catholics? (superstition, dualism, Gnosticism, Protestantism)
5. Which man was burned to death? (Innocent III, Berengarius, Peter de Bruys, Priscillian)
6. Which group did *not* claim to be Christians? (Catholics, Albigenses, Muslims, Novatians)
7. Which name is associated with Spain? (Peter Waldo, Constantine, Lyon, Priscillian)
8. Which group was named after their leader? (Flagellants, Catholics, Waldenses, Vikings)
9. The Edict of Milan was issued in (313, 1000, 1126, 1160).
10. Lyon is in (Spain, France, Italy, Greece).

Matching

A. *For each clue, write the correct term from the right-hand column.*

1. A person who disagrees with an established church	Berengarius
2. Follower of Peter de Bruys	crusader
3. Beat each other	dissenter
4. Follower of false doctrine	Flagellant
5. Another name for Waldenses	heretic
6. Waldensian leader	Innocent III

7. Met death by beheading — Peter Waldo
8. Claimed to be a soldier of the cross — Petrobrusian
9. Repented for giving up his beliefs — Poor Men of Lyon
10. Pope who sent armies to crush dissenters — Priscillian

B. *Match as in Part A.*

1. Forbidden by certain heretics	excommunication
2. Shunned by Waldenses	illiteracy
3. A power used by Catholic Church	marriage
4. Communion observance by Catholics	mass
5. Wrongly prayed to by Catholics	nonresistance
6. Did not yet exist	pagan
7. Inability to read	printing
8. Language of the common people	saint
9. Practiced by the Waldenses	vernacular
10. One who does not believe in the true God	wealth

Completion

1. Montanists head the historical lists;
   Then the Novatians, and then ———.
2. Just being church members has never sufficed;
   Members are saved if obedient to ———.
3. Seeker and teacher and Spanish civilian,
   Bishop and martyr: his name was ———.
4. Living contented with food, drink, and health,
   Faithful Waldenses would never seek ———.
5. Cruel crusaders and torture inventors
   Tried to exterminate all the ———.
6. Fierce persecution was prompted and stirred
   By the commands of Pope ———.

Thought Questions

1. We do not call a person lost just because he does not belong to our own church group. Neither do we say he is saved just because he calls himself a Christian. What determines whether a person is saved?
2. Why did many of those who desired a pure church eventually leave the Catholic Church?
3. Can you give an illustration of people today who use their work or their business to help spread the Gospel?
4. Which name (or names) given to the Waldenses seems like a compliment? Why?
5. You do not face the problem of lacking copies of the written Word or being unable to read. Why is it still important to memorize Bible passages?

Further Study

1. What other facts can you find about the Albigenses and Waldenses, besides those mentioned in this chapter?
2. How rich should a person be? (See Proverbs 30:8, 9.) What do you know about the Waldenses that shows they came close to this standard?

Marco Polo, a European explorer and trader, kneels before a Chinese emperor. Marco traveled and worked in China with his father and uncle for many years. When he returned to Italy (his native land), he published an account of his travels, which many people regarded as fiction. Some of it may have been embellished, but the Europeans' attitudes were probably also caused by their lack of knowledge about Asia.

25 Africa, India, and China Through the Middle Ages

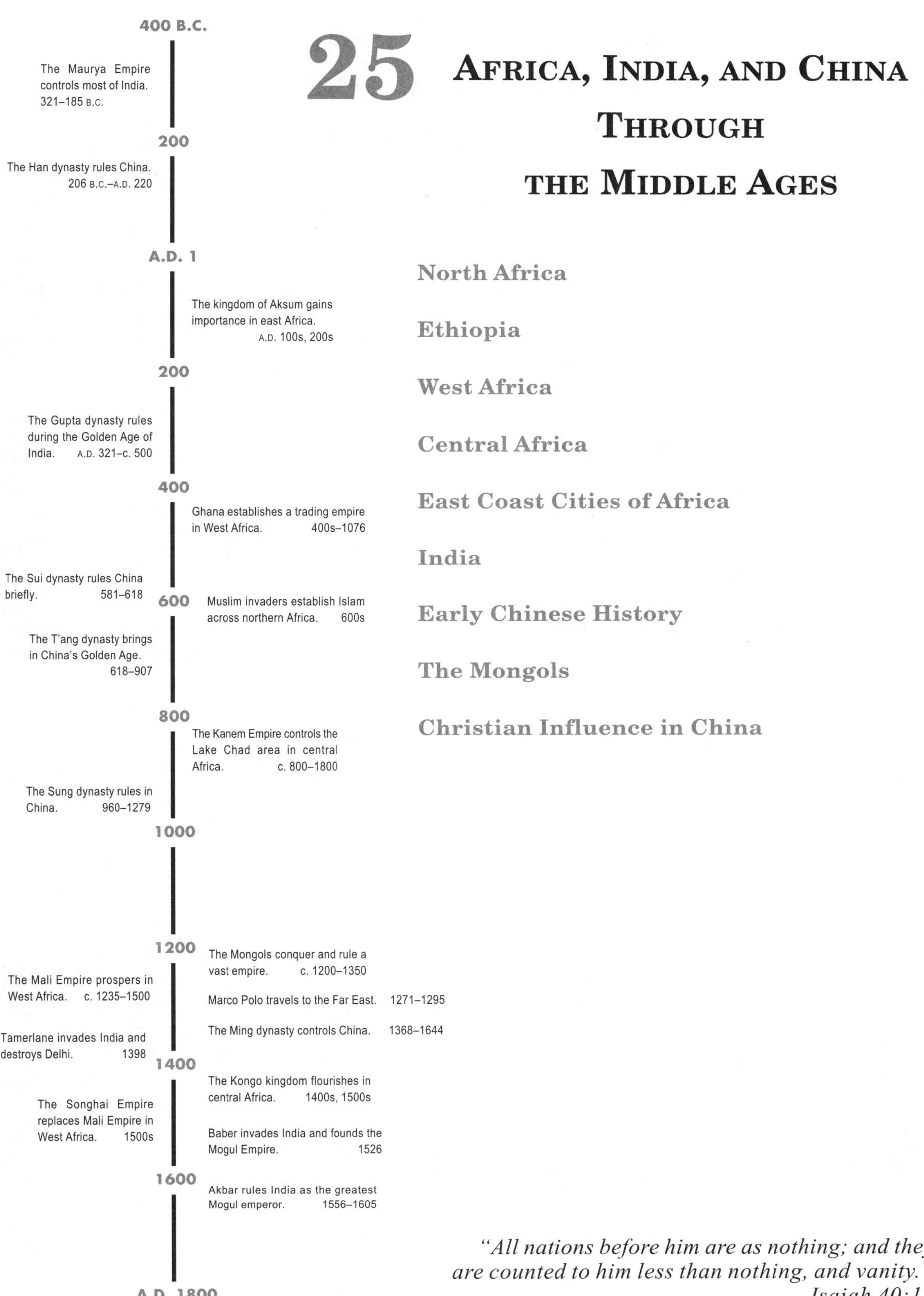
400 B.C.
The Maurya Empire controls most of India. 321–185 B.C.
200
The Han dynasty rules China. 206 B.C.–A.D. 220
A.D. 1
The kingdom of Aksum gains importance in east Africa. A.D. 100s, 200s
200
The Gupta dynasty rules during the Golden Age of India. A.D. 321–c. 500
400
Ghana establishes a trading empire in West Africa. 400s–1076
The Sui dynasty rules China briefly. 581–618
600
Muslim invaders establish Islam across northern Africa. 600s
The T'ang dynasty brings in China's Golden Age. 618–907
800
The Kanem Empire controls the Lake Chad area in central Africa. c. 800–1800
The Sung dynasty rules in China. 960–1279
1000
1200
The Mongols conquer and rule a vast empire. c. 1200–1350
The Mali Empire prospers in West Africa. c. 1235–1500
Marco Polo travels to the Far East. 1271–1295
The Ming dynasty controls China. 1368–1644
Tamerlane invades India and destroys Delhi. 1398
1400
The Kongo kingdom flourishes in central Africa. 1400s, 1500s
The Songhai Empire replaces Mali Empire in West Africa. 1500s
Baber invades India and founds the Mogul Empire. 1526
1600
Akbar rules India as the greatest Mogul emperor. 1556–1605
A.D. 1800

North Africa

Ethiopia

West Africa

Central Africa

East Coast Cities of Africa

India

Early Chinese History

The Mongols

Christian Influence in China

"All nations before him are as nothing; and they are counted to him less than nothing, and vanity."
Isaiah 40:17

Africa, India, and China Through the Middle Ages

North Africa

The history of northern Africa has names that should be familiar to you. The Roman Empire had taken control of this region before the time of Christ. In A.D. 429, as Rome was slowly crumbling, Vandals from Europe invaded northern Africa and controlled it for one hundred years. But then the Byzantine army moved in and took control.

In the 600s, Islam began its march across northern Africa. The North Africans who accepted the new religion took on Arab customs and adopted the Arabic language. Some of them married Arabs, and the children of those mixed marriages and their descendents were and still are generally referred to by the name *Moors.* By the year 711, Arabic Muslims and Moors were ready to invade Spain.

You have learned that during much of the Middle Ages, Muslim culture was more advanced than European culture. But in the centuries after the Crusades, the Arab world gradually lost interest in fresh ideas. Other parts of the world moved ahead without them. Today the Arab culture is still suffering from this lost period of time.

Ethiopia

Not everyone in northern Africa became a Muslim. Long before, in the second and third centuries A.D., the kingdom of Aksum had gained importance. Aksum was located along the southern shore of the Red Sea, in what is now Ethiopia.

The kingdom of Aksum was established about the time of Christ. The people who

The buildings of this town in northern Africa reveal that its history involves other peoples. In the center of the picture, a Muslim mosque stands, dating back to the days of Muslim control. A French fort stands on the hill, a symbol of later European control of this area.

The mountainous highlands of central Ethiopia were once controlled by the kingdom of Aksum. Many of these stony peaks rise more than 12,000 feet (3,658 m). Notice the patches of fields and the houses below the hills.

lived there set up a brisk trade with merchants from many places, such as Greece and Rome on the Mediterranean and India in the East. The visiting merchants were eager to trade for gold, ivory, and other African products.

The Gospel was probably first brought to this area by Christians such as the Ethiopian eunuch whom Philip baptized. In the 300s, a Christian slave who served the king helped to establish Christianity as the state religion of Aksum. (This took place soon after Christianity became the state religion of the Roman Empire.) Later, when Muslim lands surrounded Aksum, the people of Aksum fought them off for a time. The rulers of Aksum lost their power around 1100, but the people did not lose their habits and way of thinking. Ethiopia later became known as the oldest "Christian" nation in Africa.

The state churches of Ethiopia, which became known as Ethiopian Orthodox, developed beliefs similar to those held by the Coptic churches of Egypt. Like the Catholic Church, Ethiopian Orthodox and Coptic churches include many rituals and ceremonies in their worship. Millions of

Symbols of the triumphant past, the giant stone steles of the capital city of Aksum rise skyward up to 110 feet (33.5 m). They were probably erected several hundred years after Christ, but no one is really sure of their purpose. Some of them have altars at their bases, which suggests that they may have been used for pagan religious rites.

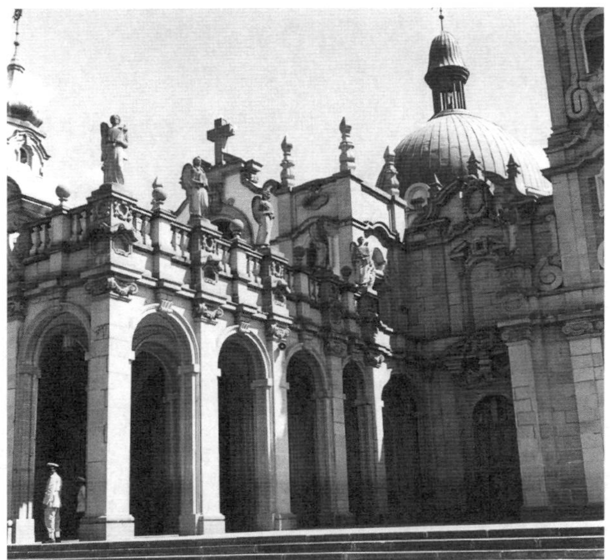

This Ethiopian Orthodox church in Addis Ababa demonstrates that this religion has some of the same basic problems that Catholicism has—both place much significance on external rituals and elaborate buildings rather than stressing the need for converted, sanctified hearts.

Ethiopians belong to the Ethiopian Orthodox Church today.

Study Exercises

1. What empire controlled northern Africa between the time of the Vandals and the time of the Muslims?
2. Why did the Muslim world lose its advanced culture?
3. What brought prosperity to Aksum?

West Africa

During the early 700s, when some Muslims were heading north into Spain, other Muslims pushed south into the bulge of West Africa. Beyond the vast, empty Sahara, they came to the savanna, where rain falls and grass grows. To their surprise, the people they found there did not belong to scattered, ignorant tribes. Instead, they were resourceful people who had iron tools and weapons—a sign of advanced culture in those days.

Instead of conquering these people, the Muslims began to trade with them. At that time the most powerful empire in West Africa was called Ghana (GAH nuh). Many people of Ghana were farmers and herdsmen. That in itself would not have given them great wealth. But they had several major advantages.

One advantage was that they had iron ore and knew how to smelt it. With iron farm tools, they could till the ground efficiently and raise enough food for the people. With their iron weapons, they could subdue neighboring tribes and govern them.

Another great advantage lay in their geographical position. In the Sahara to the north, workers dug salt from the ground in solid blocks. In the rain forests to the south, other people found gold. Arab traders who came to Ghana helped to get the salt to buyers in the south and the gold to buyers in the north. They made this a profitable business. The trade routes that ran through Ghana made the empire rich.

Arab traders expanded their business in Ghana to include many goods. From Europe, from the Middle East, and from northern Africa, they brought tools, clothing, dried fruit, salt, copper, and many other products. These they exchanged for kola nuts, gold, ivory, and slaves from the rain forests to the south; and for hides from the nearby grasslands.

Ghana had a strong government, with a power pyramid that resembled the feudal system in Europe. The king taxed the traders to enrich his empire. A strong army kept order and protected the empire from enemies. However, Ghana declined during the 1000s. Invaders from the Sahara to the north put an end to the empire in 1076.

Two other empires followed Ghana.

A member of the Songhai tribe near Timbuktu, Mali, wears a typical native straw hat.

An African farmer prepares soil for planting on the banks of the Niger River near Timbuktu.

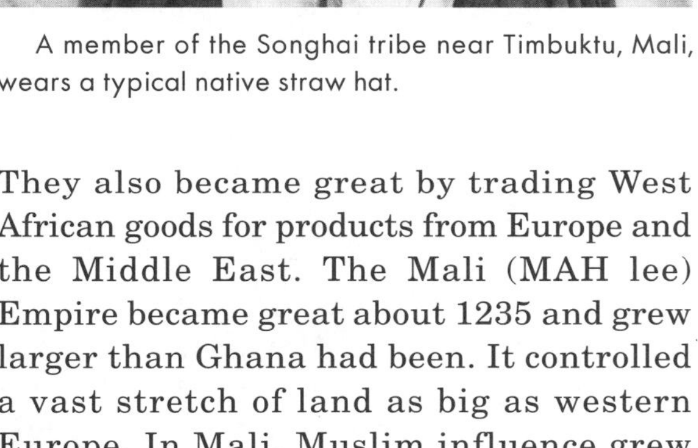

They also became great by trading West African goods for products from Europe and the Middle East. The Mali (MAH lee) Empire became great about 1235 and grew larger than Ghana had been. It controlled a vast stretch of land as big as western Europe. In Mali, Muslim influence grew very strong.

Trade was strong too. Hundreds of camel caravans came and went. It is said that around 1400, twelve thousand camels a year were crossing the desert to Mali.

Later rulers in Mali were not skillful enough to control such an enormous territory. People in outlying areas began to grow restless. The empire broke up piece by piece, and by 1500 it was of little importance.

As Mali declined, an empire called Songhai (SAHNG hy) arose and lasted until

A caravan approaches Timbuktu, the intellectual and trading center of the Songhai Empire.

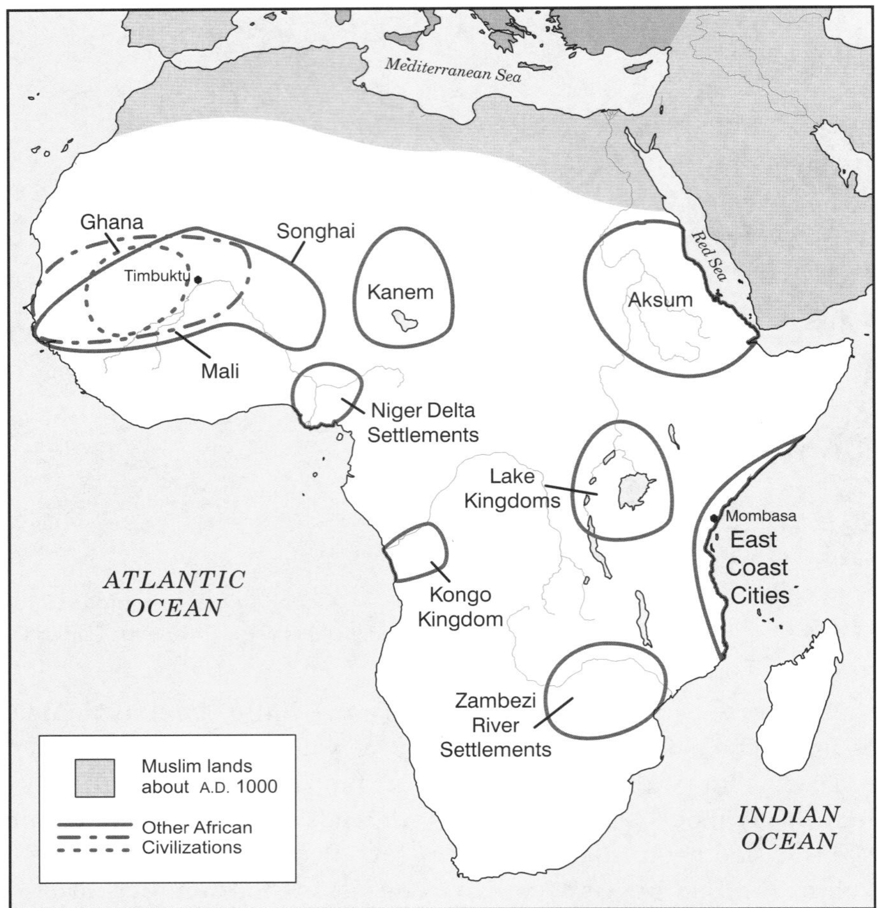

Figure 25:1. African Civilizations During the Middle Ages

almost 1600. One of its cities, Timbuktu (tihm buhk TOO), had already been important in the Mali Empire. Timbuktu was famous not only for its trade but also for its scholars and university.

Today the grassland empires are gone. Timbuktu has lost its bustling importance and is just a small trading town. But the Arab influence remains. Many people speak Arabic and follow the Islamic religion. And some old names remain. Ghana and Mali are the names of two nations in West Africa.

The Kanem (KAH nehm) Empire began around A.D. 800 and lasted about a thousand years. That is longer than most empires of the world can claim. It lay just south of the Sahara, like the other grassland empires, but it was further east near Lake Chad. It is mentioned here because, like Ghana and Mali, it depended on trade of salt, copper, ivory, kola nuts, and similar products.

Study Exercises

4. What useful metal helped to make African farmers successful?
5. Some trading cities lie on the edge of an ocean. The African trading empires lay on the edge of what desert?
6. What foreigners helped to set up trade in Ghana?
7. What empires besides Ghana arose in West Africa?

Central Africa

Historians have had difficulty in tracing what took place in Africa many centuries ago, for the Africans of that time did not know how to write. But students of African history have interviewed hundreds of people who knew old stories and traditions. Historians try to sift out the facts from the legends. As they compare the stories, a picture of African history begins to emerge.

It seems that the ancestors of today's Bantu (BAN too) Africans lived in what is now Cameroon (kam uh ROON), just east of the Niger River delta. About the time of Christ, they began to migrate to new areas. Over the centuries, groups of them met other African tribes. They sometimes fought with them, but they also intermarried with them.

These Africans shared their knowledge with other Africans. They brought the secret of iron making to the various regions that they gradually settled. They learned how to raise cattle. Bantu herdsmen down to modern times treasure cattle and count them as a sign of wealth. But because they were so far away from Europe and the Middle East, they missed learning about discoveries and inventions in that part of the world.

Many wandering tribes finally settled near the shore of Lake Victoria. Others settled on the good land near the other great lakes in eastern Africa. By the time William the Conqueror invaded England in 1066, this region was likely well populated with Bantu-speaking people.

Feeling crowded, some tribes began to push southward. They fought against the San and Khoikhoin (KOY koy ihn) they found, killing some and forcing others to move to other areas. Some of the Bantu-speaking pioneers found land that they liked along the east African coast. Others pushed farther south to the Zambezi River.

Though it was frightening to think of swimming the rolling brown Zambezi current, some of the pioneers tried it. People and cattle drowned, but the survivors pushed on. Groups of them settled here and there in southern Africa. Other tribes stopped at the Zambezi and made their homes there.

Later, people from northern Africa invaded southern Africa, and vice versa. Restless Bantu tribes moved here and there, conquering and being conquered. Finally they roamed less and settled in the areas where European explorers later found them. The Kongo kingdom, for example, flourished during the 1400s and 1500s.

Today Bantu-speaking people make up about two-thirds of all Africans. They consist of many separate tribes that speak hundreds of different languages and dialects.

East Coast Cities of Africa

Before the time of Christ, cities existed along the east coast of Africa. Arab shipmen traded with the black Africans who lived there. A few Arab merchants settled on the African coast, where they influenced the natives to accept some Arabic customs and beliefs. It appears that by the 700s the Arabs had gained some control of the government. By the end of the next few centuries, there were perhaps thirty trading colonies along the coast.

Trading ships came from far away to load ivory, gold, palm oil, iron, and slaves. They took goods as far away as northern China. In fact, by the early 1400s, the Chinese were coming in their own junks to trade.

Many Africans in the eastern coastal cities took on Arab ways and accepted Islam. They blended many Arabic words with their own words. Out of this grew a language called Swahili, (swah HEE lee) which is one of the Bantu languages. Since so many modern Africans use this language, they can usually understand each other even if they are strangers and do not know each other's tribal languages.

In the 1500s, Portuguese sailors came too—but not to trade. They knew that it was quicker to get rich by robbing the cities. Not content with that, they slaughtered many people and burned some cities, hoping to control east African trade for their own profit. Today a few of the old cities have been rebuilt. One of them is Mombasa (mahm BAS uh), on the coast of Kenya.

Study Exercises

8. How do historians know about past African civilizations that left no written records?
9. What large African country lies just west of Cameroon? (See the map on page 82.)
10. What valuable animals did Bantu-speaking people learn to care for?
11. What two non-African peoples greatly affected the coastal cities?

India

In Chapter 13 you studied India before the time of Christ. Now you will study the history of India from just before the time of Christ through the Middle Ages.

Around 321 B.C., soon after the death of Alexander the Great, an Indian leader set up a government known as the Maurya (MOW ur yuh) Empire. The traditional religion of India had been Hinduism, but one of the Maurya kings was converted to Buddhism. This happened after the king fought in a terrible battle in which a hundred thousand people were killed. The king was overcome with remorse and chose to become a Buddhist, for Buddhism teaches against violence. Because of his influence, many people in India and neighboring countries became Buddhists.

The Maurya Empire controlled nearly all of India and parts of other countries. But its last kings were not capable of holding the empire together, and it finally broke down into smaller, independent governments. The line of Maurya emperors came to an end about 185 B.C.

Christianity came to India during the first century A.D. (The first century A.D. was from A.D. 1 to 100.) Tradition says that the apostle Thomas brought the good news and won many to the faith, and that finally he was martyred in India.

A later empire began about A.D. 320 under the Gupta dynasty. It ruled northern India and parts of present-day Pakistan. The country began to return to the Hindu religion. History students sometimes call the time of the Gupta dynasty the Golden Age of India because at that time some people of India had great knowledge. India had libraries and universities. Doctors knew much about how to treat illnesses. Indian artists and writers performed so well that no age in India since then has surpassed them.

Perhaps it was during the Gupta dynasty that Hindu mathematicians developed the Hindu-Arabic numerals and invented the zero.

During the late 400s, the barbarian Huns, who attacked Europe, also invaded India. The Gupta Empire fell about 500, near the time that Rome fell. While Europe was going through its Middle Ages, India suffered many invasions. The most significant invaders were the Muslims. The first Muslims came to India during the 700s, the same century when other Muslims were invading Spain.

Just as the so-called Christians in Europe called the Muslims infidels, the Muslims called the Hindus infidels. They believed it was their sacred duty to conquer the enemies of Allah. They considered the treasures they seized as their reward from Allah.

It is said that one Muslim ruler raided India seventeen times. Once he destroyed a fabulously rich temple, killing fifty thousand Hindus. The defeated people begged him to spare the temple idol, promising him more riches than he had already gotten by robbing the city. But he refused and had it smashed.

Incidents like these built much hatred between Muslims and Hindus, a hatred that lasts to this day. The Bible says that "hatred stirreth up strifes" (Proverbs 10:12). Each incident of strife between the Muslims and Hindus has stirred up more hatred, and so the vicious cycle has continued over the centuries.

India's worst experience came in 1398, when the country was invaded by a famous Mongol Turk named Tamerlane. This man, who came from what is now Uzbekistan (uhz BEHK ih stan), had already conquered much of Asia. Although a Muslim, Tamerlane fought the Muslims who ruled in India. But he also killed many Hindus. His vicious army looted the capital city of Delhi (DEHL ee) and killed most of the people. An old legend says that not even birds flew over the city for two months.

In 1526, yet another strong Muslim conqueror invaded India. Baber (BAH bur), who was from what is now Afghanistan, marched his men through the Khyber Pass. They were equipped with cannons and muskets, which were new in India. Baber defeated the ***sultan*** of Delhi. Although he lived only four more years, Baber founded the Mogul Empire, which lasted two hundred years.

Baber's grandson, Akbar, is called the greatest of the Mogul emperors. He was a thinking man who wanted to learn more about different religions and about God. He stopped persecuting Hindus. He called Muslim leaders to help him understand the Islamic faith and explain why not all Muslims could agree. But the Muslim leaders argued with each other. Once they got so noisy that the record says, "His Majesty became very angry at the rude behavior of those he had summoned to speak about God."

In this scene, a member of Indian royalty is transported in a luxurious conveyance carried by servants. As she rests, probably in a village, the people of the area bring gifts and play musical instruments in her honor.

Akbar talked to Hindus. He talked to

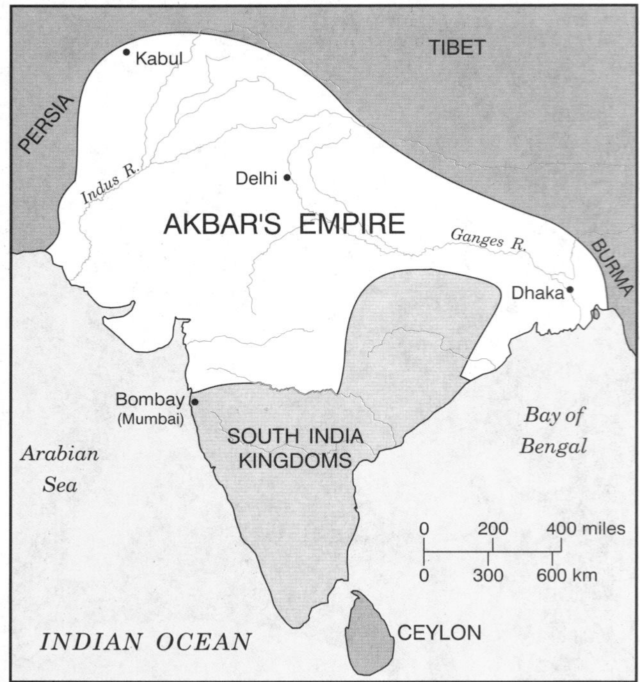

Figure 25:2. Akbar's Indian Empire

Catholics. Finally he decided to take the best of all these religions and mix it into a religion of his own. Hardly anyone accepted his new philosophy, and few people today know anything about it.

Perhaps if Akbar had read the Bible for himself, he could have found salvation. But Akbar had a handicap. When he was young, he had been allowed to hunt and play. He had never learned to read.

Because southern India was farther from the warring nations of Asia, it experienced fewer invasions than northern India did. Hinduism remained strong in the south even after Muslim invaders had brought Islam to northern India. This explains why certain northern sections broke away from India and established the Muslim nations of Pakistan (in 1947) and Bangladesh (in 1971).

Study Exercises

12. What two major religions did most Indians accept?
13. Between which empires did Christianity first come to India?
14. The main invaders of India were of what religion?
15. About how many years later than the Huns did Tamerlane come?
16. Who is said to be greatest of the Mogul emperors?

Early Chinese History

In Chapter 13 you studied the history of China long before the birth of Christ. You may recall that China was ruled by a series of dynasties. The Han dynasty is easy to remember because it began about two hundred years before Christ and ended about two hundred years after. China prospered during this time. It conquered neighboring territories and made its empire as big as the Roman Empire itself.

China had a thriving trade with Rome. Caravans took Chinese products along the Great Silk Road from China to the Middle East. Famous as it was, the road was dangerous with robbers, and land travel was expensive. Many goods traveled part of the way by ship.

The Chinese of that time had a high level of civilization. While the early Christians were still writing Scriptures on animal-skin parchments, the Chinese developed a better way. During the Han

A model of a Chinese farmer's hut, from about A.D. 200.

Tai Tsung, the second T'ang ruler in China, receives European ambassadors. The ambassadors are presenting him with gifts, no doubt hoping to receive trading privileges with his country. The T'ang dynasty lasted from A.D. 618 to 907.

dynasty, they invented the first real paper. Even today, Chinese people sometimes call themselves "sons of Han."

Han rulers ended up quarreling among themselves, and finally the empire broke up. Nearly four hundred years of disorder followed. Men from different parts of China fought among themselves.

The Sui (SWAY) dynasty, which brought China back under one government, did not last very long. The government did some good, but it overspent on too many grand projects and too many luxuries for the rulers. The rulers forced many people to be laborers and soldiers. A rebellion finally brought the Sui dynasty to an end.

The T'ang (TAHNG) dynasty began in 618. It built a strong central government. China had writers, artists, musicians, and scientists. Trade with other countries prospered. Missionaries from the Middle East traveled to China. Historians sometimes refer to the time of the T'ang dynasty as China's Golden Age.

About this time, block printing was invented. In block printing, craftsmen would

In an ancient Chinese village market, venders sell fish, ducks, grain, and produce. A shopkeeper at the right is weighing something delicate, possibly medicine or spice.

A Chinese farmer plows his rice seedbed, using a water buffalo. A scholar in a long-gown watches from a bank nearby, and a small boy brings food and drink on the pole carried on his shoulder. This illustration was drawn several hundred years ago.

carve pictures and words onto a block of wood. Then they would ink the raised part and press the block onto a piece of paper. The block printed a whole sheet of paper at one time.

The T'ang dynasty lasted almost three hundred years, but it was weakened by constant warfare. Rebellions within China itself also helped to bring the dynasty to an end.

The Sung dynasty arose about 960. It was around the time of the Sung dynasty that the Chinese invented gunpowder and movable type. Instead of carving out whole pages of type for printing, craftsmen made a separate piece of type for each word and fastened the pieces together to print. The Chinese may also have been the first to develop the magnetic compass.

In the next section you will read how the Sung Empire was eventually overthrown by one of the most terrible armies the world had yet seen.

Study Exercises

17. About how long did the Han dynasty last?
18. Name the overland route from the Middle East to China.
19. Name in order the four dynasties mentioned in this section.
20. The Golden Age of China came during which dynasty?

The Mongols

The Chinese lived in the eastern part of Asia. West of China lay desert lands and flat, dry grasslands where not many people lived. These prairies in Asia are called steppes.

Life is hard on the steppes. Strong winds sweep across the open country. The summers are short but hot, and the winters are long and cold. Many people live just as their ancestors did centuries ago, in round felt tents called ***yurts.*** They are

Nomadic Mongols set up a yurt. Having walls made of sticks that fold together and roofs made of removable sticks, yurts are easy to set up and take down for transport. Thick felt made of sheep wool covers the sticks; the natural oil in the wool makes the felt waterproof. These tents are cool under hot sun and warm in the wintertime.

expert horsemen, and they tend flocks of cattle, sheep, goats, and camels. The animals turn the short wilderness grass into meat and milk for the people.

Today Mongolia lies in this area, and the people are called Mongols. Centuries ago, the Mongol tribes fought among themselves. But about the year 1200, a strong ruler arose who came to be called Genghis Khan (JEHNG gihs KAHN). He gained control of all the Mongol tribes and established the Mongol Empire. The united Mongol army was very powerful.

Since the Mongol men spent much of their time fighting, they had great skill in warfare. At first the Chinese emperor refused to believe that the Mongols could be a threat to him. But they soon crossed the Great Wall and ravaged the rich land and cities in northern China.

The Mongols had an advantage because many poor people were oppressed by the Chinese government. These people were glad to cooperate with the invaders.

After conquering part of China, Genghis Khan led his huge army westward. His men on horseback moved swiftly, and they defeated every Muslim army they met. Whenever people offered resistance, the Mongols destroyed them. By the time Genghis Khan died, he was controlling an enormous territory.

Under his son, the next khan, the conquests went still farther—all the way into Hungary and southern Poland. (They had conquered parts of eastern Europe before this.) Polish, Hungarian, and German knights fell before the Mongols. It is hard to tell what might have happened to all of Europe if the khan had not suddenly died in 1241. The Mongols withdrew to choose a new khan and never came back to threaten western Europe.

The greatest of khans was Kublai Khan (KOO bly KAHN). He was only a child when his grandfather Genghis Khan died. Under his reign, the empire grew and took in southern China. It was the largest empire under one man that the world had ever seen. However, Kublai Khan spent most of his time strengthening his control of China. Many of the far-flung areas of his empire were almost independent. Kublai Khan made his capital at Peking (PEE KIHNG), now called Beijing (BAY JIHNG), which is the capital of China today.

Since the Mongol Empire was so huge, why do history books say so little about it?

For one thing, the empire did not last

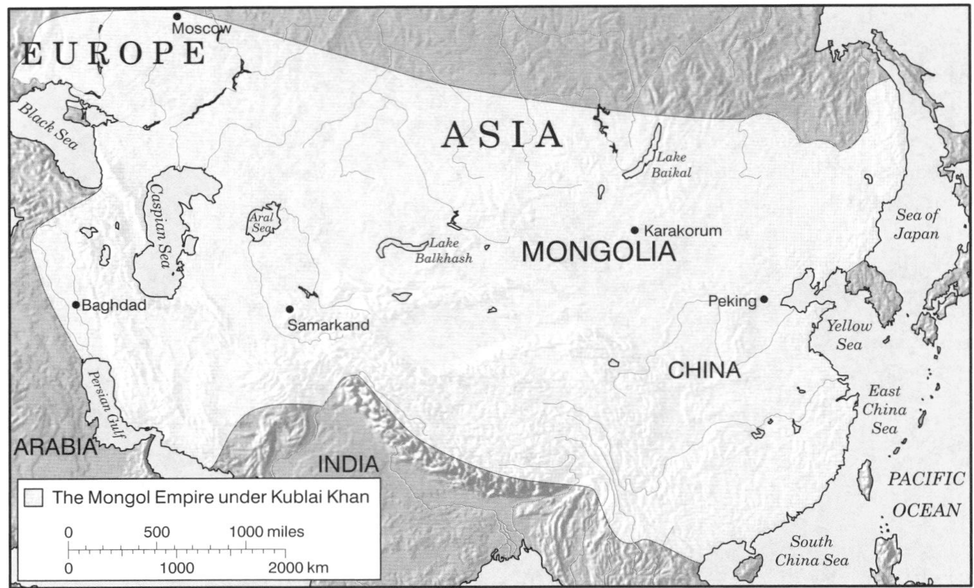

Figure 25:3. Kublai Khan's Mongal Empire

long. Such a huge empire was hard to rule, especially since the conquerors were more skilled in fighting than in governing. The great power of the Mongols lasted only during the 1200s and then shriveled. During the 1300s, the Chinese drove out the Mongols and established the Ming dynasty.

The Mongols themselves seemed to have little interest in new ideas; their main goal was to conquer and destroy. But they did promote the exchange of ideas in a different way. Because they took so many far-flung lands into their empire, different nations learned more about each other. People came into contact with each other who would never have met if the Mongols had not conquered them all. Much trade developed, and Europeans learned new ideas from Asia.

During the reign of Kublai Khan, a family of traders paid a visit to the Mongol Empire and stayed about twenty years. After they returned to Europe, one of them (Marco Polo) described his adventures in a book.

Because Marco Polo's descriptions of the Far East were so strange to Europeans,

A Mongol in his traditional warm winter clothing.

some people thought he must have made them up. Perhaps they found it especially hard to believe that Chinese culture was more advanced than their own. Remember, those were the days when many Chinese people took baths every day. Europeans seldom took baths.

Marco told of black stones that Chinese people burned to heat their houses. (Europeans knew nothing about coal.) He reported that the people used paper money, whereas Europeans had always used coins. Marco also told of how rich the rulers of the country were. He had gifts of jewels, porcelain, and fine clothes from Kublai Khan to prove it.

Marco Polo's book was widely read in Europe. Just as the Crusades and the Mongol invasions had brought strangers together, his book brought people's minds into contact with faraway places. It made them eager to learn more.

Christian Influence in China

Do you suppose Marco Polo found any Christians when he visited China? After all, they had had twelve hundred years to get there.

China did have Christians of a sort, called Nestorians. Long before, the Nestorians had broken away from the Catholic Church. During the T'ang dynasty, Nestorian missionaries began spreading their beliefs in China. Nestorians were well known in the Mongol Empire; in fact, Kublai Khan's mother was one.

But the Nestorians had mixed many ideas from old Chinese philosophers with Christian teachings. Although they knew about God and Jesus, it is questionable whether they knew enough to be born again and be saved from sin.

It is said that when Marco Polo's Catholic father and uncle met Kublai Khan on their first visit to China, Kublai Khan gave them a challenge. He said the pope should send one hundred missionaries to Peking and prove that Christianity was better than the religions he already knew. But no missionaries came. The first Catholic priests arrived many years later, and by that time Kublai Khan was dead.

Study Exercises

21. What vegetation grows on the steppes?
22. How did the Chinese government's treatment of its people weaken it when invaders came?
23. What important region was threatened but not conquered by the Mongols?
24. In what way was the Mongol Empire greater than the Roman Empire?
25. In what way was the Mongol Empire inferior to many other empires?

Clinching the Chapter

Multiple Choice

A. *Write the word or phrase* least *associated with the first item.*

1. Empire: Mongol, Byzantine, Timbuktu, Ghana
2. Bantu: cattle, silk, Victoria, Zambezi
3. Sung: paper, compass, gunpowder, movable type
4. Muslims: Turks, Delhi, Coptic, Mali
5. Mongol: khan, Peking, Tamerlane, Mediterranean
6. Invaders: Vandals, Huns, Mongols, Nestorians

7. African products: porcelain, ivory, salt, gold
8. China: Maurya, Han, Sui, T'ang
9. Invaders of India: Akbar, Baber, Kublai Khan, Tamerlane
10. River: Songhai, Niger, Congo, Zambezi

B. *Write the correct words.*

1. Ethiopian Orthodox churches developed in (Africa, China, India, Europe).
2. Muslims invaded both Europe and India during the (400s, 500s, 600s, 700s).
3. The language that resulted from mixing languages in eastern Africa is (Arabic, Swahili, Chinese, Coptic).
4. The great barrier separating northern Africa from central Africa is (the Sahara, the Congo, the Khyber Pass, the Red Sea).
5. What comes between Ghana and Songhai in order of time? (Aksum, Mali, Vandals, Gupta)
6. Name the former capital of India. (Peking, Delhi, Timbuktu, Bangladesh)
7. Who visited the Mongol Empire during the 1200s? (the apostle Thomas, Tamerlane, Marco Polo, Baber)
8. Southern India remained a stronghold of (Hindus, Muslims, Christians, Khoikhoin).
9. The sultans were (Muslim rulers, Vandal invaders, Roman emperors, Nestorian Christians).
10. The emperor of the Mongols was called a (yurt, khan, Genghis, Khoikhoin).

Matching

A. *For each clue, write the correct name from the right-hand column.*

1. Suffered from many Muslim invasions	Bantus
2. Were first to be conquered by Mongols	San
3. Egyptian church similar to Ethiopian Orthodox	Chinese
4. Were defeated by migrating Bantus	Coptic
5. Missionaries in China during the Middle Ages	Hindus
6. Raided east African port cities	Mongols
7. Terrorized most of Asia	Muslims
8. Two-thirds of today's Africans	Nestorians
9. Influenced northern India	Portuguese
10. Controlled northern Africa after the fall of Rome	Vandals

B. *Match as in Part A.*

1. Home of Baber	Afghanistan
2. Survives on east African coast	Cameroon
3. Kublai Khan's capital	China
4. Sultan's capital in India	Delhi
5. Known as oldest "Christian" nation in Africa	Ethiopia
6. Threatened but not conquered by Mongols	western Europe
7. Where Bantu history began	Mombasa
8. Home of Genghis Khan	Mongolia
9. Country of Marco Polo's tales	Pakistan
10. Modern Muslim country once part of India	Peking

Completion

1. From the desert came copper and salt, which were sold
   In the rich Ghana markets for nuts, slaves, and ———.
2. Coastal African cities supplied the Chinese,
   But the cities were sacked by the cruel ———.
3. He's unknown—a Hindu—no world-famous hero,
   But he wisely invented the numeral ———.
4. "Yet another invader!"—Repeat the refrain.
   And the worst of them all was the Turk ———.
5. In response to the Saviour's commandment and promise,
   Off to India's Buddhists and Hindus went ———.
6. When the Han dynasty toppled, and wars brought decay,
   Other rulers established the dynasty called ———.
7. If a floor of thin grass keeps you out of the dirt,
   And your felt roof is round, then you live in a ———.
8. Europeans thought China was strange, on the whole.
   Who would use paper money, or want to burn ———?
9. Moving backward in time from the great Genghis Khan,
   Think of Sung, then of T'ang, then of Sui, and then ———.

Thought Questions

1. You read that Christianity became the state religion of Aksum. What kind of Christianity do you think it was by that time?
2. There was a time when both the Arab and the Chinese cultures were more advanced than the European culture. Do you think it would be possible for modern western cultures to decline? Why or why not?
3. If a country is in a good geographical position, it can prosper even though it has few natural resources. How?
4. Why do huge empires tend to fall apart quickly?
5. Wars hinder trade and cause many other disruptions. In what way do wars sometimes promote trade?

Geographical Skills

1. On your map entitled "Large Rivers of Africa," draw and label the following rivers on your map: Congo, Zambezi, Orange, and Niger.
2. Name a main city in the Western Hemisphere that has about the same latitude as each of these African cities.
   a. Dakar, Senegal
   b. Cape Town, South Africa
   c. Cairo, Egypt
   d. Monrovia, Liberia
   e. Tunis, Tunisia
   f. Nairobi, Kenya
3. What do Lake Victoria in Africa and the mouth of the Amazon River in South America have in common on a map showing latitude and longitude?
4. Name three great rivers of India, Bangladesh, and Pakistan that have their sources in the Himalayas.

Further Study

1. What are kola nuts used for today?
2. You read that China traded with other countries. What products besides silk would China have had to trade? (See Chapter 13 and other sources.)

Time Line

Below is a list of important events described in this chapter. The events for each country are already in order. Copy the table, and place each event in the proper century and column. (Many blocks will not be used.)

Africa

Vandals invade northern Africa.
Muslims take control of northern Africa.
Muslims push south in West Africa and also take control of east coast cities.
Bantu speakers fill lakes area.
Ghana Empire comes to an end.
Mali builds up great trade.
Portuguese sailors rob east African cities.

India

Gupta dynasty begins.
Gupta Empire ends.
Muslims begin to invade India.
Tamerlane destroys Delhi.
Mogul Empire begins.

China

Han dynasty ends.
T'ang dynasty begins.
Sung dynasty arises.
Mongols build a huge empire.
Mongols are driven out; Ming dynasty begins.

	Africa	India	China
A.D. 100s			
200s			
300s			
400s			
500s			
600s			
700s			
800s			
900s			
1000s			
1100s			
1200s			
1300s			
1400s			
1500s			

Be Sure You Know

Can you answer all these questions? If not, study Chapters 24 and 25 to find the answers.

A. What

1. were three groups that broke away from the early Catholic Church?
2. bishop in Spain suffered martyrdom in 385 for faithfully teaching the Word of God?
3. two church leaders were among the first to teach against infant baptism?
4. people tried to deal with guilt by beating each other?
5. (*a*) people of the 1100s were zealous for memorizing Scriptures and for evangelizing? (*b*) was their leader's name?
6. religion spread across northern Africa during the 600s?
7. nation is known as the oldest "Christian" nation in Africa?
8. (*a*) were three important empires of western Africa? (*b*) dealings did the Muslims have with these empires?
9. is the most widely used African language?
10. apostle is thought to have visited India?
11. major contribution did the Hindus make to mathematics?
12. Muslim conqueror invaded India and destroyed Delhi in 1398?
13. were two of the main rulers in the Mogul Empire?
14. were four important inventions that the Chinese were using by about A.D. 1000?
15. (*a*) oriental people developed the largest empire ever known up to that time, and threatened to conquer western Europe? (*b*) was the name of their greatest leader? (*c*) caused them to be inferior to some other empires?
16. European traveled to China around 1300 and wrote a famous book about his visit?
17. kind of Christians lived in China around 1300?

B. What do these words mean?

18. Anabaptist
19. dissenter
20. dualism
21. sultan
22. yurt

C. How

23. have scholars learned about the history of African people that do not have written records?
24. can a nation prosper even though it has few natural resources?

D. Why

25. is it hard to know exactly what some early "heretics" believed?
26. do most historians give little attention to the large Mongol Empire?

So Far This Year

See how many answers you can give from Chapters 1–25 without looking back.

A. *Match the letters on the map to the names below. You will not use all the letters.*

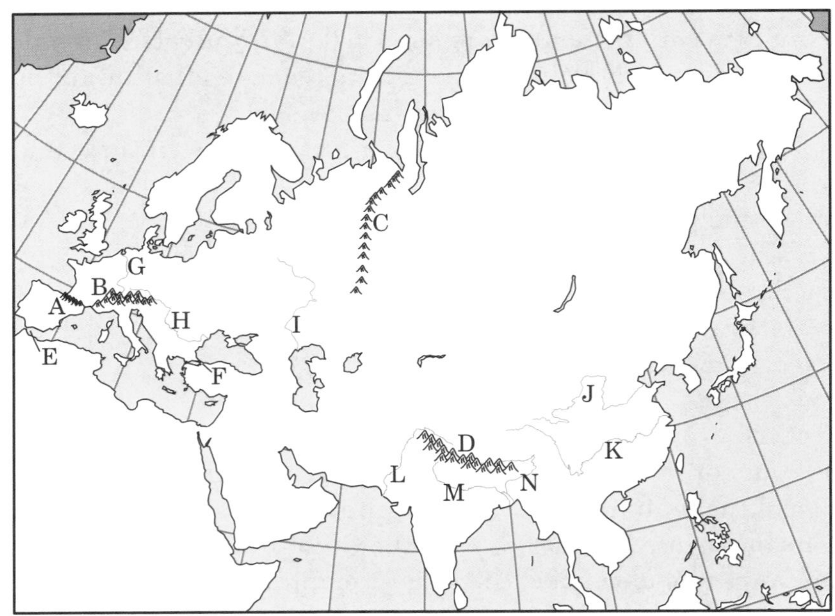

_____ 1. Alps
_____ 2. Danube River
_____ 3. Ganges River
_____ 4. Himalayas
_____ 5. Huang He River
_____ 6. Indus River
_____ 7. Pyrenees
_____ 8. Rhine River
_____ 9. Strait of Gibraltar
_____ 10. Volga River
_____ 11. Yangtze River

B. *Give the correct answers.*

12. Evidences of the Flood include all the following *except* (fossils, canyons, layers of sedimentary rock, remains of ancient civilizations).
13. Of the kings named below, which one is associated with (*a*) the first Babylonian Empire? (*b*) the Neo-Babylonian Empire?
    Sargon, Hammurabi, Ashurbanipal, Nebuchadnezzar, Xerxes
14. After the temple was destroyed, the (marketplace, synagogue, Jewish feasts) became the center of Jewish religious life.
15. Well-known products of China include all the following *except* (tea, silk, jade, rubber, soybeans).
16. The Romans helped to prepare the world for Christianity in all the following ways *except* by (building good roads, maintaining a peaceful empire, making a translation of the Hebrew Scriptures).
17. People who spoke against Catholic errors included all *except* (Priscillian, Berengarius, Peter de Bruys, Tamerlane).

18. The (Donatists, Montanists, Novatians, Waldenses) were nonresistant Christians of France during the 1100s.
19. (Egypt, Ethiopia, Kenya) is known as the oldest "Christian" nation in Africa.
20. Oriental conquerors known as (Guptas, Mongols, Nestorians) threatened all of western Europe in the 1200s but then withdrew.

C. *Choose the correct name for each clue. You will not use all the names.*

21. Roman emperor who made Christianity the state religion	Ambrose
22. Leader who translated the Bible into Latin	Augustine
23. Roman emperor who made Christianity legal	Constantine
24. Founder of Islam	Jerome
25. Leader who taught that man is too evil to choose to be saved	Muhammad
	Theodosius

The Polish astronomer Copernicus (1473–1543) was one of the first men to realize that the planets, including the earth, revolve around the sun. In his day, people thought the sun and other heavenly bodies revolved around the earth.

26 The Renaissance

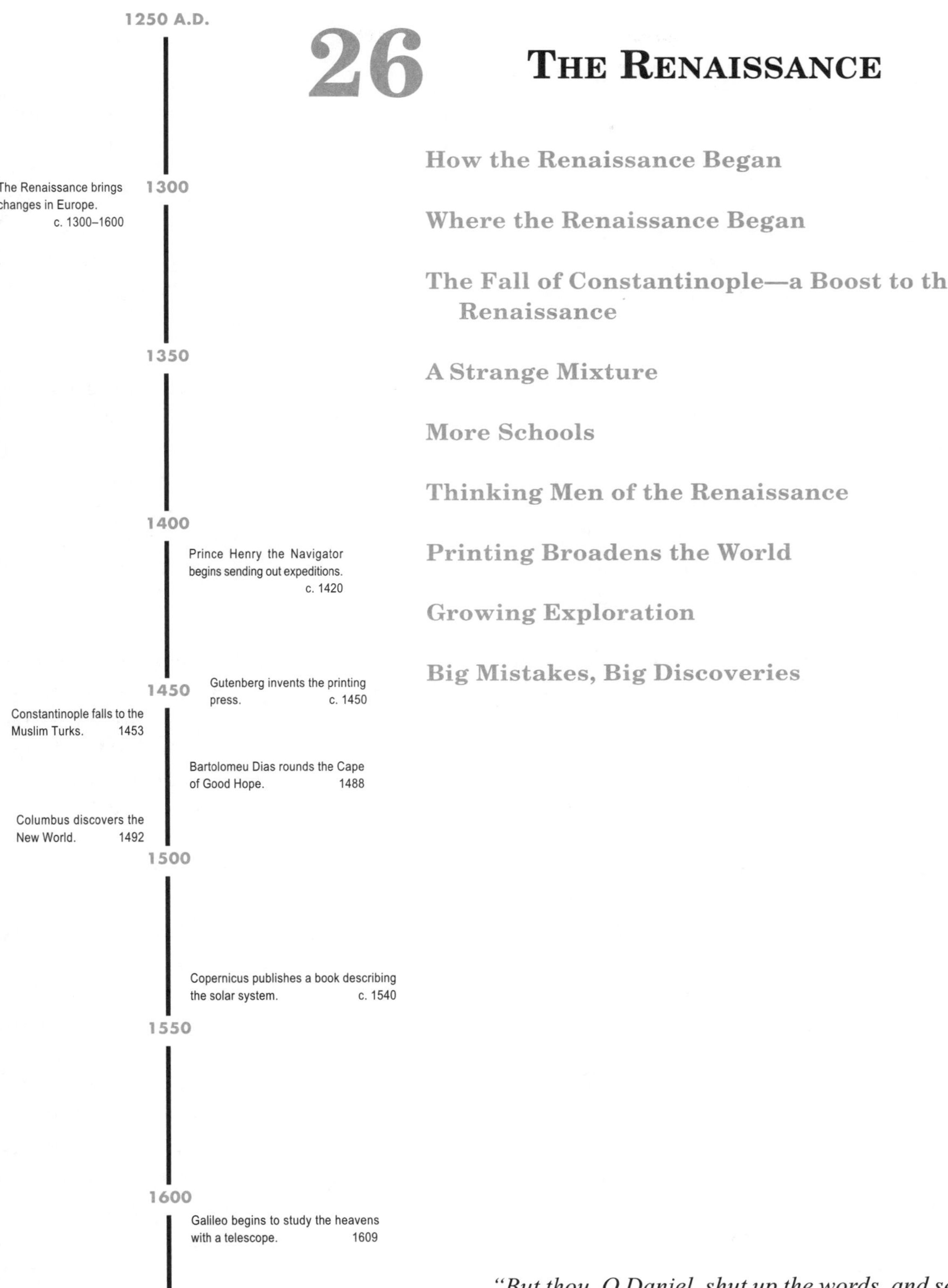

1250 A.D.
1300
The Renaissance brings changes in Europe. c. 1300–1600
1350
1400
Prince Henry the Navigator begins sending out expeditions. c. 1420
1450
Gutenberg invents the printing press. c. 1450
Constantinople falls to the Muslim Turks. 1453
Bartolomeu Dias rounds the Cape of Good Hope. 1488
Columbus discovers the New World. 1492
1500
Copernicus publishes a book describing the solar system. c. 1540
1550
1600
Galileo begins to study the heavens with a telescope. 1609
1650 A.D.

"But thou, O Daniel, shut up the words, and seal the book, even to the time of the end: many shall run to and fro, and knowledge shall be increased."
Daniel 12:4

The Renaissance

How the Renaissance Began

The word ***Renaissance*** is not as difficult as it looks. Pronounce it (REHN ih sahns), and remember that it is a French word meaning "rebirth." During the Renaissance in Europe, some long-forgotten ideas were reborn. These new-yet-old ideas changed people's way of looking at life. People began to study subjects such as art, science, and religion. What they learned and taught has affected people's thinking during all the centuries since then. Some of the changes brought by these new ideas have been good, but others have led men away from God.

The Renaissance began about 1300, during the last centuries of the Middle Ages. By the time the Renaissance ended about 1600, the Middle Ages were a hundred years past.

What started the Renaissance in Europe, where people had lived the medieval way for so many centuries? Changes had slowly taken place, even before the Renaissance. Perhaps you remember some of them.

During the Middle Ages, Muslims had pushed out from the Middle East, conquering as they went. They had a great zest for learning. When city libraries fell into their hands, they discovered many old books and manuscripts. They had these old writings translated into Arabic so that they could read them. In this way they learned and preserved much from the teachings of the ancient Greeks and Romans. They also learned from other cultures, such as that of India.

The Crusades had brought Europeans into contact with the Muslim culture in the Middle East. Europeans learned much from the Muslims. In this way they benefited from what the Muslims had learned from others. Even before the Crusades, Europeans had obtained Arabic translations of Greek writings. They, in turn, translated them into Latin. Latin was the language that educated Europeans used.

The Crusades had also encouraged trade. Towns, the centers of trade, were growing. Money was coming back into use. As a result of their new prosperity, Europeans had more money to spend on education. They had more time for thinking.

Where the Renaissance Began

The city of Florence, Italy, prospered greatly during the early years of the Renaissance. Its people did many things to make their city beautiful. They encouraged architects to design stately buildings. They spent much money on paintings and statues.

Italian architects, artists, and writers experimented with Greek ways of building, carving, painting, and writing. Long ago, Greek artists had produced statues and pictures that looked realistic. Much of that had been forgotten during the Middle Ages. Now, artists took a new interest in making the people they drew look solid rather than flat. They practiced perspective drawing.

Renaissance artists painted many religious subjects. Leonardo da Vinci (lee uh NAHR doh duh VIHN chee), an Italian artist who lived during the Renaissance, painted a well-known picture called "The Last Supper." You may have seen this picture of Jesus and His disciples. Leonardo da Vinci noticed many Bible details such as Peter motioning to John to ask Jesus who would betray Him (John 13:24). However, Leonardo da Vinci and other Renaissance artists often painted in a way that wrongly glorified human beauty and strength. They borrowed their ideas from the Greeks and Romans, who were ungodly.

This is a medieval artist's idea of the wise men following the star to Bethlehem. Only one star is shown, and it is not in the sky. The Bible does not say how many wise men came to see the young child Jesus, but many artists depict three. The Catholic Church declared there were three wise men and that these were to be honored as saints. This is shown by the use of halos in this picture.

Renaissance ideas spread from Italy across Europe. Since no telephones or trains existed in those days, this process took a long time. England did not see many changes until the late 1400s.

Study Exercises

1. What culture preserved much knowledge of the ancient Greeks and Romans for Europeans?
2. Why would extremely poor people not be well educated?
3. The Renaissance began first in which European country?
4. (*a*) What type of drawing did Renaissance artists use to make their art look more realistic? (*b*) What did they wrongly glorify?

The Fall of Constantinople—a Boost to the Renaissance

In 1453, halfway through the Renaissance, Muslim Turks conquered Constantinople. Just as scholars had fled from Rome to Constantinople a thousand years before, now scholars fled from Constantinople to Europe. They brought precious books and manuscripts with them. They also brought a knowledge of Greek, which they taught to European scholars.

This gave the scholars a useful new tool. No longer did they have to depend on writings that had been translated from Greek. They could read the ancient manuscripts themselves. They collected every manuscript they could find.

Most important, European scholars now could read and study manuscripts of the New Testament in Greek, the language used by the inspired writers. This would have far-reaching effects, as you will see in the next chapter.

A Strange Mixture

European scholars read the writings of Socrates, Plato, Aristotle, and other Greeks. The ideas of these philosophers were based on ***humanism.*** They were completely different from what European Catholics had believed for centuries.

The Greeks had emphasized that humans are the most important thing in the world. "Man is the measure of all things," they had said. But the Catholic Church in Europe taught that God is most important.

A medieval scholar in his study.

The Greeks had said that since man lives in this world, he should enjoy it. But Catholics taught that this world should be despised, and that people should spend this life getting ready for the next one.

The Greeks had said that man should ask many questions and test for himself what is right. But Catholics taught that people should simply trust their church leaders to tell them what is right.

Of course the Catholics were right that we should take more interest in God than in ourselves. We should care more about the future life than about this one. But God wants us to work heartily and to study diligently while we live on earth too. He has created many good things for us to enjoy (1 Timothy 6:17).

The Catholics were right in saying that we should trust God. And we should have the kind of church leaders we can trust. But God does not want us to blindly follow those who are "blind leaders of the blind" (Matthew 15:14). He wants us to be like the Bereans, who "received the word with all readiness of mind, and searched the scriptures daily" to see if Paul's teaching was true (Acts 17:11).

Both the Catholic ideas and the Greek philosophies had many errors. But when these two contrasting ways of thinking came together, something important happened. People began to think seriously about why they believed as they did.

Some good things came out of their thinking. Europeans became much more eager to learn about the world they lived in. They began to believe that God wanted them to learn about various subjects besides just religion. They believed more firmly that to be a human was a wonderful thing.

But much evil also came out of their thinking. Like the ancient Greeks, some Europeans began to center their thinking on man instead of on God. This caused them to care less about God's commandments. Since they no longer worried about giving account to God someday, they were not as afraid to sin. It was the same problem that Greeks and Romans had had long before.

This kind of thinking has much influence today. Many people want to avoid the old mistake of blindly accepting what others say. But often they make the opposite mistake and fail to accept teaching from good leaders. Many modern schools and textbooks teach that children should decide for themselves what is right and wrong. But God's Word teaches us to seek guidance from those who are older and wiser.

Study Exercises

5. How did the fall of Constantinople help the Renaissance?
6. What was the most important of the Greek manuscripts discovered by Europeans?

7. What did Greeks put at the center of their thinking?
8. What error is just as bad as failing to think for oneself?

More Schools

Europeans were taking a new interest in learning. Some universities were unusual, in our way of thinking. The students established them and hired the teachers! (The students were adults.) They knew that knowledge can be valuable. They certainly did not share the view that school is a place where one goes only because the government requires it.

People also took more interest in educating their children. Before this time, the Catholic Church had been teaching some of the wealthier children. Now cities and towns also began setting up schools, and more children began receiving an education. They learned in their own language and not just in Latin.

Strangely, the students and teachers of those times did not consider reading and writing as important subjects. Books were few at first. The teacher would read from a book, and the students would memorize what they heard. A student could attend a university without knowing how to read. Today, with so much written information available, knowing how to read is the foundation for most learning in school.

Around 1400, this teacher in the University of Paris leads his students in discussion. Three students stand, holding scepters that may contain things considered holy to Catholics. All the students are wearing a typical scholar's cap and gown.

Thinking Men of the Renaissance

Scientists and doctors made important discoveries during the Renaissance. In the earlier Middle Ages, people had not made many discoveries. They had simply accepted the writings of respected men of the past, such as Aristotle. But now, men were not only reading but also testing old ideas and discovering new ones.

An ancient astronomer named Ptolemy (TAHL uh mee) had correctly written that the stars are farther away than the planets. But he had also written that the earth stands still, and that the sun, moon, and planets all revolve around the earth. Thoughtful men of the Renaissance observed the heavens carefully and realized that the earth actually moves around the sun.

One such man was a Polish astronomer named Copernicus (koh PUR nuh kuhs). He wrote a book describing how the planets, including the earth, revolve around the sun. But he was afraid to publish the book until shortly before he died.

Galileo demonstrates his telescope to the government leaders of Venice, Italy.

Another such man was Galileo (gal uh LEE oh). He was an Italian born in 1564, near the end of the Renaissance. To test the old idea that heavy objects fall faster than light ones, he took two iron balls, a big one and a small one, to the top of the Leaning Tower of Pisa (PEE zuh). He dropped them both at the same time to see which would fall faster. They both hit the ground at the same moment. His experiment proved that the old idea was wrong. (Some people say this incident never really happened. But at least it illustrates Galileo's way of testing ideas to learn facts.)

Galileo explains his beliefs about science to the Catholic Church Inquisition.

Galileo built a telescope of his own to study the heavens. He found evidence that Copernicus had been right. He showed that some of the guesses other men had made about the heavens were wrong, and he wrote articles about his discoveries.

This brought Galileo into trouble with the Catholic Church leaders. They believed that Galileo's writings contradicted the Bible. They held a trial and put much pressure on him to deny what he had taught.

Galileo finally gave in, and on his knees he denied that the earth moves. An old story says that after he made his denial, he whispered, "Nevertheless, the earth does move." If he did not actually say that, he knew it was true.

Besides wooden printing blocks, the Chinese also used bronze. This bronze block was used to print money around 1287, in the time of Kublai Khan.

Printing Broadens the World

Until the mid-1400s, books were rare—and expensive. Bibles were chained to church pulpits to make sure they stayed there.

Then a German metalworker named Johann Gutenberg (yoh HAHN GOOT uhn burg) began to experiment with a fascinating idea. The Chinese had carved words onto wooden blocks or shaped them in clay. They could ink the words and press them against paper, making a neat copy. To make many copies, this method was much faster than handwriting.

But Chinese printers were handicapped because their language has thousands of different characters—one for each word. When Gutenberg invented movable type for Europe, he went one step further. He molded many pieces of metal, each with the shape of one letter in the alphabet. This task was much simpler than that of the Chinese because European alphabets have a fairly small number of letters.

Gutenberg fastened his letters together in a frame to make words and sentences. Borrowing the idea of a wine or cheese press, he made a printing press. This device had a big screw that could be turned to press the letters against a piece of paper. (Letters on a printing press must be reversed so that when they are pressed against paper, the writing looks correct.)

With his simple press, Gutenberg could print only about three hundred one-sided pages a day. But he did a very neat job. In 1456, he and his helpers produced two hundred Bibles.

Because printers could print books much faster than scribes could write them by hand, the supply of books increased greatly. Faster production reduced the cost of Bibles and other books, making them more affordable. People began reading about many subjects. By the year 1500,

Johann Gutenberg and his men look at one of their first printed sheets.

several million books had been printed. The printing press was a powerful tool to bring the ignorance of the Middle Ages to an end.

Study Exercises

9. How did medieval schools deal with the problem of having few books?
10. Why did medieval people fail to make many new discoveries?
11. Name two astronomers who contradicted some of Ptolemy's ideas.
12. Why is *press* a good name for the first printing machine?

Growing Exploration

During the 1400s, Portugal became a great exploring nation. The Portuguese explored for more reasons than just curiosity and adventure. They had riches in mind.

In those days, Europeans bought many spices and other goods from India and the islands of the Far East. Spices did more than make good food taste better. Europeans had no refrigerators, so sometimes they needed spices to improve the flavor of food that was starting to taste bad.

But direct trade with the Far East was becoming almost impossible. Ottoman Turks had seized the Middle East, and they would not let European traders go through their territory. They wanted all the Far Eastern trade for themselves. These Muslims would buy spices and other goods from the Far East. Then they would bring them to the Mediterranean and sell them to the Italians. The Italians in turn would sell goods from the East to the rest of Europe.

The Muslims and the Italians enjoyed being ***middlemen.*** Each merchant earned a profit as he passed the goods on to the next merchant. The Italian trading cities of Venice (VEHN ihs) and Genoa (JEHN oh uh) became quite wealthy.

But people in other European countries were not happy. They had to pay high prices to support all the middlemen between the Far East and themselves. If only they could go straight to lands where pepper and other spices were grown! Then they could buy directly from the producers.

Prince Henry of Portugal had an exciting idea. Since the Portuguese could not travel through the Middle East, why could they not travel to the Far East by sailing around Africa?

A modern world map quickly shows that this could be done. But the Portuguese had no maps of Africa. They had no idea how large a mass of land they would have to sail around. Furthermore, their ships were small. They did not have modern instruments by which to find their exact latitude and longitude. Sailors were frightened at the thought of sailing into unknown waters.

Prince Henry did not give up. He started a school and brought scholars and sailors to teach in it. Working together, these thinkers produced useful ideas. Because of his interest in sailing, Prince Henry became known as the Navigator. (An actual ***navigator*** directs a ship or an airplane as it travels.)

Europeans built bigger, stronger ships with a narrow prow that could slice easily through the water. They found that for steering a ship, a rudder works better than does the old-fashioned steering oar.

Europeans used the compass, which may have been a Chinese invention, to tell which direction a ship was going. But they also needed some way to tell their latitude—how far north or south the ship was. For this they used an instrument that ancient sailors had devised, called an ***astrolabe*** (AS truh layb).

If you have traveled long distances north and south, you may have noticed that the farther north you go, the higher in the sky the North Star is. An astrolabe helped sailors to measure exactly how high above the horizon a star was. Then they could find their exact latitude.

Prince Henry's sailors began traveling south along the coast of Africa. When a Portuguese sea captain had sailed as far as he dared, he would return to Portugal and report on his voyage. Shipmen ventured farther and farther until finally in 1488 Bartolomeu Dias (bahr TAHL uh myoo DEE uhs) hurried back to Portugal with

Prince Henry the Navigator lived from 1394 to 1460.

A gold-plated copper astrolabe from the 1200s.

Pepper

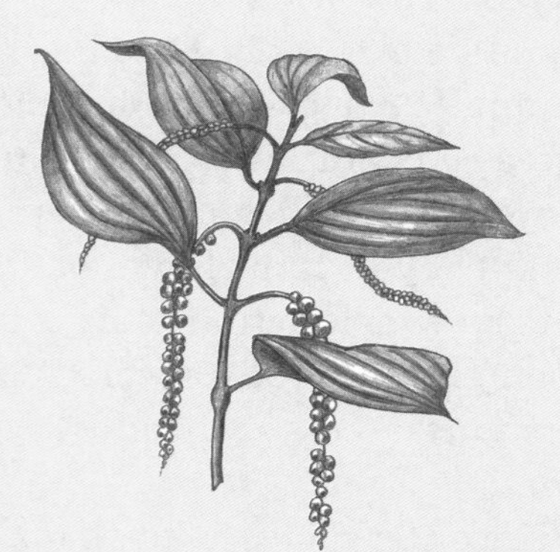

No direct reference to pepper is found in the Bible, but black pepper is discussed here as representative of the many valuable spices. The desire for spices changed the course of history. During the Middle Ages, the high price of pepper was one of the main reasons that countries tried to find a sea route to India.

Pepper was one of the earliest spices known, and the dried fruit of the pepper plant (Piper nigrum) is probably the most widely used spice in the world today. Dried pepper contains a pungent oil that is prized as a food seasoning. Black and white pepper both come from the same plant, but white pepper is the ground-up seed, which is processed differently than black pepper and is usually bleached. White pepper has a milder flavor than the black because the oil is concentrated more in the covering of the berry than in the seed.

Pepper is a woody climbing plant that can grow about 30 feet (10 m) by means of its aerial roots. It is usually supported and shaded by trees that are planted for these purposes. Some pepper plants are grown in tea or coffee plantations, so two cash crops can benefit the landowner. New pepper plants are started by cuttings, which do not produce any fruit until the second to fourth year. They yield more and more berries each year until their eighth year, and then the yield begins to decline. Two crops a year are normal for healthy pepper plants. Each plant may produce as much as 6 or 7 pounds (3 kg) of pepper in a year.

Dark-colored branches produce spikes of green flowers that develop into bright red pea-sized berries. To obtain the best flavor, the berries are gathered as they change from green to red. They are put in boiling water for about ten minutes, which causes them to turn dark brown or black in a short while; then they are spread out to dry in the sun for three or four days. When dry, they are ready to use or to sell as peppercorns. For the best taste, peppercorns should be freshly ground in a pepper mill.

The pepper plant grows wild in the East Indies, and is cultivated in India and the Philippines and other island countries of Southeast Asia.

good news. He had rounded the southern tip of Africa!

The explorations had taken a long time. By now, Prince Henry the Navigator had been dead for nearly thirty years. But Portugal started a thriving trade because of his farsightedness.

Big Mistakes, Big Discoveries

While the Portuguese were getting closer and closer to their goal, a sailor from Genoa had a startling idea. Suppose the Portuguese were taking the long way around when there might be a shorter way? Why not go straight to the Far East by sailing west?

Columbus was right that by going west from Europe, you finally arrive in the East. But he believed Asia to be bigger than it is and the earth to be smaller than it is. Asia does not wrap as far around the globe as Columbus thought. It is farther away from Europe's western shore than he realized.

To see if Columbus was right would be no small experiment. It would take somebody

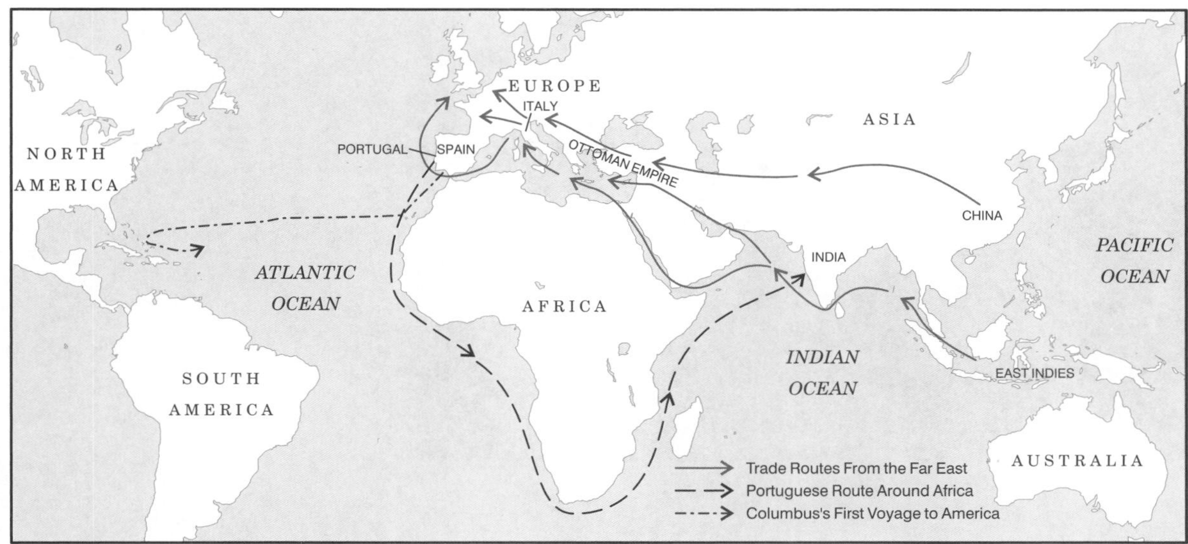

Figure 26:1. Trade and Exploration Routes

rich, such as a king, to provide the ships, men, and money for the voyage.

The king of Portugal took no interest in Columbus's idea. Columbus tried Ferdinand (FUR duh nand) and Isabella, the king and queen of Spain. They were too busy fighting the Moors, and put him off. After waiting for years, Columbus was at the point of looking elsewhere for help. But early in 1492, the last Moors in Spain surrendered to the Spaniards. Ferdinand and Isabella said they would support Columbus.

Ships such as these Portuguese vessels were known as carracks or galleons. A galleon had several masts and usually two or more decks.

Columbus and his crew sight land.

With three ships, tiny compared to today's ships, Columbus and his crew sailed out into the unknown ocean. It was a bold move in those days when ships stayed close to the coast. Columbus's men became more and more frightened as they sailed farther west.

Finally, after Columbus promised to turn back if they did not sight land soon, a lookout saw a dim shoreline ahead. Columbus believed that they had reached the Far East.

Columbus thought it strange that he could not find the Japanese cities he was looking for. Where were the silks and spices he wanted to bring back to Europe? He refused to admit that he had not reached the Far East, but later men suspected the truth. Columbus had found something that would prove more valuable for Europe than spices. He had discovered the New World.

Study Exercises

13. What is a middleman?
14. Which country in Europe made much profit from trade through the Middle East?
15. A navigator travels on a ship and directs it to its destination. Prince Henry did not do this, so why is he called "the Navigator"?
16. What misunderstandings led Columbus to mistake America for Asia?

Clinching the Chapter

Multiple Choice

A. *Write the word or phrase* least *associated with the first item.*

1. Prosperity: trade, towns, education, perspective
2. Renaissance: 1300s, 1400s, 1500s, 1600s
3. Astronomer: Ptolemy, Henry, Copernicus, Galileo
4. Middle Ages: religion, discovery, ignorance, superstition
5. Renaissance: Ptolemy, Galileo, da Vinci, Gutenberg

6. Middlemen: Muslims, Genoa, Venice, Portugal
7. Constantinople: pope, Turks, 1453, scholars
8. Greeks: Socrates, Plato, Galileo, Aristotle
9. Printing press: Gutenberg, Germany, 1456, 1492
10. Far East: spices, books, Japan, silks

B. *Write the correct words.*

1. The Renaissance took place in (Europe, Asia, Africa, North America).
2. The language of educated Europeans was (Greek, Hebrew, Latin, English).
3. Leonardo da Vinci lived in (Greece, Italy, Germany, France).
4. The ancient manuscripts from Constantinople were written in (Greek, French, German, Arabic).
5. One thing basic to learning in Renaissance schools was (reading, memorizing, writing, calculating).
6. Venice, Genoa, and Florence are all found in (Spain, Portugal, France, Italy).
7. To determine their latitude, sailors used (a compass, an astrolabe, a rudder, a navigator).
8. Ferdinand and Isabella defeated the (Turks, Moors, Greeks, Vikings).
9. Simple printing with wooden or clay type was probably done first in (Germany, China, India, northern Africa).
10. The leaders in exploring around the coast of Africa were the (Spanish, Portuguese, Muslims, English).

Matching

A. *For each clue, write the correct name from the right-hand column.*

1. Greek philosopher	Chinese
2. Ancient astronomer	Columbus
3. Tried to reach the East by sailing west	Galileo
4. Encouraged Portuguese explorers	Gutenberg
5. Painted "The Last Supper"	Leonardo da Vinci
6. Experimented with falling weights	Moors
7. Conquered Constantinople	Plato
8. Surrendered to the Spanish in 1492	Prince Henry
9. German who invented movable type	Ptolemy
10. May have invented the compass	Turks

B. *Match as in Part A.*

1. Distance north or south	arts
2. Makes paintings look realistic	humanism
3. Used by Galileo	latitude
4. Earned profits that raised prices	middleman
5. Idea borrowed from wine makers	perspective
6. Often brings prosperity	press
7. Basis of Greek thinking	religion
8. Basis of Catholic thinking	rudder
9. Blossomed in Florence	telescope
10. Better than steering oar	trade

Completion

1. The Renaissance brought change to earth.
   The term is French; it means "———."
2. A drawing might be ineffective
   Without the use of good ———.
3. The old Greek art was steeped in vanity;
   It wrongly glorified ———.
4. The students drank, as from a bottle,
   The ancient words of ———.
5. Are Bibles costly to possess?
   Not since we have the ——— ———.
6. The Muslim Turks made scholars flee
   In fourteen hundred ———.
7. A sea route to the Japanese
   Was opened by the ———.
8. Europeans paid high prices
   For Far Eastern silks and ———.

Thought Questions

1. Why is no exact year given for the beginning of the Renaissance?
2. You learned in Chapter 10 what a monopoly is. In the 1400s, what European nation had a monopoly on trade between the Far East and Europe?
3. Can you give any advantage of much memorization, such as that of the students described in this chapter?
4. Why was Copernicus afraid to publish his book?
5. People often think of a middleman as someone who helps to cause high prices. What important services do middlemen provide?

Geographical Skills

1. (*a*) Why was Constantinople well situated for trade? (*b*) What is the name of the present-day city at the same location?
2. (*a*) Bartolomeu Dias probably sailed close to the coast of Africa during much of his famous journey to the southern tip of Africa. If he had taken the shortest route, approximately how far would he have needed to sail from Lisbon, Portugal, to reach the Cape of Good Hope? (*b*) How much farther would he have needed to sail to reach Kozhikode (Calicut), India? (Round both answers to the nearest 1,000 miles.)
3. Challenge Question. Today ships sailing from Europe to Southeast Asia can sail through the Suez Canal, which connects the Mediterranean and Red seas. How many miles (kilometers) can a ship sailing from Lisbon, Portugal, to Kozhikode (Calicut), India, save by using the Suez Canal? (Round answer to the nearest 1,000 miles.)

Further Study

1. Erasmus (ih RAZ muhs) was a well-known humanist of Renaissance times. He studied the New Testament and the writings of early Christians, and he criticized many corrupt Catholic practices. Though he did much to bring the ignorance of the Middle Ages to an end, he seemed to be more motivated by human wisdom than by the fear of God, and he himself remained a Catholic. What text did Erasmus publish that greatly influenced the study of the Bible?
2. Who was the first Portuguese sea captain to sail to India and back? What adventures did he have along the way?

Martin Luther (in brown robe) defends his belief in the Bible before a group of Catholic church leaders and government leaders at the Diet of Worms.

27 The Reformation

Changes Leading to the Reformation

Men Leading Toward Reformation

Men of the Reformation

1000 A.D.

A schism permanently separates the Roman Catholic and Eastern Orthodox churches. 1054

1100

1200

1300

John Wycliffe translates the Bible into English. c. 1380

Two or three men each claim to be pope during the Great Schism. 1378–1417

1400

John Huss is charged with heresy and burned at the stake. 1415

1500

Martin Luther posts his Ninety-five Theses on a church door. 1517

Ulrich Zwingli begins reforming the church at Zurich. c. 1520

William Tyndale translates the New Testament into English. 1525

John Calvin is established at Geneva, where he promotes his teachings. 1541

John Knox leads the Protestants in victory over the Catholics. 1560

1600 A.D.

"For I am not ashamed of the gospel of Christ: for it is the power of God unto salvation to every one that believeth; to the Jew first, and also to the Greek. For therein is the righteousness of God revealed from faith to faith: as it is written, The just shall live by faith."

Romans 1:16, 17

THE REFORMATION

Changes Leading to the Reformation

What had been happening to people's thinking as the Middle Ages drew to a close? Let us review briefly.

Trade and prosperity had increased. People had more time and money for education and thinking. They depended less on the medieval church to do their thinking for them.

Printing put thousands of books and pamphlets into the hands of the people. This made them less dependent on church leaders for their information.

People were rediscovering the Bible. They read the New Testament and compared it with what they had always been taught. They began to realize that on various points, they had been wrong.

Explorers for Portugal had discovered a new source of riches by sailing around Africa. Columbus, exploring for Spain, had discovered a new world. These discoveries increased the wealth and power of nations in western Europe.

Corruption in the Catholic Church was widely known. One of the most embarrassing times was the schism of 1054, which permanently separated the Roman Catholic and Eastern Orthodox churches. Another division was the Great Schism, which lasted from 1378 to 1417. During those years, two and later three men each claimed to be pope, and they bitterly opposed each other.

All these developments weakened the control of the Catholic Church over people's minds and made them open to other ideas. People began to listen more to their kings and to church reformers, and they paid less attention to the power of the pope.

Men Leading Toward Reformation

Rarely do great movements among men happen all at once. Rather, individuals appear here and there like the first patterings of rain before a storm. They bring an idea that most people have never heard or else have forgotten. Others follow them, until thousands of people believe what only a few people stood for at first.

John Wycliffe (1330?–1384) stands trial for teaching against Catholic doctrines. He also instigated the first English translation of the Bible.

The Reformation (rehf ur MAY shuhn) was like that. First you will meet a man who lived in the 1300s and was called the "Morning Star of the Reformation."

John Wycliffe. In England, a priest and teacher named John Wycliffe (WIHK lihf) taught that people should look to God and His Word rather than to the pope as the final authority on how to live. He taught that Christ, not the pope, is the head of the church. He also stated that ***transubstantiation*** (tran suhb stan shee AY shuhn) is a false doctrine. This is the doctrine that the bread and wine of the mass are changed into the actual body and blood of Christ.

John Wycliffe thought the Word of God is so important that everyone should be able to read it for himself. He decided to translate the Bible into English, the language of the common people. He did not know Greek and Hebrew, the original languages of the Bible. But that did not stop him; he and his helpers translated from the Latin Vulgate.

John Wycliffe sent out men who tramped all over the land, carrying tracts and portions of the Scriptures. They preached wherever they went. Because they wore simple brown clothes and did not carry supplies with them, they were called "poor preachers." They became known as Lollards (LAHL urdz).

Church leaders frowned. They had learned that people who contradicted the Catholic Church would go to the Scriptures to prove that they were right. They believed the best way to keep people from breaking away from the church was to keep the Scriptures out of their hands. They denounced John Wycliffe as a heretic.

Because the king and many other Englishmen agreed with at least some of John Wycliffe's teachings, the church found it difficult to persecute him very much. He died a natural death in 1384. But later, the church ordered his bones dug up and burned. They ordered his writings and his followers to be burned too. Lollards died at the stake all over England. In later years, the Lollards that were left worked in secret.

Wycliffe's Bible did what Catholic leaders feared. It helped people to study the Bible for themselves. Men no longer depended only on the Catholic Church to tell them what to believe.

Study Exercises

1. A morning star is a bright star (actually a planet) that rises in the east just before sunrise. How was John Wycliffe like a morning star?
2. How was the Great Schism different from the schism of 1054, which is described in Chapter 19?
3. What did John Wycliffe do in addition to translating the Bible that showed his high esteem for the Word of God?
4. What was the greatest benefit that Wycliffe's Bible gave the people?

John Huss. Wycliffe's teachings spread from England to other countries. In Prague (PRAHG), which is now the capital of the Czech Republic (CHEHK), a religious school director named John Huss eagerly learned all he could. Huss preached that forgiveness of sins must come from God, not through a priest. He condemned the selling of ***indulgences.*** The Catholic Church claimed that indulgences were pardons for sin. People bought them instead of trusting in the blood of Christ.

A pope excommunicated John Huss, but John kept on with his preaching. Then in 1414 the Council of Constance was held to discuss various important matters. One thing

John Huss (1372?–1415) of Bohemia defends his teachings before the Council of Constance.

the Council discussed was the problem that John Huss was causing the Catholic Church.

The emperor promised Huss that if he came and explained his views to the Council, he would be allowed to go away safely again. John Huss thought it was only right to give his testimony. But while he was there, church officials arrested him.

John Huss protested. The emperor himself was displeased. What about the guarantee that he could come and go unmolested?

That was no problem, the church leaders said. Was not John Huss a heretic? It was perfectly all right, they said, to trick a heretic to catch him.

For eight months John Huss stayed in the dungeon. Then he was led out to die. One of the insults his persecutors placed on him was a paper hat picturing three devils. On it was written, "Here is the arch-heretic." There, tied to a post, John Huss was burned, never wavering in his convictions.

But not everybody took the news of his death calmly. In his home territory of Bohemia, John Huss had been well known and liked. People were outraged at the dishonest trick and the execution. Fighting broke out between the Catholics and the followers of John Huss. Bohemia suffered much from war damage.

In the end, Huss's followers could not win the struggle by using the sword. Besides, their fighting was a poor testimony. But John Huss's influence lived on. Some of his followers established the Moravian Church. Moravians still exist and are found today in the United States.

Men of the Reformation

Some men who led the Reformation of the 1500s were far from perfect. But God used them the way a farmer uses a plow, to break up old habits and attitudes. Some heretics, like weeds, sprang up where the reformers had worked. But good grain—Bible-obeying Christians—also prospered where the old ground had been broken.

William Tyndale. About a hundred years after John Huss, William Tyndale lived with a wealthy Englishman's family, tutoring their children. From time to time, distinguished company came to visit. High-ranking churchmen got into disputes with William Tyndale. William was shocked to realize how little of the Bible they knew—not even things like the Lord's Prayer. He told one of them, "If

William Tyndale (1492–1536) with a page of his translation of the Bible.

S. Mathew. Fo.xviij

cromes/which fall from there masters table. Then Jesus answered and sayde vnto her. O woman greate is thy fayth./ be hit to the/even as thou desyrest. And her deughter was made whole even at that same tyme.

¶ Then Jesus went awaye from thence / and cam nye vnto the see of galyle/and went vppe in to a mountayne/and sat doune there. And moche people cam vnto hym havynge with them/halt/blynde/dom/maymed/ and other many: and cast them doune at Jesus fete. And he healed them / in so moche that the people wondred / to se the dom speake / the maymed whole / and the halt to go / the blynde to se/ and glorifyed the god of israhel.

Mar. viij. ¶ Jhesus called his disciples to him and sayde: I have compassion on the people/be cause they have contynued with me nowe iij. dayes/and have nothinge to eate: and I wyll not let them departe fastinge leste they perysshe in the waye. And his disciples said vnto him: whence shuld we get so moche breed in the wyldernes as shulde suffyse so greate a multitude? and Jesus saide vnto the: howe many loves have ye? and they seyde: seve and a feawe fysshes. And he comaunded the people to syt doune on the grounde. and toke the seve loves/and the fysshes and gave thank/ and brake them/and gave to hys disciples/ and hys disciples gave the to the people. And they all ate/and were suffysed and they toke vppe of the broke meate that was lefte vij. basketsfull. They that ate were iiij. M. men/ besyde wemen and chyldren. And he sent awaye the people/and toke shyppe and cam in to the partes of magdala:

The xvi. Chapter.

Mar. viij. Luc. xi. Then cam to him the pharises with the saduces also /and dyd tepte him / desyringe that he wolde shewe the some sygne fro heven. He answered and saide vnto them: At even ye saye/we shall have fayre wedder. and that be cause the skye ys reed: and in the mornige: ye saye/to daye shalbe foule wedder/ and that because the skye is trobelous and reed. O ye ypocrytes/ye

Luc. xij.

G ii

God spares my life, ere many years I will take care that a plowboy shall know more of the Scriptures than you do." To help the common people understand the Bible, he began a new English translation of the New Testament.

Later, Tyndale had to flee from England to Germany. There he finished translating the New Testament into English in 1525. It was a better work than Wycliffe's because Tyndale translated from Hebrew and Greek, the Bible languages, rather than from Latin.

Word leaked out that an English translation of the New Testament was being printed. Authorities tried hard to stop it. They searched merchant ships sailing from Germany to England. They invaded the shop of Tyndale's printer, but the partly printed Testaments were gone by the time the authorities got there. So was Tyndale.

In spite of all the enemies could do, the Testaments slipped into England—some in bales of cloth, some in barrels of grain. Catholic officials searched homes. They seized copies of the English translation and arrested their owners. They burned the books publicly.

The bishop of London saw that he could not seize all the copies of Tyndale's hated translation. So he decided to buy all he could and then burn them. That scheme worked out poorly for the bishop. All over England, people heard that the authorities had burned God's Word. Many of them were displeased at this, and instead of opposing Tyndale's translation, they wanted a copy of their own.

Furthermore, the bishop did not realize that the merchant who delivered most of the books to be burned was Tyndale's friend. The merchant sent the money to Tyndale,

Tyndale's Bibles were packed into bales of cloth and sometimes passed right under the noses of the authorities searching for them.

who used it to print an even better translation. So it turned out that one of Tyndale's greatest helpers was the bishop of London. Soon New Testaments flooded into England faster than ever.

Tyndale was finally arrested. But during his long months in prison, he translated as much of the Old Testament as he could. His prison keeper was friendly and gave him materials he needed. In 1535, a bishop in England named Miles Coverdale produced a Bible based largely on Tyndale's work.

At last, in 1536, William Tyndale was led out to be executed publicly. He was strangled and his body was burned. It is said that just before he died, he prayed,

Miles Coverdale was the first to translate the entire Bible into English in 1535.

"Lord, open the King of England's eyes."

William Tyndale was an excellent translator. The scholars who made the King James Version of the Bible used Tyndale's translation to help them in their work.

Study Exercises

5. In what modern country is Bohemia?
6. How do we know that not all of Huss's followers understood all of Christ's teachings?
7. How did William Tyndale intend to make plowboys learn the Scriptures?
8. Give an example of something intended to hinder William Tyndale's work that turned out for the good.
9. How do we benefit from Tyndale's translation today?

Martin Luther. Martin Luther was born in 1483 in eastern Germany. As a young man, he studied to be a lawyer. But at the same time, he was asking himself hard questions. Was he really saved and on his way to heaven? He was not sure.

Caught in a violent thunderstorm one day, Luther became terrified. "Saint Anne!" he cried. "Save me, and I will become a monk." That is not a good way to pray, but Luther prayed the best way he knew. God spared his life, and Luther kept his promise.

Luther hoped he could please God by living in a monastery. But somehow, no matter how hard he worked, no matter how many sins he confessed, no matter how cold and hungry and sleepless he forced himself to be, he was afraid. God seemed far away and unforgiving.

A little light began to dawn in his mind through what he read and through advice he received. But most important, he studied the Bible. A great breakthrough came when he read in Romans, "The just shall live by faith." So, thought Luther, that is the key to finding peace with God—trusting Him to give salvation rather than trying to earn it.

Martin Luther began to preach and teach the ideas he gathered from the Bible. These ideas excited other people who were troubled by the corruption in the Catholic Church.

Luther was still a Catholic. He was not planning to start a great upheaval in the church. But then Johann Tetzel (TEHT suhl), another monk, showed up at Wittenberg. He was selling indulgences.

Indulgences had been invented by the church. Usually when people confessed their sins to a priest, he would assign them something to do to show that they were sorry. They might have to fast, recite many prayers, or take a pilgrimage. Catholics did this because they had long departed from the truth that the blood of Jesus alone makes atonement for sin. But someone had come up with a new idea. Why not simply have people pay money as their punishment? The people liked this idea because paying was much handier than praying—especially the many prayers that would have been assigned to them. The Catholic Church liked it too, because it brought in money the church could use to build cathedrals or make life pleasant for high-ranking church officials.

In return for the money they paid, people would receive a paper declaring that they were pardoned. This was called an indulgence. It was supposed to guarantee that the person who bought it would spend less time in ***purgatory*** (PUR guh tor ee) after he died.

At a county fair in Germany, people purchase indulgences from a Catholic church official. The real reason for selling indulgences sits on the table beside the seller—bags of money for the Catholic Church.

Because there were few Bibles and most people could not read the few that were available, they did not know that the apostle Paul gave the following warning: "For there are many unruly and vain talkers and deceivers, . . . who subvert whole houses, teaching things which they ought not, for filthy lucre's sake" (Titus 1:10, 11).

Purgatory was also a Catholic invention. The church taught that there is not only a heaven and a hell, but also a special place where people go who are not bad enough for hell but not good enough for heaven. There they must suffer in the fire until their sins are purged away. After that they may go to heaven. But the Bible teaches that all who are not prepared to enter heaven when they die will suffer forever in hell.

Tetzel taught that people could buy indulgences for their dead relatives as well as for themselves. Many bought indulgences, believing that this would release their loved ones from the flames of purgatory.

Martin Luther was shocked. He had learned, after much agony, that "the just shall live by faith." Here was Tetzel, preaching, in effect, that people get into heaven by buying indulgences!

Today if someone wants to make a public announcement, he might have it printed in a newspaper or put up copies in supermarkets. In Wittenberg, people attached their announcements to the church door. So Luther wrote his arguments against indulgences in ninety-five statements, called ***theses*** (THEE seez), and nailed them to the door.

Many people stopped to read what Luther had posted. Always hungry for news at a time when news traveled slowly, they soon saw that this was no ordinary announcement. Martin Luther, a respected church leader, had openly challenged the practice of selling indulgences! He had even asked why the pope, who was rich, needed money from selling indulgences to common people, who were poor.

The people went home and told others. Printers published the Ninety-five Theses and translations of them. Soon all western Europe knew about them.

Martin Luther posted his Ninety-five Theses in 1517. He did not realize that historians would later point back to 1517 as the beginning of the Reformation.

Some men argued against Luther. Luther argued back. He discovered still more reasons for disagreeing with the pope. He made even stronger statements.

The pope had not worried too much about Luther at first, but now he threatened to excommunicate him. He gave Luther sixty days to recant, but Luther

Martin Luther (1483–1546) nails his theses to the church door in Wittenberg.

Pope Leo X excommunicated Martin Luther in 1521. In defiance, Luther burned the pope's letter before a crowd.

would not give up. While a crowd watched, he lit a bonfire. Then he burned the pope's threatening letter and a number of Catholic writings. The pope excommunicated Luther a few weeks later.

Luther was called to answer for his views before the emperor of the Holy Roman Empire. The emperor, Charles V, was a staunch Catholic. Luther feared for his life, but he went to the city of Worms, Germany. There he appeared before the emperor and a group of officials, which was called a ***diet.***

An official asked if Luther would take back the statements he had written. Luther answered that he could not go against his conscience. He would change his mind only if the Scriptures proved him wrong. He ended his reply with what is probably the most famous statement of his life: "Here I stand. I cannot do otherwise. God help me! Amen!"

The emperor wanted to get rid of Luther, but he had been promised safety when he came to the diet. Besides, some of the powerful German princes sided with Luther. Charles outlawed Luther and banned his writings. He also demanded that Luther be turned over to the authorities when his promise of safety was over.

A few days after his appearance at the diet, Luther mysteriously disappeared. His friends were troubled, but his enemies rejoiced. They did not know that Luther had been secretly carried off to safety in a castle. For the next ten months, Luther quietly stayed there, translating the New Testament into German. Later he also translated the Old Testament into German. Luther's German translation of the Bible is still used by some German-speaking people today.

While staying at the castle, Martin Luther made a major mistake. He decided not to call for an end to the mass until the government leaders agreed to abolish it. This meant that he accepted the government as having authority over the church.

Luther's influence extended beyond Germany. Denmark, Norway, and Sweden became Lutheran countries. In fact, his influence went far beyond the Lutheran Church. Around the world, people still sing "A Mighty Fortress Is Our God"—a hymn written by Martin Luther.

Luther's Bible translation also gave Germany a valuable side benefit. At this time, the Germans spoke many different dialects. But after Luther's translation became widely used throughout Germany, other Germans began to use Luther's dialect as the standard written language of Germany.

It was in 1529 that the new movement received the name *Protestant.* The Catholic leaders had passed a law saying that Lutheran teaching should be suppressed. When some German nobles objected to the law by issuing a "Protestatio," the Catholics called them "Protestants."

Study Exercises

10. In what wrong way did Luther try to find peace with God?
11. What chapter and verse in Romans says that the just shall live by faith?
12. What famous act in 1517 signaled the beginning of the Reformation?
13. Besides the pope, who was Luther's most powerful Catholic enemy?
14. "A Mighty Fortress Is Our God" evidently was translated into English from what language?
15. How did Protestants receive their name?

Ulrich Zwingli. While Martin Luther was growing up in Germany, another boy of his age was living in Switzerland. Ulrich Zwingli (UHL rihk ZWING lee) never went through the great spiritual struggles that Luther did. But as he grew older, he took a great interest in spiritual things. Once he copied most of Paul's epistles by hand. He spent much time reading the New Testament, and he memorized large portions of it.

Zwingli became convinced that much of what the Catholic Church taught was wrong. He was encouraged by Luther's writings and went even further in reforming the church than Luther did. Martin Luther had tried to get rid of anything in the church that the Bible spoke against. Zwingli wanted to get rid of anything the Bible did not specifically command.

At the time, Switzerland was divided into separate governments, called cantons. Each canton was ruled by a council. As priest in the church at Zurich, Zwingli wanted permission from the Zurich council to make changes in the church. He wanted the council to support his plans for reform and to grant protection from rulers who opposed him.

This was perhaps Zwingli's biggest mistake. Scriptural churches do not wait for permission from the government to decide spiritual matters. Government leaders often oppose what good leaders know is right. Just as churches should not direct the government, the government should not direct churches. Even if the council said yes to Zwingli, he was telling them by his actions that he would obey them if they said no.

As it turned out, the council said yes to many things that Zwingli wanted. He threw out the images, closed monasteries, and

Ulrich Zwingli (1484–1531) died on the battlefield, fighting Catholics. He was not obeying what Jesus taught in Matthew 5:9, 39, 44.

dropped the rule that ordained men must not marry.

A number of German-speaking cantons became followers of Zwingli's reforms. But other cantons remained Catholic. Zwingli thought these others were dangerous. He hoped that he and Luther could work together against them. But when the two reformers talked things over, they could not agree on the meaning of Communion. They never did work together very well.

In 1531, while Zwingli was serving with the Protestant armed forces who were fighting Catholics, he was killed. A statue of Zwingli in Zurich shows him holding a Bible and a big sword.

John Calvin (1509–1564)

Study Exercises

16. In what country did Zwingli center his activities?
17. Why should a church not allow a government to direct its policies?
18. What language is spoken in much of Switzerland?

John Calvin. You may have heard of Calvinism. The founder of Calvinism was John Calvin, a Frenchman who was born near Paris in 1509. Calvin was just a boy when the Reformation began in 1517. As a young man he became a student at the university in Paris, a Catholic city, and there he became a Protestant. When local authorities came to arrest him, Calvin escaped through a back window and fled.

Protestants were being blamed for many things that were not true, such as rebelling against the government. John Calvin wanted to set the facts straight. So he wrote a book called *Institutes of the Christian Religion.* It stated clearly what many Protestants believed. The book became widely known, even though Calvin was only twenty-six when the first edition was published.

Soon afterward while traveling, John Calvin stayed overnight in Geneva (juh NEE vuh), a city in the southwest corner of Switzerland. To Calvin's surprise, a noted Reformation preacher named Farel came to see him.

Geneva had become a Protestant city. The people had thrown images out of the churches and forced monks and nuns to

William Farel (1489–1565) promoted Calvinism in Switzerland.

John Calvin preaches a farewell sermon to a large crowd in a Geneva cathedral. He expected to be banished.

leave. But Farel told Calvin that the city was in turmoil and the people lived in much sin. Would Calvin be willing to help restore peace and order?

"No," replied Calvin. He wanted to travel on to Strasbourg (STRAHS burg), in what is now France, and bury himself in his studies. Besides, he thought he was too young and inexperienced to try to help reform the city. But Farel kept insisting, and finally Calvin agreed to stay in Geneva.

His first several months in Geneva were discouraging. Many people did not like Calvin's strict ideas. In less than two years, Calvin and Farel were banished from the city.

Later Calvin was asked to return, which he did reluctantly. But he insisted on such strict discipline among the people that some tried to banish him a second time. Though Calvin was of frail health, he had an iron will. In the end, the people accepted his authority, and Geneva became a more respectable city. Calvin stayed there for the rest of his life.

Besides making rules, John Calvin also established a school. He trained preachers who spread Protestant ideas in various countries. He wrote letters to other church leaders in Europe. Because of his widespread influence, the Reformation grew in areas where he himself had never been.

In spite of some good that John Calvin

Geneva is no longer the center of Calvinism. Rather, it is a financial center and an international meeting place for many associations and for government and military leaders.

Although the European headquarters for the United Nations is located in Geneva, Switzerland is not a member of the organization. Becoming a member of the United Nations could threaten the beneficial, longstanding Swiss policy of neutrality.

did, he made some mistakes and taught some false doctrines. One of Calvin's failures was his use of the city government to enforce his rules. A government can use force to keep people from doing wrong, but it can never lead people to spiritual life. Calvin was a church leader, but he found himself doing what only a government should do.

In at least one case, Calvin became a persecutor because of his involvement in government. A Spanish doctor named Servetus (sur VEE tuhs), who had taught false ideas about the Trinity, was captured while he was in Geneva. Calvin was part of the council that found Servetus guilty of heresy and had him burned at the stake.

Calvin taught that God decreed beforehand exactly who will be saved and who will be lost, and that nothing that man does can change his destiny. Augustine, a Catholic, had taught this false doctrine around A.D. 400. The Bible teaches that God is "not willing that any should perish, but that all should come to repentance" (2 Peter 3:9). John Calvin's teachings became known as Calvinism, which some churches still promote today.

Study Exercises

19. Name a well-known book written by John Calvin.
20. Why did Geneva need a strong reformer even though it had already become Protestant?
21. (*a*) Name the country of Calvin's birth. (*b*) of his death.
22. What is probably the worst blot on Calvin's life as a religious leader?

John Knox. When Luther nailed up his Ninety-five Theses in Germany, John Knox, like John Calvin, was only a boy. He was born in Scotland.

Scotland was a poor country, ruled by a weak king and quarreling nobles. The ordained leaders of the Catholic Church lived disgraceful lives, worse than almost anywhere else. So when Protestant teachers began to arrive in Scotland, a number of people received them gladly.

When a French Catholic fleet captured a town of Scotland and took some Protestants as prisoners, Knox was among the captives. For nineteen miserable months he had to

John Knox (1514?–1572) preaches to his Scottish countrymen.

Figure 27:1. Religious Groups in Europe, About 1600

help row a French ship as a galley slave. Released at last, he went to England and later to Geneva in Switzerland.

Knox learned much from John Calvin. He wrote letters to his fellow Protestants living in Scotland, giving them advice. In time, they asked him to come back to Scotland.

John Knox was a fiery, plain-speaking preacher. When he preached, people became excited. They would destroy Catholic images and threaten to kill priests that insisted on giving the mass.

In Scotland, John Knox asked English armed forces for help against the Catholics. Fighting together, the Protestants drove out the Catholics. The Scottish parliament made Protestantism the official religion of Scotland. The form it took in Scotland is called Presbyterianism (prehz bih TIHR ee uhn izm).

Then Mary, Queen of Scots, took the

Mary Stuart, Queen of Scots (1542–1587), reigned in Scotland from age 18 until she abdicated the throne in 1567. She was later beheaded by Queen Elizabeth of England.

throne. Being a strong Catholic, she tried to restore Catholicism in Scotland. But John Knox and his followers stood against her wishes. Mary finally ***abdicated,*** and John Knox had his way. The Presbyterian Church became the established church of Scotland.

Since John Knox took his ideas from John Calvin, he repeated many of Calvin's mistakes. The church and the government worked closely together; in fact, Presbyterian preachers were paid by the government. Thus the same pattern prevailed in Scotland as in other Protestant countries.

Study Exercises

23. From whom did Knox get many of his Protestant ideas?
24. What country gave Scotland military help against Catholics?

Clinching the Chapter

Multiple Choice

A. *Write the word or phrase* least *associated with the first item.*

1. John Wycliffe: Lollards, 1500s, English, the Scriptures
2. John Huss: Prague, Moravia, Czech Republic, London
3. John Knox: Scotland, Switzerland, Geneva, Paris
4. John Calvin: Scotland, Switzerland, Geneva, Paris
5. William Tyndale: Latin, English, Hebrew, Greek
6. Johann Tetzel: Wittenberg, indulgences, Protestant, Catholic
7. Martin Luther: Wittenberg, Germany, Worms, Geneva
8. Miles Coverdale: England, bishop, Constance, Bible
9. Charles V: emperor, translator, Catholic, Worms
10. Mary: Protestant, Scotland, queen, abdication

B. *Write the correct words.*

1. During the Great Schism, the Catholic Church had too many (merchants, popes, dissenters, Bibles).
2. Rising powerful nations paid less attention to the power of (the pope, their own kings, church reformers, the translators).
3. Participants in the Catholic mass believe in (simony, indulgences, transubstantiation, abdication).
4. John Wycliffe's missionaries were called (Hussites, Protestants, Lollards, Scots).
5. In spite of the emperor's promise of safety, John Huss was burned at (Constance, Worms, Rome, Geneva).
6. At one time or another, Huss, Knox, and Tyndale were all (Bible translators, prisoners, martyrs, popes).
7. Catholics paid much to get souls out of (ignorance, purgatory, monasteries, Wittenberg).
8. The reformers in this chapter began as (Calvinists, Lutherans, Lollards, Catholics).
9. The sale of indulgences produced (forgiveness, peace, education, money).
10. John Knox was a follower of (Tyndale, Charles, Calvin, Mary).

Matching

A. *For each clue, write the correct term from the right-hand column.*

Clue	Term
1. Supposed to purify souls for heaven	canton
2. One way Catholics tried to make up for sinning	corruption
3. A regional form of a spoken language	dialect
4. Ship propelled by rowers	edict
5. King's commandment	excommunication
6. Local Swiss government	faith
7. Damaged respect for Catholic Church	galley
8. What the just live by	pilgrimage
9. False doctrine stating that bread and wine become Christ's body and blood	purgatory
	transubstantiation
10. Cutting off church membership	

B. *Match as in Part A.*

Clue	Term
1. Hymn written by Luther	"A Mighty Fortress Is Our God"
2. Produced by young John Calvin	diet
3. Nailed to church door in Wittenberg	*Institutes of the Christian Religion*
4. Assembly of officials	King James Version
5. Based on Tyndale's work	Lollards
6. Church in Scotland	Morning Star
7. Where Calvin wanted to study	Presbyterian
8. Doctor burned as heretic	Servetus
9. What Wycliffe is sometimes called	Strasbourg
10. Sent out by Wycliffe	Ninety-five Theses

Completion

1. Wycliffe and his new translation
   Pointed toward the ———.
2. Bibles from a man in jail
   Influenced Bishop ———.
3. What he could not well discuss,
   He could burn for. He was ———.
4. People thought a pardon theirs
   If they mumbled many ———.
5. Scotland's pastors and their flocks
   Found a leader in ——— ———.
6. Christians on their way to glory
   Do not burn in ———.
7. Scottish Presbyterianism
   Has its roots in ———.

Thought Questions

1. What is probably the most important year in the time span of this chapter? Why?
2. How did Luther's Bible help the German language?
3. What did various reformers do that made their influence last much longer than preaching would have?
4. How does the idea of purgatory insult Christ's work on the cross?
5. Doctrines like purgatory and transubstantiation are dangerous as well as false. How are they dangerous?

Geographical Skills

1. Trace Map H, and label it "Where the Reformers Worked."
2. Label the following cities on your map: London (England), Prague (Czech Republic), Wittenberg (Germany), Zurich (Switzerland), Geneva (Switzerland), and Edinburgh (Scotland).
3. Choose a different color for each of the following reformers, and underline the name of the city in or near where each of them worked. Make a legend for your map that matches the color you chose for each reformer's name.
   a. John Wycliffe
   b. John Huss
   c. William Tyndale
   d. Martin Luther
   e. Ulrich Zwingli
   f. John Calvin
   g. John Knox

Further Study

1. Copy this time line on graph paper, and draw lines to show the life spans of the men listed below. Each square on your graph should represent ten years. The first one is done for you.

   Wycliffe 1320?–1384
   Huss 1369?–1415
   Luther 1483–1546
   Tyndale 1492?–1536
   Charles V 1500–1558
   Calvin 1509–1564
   Knox 1515?–1572

1300	1350	1400	1450	1500	1550	1600

Wycliffe 1320?–1384

This is an artist's idea of Anabaptist leader Michael Sattler. Though condemned to a horrible death for his faith, and though some of the brethren with him recanted under the pressure, he remained unshakable to the end.

28 The Anabaptists

1520 A.D.

Zwingli agreed to let the Zurich council decide when to abolish the Catholic mass. 1523

Grebel, Manz, Blaurock, and others rebaptize each other and establish a church of true believers. 1525

Felix Manz is condemned and martyred by Protestants; Anabaptist leaders draw up the Schleitheim Confession; Michael Sattler is arrested and martyred for his faith. 1527

The Hutterites start practicing their belief of having all things in common. 1528

1530

Melchoir Hofmann teaches strange ideas about the Lord's return. 1530–1533

Anabaptist fanatics set themselves up as rulers in Münster. 1534

Menno Simons renounces the Roman Catholic Church and is rebaptized. 1536

Jacob Hutter is burned at the stake. 1536

1540

1550

1560

Menno Simons dies a natural death. 1561

1570 A.D.

"Having your conversation honest among the Gentiles: that, whereas they speak against you as evildoers, they may by your good works, which they shall behold, glorify God in the day of visitation."
1 Peter 2:12

The Anabaptists

Partial Reformers

Luther, Zwingli, Calvin, Knox! Like kings and conquerors, they were great. They set forth new ideas that shook the religious world in Europe.

But these reformers fell short in some important ways. Although they held the Bible high as no Catholic had done for many years, they failed to understand and practice some important Bible doctrines. They made serious errors.

They worked hand in hand with the government. Sometimes they waited for government permission to make reforms in the church. Sometimes they helped to direct the government. Either way, they were like David when he started out to fight Goliath, wearing Saul's armor. The armor of government does not fit on a church leader.

They did not love their enemies as Jesus commanded His followers to do (Matthew 5:44). If they had, the Protestants would not have fought the Catholics, and Zwingli would not have died on the battlefield.

The reformers did not allow religious freedom. They insisted that everyone living in their territories be a Protestant. To make sure everyone was included, they baptized babies into the Protestant Church. They persecuted non-Protestants.

Because they thought their church should include the whole population, they could not insist that their members live holy lives. To Luther's great disappointment, many of his followers decided that since "the just shall live by faith," faith alone was all they needed. Some of them thought obeying the Bible had nothing to do with getting to heaven. Often sin and crime were worse in regions that had accepted Lutheran doctrines than in regions that were still Catholic.

Luther did not know what to do about the sin in his church. He thought that if he expelled all the unholy members, hardly anyone would be left. Then what would happen to his dream of a Lutheran Germany?

In Geneva, John Calvin did better at suppressing open sin. But none of the reformers were able to establish churches that included only born-again believers, for they clung to the unscriptural idea that the whole population must belong to their churches.

Study Exercises

1. What must a Christian leader emphasize besides the fact that "the just shall live by faith"?
2. What problem arises when everyone in a country must belong to the church?

Note: *Some historical illustrations show appearances and clothing that do not seem to meet the Biblical standards of simplicity and modesty. These paintings and drawings are often artists' conceptions, sometimes drawn many years after the historical figure had died. Therefore we cannot always be sure exactly how these historical figures appeared or dressed. Nor do we know what stage in these people's lives is being portrayed.*

We should evaluate their application of separation from the world by their statements of faith and practice instead of by how artists portrayed them. In 1568, the Swiss Brethren stated: "Tailors and seamstresses shall hold to the plain and simple style and shall make nothing at all for pride's sake."

Early Anabaptist Leaders

The name *Anabaptist* means "rebaptizer." This word was first used by the enemies of the Anabaptists as a nickname—and it stuck!

This chapter cannot mention all the gifted leaders and dedicated followers who served the Lord during this time. Only a few of the more outstanding leaders will be discussed.

Conrad Grebel. Conrad Grebel grew up in Switzerland as the son of a respected town leader. But as he grew up and studied in various universities, he joined bad company. He got into fights and lived so sinfully that he ruined his health. For the rest of his life, he suffered from the sins of his youth.

Conrad's parents were unhappy with him. Although he was attending universities, for a time he did not accomplish much that was worthwhile. But an important turning point in his life came when he joined a group of men who were studying Greek writings. Their leader, Ulrich Zwingli, started them studying the Greek New Testament.

Conrad Grebel was struck by the truths he found in God's Word. Soon he became converted. His whole attitude toward life changed. Instead of quoting the Greek philosophers, he began to fill his talk and his writing with the Word of God.

Felix Manz. Another young man who took part in Zwingli's meetings was Felix Manz. He knew Hebrew, Greek, and Latin. Both Manz and Grebel agreed with Zwingli that the Bible pointed to a better Christian life than the Catholic Church was providing. Some changes would have to be made.

Not content just to talk among themselves, Grebel, Manz, and others organized meetings for Bible study with community people. Soon concerned men were leading study groups in various places in Switzerland and southern Germany.

Zwingli, Grebel, and Manz agreed that the Catholic mass should be abolished. In 1523, Zwingli argued against the mass before the Zurich council. But when the council made it plain that they were not ready to abolish the mass, Zwingli backed down. He agreed to wait until the council decided in his favor.

After Zwingli made this decision, Grebel and Manz began to separate from him. They urged Zwingli to make a complete break with the ***state church.*** They told him that he should organize a church like the one in the Book of Acts. The apostles had not tried to make their church include everyone in the country; they baptized only those who were saved.

George Blaurock. A tall, black-haired priest named George Blaurock came to Zurich about this time, asking questions. He was looking for reformers who truly followed the Bible. After talking to Zwingli, he kept looking and finally met Conrad Grebel and his friends. They satisfied his earnest heart, and he joined them.

In January 1525, Conrad Grebel and other leaders had a public debate with Ulrich Zwingli about infant baptism. Since Zwingli and the city council controlled the official decision, the debate could have only one outcome. The city council knew well enough that they had to baptize babies if they wanted a state church. The day after the debate, the council ordered that any parents who had not baptized their babies should do so immediately.

Grebel, Manz, Blaurock, and others came to the sad realization that they had no hope of reaching an agreement with Zwingli and the council. Those who wanted to follow the Bible regardless of the cost met a few nights later on January 21, 1525. After fervent prayer, George Blaurock asked Conrad Grebel to baptize him. Then Blaurock baptized the others. That night was the birthday of the group

The Rudi Thomann house at Zollikon, a village near Zurich, is where the first Anabaptist church was formed on January 25, 1525. But soon most of the Zollikon brethren gave up the faith under pressure from the Zurich authorities.

This is an artist's idea of Anabaptist leader George Blaurock (1492?–1529). In the background lie the rugged mountains of eastern Switzerland, where Blaurock grew up. He faithfully evangelized this area until he was banished to Austria, where he was captured and burned.

Felix Manz was drowned for his faith in the Limmat River at this site in Zurich.

that became known as the Swiss Brethren.

Within a few weeks, the leaders of this new movement were seized and put in jail. Although they were soon released, this was only the first of many prison experiences for the Swiss Brethren.

Within another year and a half, Conrad Grebel died of the plague. He was not yet thirty years old and had been a leader among the Swiss Brethren for a very short time. Much of that time he had spent in prison. Yet by God's grace, he had helped to light a fire that has never gone out.

The following January, in 1527, Felix Manz was taken from prison to the Limmat River. He resisted the pleadings of Zwingli's reformed preachers, listening instead to his friends as they shouted encouragement. Then his enemies bound him and cast him into the river. Felix Manz was the first of the Swiss Brethren to be killed by Protestants. The same day, George Blaurock was severely beaten and expelled from Zurich.

Anabaptists are sometimes classed as Protestants, but plainly there was a big difference between the two groups.

Study Exercises

3. What reformer did Felix Manz and Conrad Grebel follow at first?
4. On what issue did Zwingli first go wrong?
5. Why did the Zurich council insist that babies must be baptized?
6. What year was to the Anabaptist movement as 1517 was to the Reformation?
7. (*a*) In what year did Conrad Grebel die? (*b*) Felix Manz?

Michael Sattler and the Schleitheim Confession

Michael Sattler became the most outstanding leader of the Swiss Brethren after the death of Felix Manz. However, he outlived Manz by only a few months.

Like Manz and Blaurock, Michael Sattler was born in the 1490s. He joined a Catholic monastery in his youth, but he was soon disappointed to see the sinful lives of his fellow monks. After reading the epistles of Paul, he became even more dissatisfied and left the monastery.

Sattler lived in Austria, which was not a safe place for those who questioned Catholic doctrines. So he fled to Switzerland. There he met Anabaptists who helped him become one of the Swiss Brethren.

Michael Sattler served well as a hardworking, enthusiastic preacher. But in 1527, Sattler and his wife were arrested in Germany. He was placed on trial with a number of other Anabaptists.

The court confronted Sattler and his group with a list of accusations. Some charges were true, such as the fact that they believed in baptizing believers and not babies. Other charges were false.

Michael Sattler calmly answered the accusations. His calmness only seemed to make his accusers more angry. One of them said that if there were no hangman to kill Sattler, he would do it himself.

Sattler was sentenced to death by torture and burning. Two days later, after horrible suffering, he was bound to a ladder and pushed into the fire. But when the ropes burned off his wrists, he raised the forefingers of both his hands. This was a promised signal to show the brethren that a martyr's death was bearable and that he was faithful to the end.

One of Michael Sattler's most important contributions was to preside over a special meeting at Schleitheim (SHLYT hym) in northern Switzerland. The Anabaptist church leaders who met at this meeting in February, 1527, drew up the ***Schleitheim Confession.*** It was not like the Apostles' Creed, which briefly states the most basic Christian doctrines. Rather, it clarified the Anabaptists' position on a number of doctrines that people were raising questions about. Here are some of the things it said.

- Only those who believe and obey Jesus Christ shall be baptized.
- Persons who practice sin shall not be part of the church.
- Christians shall be separated from the world.
- Christians shall not fight their enemies. (This is the doctrine of nonresistance.)
- Congregations shall support their

An ancient German copy of the Schleitheim Confession of 1527.

ministers with goods and money when necessary.

- Christians shall not swear oaths.

The Schleitheim Confession was printed and was passed around wherever there were Anabaptists. It helped them to be unified in their doctrines.

Study Exercises

8. What did Michael Sattler read that persuaded him to leave the Catholic Church?
9. What was Sattler before he became an Anabaptist?
10. Name three countries in which Michael Sattler lived.
11. What term refers to the doctrine that Christians must not fight?
12. Why was the Schleitheim Confession important to Anabaptists?

Anabaptist Fanatics

In any great movement, even a good one, some false doctrines or wrong motives will appear. Not every Anabaptist was a good man just because he taught that believers instead of babies should be baptized. Some were sinners of the worst sort.

Melchior Hofmann lived from 1495? to 1543.

Melchior Hofmann (MEHL kee or HAHF muhn) was one man who taught believers' baptism but was deceived about some other doctrines. He had strange ideas about the Lord's return. He believed that Christ would return to Strasbourg and make it His New Jerusalem. He also believed a prophecy that after he had spent six months in prison, he would be released and a wonderful time of peace without persecution would come to the world.

Melchior Hofmann cheerfully turned himself in to the authorities, who placed him in prison. He thought he would be in prison only half a year. But as the time stretched out longer and longer, Hofmann realized that the prophecy had been wrong. He died in prison about ten years later, sorry for his earlier views.

Jan van Leyden was also known as "King David." He and his friend "Enoch" believed that God was soon going to set up the New Jerusalem on earth. They tried to set up this kingdom themselves. The confusion that resulted is an example of what happens when professing Christians do not understand that the Old Testament way of fighting is not for the New Testament Christian. John 18:36 says: "Jesus answered, My kingdom is not of this world: if my kingdom were of this world, then would my servants fight . . . but now is my kingdom not from hence."

While Hofmann was in prison, two men decided that the New Jerusalem would not be in Strasbourg, but at Münster (MUHN stur), Germany. They set themselves up as rulers in Münster. One called himself Enoch; the other called himself King David. Actually, their names were both Jan.

When enemies besieged the city, one of the Jans marched out and fought them until he was killed. The other ruled inside the city like a madman, living in great sin and executing anyone who stood in his way. While supplies in the city ran short and people were starving, he lived in luxury and plenty. The besiegers finally broke into the city, killed many people on the spot, and tortured the leaders.

Some historians seem to think all Anabaptists were like those at Münster. That of course is not true. Most Anabaptists were quiet, respectable people, displeased and shocked at the report from Münster. Nevertheless, the faithful Anabaptists suffered because of the bad reputation the Münster fanatics gave to Anabaptism.

The Spread of Anabaptism

Because of persecution, many people who sympathized with the Biblical Anabaptists made a serious mistake. They decided God wanted them to wait for persecution to die down before they obeyed the Bible. They continued to baptize their babies even though they did not believe in it, thinking that sometime the situation would change so that they would be free to do otherwise. Historians call these people the ***Halfway-Anabaptists.***

But the true, God-fearing Anabaptists waited for nothing. Because they obeyed God in spite of opposition, the church grew.

This cave in Switzerland is known as the cave of the Anabaptists. It was a secret Anabaptist meeting site in the early years of persecution.

They proved the old statement true again: "The blood of the martyrs is the seed of the church."

The faithful Anabaptists were savagely persecuted—more severely, some historians say, than Christians were persecuted by the ancient Romans. They were jailed, branded, burned, tortured, beheaded, and drowned. Sometimes the children of Anabaptists were not allowed to inherit their parents' property. Many Anabaptists had little or no property anyway, for they were driven from place to place.

Everywhere they went, they shared their faith as neighbor to neighbor. They simply told how the Lord Jesus had saved them from their old sinful lives. They especially liked to share the Gospel with common people like themselves.

Their neighbors had no trouble believing them, for the Anabaptists were not slaves to sin as many other people were. Even the enemies of the Anabaptists admitted that they avoided evil, but they said that just showed what great hypocrites the Anabaptists were.

However, the truth cannot be squelched. People could easily see that "he that *doeth* righteousness *is* righteous" (1 John 3:7). The Anabaptists' neighbors wanted the same kind of faith—the kind worth dying for. Although thousands of Anabaptists were killed for their faith, even more thousands of people were baptized. One ruler said, "What shall I do? The more I execute, the more they increase."

Study Exercises

13. How can you tell that Melchior Hofmann actually believed the false prophecy that he would be released from prison in half a year?
14. Name two false prophecies given by Anabaptist fanatics that contradicted each other.
15. What mistake did the Halfway-Anabaptists make?
16. What class of people were most Anabaptists?
17. How did the enemies of the Anabaptists explain away the fact that they lived upright lives?

The Mennonites

While the Swiss Brethren movement was growing, Menno Simons was serving as a Roman Catholic priest in the Netherlands. One day a nagging doubt came to him. Suppose the bread and the wine he handled in the mass were not really the body and blood of Christ?

The thought kept bothering Menno even after he had confessed his doubts to another priest. In desperation, Menno decided to do what he had never done before—study the Bible. As he searched it, he discovered that the Catholic Church was wrong.

Menno Simons (1496–1561)

But at first he did nothing about it. He did not intend to quit his life of drinking, gambling, and reveling with his friends.

Some time later, he heard that a man named Sicke Snyder had been beheaded for being baptized a second time. That sounded strange to Menno. This time he knew what to do. He examined the Bible and found that the church he belonged to was also wrong in its teaching on infant baptism.

Still he clung to his old life. Although he began to include Scripture verses in his sermons, he continued living in sin. But Menno felt very guilty. He felt even worse when he heard about a group of Anabaptists who had tried to fight their enemies and were killed. One of them was Menno's brother.

Menno saw where these Anabaptists were wrong. Yet he admired their willingness to stand up for what they did know. Although he knew better, he did not do better!

Menno Simons ordained Leenaert Bouwens (1515–1582), who became a strong Dutch Anabaptist leader. Here he preaches at a secret meeting in a house.

Finally Menno gave up. He knelt before God in sincere repentance from his old life. He began preaching as he never had before—still in the Catholic pulpit. But he realized more and more that if someone believed as he did, he should break his ties with the Catholics. He did, and he found some Biblical Anabaptists. They baptized him in 1536, when he was about forty years old.

Later, Menno was ordained as a minister. He did much writing; but even more important, he had a godly character and was a strong leader. He helped the Anabaptists to grow in numbers and in unity. People began to call the main groups of Anabaptists ***Mennonites.***

The authorities tried hard to catch Menno. They knew that as long as he was alive, they could not get rid of the Mennonites. Emperor Charles V even offered a reward of one hundred gold guilders for catching him. Menno and his family had to flee here and there, even though his wife Gertrude was often sick. Menno wrote that they had to be on guard when a dog barked for fear the arresting officers had come.

Yet in spite of all his enemies, Menno Simons was never caught. God protected him and allowed him to lead the church for nearly twenty-five years. He died a natural death in 1561.

Study Exercises

18. Menno was a native of what country?
19. What always settled Menno Simons's doubts about right and wrong?
20. Why did Menno not immediately leave the Catholic Church?
21. Why did the largest group of Anabaptists become known as Mennonites rather than as Swiss Brethren?

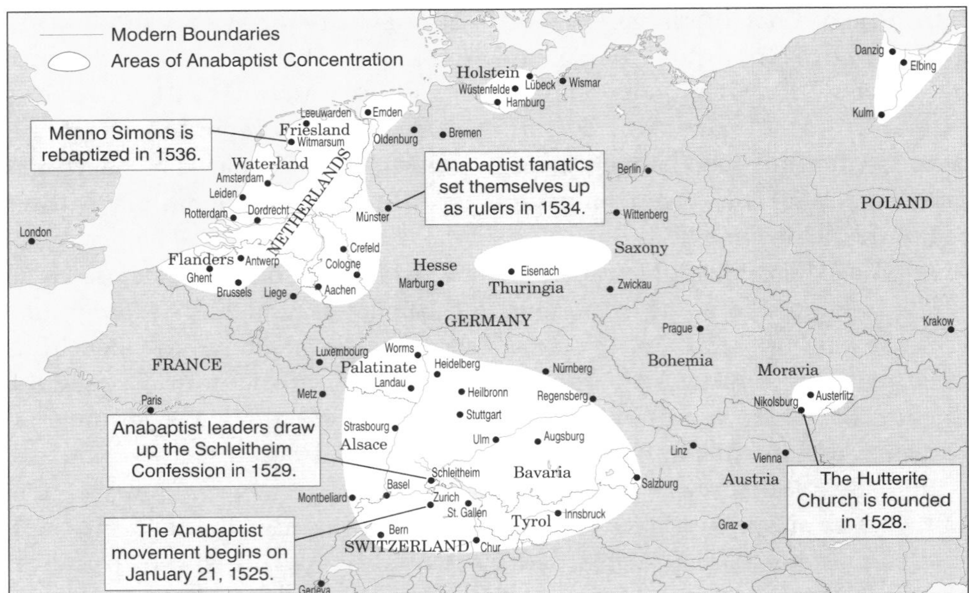

Figure 28:1. Anabaptists in Europe

The Hutterites

Many Anabaptists lived in Moravia (muh RAY vee uh), an area in what is now eastern Czech Republic. Not all of them believed alike, however. In Nikolsburg, quite a few Anabaptists believed that it was right to fight their enemies. Others disagreed. Besides, they believed that the Bible teaches Christians to share alike with other Christians in their group.

Old Hutterite buildings have been well preserved in present-day Slovakia. Notice the thatch roofs. This was a potter's home in this typical Moravian Hutterite village.

In 1528, these dissenters were finally told to leave the city. Camped in a deserted village nearby, they agreed to start practicing their belief of having all things in common. Someone spread a cloak on the ground, and on it everyone willingly placed what few possessions he had. The leaders then shared with those who had nothing.

Living so closely like a big family sometimes caused problems and disagreements. But a strong leader named Jacob Hutter joined the group. He helped these Anabaptists to work together. Hutter's ministry among the group did not last long; in less than three years he was arrested, tortured, and burned at the stake. But because of his strong leadership, the Anabaptists that he had led were named after him—***Hutterites.***

The Hutterites were very mission-minded. But to be a missionary in those days was extremely dangerous. It has been estimated that 80 percent of the Hutterite missionaries lost their lives through persecution.

The rulers disagreed on what to do with the Anabaptists in Moravia. One ruler was King Ferdinand of Austria, who later replaced his brother Charles V as emperor of the Holy Roman Empire. A strong Catholic, he urged the nobles of Moravia to get rid of the Anabaptists. But the nobles argued that to kill or chase out the Hutterites would hurt Moravia. These people, they said, were expert craftsmen, whether they made barrels, watches, shoes, or wagons. Furthermore, the Hutterites were honest.

For a time the Moravian rulers had their way, and the Hutterites lived in peace. They established many colonies, which they called ***Bruderhofs*** (BROO dehr hohfs). Since they believed that educating children was necessary to keep their way of life alive, they established schools for their children. They made sure the children were thoroughly taught in the Christian faith.

But later the rulers who called for persecution had their way. The Hutterites were forced to flee to Hungary. Then they were forced back to Moravia, and before long they had to flee again. As they traveled, robbers sometimes attacked them and stripped them of what little they had. Some Hutterites had to live in forests and caves.

Despite bitter persecution, the Hutterites were never completely stamped out. Hutterite *Bruderhofs* can be found today in the United States and Canada, most of them on the central plains. As their forefathers did, they have all their goods in common.

Study Exercises

22. In what modern country was the region of Moravia?
23. How are Hutterites different from most other Anabaptists?
24. Why did some Moravian nobles not want to persecute the Hutterites?
25. What did the Hutterites do to prepare their children for life?

Clinching the Chapter

Multiple Choice

A. *Write the word or phrase* least *associated with the first item.*

1. Conrad Grebel: Greek, Switzerland, education, Lutheran
2. Anabaptist: "rebaptizer," Zwingli, Manz, Hutter
3. Zurich: Manz, Blaurock, Simons, Zwingli
4. Zurich council: mass, infant baptism, government, fanatics
5. First Swiss Brethren leaders: Manz, Simons, Grebel, Blaurock
6. Michael Sattler: monk, martyr, priest, minister
7. Schleitheim: baptism, nonresistance, obedience, colonies
8. Fanatics: Münster, Grebel, two Jans, Hofmann
9. Hutterites: huts, *Bruderhofs,* crafts, missions
10. Menno Simons: Netherlands, Catholic, Protestant, Anabaptist

B. *Write the correct words.*

1. The Protestant reformers practiced (nonresistance, religious freedom, infant baptism, love for enemies).
2. One of the Protestant enemies of the Anabaptists was (Charles, Ferdinand, Hofmann, Zwingli).
3. The first Swiss Brethren baptized each other at a prayer meeting in (1517, 1525, 1527, 1536).
4. Who was a later Anabaptist leader? (Conrad Grebel, Felix Manz, George Blaurock, Menno Simons)
5. Zwingli backed down on his view of the mass because of the (Anabaptists, Zurich council, Hutterites, Münsterites).
6. In 1528, the founders of the Hutterites began having their goods in common after leaving (Münster, Zurich, Nikolsburg, Strasbourg).
7. Some fanatics were called Anabaptists because they (baptized adults, were persecuted, shared their goods, prophesied).
8. To what class did most Anabaptists belong? (upper class, common people, merchants, rulers)
9. Who died a natural death? (Felix Manz, Menno Simons, Michael Sattler, Jacob Hutter)
10. No religious group is named after (Sattler, Simons, Luther, Hutter).

Matching

A. *For each clue, write the correct name from the right-hand column.*

1. First Anabaptist martyr at Protestant hands	Blaurock
2. Died before age thirty	Ferdinand
3. First one baptized at meeting on January 21	Grebel
4. Former monk from Austria	Hofmann
5. Spent his last ten years in prison	Hutter
6. Fanatic at Münster	Jan
7. Made Menno Simons think seriously	Manz
8. King of Austria	Sattler
9. Greatest Mennonite leader	Sicke Snyder
10. Anabaptist leader in Moravia	Simons

B. *Match as in Part A.*

1. Home of Menno Simons	Germany
2. Land of Zwingli and early Anabaptists	Limmat
3. Anabaptist confession drawn up	Moravia
4. Hofmann's "New Jerusalem"	Münster
5. City of worst "Anabaptist" fanatics	Netherlands
6. City of first Anabaptist-Protestant conflict	Nikolsburg
7. Eastern area of Czech Republic	Schleitheim
8. River where Felix Manz was drowned	Strasbourg
9. First city in Hutterite story	Switzerland
10. Land of Sattler's death	Zurich

Completion

1. The beliefs of the brethren found written expression
   Under Sattler's advice in the ——— ———.
2. All relations with Zwinglians came to a schism
   When the council had reaffirmed ——— ———.
3. Though the Jan called "King David" looked very dramatic,
   He was only a misguided Münster ———.
4. Anabaptists were frequently drowned in a lake;
   They were jailed, whipped, beheaded, and ——— ——— ——— ———
   .
5. While not yet a seeker, and still an outsider,
   Menno heard of the burning of faithful ——— ———.
6. Menno's fatherly love and his spiritual sight
   Led the way for the church that is called ———.
7. They were chased from their homes and deprived of their rights,
   But they all shared alike and were called ———.
8. Though the Hutterites seemed to the world to be fools,
   They were known for their missions and well-ordered ———.
9. Even though they were urged to take matters in hand,
   Moravian nobles resisted King ———.

Thought Questions

1. Could Menno Simons be called a martyr?
2. Is faith without works really faith? Explain. (See James 2:14–26.)
3. Some historians seem to consider the whole Anabaptist movement to be something like what happened at Münster. What is a likely reason for this?
4. It has been said that many great truths begin as heresies. How would this chapter illustrate that idea?
5. If Menno Simons looked back over his life on his dying day, what do you think was his greatest regret?

Geographical Skills

1. The Hutterites lived near the Danube River. The source of the Danube is in the (*a*) ——— Forest region of Germany. The mouth of the river is at the (*b*) ——— Sea. (*c*) What present-day countries does the Danube River flow through or border?
2. Felix Manz was drowned in the Limmat River, which is a tributary of the Rhine River. The two sources of the Rhine are both in the (*a*) ——— (mountains) of Switzerland. The mouth of the Rhine is at the (*b*) ——— Sea. (*c*) What present-day countries does the Rhine River flow through or border?
3. If you had been a Swiss Anabaptist immigrant to the New World, you probably would have traveled by boat from Basel, Switzerland, to Rotterdam, Netherlands. About how long would such a river journey be? (Hint: Using a string to follow the course of rivers makes measuring easier.)

Further Study

1. Page 452 of *Martyrs Mirror* tells about Anabaptists from Austria who were sentenced to be galley slaves. What did they do as they passed from city to city on their way to the sea? What finally happened to them?
2. What Bible verse did Menno Simons place at the beginning of all his writings?

Be Sure You Know

Can you answer all these questions? If not, study Chapters 26–28 to find the answers.

A. What

1. Italian artist produced "The Last Supper" and other famous works of art?
2. Polish astronomer wrote a book saying that the planets move around the sun?
3. Italian built a telescope and found evidence that many old ideas about the heavens were wrong?
4. man in Germany built the first printing press that used movable type?
5. Italian sailor thought he could reach the Far East by sailing west across the Atlantic Ocean?
6. was the Great Schism?
7. man of the 1300s translated the Bible from Latin into English?
8. teacher of Prague was burned for heresy even though the emperor had promised that he would not be harmed?
9. man of the 1500s translated the Bible from Hebrew and Greek into English?
10. German priest wrote ninety-five statements opposing the sale of indulgences and later translated the Bible into German?
11. Swiss reformer allowed the Zurich council to make the final decision about any changes?
12. French reformer helped to govern Geneva and later had Servetus burned for heresy?
13. Scottish reformer used military force to drive out the Catholics?
14. three men started the group known as the Swiss Brethren?
15. were some of the doctrines upheld by the Schleitheim Confession?
16. German city was the place where a group of fanatics brought great disgrace on the Anabaptist name?

B. What do these words mean?

17. astrolabe
18. diet
19. Halfway-Anabaptist
20. humanism
21. Hutterite
22. indulgence
23. Mennonite
24. navigator
25. purgatory
26. Renaissance
27. Schleitheim Confession
28. state church
29. theses
30. transubstantiation

C. How

31. was the fall of Constantinople a boost to the Renaissance?
32. was humanism an evil influence, even though it encouraged people to think for themselves?

D. Why

33. were the Protestants called by that name?
34. were the Protestant reformers unable to establish churches that included only born-again believers?
35. were the Anabaptists called by that name?

God allowed the destruction of the Spanish Armada in 1588, which broke Spain's power on the seas and in exploration. Here, the center ship is an English ship battling with a large Spanish galleon on either side. The Spanish ships were too large to be maneuvered quickly, and could not keep up with the swift tactics of the smaller English vessels.

29

The Rise of Modern Nations

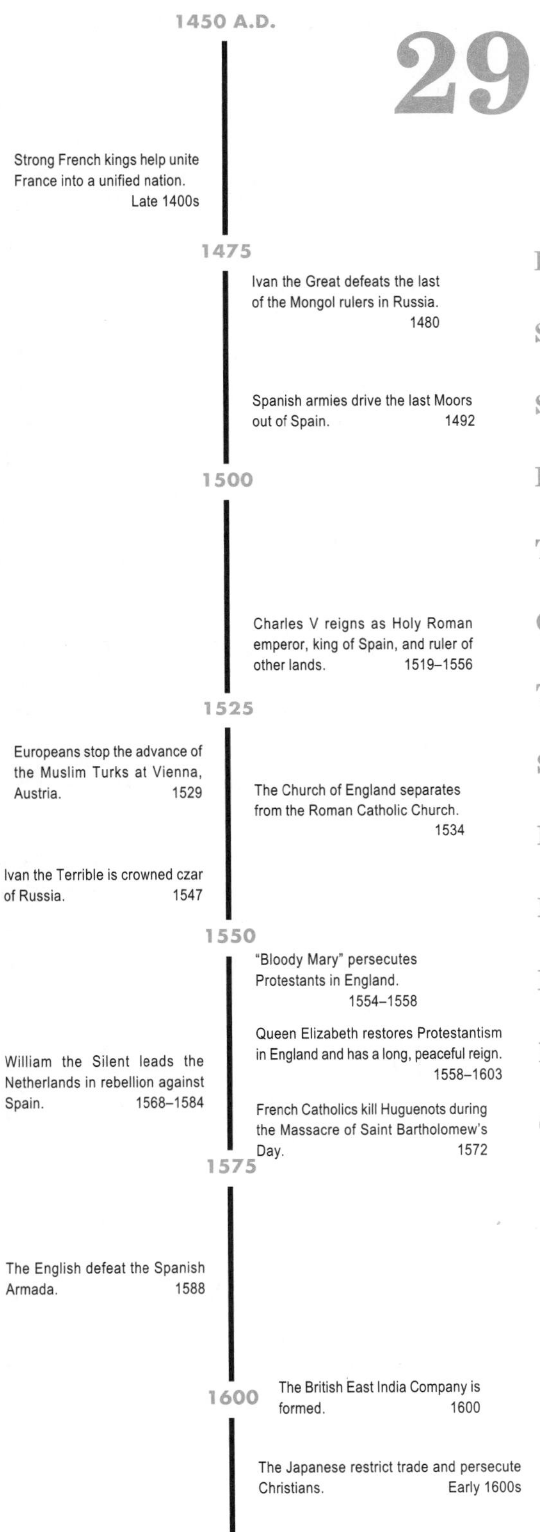

1450 A.D.
Strong French kings help unite France into a unified nation. Late 1400s
1475
Ivan the Great defeats the last of the Mongol rulers in Russia. 1480
Spanish armies drive the last Moors out of Spain. 1492
1500
Charles V reigns as Holy Roman emperor, king of Spain, and ruler of other lands. 1519–1556
1525
Europeans stop the advance of the Muslim Turks at Vienna, Austria. 1529
The Church of England separates from the Roman Catholic Church. 1534
Ivan the Terrible is crowned czar of Russia. 1547
1550
"Bloody Mary" persecutes Protestants in England. 1554–1558
Queen Elizabeth restores Protestantism in England and has a long, peaceful reign. 1558–1603
William the Silent leads the Netherlands in rebellion against Spain. 1568–1584
French Catholics kill Huguenots during the Massacre of Saint Bartholomew's Day. 1572
1575
The English defeat the Spanish Armada. 1588
1600
The British East India Company is formed. 1600
The Japanese restrict trade and persecute Christians. Early 1600s
1625 A.D.

"Let every soul be subject unto the higher powers. For there is no power but of God: the powers that be are ordained of God." *Romans 13:1*

The Rise of Modern Nations

One reason we study history is to find out how the world became the way it is. North Americans study the countries of western Europe with special attention because European influence spread over the parts of the world that North Americans know best. What happened in Europe a few hundred years ago helps us to understand why people in North America think and act as they do.

As you study various cruel and crafty characters in this chapter, remember that God was working behind the scenes. God is not always pleased with what humans do. Sometimes He allows the world to suffer because of mistakes people make. But He always has certain purposes of His own, and He works through both good and bad people to bring them about.

Previewing the 1500s

Two important systems controlled Europe during the Middle Ages. One was the feudal system, and the other was the Catholic Church. As the Middle Ages came to an end, the feudal system died out. There were several reasons for this.

You recall that money had begun to flow again in Europe. Workers who had depended on a noble for food and shelter found that now they could earn money and buy their own supplies. They could live in towns instead of on a manor. Instead of being under the authority of a local noble, they could be responsible only to the king. As more and more people transferred their loyalty to the king of their country, kings gained power.

Inventions had also weakened the feudal system—especially the invention of gunpowder. A bullet could pierce a knight's armor, and cannonballs could shatter castle walls. The new weapons that used gunpowder were expensive. Because kings could buy them more easily than feudal lords, the new weapons helped the kings build stronger armies.

The Catholic Church was also losing ground. Some of the reasons for this are listed at the beginning of Chapter 27. Another reason was that popes of this time were interested more in worldly matters and riches than in guiding the church. To people of nations such as France and England, it seemed that the money they gave to the church just went to another "king"—the foreign pope in faraway Italy.

As the 1500s progressed, people took more and more pride in belonging to their own nation. This feeling is called ***nationalism.*** They took less satisfaction in belonging to "Christendom"—Europe under Catholic control. Some lands developed into nations more quickly than other lands did.

Some countries broke completely with Rome and became Protestant countries. But even loyal Catholic rulers wanted more authority of their own and less control by the pope.

Spain Unites

Ferdinand and Isabella, the king and queen who financed Columbus's voyage, began ruling in the 1400s. As a young man, Ferdinand was prince of one part of Spain; Isabella was princess of another. When they married, they combined their powers and made a strong country.

During their reign, Ferdinand and Isabella's army drove the Moors from their last stronghold in Spain. Later another section of land was added, making what is known as modern Spain. Spain was the first great power in modern Europe.

Ferdinand and Isabella were famous, intelligent, and in some ways wise. But

Young King Ferdinand and Queen Isabella give audience to a group of suffering Jews. A Catholic church leader on the right tries to persuade the king and queen to deal harshly with them.

Isabella was a fanatical Catholic. She considered it her duty to convert or drive out all Muslims, Jews, and those she considered heretics. Under Ferdinand and Isabella, the ***Spanish Inquisition*** was developed. People still shudder to hear of the tortures that suspected persons went through.

Persecuting the people was hard on the country. Many talented people were killed or driven away. Spain would have prospered more if the government had been more tolerant.

Portugal also persecuted non-Catholics, including many Jews. The country suffered when they fled. Portugal did not long remain a powerful country.

Study Exercises

1. Why do North Americans study the history of European nations more than the history of Asia or Africa?
2. Give two reasons why the feudal system came to an end in Europe.
3. What is nationalism?
4. What were the political results of Ferdinand and Isabella's marriage?
5. How did persecution of non-Catholics turn out to be bad for Spain and Portugal?

Switzerland Takes a Stand

Switzerland began as a tiny country in the Alps. The Swiss were a freedom-loving people, and they fought off neighbors who wanted to add Swiss land to their own. Switzerland became larger as nearby areas joined it.

The Swiss sometimes became involved in foreign wars, both to gain land and to protect themselves. But after a terrible battle in 1515 when thousands of Swiss soldiers were killed, the Swiss people began to talk against being involved in other countries' wars. Switzerland soon became a ***neutral*** country.

Being a neutral country did not keep the Swiss from fighting each other from time to time, since some of them became Protestant while others stayed Catholic. But in recent times, the policy of staying out of foreign wars kept Switzerland neutral during terrible European wars.

Because of Switzerland's neutral policy, Swiss banks are considered safer than banks in some other countries. Also for this reason, leaders of disputing nations sometimes meet in Switzerland for discussions. This illustrates how a knowledge of history can help us understand a modern nation. Switzerland's present neutral policy is based on a decision that the Swiss made almost five hundred years ago!

England Sets Up Her Own Church

Ferdinand and Isabella had a daughter Catherine who married the new king of England, Henry VIII. In those days, it was like a peace treaty for a prince from one country to marry a princess from another.

But after eighteen years of marriage with Catherine, Henry was dissatisfied. They had only one living child, a girl named Mary. What would happen to England if the king had no sons? Mary might marry a foreign prince. Then a foreign country might gain power in England.

"Bloody Mary" caused nearly 300 people to be burned during her short reign from 1553 to 1558. She tried to totally destroy Protestant leanings in England, but instead her actions aroused fervent anti-Catholic sentiments.

Henry VIII was king of England from age 18 until his death in 1547.

Besides, Henry wanted to marry someone else. So he asked the pope to grant him a divorce. The pope refused, but Henry VIII did not like to be told no. He counted on the English people to support him more than they supported the pope.

Henry pressured English church leaders and Parliament until in 1534 they declared him supreme head of the Church of England. Now he was replacing the pope in England and could do as he pleased. And England had a new church, often called the Anglican Church.

Henry and his second wife, Anne, looked forward to the birth of their first child. Surely they would have a son! The royal announcement was ready to inform

Queen Elizabeth I ruled England from 1558 to 1603. Here, during a visit on June 16, 1600, she rides under an embroidered canopy being carried by courtiers.

Europe's dignitaries that a new English prince had been born.

Later, people said that the earth trembled on the day Elizabeth was born. When two more years passed and Anne still did not have a son, Henry accused her of unfaithfulness and had her beheaded. Then he married a third time, and finally a son, Edward, was born.

But even though Henry at last had his boy, he did not get his way. Henry died when Edward was only ten, and Edward died of tuberculosis six years later after a short reign in which his tutors held most of the power. Then Henry's daughter Mary took the throne.

Queen Mary was a strong Catholic who persecuted Protestants. Because she had hundreds of people burned at the stake, the English people called her "Bloody Mary." Protestant feeling in England became stronger than ever. But Mary died after reigning about five years, and Elizabeth became queen.

Queen Elizabeth I had a long, peaceful reign. People called her "Good Queen Bess." She favored the Church of England, but she showed some tolerance toward the Catholics in England as long as they obeyed the laws of the land and remained loyal to her. However, she did persecute others, such as Anabaptists and Puritans.

Trouble Develops in Ireland

During the 1100s and 1200s, Normans from England had taken over part of Ireland. As time went on, they began to lose their English ways and to take on the Irish language and customs.

In the 1500s, Henry VIII of England tried to win back English power in Ireland. He forced the Irish Parliament to declare him their king. As head of the Church of England, he also tried to force the Irish to drop their Catholic faith and accept the Anglican Church.

Elizabeth I persecuted Catholics in Ireland. She had some church leaders executed. Because of her harsh policies, the Irish revolted a number of times, but she was always able to put them down.

Later English rulers also mistreated the Irish. Much resentment against England built up in Ireland. To this day, Protestants and Catholics in Ireland struggle against each other. From time to time, violence breaks out and gets into the news.

Remember, though, that most Irish people are opposed to the extreme acts of fanatics and might not even live close to where fighting occurs.

Study Exercises

6. Did the Swiss become neutral because they believed that fighting is wrong? How do you know?
7. Why did Henry VIII want a son so badly?
8. Name the two Catholic queens in this chapter who persecuted non-Catholics.
9. What was the traditional religion of Ireland?

Germany Waits to Unite

Ferdinand and Isabella had another daughter who married the son of the Holy Roman Emperor. This couple had a son named Charles, who would grow up to rule more countries than any other king in Europe.

Emperor Charles V lived from 1500 to 1558.

Charles began as ruler of the Netherlands and other areas. In 1516, because he belonged to the family of Spanish rulers, he also became King Charles I of Spain. Still later, he was elected Emperor Charles V of the Holy Roman Empire. He was the one who heard Martin Luther declare, "Here I stand!"

Germany made up much of the Holy Roman Empire. Nobles and princes held much power, and the emperor could not always make them submit to him. Some German rulers were Catholics; others were Protestants. Sometimes they worked against each other.

Emperor Charles V worked and fought hard to crush the Protestants, but he could not overcome them. Discouraged with the religious war and faced with economic and health problems, he gave up his throne and went to spend his last days in a monastery. His title of Holy Roman Emperor went to his brother. His rule of Spain and the Netherlands went to his son Philip II.

Germany did finally become a single strong nation, but not until several hundred years later.

The Netherlands Shakes Off Spanish Rule

Philip II, a strong Catholic like his father, tried hard to free the Netherlands of Protestantism. But Philip's way was blocked by rulers in the Netherlands. One of them was called William of Orange (also called William the Silent). When Philip's army marched into the land, the Dutch fought them with everything they could—even boiling water.

But the Spanish army was strong. City after city fell. Then the Spanish army besieged Leiden (LY duhn). The people of Leiden held out as long as they could, but they were beginning to starve. In 1574, William of Orange ordered his men to open

During the siege of Leiden in 1574, the bubonic plague broke out in the city, bringing additional suffering to the starving people.

William of Orange (1533–1584) supported religious freedom in the Netherlands. He is considered the founder of the Dutch Republic. When the Netherlands became independent of Spain, the Dutch Anabaptists benefited from this freedom.

the dikes. Seawater poured in, ruining the farmland but chasing the Spanish army away. Then supply ships sailed in across the Dutch countryside right up to Leiden, bringing food for the hungry people.

Eighty years after the Netherlands rebelled in 1568, Spain finally recognized Dutch independence. However, the southern part of the Netherlands did not gain independence from Spain at the same time. Today this land is called Belgium, and most Belgians are still Catholics.

Spain Begins to Decline

Philip II of Spain had been married to Mary I of England. After she died, he tried to arrange a marriage with Queen Elizabeth. He had no particular affection for her; he simply wanted to maintain the power that he had in England. But Elizabeth remained single. Philip, a Catholic, finally became a bitter enemy of Elizabeth, who was a Protestant.

King Philip II ruled Spain from 1556 to 1598.

Philip ruled Spain at the peak of her power. He was earnest and hard-working, but he wanted all the power in his own hands. He did not let others make many decisions. They made recommendations to him, and he made the final decisions. Sometimes he made this a very slow process.

Philip also failed to understand that it takes more than gold and silver to make a country rich. Spanish ships were bringing millions of dollars' worth of treasures from Spanish mines in the New World. But Philip did not use these riches to improve farms, highways, schools, and industries in Spain. Instead, he used the money to build warships and improve his army. Spanish people who had gold could not buy goods produced in Spain because Spain was not producing many goods. So they bought goods produced in other countries—and the Spanish gold went out of the country to pay for them.

English and Spanish ships fought each other from time to time. Philip became exasperated at the victories that the English won. He assembled a great fleet of 130 warships and called it the Invincible Armada (ahr MAH duh). In 1588, this fleet sailed toward England.

The English knew about Philip's plans and were waiting for him. Living on an island, they knew something about water transportation too. The English ships were smaller than the tall Spanish ships, but they were quicker.

The battle went badly for the Spanish.

An artist pictures the 1588 fight between the supposedly invincible fleet of Spanish warships and the smaller English ships in the English Channel. Bigger is not always better—the Spanish were defeated.

The English battered them so severely that they were forced to flee. But a strong wind blew from the south, making it impossible for the Spanish to sail straight for home. They had to sail north through the English Channel and around Scotland. Winds and waves opposed them. Some ships were wrecked along the coasts of Scotland and Ireland. Only about half of the great Armada came back to Spain.

The defeat of the Spanish Armada stands alongside the Battle of Tours as one of the turning points in world history. Had the Spanish won that battle, England might have had little chance to spread her culture in the New World. Not only might most of North America have become Spanish-speaking but it might also all have come under Catholic control. But as noted before, there are no might-have-beens with God.

Little England was rising and would eventually become a great world power. But Spain was weakening. It never regained the power it once had, and today it is one of the poorer countries of Europe.

Study Exercises

10. How could Charles I be Charles V at the same time?
11. How did Holland's low-lying land turn out to be helpful in the Netherlands' war with Spain?
12. Who was the father of Philip II?
13. In what way could Philip II have better invested his money?
14. About how many ships of the Spanish Armada returned to Spain?

France Struggles Within

You have already studied the history of France up to the Hundred Years' War, which ended in 1453. By the end of the war, various nobles of France had seized power for themselves, leaving the king with little power of his own.

But in the late 1400s, several strong kings arose. They helped France to become a powerful, unified nation. One king was called "the Spider" because he was crafty in dealing with the French nobles. He "caught" them and made them submit to him.

France could have become even stronger, but a religious struggle soon developed. In the 1500s, John Calvin's teachings began to spread in France until about a sixth of the French people were Protestants. The Catholic rulers raised persecution against them.

But the French Protestants, who were called ***Huguenots*** (HYOO guh nahts), fought back against their persecutors. A number of them were nobles, and they were not used to being pushed down.

In 1572, during a time of peace, a leading Huguenot named Henry planned a big wedding in Paris. All the important Huguenots were invited. But their enemies feared that Henry might plot to become king. So in the early morning they made a sudden attack and killed a number of leading Huguenots in Paris.

The slaughter, now called the Massacre of Saint Bartholomew's Day, went on for three days and nights. Thousands of Huguenots in Paris were tortured and killed, including most of the leaders. In massacres elsewhere in France, more thousands of Huguenots were killed.

The bridegroom Henry escaped, and the remaining Huguenots fought on. Henry later decided to become a Catholic so that the French Catholics would accept him as king. Of course it is not noble for any man to change his religion for such a reason. But Henry did make some wise moves as king. Under Henry IV, as he was called, both Catholics and Protestants had freedom.

Catherine de Médicis (in black) views victims of the Saint Bartholomew's Day massacre. Catherine was the mother of the young French king. The Catholic extremists convinced her that the Huguenots were planning to take the throne, so she helped form a plot for the wholesale slaughter.

Henry IV was the Protestant who became a Catholic so that he could become king of France. He ruled from 1589–1610.

The next French kings generally tolerated the Huguenots, although they placed some restrictions on them and fought against them at times. During the periods when the Frenchmen were not fighting each other, they could work together to make a more prosperous country. But in 1685, King Louis XIV removed all the freedoms that Henry IV had given to the Huguenots, and severe persecution resumed.

Russia Stretches but Slumbers

Russia came under the power of the Mongols when they made their great raids from the Far East. They ruled the country for nearly two and a half centuries. During this time, the Russians had little contact with Europe and missed learning many new ideas. Russia was a backward nation.

But strong Russian leaders began to come forward. Ivan the Great, who lived in the 1400s, defeated the last of the Mongol rulers in Russia. At that point,

Ivan the Terrible was czar of Russia from 1547 to 1584. A popular legend says that Ivan had the architect of the Saint Basil Cathedral (shown in the background) blinded so that he could never again build anything that was equal to it.

Russia was not yet the huge, sprawling land that it is today, but Ivan the Great helped to expand it.

During the 1500s, Ivan the Terrible expanded Russia still more. He was the first Russian ruler to be officially crowned ***czar*** (ZAHR). Although he made contacts with Europe, Russia was still mainly a sleeping giant.

Ivan the Terrible is also remembered for his cruelty and for his use of secret police. While serfs in western Europe were breaking away from the old feudal system, Ivan made sure the ones in Russia remained serfs. He gave them no freedom. Later czars followed his example.

Knowing the history of Russia helps us understand why communism took over Russia in the 1900s. The people had lived with poverty and oppression so long that they welcomed any change which they thought might improve their lives.

Eastern Europe Trembles

While western European nations like France and England were watching each other suspiciously, the Holy Roman emperor was looking over his shoulder at the back door of Europe. To the east was an empire more frightening to him than most countries to the west. The Ottoman Turks, who had mastered the Middle East and northern Africa, were advancing.

Europeans remembered that in 1453 the Muslim Turks had conquered Constantinople. Before then, they had conquered most of Greece and some lands even nearer than Constantinople. In the early 1500s the Turks advanced as far as the border of Italy and seized parts of Romania. They defeated Hungary in a great battle in 1526. Then they headed into Austria.

But Vienna, Austria, was the high-water mark of the Turkish invasion. The Turks tried to capture it in 1529, but then retreated.

Not until the late 1600s did the Turks stop being a threat to the Holy Roman Empire. The Turks were probably no worse than most other conquerors, but what town or city wanted to be overrun by robbing, smashing, murdering foreigners? The Hutterites suffered much from wars between Europeans and Turks.

Michael Sattler said that Christians should not fight the Turks, and at his trial, his accusers made sure to mention it. They wanted to turn people against him. Knowing about the Turks helps us understand why Europeans of these centuries became agitated when the word *Turk* was mentioned.

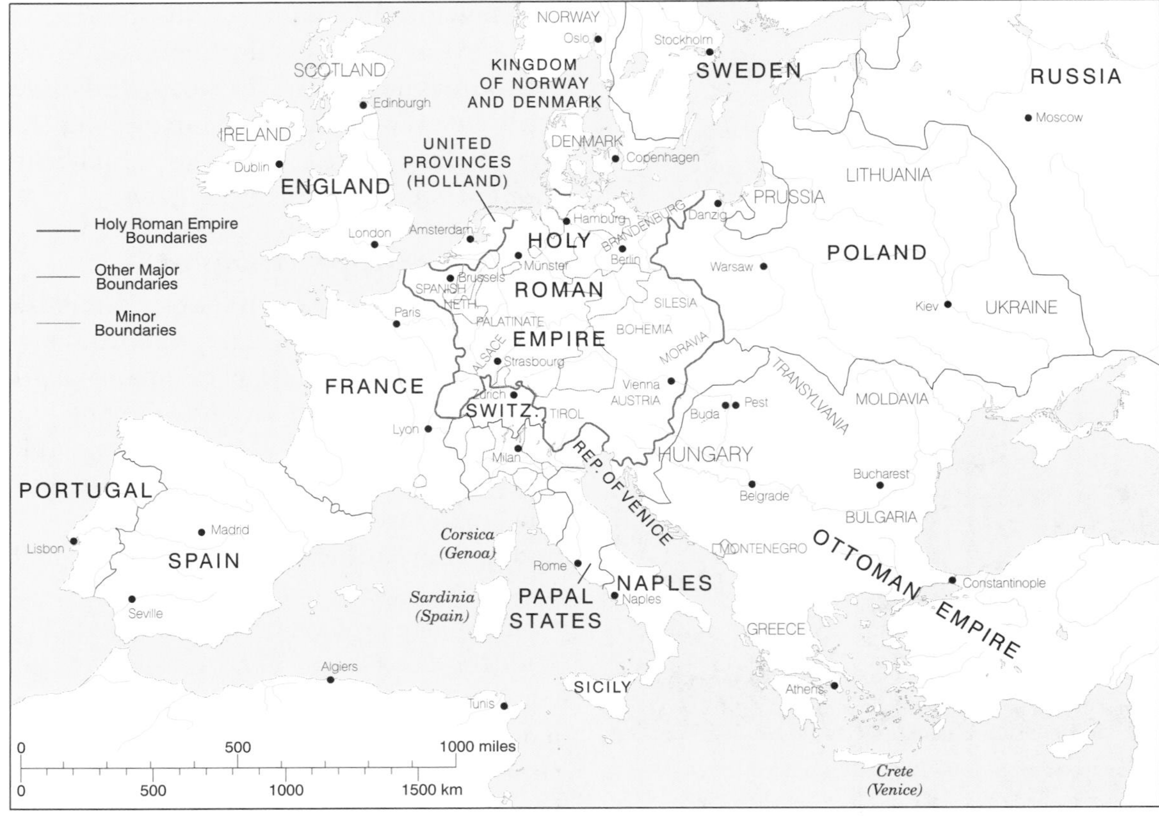

Figure 29:1. Europe in 1648

Study Exercises

15. Were the Huguenots a majority or a minority in France?
16. What East Asian people controlled Russia for several centuries and hindered it from becoming a modern country?
17. What was terrible about Ivan the Terrible?
18. What religion did the Turks profess?
19. How far did the Turks advance into Europe?

Foreign Trade Comes to India and Africa

During most of the 1500s, India was ruled by the Mogul Empire. Moguls were Muslims, but these Muslims were different from the Ottoman Turks who threatened eastern Europe. Maybe you remember reading in Chapter 25 about Akbar, the greatest of the Mogul rulers. He ruled wisely and won the loyalty of his subjects instead of ruining their cities.

After Vasco da Gama first visited India, Portuguese shippers developed trade with India. Soon England, France, and the Netherlands were also trading there. They fought each other for trading privileges.

It was the British who finally gained the strongest foothold in India. The British East India Company was formed in 1600; and over the next several decades, men from this company took control over large sections of India. Later India became part of the British Empire for a time.

India still shows some British influence.

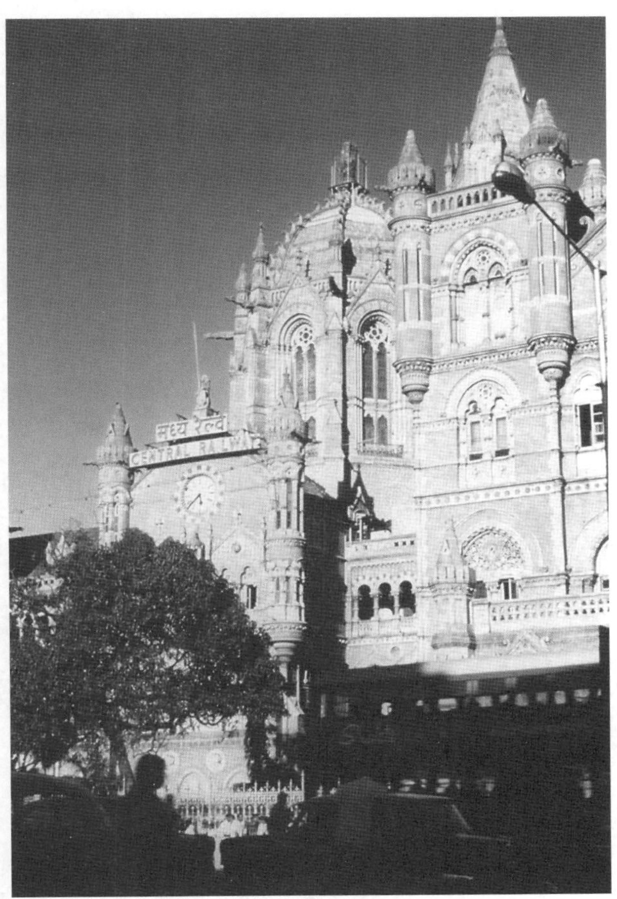

The British built this huge railway station in Mumbai (Bombay), India.

Many well-educated Indians can speak English. Some of the rich live in houses built by the British.

During the 1500s, Africa also was visited by the Portuguese. But European explorers learned that much of Africa south of the Sahara was dangerous to visit. Insect-carried diseases brought fever and death to white men. So they came to the African coasts only to trade in what brought them the most money, such as slaves and gold.

Europeans would eventually roam all over Africa and carve up the land for their own possessions. But that would not happen until several hundred years later.

China and Japan Fall Behind Europe

Perhaps you remember that the Mongols who controlled China were defeated by Chinese people called the Ming. The Ming dynasty was in control during the 1500s when the Portuguese sailed all the way to China and wanted to trade.

The European sailors looked uncivilized to the Chinese. Although the Chinese sold them some silk, porcelain, and tea, they did not see much benefit in trading more than that. Did they not have everything they wanted in their own country? They allowed the Portuguese to visit only one small part of China. Other countries could not trade with China at all.

The Japanese, on the other hand, welcomed Europeans for a while. Missionaries came to Japan. Trade with Japan lasted for about a hundred years.

But in the early 1600s, the Japanese rulers began to fear the new influences. They wanted Japan to stay as it had been. They worried that European countries might try to conquer Japan. So Japan cut down trade with other countries. They ordered European missionaries to leave and massacred Japanese Christians. Japanese sailors were forbidden to go far from home. Only one Dutch ship a year was allowed to visit Japan.

Although the Japanese made some changes, they still lived under a feudal arrangement. They still had castles, as the Europeans had had a hundred years before. The Japanese did not open their doors to the outside world again until the 1800s.

Study Exercises

20. Who were the first European traders to visit India?
21. What European country influenced India most?

22. Which country—China or Japan—seemed more open to foreign trade at first?

23. Why did the Japanese close their doors to the outside world in the early 1600s?

Clinching the Chapter

Multiple Choice

A. *Write the word or phrase* least *associated with the first item.*

1. Persecuted in Spain: Jews, Catholics, Protestants, Muslims
2. Henry VIII: Lutheran, Anglican, several wives, king of England
3. Children of Henry: Mary, Edward, Philip, Elizabeth
4. Charles: Netherlands, Spain, Germany, England
5. Unified nation: Germany, France, Spain, England
6. Muslims: Turks, Moguls, Mongols, Moors
7. Russia: Mongols, peasants, czars, Ming
8. Turkish conquests: Belgium, Romania, Hungary, Greece
9. Ruled Netherlands: Philip, Henry, William, Charles
10. Far East: Mongols, Ming, feudal system, Huguenots

B. *Write the correct words.*

1. The culture of most North Americans comes mainly from (northern, southern, eastern, western) Europe.
2. At the end of the Middle Ages, more power was in the hands of (kings, nobles, popes, knights).
3. Henry VIII took away the authority of the (pope, Parliament, navigator, emperor) in England.
4. Spain, France, and Portugal suffered from their own policy of (neutrality, persecution, independence, exploration).
5. The Spanish army was driven away from (Vienna, Constantinople, Leiden, Paris) by seawater.
6. Which of the following dates was an important turning point in world history? (1534, 1572, 1574, 1588)
7. Most frightening to eastern Europeans were the (Turks, communists, Irish, Huguenots).
8. What was the most dangerous place for Europeans to visit? (Asia, Africa, North America, India)
9. What country eventually held the greatest power in India? (Netherlands, England, France, Portugal)
10. The Chinese traded only with the (Dutch, Portuguese, English, Spanish).

Matching

A. *For each clue, write the correct name from the right-hand column.*

1. Forced his rule on Irish parliament	Elizabeth
2. Opposed Spanish rule in the Netherlands	Henry IV
3. Helped establish Spanish Inquisition	Henry VIII
4. Gave freedom to two religions in France	Isabella
5. Laid foundation for Huguenot beliefs	Ivan the Great
6. Sent out the Spanish Armada	John Calvin
7. Freed his country of Mongol rule	Mary
8. French king in the 1400s	Philip II
9. Persecuted Catholics in Ireland	"the Spider"
10. Was called "Bloody"	William of Orange

B. *Match as in Part A.*

1. Resented English rule	Africa
2. Conquered by Turks	English Channel
3. Turkish invaders turned back	Europe
4. Dangerous for Europeans to visit	Greece
5. Huguenots massacred	India
6. Hindu country ruled by Muslims	Ireland
7. Country famous for its Alps	Paris
8. Source of North American culture	Russia
9. Oppressed by czars	Switzerland
10. Spanish Armada defeated	Vienna

Completion

1. Castles and armor made no one the prouder,
   Weak as they were in the face of ———.
2. Who would let Protestants stay in the land?
   Not Isabella, and not ———.
3. Nationalism helped people at home
   Feel less responsive to faraway ———.
4. Daring King Henry defied the pope's ban,
   Wishing to marry a woman named ———.
5. Switzerland, weary of fighting and gore,
   Chose to be neutral, not looking for ———.
6. Charles quit ruling when all seemed in vain;
   Philip, his son, would take Holland and ———.
7. Born as a daughter, in spite of each guess,
   She would become the beloved ——— ———.
8. First of the sailors to reach the Chinese
   Were the adventurous, brave ———.
9. Europe's artistic and scholarly works
   Could have been lost to Muhammadan ———.

Thought Questions

1. Henry VIII officially broke England away from the Catholic Church. In spite of this, why is it not accurate to give him credit for being a great Reformation leader in England?
2. How was Germany behind the times in comparison to England, Spain, and France at this time?
3. To succeed better than Philip II, what should one do besides working hard?
4. Why would it have been helpful for the Chinese to trade, even with people they considered less civilized than themselves?
5. In Daniel 7, the Bible portrays empires as beasts. In what way or ways is that description suitable for the nations you have studied in this chapter?

Geographical Skills

1. About how far did the Spanish Armada travel from Lisbon, Portugal, to fight the English forces in the English Channel?
2. Find a map showing world time zones in an encyclopedia. How many time zones would you cross if you flew from Moscow to Vladivostok?
3. (*a*) Give the northernmost and southernmost latitude degrees for the country of Japan (including only the four main islands). (*b*) What difference in climate would you expect between the northernmost and southernmost points of Japan?

Further Study

1. How and when did Germany finally become one nation?
2. Use encyclopedias or other sources to find additional information about the various czars and empresses of Russia. Write a list or a paragraph giving interesting facts about them.

Sir Isaac Newton experiments with light. Newton was one of the most outstanding scientists of the 1600s. He developed a number of theories, now called Newton's laws, explaining inertia, gravitation, and motion. He was a brilliant mathematician and also studied theology.

30 Society Moves Into Modern Times

1500 A.D.
Europeans explore and settle the New World. 1500s, 1600s
1525
Ignatius of Loyola organizes the Jesuits. 1534
Catholic leaders begin the Council of Trent to clarify Roman Catholic teachings. 1545
1550
Michael Servetus describes the blood circulation system. 1553
1575
1600
The King James Version of the Bible is published. 1611
The Thirty Years' War devastates Europe. 1618–1648
1625
1650
Marcello Malpighi proves that blood flows through capillaries. 1661
The bubonic plague strikes London. 1665
Isaac Newton studies light, universal gravitation, and the laws of motion. 1665–1686
Anton von Leeuwenhoek observes bacteria through his microscope. 1674
1675
The Pilgrim's Progress is published. 1678
1700 A.D.

Progress: Fast or Slow?

Old Problems

Old Hatreds

Changes Nevertheless

New Commerce

New Scientific Discoveries

New Freedoms

A New World and How Europe Affected It

How the New World Affected Europe

New Developments in the Catholic Church

New Writings

An Old, Old Book

The Christian's Place in Modern Society

"Come near, ye nations, to hear; and hearken, ye people: let the earth hear, and all that is therein; the world, and all things that come forth of it."
Isaiah 34:1

Society Moves Into Modern Times

Progress: Fast or Slow?

When reading history, one can get the feeling that changes came suddenly, almost like an explosion. A few pages after reading about medieval times, we read about the Renaissance and then about modern times.

But remember, the Renaissance took place over several hundred years. From year to year, Europeans could not usually see much change. Boys and girls probably felt that time was moving slowly, just as you often do.

Remember also that society did not stop changing after modern times began. Far from it. You might find it helpful to think of the Renaissance as a ramp leading from a small country road onto an expressway. The Middle Ages are the small country road, and modern times are the expressway. Yet the Renaissance did not come between medieval and modern times; it overlapped the two.

On the modern highway, time seems to go faster and faster. People today must adjust to more changes than they did when modern times began.

Old Problems

The Middle Ages are usually considered to have ended in the 1400s or 1500s. Yet in many ways, cities of the 1600s still resembled cities of one or two hundred years before. Streets were narrow and dirty. Houses were crowded together.

The times were violent. People flocked to see criminals and traitors tortured, hanged, and beheaded.

Travel was slow and dangerous. ***Highwaymen*** robbed travelers. Mud holes and dangerous ditches abounded. To travel 35 miles (56 km) even by coach might take a whole day. But most roads were not fit for coaches. People going long distances usually went on horseback.

Knowledge in some areas was quite limited. Although schools emphasized knowledge of languages, which is a good thing, multiplication was thought to be difficult. Only skilled mathematicians tried to divide numbers.

People were poor. Once it was estimated that half the people in France lived in great poverty and that only one person in ten was living comfortably. Townspeople thought peasants were dull—and perhaps they were, for they lived a dull life. They could not afford the little things that make life pleasant. Their long days of hand labor in the fields earned them barely enough to live on.

In medieval times, there was no good way to get rid of waste water in the cities. People threw waste and sewage out their windows and into the streets.

This medieval hospital of the 1500s has all its patients in one room. Notice the man in the lower left corner having his leg amputated. We should be thankful for the pain-relieving medications God has directed scientists to discover. Even aspirin, which we might take for granted, was not available in the Middle Ages.

Doctors were ignorant and hospitals dirty. Often several patients needed to share the same bed. Others lay on the straw-covered floor, where insects crawled and hopped. Surgeons did not know how to relieve the pain of an operation. Most surgical patients died.

People had little idea of public sanitation. In 1665, the bubonic plague struck London hard. At least one out of every seven persons died.

Public safety received little attention. The year after the great plague in London, a fire got out of hand. It spread among the wooden buildings, and more than thirteen thousand houses burned. Although few if any people were killed, about 200,000 Londoners had to camp out that winter.

Besides all this, not everybody wanted progress. Some people benefited from the old, ineffective ways. Others feared all change, whether good or bad.

Old Hatreds

During the 1500s and 1600s, various European nations fought first one neighbor and then another. Some wars had religious causes; others were fought because kings or emperors wanted more power and land. Spain, France, England, the Holy Roman Empire, and other powers sometimes fought a series of wars before peace was made. Sometimes several nations formed alliances to keep an especially strong nation from conquering too much.

There were other kinds of armed conflict.

The Peasants' War took place when oppressed peasants mistakenly thought Martin Luther would support them if they tried to overthrow their rulers. They were crushed. The War of the Three Henrys took place when several men tried to gain the throne of France. So many large and small wars took place in Europe that it is hard to assign names to them all.

Many people were killed in the name of religion. One source speaks of "a century and a half of religious wars."

The Thirty Years' War began as a struggle between Catholics and Protestants in the Holy Roman Empire. For the first while, the Catholics defeated the Protestants. The next while, the tide ran against the Catholics.

By the time the war ended, most European countries had been involved in it. The war had begun as a religious war, but by the end the focus had shifted to other issues. Various countries fought for power and property for themselves. During the war, foreign armies repeatedly tramped across Germany, intent on fighting for things that had little to do with Germany.

Catholic acts of repression against the Protestants, such as these Catholics boarding up a Protestant church door, helped to ignite the Thirty Years' War.

European leaders conclude the Peace of Westphalia, an agreement that ended the Thirty Years' War.

In the end, very few people gained what they wanted. The war—actually a series of wars—had dragged on from 1618 to 1648. Farms had been ruined, towns destroyed, and fathers and older brothers had been slaughtered. It took Germany a long time to recover.

One important effect of the Thirty Years' War was that many people left Europe to make a better home in the New World. Also, the Catholic Church lost much of its political influence and power.

Study Exercises

1. Compared to several hundred years ago, are changes taking place more rapidly or more slowly today?
2. Name one school subject that pupils commonly studied in the 1500s.
3. Why did people avoid going to hospitals?
4. Why did nations form alliances?
5. What country received the worst battering during the Thirty Years' War?

Changes Nevertheless

Although Europeans seemed to be taking one step back for every two steps forward, Europe was advancing in some ways. People learned from past disasters. After the Great Fire of London in 1666, the people rebuilt their city. They planned wider streets, brick and stone buildings, and a better water supply. They organized the first real fire department.

Between 1450 and 1600, the population of Europe grew. In this chapter, you will read about the trade, exploration, and scientific discoveries of this period.

New Commerce

Trade was improving between countries in Europe. Dutch ships carried much of the trade. Not only did they transport goods between the Netherlands and other countries; they brought goods from one foreign country to another, such as from Poland to Italy.

River and canal transportation improved. In the 1600s, the French government built a great canal having a hundred locks and supplied with water by three aqueducts. A tunnel for the canal was blasted open with gunpowder, the first time gunpowder was used for such a purpose.

The Great Fire of London in 1666 destroyed about 13,000 homes, besides numerous churches and government buildings. Four-fifths of the city was destroyed. People fled with as many of their belongings as they could save.

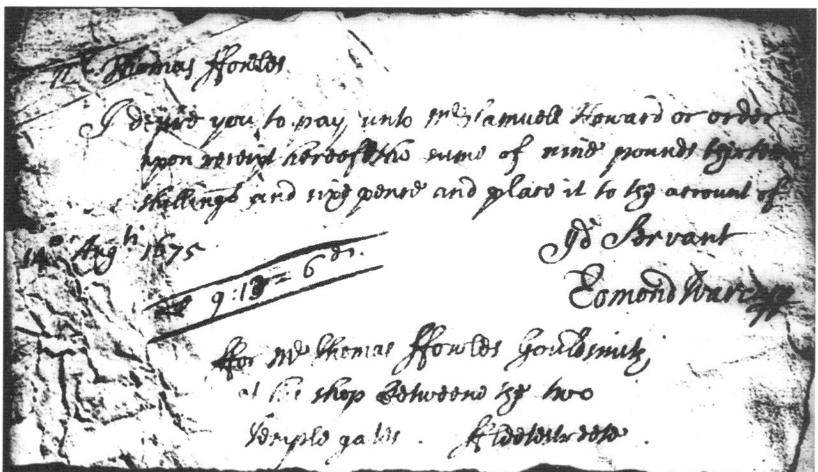

Dated in the late 1600s, this is one of the earliest written checks. If you look carefully, you may be able to read some of the writing. This check was drawn by Edmond Warcupp from his banker Thomas Ffoulds, a goldsmith, and was payable to Mr. Samuel Howard.

Banks were beginning to serve businessmen. Although the first bankers kept very simple street-side shops and used the abacus (AB uh kuhs) for calculations, banks were more important than they appeared. They helped merchants to trade with foreign countries by making it safer to transfer large sums of money over long distances.

For example, if a man in Italy owed money to a merchant in France, he would give the money to an Italian banker. The Italian banker would then ask a French banker to pay the French merchant. In return, the French banker would sometimes ask the Italian banker to pay a bill for him. In this way, banking transactions were done on paper, without much money needing to travel long distances.

People began to use paper money. In England, they would sometimes give valuable possessions to a goldsmith to keep safe for them. The goldsmith would give them a paper stating the value of what they had placed in his hands. When these people needed to pay a debt, rather than paying with gold they had left with the goldsmith, they paid with the paper. The next person knew he could go and get the valuables any time, so he was satisfied with the paper.

New Scientific Discoveries

Doctors were learning more about the human body. It was not true, after all, that blood seeped through the wall of the heart to get from one side to the other. Michael Servetus explained that the blood is pumped to the lungs by one side of the heart and flows back from the lungs to the other side.

Neither was it true that blood flowed back and forth in the body. William Harvey showed that it moves in a circle, from the heart through the arteries and back to the heart through the veins. Another doctor named Marcello Malpighi (mal PEE gee), with the newly invented microscope, proved that blood travels through tiny tubes now called capillaries.

In the Netherlands a businessman named Anton von Leeuwenhoek (LAY vuhn hook), who ground lenses as a sideline, was amazed when he looked at some plaque from his teeth under one of his lenses. He wrote that he saw "little animals, more numerous than all the people in the Netherlands, and moving about in the most delightful manner!" Still, people had little inkling that microscopic creatures might cause disease.

Until these times, surgery was often done by barbers. (The red stripes on a barber's pole stand for the blood that was part of a barber's business.) But a new law in England was passed during the reign of Henry VIII, forbidding barbers to perform operations.

Perhaps the most outstanding scientist and mathematician of the 1600s was Isaac Newton. Though he was an absent-minded professor who cut two holes in his door—one for his big cat and one for his small cat—Newton was nevertheless a profound thinker. One day, seeing an apple drop from a tree in a garden, it struck him that he was seeing an illustration of a very important law—the law of universal gravitation. Just as the gravity of the earth pulled on the apple, it pulls on the moon, keeping it in place as it speeds around the earth.

Sir Isaac Newton (1642–1727) was an English physicist and mathematician.

Isaac Newton also experimented with light, using a prism to break a beam of sunlight into a rainbow and demonstrating that white light is a combination of all colors. He studied the law of action and reaction, which is the basis of modern jet and rocket engines. These are just a few examples of his interests and discoveries.

But Newton was quick to point out that he had used the discoveries of other men to guide his own thinking. He modestly remarked, "If I have seen farther than other men, it is because I have stood on the shoulders of giants."

Study Exercises

6. What problem of trade did bankers help to solve?
7. What finally happened to Michael Servetus? (See Chapter 27.)
8. (*a*) What did Malpighi discover? (*b*) What did Leeuwenhoek discover?
9. Gravitation is universal—it works everywhere in the universe as far as we can see. What man first realized this?

New Freedoms

When the Catholic Church had controlled all Europe, it was fairly easy to keep most of the population under one church government. But now it was different. Government leaders began to see that people having a faith different from their own could be valuable, hard-working citizens. They respected these citizens and decided not to persecute them. Others decided that with so many people of various beliefs, they might as well not try to force everyone to believe as rulers did. Slowly religious freedom was growing.

Religious refugees fled from countries where persecution continued to other countries such as the Netherlands. They brought their talents with them and helped to make their new homeland prosperous.

The Netherlands, where dissenters had once been hotly persecuted, became the first European country to allow much religious freedom. Her people had other freedoms too, such as freedom of the press. Dutch printers published books that could not be printed in any other country.

A New World and How Europe Affected It

Cabot, Cortés, Balboa, Pizarro, Ponce de Leon—perhaps you could name even more explorers of the New World. After them came a flood of men, women, and children who helped to bring European ideas. Because Europe in the 1500s and 1600s was the way it was, explorers and settlers who came from there helped to make the New World the way it is.

Eager workers came from Europe because many of them had been unable to make a living. In England, for example, poor farmers were ordered to move off the farms they were renting because the owners wanted to use the property for sheep instead. This made the farmers even poorer. They could not buy land, for the landowners did not want to sell.

Also, some poor Europeans sat in prison because they had fallen into debt. The poor looked to the New World as a place where they could work their way out of problems. The New World had much work to do, and Europe supplied willing hands to do it.

Many people left Europe with ambitions to improve their social standing. Old customs in Europe kept each man in his place.

The Pilgrims pray and read the Bible just before embarking for their voyage to America.

A lower-class boy could expect to become a lower-class man. There was little he could do to change that. But in the New World, any man who worked hard and managed well could become prosperous and well respected.

Ideas about government came from Europe. Englishmen remembered the Magna Carta and other important decisions that gave rights and freedoms to the citizens. They wanted just as many freedoms in the New World, and maybe a few more. They wanted courts and legislatures and laws like the ones they had known at home. That is why the governments of the United States and Canada have many ideas based on English law.

Those who crossed the ocean to the New World usually brought a love for their old countries with them. Sometimes that meant that when England and France fought in Europe, the English and French also fought in America. Understanding European history helps us understand North American history.

Various religious beliefs came from Europe. Among the first Europeans to sail to the New World were Catholic priests. But though these priests worked zealously to evangelize the American Indians, they carried their mistaken ideas with them. They considered the Indians to be Christians if they received Baptism. They had little concern about teaching the Indians to obey all things as Christ had commanded.

Many people came to the New World to escape persecution, for the idea of religious freedom was growing too slowly in Europe. Even in England, King James was heard to say of dissenters, "I will make them conform, or I will harry them out of the land." Dissenters who are remembered as Pilgrims fled to the Netherlands, and then to America in the *Mayflower*.

Huguenots fled from France, Quakers from England, and Lutherans from war in Germany. Anabaptists, Catholics, and Jews migrated from various places. All these people brought their energy, knowledge, and skills to the New World.

Study Exercises

10. What European country was the first to allow much religious freedom?
11. What fact encouraged lower-class Europeans to move to the New World?
12. From what country in Europe did Canada and the United States get many ideas on how a government should operate?
13. How did wars in Europe harm the New World?
14. How did religious persecution in Europe help the New World?

The *Mayflower,* in which the Pilgrims came to America, floats in Plymouth harbor during the winter of 1620. The approximately 90-foot (27 m) vessel made the journey in 66 days.

How the New World Affected Europe

People of the Western Hemisphere tend to read history as if explorers and settlers came to bring great changes to the American homeland. But remember that while they brought changes to the Americas, they also took changes back to Europe.

Try to imagine being a European and watching your friends sail away to cross the Atlantic. How eagerly you would listen to stories and rumors about the New World! Some stories in those days were exaggerated. There was not nearly as much gold in the New World as some people would have liked to think. But other stories were true.

John Cabot, sent by the king of England, found so many fish off the shores of Newfoundland that his men could catch fish by lowering baskets into the ocean. European ships soon headed for these new fishing grounds. Explorers also noted the many fur-bearing animals in the New World. Trappers set up a highly profitable fur trade.

New foods, such as corn, tomatoes, and potatoes, came from the New World. Potatoes, discovered by Spanish explorers in South America, grew especially well in mild, damp Ireland. In later years, most of the Irish people depended on potatoes as much as the Chinese depended on rice.

Tobacco was discovered, and many Europeans began to smoke. Tobacco can hardly be called a gift from the New World. Yet it enriched traders who did not care how they earned money.

Gold and silver flooded into Europe from conquered Indian cities and Spanish mines in the New World. This made certain people rich for a time. But since precious metals had become more common, they were less valuable than before. This helped to bring on ***inflation,*** a problem in which money loses its value. Customers needed more money to buy the same goods.

New Developments in the Catholic Church

About the time of the Reformation, many Catholics realized there were serious disgraces in the church. They tried to improve the church and strengthen it against the Protestants, who were drawing many people away from the Catholic Church. This movement among the Catholics is called the ***Counter Reformation.*** Several important persons and events helped to boost the Counter Reformation.

During the early 1500s, a Spanish soldier named Ignatius of Loyola (ihg NAY shuhs; loy OH luh) wanted to win fame for

Ignatius of Loyola (1491–1556) was the founder of the Society of Jesus (Jesuits).

himself. But he was severely wounded in battle and needed a long time to recover. During his long, quiet days, he read a book called *Lives of the Saints.* He decided that he would dedicate his life to religion.

In 1534 Ignatius of Loyola organized a small group of loyal Catholics. Later the group expanded. This organization was called the Society of Jesus, and its members were nicknamed the ***Jesuits*** (JEHZ oo ihts). They began working hard to win people for the Catholic Church.

The Jesuits knew that schools have a great influence on society. They established many schools in Europe and in the New World. These schools helped children to become staunch Catholics.

By their efforts, Jesuits strengthened the Catholic religion in Austria, Poland, Ireland, Belgium, France, and other countries. In Spain and Italy, of course, the church already had an iron grip on the people.

The Jesuits did some good, but they also did much harm. When explorers and conquerors oppressed the Indians, Jesuit missionaries spoke against it. But they also were responsible for helping to send many non-Catholics to a cruel death.

From 1545 to 1563, Catholic leaders had a series of conferences called the Council of Trent. This council made various decisions that clarified what the Catholic Church taught. The Council also drew up a list of books that Catholics were forbidden to read. Catholics who refused to read these books were harder to win to another faith.

Study Exercises

15. Name two important foods unknown to Europeans before the discovery of America.
16. Why is inflation considered to be a problem?
17. What was the Counter Reformation?
18. Who was the founder of the Jesuits?
19. Why did Jesuits emphasize the importance of schools?

New Writings

In every age, writers produce work that is soon forgotten. But one writer in Queen Elizabeth's time is well remembered to this day. He was William Shakespeare, a writer with a knack for expressing human feelings clearly. For example, he wrote, "Love is not love which alters when it alteration finds." He meant that if you stop loving someone because he is no longer rich or strong or good-looking, you never did love him very much.

But Shakespeare also used his talent to express ungodly feelings. He wrote many plays for the theater, and he acted in some of them. He is not remembered for upholding Christian standards and values.

William Shakespeare (1564–1616) was a famous writer of English literature.

Young poet John Milton peers through a telescope in Galileo's observatory in the early 1600s.

THE
Pilgrim's Progreſs.
FROM
THIS WORLD
TO
That which is to come.
The Second Part.
Delivered under the Similitude of a
DREAM,
Wherein is ſet forth
The manner of the ſetting out of *Chriſtian's* Wife and Children, their Dangerous JOURNEY,
AND
Safe Arrival at the Deſired Country.

By *JOHN BUNYAN*,

I have uſed Similitudes, Hoſ. 12. 10.

LONDON,
Printed for *Nathaniel Ponder* at the *Peacock*, in the *Poultry*, near the Church, 1684.

John Bunyan wrote the two parts of *The Pilgrim's Progress* at different times. The first part of this well-known book was published in 1678 and tells the story of Christian, a pilgrim journeying to the Celestial City. The second part was published in 1684 and tells the story of Christian's wife and children, who, along with a friend, start on their journey to the Celestial City.

This page spread from the second part shows the author dreaming of the journey.

John Milton, who lived during the next century, is another well-remembered writer. Milton became blind when he was forty-three. But he kept on with his writing by dictating to his daughters, who wrote for him. In a poem about being blind, he made a statement that people still quote today: "They also serve who only stand and wait."

One man, John Bunyan, probably had a greater godly influence than any other writer of the 1600s. A recent writer called him "a common man lumpy with talent."

As a young man, John Bunyan was not godly. When he did try to live a better life and please God, he was frightened because he did not know how. Then he met a few Christians who talked of God as if He were a friend. That was a new thought to John, for he had been trying to serve God as if He were a stern master. John finally learned that God has "grace abounding to the chief of sinners." Later he wrote a book with that title.

The Church of England did not approve of the religious services John Bunyan attended. He was imprisoned several times for preaching without a license. It was during one of his prison terms that John Bunyan began writing his greatest book, *The Pilgrim's Progress.*

This book is the story of Christian, who started out for heaven, carrying a great load of guilt on his back. It tells how he entered the Wicket Gate, how his burden fell off, and how he struggled up the Hill Difficulty. On his journey he met characters like Talkative, Ignorance, and Atheist, and finally he waded the last dark river with his friend Hopeful and entered the Celestial City. *The Pilgrim's Progress* became very well known, even during Bunyan's lifetime. It has been translated into many, many languages and has traveled all over the world.

An Old, Old Book

But a greater work than Bunyan's had already been printed. Someone had suggested to King James I that a standard version of the Bible be made. Up to this time, there had been a number of translations. Sometimes translators added notes to support their own point of view. King James liked the idea of a new Bible version.

About fifty scholars and ordained men worked on the project. They divided into six committees. Each committee would translate a portion of the Bible, and then send it to the other committees for examination. When this stage of translation was done, twelve men formed a committee to make final decisions on the wording of the Scriptures.

The King James Version, sometimes called the Authorized Version, was completed and published in 1611. Although some objected to it, this translation became more and more accepted. The King James Version not only gives us the Scriptures but it also says things in a graceful, often musical way. It uses forceful words. Eventually it gained such high esteem that no significant new translation was produced for over two hundred years.

The Christian's Place in Modern Society

You are reaching the end of this book, but not the end of history. Other textbooks have been written to cover the most recent centuries.

As you study the recent past, you will learn about ever faster-moving times. Radios, satellites, computers, and jet airplanes are speeding the pace of modern life. Greater affluence (flow of money), booming industry, and rapidly increasing knowledge are changing the world.

At the same time, you will also learn

about modern problems—unemployment, wars, violence, oppression, persecution, and corruption. Perhaps it will dawn on you then in a new way that modern problems are much the same as ancient problems. "The more things change," someone has said, "the more they stay the same." Human nature does not change, except that "evil men and seducers shall wax worse and worse" (2 Timothy 3:13).

Neither does God's Word change. The answers that men and women found in the Bible throughout history are the answers that people are still discovering in the Bible today. God's Word directs us as well in the day of telephones and atomic bombs as it guided people thousands of years ago.

In this time of "men's hearts failing them for fear" (Luke 21:26), remember that what held men steady down through the years can hold us steady now. Think again of the nonresistant love of Jesus and of Michael Sattler, the brave honesty of Daniel and of Menno Simons, the prisoner's endurance of John the Baptist and John Bunyan. What was right for them is still right for every young person growing up today.

Study Exercises

20. What do people admire about Shakespeare's writings?
21. What can be admired about John Milton's character?
22. Name two books that John Bunyan wrote.
23. (*a*) When was the King James Version first printed? (*b*) Why was it named after King James?
24. Name two things that stay the same in every age.

Clinching the Chapter

Multiple Choice

A. *Write the word or phrase* least *associated with the first item.*

1. Results of Thirty Years' War: many immigrated to the New World, Catholic Church lost power, Germany was strengthened, farms and towns were ruined
2. Science: Servetus, Harvey, Newton, Balboa
3. Newton: surgery, gravity, light, reactions
4. Explorers: Milton, Cabot, Cortés, Pizarro
5. From New World: fish, furs, tobacco, microscopes
6. Notable writers: Bunyan, King James, Shakespeare, Milton
7. Counter Reformation: Jesuits, Loyola, Bunyan, Council of Trent
8. Shakespeare: actor, expressive, blind, observant
9. Persecution: England, Netherlands, France, Spain
10. *The Pilgrim's Progress:* England, 1500s, Bunyan, prison

B. *Write the correct words.*

1. The Renaissance (overlapped, came between, followed, preceded) medieval and modern times.
2. Schools emphasized (mathematics, languages, sanitation, writing).
3. The Thirty Years' War began as a fight over (land, language, religion, commerce).
4. Barbers were also (surgeons, scientists, adventurers, professors).

5. Because of (Dutch shipping, canals, banks, writers), it became possible to pay debts without needing to send money long distances.
6. The microscope helped to prove the existence of (gravity, capillaries, lenses, colored light).
7. Who studied the law of action and reaction? (Servetus, Harvey, King James, Newton)
8. A kind of paper money in Europe was introduced by (goldsmiths, the government, traders, surgeons).
9. The "Irish" potato was actually discovered in (Ireland, England, South America, China).
10. Notable first missionaries to the New World were (Anglicans, Lutherans, Jews, Catholics).

Matching

A. *For each clue, write the correct name from the right-hand column.*

1. Thought much while recuperating	Ignatius of Loyola
2. Thought much while in prison	Isaac Newton
3. "Love is not love which alters . . ."	Jesuit
4. Explained heart-lung blood circulation	John Bunyan
5. Explained artery-vein blood circulation	John Cabot
6. "They also serve who . . . wait."	John Milton
7. Scientist and mathematician	King James
8. Approved new Bible version that was completed in 1611	Michael Servetus
9. Member of zealous Catholic group	William Harvey
10. Discovered North American fish	William Shakespeare

B. *Match as in Part A.*

1. Hard on Germany	alliance
2. Found freedom in the Netherlands	Counter Reformation
3. Improving of Catholic Church	fur
4. What Bunyan did not have	grace
5. Shakespeare's interest	inflation
6. Abounds to the chief of sinners	license
7. Found plentifully in New World	plague
8. Hard on London	printers
9. Decrease in the value of money	theater
10. Agreement among nations	Thirty Years' War

Completion

1. Disease ran free in every nation
Because of little ———.
2. The richest European born
Had never known the taste of ———.
3. A German war caused blood and tears;
And worse, it lasted ——— ———.

4. For distant payments, we may thank
   The careful workers in a ———.
5. What richer place could Cabot wish
   Than where a basket catches ———?
6. The ships sailed west where trappers were
   And traded guns and tools for ———.
7. Those Jesuits—they knew their tools!
   They drilled false doctrines in their ———.
8. A good, hard worker may surpass
   The others of his social ———.
9. What Bunyan learned is still astounding:
   For sinners God has ——— ———.

Thought Questions

1. What did Isaac Newton mean by saying he had stood on the shoulders of giants?
2. Many people besides Newton had seen apples fall, and many had seen the moon in the sky. What did Newton understand that others did not?
3. Why is it important in our time that people know mathematics better than they did four hundred years ago?
4. We know that no one can be right without being dedicated to his faith. Can anyone be dedicated to his faith and still be wrong? Support your answer from what you have read.
5. Consider the statement, "The more things change, the more they stay the same." How would you explain it in your own words?

Geographical Skills

1. Trace Map H, and label it "Modern European Nations."
2. Label the countries and color them lightly. (If you have time, make similar maps for Africa and Asia.)

Further Study

1. How does the current violence in North America compare with the 1600s, when the times were violent?
2. Give some other information about the life of John Bunyan.

BE SURE YOU KNOW

Can you answer all these questions? If not, study Chapters 29 and 30 to find the answers.

A. What

1. European nation is known for its policy of being neutral?
2. (*a*) king of England became the head of the Anglican Church? (*b*) were the names of his three children?
3. German ruler was the Holy Roman Emperor when the Reformation began?
4. struggles within France kept that nation from becoming strong for many years?
5. (*a*) Russian leader freed his country from the rule of the Mongols? (*b*) Russian leader kept the serfs under the old feudal system?
6. European city were the Turks attacking when they were turned back in 1529?
7. Europeans gained power over India during the 1600s?
8. were two results of the Thirty Years' War?
9. doctor developed a correct theory of blood circulation through the arteries and veins?
10. man discovered important scientific principles such as the law of gravitation and the law of action and reaction?
11. European country was the first to grant much religious freedom?
12. (*a*) were some effects of Europe on the New World? (*b*) were some effects of the New World on Europe?
13. writer of the late 1500s became famous for his ability to express human feelings?
14. (*a*) English king authorized a well-known Bible translation? (*b*) year was it completed?

B. What do these words mean?

15. Counter Reformation
16. czar
17. highwayman
18. Huguenot
19. inflation
20. Jesuit
21. nationalism
22. neutral
23. Spanish Inquisition

C. How

24. did Spain become a united kingdom?
25. was the Dutch city of Leiden delivered when Spanish soldiers besieged it?

D. Why

26. did feudalism in Europe come to an end?
27. did hostility develop between the people of Ireland and England?
28. was the defeat of the Spanish Armada a major turning point in history?
29. (*a*) was China not eager to deal with Europeans? (*b*) was Japan not eager to deal with Europeans after a while?

So Far This Year

See how many answers you can give from Chapters 1–30 without looking back.

A. *Match the letters on the map to the names below. You will not use all the letters.*

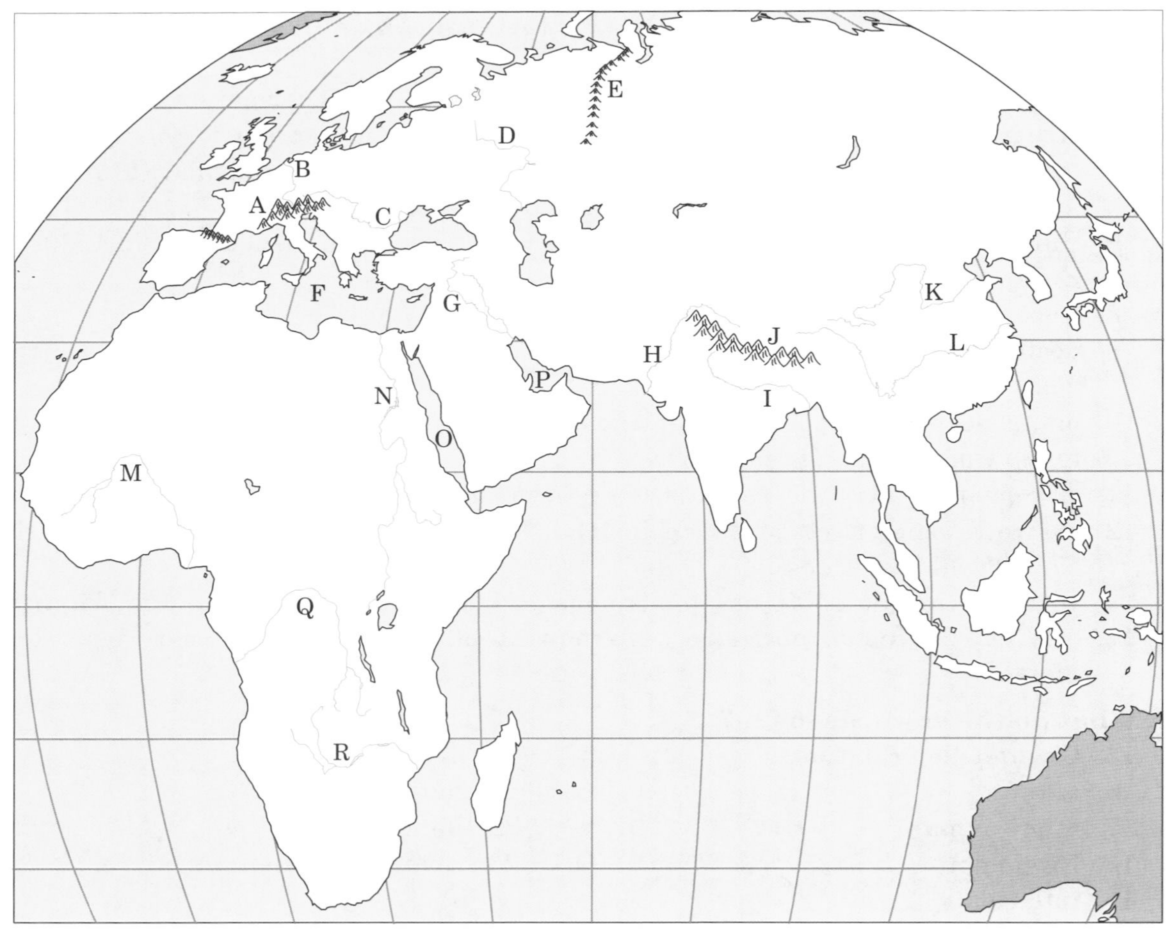

_____ 1. Congo River
_____ 2. Danube River
_____ 3. Euphrates River
_____ 4. Ganges River
_____ 5. Huang He River
_____ 6. Indus River
_____ 7. Niger River
_____ 8. Nile River
_____ 9. Rhine River
_____10. Yangtze River
_____11. Mediterranean Sea
_____12. Persian Gulf
_____13. Red Sea
_____14. Alps
_____15. Himalayas

B. *Give the correct answers.*

16. The earliest civilizations began (along seacoasts, along rivers, on broad plains).
17. The Hittites' way of dealing with conquered people was (deporting them, enslaving them, allowing them to continue living much as before).

18. Many battles were fought in Canaan because (the inhabitants were unusually warlike, Canaan was a buffer between strong nations, the landscape of Canaan made it an excellent battlefield).
19. The Behistun Rock is important because it provided the key to ancient (hieroglyphic, cuneiform, Phoenician) writing.
20. Ideals of the Greeks included all the following *except* (freedom, justice, democracy, national unity, new ideas).
21. Alexander the Great was eager to spread (Gnosticism, Hellenism, Zoroastrianism) throughout his empire.
22. Jerusalem was destroyed in (A.D. 30, A.D. 40, A.D. 70).
23. Muslims fast during the month (Hegira, Ramadan, Koran).
24. The system of land ownership known as (feudalism, Christendom, parliament) was common in the Middle Ages.
25. The (Huguenots, Hutterites, Waldenses) were nonresistant Christians of France during the 1100s.
26. Oriental conquerors known as (Guptas, Mongols, Turks) threatened western Europe in the 1200s but then withdrew.
27. Even though the Münsterites differed radically from most Anabaptists, they were called Anabaptists because they practiced (adult baptism, infant baptism, nonresistance).

C. *Choose the correct name for each clue. You will not use all the names.*

Clue	Names
28. Leader who translated the Bible into Latin	Ambrose
29. Roman emperor who made Christianity legal	Augustine
30. Leader who taught that man is too evil to choose to be saved	Charles V
31. Holy Roman Emperor when the Reformation began	Constantine
32. Writer who was famous for his ability to express human feelings	Henry VIII
	Jerome
33. Famous scientist who studied things such as light and gravitation	Milton
	Newton
	Shakespeare

Guidelines for Neat Maps

1. Use printing, not cursive writing, for all words on the map.
2. As space allows, print all words horizontally except the names of rivers and mountain ranges. A river or mountain range name should follow the course of the river or mountain range.
3. Use all capital letters for the names of countries, states, provinces, and large bodies of water. Capitalize only the first letter of each word for cities, lakes, rivers, and land regions.
4. Color bodies of water blue. Make all coloring strokes horizontal, not vertical or in every direction.
5. To color countries, states, or provinces, use a color that is different from the color of any area beside it. Do not use any color that is too dark for the lettering to show.

Table of Contents

Map A (Middle East)

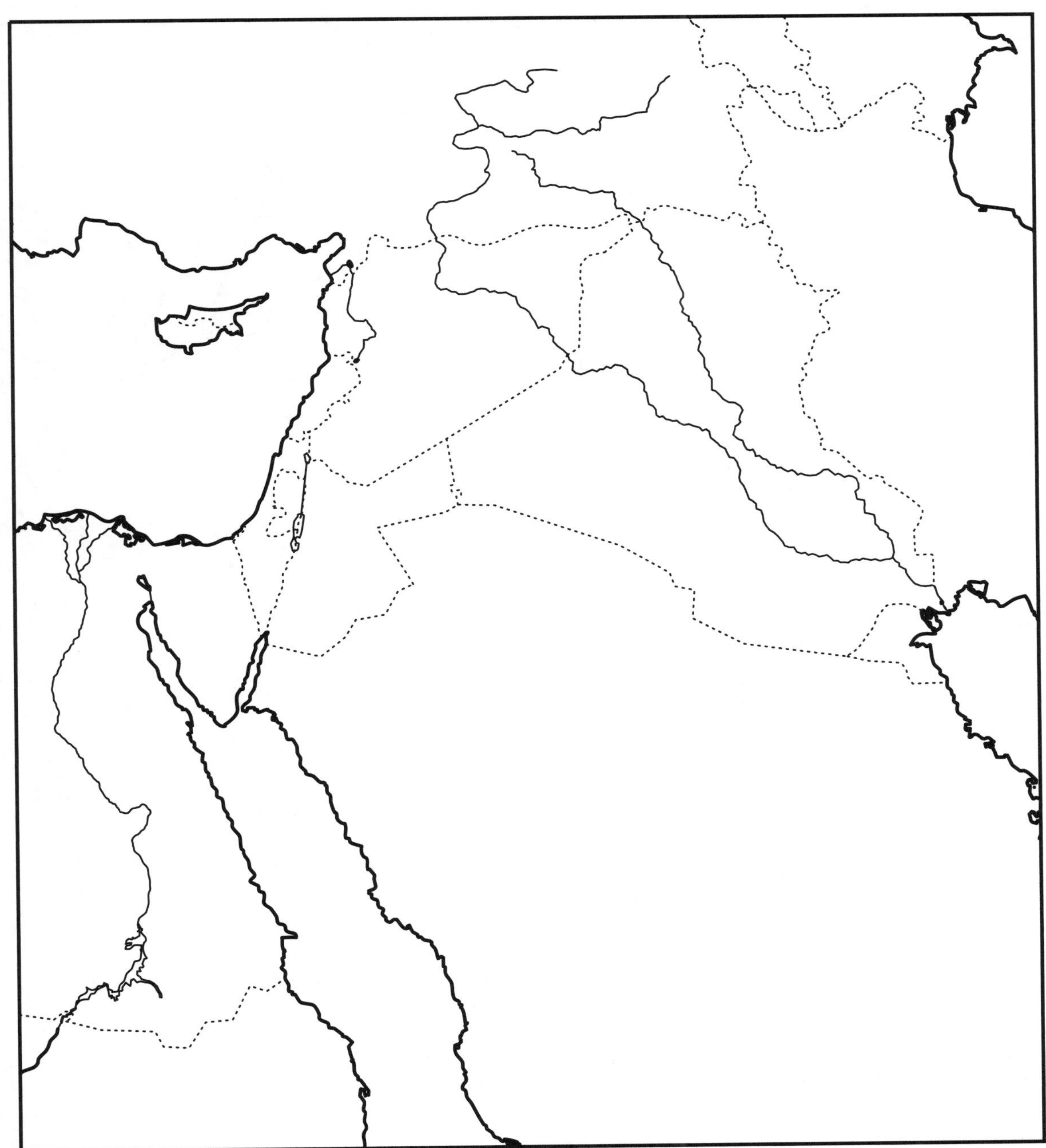

Map B (Africa)

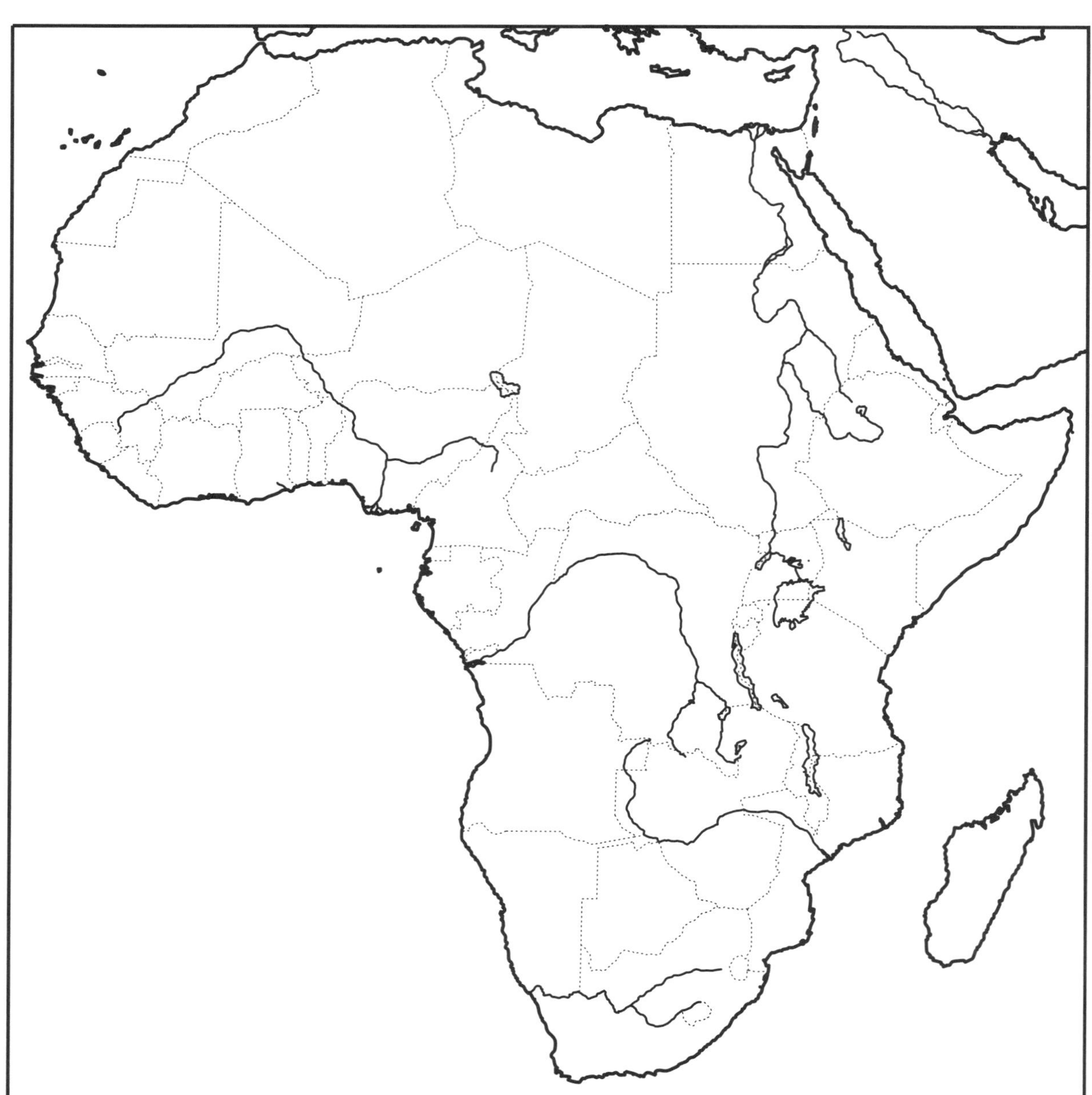

Map C (Canaan)

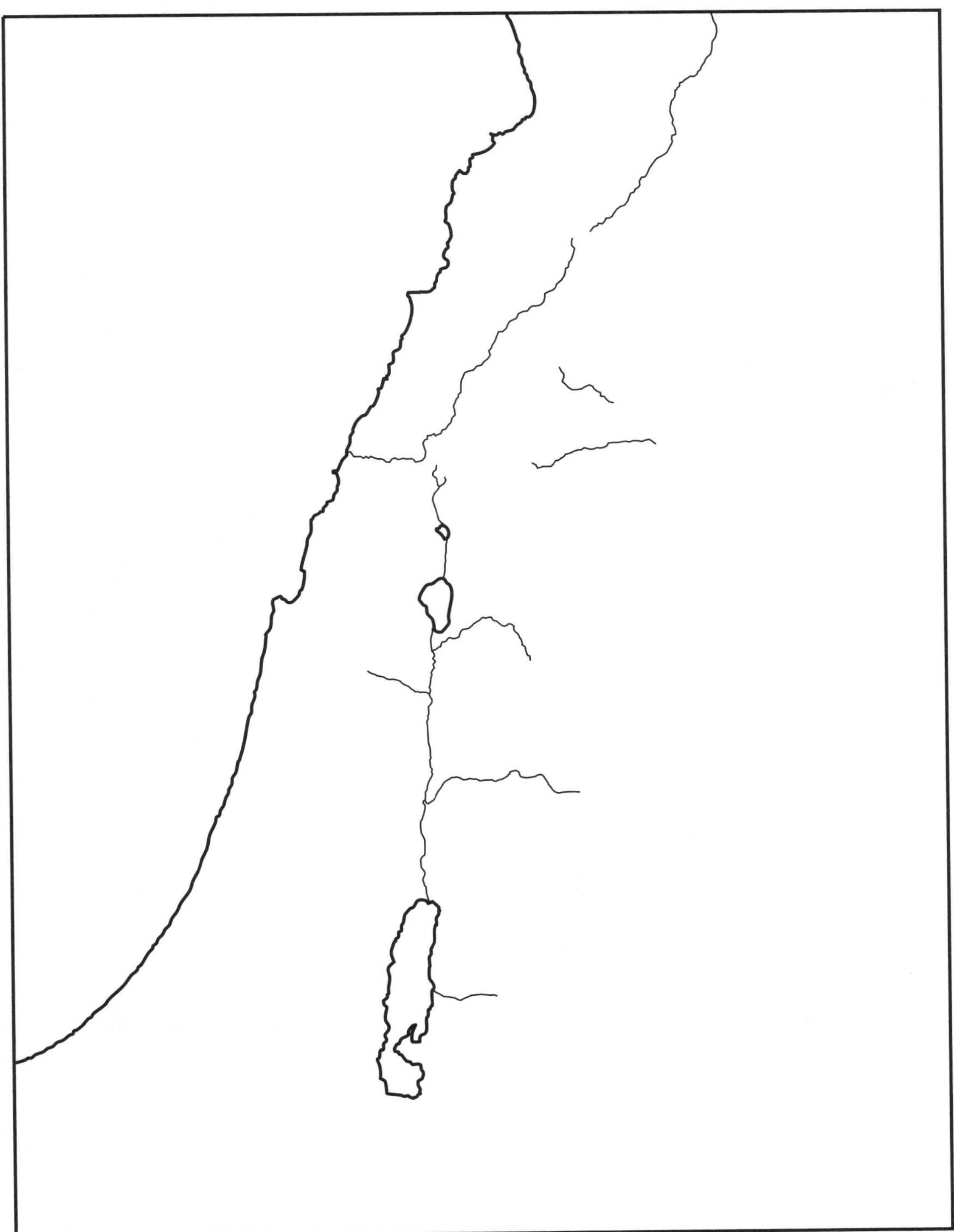

Map D (India)

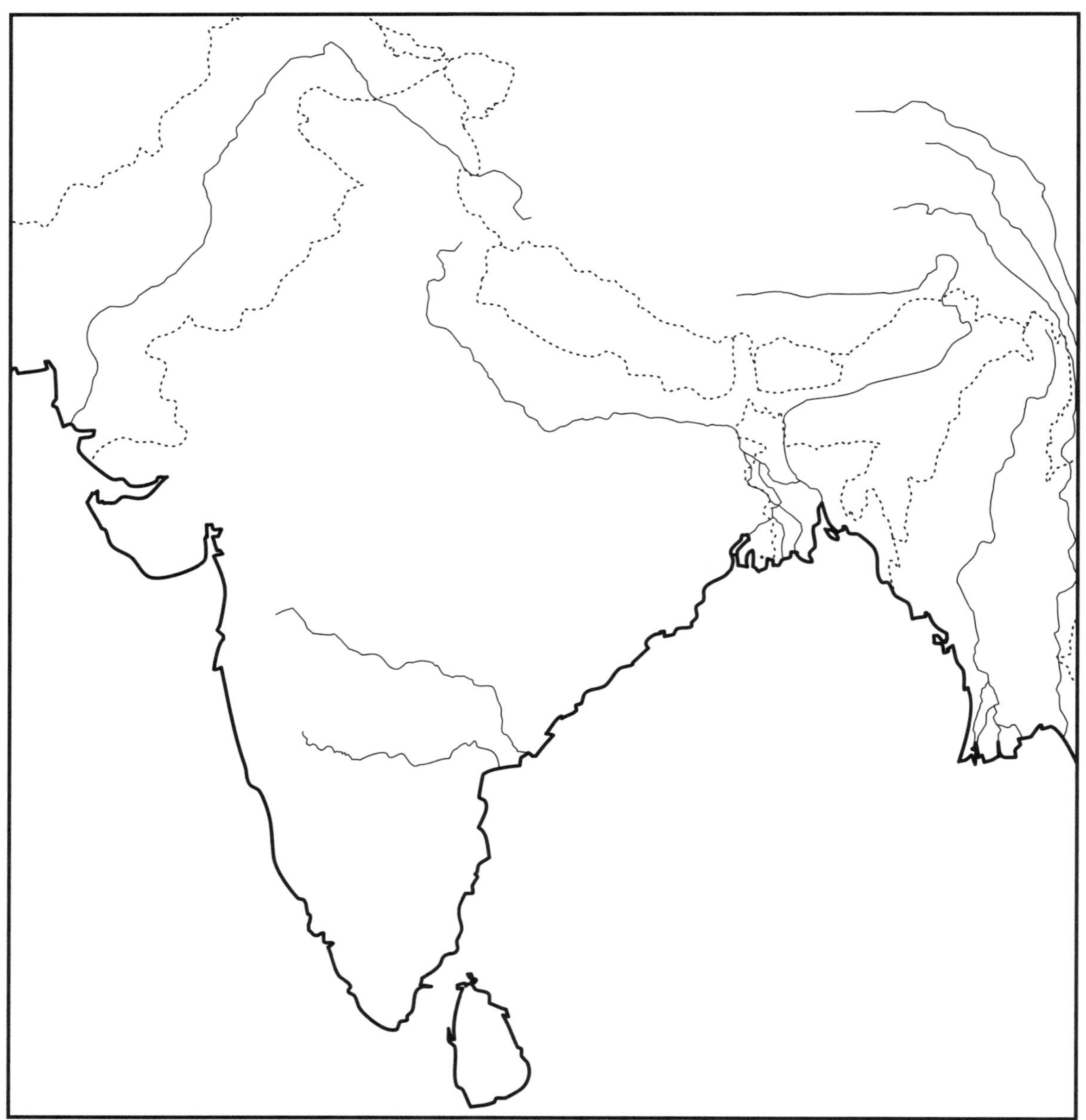

Map E (China)

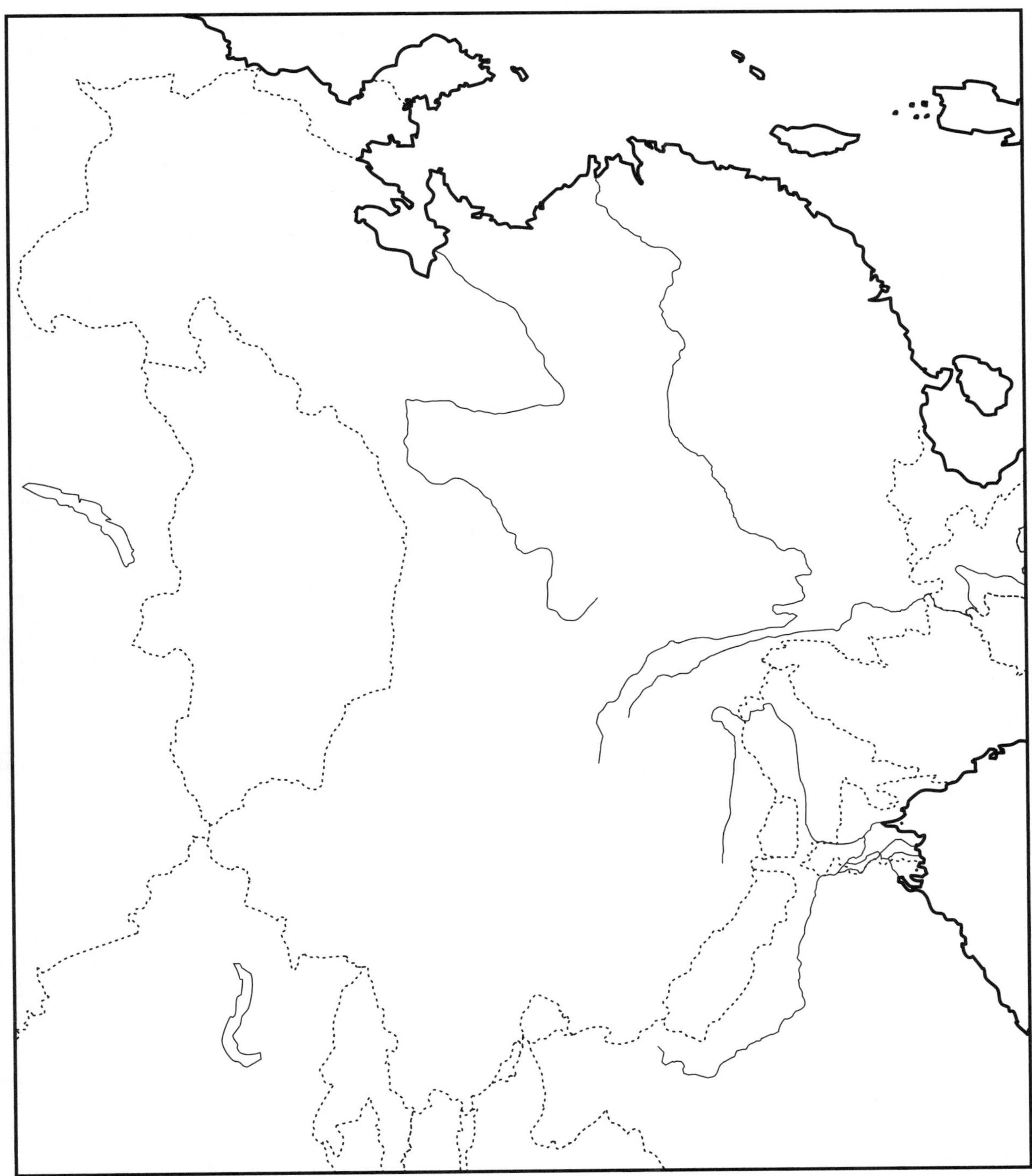

Map F (Italy to India)

Map G (Mediterranean Lands)

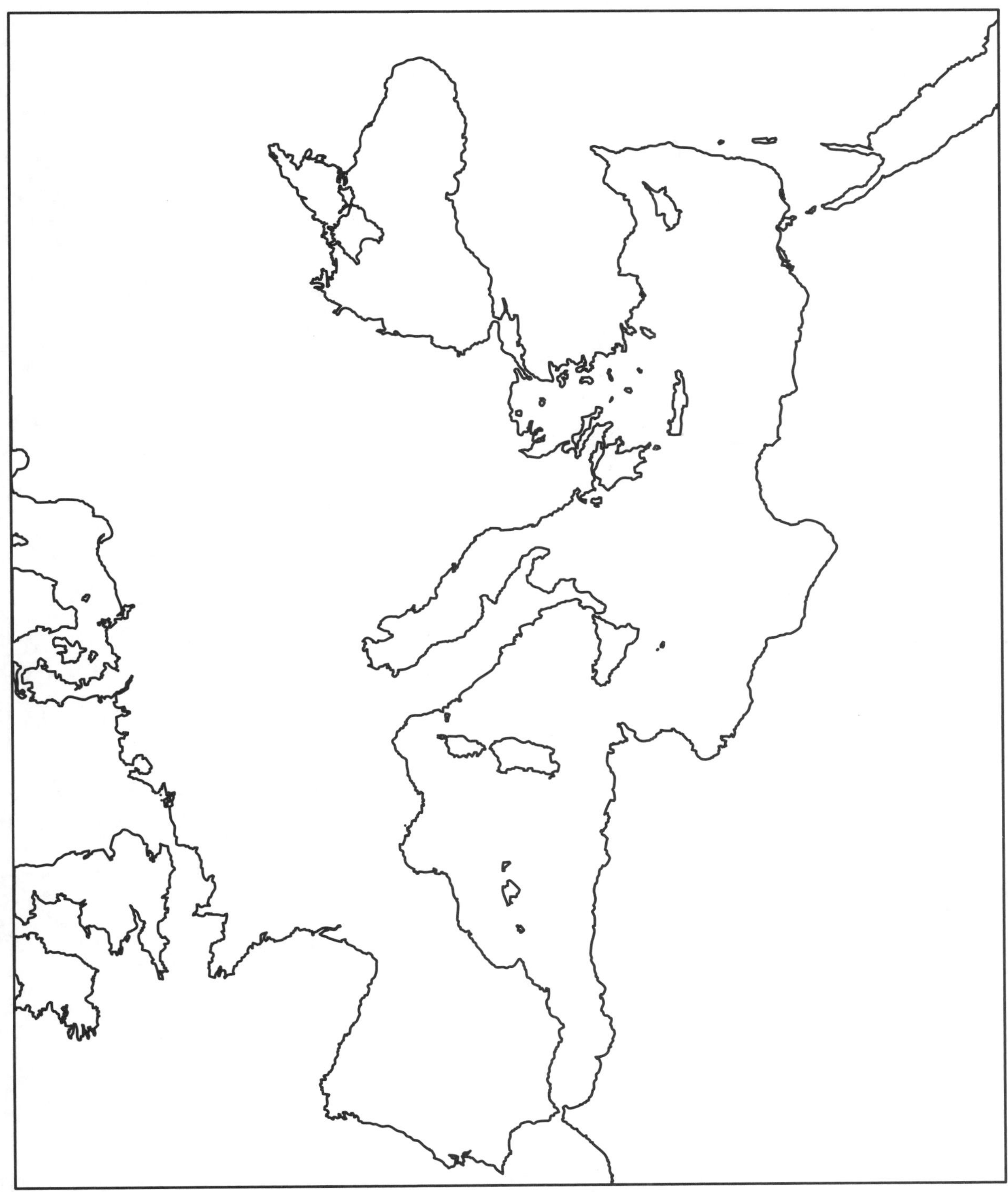

Map H (Europe)

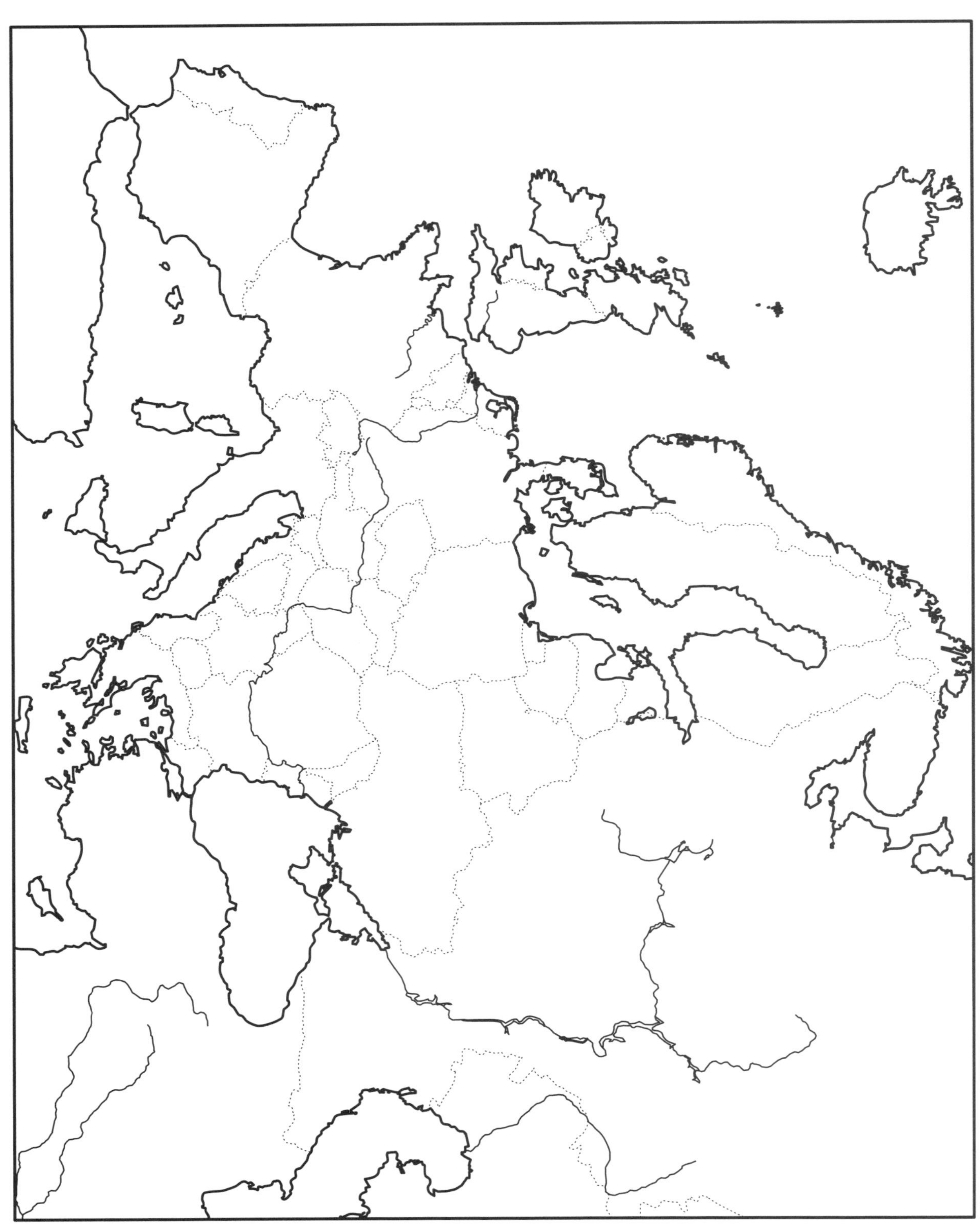

Map I (Asia)

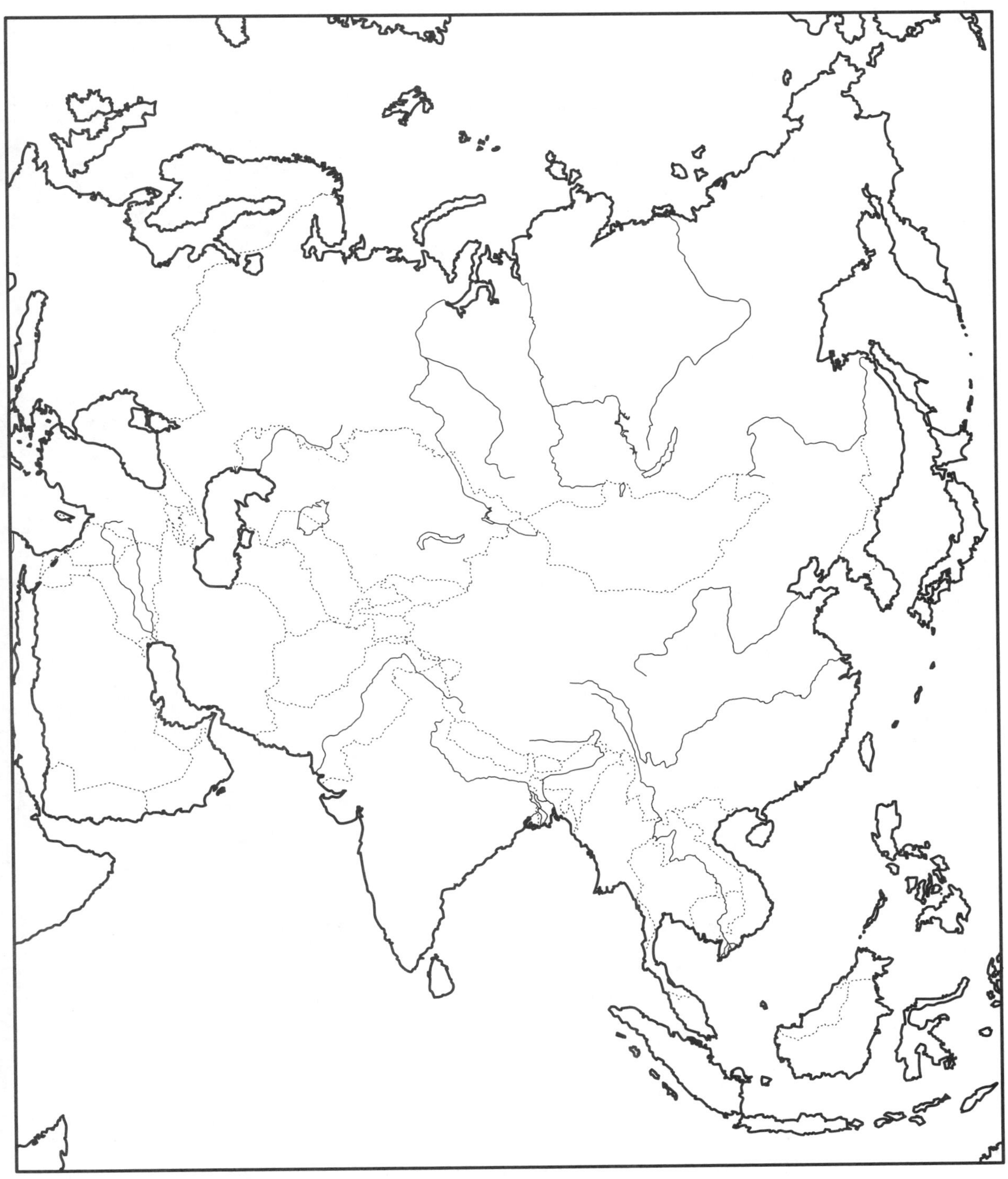

Important Events in History

The text mentions these events but does not give dates for all of them. Dates before Israel's sojourn in Egypt are labeled "about," since it is difficult to determine for sure whether the 430 years in Exodus 12:40 include the 215 years of sojourn in Canaan. Question marks indicate that the date is very uncertain. Some dates given in various sources vary a year or so.

The dates for early Mesopotamian and Egyptian history give a very approximate sequence of events based on a Flood date of 2304 B.C. The more common dates found in most reference sources are based on the shaky Sothic dating system, which pushes the beginning of these civilizations back before a Biblical Flood date.

God creates the earth.	*About 3960 B.C.*
The Fall of Man	*About 3959*
God destroys the earth with the Flood.	*About 2304*
Noah's descendants are scattered from the Tower of Babel.	*About 2150 (?)*
Abram enters Canaan.	*About 1877*
God delivers the Israelites from Egypt.	*1447*
Moses receives God's Law on Mount Sinai.	*About 1447*
Solomon begins to build the temple.	*967*
Samaria falls to the Assyrians.	*About 722*
Nineveh is destroyed by the Babylonians and the Medes.	*612*
Jerusalem falls to the Babylonians.	*586*
Babylon falls to the Medes and the Persians.	*539*
Cyrus allows the Jews to return to Jerusalem.	*537*
The Romans overthrow their Etruscan king and set up a republic.	*About 509*
The Greeks hold off the Persians at the battles of Marathon and Salamis.	*490, 480*
The Persian Empire falls to Alexander the Great.	*334–323*
The Ch'in dynasty unites China and builds the Great Wall.	*221–206*
The Maccabees fight the Seleucids in Palestine.	*167*
The Romans destroy Carthage in the third Punic War.	*149–146*
Jesus Christ is born.	*5 B.C.*
Jesus is crucified and rises again.	*About A.D. 30*
God sends His Holy Spirit; and the church is born.	*About 30*
The Romans destroy Jerusalem and the temple.	*70*
The apostle John dies a natural death after suffering for his faith.	*About 100*

Constantine legalizes Christianity.	*313*
Barbarians overthrow the last Roman emperor.	*476*
Muslims invade Spain.	*711*
The Muslims are defeated at the Battle of Tours.	*732*
King Alfred conquers London.	*886*
A schism permanently separates the Roman Catholic and Eastern Orthodox churches.	*1054*
William the Conqueror wins the Battle of Hastings and is crowned king of England.	*1066*
European Catholics fight Muslims in the First Crusade.	*1095–1099*
Peter Waldo is converted and becomes a leader of the Waldenses.	*1160*
The Mongols conquer and rule a vast empire.	*About 1200–1350*
King John of England signs the Magna Carta.	*1215*
Marco Polo travels to the Far East.	*1271–1295*
Gutenberg invents the printing press.	*About 1450*
Constantinople falls to the Muslim Turks.	*1453*
Columbus discovers the New World.	*1492*
Europeans explore and settle the New World.	*1500s, 1600s*
Martin Luther posts his Ninety-five Theses on a church door.	*1517*
Grebel, Manz, Blaurock, and others rebaptize each other and establish a church of true believers.	*1525*
Baber invades India and founds the Mogul Empire.	*1526*
Menno Simons renounces the Roman Catholic Church and is rebaptized.	*1536*
The English defeat the Spanish Armada.	*1588*
The King James Version of the Bible is published.	*1611*

Glossary

This glossary gives the meanings and pronunciations of the vocabulary words listed in each lesson. The numbers in brackets indicate the chapters where words are introduced.

The definitions tell only how the words are used in this book. Use a dictionary if you want to find other meanings for the words.

Most of the words have been respelled within parentheses to show how they are usually pronounced. Accented syllables are printed in capital letters.

abbot (AB uht) The man in charge of a monastery. [22]

abdicate (AB dih kayt) To formally give up or renounce the right to a throne, high office, or responsibility. [27]

alliance (uh LY uhns) A joining together by several parties; league. [10]

alloy (AL oi) A mixture of two or more metals. [9]

Anabaptist (an uh BAP tihst) A member of a church organized in 1525, whose doctrines included adult baptism, love for enemies, refusal of oaths, and nonparticipation in civil government. [24]

apartheid (uh PAHRT hyt) A policy requiring black people to stay separate from white people, practiced especially in South Africa; racial segregation and discrimination. [4]

apostolic father (ap uh STAHL ihk) An early church leader who had personally known the apostles of Christ. [18]

apprentice (uh PREHN tihs) A person who agrees to work under a master without pay for a certain time, in order to learn a craft. [23]

aqueduct (AK wih duhkt) A manmade channel for bringing water from a distance. [11]

Arab (AR uhb) 1. A native or inhabitant of Arabia. 2. Any of the Arabic-speaking people of the Middle East and North Africa who descended from Ishmael, Lot, Esau, Keturah's sons, and other Arabian tribes.[5]

archaeology (ahr kee AHL uh jee) Scientific study of the remains of past civilizations. [6]

archipelago (ahr kuh PEHL uh goh) A large group of islands. [3]

architecture (AHR kih tehk chur) A manner or style of building. [11]

artesian well (ahr TEE zhuhn) A well from which water flows without being pumped. [4]

artifact (AHR tuh fakt) A manmade object such as a tool or utensil, which is of interest in archaeology. [6]

ascetic (uh SEHT ihk) A person who tries to please God by denying himself of all pleasant things. [19]

assassination (uh sas uh NAY shuhn) The murder of a high-ranking person by a sudden attack, usually for political reasons. [12]

astrolabe (AS truh layb) An instrument used by medieval sailors to determine latitude, now replaced by the sextant. [26]

astrology (uh STRAHL uh jee) A system by which people try to predict the future by studying the positions of heavenly bodies. [7]

barbarian (bahr BAIR ee uhn) A member of a people or group considered to be uncivilized, crude, or brutal. [13]

barter The trading of goods or services without exchanging money. [7]

bauxite (BAWK syt) The ore from which aluminum is obtained. [2]

bazaar (buh ZAHR) A market consisting of a street lined with booths and small shops, especially in the Middle East. [5]

Bedouin (BEHD oo ihn) An Arab of certain nomadic tribes living in the deserts of the Middle East. [5]

bribe A favor (usually money) given to persuade a person to do something dishonest or illegal. [16]

bronze An alloy made by mixing copper and tin. [9]

Bruderhof (BROO dehr hohf) A farm or colony operated by Hutterites, on which they practice community of goods (see *Hutterite*). [28]

bubonic plague (boo BAHN ihk) A serious disease carried by fleas and rats, so named because of the buboes (swellings of lymph nodes) associated with it; also called Black Death. [23]

buffer An area between two enemy nations that helps to reduce the likelihood of conflict. [9]

cacao (kuh KAH oh) 1. A small tropical tree that produces beans which are used to make cocoa and chocolate. 2. The beans of this tree. [4]

capital Money or property that can be used to produce more goods or wealth. [4]

caravan (KAIR uh van) A company of people traveling together for safety, such as through a desert. [9]

cassava (kuh SAH vuh) A plant that produces large, starchy roots shaped like sweet potatoes. [4]

caste (KAST) A fixed social class, especially in Hindu society. [3]

catacombs (KAT uh kohmz) A system of passages and caves under the city of Rome used as a refuge and burial place by the early Christians. [18]

cataract (KAT ur akt) A swift, heavy flow of water, as at large falls or steep rapids. [8]

cathedral (kuh THEE druhl) One of the large, elaborate churches built during the Middle Ages, usually in the shape of a cross. [22]

causeway A raised roadway through water or wet land. [15]

centurion (sehn TUR ee uhn) A Roman officer in charge of one hundred soldiers. [17]

citizen A person who belongs to a given nation and therefore has certain rights. [17]

city-state An independent territory consisting of a city and the surrounding land under its control. [7]

coat of arms A design painted on the shield of a medieval knight as a means of identification. [22]

code A systematic collection of laws. [7]

communist (KAHM yuh nihst) Pertaining to a system in which most of the land, factories, and resources are owned and controlled by the government rather than by individual citizens. [2]

coniferous (koh NIHF ur uhs) Cone-bearing; pertaining to the group of trees that are mostly evergreen. [2]

consul (KAHN suhl) One of two rulers in the republic of Rome, each of which was elected for a one-year term. [16]

continental shelf An underwater ledge along the coast of a continent, extending some distance out into the ocean. [2]

Counter Reformation A movement in the 1500s and 1600s whose goal was to improve the Catholic Church and strengthen it against the Protestants. [30]

cradle of civilization A place where one of the earliest civilizations in the world began. [7]

Crusade (kroo SAYD) One of the military expeditions made by Europeans in the 1100s and 1200s to recover Palestine from the Muslims. [23]

culture A distinctive set of customs and values associated with a certain group of people. [2]

cuneiform (kyoo NEE uh form) Writing done by making wedge-shaped impressions in clay, used by Sumerians and other ancient people. [7]

czar (ZAHR) An emperor who ruled in Russia. [29]

Dark Ages The first part of the Middle Ages, from the 400s to the 1000s or 1100s. [19]

deity (DEE ih tee) Divine nature or status of being God; (*Deity,* when it is capitalized, means "God".) [19]

delta A fertile deposit of earth, usually triangular, that builds up at the mouth of some rivers. [3]

democracy (dih MAHK ruh see) A government controlled by the people. [14]

deport (dih PORT) To force (people) to move from their homeland and settle in a different place. [11]

desertification (dih zurt uh fih KAY shuhn) The changing of useful land to desert, as by overgrazing or by removing forests. [4]

Diaspora (dy AS pur uh) The Jews scattered among the Gentiles of other nations after the destruction of Jerusalem. [17]

dictator In Rome, a ruler appointed temporarily to deal with an emergency. [16]

diet A formal assembly of officials in the Holy Roman Empire. [27]

dissenter (dih SEHN tur) A person who disagrees with the teachings of an established church. [24]

distortion A pulling or twisting out of a normal shape. [1]

domestic (duh MEHS tihk) Tame; not wild (said of animals). [7]

dualism (DOO uh lihz uhm) The false doctrine that there is a good and an evil god, and that the evil god keeps souls imprisoned in his "evil" realm (the physical world) to keep them from going to the "good" realm (the spirit world). [24]

duke A nobleman ranking next to a king, who ruled a local region during the Middle Ages. [21]

dynasty (DY nuh stee) A succession of kings from the same family. [8]

empire An extensive territory composed of various nations ruled by a single government. [7]

epic (EHP ihk) A long poem that celebrates the heroic deeds of a famous person. [13]

excommunicate To expel (a person) from a church. [21]

fallow Idle farmland; not used for raising a crop. [16]

Fertile Crescent A crescent-shaped strip of fertile land extending from the land of Canaan to the Persian Gulf. [7]

feudalism (FYOO duhl ihz uhm) The system of land ownership in the Middle Ages, by which vassals received land from lords in exchange for the promise of their loyalty. [22]

fief (FEEF) The land held by a nobleman of medieval times; also called a feud. [22]

fiord (FYAWRD) A long, narrow, steep-sided inlet of the sea, especially common in Norway. [2]

fossil The hardened remains of an ancient plant or animal, embedded in rock. [6]

friar (FRY ur) A Catholic "brother" who teaches Catholicism to others. [22]

geometry (jee AHM ih tree) The branch of mathematics that deals with lines, angles, planes, and so forth. [8]

Gnosticism (NAHS tih sihz uhm) A false doctrine of early Christian times, which included the idea that spirit is good and matter is bad and which led to the denial of Christ's humanity and resurrection. [19]

great-circle route 1. The shortest route between two points on the earth's surface. 2. A route that follows a great circle of the earth (that is, a circle lying on the earth's surface and having the same center as that of the earth). [1]

Halfway-Anabaptist (German *Halb-taufer*) A person who claimed to accept Anabaptist doctrines but decided to wait until persecution ended before acting on his beliefs. [28]

Hanukkah (HAH nuh kuh) A Jewish festival celebrating the purification of the temple by Judas the Maccabee, also called the Feast of Dedication and the Feast of Lights. [15]

heavy industry The manufacture of large steel products such as cars, trucks, and locomotives. [2]

Hegira (hih JY ruh) The flight of Muhammad from his hometown of Mecca to Medina. [20]

Hellenism (HEHL uh nihz uhm) The culture of the ancient Greeks. [15]

hemisphere (HEHM ih sfihr) Half of a sphere, usually referring to half of the earth. [1]

heretic (HEHR ih tihk) A person who adheres to a doctrine, usually false, that is contrary to the teaching of an established church. [18]

hermit A person who tries to serve God by withdrawing from society and spending much time alone in religious exercises. [19]

hieroglyphics (hy ur uh GLIHF ihks) Simple pictures and other symbols that stand for words; picture writing. [8]

highwayman A man who lurks along roads and robs travelers. [30]

Holy Roman Empire The empire in central and western Europe that was governed by German kings and that lasted from A.D. 962 until 1806. [21]

Huguenot (HYOO guh naht) A French Protestant of the 1500s and 1600s. [29]

humanism (HYOO muh nihz uhm) The idea that man is the highest being of the universe and that he is accountable to no one but himself. [26]

Hutterite A member of the branch of Anabaptists that began to practice the community of goods under the leadership of Jacob Hutter. [28]

hydroelectricity (hy droh ih lehk TRIHS ih tee) Electricity generated by waterpower. [2]

illiterate (ih LIHT ur iht) Unable to read and write. [4, 19]

indulgence (ihn DUHL juhns) A paper issued by the pope and purchased by the people to obtain pardon for sin. [27]

inflation A decrease in the worth of money, which results in rising prices. [30]

Inquisition (ihn kwih ZIHSH uhn) A court established by the Catholic Church in 1231 to discover and punish persons thought to be guilty of heresy. [23]

interdependent Dependent on each other, as opposed to being self-sufficient. [23]

interdict (IHN tur dihkt) A command issued by the pope, forbidding the administration of sacraments in a certain region. [21]

International Date Line An imaginary line passing through the Pacific Ocean about 180º from the prime meridian, to the east of which the calendar date is one day earlier than to the west. [1]

Iron Curtain The heavily guarded border between communist countries and free countries. [2]

jade A hard, greenish or white stone used as a gem and in carving. [13]

Jesuit (JEHZ oo iht) A member of the Society of Jesus, which was organized in 1534 to promote education and the spreading of the Catholic faith. [30]

journeyman A person who had completed an apprenticeship and could work for wages but was not yet recognized as a master. [23]

jury A group of citizens (usually twelve) who are appointed to determine whether an accused person is innocent or guilty. [14]

jute 1. A plant that produces fibers used in making ropes and burlap. 2. The fibers of this plant. [3]

knight A medieval nobleman who served as a soldier under a nobleman of higher rank. [22]

Koran (koh RAHN) The book of writings considered holy by Muslims. [5]

kosher (KOH shur) Meeting the requirements of Jewish dietary laws; ceremonially clean. [5]

landlocked Entirely surrounded by land; having no seacoast. [4]

latitude (LAT ih tood) Distance north or south of the equator, measured in degrees. [1]

league (LEEG) A joining together by several parties; alliance. [16]

legend A list of map symbols and their meanings; key. [1]

legion (LEE juhn) A group of four thousand to six thousand Roman soldiers. [17]

light industry The production of goods such as food, textiles, and electrical appliances. [2]

loess (LOH uhs) A fine, yellowish-brown soil, usually deposited by the wind. [3]

longitude (LAHN jih tood) Distance east or west of the prime meridian, measured in degrees. [1]

lord A nobleman who granted land to a vassal in exchange for his promise of loyalty. [22]

Magna Carta The "Great Charter" by which King John granted various freedoms to English noblemen in 1215. [23]

malaria (muh LAIR ee uh) A serious disease carried by mosquitoes, which causes periodic chills, fever, and sweating. [4]

manor (MAN ur) One of the large farms of medieval Europe, owned by a lord and worked by serfs. [22]

Martyrs Mirror A large book first published in 1660 as a record of the sufferings that Anabaptists and other Christians endured for their faith. [18]

mass The Communion service as observed by Catholics, who believe that the bread and wine are changed into the actual body and blood of Christ. [22]

master An independent craftsman who is qualified to teach his trade to apprentices. [23]

masterpiece A good example of a craftsman's skill, used to seek recognition as a master. [23]

medieval (mee dee EE vuhl) Pertaining to the Middle Ages. [21]

Mediterranean climate (mehd ih tuh RAY nee uhn) A climate with hot, dry summers and mild, rainy winters, so named because it is the climate of lands around the Mediterranean Sea. [2]

melting pot A place where people of different nationalities blend into one society. [11]

Mennonite (MEHN uh nyt) A member of the branch of Anabaptists that came under the leadership of Menno Simons. [28]

meridian (muh RIHD ee uhn) An imaginary line running north and south, used to indicate longitude. [1]
metropolis (mih TRAHP uh lihs) A major or chief city. [5]
Middle Ages The period of history from about A.D. 500 to 1500. [19]
middleman A trader between the producer and the final buyer. [26]
moat A deep, wide ditch, usually filled with water, which forms a defense around a castle or city. [11]
monastery (MAHN uh stehr ee) An establishment where a group of monks live together. [19]
monk A man who has entered a monastery and taken the vows of its members. [19]
monopoly (muh NAHP uh lee) Exclusive control over something, such as a certain product or service. [10]
monotheism (MAHN uh thee ihz uhm) The belief that there is only one God. [3]
monsoon (mahn SOON) A seasonal wind of southern Asia, bringing dry air from the northeast during winter and bringing heavy rainfall from the southwest during summer. [3]
mortuary temple (MAWR choo air ee) A temple built in honor of a dead king or queen, sometimes near the burial site. [8]
mosque (MAHSK) A Muslim building of worship, often having a pointed dome. [4, 20]
mummy (MUHM ee) A human or animal body embalmed according to ancient Egyptian practice. [8]
mythology (mih THAHL uh jee) A collection of traditional stories, usually involving supernatural characters, which are supposed to explain things in nature (like the four seasons and the origin of life). [14]
nationalism (NASH uh nuh lihz uhm) Pride in belonging to one's nation; patriotism. [29]
navigator (NAV ih gay tur) A person who guides a ship or an airplane as it travels. [26]
neutral (NOO truhl) Supporting neither of two sides in a conflict. [29]
nomad (NOH mad) A person of a group that lives in movable dwellings and moves frequently from one place to another. [3]
nonresistance (nahn rih ZIHS tuhns) The doctrine of refusing to retaliate for wrong, but returning good instead. [20]
North Atlantic Drift A warm ocean current that flows northeastward across the Atlantic Ocean and brings mild temperatures to western Europe. [2]
oasis (oh AY sihs) A green, watered area surrounded by a desert. [4]
Orient (AWR ee uhnt) Lands of Asia, especially eastern Asia. [3]
orthodox (AWR thuh dahks) Adhering firmly to the established doctrines and practices of a religion. [5]
papyrus (puh PY ruhs) 1. A water plant used to make a writing material that was the forerunner of modern paper. 2. The writing material itself. [8]
parallel (PAR uh lehl) An imaginary line running parallel to the equator, used to indicate latitude. [1]
parliament (PAHR luh muhnt) The lawmaking body of England and certain other nations. [23]
pass A relatively low place that allows passage through a mountain range. [3]
patriarch (PAY tree ahrk) 1. A father and leader of a family or tribe. 2. One of the five

main bishops of the period several centuries after the apostles' time. [10, 19]

patrician (puh TRIHSH uhn) A person of the upper class in Roman society. [16]

Pentateuch (PEHN tuh took) The first five books of the Old Testament, written mostly by Moses. [5]

permafrost Ground that is permanently frozen. [3]

philosopher (fih LAHS uh fur) A person who studies the basic causes and principles that operate in the universe. [14]

physical relief map A map showing natural features such as mountains, lakes, and rivers, along with the different elevations of land. [1]

plateau (pla TOH) A large, elevated area of the same general height; tableland. [3]

plebeian (plih BEE uhn) A person of the lower class in Roman society. [16]

plunder To take valuable things from (a place) especially during war. [12]

poacher (POHCH ur) A person who hunts game illegally. [4]

political map A map showing manmade features such as countries, provinces, cities, and roads. [1]

polytheism (PAHL ee thee ihz uhm) The belief that there are many gods. [3]

pope The bishop of Rome and "father" of the Roman Catholic Church. [19]

prime meridian (muh RIHD ee uhn) The meridian running through an observatory in Greenwich, England, which is the beginning point for measuring degrees of longitude. [1]

publican (PUHB lih kuhn) A tax collector for the government of the Roman Empire. [17]

purgatory (PUR guh tawr ee) An imaginary place of suffering where people are supposedly purged from their sins before entering heaven. [27]

rabbi (RAB eye) A man who is authorized as a leader of a Jewish congregation. [5]

Ramadan (ram uh DAHN) 1. The ninth month on the Muslim calendar. 2. The fast that is held from sunrise to sunset on each day of this month. [5]

rapids A part of a river where the water flows swiftly, often over rocks just beneath the surface. [4]

Renaissance (REHN ih sahns) The "rebirth" of learning that began in Europe around 1300. [26]

republic (rih PUHB lihk) A form of democracy in which the people elect officials to represent themselves and manage government affairs. [16]

rift A deep, narrow crack in the rock layers of the earth's surface. [4]

sacrament (SAK ruh muhnt) A religious ceremony such as Baptism or Communion, which is thought to provide a spiritual benefit to anyone who observes it. [22]

safari (suh FAHR ee) A trip for hunting or exploration, especially in Africa. [4]

Sanhedrin (san HEE drihn) The highest court of the Jewish nation, consisting of about seventy men. [17]

satellite (SAT uhl yt) A nation that is supposedly independent but is actually controlled by a stronger nation. [2]

savanna (suh VAN uh) A large tropical grassland, sometimes with a few trees or shrubs. [4]

schism (SIHZ uhm) A division; separation. [19]

Schleitheim Confession (SHLYT hym) A confession of faith drawn up by Michael Sattler and other Anabaptist leaders at Schleitheim, Switzerland, in 1527. [28]

secede (sih SEED) To withdraw from a nation or other association. [10]

sedimentary (sehd uh MEHN tuh ree) Made of sediments deposited by water. [6]

Semite (SEH myt) One of the descendants of Shem, including Hebrews, Arabs, Syrians, Babylonians, and other groups. [7]

Septuagint (SEHP too uh jihnt) The Greek translation of the Hebrew Scriptures made by about seventy Jewish scholars. [15]

serf One of the common people who tilled the soil in medieval times. [22]

shrine A place that is considered sacred, usually because an object of adoration is there. [5]

simony (SY muh nee) The buying or selling of a church office. [22]

site In archaeology, a place where excavations are done. [6]

skeptic A person who tends to disbelieve generally accepted ideas, especially in religious matters. [9]

smelt To obtain (metal) from ore by melting. [2, 9]

Spanish Inquisition An inquisition under the control of Spain, established in 1483 to suppress non-Catholics. [29]

specialization (spehsh uh lih ZAY shuhn) The earning of an income by producing only one kind of goods or service, as opposed to producing everything for oneself. [7, 23]

sphere (SFIHR) An object shaped like a ball. [1]

state church A church that is supported and controlled by the civil government, and that may persecute those who do not accept its doctrines. [28]

stele (STEE lee) A stone shaft bearing an inscription and used as a monument. [7]

steppe (STEHP) A vast, open plain in Russia. [2]

strait A narrow stretch of water between two areas of land. [2]

subsistence farmer A farmer who produces only enough to support his family, usually with little extra. [4]

sultan (SUHL tuhn) A ruler in a Muslim country. [25]

synagogue (SIHN uh gahg) 1. A meeting place for Jewish worship or religious instruction. 2. The congregation of Jews who meet in the place of worship [5, 12]

synthetic (sihn THEHT ihk) Not natural, but made artificially; manmade. [3]

taiga (TY guh) A vast belt of evergreen trees stretching across Russia. [2]

Talmud (TAL muhd) An ancient commentary on the Law of Moses, considered one of the holy books of Judaism. [5]

tell A mound that was formed by building successive cities on the ruins of previous cities. [6]

terrace (TEHR ihs) One of a series of "steps" built along a steep hillside to make possible the raising of crops. [3]

tetrarch (TEHT rahrk) A governor of a fourth part of a Roman province. [17]

textile (TEHKS tyl) A fabric; cloth. [2]

theocracy (thee AHK ruh see) A country that is ruled by God. [10]

theses (THEE seez) *Plural of* **thesis**. Formal statements; propositions. [27]

tournament (TUR nuh muhnt) A mock battle fought between knights for entertainment. [22]

transubstantiation (tran suhb stan shee AY shuhn) The false doctrine that in the Communion service, the bread and wine change into the actual body and blood of Christ. [27]

tribute Money or goods that conquered people pay to their conquerors. [11]

tsetse fly (TSEHT see) A fly of Africa whose bite transmits sleeping sickness and other diseases. [4]

tundra A treeless plain in the Arctic regions, where the topsoil thaws in summer but the ground underneath is permanently frozen. [3]

Turk One of the Muslim groups of central Asia who took control of Palestine and nearby lands during the Middle Ages, and who were long-time adversaries of European nations and the Catholic Church. [23]

usurper (yoo SURP ur) A person who seizes power by force, without the proper right to do so. [10]

vassal (VAS uhl) A nobleman who received land from a lord in exchange for his promise of loyalty. [22]

vizier (vih ZIHR) A man appointed by an Egyptian king to see that the king's commands were actually carried out; a prime minister. [8]

yurt A round felt tent used by people on the prairies of Asia. [25]

ziggurat (ZIHG uh rat) A temple tower of the Sumerians and other ancient people, built in the form of a terraced pyramid. [7]

MAP INDEX

General Index

C

F

G

H

I

N

Photograph Credits

Agence France Presse/Corbis-Bettmann: 64 (top), 141 (right), 142 (top), 318 (top), 350
Air-India Library: 74, 513
American Heritage Collection: 431 (top)
Anton Geisser/Corbis-Bettmann: 38
Barth, *Travels in Central Africa:* 1857, 433 (bottom)
British Information Services New York: 41 (bottom)
Christian Light Publishers, Inc., 492
Clark Dana/Corbis-Bettmann: 371 (top)
Columbia University (from the collection of C.V. Starr East Asian Library): 457
Corbis-Bettmann: 73 (top), 93, 116 (bottom), 126, 141 (left), 146, 151, 153, 155 (top), 156, 169, 170 (top), 172, 174 (both), 175, 188, 189, 191 (both), 192, 204, 216 (bottom), 217 (top), 218, 219, 220, 221, 230, 232 (both), 233 (both), 235, 239, 251, 254 (both), 255, 263, 268 (bottom), 269 (both), 270, 271, 276, 278, 279 (both), 293, 295, 296, 297, 300 (both), 301 (both), 314 (both), 315, 316, 317 (both), 319 (both), 322, 324, 326 (left), 329, 330 (both), 331, 336, 338, 339, 340, 341, 342 (both), 343, 344 (both), 345, 347, 352, 354, 355 (both), 356, 357, 366, 371 (bottom), 372, 373, 374, 375, 378, 379 (both), 384, 386, 387, 388, 389, 390 (both), 391, 392, 393, 396 (both at top), 400, 402, 403, 404, 406 (both), 408, 409, 410, 411, 413, 418, 428, 433 (top left), 439 (top), 450, 454, 455, 456 (both), 458, 459 (both), 461, 462, 466, 468, 470, 471, 472 (both), 473, 474, 475, 476, 477 (both), 478 (top), 479, 500, 503, 504 (both), 505, 506, 507 (both), 508 (both), 510 (both), 511, 518, 520, 521, 522 (both), 523, 524, 525, 526, 527, 528, 529, 530 (both)
Corel: 1, 395, back cover
Ecuadorian Foundation for the Promotion of Tourism: 19 (left)
Fairbank, John King. *China: A New History,* Harvard University Press, 1992. From *Peiwenzhai gengzhitu* (1808 edition): 439 (bottom), 440
Fisher, Martha: 64 (bottom)
Frohman; Col. Louis/Corbis-Bettmann: 376
Gleysteen, Jan: 421, 422, 423, 484, 488 (all), 490 (both), 491 (both), 493, 494
Graphic House/Corbis-Bettmann: 202, 268 (left)
Gustavo Tomsich/Corbis-Bettmann: 480
Harvest Time Books: 424, 425
Horst, Melvin: 99
Italian Government Tourist Office: 294
Jay Pasachoff/Corbis-Bettmann: 268 (top right)
Kaschub, Norma, front cover, 41 (top), 44 (both), 80, 92, 260, 262 (left), 292, 299, 358
Korea National Tourist Organization: 71, 72, 73 (bottom)
Library of Congress: 62, 119, 120, 136, 137 (bottom), 139 (both), 148, 152, 160, 163 (both), 168, 170 (bottom), 171, 173, 183, 184, 198, 199, 200, 201, 214, 216 (top), 223, 225, 249, 283 (both), 311, 437, 438, 442
Luyken, Jan, *Martyrs Mirror:* 326 (right), 328
Mano Orel/Corbis-Bettmann: 185
Miller, Lester: 63 (top, middle, and bottom right)
Norwegian Tourist Board: 35 (top)
Oriental Institute of the University of Chicago, The: 149, 155 (bottom), 187, 212
P. Gendreau Collection/Corbis-Bettmann: 394

Photri: 8, 19 (right), 26 (both), 32, 33, 34 (both), 35 (bottom), 40 (both), 46, 47, 52, 58, 59, 60, 61, 63 (left), 65, 85, 86 (both), 87, 94, 95, 98, 100, 106, 112, 117, 118, 121, 123 (both), 125, 134, 140, 180, 182, 265 (both), 280, 290, 478 (bottom)

Photri/© Bachmann: 262 (right)

Photri/© Nowitz: 124

Raymond V. Schroder/Corbis-Bettmann: 396 (bottom)

Reid Rossman/Corbis-Bettmann: 164

Reuters/Corbis-Bettmann: 101, 116 (top), 244, 318 (bottom)

Stock Montage, Inc.: 10

The Metropolitan Museum of Art, Gift of John D. Rockefeller, 1932. (32.143.1): 217 (bottom)

The Metropolitan Museum of Art, Maitland F. Griggs Collection, Bequest of Maitland F. Griggs. (43.98.1): 453

Underwood & Underwood/Corbis-Bettmann: 237

UPI/Corbis-Bettmann: 162, 238, 252, 353, 369, 432, 441

Wheeler, Sir Mortimer, from *The Indus Civilization*, (London, England: Cambridge University Press, 1968): 247, 248

Woodfin Camp and Associates: 306

Zook, Miriam: 137 (top)

Graph and Map Credits

Britannica: 37 (Brother Lester Miller drew a replica of a chart found on Britannica CD, Version 99 © 1994-1999. Encyclopædia Britannica, Inc.)

The maps on the following pages are based on map images from **Cartesia:** 11, 12 (top, bottom left, bottom right), 14, 15 (bottom), 19 (both), 21 (top, both), 31, 84 (all), 87, 110 (all), 127, 132, 154, 164, 184, 185, 205, 210, 215, 231, 236, 280, 282, 288, 298, 311, 356, 363, 374, 377, 405, 434, 438, 448, 461, 480, 494, 536, front and back endsheets

Hostetler, Bennie: 222

The maps on the following pages are based on map images from **Mountain High Maps ® Copyright © 1993 Digital Wisdom, Inc.:** 12 (middle), 15 (top), 16, 18 (bottom), 20, 21 (bottom, both), 28, 29, 30 (all), 54, 55, 56 (all), 82, 83, 108, 109, 246, 247, 253, 263, 295, 327, 346, 369, 402, 442, 512

Yoder, Dale: 539, 540, 541, 542, 543, 544, 545, 546, 547

ARCTIC
Beaufort Sea
Arctic Islands
Baffin Bay
Greenland
Great Bear Lake
Great Slave Lake
Hudson Bay
Bering Sea
Gulf of Alaska
Aleutian Islands
Canadian Shield
Coast Ranges
Rocky Mountains
NORTH AMERICA
Central Plains
Great Lakes
Appalachian Mts.
Coastal Plain
ATLANTIC
PACIFIC
Canary Islands
Gulf of Mexico
West Indies
Hawaiian Islands
Caribbean Sea
Cape Verde
Guiana Highlands
165°W
150°W
135°W
120°W
105°W
90°W
45°W
30°W
15°W
Galápagos Islands
SOUTH AMERICA
Amazon Basin
Andes Mountains
OCEA
Polynesia
Brazilian Highlands
Gran Chaco
OCEAN
Pampas
Falkland Islands
Bellingshausen Sea
Weddell Sea
Ross Sea
ANT